TQ 20

Twenty Years of the Best Contemporary Writing
and Graphics from *TriQuarterly* magazine

Edited by Reginald Gibbons and Susan Hahn

A special issue of *TriQuarterly* magazine

Northwestern University

1985

TriQuarterly 63

Spring/Summer
1985

Editor	**Reginald Gibbons**
Executive Editor	**Bob Perlongo**
Managing Editor	**Joseph LaRusso**
Fiction Editor	**Susan Hahn**
Special Projects Editor	**Fred Shafer**
Design Director	**Gini Kondziolka**
TriQuarterly Fellow	**Doug Clayton**
Editorial Assistants	**Brian Bouldrey, James Bryant, T.R. Johnson, Sheelagh McCaughey**
Advisory Editors	**Robert Alter, Michael Anania, Elliott Anderson, Terrence Des Pres, Gloria Emerson, Richard Ford, George Garrett, Gerald Graff, Francine du Plessix Gray, Michael S. Harper, David Hayman, Bill Henderson, Maxine Kumin, Elizabeth Pochoda, Michael Ryan**

TRIQUARTERLY IS AN INTERNATIONAL JOURNAL OF ART, WRITING AND CULTURAL INQUIRY PUBLISHED IN THE FALL, WINTER AND SPRING AT **NORTHWESTERN UNIVERSITY**, EVANSTON, ILLINOIS 60201.

Subscription rates—Individuals: one year $16; two years $28; life $100. Institutions: one year $22; two years $40; life $200. Foreign subscriptions $4 per year additional. Single copies usually $6.95. Sample copies $3. Correspondence and subscriptions should be addressed to **TriQuarterly**, NORTHWESTERN UNIVERSITY, 1735 Benson Avenue, Evanston, Illinois 60201. Phone: (312) 491-3490. The editors invite submissions of fiction, poetry and literary essays. No manuscripts will be returned unless accompanied by a stamped, self-addressed envelope. All manuscripts accepted for publication become the property of **TriQuarterly**, unless otherwise indicated. Copyright © 1985 by **TriQuarterly**. All rights reserved. The views expressed in this magazine are to be attributed to the writers, not the editors or sponsors. Printed in the United States of America.

National distributor to retail trade: B. DeBoer, 113 East Central Street-Rear, Nutley, New Jersey 07110. Distributor for West Coast trade: Bookpeople, 2929 Fifth Street, Berkeley, California 94710. Midwest: Bookslinger, 213 East Fourth Street, St. Paul, Minnesota 55101 and Prairie News Agency, 2404 West Hirsch Street, Chicago, Illinois 60622.

Reprints of issues #1–15 of **TriQuarterly** are available in full format from Kraus Reprint Company, Route 100, Millwood, New York 10546, and all issues in microfilm from University Microfilms International, 300 North Zeeb Road, Ann Arbor, Michigan 48106. ISSN: 0041-3097.

Publication of this issue of *TriQuarterly* has been made possible in part by generous aid from the Joyce Foundation and the Atlantic Richfield Foundation, as well as the Illinois Arts Council and the National Endowment for the Arts.

Contents

4

7

Cover design by Gini Kondziolka

Preface/1964 -- 1984

To read through the nearly 12,000 pages of *TriQuarterly*'s twenty years is inevitably to trace a literary trajectory of writing in America. The founding editor, Charles Newman, and his successor Elliott Anderson, seem to have had prescience as well as acumen in seeking new writing and recognizing its merits, for many writers new to *TQ* and the American scene were later to find wide readership.

Fiction had a central place in the magazine almost from the beginning, perhaps because both editors were sensitive to the difficulty faced by writers of short stories during a period when neither commercial magazines nor trade publishers were generous with space or money. (That situation has changed now, let us hope, perhaps partly thanks to magazines like *TriQuarterly* that have steadfastly devoted space to what some call "literary" fiction.) The range of fiction in *TQ* has been wide—from the "postmodern" works of Coover, Gass, Barth, Hawkes and others, to the "boom" writers of Latin America and the most gifted and forceful writers of a more traditional sort. Perhaps *TQ*, more than many literary magazines, has also given its readers the irreverent and questioning, the experimental and artistically self-conscious, alongside the best work—including the literary essay—from other realms, Stanley Elkin and Richard Brautigan to Julio Cortázar and Roland Barthes to Raymond Carver and Susan Sontag.

Some history: Charles Newman launched *TQ* from the base of its earlier history as a modest, staple-bound campus magazine at Northwestern University. His issues presented a great range of authors and literary concerns, from considerations of Yeats on the centenary of his birth to recent writings from Eastern Europe and the Soviet Union, from the first sizable critical consideration of Sylvia Plath's work to the first volume in English on Jorge Luis Borges. Immediately the magazine's participation in the larger issues of literary culture was notable— Newman published a great number of critical articles on contemporary

9

writing, a sizable variety of contemporary European literature (in fact, numerous works in translation, including Asian) and essays on the theater, philosophical questions, literary imagination and history. He repeatedly demonstrated that he intended *TriQuarterly* to be a national magazine of international range. He published fiction generously—and in an especially interesting way, often presenting critical articles that questioned or explored theoretical issues side by side with imaginative works of the sort under scrutiny.

Newman's special issues included two volumes of writings by Russian émigré writers in the west, a volume dedicated to Nabokov, a Latin American anthology and an issue devoted entirely to conceptual art, besides the special issues mentioned above. He resigned as editor in 1975 and was succeeded by Elliott Anderson, who devoted even more space to fiction (but by sacrificing poetry and reviews) and continued *TQ*'s special issues. Anderson published the monumental documentary volume *The Little Magazine in America* (*TQ* #43) and a collection of Israeli writing, but also all-fiction issues with titles like *Love and Death*, *War Stories* and *Western Stories*. One impressive aspect of many of the special issues of both editors—which the present editor has tried to emulate— was the way in which they did not wish merely to collect miscellaneous works around a theme, but tried to create a context within which each individual work had greater significance for the American reader. Often the special issue was itself a whole with the integrity of a book. (This very virtue, which gave many of the issues their continuing interest when they were republished by trade and university houses, has worked against our selection of excerpts for reprinting.)

The partisanship of the first two editors allows a reader of the whole bulk of *TQ* to see how an artistic trend like postmodern fiction appears both in the context of its contemporary excitement and comment, and in our own moment, which has made it seem more an experiment somewhat limited to a certain time and certain writers. Reprinting individual works from that period often shows too little of their own context; thus deprived, many of them seem less readable now. But lively and interesting these works certainly were, and *TQ* built a good portion of its reputation on them. The inclusion in this volume of a few of the best such pieces and what we believe is a very wide range of other sorts of fiction is part of our hope to show that much of *TriQuarterly*'s history is not only lively and interesting, but also of enduring importance to the life of writing in this country; thereby we hope to show also that the literary magazine, in general, need not be a marginal or dispossessed or merely self-absorbed creature of its time. Indeed, it is not, except of necessity in the economic conditions that limit its circulation. Its contents, in contrast—and this is true of *TQ* despite or even partly because of its occasional partisanship—can be as vital and central to national cultural life as anything whatsoever of greater currency. Indeed, in both

Charles Newman's first-issue foreword and the present editor's editorial in 1982, readers of this volume will find the intention of conceiving the literary magazine in the largest terms possible, though it will be for those same readers to judge whether the editors of *TQ* or any magazine manage to succeed. The several editors of TQ, anyway, would argue that the "little" magazine works reprinted here introduce and reiterate, examine and embody, many ideas, causes, concerns, arguments, dilemmas and situations of the "big" world of our time.

To our minds, there is a great feast of wonderful writing in the magazine's twenty-year run, so much so that of necessity a huge portion of it has had to be excluded because of the unavoidable limitations we face. This volume too is a little-magazine publication, and can reach only a few thousand readers and gather only some hundreds of pages. These are economic restrictions imposed on all literary magazines by the nature of publishing in this country. And it's in this context that we lament all the more not being able to reprint more work from *TriQuarterly*. We have judged individual pieces on the basis of their enduring value and vitality rather than either their documentary interest or their standing as evidence of a writer's presence in the pages of *TQ*. In fiction and poetry, we chose works that seemed to us extraordinarily strong and fresh, and which we were proud to point to as contributions to *TQ* before they became better known, or their authors did. We would have liked to add another two hundred pages of distinguished fiction, especially, if we could have published an even larger book. With regard to essays, the standard for inclusion has been general appeal, although here there was also a remarkable range of powerful, original and important works, not at all academic in the worst sense. (The best of the more specialized literary essays from the magazine's history will indeed be collected in the future, as the second volume in the new *TriQuarterly* Series on Criticism and Culture, published by Northwestern University Press.)

And after all this has been said, we should add that other editors might well produce, from these same issues of *TQ*, a very different anthology to celebrate the same twenty years of an existence usually precarious but—we feel, looking back on our predecessors—consistently valuable.

Not just pride, then, prompts our publication of this book. There's also the hope of response, once again, to these works which in the past found their first response among readers of *TQ*. These are writings which are—as good and great works should be—still speaking to us, whose business is still unfinished, and will remain actively unfinished as long as there are serious readers. Readers whose habit it is to read imaginative writing will not be surprised to hear a plea for attention to the works in literary magazines, because for them the value of fiction and poetry is self-evident, confirmed a thousand times by experience. But those to whom a book like this comes as a less usual occasion, and whom the literary magazines generally hope to add to their audience, will hear us also entering a plea at this point. It is in favor of what perhaps is all too obvious but which seems all the more to need saying, at a time when the success – in numbers – of literary culture (numbers of writers, or books, of magazines) belies the continuing marginality of literary endeavor in our time: stories, poems, and essays can remind us that our lives are not a series of problems to be solved, but a plight or triumph common to others as well, a continuum of experience to be shaped and understood as best we can – however provisionally. We are joined in a community of others. Perhaps those others are not many, compared to the number of persons who do no living, or very little, in their imaginations.

But those who do enter the realm of literary works perhaps find there a fuller expression of the possibilities of life and the fact of death than can be found elsewhere. They find pleasure and exhilaration in artistic mastery and craft, in language, in the creation of meaning – whether that meaning is joyous or painful. If some would say that an acknowledgment of meaninglessness is the accepted intellectual, perhaps even universal, credential of our day (however it is disguised by the images of religion, politics, or individualistic pursuits), most writers would answer that to experience personal powerlessness in life, whether privately you face that powerlessness honestly or not, is not to abandon either hope or the appetite for meaning in art *or* life.

No less than in earlier times, the literary magazines offer readers many of the best works by the best writers, and perhaps this anthology will argue for the value and validity of such publications. To write at all, as Flannery O'Connor said, is an act of hope. So, it may be, is reading. More than anything, this celebratory anthology of *some* of the best works from *TriQuarterly*'s twenty years is an affirmation of faith in both. Here, then, presented almost exactly as originally printed, is our guided tour through *TQ*. May it take you past some familiar places you are glad to see again, and introduce you to some you missed and are pleased to discover now. May it entertain and solace, shock and reassure, transport and occupy you. May it suggest not only a route through the recent past, but a map into the future.

Reginald Gibbons
Susan Hahn
May 1985

FOREWORD

"As for the future, it cannot possibly shock us, since we have already done everything possible to scandalize ourselves. We have so completely debunked the old idea of the Self that we can hardly continue in the same way. Perhaps some power within us will tell us what we are, now that the old misconceptions have been laid low. Undeniably the human being is not what we commonly thought a century ago. The question nevertheless remains. He is something. What is he?" — SAUL BELLOW

There are two kinds of magazines — those which fascinate with nouns, and those which delight in verbs. The former are more proper: dealing modestly with time and life, they assert rather than explain; to sell things, they *name* things. The latter, more common, more active, tend to make a statement, ask a question, give a command. Their tenses are generally more progressive and less tangible. This is a perfect situation for dialectic, but there isn't one. It is not at all as simple as that. This accounts for the ambiguity of the title — *Tri-Quarterly*. We read it as an adverb — a modified occurrence, in which *action* and *naming* are indivisible. It may tell place, sense, manner, frequency, degree, direction. Yes and No are also adverbs.

Pluralism

When Dos Passos said, "All right! Now we are two nations", he was right save in one particular — the number. Dualism for his generation dramatized a final disgust with the oneness, the phony unities of the modern world. We have since learned that even something elemental as disgust is not easy to come by. In a society where poets use the marketing techniques of advertising, where businessmen hire poets to sensitize their images, where radicals captivate the very audience they are pledged to destroy, where the bourgeois find anarchism fashionable, where the ethics of corporations and universities appear interchangeable, it is difficult to draw that old dialectic taut again. Heaven and Hell are no longer popular concepts in an affluent democracy. The social scientists have given us another, less pejorative vocabulary to explain ourselves. What De Tocqueville noted as the tyranny of equality, what Jefferson envisioned as the chance for each talent to find its own authority, we call now Pluralism — which is both the fear and promise of unlimited possibility. Now we are x nations.

It is possible, of course, that we simply cannot calculate fast enough, that a machine will come up with that number and set us straight again. But that is to assume that mere *naming* will again suffice. It is who makes use of that pure mathematics, and how, which concerns us. Pluralism means that the number in Dos Passos' retort is an unknown integer. It does not mean that any single reply is inadmissible — but that answers are viable, dangerously so, precisely because they are mutable. Pluralism means that the stuff of each choice is a genuine confusion, and that order may be as various as the unique personalities which lay claim to it.

Order is perverse then, when a personality is absent or synthetic. Modern journalism is awesomely adept in avoiding the price of order. In collective editorializing, the personality is subsumed by committee for the sake of consistency. The voice must never catch or waver; that would complicate things. There are the 'Objectivists', on the other hand, who would let the "images speak for themselves". Thus, we are treated, in successive exposures, to a president, a quadruple amputee, tomato soup, a debutante, an earthquake — bound together simply because they are all "news". In one case, the perspective is synthetic; in the other it is non-existent. Both lack the unity of personal vision, and the courage implicit. Commercialism is only one kind of cowardice, however. Who knows what to make of that president, that cripple, that girlie, that soup, that disaster?

Art

Modern art is the creative personality's confrontation with pluralism — the sharing of the spectrum. There is an old and engaging ideal that art, literature particularly, might structure reality in such a way as to develop human sensitivity, and if not create values, at least indicate alternatives. A figure as recent as James Joyce is said to have thought that the worst thing about World War II is that it kept people from reading *Ulysses*. The *Sturm und Drang* literary reviews at the time of "two nations" believed that after that blasting, what floated back to earth would find new roots, grow new patterns. It is no secret that all the pieces did not fit together. The tradition that Art might affect Life, even uplift it, is now carried on, not so much by artists, but by the profession of criticism, which — whatever its merits as a discipline in itself — must be considered a rear guard action in terms of art.

A most compelling fact of modern life is that much of modern art seems to repudiate it. It is the old debate between Jefferson and De Tocqueville again; whether you choose to celebrate the dynamism or the vulgarity of a pluralistic world. The cultural elite used to allow that people get along pretty well without art. It has taken them the last half-century to say that art gets along pretty well without people — since the people confuse their capacity to react with the artist's ability to explore.

It is not for us to gauge the proper relationship between art and society, or even to bring the mind and marketplace together. They are already too close for comfort. The idea that art should serve society is impractical, not because some societies, like ours, have failed at it, or others like Russia, have succeeded all too well — but simply because it is impossible to harness the creative personality to a phenomenon which is more or less than himself. It takes too much out of everybody concerned.

But what if society should serve art? The artist's task, we have often been told, is to question without regard to the consequences. Society's task is less newsworthy, but no less compelling — for they must have the courage to confront questions which not only don't occur to them, but which they could not answer if they did. In that sense, appreciation is a selfless act. It is the audience, themselves, who must reject the synthetic order of those who serve their needs or presume to create them. In the supermarket, the consumer must provide his own synthesis.

The necessity for the artist's personal vision, the value of his partiality is clear. The creative individual has his place, such as it is. Art, and what passes for it, is surely taken seriously enough. Perhaps it is the audience in which we no longer believe.

The University

Proof of pluralism is that we can now talk of the university in the same breath with art and society. Higher education has come in for a good share of attention lately. It has been criticized both for a willful aloofness from society and its needs, and for a fatally perfect adaptation to society and its impositions. One thing is clear — its scope has been immeasurably increased — not only does everyone end up at college, but as institutions, universities have been made responsible for everything from driver training to the preservation of grand opera. Given modern military and technological goals, some have **acquired a power, prestige, and concomitant awe, once reserved for nation-states. The** competition between them is purer than between our oligopolies; the politics within them as proselytizing as in any of our parties. They insist upon tangible credentials from a society whose motive force has always been a pragmatic test of talent. They talk among themselves in specialized languages provocative as any underground, yet justify themselves to society in a common counter-revolutionary rhetoric. They are becoming a sub-culture unto themselves.

Most importantly, perhaps, is the number of artists who are not only educated in universities, but make their subsequent living off them. What this relocation of dissent will cost us is not yet clear. It has gone far enough, however, that the old Bohemian/Bourgeois debate has been set along new lines; the "academic" and the "beat", or in Robert Lowell's words, between the "cooked" and the "uncooked". We want to elaborate that debate — make the dialectic something more than the rejection of some foul unity. We are not interested in making anybody's career, although we hope our existence may dignify many. We hope to search out new talent, and encourage the established to venture beyond their reputations.

One recalls, however, that universities, like all institutions dependent upon the good will of the community, have not always been receptive to the kind of questions good artists ask. One can then tell artists to avoid such institutions, or demand that the institutions become more accountable. It may be that in the expanding university, we are witnessing an affluent democracy's oblique answer to the patronage system of the old world — although we could not afford to call it that yet. Still, leisure does strange things to people. And the university's function, most magnificently conceived, has after all been roughly akin to the artist's, in that it is pledged to the damnation of spurious order, and devoted to questions that society will not, alone, ask itself. This does not negate synthesis; it simply enhances its value. The university serves art by witnessing the pluralism of society.

All this implies the concept of limited revolution; revolution in the American tradition by chance, in that it makes use of the Establishment. We believe that to be more in accord with both the ideal and the real. This is not the time to profess loyalty to institutions, but to the discipline which keeps institutions alive.

Our task is to assemble. Literary reviews provide no more viable standards than I.Q. tests or annual income. They are simply another alternative; an attempt to bind temperament and action through language. Without resorting to epilogues or manifestoes, we want to embellish those proper nouns and common verbs which have made our culture too often a vehicle for minor aspirations and mock debate. It will be a modern enterprise, perhaps embarrassingly so, in that we are justified by little save our own potential. We're getting dressed up to celebrate the fact we're still looking.

CHARLES NEWMAN

Fragments from the unpublished
death fantasy sequence
of *Judgment Day*

JAMES T. FARRELL

. . . AND HIS CHEEKS BURNED, his legs were on fire, his chest was heavy, crossed by pains, warm, burning, all over him, there was a fire consuming his skin, and his nerves. His bones ached. His back ached. In his backbone at the base of his spine, there was pain. There was fire and weariness in the thin arms beneath the covers of his bed. There was pain and fire in his sunken cheeks. There was fever in his glazed half-opened eyes, and in the lids that pressed them down. He tried to speak. . . . The strange white woman, her white soothing and . . . cool, bent towards him. In his mind, there formed the words

I'm afraid.

They travelled to his tongue and issued as sounds that the strange white woman bent to hear.

The sick eyes closed. Blackness came . . . certain objects in the misty room bound . . . crossed in front of the blackness . . . through the colors, and a cool . . . surrounded by grass . . . large tree, and seemed to be propelled away from him fast and faster and faster, and he suddenly broke into a run after the tree, and he felt that if he caught that tree, touched it, stood under it, climbed it, only caught up with it, he would not die, and he felt that he was dying. And the tree disappeared. . . .

Instead of finding himself dead, he found himself to be only a boy, and he could not understand it. He was a boy, in short pants, and he was walking down Indiana Avenue, and there were new houses on Indiana Avenue, and he couldn't understand how there could be new houses on Indiana Avenue, today, when there had been only the old houses on Indiana . . . and he looked to glance into the window of the stone house where Lucy lived. And it was not there. In its place, there was a tall apartment building; out of it, people walked, strangers, who did . . . men and women whose faces were not clear . . . a woman he felt he must have seen somewhere . . . some place before, and he could not remember what . . . Helen Shires came along and said. . . .

Helen was gone. Indiana Avenue was gone. Studs had been propelled away

16

from Indiana Avenue, and he was riding in an aeroplane, regretful, thinking of Indiana Avenue, and wondering why he had been carried way, how, where he was going to, and he fell over trees, and he looked down, and he thought that he recognized Washington Park, and he did not know, and he carried with him, in this aeroplane, the regret, and kept asking himself why he had been carried away. He shouted to the driver

Hey!

The driver did not answer him, and a pain began to spread over him, a pain of regret, of . . . unsatisfied.

And he was no longer in the aeroplane. He did not know where he was. He saw shapes that he . . . therefore, phallic, shapes, twisted, gargoyles . . . similar objects, chairs and stoves, and buildings . . . twisted and torn, and he felt sorry and sick . . . felt that he was dying, and that he was . . . many things.

Behind them, the fires of Hell burning with terrific heat, and he stood facing them helplessly, a terrific heat parching his body, causing the perspiration to drip from him in large warm drops that caused small and prickling irritations . . . little fires amongst dried grass at his feet. And with the face of Weary Reilley, the devil bobbed up and down in the flames, and shouted each time his face appeared

You're coming to me, you bastard!

Above the fires of Hell, the Sacred Heart of Jesus hung, blood dripping from it, to sizzling sizzle in the flames.

"The wages of sin is death, you skunk," the Pope of Rome dourly said to Studs.

"Give me a nickel to save your soul . . . for the Church commands you to contribute to the . . . pastor," Father Gilhooley said, extending his hand.

". . . jazzed whores, and now you're going to get . . . our life in Hell. Ha! Ha! Ha!" Father Shannon told him.

"Thou shalt not take the name of the Lord Thy God in vain," the Pope of Rome said.

"In your life you spent three times as much on whores as you did on the salvation of your immortal soul," said Father Gilhooley.

"Woe unto you, you who disregarded my word in my missions, you in whom I placed confidence," said Father Shannon.

"You're coming here, you bastard, and these flames go up your brown," the devil with the face of Weary Reilley said.

Hell, give me a break. Fathers forgive me for I have sinned. I'm heartily sorry. Hell, give me a break. Jesus Christ give me a break and a drink. I'm dying, I'm dying, I'm burning, for Christ sake give me some water and put out the fire. I'm dying. Goddamn it! I'm dying. I'm a goddamn fool, and I'm dying.

"Well, hurry up about it, you fatheaded slob . . . can't wait all eternity for a measly bastard with a . . . damned soul like yours to die," the devil with the face of Weary Reilley called out to him.

". . . you had the water of faith to . . ." Father Gillhooley said sternly, rubbing his bay front, just as he had comfortably rubbed it when he stood speaking on the stage that night in June 1916 when Studs Lonigan had graduated from St. Patrick's grammar school.

"Drink some moonshine now, and be damned with it," said Father Shannon.

Studs rubbed his hand across his sweating, heat-tortured brow, and looking at his hand, he saw blood on it, and his fear and horror again spread through him, until he felt like a boil ready to burst in pain and pus.

The Pope of Rome turned and pointed at the bleeding Sacred Heart of Jesus, and the blood dripped drop by drop from it to sizzle and dry in the fires of Hell.

"Each drop of that precious blood is shed because of the mortal sin you committed with whores, William . . . son of Lonigan," the Pope of Rome said.

I didn't know no better. Forgive me, give me absolution . . . must I die like a goddamn dog, said Studs.

"You sonofabitch, you ain't begun to suffer yet," the devil with the face of Weary Reilley said.

"Suffer little louse to come unto me and I will burn thee in the fires of Hell and damnation," said Father Shannon, and brimstone, like firecrackers, shot up from the fires of Hell, and fell all around the burning bare feet of Studs Lonigan.

He fell on his knees and cried.

Drink. A drink of water. For Christ sake give me a drink of water.

The Pope of Rome came forward and placed a bottle of fire to the lips of kneeling Studs Lonigan, and poured liquid fire down his throat, the fire burning a path into his stomach, and Studs Lonigan let out a terrified yell.

Mrs. Lonigan rushed into the bedroom, and looked at the tossing, fire-burned, sick and wasting body of her son, and amidst a dribble of inarticulate sounds and disconnected words, he emitted a weak and painful cry. She screamed, and shouted, "He's dying."

The nurse came over to Studs' bed; wiping his face with a wet washrag, she asked her to be quiet. . . .

"He's in a very critical condition, and he is in a restless coma. His fever is very high too," the nurse said.

Fighting back tears and sniffling, the mother looked down at her son. Unable to hold back her tears any more, she burst forth in a deluge, and the tears ran hot down her cheeks.

"I'll call the doctor," the nurse said.

She energetically left the room.

II

Lonigan sat drunk by the kitchen table. He hiccuped. He put his head down and cried, babyishly. He got up and told himself, Paddy, buck up and be a man. Then he walked unsteadily to the stove, and lit the gas under the coffee pot. He staggered over the coffee pot, and looked down at it, and at the gas flame.

He turned from the coffee pot and walked to the cupboard, drew out a cup and saucer, and set it on the table. Then he sat down at the table, looking at the cup and saucer.

Buck up Paddy, be a man, brace yourself, Paddy, my boy, he told himself.

My son is dying, he tearfully informed himself.

He lowered his head on the table, thinking that he might close his eyes a minute while the coffee heated. He raised his head. He thought dully, stupefied, of himself as a ruined man, and of his son on his death bed. Any minute Bill would die. He had a sense of there being so many things that might have been averted, but that were now too late! His dullness persisting, he reflected, like a man in a stupor, of how so much had passed by. He looked at the clock on the window beyond the stove, and listened to its ticking . . . afraid of what the clock signified, the passage of seconds that all added up, in minutes, and hours, and days. He looked at the clock, acutely aware of the ticking of seconds in a quiet house, feeling that these ticking seconds meant the approach of a catastrophe. He looked at the clock hands which read a quarter to eight, and wished that they would stop, that time would stop for a while. The ticking of these seconds, the slow change of the minute hand from notch to notch, was indissolubly tied up for him with the death of his son. He was tense, and stared evenly at the table and the dishes he had laid out on it. The coffee boiled steadily in the percolator on the stove, and he was heedless of it. He felt completely powerless. He could do nothing for Bill. He could do nothing to check the downward swing of business that had taken his money from him, and was ruining him. He was sobering up also, and he felt lassitudinous. He commenced to have a sick headache, and he realized how tired and worn out he was. And he feared sleep, feared lest, if he go to sleep, he should wake up and find his son dead. He leaned his left elbow on the enameled table, and laid his forehead against the palm of his left hand. He snapped his right fingers. He ran his right hand through his thinning hair. The coffee pot began to burn, and a burning odor started to pervade the kitchen. He was unaware of it, and sat in a stupor.

"Goodness, Patrick, what's this? Is the house on fire?" Mrs. Lonigan exclaimed, rushing into the kitchen, making a face as she raised her nose to smell, and her nostrils twitched.

He looked up at her, like one aroused from an absorbing internal distraction.

"What, Mary? Oh, hello," he said vacantly.

He was merely a voiceless body, and the words came listlessly through his lips.

She rushed to the stove and turned the gas out. He realized that he had let the coffee pot burn, and was aware of the burning smell in the kitchen. He looked at her, a look which seemed to her like that of a guilty small boy, and immediately she thought of her dying son, and saw in his abashed and guilty expression, her son William in short pants, after being caught in some domestic misadventure. She commenced to cry. Seeing her drop her head, Lonigan appeared to wince. He moved clumsily to her, and awkwardly put his arms around her shoulder, and drew her against him.

"Father," she said in a moan.

"Now Mary, we got to be brave, you and me, and face whatever the Lord gives us. I know it's hard, but Mary, now you and me, we've come through a lot together, and we've still got each other," he said, and her body shook as she cried against his shoulder. She seemed not to have heard what he had said, and continued to choke and gasp out in moans.

1965   19

He patted her back, stroked her hair. . . .

He had nothing to say, and he looked aside. He felt like crying also. She finally turned from him and busied herself with washing out the burned coffee pot, and he stood helplessly by her side.

III

The white-garbed nurse looked down at the form of Studs Lonigan and smiled. He was resting easily now, and that was a hopeful sign. She sat back in her chair by the bedside, and yawned. There was a tremor in the body on the bed, and she dropped into a snooze.

Studs lay on the bed, and his body twitched. There was a twitch in his wasted face, a slight motion of a hand under the cover, the movement of his breathing beneath the sheet.

And Studs Lonigan walked along a strange street with a gun, and he said to himself

Al Capone Lonigan.

He pulled the gun out and shot at a man on the opposite side of the street who looked like Weary Reilley. He calmly walked along, and three policemen intruded on him, looking like Bull Mac Namara, the cop around Fifty-Eighth Street, used to look, and he pot-shotted them, and they dropped like felled logs.

Al Capone Lonigan.

He walked along, and he forgot that he was Al Capone Lonigan, and he thought to himself

I'm Jack Dempsey Lonigan.

He was no longer walking along a street, but he was entering a ring with two million people looking on, and he was the heavyweight champion of the world, and across from him, seated in the ring, there was Jim Jeffries, Jack Johnson, Jess Willard, Jack Dempsey, Gene Tunney, and Jack Sharkey, and he thought it funny that he would be fighting six men. And he thought, could they all be fighting at the same time, when they were not of the same age and some were old timers? He returned to his handler and manager, Lucy Scanlan, and he asked

How come?

They're fighting you. You can beat them. You can beat them because I have confidence in you, and I've always loved you.

He walked into the ring and he knocked. . . .

The nurse awakened from her snooze, and looked at him. He seemed to be resting, and again she heard him call out something in a feeble voice.

She felt his pulse, and bent down to listen to his heart, and then sat down again by his bedside.

Studs Lonigan rode on a railroad train, thinking that Lucy would be in the next town, and he would meet her. He had something to tell her, and he forgot what it was, but he felt that if he saw her, he would remember all over again what he had to tell her. The train was drawing near to the city where he would see Lucy, and it gathered speed, and shot right through, and Studs ran up and down the aisle yelling

Hey, stop the train!

The conductor came to him and said,

"This is a through train."

Well, stop it. I got to get off. I got to get off. I got to get off.

The conductor looked at him.

"Get off then," the conductor said. . . .

Studs ran to the end of the train, and . . . the last step, and there was Lucy. . . . He stood on the platform of the last car, knowing that he was a coward, and that out of cowardice, he had failed to see Lucy, and he felt that he had forever lost something.

Studs Lonigan walked through a jungle looking for Lucy. About him were lions and tigers, and he was constricted by a fear within him. Out of this fear, he lost suddenly his motive power, and he stood still, and felt himself to be shrinking, shrivelling up within, growing smaller, and if he did not check this growing smaller because of his fear, he would shrink to a pinpoint, or bust with fear. He saw Red Kelly walking by, unafraid, and he called

Oh, Red.

Red Kelly walked on, dressed like a hunter with a sunshade, puttees, white shorts, shirt, and long rifle. He saw Red disappear through a snarling group of lions and tigers.

Fly, he told himself. He raised his arms, and like a bird he floated through the air, without arms, over snarling packs of hungry carnivorous animals. He floated on, and. . . .

He seemed to float and fly, flapping armwings for a long indefinite period, and the pleasure he had derived from it changed to boredom, and then to fear, and looking down at the blue water, a terrible thirst burning in his body, his tongue dropping parched from his dry mouth, he wondered would he ever touch land, and would he ever again have a drink of water. A fear of unknown and threatening consequence blotted from his mind other things that stood in the part of his . . . and on and on he flew, parched and dry and afraid . . . he knew unless it stopped, unless he received water, unless his feet touched land, and he knew when and why he was there, he would come to some unhappy end. Clarity came to him, a clarity that told him that unless such a thing happened, he would die. Floating still, he knew that he was flying to death, and he knew that he did not want to die, and he . . . a deep and mournful sadness that he did not articulate in words, but that he felt vaguely. He looked at the water beneath him and around him, water running. . . .

I'm dying, he told himself.

On and on he flew, and suddenly, he was flying no more. He was standing in sand, and every step he took, his feet sank in sand, so that walking was slow and difficult. He walked on slowly, difficultly, tortured, directionless. He looked up at a sky in which there was a blazing hot sun, and he wondered, was he in Africa? He looked off, and beyond the stretch of sand he was crossing, in a far distance, there were trees, some kind of shrubbery and vegetable growth. He knew that he wanted to get there, and walking was slow. He went along in sand, and he could not remember where he was and where he was going to. All that he knew was . . . he was himself. He said to himself as he travelled

I am Studs Lonigan, the great Ham What Am!

He walked on. He had come from some place . . . pain. He was glad to be away from him. He could remember how there had been pain for him in the place from which he had come, and it lingered from him . . . he stood for a moment, his feet sinking in sand. . . .

He could not remember it, or what it was. He did not know where he was going, he knew nothing, and he walked tiredly forward, and again he was thirsty.

He fell down. He crawled on his hands and knees, feeling that it was a compulsion. He crawled feeling that he did not no more know how to walk, and ahead of him he saw a man walking, a man with his back turned, but with a walk and a figure and build that seemed to him familiar. He stopped and looked as the man moved ahead of him, unimpeded, with ease. He was awed that a man should be able to walk on his legs, instead of having to crawl. He was envious . . . a man could do that. He moved to catch up with the man to ask him how he could do such an astounding thing . . . walk on his legs. He crawled swiftly, and overtook the man, and he was Red Kelly, and Studs recognized him.

Red Kelly, why can you walk on your legs?

Your small fry brother, Red Kelly said, walked . . . leaving Studs alone and sad and envious and he crawled slowly with lowered head. . . .

In pain, Studs Lonigan sensed mistiness, and in this mistiness terror and danger. He sensed a sickness through a surrounding realm of this grayish blue mistiness, as if it were to attack him, to transport its danger from outside him to his body, his mind, his soul. He knew he was sick, and his soul was sick, and the world was unhappy, and he was unhappy, and he standing in it alone. If only he could hear a voice. If only he could see someone. If only he could see Lucy. Hear Lucy. Speak to Lucy. Or if not Lucy, then Catherine. Yes Catherine. Now he remembered. He had loved Lucy, and he had loved Catherine. He had loved and laid Catherine, and she had said to him, Studs jazz me when you want me, anytime, anywhere, anyplace . . . he had led her into sin, and the sin black on her soul was blacker on his own soul, and now he was . . . and sick in a sick world, unhappy in an unhappy world, sinful in a world of black sin, and around him there was mist, mist and no one, no voice, no voice of . . . no voice from Lucy, from Catherine, from friends or enemies, or angels.

He sat down. He was too sick and too fatigued. . . .

And Studs Lonigan understood. Clarity came to him, and the voice of his conscience said to him

Die, goddamn you, die, die like a dog. Die, you Lonigan louse, die like a mangy cur dog.

He sat there, looking from right to left, forward and behind him, his face distorted with terror and fear, and he knew something was happening to him. He sat there.

He took mist in his hand, and formed it, and he realized, in terror and abjectness, that he was anti-Christ. Anti-Christ Lonigan arose. He was afraid and knew that he was sinning, and he heard from beyond the mist, the powerful voice of God.

I am the Lord Thy God, and Thou shalt not have graven images before me!

He knew that he must not defy God, and Anti-Christ Lonigan was forced to defy God. He was compelled to stand up as the rival of God. He held the mist in his hands, and he said

. . . there be a sinful black world of orangemen . . .

. . . saw the mist spread . . .

. . . before him there was a . . .

. . . urine at his feet, and blessed himself lefthanded, and then, over the world, with his left hand, he spread the filthy holy water of his own urine, and said

As Anti-Christ, I say, let there be sin. Let there be birds and beasts, and flowers, and trees, and let there be males, and let there be females, and let the males be like tomcats, and let the females be like she bitch dogs, and let them jazz morning, and noon, and night, and let them jazz until their sin rises to heaven in a great and powerful stink like that of the Chicago stockyards.

And Anti-Christ on the fifth Sunday of February after Pentecost went on into the world of his own sinful creation, and Anti-Christ Lonigan walked amongst . . . cities, and over the plains, and across the mountains and down into the seas, and on the waters that were his own urine, and everywhere, amongst the birds and amongst the bees, and amongst the fishes, and . . . and cows, and cats, and men and women, he went, jazzing, and he said, everywhere he went

Let Heaven stink with the jazzing of my own . . .

. . . stink rose from the world of . . .

. . . the duty of leading his people in sin, and he jazzed in the mountains, and in the valleys, in the hills and in the dales, in the cities and in the villages, towns and hamlets, and on the plains, and the plateaus, and on the oceans, and he jazzed the fishes and the beasts of the fields, and the birds of the air, and he jazzed Lucy Scanlan, and he jazzed his sisters and his mother and his cousin, and he jazzed Catherine, and he jazzed Helen Shires, and Helen Borax, and he jazzed the sister of Weary Reilley, and the sister of Lucy Scanlan, and the sister of Helen Shires, and he jazzed until . . . God could no longer stand the stockyard stench . . . in his nostrils, and he turned his face away, and . . .

Amen, amen, verily I say unto you, I cannot stand the sinful smell of Studs Anti-Christ Lonigan, and he . . . and the world of his creation must die, and that . . . be death unto this world, for verily, verily, he is black with sin.

And Anti-Christ Lonigan flung himself on his knees . . . and looked up to high heavens where God . . .

Father, I say unto you, forgive me for I have jazzed. Father forgive me, and if you must, kill me, but let me die in the state of grace, and with the last Sacraments of the one holy true and apostolic church that takes up a collection every Sunday under the auspices of Father Gilhooley, who is known as the one and only Gilly Himself.

And God looked down upon Studs Anti-Christ Lonigan who knelt humbly in his own defecation, and God said unto him,

Verily, verily, go take a flying jazz at the moon and die!

And Studs Anti-Christ Lonigan knelt in his own defecation, and he lowered his head, and said unto himself

Verily, verily, verily, I must take a flying jazz at the moon and die.

And he raised himself, and said aloud

I go forth as I am told to jazz the moon.

He walked over the hills and over the dales . . . climbed up ladders of air to the moon . . . and he jazzed the moon, and then he stood again alone in a mist, and he knew that he must die. And he felt that if only he could have a drink of water, he would die. His throat dried. Parched, he tore at his hair, and cried out

Save me! Save me!

IV

The doctor looked at Studs. Studs lay there, wasted and breathing rapidly. He felt the pulse and found it feeble, 110 a minute. He talked in delirium, unascertainable . . . ugly sounds, out of which there were audible the words

Save me! Save me!

The doctor found that Studs had a high fever and an indication of pus in the lungs . . .

V

Studs Lonigan again seemed resting quietly. He saw himself clearly as a boy around Fifty-Eighth Street, the morning sunny, walking down Indiana Avenue. He felt that he should be happy, and he was unhappy. Sadly, his face moody, he walked slowly along, looking at the buildings, looking in at the building where Lucy Scanlan should live, but where he was sure she did not live, and seeing through dusty windows the interior of a furnitureless parlor.

He walked on. The buildings, all of them, he realized, were untenanted, and this was funny . . . none of the old people were there . . .

An awful loneliness was in him like some great thwarting obstacle.

Well, you got your wish, a voice told him.

What wish? he asked, seeing no one.

You wanted to be back here. Riding home from the wake of Shrimp Haggerty, you asked for your wish, and here it is, here is your wish. You're back on Fifty-Eighth Street, back on Indiana Avenue, back in the old neighborhood. You got what you want, I hope you're satisfied, the voice said.

Where is the old gang, said Studs.

All right, the voice said.

Studs turned, and saw walking toward him a procession of people, walking one by one. As they approached, a stout woman with four double chins smiled, walked up to him, kissed him, and he felt. . . .

Studs, you darling boy, said the woman.

Who are you? asked Studs.

I'm Lucy Scanlan, the woman said.

Studs looked at her. She walked on, and Studs saw in back of her a crummy little runt, who looked like a bum on West Madison Street.

Got a butt, Studs asked the crummy . . .

. . . Phil Rolfe, dressed in a jockey suit.

Studs, the riding is fine. I'm riding your kid sister, and Studs no man else ever rode her, and she was good riding in her day. But now I want some new riding, said Phil Rolfe, laughing lewdly.

Studs stood at the edge of the sidewalk, speechless.

Joe Thomas passed, small, and looking like hell, and he said

Studs, don't ever get without a job.

Studs, how you like my new suit, said Johnny O'Brien.

Studs, go wash your dirty mouth, said Helen Borax, a fat woman with a lorgnette.

Look at Studs, he hasn't changed, said Dan O'Neill, dressed in a gray suit.

Studs, go hop in, and stay hopped, said Weary Reilley in convict's stripes.

Studs, don't have crippled kids. When you have crippled kids, even jazzing doesn't pay, said . . . Simonsky.

Come on back in the alley and bend your . . . over a barrel, little boy, said Leon, the man . . . with a breast hanging through his shirt.

Studs turned. He did not want to see. . . .

Studs knew that he was in some unhappy and dangerous state, and something was happening to him, and he did not know what it was, and if his wish came true, it would not happen. He walked through an alley, down to Michigan, back along Fifty-Eighth Street to Prairie, and there he saw Barney Keefe, his pecker hanging out, with his false teeth tied to them.

Go home, you lousy Lonigan little brat, Barney said.

Studs looked at Barney, and walked on, saying nothing. He turned in the alley in back of the elevated, and there saw Father Gilhooley on an ash wagon, emptying ash cans, and he asked

Father, what's all the ashes?

Remember oh man that thou art dirty dust and to dirtier dust thou shalt return. Come on in, and give me your dirty ashes, the priest, dressed like an ash man, said, and Studs knew that he was dying, and that his wish was to live, and he wanted life.

He ran from the priest, feeling that in running from the priest dressed like an ash man, he was running from death, and he ran, but when he stopped . . . ashes, and he knew that he could not run. . . .

. . . and dirty, and the world was full of them, and they pelted Studs Lonigan.

Wherever he went, they pelted him, and he had no escape, and he stood, stormed under by them, choking, crying out

Help!

Mrs. Lonigan rushed sobbing into the room, and saw her son on the bed, and heard his feeble delirious cry of

Help!

Oh God! she loudly cried.

"Mrs. Lonigan, please be patient," the nurse said, moving toward her.

"Oh, God! Jesus, Mary and Joseph! Jesus, Mary and Joseph! He's dying, he's dying," she loudly cried.

"Mrs. Lonigan, please, please. Now you go and stop fretting yourself. He is not dying . . .

Disregarding the nurse, Mrs. Lonigan flung herself on her knees beside the bed, and looked through her teary eyes at her son, seeing him as in a fog . . .

Lonigan, having heard the cries from the kitchen, where he had been slumped over the table with his head down, asleep, appeared in the doorway, and winced, seeing Mary flung on the bed looking at Studs, and sighing from the sight of her boy. He moved slowly toward her. The will was out of him.

"Mary," he said.

"My son," she murmured, ignoring her husband's gentle word.

He patted her. He looked at his son, a sight which, he told himself, was scarcely bearable.

"Now Mary, come, you must get some sleep."

"My son," she said.

She arose, went to the dresser, and lit a holy candle. She walked from the room, and he followed her, a helpless man, looking on at a woman's, a mother's over-stimulated sorrow. She went to the dresser drawer, fished out . . .

She blessed herself with it, and knelt down to pray before the holy candle.

VI

Before him stood a thin woman, and for a moment, he knew not who she was. She was familiar, and old enough to be dried up. Her skin was tight against her bones. He looked at her. He realized that it was his mother. He did not want her there before him like that, a figure standing alone, with nothing else in sight, and she not plain, but shifting, her features and form becoming clear, and then unclear, as if he was drunk and seeing her drunk, or as if she was drunk, and not steady on her feet before him. She was nervous and excited.

"Honor thy God and thy mother!" she said, pointing an accusing finger at him.

"Your mother is your best friend," she then said, and he felt that her long, talon-like finger would be dug into his eye.

Yes, he said, meekly, wishing she would go away, not wanting her there.

Jesus Christ, he exclaimed to himself.

"You'll only have one mother," she said.

. . .

"When your mother dies, you'll never have another."

Thank God!

"No one loves you like your mother."

"God punishes a son who dishonors his mother."

Does God punish a son who jazzes his mother? Studs asked.

"If a son gives a mother one gray hair, he will merit the punishment of God," said his mother. His father pointed an accusing finger at him and said solemnly:

"Honor thy father and thy mother."

Screw you, said Studs.

"Nothing is as sacred as the home," the father and mother said.

And as goddamn unadulterated dull, said Studs.

"You'll never have a second home, and when you have your own home, and your own children, you will know the truth of what we say. You'll remember then, and say Mother and Dad were right, if I only had listened to them when I had the chance."

If I listened to them, where in the name of Christ would I be now? Shut up. Shut up, for Christ sake, shut up, you make my head dizzy and my ears go around, said Studs.

"The home is next to heaven, your father is next to God, and your mother is next to the Blessed Virgin Mary."

Whoops! said Studs, feeling a strangeness, feeling brave at saying things he had never had the heart to say and he only wished that people, some of the fellows were there, to hear him say these things.

. . .

S ing 'em, sing 'em, sing them blues, said Studs.

M is the million things she did for you.

O means only that she's growing older

T is for the tears she shed to save you.

H is for her heart of purest gold

E is for her eyes with lovelight shining

R is right and right she'll always be.

P ut them all together, they spell Mother

A word that means the world to me.

1965

27

To Friends in East and West

"A New Year's Greeting"

BORIS PASTERNAK

SOME JOURNALISTS were gathered in a certain newspaper office. They were talking about the imminent New Year's celebrations, and the usual New Year's wishes that would appear in the press. Everyone finally agreed that the best New Year's wish for 1958 would be one of peace for all the world,—as in the old prayers.

Must we remind ourselves how needful peace is and how sweet, and how irreparably terrible is war? It is almost embarrassing to pronounce these truisms, to have more or less the same thoughts as everyone else in the world, but—unlike most of them—instead of modestly keeping these truths to oneself, to publish them over one's signature, and get a fee for it.

In ancient times people saw nothing wrong with the use of armed force. But almost from earliest Christian times, war—the destruction of people—has come to be considered sinful and criminal. The idea of an international court of justice, to settle quarrels between different countries through goodwill instead of force, was first conceived in France, in the mediaeval urban communities of the twelfth century. Since then, through the centuries, philosophers have gone on writing about everlasting peace; and to tell the story of this dream is to recite the names of all the moral philosophers from Augustine to Kant and Tolstoy. But we will approach the question more simply, without too much learning; like an ordinary everyday matter.

People usually think something like this—"Life is heaven just now; we've got no worries—except maybe that a fly might settle on us. Don't trouble our bliss; go away and don't disturb us."

I think the opposite argument carries far more conviction. It is precisely because Heaven is still so far away (and who wants it anyway—this imaginary, unreal

---

This article was published in *Literaturnaya Rossiya* (Literary Russia) January 1st, 1965. The editor's note stated that the manuscript was found in Pasternak's archive, dated December 20th, 1957, and that it was now being published (with slight omissions) as the ideas and wishes were "still of interest for the reader."

Heaven, boring as everything that does not exist)—it is precisely because you are displeased with us, annoyed with us about something—and because we are none too pleased with ourselves—that you should leave us alone.

*Let Life itself patiently and naturally round off and smooth out what was begun in storm and violence. Don't meddle with its transformations. Don't hinder it. Because not a single war has ever taken away the evil it was supposedly started against; the evil has always been strengthened and perpetuated.**—Or do you expect no changes from us, do you think we have begun to stagnate? That all we can do is re-name our cities and streets, that we are incapable of any further change or improvement? But perhaps we were so impoverished and so overwhelmed by the labour of destruction and transformation—which your prophets of enlightenment had been preaching for the last hundred years, and which we alone undertook for the whole world—that we do not want any more upheavals yet, we haven't yet come to our senses, we haven't got our breath back.

To think back on it, it really might have seemed for a long time that these mirages and prophecies, this flower of nineteenth-century thought, this socialist dream would always remain an adornment of political journalism, would never come out of the books, would never actually come true.

But here was a country where people, pure in heart as children, did not trifle with their words. They took everything seriously, and words were laws for them; they considered that if something was said, it had to be done. And they plunged recklessly, without thinking twice, into the maelstrom of their (and—mainly—your) theories. They achieved the new political maturity you had proclaimed, and they alone in all the world have passed through it. What had been so long planned, prepared and postponed, came to pass. Thank us that this is done; that it is behind us.

And thank us for this too. Our revolution set the tone for yours, however great the difference between them; it filled this century with sense and meaning. Not only we, and our younger generation—even your banker's son is not the same as his father and grandfather were before him. He may be more cynical and less well-educated than they were, but he is simpler and less long-winded, his spirit is wiser and closer to the truth. He no longer believes in the divine origin of property, nor thinks that with his savings he can conquer death. He enters life unencumbered, as a man should: he comes as a guest to the feast of existence, and knows that what matters is not how much he inherits but how he behaves at the feast, and what people remember and love him for.

Thank us then for this new man, even in your old society; thank us that he is livelier, finer-witted and more gifted than his heavy and pompous predecessors; for this child of the century was delivered in the maternity home called Russia.

So should we not rather peacefully exchange good wishes for the coming New Year, and hope that no echoes of warlike thunder mingle with the popping of corks as it comes in, nor are heard later in the course of it, or in succeeding years.

But if fate has decreed a disaster, then remember the events that formed us, and what a severe and hardening school they were. There is no-one more desperate

---

*..........**The lines between the asterisks were left out in the Russian publication.

than we, no-one more prepared to do the impossible and unbelievable; and any challenge to war will turn us all into so many heroes, as our recent ordeal has shown.

Translated by NICHOLAS SLATER

LEONARD BASKIN. *JOB.* (*TQ* #4)

Three essays

ROLAND BARTHES

Strip-Tease

THE STRIP-TEASE—at least the Parisian variety—is based on a contradiction: woman desexualized even as she is denuded. Hence we are offered a terrorist spectacle, or rather, a "frighten-me" one—as if eroticism here remained a kind of delicious alarm, whose ritual signs suffice to provoke both the notion of sex and its exorcism.

The mere duration of the undressing turns the public into voyeurs; but here, as in any spectacle of mystification, the decor, the accessories, and the stereotypes contradict the initial provocation of the enterprise and end by engulfing it in insignificance: sin is *paraded* the better to embarrass and exorcise it. The French strip-tease seems to utilize what I have elsewhere called Operation Astra, a method of mystification which consists in vaccinating the public with a drop of sin, the better to plunge that public, subsequently, into a henceforth immunized Morality: a few atoms of eroticism, designated by the very situation of the spectacle, are in fact absorbed into a reassuring ritual which effaces the flesh as surely as a vaccine or a taboo arrest and contain a disease or a transgression.

Hence we get, in the strip-tease, a whole series of screens set before the woman's body, even as she pretends to undress that body. Exoticism is the first of these distances, for there is always a frozen exoticism involved, one which alienates the body into the fabulous or the fictional: the Chinese Siren armed with an opium pipe (that obligatory symbol of Sinicism), the undulating Vamp with her gigantic cigarette-holder, the Venetian courtesan with her gondola and serenading gondolier —all these aim at constituting woman, *from the start*, as a disguised object; the goal of the strip-tease is thus no longer to draw out into the light a secret depth, but to signify nakedness, through the removal of a baroque and artificial vesture, as the *natural* clothing of woman, in other words, to rediscover, finally, a perfectly modest state of the flesh.

The classic accessories of the burlesque-theater and the music-hall, mobilized here without exception, also alienate the undressed body at every moment, forcing it into the enveloping comfort of a familiar rite: furs, fans, gloves, feathers, net-stockings—in a word, the entire range of adornment—constantly reintegrate the living body into the category of those luxurious objects which surround man with a magical decor. Furred or gloved, a woman parades herself here as a frozen music-hall element; and to strip herself of such ritual objects now has nothing to do with a new divesting: furs, feathers, and gloves continue to impregnate her with their magical virtue even once they are removed, afford a kind of enveloping memory of a luxurious carapace, for it is an obvious law that the entire strip-tease is *given* in the very nature of the initial garment. If the latter is improbable, as in the case of the Chinese Siren or the Venus in Furs, the ensuing nude remains quite unreal herself, as smooth and impenetrable as a lovely, slippery object, alienated by its very extravagance from human use: this is the profound meaning of the diamond- or sequin-sewn G-string, which is the very goal of the strip-tease: that ultimate triangle, but whose pure and geometric form, by its hard, glittering substance, bars the sex like a chastity belt and definitively ejects woman into a mineralogical universe, the (precious) stone here constituting the irrefutable theme of the total and useless object.

Contrary to common prejudice, the dance which accompanies the whole of the strip-tease is not an erotic factor at all; it is probably, in fact, quite the opposite. The more or less rhythmic undulation here exorcises the terror of immobility; not only does it afford the spectacle the guarantee of Art (burlesque dances are always "artistic"), but above all it constitutes the last and the most effective screen: the dance, consisting of ritual gestures seen a thousand times, functions as a cosmetic of movements, conceals nudity, coats the spectacle with a glaze of useless and yet leading gestures, for here undressing is relegated to the rank of a parasitical operation conducted in an improbable distance. Thus we see the professionals of strip-tease cloak themselves in a miraculous ease which ceaselessly envelops them, removes them, gives them the icy indifference of skillful practitioners, arrogantly taking refuge in the certitude of their technique: their dexterity clothes them like a garment.

All this scrupulous exorcism of sex can be verified *a contrario* in amateur strip-tease contests: the "beginners" remove their clothes before several hundred spectators without resorting, or resorting very clumsily, to magic, which incontestably reestablishes the erotic power of the spectacle. Here, at the start, we find nowhere near so many Chinese or Spanish numbers, neither feathers nor furs (simple outfits, street wear), few original disguises: clumsy steps, inadequate dances, the girl continually trapped by immobility and, above all, a "technical" embarrassment (resistance of panties, the dress catching on the bra, etc.) which gives the gestures of revelation an unexpected importance, denying the woman the alibi of art and the refuge of the object, confining her within a condition of weakness and timidity.

Yet, at the *Moulin Rouge*, an exorcism of another kind appears, probably typically French, an exorcism which seeks, moreover, to domesticate rather than to abolish eroticism: the master of ceremonies attempts to give the strip-tease a reassuring *petit-bourgeois* status. First of all, the strip-tease is a *sport*—there is a Strip-Tease Club, which organizes healthy competitions whose prizewinners emerge crowned, rewarded by edifying prizes (a course of physical-culture treatments), a novel (which *has* to be Robbe-Grillet's *Voyeur*), or useful trophies (a pair of nylons, five-hundred francs). Then, the strip-tease is identified with a *career* (beginners, semi-professionals, pros), that is, with the honorable exercise of a specialty (the strip-tease "artists" are qualified workers); even the magical alibi of work can be accorded: *vocation* (one girl is "on her way" or "likely to fulfill her promise", or else "taking her first steps" on the arduous runway of strip-tease). Finally, and especially, the competitors are placed socially: one is a salesgirl, another a secretary (there are a great many secretaries in the Strip-Tease Club). Thus the strip-tease reunites the hall, acclimatizes itself, turns bourgeois, as if the French, unlike the American public (at least from what I have been told), and following an irrepressible tendency of their social status, could conceive of eroticism only as a household property, "covered" by the alibi of a bi-weekly sport, much more than by that of the magical spectacle: this is how, in France, the strip-tease is nationalized.

Billy Graham Comes to Paris

So MANY MISSIONARIES have reported on the religious customs of "Primitives" that it is really too bad there wasn't a Papuan witch-doctor at the Vel' d'Hiv' the other night to tell us about the ceremony Doctor Graham conducted under the name of an evangelical campaign. For there is some splendid anthropological material here which seems, moreover, inherited from certain "savage" cultures, presenting as it does, under an immediate aspect, the three great phases of every religious act: Expectation, Suggestion, Initiation.

Billy Graham makes us wait for him: hymns, invocations, a thousand futile little talks entrusted to walk-on pastors or to American impresarios (the jolly introduction of the troupe: Smith the pianist from Toronto, Beverly the soprano from Chicago, "a star of American radio and television, a truly wonderful Gospel singer")–a long spiel precedes Doctor Graham, who is continuously being announced and who never appears. At last he is with us, but only to transfer our curiosity all the more effectively, for his first speech is not *the good one:* he is only preparing us for the coming of the *Message.* And more interludes prolong our expectation, warm up the house, assign in advance a prophetic importance to this message, which according to the theater's best traditions begins by making itself desired in order to exist all the more readily afterwards.

In this first phase of the ceremony we recognize that great sociological resource called Expectation (*Waiting on God*), of which the recent demonstrations of the hypnotist Le Grand Robert have already furnished a modern example in Paris. Here too the Mage's appearance was postponed as long as possible, and by repeated artifices the public was worked up to that pitch of anxious curiosity which is quite ready to see in fact what it is made to expect. Similarly, from the first moment, Billy Graham is presented as a true prophet, through whom we entreat the Spirit of God to be so good as to descend, this evening in particular: it is an Inspired

Prophet who will speak to us, the public is invited to observe the spectacle of a man possessed: we are asked in advance to take the words of Billy Graham as literally divine.

If God does speak through Dr. Graham's mouth, it must be confessed that God is a dunce: the Message is astonishing for its banality, its childishness. In any case, God is certainly no longer a Thomist, he avoids logic like the plague: the Message consists of a kind of buckshot of broken affirmations which are quite unrelated to each other, and which have as their sole content the tautology God is God. The dullest Marist Brother, the most academic pastor would look like a decadent intellectual beside Dr. Graham. Reporters, deceived by the Huguenot decor of the ceremony (hymns, prayer, sermon, benediction), lulled by the soothing compunction of Protestant worship, have praised Dr. Graham and his troupe for their restraint: we expected some form of *outré* Americanism, girls, jazz, and a few red-hot metaphors (there were two or three of these, at least). Billy Graham has no doubt filtered everything picturesque out of his sessions, and French Protestants found them quite acceptable. Nonetheless Billy Graham's manner breaks a whole tradition of the sermon, whether Catholic or Protestant, inherited from classical culture, and which is that of a need *to persuade*. Western Christianity has always submitted itself, in its exposition, to the general form of Aristotelian thought, it has always agreed to come to terms with reason, even when it was accrediting the irrationality of faith. Breaking with centuries of humanism (even if the forms may have been hollow and rigid, the concern for the Other, the audience, has rarely been absent from Christian didacticism), Dr. Graham brings us a method of magical transformation: he substitutes suggestion for persuasion: the pressure of the argument, the systematic elimination of any rational content from the proposition, the constant breaking-off of logical trains of thought, the verbal repetitions, the grandiloquent designation of the Bible held in an outstretched hand like some universal snake-oil remedy, and above all the absence of warmth, the manifest contempt for the audience's presence—all these operations are part of the classical material of the music-hall hypnotist: as I said, there is no difference between Billy Graham and Le Grand Robert.

And just as Le Grand Robert ended the preparation of his public by a special selection, calling up to the stage the Chosen People of hypnosis, entrusting certain privileged beings with the burden of a spectacular capacity for torpor, Billy Graham crowns his Message by a material segregation of the Elect: the neophytes who the other evening at the Vel' d'Hiv, among the advertisements for Super Dissolution and Cognac Polignac, "received Christ" under the influence of the magical Message were herded to a room apart, and if they spoke English, to a still more secret crypt: it matters little enough what happened there—whether inscription on the conversion lists, new sermons, spiritual conferences with the "counsellors", or collections—this new episode is the formal ersatz of Initiation.

All this concerns us quite directly: first of all, Billy Graham's "success" manifests the mental fragility of the French *petite bourgeoisie*, a class from which the public of these sessions appears to be chiefly recruited: the plasticity of this public to alogical and hypnotic forms of thought suggests that there exists in this social group what one might call a situation of risk: a part of the French *petite bourgeoisie* is no longer even protected by its famous *bon sens*, which is the aggressive form of its class consciousness. But that is not all: Billy Graham and his troupe have heavily and repeatedly emphasized the purpose of their campaign: "to awaken" France ("We have seen God do great things in America; an awakening, in Paris, would produce a tremendous influence the whole world over." "What we want is for something to happen in Paris which will have repercussions throughout the entire world."). Apparently the point of view is the same as President Eisenhower's in his remarks on French atheism. France is distinguished by her rationalism, her indifference to faith and the irreligion of her intellectuals (a theme common to America and the Vatican; moreover, a theme greatly overrated): it is from this bad dream that she must be awakened. The "conversion" of Paris would obviously have the value of a world-wide example: Atheism KO'd in its very stronghold.

Obviously we are dealing here with a political theme: France's atheism interests America because it appears to be the preliminary face of Communism. "To awaken" France from atheism is to awaken her from the Communist spell. Billy Graham's campaign has been nothing more than a McCarthyist episode.

Einstein's Brain

EINSTEIN'S BRAIN is a mythical object: paradoxically, our image of supreme intelligence is that of a perfected mechanism; when man is too powerful, we isolate him from psychology and install him in a world of robots (science fiction shows that there is always something reified about supermen). Einstein too: he is ordinarily expressed by his brain, an anthological organ, a true museum-piece. Perhaps because of his mathematical specialization, the superman Einstein is divested of any magical character; he has no diffuse potency, no mystery save the mechanical: he *is* a superior organ, prodigious but real, even physiological. In terms of myth, Einstein is matter, his power does not spontaneously produce spirituality, but requires the assistance of an independent morality, the remedy of the savant's "conscience" (*science without conscience*, the saying goes . . .)

Einstein himself contributed something to the legend by bequeathing his brain, which two hospitals fought over as though it were some unheard-of machine that could at last be dismantled. One photograph shows him lying down, his head bristling with electric wires: his brain waves are being registered while he is asked to "think about relativity". (But as a matter of fact, what does "think about" mean?) We are doubtless meant to assume that the seismograms will be all the more violent since "relativity" is a difficult subject. Thought itself is thus represented as an energetic substance, the measurable product of a complex (virtually electric) apparatus which transforms the cerebral matter into power. The mythology of Einstein makes him so un-magical a genius that we speak of his thought as of some functional labor, analogous to the mechanical manufacture of sausages, the milling of grain or the smelting of ore: Einstein produced thought, continuously, as the mill produces flour, and death, for him, was above all the cessation of a localized function: *"the world's most powerful brain has stopped thinking."*

What this mechanism of genius was supposed to produce was equations. With the help of the Einstein mythology, the world delightedly recovered the image of a formulated knowledge. Paradoxically, the more the man's genius was materialized in the nature of his brain, the closer the product of its invention approached a magical condition, reincarnated the old esoteric image of a *scientia* compassed in a few letters. There is a secret that explains the world, and this secret is contained in a formula, the universe is a safe whose combination humanity is searching for: Einstein almost found it—that is the myth of Einstein; in it we rediscover all the Gnostic themes: the unity of nature, the ideal possibility of a fundamental reduction of the world, the open-sesame of a formula, the ancestral conflict between a secret and a magic word, the notion that total knowledge can be had only at a single stroke, like a lock that suddenly yields after a thousand fruitless fumblings. The historic equation $E = mc^2$, by its unexpected simplicity, virtually realized the pure idea of the key—naked, linear, made of a single metal, opening with magical ease a door with which Humanity had struggled for centuries. The iconography shows this clearly: in *photographs*, Einstein stands beside a blackboard covered with mathematical symbols of an evident complexity; but in *drawings* (that is, in legend), the chalk still in his hand, he has just written on an empty slate, as though without any preparation whatever, the world's magic formula. Thus mythology respects the nature of various tasks: research proper mobilizes mechanical means and its seat is a material organ monstrous only in its cybernetic complication; discovery, on the contrary, is of a magical essence, is simple as a primordial, principial body, the Philosopher's Stone of the Hermetics, Berkeley's tarwater, Schelling's oxygen.

But since the world continues, since research still proliferates and since, too, God's share must be secured, Einstein must suffer a certain failure: Einstein died, we are told, without having been able to verify *"the equation for the secret of the universe."* In other words, the world resisted him; no sooner broached than the secret closed up again, the cipher was incomplete. Thus Einstein fully satisfies the myth, which brooks any contradiction provided it establishes its euphoriac security: both mage and machine, eternal seeker and unfulfilled finder, releasing the best and the worst upon us, brain and conscience, Einstein satisfies the most contradictory dreams, mythically reconciles man's infinite power over nature with the "fatality" of the sacred which he still cannot reject.

translated by Richard Howard

Two stories

RICHARD BRAUTIGAN

Revenge of the lawn

MY GRANDMOTHER, in her own way, shines like a beacon down the stormy American past. She was a bootlegger in a little county up in the state of Washington. She was also a handsome woman, close to six feet tall who carried 190 pounds in the grand operatic manner of the early 1900s. And her specialty was bourbon, a little raw but a welcomed refreshment in those Volstead Act days.

She of course was no female Al Capone, but her bootlegging feats were the cornucopia of legend in her neck of the woods, as they say. She had the county in her pocket for years. The sheriff used to call her up every morning and give her the weather report and tell her how the chickens were laying.

I can imagine her talking to the sheriff: "Well, Sheriff, I hope your mother gets better soon. I had a cold and a bad sore throat last week myself. I've still got the sniffles. Tell her hello for me and to drop by the next time she's down this way. And if you want that case, you can pick it up or I can have it sent over as soon as Jack gets back with the car.

"No, I don't know if I'm going to the firemen's ball this year, but you know that my heart is with the firemen. If you don't see me there tonight, you tell the boys that. No, I'll try to get there, but I'm still not fully recovered from my cold. It kind of climbs on me in the evening."

My grandmother lived in a three-story house that was old even in those days. There was a pear tree in the front yard which was heavily eroded by rain from years of not having any lawn.

The picket fence that once enclosed the lawn was gone too, and people just drove their cars right up to the porch. In the winter the front yard was a mud hole and in the summer it was hard as a rock.

Jack used to curse the front yard as if it were a living thing. He was the man who lived with my grandmother for thirty years. He was not my grandfather, but an Italian who came down the road one day selling lots in Florida.

He was selling a vision of eternal oranges and sunshine door to door in a land where people ate apples and it rained a lot.

Jack stopped at my grandmother's house to sell her a lot just a stone's throw from downtown Miami, and he was delivering her whiskey a week later. He stayed for thirty years and Florida went on without him.

Jack hated the front yard because he thought it was against him. There had been a beautiful lawn there when Jack came along, but he let it wander off into nothing. He refused to water it or take care of it in any way.

Now the ground was so hard that it gave his car flat tires in the summer. The yard was always finding a nail to put in one of his tires or the car was always sinking out of sight in the winter when the rains came on.

The lawn had belonged to my grandfather who lived out the end of his life in an insane asylum. It had been his pride and joy and was said to be the place where his powers came from.

My grandfather was a minor Washington mystic who in 1911 prophesied the exact date when World War I would start: June 28, 1914, but it had been too much for him. He never got to enjoy the fruit of his labor because they had to put him away in 1913 and he spent seventeen years in the state insane asylum believing he was a child and it was actually May 3, 1872.

He believed that he was six years old and it was a cloudy day about to rain and his mother was baking a chocolate cake. It stayed May 3, 1872 for my grandfather until he died in 1930. It took seventeen years for that chocolate cake to be baked.

There was a photograph of my grandfather. I look a great deal like him. The only difference being that I am over six feet tall and he was not quite five feet tall. He had a dark idea that being so short, so close to the earth and his lawn would help to prophesy the exact date when World War I would start.

It was a shame that the war started without him. If only he could have held back his childhood for another year, avoided that chocolate cake, all of his dreams would have come true.

There were always two large dents in my grandmother's house that had never been repaired and one of them came about this way: In the autumn the pears would get ripe on the tree in the front yard and the pears would fall on the ground and rot and bees would gather by the hundreds to swarm on them.

The bees somewhere along the line had picked up the habit of stinging Jack two or three times a year. They would sting him in the most ingenious ways.

Once a bee got in his wallet and he went down to the store to buy some food for dinner, not knowing the mischief that he carried in his pocket.

He took out his wallet to pay for the food.

"That will be 72 cents," the grocer said.

"AAAAAAAAAAAAAAAAAAAAA!" Jack replied, looking down to see a bee busy stinging him on the little finger.

The first large dent in the house was brought about by still another bee landing on Jack's cigar as he was driving the car into the front yard that peary autumn the stock market crashed.

The bee ran down the cigar, Jack could only stare at it cross eyed in terror, and stung him on the upper lip. His reaction to this was to drive the car immediately into the house.

That front yard had quite a history after Jack let the lawn go to hell. One day in 1932 Jack was off running an errand or delivering something for my grandmother. She wanted to dump the old mash and get a new batch going.

Because Jack was gone, she decided to do it herself. Grandmother put on a pair of railroad overalls that she used for working around the still and filled a wheelbarrow with mash and dumped it out in the front yard.

She had a flock of snow-white geese that roamed outside the house and nested in the garage that had not been used to park the car since the time Jack had come along selling futures in Florida.

Jack had some kind of idea that it was all wrong for a car to have a house. I think it was something that he had learned in the old country. The answer was in Italian because that was the only language Jack used when he talked about the garage. For everything else he used English, but it was only Italian for the garage.

After Grandmother had dumped the mash on the ground near the pear tree, she went back to the still down in the basement and the geese all gathered around the mash and started talking it over.

I guess they came to a mutually agreeable decision because they all started eating the mash. As they ate the mash their eyes got brighter and brighter and their voices, in appreciation of the mash, got louder and louder.

After a while one of the geese stuck his head in the mash and forgot to take it out. Another one of the geese cackled madly and tried to stand on one leg and give a W. C. Field's imitation of a stork. He maintained that position for about a minute before he fell on his tail feathers.

My grandmother found them all lying around the mash in the positions that they had fallen. They looked as if they had been machine-gunned. From the height of her operatic splendor she thought that they were all dead.

She responded to this by plucking all their feathers and piling their bald bodies in the wheelbarrow and wheeling them down to the basement. She had to make five trips to accommodate them.

She stacked them like cordwood near the still and waited for Jack to return and dispose of them in a way that would provide a goose for dinner and a small profit by selling the rest of the flock in town. She went upstairs to take a nap after finishing with the still.

It was about an hour later that the geese woke up. They had devastating hangovers. They had all kind of gathered themselves uselessly to their feet when suddenly one of the geese noticed that he did not have any feathers. He informed the other geese of their condition, too. They were all in despair.

They paraded out of the basement in a forlorn and wobbly gang. They were all standing in a cluster near the pear tree when Jack drove into the front yard.

The memory of the time he had been stung on the mouth by that bee must have come back to his mind when he saw the defeathered geese standing there, because suddenly like a madman he tore out the cigar he had stuck in his mouth and threw it away from him as hard as he could. This caused his hand to travel through the windshield. A feat that cost him 32 stitches.

The geese stood by staring on like some helpless, primitive American advertisement for aspirin under the pear tree as Jack drove his car into the house for the second and last time in the Twentieth Century.

* * *

The first time I remember anything in life occurred in my grandmother's front yard. The year was either 1936 or 1937. I remember a man, probably Jack, cutting down the pear tree and soaking it with kerosene.

It looked strange, even for a first memory of life, to watch a man pour gallons and gallons of kerosene all over a tree lying stretched out thirty feet or so on the ground, and then to set fire to it while the fruit was still green on the branches.

A short history of religion in California

THERE'S ONLY one way to get into it: we saw the deer in the meadow. The deer turned in a slow circle and then broke the circle and went toward some trees.

There were three deer in the meadow and we were three people. I, a friend and my daughter 3½ years old. "See the deer," I said, pointing the way to the deer.

"Look the deer! There! There!" she said and surged against me as I held her in the front seat. A little jolt of electricity had come to her from the deer. Three little gray dams went away into the trees, celebrating a TVA of hoofs.

She talked about the deer as we drove back to our camp in Yosemite. "Those deer are really something," she said. "I'd like to be a deer."

When we turned into our campground there were three deer standing at the entrance, looking at us. They were the same three deer or they were three different ones.

"Look the deer!" and the same electrical surge against me, enough perhaps to light a couple of Christmas tree lights or make a fan turn for a minute or toast half-a-slice of bread.

The deer followed close behind the car as we drove at deer speed into the camp. When we got out of the car, the deer were there. My daughter took out after them. Wow! The deer!

I slowed her down. "Wait," I said. "Let Daddy take your hand." I didn't want her to scare them or get hurt by them either, in case they should panic and run over her, a next to impossible thing.

We followed after the deer, a little ways behind and then stopped to watch them cross the river. The river was shallow and the deer stopped in the middle and looked in three different directions.

She stared at them, not saying anything for a while. How quiet and beautiful they looked and then she said, "Daddy, take off the deer's head and put it on my head. Take off the deer's feet, put them on my feet. And I'll be the deer."

The deer stopped looking in three different directions. They all looked in one direction toward the trees on the other side of the river and moved off into those trees.

So the next morning there was a band of Christians camping beside us because it was Sunday. There were about twenty or thirty of them seated at a long wooden table. They were singing hymns while we were taking down our tent.

My daughter watched them very carefully and then walked over to peek out at them from behind a tree as they sang on. There was a man leading them. He waved his hands in the air. Probably their minister.

My daughter watched them very carefully and then moved out from behind the tree and slowly advanced until she was right behind their minister, looking up at him. He was standing out there alone and she was standing out there alone with him.

I pulled the metal tent stakes out of the ground and put them together in a neat pile, and I folded the tent and put it beside the tent stakes.

Then one of the Christian women got up from the long table and walked over to my daughter. I was watching this. She gave her a piece of cake and asked her if she wanted to sit down and listen to the singing. They were busy singing something about Jesus doing something good for them.

My daughter nodded her head and sat down on the ground. She held the piece of cake in her lap. She sat there for five minutes. She did not take a bite out of the piece of cake.

They were now singing something about Mary and Joseph doing something. In the song it was winter and cold and there was straw in the barn. It smelled good.

She listened for about five minutes and then she got up, waved good-bye in the middle of *We Three Kings of Orient Are* and came back with the piece of cake.

"Well, how was that?" I said.

"Singing," she said, pointing they are singing.

"How's the cake?" I said.

"I don't know," she said and threw it on the ground. "I've already had breakfast." It lay there.

I thought about the three deer and the Christians singing. I looked at the piece of cake and to the river where the deer had been gone for a day.

The cake was very small on the ground. The water flowed over the rocks. A bird or an animal would eat the cake later on and then go down to the river for a drink of water.

A little thing came to my mind and having no other choice: it pleased me, so I hugged my arms around a tree and my cheek sailed to the sweet bark and floated there for a few gentle moments in the calm.

1966

LEONARD BASKIN. *DOG IN THE MEADOW.* (*TQ* #5)

In a hole

GEORGE P. ELLIOTT

I AM IN A HOLE. At first I did not want to get out of the hole. It was a sort of relief to be in it. In my city we are prepared for cataclysms. You cannot be sure which kind of destruction is going to catch you, but one or another is pretty sure to. In fact, I am lucky. I am nearly forty and this is the first one to catch me. Properly speaking, I am not caught yet, for I am still alive and not even injured. When I first came to in this hole and realized what had happened and where I was, I had no impulse to get out. I was afraid of finding the city in rubble, even though I knew we were a tough people and would rebuild it as we had done more than once before. My first thought was: caught at last. Perhaps the shock had stunned me. In any case, I certainly felt relieved of anxiety, my worry about how and when trouble was going to find me was over.

Our city is great and strong. Yet when it was founded over three hundred years ago, our forefathers were warned against the location. We are at the tip of a promontory at the extreme west of the continent, situated on a geological fault—typhoons rake us—the land is sterile, everything worth having must be brought to us from outside—our people are immigrants, dissatisfied and ambitious, we have not brought many of our ancestors' myths with us, we are eager to rid ourselves of customs, we are unruly and rely on police to keep us in order—no matter how rich we are, no matter how hard we work, we are always overcrowded—despite the researches of our dieticians, we have many nutritional ailments, new ones springing up among us as fast as the old ones are cured. Perhaps the hardships of our location have tested us and made us tough, and our founding fathers knew this would be the case. They were stubborn in choosing this raw location. We question their wisdom, we grumble, we analyze the possibilities. But we do not seriously complain, we have no real intention of rebelling, even if we did it is dangerous to say anything but what is expected. We are too rich from trade, we are richer than we can explain, we are envied by outsiders who do not appreciate the extent and nature of our troubles. They have no idea how troubling it is not to know when and how you will be caught. One can never forget it here for long. Perhaps because of our difficulty with food, threats are always alive in our minds, ready to leap at us. No matter how much we eat, no matter what our dieticians do, no matter what chefs we import to make our food savory, we suffer from malnutrition. We are fat and undernourished. The stupid are luckiest for they do not know they lack. The wise suffer most. There are a few who make a virtue of fasting and austerity; they say they are at peace; but I have never seen one look me in the eye when he said it. They look up at the sky or out to sea, and talk of love and peace and truth. Their strict diet makes their skin rough and scaly, their nails thicken and turn blue, their eyes become vague. They do not bother people much, nobody cares enough to restrain them. We keep on trying to improve our diet, we hold conferences and symposiums on the subject, it has become the subject of our most intensive experiments.

An earthquake caught me. It was quite a severe one, but I don't think it was as bad as the one that killed a third of our people when I was a young man. I was nimble and quick, and came through with nothing worse than a few bruises. In that one, great chasms opened, whereas the hole I am in now is not more than twenty feet deep. This one caught me just as I was coming out of the telephone building.

I had gone there to argue about a mistake on my bill. They had charged me for two long distance calls to Rome the month before. Absurd! Neither my wife nor I would dream of talking with anyone at such a distance. Overseas connections are notoriously unreliable, even with our communications system, our greatest civic pride—we would be able to talk with the moon if there were anyone there to talk to. Neither my wife nor I have any friends in Rome. It is true that I have corresponded for years with a numismatist in Rome — I collect old coins — but our common interest conceals the profoundest disagreement. I would do much to avoid meeting him in person, should he ever propose such a thing, as he has never shown the slightest sign of doing. To him ancient coins are objects of trade, their value varies from time to time but at any given moment it can be agreed upon, they are commodities. I would never expose to him the slightest edge of what they mean to me, of the speculations they excite in me. (A drachma which was worth many loaves of bread two thousand years ago is now worth nothing— except to a few antiquarians like me, to whom it means a hundred times more than it did then. I look at it unable to comprehend. If I did comprehend, it would cease to be worth even a slice of bread to me. Do all those to whom it is worthless understand something that eludes me?) The numismatist and I share no language but the code of catalogues. We would not be able to talk to one another face to face, much less over the telephone. And the length of time these supposed long distance calls went on! One lasted an hour, the other nearly as long. I went to the telephone building to complain, politely of course, but firmly. They had to prove that my wife or I had made such preposterous calls. They said they would find out who it was the call had gone to—both calls to Rome were to the same number. I saw they did not believe me. I knew that legally they could not force me to pay if I denied responsibility. All the same, I was not feeling cleanly victorious as I left the building.

I was thrown to the street. I remember seeing the façade of the telephone building topple out towards me in one slab, then crack and buckle. When I came to my senses, I was in this hole. There was still dust in the air. I stood up. coughed, and wiped my eyes. The rubble at the bottom of the hole was all small stuff, no boulders or big chunks of material. There was a good deal of light coming down the chimney above me; it could not be late in the day; I had not been out long. I got up, stiff, creaking a bit, but uninjured, and I inspected the hole I was in. It was shaped like a funnel, big end down. The bottom of the chimney was at least five feet above my head, and the chimney itself appeared to extend up another eight or nine feet. The walls of the cone I was in were of chunks of rock propped on one another. To remove one would risk making the whole haphazard structure fall in. I yelled. There was no answer, no answering noise, no noise of any sort. I whistled and shouted. The echo hurt my ears. I collapsed. At that moment I realized I did not want to get out. Not till light returned next morning did my forces rally.

Hunger drove me. At first, choked with dust, I suffered badly from thirst. But during the night it rained, and enough rain water dripped down for me to refresh my mouth and rinse my face. Then hunger pulled me up from my lethargy. I determined not to die alone. I would get out if I could.

But how? I yelled for help, there was no response. Once I got up into the chimney above me, I would be able to brace myself back and knees like a mountain climber and inch my way up. But getting myself into the chimney, that was the problem. The walls sloped back, only an experienced mountain climber with equipment would even try to climb them. There was nothing else to be done— I would have to build a pile of rocks to climb up on so that I could insert my body into the chimney. I tried to pull one of the boulders free but it was lodged too tight to budge. Another was as tight; another, another. Then one moved a little as I pulled and pushed. But when it moved, there were ominous shiftings in the wall above me, and a stone as big as my fist sprang out from just over my head, narrowly missing me. All the other boulders I could reach were wedged tight. I pulled at the loose one again. Suddenly half of it broke free and I fell on my back. It was of rotten stone, it crumbled, I had gained nothing.

I complained. If there had been anyone to hear me I would never have been so self-indulgent as to complain. But I was alone and not quite hopeless. I stood with legs spread, raised my fists, and spoke in a loud clear voice as though I were addressing myself to someone who would have understood me if he had heard me. "I have not been unwilling to be destroyed, I know how to resign myself to destruction. But why must I exhaust myself laboring to return to a world which may be in ruins and where, if it is still standing, I will be even more fearful than I was before?" As I finished speaking, a fair-sized piece of stone fell from the wall high above me onto the floor of the hole. I waited to see what else might happen. Nothing happened. I complained again, watchfully. Another rock fell. The sound of my voice was dislodging some of the upper rocks without causing the whole pile to shatter down onto me. I sang, hummed, yelled, whooped, wailed: nothing happened. I went back to complaining, in a loud clear voice and complete, rather formal sentences. Another rock fell. One of the fallen boulders was too big for me to lift, but I could roll it into place. They were of irregular shapes and would not pile easily and securely. I was going to need a great many pieces of stone of this size. I am healthy and my gardening has kept me in good condition; nevertheless,

I felt myself weaker after each complaining and rock-piling episode and had to rest for longer and longer periods. My predicament did not allow me to complain mildly. I am reserved by temperament, I tried to hold back both out of inclination and out of a desire to save my strength, but I found that I could give each complaint nothing less than everything I could muster.

I did not dare complain during the night, for fear a dislodged stone would fall on me. In the daytime I watched when I talked, I could jump to one side in time. I kept trying to figure out which of my words had the power to dislodge the rocks; it must have something to do with vibrations, wave-lengths.

In our city we are quite experimental. Even a private citizen like myself is infected with the spirit of experiment. I live off the income from my inheritance. My wife and I love gardening above everything. Our few friends are scattered throughout the city, we make a point of being strangers to our neighbors. Our rock garden, at the edge of a cliff overlooking a northern cove, is quite remarkable. I am sure it would win prizes and be much visited if we were interested in that sort of thing. But our friends respect our wish to keep our garden private, and our neighbors, whose gardens are severely arranged and have swept paths, do not notice the perfection of our succulents (which they think of as being no more than cliff plants anyway) nor do they see any order in the way our paths and stepping-stones adapt themselves to the terrain. My wife and I have little use for most of what our city gets excited about, we are inclined to scorn prizes and fashion, I had thought I was equally indifferent to the fervor for experimentation. Now, in this hole, I have learned better.

The second night, unable to sleep well because of the discomfort of the floor, I planned experiments to try the next day. I have never heard of anyone who was in a hole like mine. Perhaps these conditions are unique. There are plenty of holes into which our citizens have been known to have fallen; sometimes they were rescued, sometimes they died before they could be got out, often no doubt they just disappeared from sight as I have done. Perhaps no one else discovered how to dislodge boulders as I did. There might be something exceptional about my voice, though no one has ever commented on it. There certainly is nothing odd about my words. They are just ordinary words used with care. Still, though I am not slovenly in my use of words, neither am I a poet. I must not let this opportunity to experiment slip from me, even though, since I need all the physical strength I have to pile the rocks up, I must work fast before I give out. During the night I planned a series of speeches to try out.

I prayed. When our city was founded, many churches had been built, strong, handsome, stone structures. Our city had originally been built with walls, to withstand the assaults of pirates. To be sure, the pirates were suppressed two centuries ago, and the city grew far beyond the walls, which are now visited by tourists as museum pieces. But our churches, the best ones, which look like and once served as fortresses, have been kept in good repair, services are held in them, the choir schools still function at public expense. I knew many prayers, having been a boy soprano for a few years till my voice cracked. Neither the prayers I recollected nor the ones I made up worked to dislodge the stones.

I delivered the patriotic speeches memorized by every schoolchild—the salute to the flag, a constitution day address, the funeral oration which had been delivered by our first prime minister after the revolution had established parliamentary government, our oath of allegiance. None of them worked.

I gave an exact and full history of how I came to be where I was. I described my condition with scientific accuracy and offered every reasonable hypothesis about why I was doing what I was doing. Nothing happened.

I recited a poem, nursery rhymes, a folk tale, the prologue of our constitution. I counted to twenty in Latin, I recited as many of Euclid's axioms as I could recall. No result.

I recited a speech from a play I had acted in when I was in college. Actually I saved this till the last because the speech had become more than the character's words for me, it had come to say what I meant or at least I had come to mean what it said. The part was a small one. I was one of the lesser court gentlemen. At a crucial moment the king gives me a vital message, his throne depends on its delivery. Halfway to the nobleman to whom I am supposed to deliver it, I decide not to, and then the playwright gives me my only important speech, a soliloquy, the great speech of the play. I have no good political reason not to deliver the message, nothing but good will befall me if I do deliver it, I have never before done such a thing as I am now doing. The longer I try to account to myself and the audience for what I am doing, the stranger my action appears; I labor to find the right words, for my court language is insufficient. Twice in the history of our city this play, one of our classics, has been proscribed because of this speech, which cannot be cut out of the play, being its keystone. I recite it now in my hole. A boulder is dislodged all right, but it almost hits me. It is too large for me to lift to the top of the pile I have made. Worst, it comes from the mouth of the chimney above, enlarging it, so that now I must build up my pile even higher than before, in order to be able to brace myself in the chimney and work my way out.

I have to use our language in my own way, I have to speak for myself.

"I am in a hole, I want to get out. I don't know what I shall find when I make my way back into the city. I long to see my wife; if she is still alive and well, she will care for me while I recuperate; if she is injured, I will do what I can for her. These stones are heavy; after I put one up onto the pile, my muscles do not leave off trembling until I raise my voice to talk another rock down from the jumble about me and then hoist it into place; each time after such effort, the trembling penetrates into me deeper. I fear I will not have strength to work my way up the chimney once I have got myself into it. I want to cry, but I must save my strength for words. I do not know why I am here, I did nothing to deserve being thrown down here alone and abandoned."

So, the rocks fall.

What would happen if I did not pretend someone is listening to what I say? I know of course that no one hears my voice, but I speak as though I were being listened to. It must be that which gives my voice the right wave-lengths to dislodge the stones. It obviously is neither the words themselves nor their arrangement; my experiments have removed those possibilities. In the interests of exact knowledge I should complain without audience. I know well enough that I have no audience, not a sound from outside has reached me. But I cannot imagine doing anything so unreasonable as to complain without any audience at all, even though that is what I am in fact doing. Besides, suppose when I did that, all the rocks should fall in on me at once? If I had more strength I would take the risk, I would try to imagine myself as I am. Meanwhile, I had better get on with my complaining while I still have strength and time.

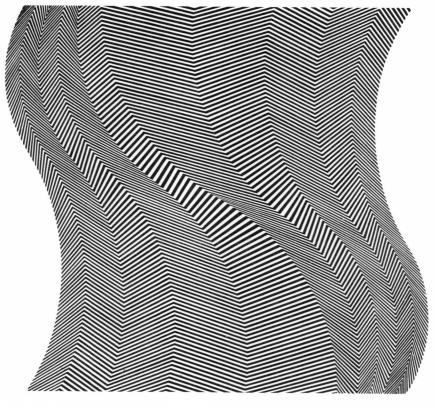

BRIDGET RILEY. *TWIST*. (*TQ* #5)

1966

Two poems

ANNE SEXTON

Man and wife

To spake of wo
  that is in mariage . . .

We are not lovers.
We do not even know each other.
We look alike
but we have nothing to say.
We are like pigeons . . .

that pair who came to the suburbs
by mistake,
forsaking Boston where they bumped
their small heads against a blind wall,
having worn out the fruit stalls in The North End,
the amethyst windows of Louisburg Square,
the seats on The Common
and the traffic that kept stamping
and stamping.

Now there is green rain for everyone
as common as eyewash.
Now they are together
like strangers in a two-seater outhouse,
eating and squatting together.

They have teeth and knees
but they do not speak.
A soldier is forced to stay with a **soldier**
because they share the same dirt
and the same blows.

They are exiles
soiled by the same sweat and the **drunkard's** dream,
As it is they can only hang on,
their red claws wound like bracelets
around the same limb.
Even their song is not a sure thing.
It is not a language;
it is a kind of breathing.
They are two asthmatics
whose breath sobs in and out
through a small fuzzy pipe.

Like them
we neither talk nor clear our throats.
Oh darling,
we gasp in unison beside our window pane,
drunk on the drunkard's dream.
Like them
we can only hang on.

But they would pierce our heart
if they could only fly the distance.

Live

Well, death's been here
for a long time—
it has a hell of a lot
to do with hell
and suspicion of the eye
and the religious objects
and how I mourned them
when they were made obscene
by my dwarf-heart's doodle.
The chief ingredient
is mutilation.
And mud, day after day,
mud like a ritual
and the baby on the platter,
cooked but still human
cooked also with little maggots,
sewn onto it maybe by somebody's mother,
the damn bitch!

Even so,
I kept right on going on,
a sort of human statement,
lugging myself as if
I were a sawed off body
in the trunk, the steamer trunk.
This became a perjury of the soul.
It became an outright lie
and even though I dressed the body
it was still naked, still killed.
It was caught
in the first place at birth,
like a fish.
But I played it, dressed it up,
dressed it up like somebody's doll.
Is life something you play?
And all the time wanting to get rid of it?
And further, everyone yelling at you
to shut up. And no wonder!

People don't like to be told
that you're sick
and then be forced
to watch
you
come
down with the hammer.

Today life opened inside me like an egg
and there inside,
after considerable digging
I found the answer.
What a bargain!
There was the sun,
her yolk moving feverishly,
tumbling her prize—
and you realize that he does this daily!
I'd known she was purifier
but I hadn't thought
she was solid,
hadn't known she was an answer.
God! It's a dream,
lovers sprouting in the yard
like celery stalks
and better,
a husband straight as a Redwood,
two daughters, two sea urchins,
picking roses off my hackles.
If I'm on fire they dance around it
and cook marshmallows.
And if I'm ice
they simply skate on me
in little ballet costumes.

1966

51

Here
all along,
thinking I was a killer,
anointing myself daily
with my little poisons.
But no.
I'm an Empress.
I wear an apron.
My typewriter writes.
It didn't break the way it warned.
Even crazy, I'm as nice
as a chocolate bar.
Even with the witches' gymnastics
they trust my incalculable city,
my corruptible bed.

O dearest three,
I make a soft reply.
The witch comes on
and you paint her pink.
I come with kisses in my hood
and the sun, the smart one,
rolling in my arms.
So I say *Live*
and turn my shadow three times round
to feed our puppies as they come,
the eight dalmations we didn't drown,
despite the warnings: The Abort! The Destroy!
despite the pails of water that waited
to drown them, to pull them down like stones,
they came, each one head first,
blowing bubbles the color of cataract-blue
and fumbling for the tiny tits.
Just last week, eight Dalmations,
¾ of a lb, lined up like cord wood
each
like a
birch tree.
I promise to love more if they come,
because in spite of cruelty
and the stuffed railroad cars for the ovens,
I am not what I expected. Not an Eichmann.
The poison just didn't take.
So I won't hang around in my hospital shift,
repeating The Black Mass and all of it.
I say *Live, Live* because of the sun,
the dream, the excitable gift.

1966

Why Is American Poetry Culturally Deprived?

KENNETH REXROTH

ANDRE MALRAUX is famous for the remark that American literature is the only contemporary literature not written by intellectuals. He points out that general ideas of any subtlety or profundity are unknown to all major American novelists, poets and dramatists. Partly of course this judgment is motivated by Malraux's own taste. The only writers acceptable to him are Faulkner, Hemingway, Tennessee Williams, Raymond Chandler, Dashiell Hammett, the militantly mindless. In fact, shortly after the war, both Malraux and Roger Caillois happened to have said to me that they considered somebody named "Orass Mikwo" America's most significant writer. It was some time before I figured out that this was the semi-literate pulp magazine writer of the blood-on-the-bikini school, Horace McCoy.

Nevertheless, Malraux's judgement is substantially correct. I have known the leading exponents of all the movements in American poetry which presumed ideological motivation, that at least attempted to assume the language of those general ideas which were part of the storm and stress of international thought. Without exception, these ideas came to their poet exponents only through the most superficial literary journalism, were never comprehended, either the simple elements or their consequences and were never in fact acted upon. Let me detail this. Carl Sandburg could stand as an example of the Social Democratic and Populist writers of 1910, a colleague of Richard Dehmel and Emile Verhaeren and Romain Rolland. Sandburg is usually considered to have bankrupt himself as an artist by betraying these ideas when America entered the first war. The fact is he didn't have any ideas to betray. His attitude toward "the people" was a compound of Chicago police court reporter sentimentality, Midwest small town Populist oratory and Hull House maidenly magnanimity. The picture of the young Sandburg breathlessly following the debates in the international Socialist movement over Bernstein's Revisionism, the Millerand crisis, Luxemburg and Kautsky disputing the questions of imperialism and the falling rate of profit is so ridiculous it is not even laughable.

The Modernist movement in verse, from the Imagists to the old masters of modern verse, first extensively published in Alfred Kreymborg's *Others,* the period of *Broom* and *The Little Review*—was a movement of technical reform of syntax and a cleaning up of the vocabulary of poetry. It has often been compared to the Symbolist movement in France. None of these poets, with the exception of Amy Lowell, John Gould Fletcher, Walter Conrad Arensberg, and T. S. Eliot, read French poetry or knew anything about it. In their French classes in college the last poet in the course had been Jules Laforgue. Therefore, in so far as they paid attention to their lessons, he represented for them the last word in French modernism. He died in 1887. He still represents the last word in French modernism for American academic versifiers. The profound revolutions of the sensibility, the climactic changes in the soul of modern man, so-called, which began with Baudelaire, Kierkegaard, Newman, Dostoievsky and Nietzsche and which represent in fact a systematic destructive criticism of the foundations of humanism and humanitarianism, and which have thrown up in the course of their ever-accelerating liquidation all the anti-humane art movements and philosophies of our time were, to judge from the evidence, totally incomprehensible to the American imitators of their stylistic innovations—even at the remove of fifty years. It should never be forgotten that H. D. was a contemporary of the Dadaists. French and German literature was falling to pieces with hearbreak. The veriest schoolboy, as Lord Macaulay used to say, in Europe knew that civilization had betrayed itself. H. D. was dedicating herself to cleaning and brightening the idiom of the Sapphic poets, Michael Field and Renée Vivien. Over against such much abused esthetes there was only Midwest Populism, whose intellectual foundations never rose higher than an editorial in a Des Moines newspaper. Out of the ranks of what were to become the classic modernists, two young men from the remote hinterland rose in revolt, T. S. Eliot and Ezra Pound. Pound most emphatically was not a member of the international community of letters, any more than any other emigré cafe sitter, then or now. Drinking pernod on the sidewalk of the Dôme then, or the Flore now, never made Pound a cubist nor has it, if you will forgive the French word, made any *foundation bum* an existentialist. Pound was under the impression that his cafe companions, Max Elskamp and Georges Fourrest, were the leaders of French poetry. This, at the height of the careers of Reverdy, Eluard, Aragon, with Apollinaire only dead a year. Eliot, on the other hand, did attach himself to an international community—the movement of virulent obscurantism and clerical fascism led by Henri Massis and Maurras and given voice in *"l'Action Française."* It should not be forgotten that the real reason for the international failure of this movement was that it was so reactionary that practical politicians like Hitler and Mussolini found it unusable. When *l'Action Française* said "We are not interested in the opinions of an obscure Jewish carpenter who met a disgraceful death two thousand years ago, but in restoring to France the order and glory (*gloire*—a bit of French slang recently restored to currency) of Richelieu and Mazarin", the Holy Office excommunicated them by telegram. This is not an idle, an unsubstantiated accusation against Mr. Eliot. He is not only on record as being an anti-Semite, but on record as being in favor of eliminating the Jews, and a surprising number of the French contributors to *The Criterion* ended up in the dock as war criminals.

Now, it so happens that if any international community recruited English and American poets in the interbellum period, it was Fascism—Pound, Yeats, Eliot are on record. This is not because American poets are exceptionally vicious men, although some of them are and have been. It is simply because Fascism is so much more easily assimilated by simple and emotionally unstable minds—you don't have to read so many books. As the economic depression deepened and their betters began talking about economics, most of this generation of American poets became money cranks, followers of the Social Credit theories of Major Douglas. This is an ancient American foolishness. I don't doubt for a moment but that, as the fur market moved inexorably westward to Michillimakinac, the Grand Sachems of the Iroquois believed they could call it back by fooling with the wampum. Funny-moneyism is precisely a symptom of the incorrigible provinciality of small town debtors in the American Outback. When the actual levers of power are so remote as to be unimaginable, their victims always result to sympathetic magic. Although Mr. Eliot is reputed to have worked in a bank, it didn't help. No one used to handling general ideas, no one familiar with the elementary facts of, to use a sound but old fashioned term, political economy, as those facts and general ideas work themselves out in the real affairs of men, would ever fall for such flimsy nonsense as Major Douglas.

Like a faint chorus of young birds in the nest, echoes of Mr. Eliot's principled reaction suddenly were heard amongst the moonshine of the Southern Hills. Mr. Ransom, Mr. Tate and their friends at Vanderbilt, meeting in the parlor of a Greek letter fraternity, launched the frail vessel of American reaction. Alas, the cargo was too slight for even so puny a ship. If Mr. Eliot's *The Criterion* carried on its manifest bales of Massis, Maurras and Maritain, as re-interpreted by Fernandez, Suarez and Bernard Fay, and Pareto and Major Douglas reinterpreted by Ezra Pound and Wyndham Lewis, and the Almighty as reinterpreted by the followers of Gurdjieff, Mr. Tate and Mr. Ransom could manage no more than the ideological residues of "Red Rock" and "The Clansman". True, there was a vague echo of the Physiocrats but an echo bounced off the surface of the thinker of the Fugitives' new agrarian group, a professor who seems to have been a ghost writer for a number of leading Southern personalities from Governor Long and Senator Bilbo to Governor Wallace. This is as near as serious thought amongst American poets ever came to the international discussions which raged throughout the interbellum period about the role of the elite, the threats of mass culture, the relations of town and country.

Many of these people were connected with the absurd Humanist movement of the pre-Crisis Twenties. Today it is obvious that this was just a power drive on the part of a number of young academicians to re-capture book reviewing jobs from the Populist disciples of H. L. Mencken, who threatened to monopolize mensely important figures if they had written in French or even German or Italian. For over a generation, they have been the think tanks from which the editors of *The Partisan Review* drew their sustenance. They are, or were (Wheelwright is long dead) very dear friends of mine, but I would never claim them as America's leading poets.

The immense popularity of the Beats in Europe on both sides of the Iron Curtain is due to the fact that, although they may not reflect the eschatological emphasis of modern philosophy, they do reflect an emotional consciousness of the fact of apocalypse. Youngsters in blue jeans read each other the poems of Ferlinghetti, Gary Snyder and LeRoi Jones to records by Thelonius Monk or Ornette Coleman in the coffee shops of Prague, Beirut and Barcelona as well as in Warsaw, London, Paris, Berlin, Rome. It is apparent why. It is also apparent why their fathers never, in a Prague Cafe called Swanee River, sat about dressed in string ties and calico shirts drinking mint juleps and listening to the poetry of Allen Tate recited to the music of Stephen Foster. This is not true of his master, T. S. Eliot. I can imagine "The Waste Land" so read although what the musical accompaniment would be I'm not sure—possibly Richard Strauss or Scriabin. What is the reason for this state of affairs? The answer is self-evident. From the death of Longfellow to the day Allen Ginsberg took off his clothes, the American poet was not an important factor in American life. He was not a factor at all. For this reason, the kind of young man who wishes to participate in the decisions of his community went into business, engineering or the professions. The boy who knew he could not or was afraid to participate wrote verse.

A generation or so ago the poet considered himself an outcast because he partook only minimally of the life of his society. Today he is very much an incast. Society has overtaken and surpassed him. Everybody gets very little out of life nowadays. The engineer who once went off in kepi, breeches and puttees to build roads through the haunts of the headhunters now lives in a garden suburb, finds his sexual outlet in Saturday night dirty movie parties and for maximized living reads *On the Road* and subscribes to the *Evergreen Review*. His indistinguishable neighbor teaches creative poetry at the local college and writes slide rule poems more indistinguishable still. What is wrong with the vast bulk of American society is that it is smug. The neurosis of the affluent society is not anxiety but *taedium vitae—accidie—*moral boredom.

Over the years since the First War there have been a number of poets who have given expression to certain general ideas of more or less social importance for our time. A list of them makes curious reading—Vachel Lindsay put into one time immensely popular doggerel the mystic Midwest Populism that had come down from the communitarian experiments of the 1840's—Robert Owen and so on, and which found final expression in the sentimental manifestos of Louis Sullivan and Frank Lloyd Wright. Eliot's "The Waste Land" is the only major work of "anxiety" in American poetry. Conrad Aiken was one of the very few writers anywhere before the surrealists to attempt to use psychoanalysis as them. It was successful, but unimportant in the arena of world thought.

Throughout the period of proletarian literature, I never knew a Communist poet who was able to read through the first, much less the third volume of *Capital*. It was looked upon as a dry, dull, excessively technical book. Of course, what's wrong with it is its highly emotional rhetoric and its elementary sleight-of-hand mathematics. God knows, it's absorbing enough reading, as absorbing as the Isaiah to which it has often been compared, but the Marxists of the Thirties judged Marx as the contributors to *Commentary* of the Fifties judged Isaiah—dry, dull, excessively technical. American poets just don't read non-fiction.

Since the Second War the literary quarterlies which started out under an alliance of Southern reactionaries and ex-Trotskyites, have, it is true, tried to give their readers some inkling of some of the intellectual currents in the maelstrom of post-war European thought. This has meant, pretty much Existentialism, but with the exception of Lionel Abel, no poet has contributed to this discussion. What is more significant, not a single, original autochthonous idea has come up in the literary quarterlies of the post War period. We live in a time of continuous revaluation. It is a time when it seems less and less possible to do anything overtly and therefore a time given over to relentless subjective subversion. There is no sign of this revaluation in America—our think pieces in our leading intellectual quarterlies never rise above the *ABC of Zen Buddhism, What is Existentialism, How to Appreciate the Theatre of the Absurd in Easy Lessons for Small Town Clergymen, Over-read Clubwomen and Candidates for Ph.D's*. Modern thought is haunted by a sense of crisis. We live in an eschatological age. Had we not invented the atom bomb, the Deity would have been forced to create it. This sense of crisis is not new. It began in the 1840's. But for the past two generations, there has solidified a tradition of crisis-thinking which is now almost universal, a true universe of discourse from which no one seems to be able to escape. Niccolo Hartmann, Scheler, Berdyaev, Buber, Tillich, Marcel, Mounier—these men are in fact anti-existentialist, but even they are swept up in the general mass movement of anguish and anxiety. I have never met an American poet who was familiar with Jean Paul Sartre's attempts at philosophy, much less with the gnarled discourse of Scheler or Heidegger.

This is not quite true. Lionel Abel is an exception. He even went to Paris and met Jean-Paul Sartre personally, and for a year could be seen on the Boulevard St. Germain eavesdropping on his conversations with Simone de Beauvoir and Jean Wahl. There's only one trouble. Although he is a pretty good playwright, Lionel Abel is not a major poet. The same is true of Paul Goodman, who not only is part of the discourse of modern international thought, but who has certainly tried hard all his life to be an honestly original thinker. Again, he's not one of our most important poets. Similarly, in the Marxist epoch, John Brooks Wheelwright, not only knew more about Marx than Earl Browder, he knew very much more about St. Thomas Aquinas than T. S. Eliot and Mortimer Adler rolled together. All three of these people—Goodman, Abel, Wheelwright and the forgotten poet disciple of Wittgenstein, Lou Grudin—would be ima basic philosophy of life. The surrealists themselves were passionate evangelists of a dogmatic world view, which presumed to use art, in the words of André Breton, "to revolutionize the human sensibility as such." Eugene Jolas, the editor of *transition,* was a more learned man and a more ambitious thinker than Breton himself. Unfortunately, the whole program was fundamentally misconceived and resulted in poetry which today seems trivial and dull. The best long surrealist poem by an American was Parker Tyler's *Granite Butterfly.* Reading it over today, it simply does not seem effective enough. Hart Crane's "Bridge" failed precisely because of its total lack of intellectual content.

Hart Crane certainly led a tortured enough life. But what tortured him was inability to hold a job, unhealthy relations with his parents, inability to accept his own homosexuality gracefully, and alcohol. He was not tortured by any failure of life to provide him with significance. On the contrary, he was a rather simple-minded man, gusty and lusty with a great appetite for crude experience. His most ambitious poem is an impressive attempt to write again the patriotic epic exhortations of Walt Whitman. Insofar as it fails, it does so for no profound reason, but simply because Hart Crane was not able to control his appetites. His intoxication with his own rhetoric defeats his gospel and his poem is devoid of general ideas entirely.

Other writers of long ruminative reveries (we used to call them philosophical epics) like Walter Lowenfels' *Some Deaths* or Louis Zukofsky's *A* or Charles Olson's *Maximum Poems*—in spite of all the avant garde rhetoric, manage to say only quite conventional things. Of no one is this more true than of Gertrude Stein. A whole generation thought she must be deep because no one believed that anybody could take so much trouble to say such fatuous things as she seemed on the face of it to be saying. Late in life she suddenly started to write conventional English and revealed herself as possessed of the most extraordinarily ordinary intellectual endowment. Properly understood, she bears a strong resemblance to her contemporary, Edgar Guest. Who reflects the age of anxiety which is so much the concern of French intellectuals, German theologians and American psychiatrists? W. H. Auden wrote a book called that. But W. H. Auden is English; his state of anxiety has conspicuously died down in the last few years and he's considered very out of date. Leonard Bernstein wrote a symphony called *The Age of Anxiety* but I don't think the things that make him anxious could be classed as ontological *angst.* It's perfectly true that George Barker, Dylan Thomas, Auden, David Gascoyne do give utterance to the kind of metaphysical terror which afflicts many people who confront the ultimate implications of the contemporary human condition. They are all British. Thomas is dead; the rest are middle-aged and not read by young English poets. "The Movement", so-called which dominates English verse is not a movement at all. It is simply a reflection of the fact that English poets in recent years, have, like their American counterparts, become well-paid professors of creative writing. Anything more flaccid and less creative it would be difficult to imagine. There are certain American poets, like Robert Lowell or Robert Creeley, whose work is haunted by anxiety, but this is, in each case, an individual psychological problem and very far from a judgment as to the meaning of life. This is the trouble with the most alienated of the Beats. Their alienation is a luxury product of the affluent society. They can afford to live in what Lawrence Lipton calls voluntary poverty (viz. No fourth T.V. set in the bathroom). Villon, Baudelaire, Van Gogh could not afford it and that's all the difference.

Does this mean that I think American poetry in the Twentieth Century is worthless? Quite the contrary. It serves society as it always has, as a symbolic criticism of value but the values it concerns itself with are not those of philosophy or a metaphysics of the conscience. The one specifically philosophic American poet of the Twentieth Century has been Wallace Stevens and his work has been a kind of versification of the philosophy of George Santayana, of what Santayana called scepticism and animal faith. But Stevens' poetry is not of the great artistic merit that it is because it versifies Santayana. If that's what we want, it's better to go to the original in Santayana's own prose. What is valuable about the poetry of Wallace Stevens is that it really does reorganize the human sensibility afresh in each poem in terms of quite simple elements of experience. This experience is never more profound than that accessible to the kind of man Wallace Stevens in fact was—a wealthy cultivated executive of a big insurance company.

So with William Carlos Williams, who for contemporary taste is the best of the generation of Classic Modernists. As a handler of general ideas, Williams is pathetic. As either esthetics or epistemology, his favorite phrase, "No ideas but in things" is infantile. He thought of his great poem *Paterson* as a philosophic epic preaching precisely that profound philosophy. What it is, of course, is a profound organization of the life experience of a small town doctor with all of a small town doctor's infinite roots into a community into which he was born, practiced medicine and never left except for vacations. To products of environments as troubled as those which produced Rilke, Maiakofsky, Paul Eluard or Dylan Thomas, even the most tormented American poet must seem singularly content, but so it is.

1967

AARON SISKIND. (*TQ* #8)

Storm Still

BROCK BROWER

IT WAS SOMETIMES WINTRY, probably in 1608, at Bankside, and he was clearly at the Globe, among the groundlings, chinned up against the front stage by the pushing of the farrier's apprentice behind him, and the garlic-breathed orangegirl on his right. Robert Armin was playing the Fool. That was why he had come. To see Armin in his motley, coxcomb, and huge ass's ears, the bladder rioting in his lunatic hand. But then Richard Burbage was also acting that afternoon. He was playing Lear. Brilliantly, he thought. "Take heed, sirrah; the whip." The steely core of kingly authority. Lear not yet mad, still regal. He suddenly wanted to tell somebody, anybody how fine an actor Burbage was. He turned smiling to the orangegirl. She smiled back coquettishly. He started to open his mouth to utter some critical *bon mot,* but closed it quickly around her wild kiss. Then she was clinging to him like a daughter. "I cannot heave my heart into my mouth," she cried. "I cannot heave my heart into my mouth, I cannot heave my heart into my mouth, I cannot heave my . . ."

Then everything turned on a great, dizzy wheel, wrenching his attention around to the stage again, away from Cordelia, the orangegirl. He was horrified. Lear *was* whipping the Fool, beating him mercilessly to the cruel, cheek-cracking tune of the thunder. The cannonball rolled back and forth behind the stage, and Armin sang to the beating of the whip.

> *He that hath but a tiny little wit,*
> > *With hey, ho, the wind and the rain,*
> > *Must make content with his fortunes fit,*
> > *Though the rain it raineth every day.*

The Fool jigged, and the whip cut.

He tried to shout out. The Fool should not be whipped, it wasn't in the play. He started to climb onto the stage. First it grew higher and higher, forcing him down and down as he climbed. Then it collapsed under him. From the three balconies around the octagonal Globe they laughed at him. "But the Fool is *not whipped,"* he shouted at them, almost defensively. "Lear must never do such a thing. Never, never, never, never, never." Then they began to disappear, laughing, behind the rising flames. He saw why the stage had collapsed. It was on fire. The great Globe itself was on fire, burning like a wooden bucket. But that was wrong too. The Globe fire was in 1613. "Stop, stop!" he cried at the flames. "You're too early. Don't burn. Don't whip the Fool. Don't burn. Don't whip the Fool." Then he woke up.

Immediately he felt his old fumbling sense of panic. He'd slipped again in some matter of the play. There was a reference he carelessly hadn't checked all the way back—some date or alternate reading he must look up this very instant, or they were going to catch him out. He knew it was something terribly minor. Some question about the colophon on the Pide Bull Quarto, or a line he'd wrongly attributed to the source play *Leir* or to Holinshed, or even some stupid quibble over the spelling of Cordelia's name. Really that picayune. It didn't affect his main argument in the slightest. But they would crucify him for it, put his whole scholarship in doubt at next spring's meeting, if he didn't find it now and burn it out like a tiny plague spot in his critical acumen.

He knew all this was nonsense, yet he still began shuffling furtively through the papers on his desk to see if he hadn't possibly made a note somewhere, perhaps in the margins of his Spenser. It was one of those involuntary things that had finally become quite voluntary. He needed something to clear his mind when he napped off, and this seemed to do the trick. One of these days, he suspected, he was going to nap off altogether. His mind would simply fail to clear. Last scene of all that ends this strange, eventful history. Second childishness and mere oblivion. But somehow that would be all right too, because, look, he was only here picking over his papers after an insignificant reference. There was nothing really important to get back to. . . .

But he was awake enough now to hear the knock. It was hard to tell whether he was hearing it now, actually at the door, or whether memory was echoing it for him. Such distinctions were becoming difficult for him to make at times. Or just not worth making.

"Yes?" he asked peevishly. He wondered if he wheezed at all. Manly voice, turning to childish treble.

His study door opened part way, and a bearded face cocked around at him, its smile still back in the door's shadow. "Busy?"

This was young Nelson's way of asking permission to come in out of the shadows. For a moment he mused on just leaving him there in the shadows. Forever. Perhaps he would eventually fade into the umbra, pulling his bearded smile in after him, and become a complete shadow, instead of the furtive, diffident half shadow he already was. But oh what silliness, he warned himself, and said pleasantly, "No, no, no. Come in, Nelson. Please."

The young instructor bowed out of the doorway, bringing in a towering pile of corrected blue books. On top of them was the marking book, stretched open to the proper page with a rubber band. Nelson seemed to come bearing them almost like a hecatomb, yet at the same time he managed somehow to be putting them aside—to ask about obviously more important work. "How are you coming along with the old fool?"

He meant Lear, of course. Almost certainly, he meant Lear.

Nelson handed him the pile, which was deceptively heavy. He lifted it the little height onto his desk, straining every chest muscle not to puff.

"All right, my boy," he laughed. "I'm having most of my trouble with the young fool. If I can settle his hash. . . ." He decided he'd better be hospitable. "Can you stay a minute?"

Nelson nodded and slipped over to the other chair by the cold fireplace. On his way he ran his fingers along the books on one shelf. Too lightly, too quickly. Looking for his poems, the older man knew. Feeling for it, actually. An absurdly thin volume, and from the spine, it really was hard to see. A two-dimensional piece of work. If that. It was silly enough to find a scholarly press going in for that sort of publishing, but it was much sillier to have it inspire a beard. An effeminate beard too, he felt, even though it covered those sallow cheeks blackly. A shadow would grow just such a beard. That plushy. His book and his whiskers had both come out far too soon, and that summed up Nelson precisely as far as he was concerned.

Nelson crossed his legs and all his fingers in one nervous motion. "You know," he said, "sometimes I think Shakespeare himself must've been a jester one time or another."

How he hated that kind of remark. Shakespeare was Marlowe, or Bacon, or the Earl of Essex, or the boy who held the horses, and now a Fool. It threw everything out of balance. *The Tragedy of Lear* by Crazy Will.

"Oh?" he said simply.

"Everything he does—well, it has the fool's wit. I was reading an article the other day, sir. You might look at it if you're working on this theme of Folly." He smiled quickly. "I suppose you've got your material down pat as it is, but this man had something really new—I mean, he puts you up against it on a couple of points. Quite up against it."

Nelson had studied a year at Oxford. It had made him an expert at malicious deference. Maddening.

Nelson mentioned where he might find the article. It was in a publication that had not been in existence before his fiftieth birthday. He'd read a few issues, and thought it all nonsense. Then he was flabbergasted to find that he had to suffer a certain amount of condescension for thinking it all nonsense. He kept silent about it nowadays, but he would certainly not read the article.

"Have you been doing anything on *Lear* yourself?" he suddenly thought to ask.

The instructor bowed low before the challenge. "No. Not at all. Nothing on *Lear* itself. I just thought you might like to hear about this man's work. Are those exams all right then?"

"Must be, my boy, if you've done them. You ought to be thanked, of course. It's very pleasant to be left free—"

"Not at all."

1967   63

Gratitude was the very cup of bitterness sometimes, he thought. But he was too old to be much surprised by the taste. That same taste crept into so many things that were supposed to be ennobling.

"But I'm afraid, sir. . . ."

"You must run along. That it?"

"Yes, I'm afraid."

"Of course. Mustn't keep you. I know better. Thank you again, Nelson. Won't keep you. Must work myself." Sometimes, he calculated, a properly self-effacing old man can lick the pants off any youth for modest demeanor.

Nelson went out, closing the door without a sound, almost as if he didn't want to wake somebody. Maddening.

He leaned back heavily in his chair, lifting the front legs about an inch off the floor, and patted his girth. His Phi Beta Kappa key, comically oversized, topped the hillock like a small tablet of laws. A back leg of the chair suddenly hobbled on its uncertain shank and brought the chair down sharply onto all fours again. The slip shook him for a moment.

So it is all happening to me, he thought. I can't even stay steady in my own chair. I shall simply have to toss up this *Lear* business and seek level ground. Unburthen'd crawl toward death.

That was why he's asked for young Nelson. Actually asked for him, absurd as that seemed now. So he could gather his thoughts in peace and produce them in final form. Which he hadn't done before, because of the pressure of . . . now, of course, with young Nelson, he'd be able . . . able now, with young Nelson.

Calling him Nelson, that was his first blunder. He'd meant to keep him kindly at a distance by using his last name without the Mister. It would've been just right. Mr. Nelson was too formal, but the last name alone, that set up just the correct balance of friendliness and seniority. Only his name wasn't Thomas R. Nelson. It was R. Nelson Thomas. He must've seen it somewhere on a list as Thomas, R. Nelson, and simply slipped the comma. Bad textual error. Trapped into familiarity. But then he seemed to recall vaguely hearing students call him Mr. Nelson. At least he assumed they were using the Mister. My God, he thought, what has happened to Degree. Take but Degree away and . . . and you get familiarity, and familiarity breeds contempt. He shook his head ruefully. Could he do no better than that innocuous cliché?

He hauled himself out of his chair, away from these thoughts—away from all thinking, in fact—and stood in front of his long, narrow Queen Anne window. Somebody else would have this window all to himself soon, and he'd be outside it. His study was on the first floor of the Library, and the campus was framed before him, cut into neat, rectangular cards by the panes. He'd be out there somewhere. Mostly bare elms, stark in the winter gloom. A five o'clock January gloom. He looked at his watch, a little loose on his wrist now. He should be hearing the Library bells, somewhere in the tower above him, ringing a knell in the gloom. Lights were already dotting on in the buildings behind the elms. The wind was coming up, bringing in the snow again.

Yes, of course, there was snow on the ground. How could he stand there and not think of the snow first thing? The white, even stretch of winter over the earth. Fresh and flocculent yesterday. Old and icy today. The hoary, arthritic, fallen snow. A crust.

Tom's a-cold, he mused. Prithee, Nuncle, be contented; 'tis a naughty night to swim in.

Then he noticed somebody running across the campus towards him, struggling hopelessly with the deep, crusted snow that broke under him at every step. Tom's a-cold, he mused again, looking out at the battling figure. Tom's adrift.

Quite suddenly, he felt himself adrift. His eyes watered and wanted to blink, only ever so slowly. He fought to keep his attention on the figure struggling in the snow, and a sensation of steepness, all about him, grew until he felt he was once again climbing onto the stage in the burning Globe to rescue the Fool. Don't whip the Fool. The whip cut, and the Fool jigged, raising the powdery underdown of snow about him like a rich mist.

He had come nearer the window now. He leaped and pirouetted and somer-saulted, playing with the snow as if it were a partner. Bells jingled. He ran to an elm tree, even nearer the window, and passionately kicked it. Immediately he was remorseful and threw his arms around the tree. A long kiss on the icy bark. Then he kicked it and laughed. The bells on his cap trembled. He looked about him inquisitively and discovered the window.

He rushed towards it and pressed his nose moistly against a pane of glass, bordered in frost. His face cocked and bobbed on his nose like the ticking moon in an ancient clock. He grinned and brayed through the glass. He shook his bells, and banged the head of the marotte that he carried against the window. And then his own head. The bells rang. The five o'clock knell rolled through the gloom.

Soberly the old man shook himself, and a certain richness of sensation deserted him. He did blink finally and reassured himself that there was no nose mark on the window pane. Outside, only the gloom. It was the first time in his life he had dozed off still on his feet. Mortifying. He forced himself back to his desk. Work.

I suppose that's really what old age is, he thought. Getting fuzzy about whether you're awake or asleep. When is Lear mad, and when is he sane? He wants to sing like a bird in a cage when he and Cordelia go off to prison. That's mad as much as it is sane. On the heath he wants the storm to strike flat the thick rotundity of the world. That's sane as much as it is mad. What's the difference?

He took the trouble to jot these ideas down in a creaky scrawl, and stuffed the paper in the corner of his blotter. After supper, he'd come back and reread them. He hadn't yet kept his promise to himself to work after supper, but tonight he would.

But already he knew what he really thought of his jottings. If he'd found them in a freshman paper, he'd have put an encouraging remark in the margin, something like, "An interesting approach, but don't rest on it. Sh. certainly intended L.'s madness and sanity to have a distinction. Same with Ham. What is it?" And in a senior thesis, he'd expect a carefully argued answer.

1967

But *was* there an answer? Could any distinction be made between madness and sanity, wisdom and folly, sleeping and waking? He stared at the clutter of papers, the underlined books, the closed Quarto interleaved with ragged note-cards, the mere inkblots before him. The impulse to plunge his head into his hands and groan helplessly tugged at his dignity like the impish pluck at the king's sleeve by the court imbecile. What were the lines? "O, let me not be mad, not mad, sweet heaven! Come in," he almost moaned. "Come in, come in, come in."

Then he realized he was saying it, and tried to remember hearing a knock. Yes, most certainly. He could distinctly remember hearing a knock. At his door. So things were back in order again, and he must immediately do the next thing. He reached out to open the door. But his hand bumped the knob long before his grasp closed, and the door moved away from him, a good foot, swinging shut.

For a long moment he did not move his hand. He frowned at the knob, trying to remember many more things, and their proper order. Time ran back and forth in his mind, but he still could put nothing between the last two closings of the study door. It was like that discrepancy in exits he'd once discovered in a bad Jacobean quarto, which forced an important extra character on stage and opened up a wholly new interpretation of the entire scene. That had made his reputation. But this shocked him. It suddenly seemed such a wretched business, trying to think things through, and he decided not to think, only listen. He heard the tunnel echo of his own strained silence, and then deep within it, bells, softened by cap and curled toes, jingling almost in a whisper, and then unmistakably, laughter. Inane laughter.

He whirled around in his chair—too quickly for his age—and a small dizziness seized him, so that the riot of color, the grotesquery, the motley patches of things possible over the chimerical fabric, all assailed his sight at once. Then he was at last able to blink again, and the cowl, braided over with a red coxcomb, dipped toward him in a mocking bow, and the bells on the comb's points shifted. Their fleeting tinkle struck at him, and his old, uncompromising body gave way before the onrush of a deep shudder.

The Fool had his motley feet drawn up in the chair. He was grinning much as he had through the window. With great, friendly inanity. Everything in the room seemed instantly to delight him. His head lolled about on his neck, an imbecile motion exaggerated by the huge ass's ears that flopped from his cowl. When he saw something that had any brightness to it, he pointed his marotte's puppet face toward it, and pretended to whisper violently in the marotte's ear.

The old man's first thought was to rush at the coxcomb and beat him from the room. Never in his life had he felt such savagery rise within him, and he sensed it was all about to burst from him with a leaping howl at the Fool's throat.

But, the Fool abruptly stopped his meandering and rounded his grin on the old man. The grin was even more imbecile. Stupidly loyal, it seemed. The Fool was waiting. Then suddenly he kicked his motley legs with a great mocking jangle of bells, and teased at the old man with groping fingers, daring him to come ahead. Then one finger only crooking at him blackly, like the dead wick in the

66

lamp of reason.

It would kill me. He saw that one fact, and then began to catch hold altogether. Oblivion was smirking at him through a Fool's grin, but he was not going to let loose from the holds of logic and age and certainty. Not yet.

His first thought—his first self-possessed thought—was whether anybody had heard or seen anything. Whether anybody anywhere in the world had heard or seen anything. That he had very nearly attacked the Fool—*admitted him*—filled him with terror. Thoughts carried. Even the silence of the mind was suspicious.

Deliberately he turned back to his desk. He picked up the Pide Bull Quarto and set painfully to work on the storm scene. He courted his powers of concentration, and counted upon them to shut out any other presence that might be —that was how he must think of it, *might be*—near him. Gradually they did. The rollings of the bells and the little chuckles merged with the rising storm outside, and together, close to either side of his window, they passed away, out of his ken.

II

He ate his supper in the upper hall of the undergraduate Commons. He frequently did this for the sake of a change from his quiet widower's meal, served up uneventfully by the bad-tempered housekeeper who had outlived his wife's patience with her. But tonight he wanted something else from the dining hall. Something almost tribal.

He listened gratefully to the tumult of undergraduate cutlery. The meal was eaten out of various triangular, oblong, and serpentine depressions in uniform aluminum trays, collected from a cafeteria line, and the din reminded him of nothing so much as the Roman legionaries going into battle, beating their shields. On top of this, there was the babble of a least two hundred youths, all talking at once, none of them yet sure how his voice should really sound. Bedlam, Jericho. Or a thousand twangling instruments.

It all had a strangely reassuring effect upon him. The noise and liveliness argued against the Fool. When he got back to work, there would only be frost at his window. In a few days he might be able to talk confidently about hallucination, or tricks of the dozing eye, the dream-fondled ear. He tidied his wrinkled mouth with a napkin, took advantage of his age to leave the tray on the table rather than face the confusing actions of the dishwasher's chute, and left the Commons, mantled in an overcoat.

The walk back to his study followed shoveled canyons through the old snow. Within the last hour, they had begun to fill up again with a new undergrowth of flakes. A good way to put it, he thought. It stings your face like nettles, it clings to your clothes like burrs, so why shouldn't it be considered some kind of uncontrollable, prickly weed? The false logic of it pleased him. It kept him warm during the rest of the cold, devious walk, barriered him against the increasing storm that whipped at him devilishly. No matter which way he bent his head, it seemed to strike him on his unprotected side.

He reached the Library. Inside, he stamped his boots in the dark corridor—managed to kick one off, but had to stoop over for the other. He walked briskly down the corridor, congratulating himself on his desire to work after supper. Even if it might be false desire. He unlocked his study door and pushed it open, but it moved too lightly ahead of him, and he caught enough glimpse of haste in the Fool to know he'd just skipped back to the fireplace chair in time.

Disappointed, he told himself. Not surprised. Not afraid. Just disappointed.

He sat down at his desk with his back again to the other chair. He would have to do a little work, make a little progress before he could safely turn around. He did not know where the feeling came from, but he was certain that to work well was his only hope against the Fool's inane grin, his seductive, will-o'-the-wisp bells. The stir of the outside world—the noisy community of the dining hall—he realized now were useless.

He decided to give up the Pide Bull Quarto for the evening, in fact, to turn away from *Lear* itself altogether and read *The Tragecall historie of Kinge Leir and his Three Daughters*. Over the years he'd read the source play in patches, little snippets for his lectures, but he'd never sat down to read the whole play through for itself. He suspected it would be dull, wretchedly jangling, and stupid. In only a few pages he was convinced he was right. But he refused to give in to boredom, to let his mind slip out of its set task. The Fool was seated too near him for that.

The verse trotted along like an old dray. He had to stop reading line by line, and rushed ahead for the sense alone. The play dragged on preposterously. Leir was arrogant, lachrymose, and stupid. Truly stupid.

His patience began to wear. He tried to stifle his irritation, but it grew into a repressed anger. Finally, he yielded to a loss of temper he could hardly understand himself, and flung the book down on his desk. The old fool, he snapped to himself. Yes, precisely. The old fool, because there is no fool worse than Lear without his Fool. And that was Leir.

Suddenly he had the feeling of tottering on the verge of some immeasurably deep but opulent unknown. It was like that quibble that always touched the unsettled edge of his waking, only he felt he was much nearer the instance this time, that it *was* important after all. Terribly important. They were right to catch him up on it. It was a reference he needed to make. Properly. He had to refer back . . . and just as he seemed to have it, something frightened him away from the very thought, and his tottering was all nonsense again.

Behind him, the Fool tittered, and in a rage the old man turned on him. Through the waves of his vision, so tired now, he saw the Fool had taken up a new attitude.

He was sitting straight up in the chair, studiously attending upon a large book in his lap. He was turning the pages as fast as he could with the dexterity of one finger, and keeping time to the flipping of the pages by bobbing his cowled head up and down like a mechanical sage. Yes. Certainly. Quite. True.

Most. Likely. Yes. Indeed. Why. Of Course. He was very soon through the book. Immediately he stuffed it back into its place on the shelf, took down another one right next to it, and began the whole burlesque again.

Ignore it, he warned himself. But he watched the bobbing head and the passing pages with utter fascination. He was horrified, but somehow the horror did not reach, could not break in upon the rhythm of the mockery itself. The Fool increased his tempo. The pages beat by as if the book had been blown open, and a shifting wind were leafing through it. The Fool began turning pages either way now, in sharp little gusts of mindlessness. It struck him suddenly that the Fool had probably been hunched over a book, clowning an intelligence this way, all the time he'd been reading *Leir*.

He got to his feet, trembling. But the Fool, the moment he rose, stopped turning the pages and slowly, patiently took up his grin again. The horror at last broke through. For the first time, he really looked into the Fool's face. It was like looking not into a mask, but *out* of one. He was not in front of the Fool's face at all. He was *behind* it, staring out of its vacant eyes and teething its ruthless, dumb, ecstatic grin.

Hastily he piled his papers, closed his books. When he took his overcoat from the hook behind the door, he leaned against the door for just a moment, not realizing that a full minute passed before he pushed away from it again. He left the office, locking it behind him. Then he hurried out of the Library, forgetting his boots in the dark corridor. Once outside, he noticed he'd also forgotten the light in his study. Unless it had been turned on again. He went back for his boots, but decided to leave the light. It would go out when it wanted to.

III

The next afternoon his retirement was announced at the faculty meeting. He came in late, and heard the announcement almost as a surprise, having forgotten that it was to be made.

He looked around at his colleagues, who were clapping tenderly and avoiding his eye. Good night, old prince, he mused foolishly, may flights of angels help you up the stairs. He was amazed at himself. For the past few months, he had been planning how to suppress uncontrollable anger at this inevitable insult to dignity, professionally disguised as a tribute. But listening to the mannerly, almost withdrawn applause around him, he wasn't at all angry. There were so many other furies in his bosom now that he was actually relieved. Good, he thought, they haven't caught me out. They don't know. Then he realized exactly what it was they did not know. That he was suddenly unburdened of them. He had begun an existence which simply did not include them among its cares. Even as he stood among them, reaching for their kind hands, he felt he was setting them aside for good and all.

Nelson was among the first to rush up to him. No longer maddening.

"Congratulations," said Nelson. "Forty-three years. That's a long time."

1967

So it is, he thought. Or said. He wasn't sure which. And forty-three on top of twenty-four makes sixty-seven years' presence of mind, and now I've chucked it all. Don't need it. Wish I'd never had it. Wish I'd never been bothered with it.

He looked carefully at Nelson's face to see if he was possibly saying these things too, not just thinking them. But Nelson's face didn't seem to know either.

"Thank you, Nelson," he made sure to say, not think.

"I wanted to mention to you," Nelson went on, "the light was on in your study this morning. I tried to get in to turn it off, but your door was locked, and I couldn't find the janitor."

It occurred to him that Nelson too said all this without thinking. Or at least without thinking of any of the rich and enchanting possibilities. The scene if they had forced the door and found the Fool asleep at his desk, sprawled out in a garish parody of the pedant adoze over his dry books. The great blot of ink on the end of the Fool's nose, making him look like a broken nib. The marotte stuck into the Variorum like a bookmark, grinning over the binding in a frozen mime of the Contents. For all this, no thought. Of course, Nelson did not have *his* knowledge to go on. But somehow that came off as only another very distinct limitation in Nelson himself. He found it easy to fault him for it and set him aside.

Why, there was even snoring. Great hawking at a burbling lip. A grand test. The Fool curled up in exactly his own napping posture, when he opened the door that morning, pretending the noise of entering had troubled his sleep, bestirring himself with a loud carillon from his cap. He'd really almost laughed out loud, but suddenly sensed the open door behind him. He fell back against it, listening hard for any approaching sound outside in the corridor. God's spies, he thought, it's broad daylight. The Fool chuckled, beaming at him over that great noseblot with blank, uncanny eyes, bright with false sleep, and he felt himself pulled another small tug away from the order of things into the clutter of that merry-andrew gaze.

Perhaps he really ought to tip Nelson off. Perhaps it would be better, even now, if he simply leaned over and whispered, "Look, there's a pest of a fellow in my office. Will you run over and tell him I won't be by today?" Only he knew he would be by, and alone, and all he could bring himself to say was, "Thank you again. Stupid of me. Getting a little careless lately. Need to be watched, don't I?"

An older friend in the English department came up to him then and had the good sense not to congratulate him.

"Working on anything now?" he asked simply.

"Yes. *Lear*. Cleaning up, really. Talked about it enough in my lifetime, haven't I? Never make a book. But a little—a little *opusculum* would do, wouldn't it? For 'A poor, infirm, weak, and despised old man' ?"

"Utter nonsense," replied his friend, staring at the floor. "You'd better save a little room in the pasture when they put you out there next spring. I'm afraid they won't give me those extra few years of grace they gave you. I'm not that tough."

"Plenty of room." He wondered if Nelson could see how graciously his friend had turned the compliment. Probably not. But then it really made no difference. They were both foolish even to try. Eptly or ineptly, they stayed nothing by it. They were only tarrying here, all three of them.

"What is it you're trying to do with *Lear?*" his friend asked, bringing back the subject.

"Oh, I'm taking up Folly. Much the same way Erasmus does. Though he's quite wrong about her, you know. She isn't a goddess at all. Only a fool."

"I'm not surprised."

"You would be. I've been spending most of my time lately on the Fool. If you stay with him long enough, he becomes a sort of familiar. A goddess is only a conception. The fool's much more than that." He said all this lightly, edging as near as he dared to his own peccant sense of the matter. The risk was titillating. "I'm really trying to decide just what his existence amounts to."

His friend frowned in a way he quite understood, but Nelson smiled in a way that escaped him. What bit of dried fungi had he managed to fire in that tinderbox this time?

Nelson seemed for a moment to want to hold it all in, but he couldn't resist. "I suppose you might even call him," he said nervously, "the existential fool."

So. That poppycock. When was he going to learn to watch every single word he used in front of this young Holofernes? He felt a wild urge to reach out with grand punctilio and pluck Nelson's velvety beard, but the deepening of his friend's frown kept him off.

"You suppose whatever you wish to suppose, young man," his friend snorted at the instructor, "but remember it's your own tomfoolery." Then he turned back again. "But I must admit I don't quite see what you're driving at either. The Fool's simply a character in the play. His existence is in his role, isn't it?"

And so. More poppycock. This was harder, riskier. "Of course," he agreed affably, "but I'm wondering if that role isn't just a bit wider than you think it is. The Fool is a character in all of sixteenth, seventeenth century life. He has a role even *off* the stage. We find Queen Elizabeth footing the bill for a huge wardrobe of motley. Read the list sometime. The fools Robert Greene, Jack Green, and Mr. Shenstone. An Italian named Monarcho. A little Blackamoor. Thomasina the Dwarf—oh, I'd like to have seen her—and Ipolyta the Tartarian. And Clod. Clod—bless him—Clod is even chided by his Queen for not criticizing her sharply enough. Royal displeasure at his failure to play his role. Not quick enough in his hits upon Glorianna, can you imagine?" He warmed to his own tired lecture style, feeling how safely he could dissemble under its fey pedantry as others gathered around him. "The Fool is with us, you see? With them, I suppose I should say," he added hastily, "but I mean, abroad. That's important. Abroad. As the Lord of Misrule, as the Comte de Permission, guilty of 'Flearing and making of mouths.' He is fed on crow's meat, they say, and monkey flesh. Or he eats only what the dogs have tasted, and so they serve the dogs great delicacies for the Fool's sake. An odd, rarified life, you realize. Terribly indulgent, but at the same time terribly mangy. It says of Will Sommers, for instance, Henry the Eighth's great fool, that he 'laid himself down among the spaniels to sleep' after he'd pleased his Harry with a riddle. A silly riddle at that. Damnably silly. 'What is it that, being borne without life, head, lip, or eye, yet doth run roaring through the world till it die?' "

He looked quickly around him hoping for someone to answer. It was so easy, but they all seemed to give up. He felt the silliness take an oddly dreadful hold upon him, and spoke as lightly as he could.

" 'Why, quoth Will, it is a fart.' "

He knew he was the only one laughing—senselessly—yet all their faces were bent up in a way that meant they might be laughing too, if he could only hear them. Desperately he fought his way out of his own shameful laughter.

"The most ridiculous bawdry. Not funny at all. Just not funny. Very weak. Very. But you see—I think we can sense in it—the Fool's familiarity." He wormed loose again. "To an Elizabethan, Jacobean audience. What I mean is, that the Fool might have more reality for these people than Lear, even though they did know kings too. They wouldn't expect to go into the narrow streets at Bankside and find Lear walking abroad. But they could very well expect to find the Fool. That, actually, is how fools were found. They existed, you see. Naturals."

He stopped, hoping he was nearer sense now. "Fascinating idea," his friend said, but he knew that was coddling. He must be more careful, he realized, much more careful, even with friends, and this suddenly enraged him.

"Do you know how to pick a fool?" he burst out. "There was one in Germany named Conrad Pocher—the Count Palatine delighted in him—he was considered ripe for the court's pleasure after he hanged a little boy from a tree. Pocher hanged the little boy because the little boy had scabs. It was a joke that Pocher would hang you if you had scabs too. Beware, all you who are scabrous—"

He felt his friend's hand grip his shoulder, as if to pinch off what he was saying. His friend said to him, "I'm afraid I still don't see what you're getting at, but good luck with it anyhow." The others hastily agreed.

He closed them out and turned abruptly to Nelson. "I'm letting you take all my classes."

The surprise of it dropped his friend's hand from his shoulder. But he couldn't bother to care. He went on to Nelson. "I'd appreciate it if you'd do the exam as well. I'm afraid I'm going to want to be left very much alone."

Now he didn't dare look at his friend. He had as good as abdicated. Nelson was in a fidget of self-effacement. He felt he wouldn't be able to stand that maggoty beard another moment longer. Other friends came up to him. They suggested delicately all the wonderful things he had done in the past, and the long life he had ahead in peace and quiet contemplation. In five more minutes, it was over, and he turned from the scattered gathering, found his coat, and went out across the frozen snow that pitched out flat before him like a white heath.

IV

He worked furiously. Everyday he was more exhausted, but he fought fatigue with anger, and anger, he found, could keep him going when all his faculties were otherwise ready to fail.

The storm wore on, running in tatters across the stiff snow, almost following his anger. After a ruthless night, it would seem to be dying away, only to regain its ferocity in the late afternoon, cutting icily against the window, closing away what little light there was in the grey sky. But he didn't mind. It kept him alone. He'd taken his card off the door, and nobody bothered him.

The Fool was always decorous. For the most part, he stayed happily in his chair, and thumbed through the books over and over again, timing his flurries to the storm. There were a few pranks. The old man would glance up from his work to find the marotte nodding methodically over his shoulder like a wizened scholar whose head had been shrunk, the Fool pressed right up against the back of his chair. It made him jump, but no more. Or he would come in to find a paper full of meaningless inkblots, almost like writing, lying among his notes. Yet he could never quite be sure it wasn't a scrap he'd used himself to test his pen. The tricks kept him on edge, but they were nothing beside the threat he felt in the Fool's patience. The fool seemed somehow able to wait without ever losing a moment. Nothing could exhaust his empty loyalty. He was there forever. Or not. It made no difference to him. Only to those in quest of differences.

But he could admit none of this. Not to himself, certainly not to the Fool. Not even by the fleet tribute of another eyeblink that might drop him into an unguarded sleep.

Instead, he settled into a fixed wakefulness, embarking on what he sensed would be some final test of his scholarship. He had already made a beginning, so it was only a matter of shifting his emphasis. Under the pretense of still pursuing his studies of _Lear_—to whom, he wondered, to whom?—he set out to study the Fool himself. He felt certain that if he could only read up on the Fool, chivvy his motley image through the bramble of source material and first mentions and oblique references and analogues, hunt him down like startled sense at bay behind a faulty and obscure text, he would save him. As simple a thing as fixing the Fool's dates properly might trap him, he was half convinced. He was depending upon his last reliable habit of mind. Somewhere among the disputed readings, the incunabula, the endless exegesis, he felt he was bound to come upon the right page. Then, all he would need to do—all he could ever do to end this gest—was somehow to rip out that page.

He began working through the literature. Other scholars had been there before him, but they had no sense of the menace—he could tell that from the bloodless measure they took in their writings—the menace that lay within the sweet hollow of folly. None of them, obviously, had ever kept a fool. Yet any simpleton writing a pet manual, would at least know his German Shepherd or his Siamese or his box turtle. He pushed impatiently through their treacly rationality to the primary sources, testimony from the great warders who had once kept real fools to fondle like favored apes.

He searched constantly for a touchstone. He picked finically even among the original Latinisms in hopes of finding a proper one. *Stultus. Morio. Fatuus. Sannio.* They all fitted, yet none quite, really. He set the legends alongside his own Fool for measure. Til Eulenspiegel, the owl glass, the wise mirror, but still a brute. At Til's graveside, a cord snapped, and his coffin tipped upright into the broken earth. "Leave him as he is, he was strange in this life, he wants to be after his death." So they buried him standing straight up and stole his estate, which proved his last mockery, being only a box of stones. His own Fool could have inherited, yes, easily inherited that owlishness, that false legacy of stones. But much more his own Fool favored Marcolf, the jester who watched Solomon dispense justice to the two women who claimed one child, and as the king calmly lowered the threatening sword to his side again and judged so wisely, jeered at him for trusting a woman's tears. Ah, how that fitted. That exactly, the same jeering laughter that so harrowed him, turning his own subtlety of mind suddenly as luggish as the clapper in a frozen bell.

Yet legend could not satisfy him. Legendary fools were vagrant in time, and his own Fool carried his days upon his back—a hunch to his motley shoulders that meant he stooped under the hour, not under a proverb. He came from a rich period. The old man relished such labor, and early on, among the many sotties he dug up, he found Robert Armin's own *Nest of Ninnies*. The actor-clown's account of the fools of his day. "Simply of themselves without Compound." Just what was wanted—"without Compound"—and reaching into that nest—down among Jemy Camber, the fat fool a yard wide and a nail high, and Jack Oates, eating a hot quince pie while standing in the moat and drinking from it to cool his tongue, and Will Sommers, capping Cardinal Woolsey's rhymes—he felt the quick flutter of his own Fool's ninny soul cross his fingertips.

He reached again, but then drew back quickly from that mock grin, the glissando that ran down the coxcomb bells in chilling welcome.

He pushed deeper into the documents. Account books of royal households, pamphlet Lives of fools, ha' penny street ballads and mock Last Wills & Testaments, extracts from court diaries, an actual letter to James I from his fool away in Spain with Philip II's court. Some of them were on microfilm, and he turned to this newfangled apparatus for momentary escape. He could leave his Fool behind, yet pursue him still, more at his ease, studying the little scrolls as they unrolled beneath the thumbing white light of the scanner. But he soon found this another mockery. The glare of the machine, blowing up the quaint Elizabethan printing into an illusory page pressed without substance against the cold, milky glass, was too much for his weak, old eyes, and somehow for his sense of reality. He could not stand the ghostliness of it. He felt he must be able to turn the actual page, crumble a chip out of its browned edge, smell its acrid, bookish dust, if he were ever going to find it. What was there to tear out here. He hated the skimping artifice that robbed him of the feel of a book, and imagined the scanner as some great Worm that had invested the castle of his learning. Like Spenser's Error, only too uncreatured a thing to spew forth black ink, or disgorge the books it had swallowed. Its only malice, a pale flush of cold light producing an incubus of a page. He knew how ridiculous he was being, possibly senile, and he drove himself to take meticulous notes, as usual. But he only breathed freely again in the staleness of his closed-up study, back within the pied *ambiance* of his Fool.

By then, he had all his facts. He was now thoroughly familiar with, something of an authority on, a good man in the field of. Oh, he understood his own qualifications all too well. It only remained for him to think things through to the entrapment, to perform the sacred rites of abstraction, and in a curious way, he sought to cleanse himself for them. He stripped away his last ragged pretenses to any venerability, all the shoddy of his professorial airs, and bared himself, in all but intellect, for a naked, failing old man.

It ended so many qualms. He could talk to himself freely. He mumbled and muttered as he pleased, and if his mouth grew wet, he wiped it on his sleeve without shame. When he caught the Fool imitating him in some palsied fumble, he hardly cared. Once he watched the Fool's great, dirty tongue loll almost to the floor before he sensed the coldness at his own cheek and brushed away a long, loose string of saliva. Unimportant. All that mattered was the careful tightening of his logic as it closed around the Fool.

"Decide whether natural or artificial," he thought or said or wrote down somewhere. "Could be a mute. Idiot boy sold by a rustic to some great house in exchange for a few acres grazing land free of enclosure. Such happens. But looks brighter than that. Silence too sly. Vacancy too coy. Hidden wits. I see him offering the egg. Like Will Sommers again, asking the King to let him give an egg to every cuckold in England, and permission granted, hands the first egg to Harry himself. What is he here to hand me? What's in his hand? What's in my hand? A page? A page?"

He glanced down at his hand, but there was only the back of it, covered with liver spots, and he realized that the ambuscado, so carefully laid up in his notes, had missed its elusive quarry yet again.

But he started once more, reciting a tale. "Will Sommers loudly broke wind, and glared at the lady by his side. Then he smiled at her and said for all to hear, 'Don't worry. I'll say it was me.' Clever fool. Rich fool. But this is a poor fool. Violent? Often they are insane. No attack yet. But if it comes. . . . Bawdry? A scurrilous fool? Behind that dumbshow, what cess of mind, waiting to pour over me like a chamber pot? Gardyloo!" And then an old man's decrepit giggle, like beans rattling in a bladder, caught him off guard, sucked up from some grossness he'd suddenly remembered from his long study of folly. Again and again, he broke away from that giggle, forcing his way back to the needed date or reference that would repair the break where flatulence and scurrility had escaped from his thinking.

He even allowed himself little threats now. Never quite to the Fool's face, but, "Take heed," he would mumble, "the whip. The whip."

Then suddenly he felt the grip of it in his hand.

Carefully he let go, and gathered up his notecards to give his hands something else to do. He tried to reshuffle them for the hundredth time, but found that they were at last, by some fluke, in a correct order. Irrefutably that order imposed itself upon him. Sequential, exact, conclusive. This time, all his learning told him, there was no escape. Tapping each card nervously on his blotter, searching for error, he tried to think how many days it had been, how many stormy hours had hawked at his chill window to tumble this sudden, random knowledge upon him. He counted slowly—days, hours, cards—and imagined the Fool at his back, counting too, with great pulls at his gross fingers, unable, like himself, to arrive at any sensible number.

But he did not turn around. He saw that he could corner the Fool now with a mere glance, that he could positively identify him beyond any quibble to his colleagues, much more, that he could whip him, rip him out, do with him as he pleased. He had all that certainty, but once again it seemed to be forcing him to the verge of that same opulent unknown over which he had tottered so often, so perilously. . . .

Only now, at the Fool's warning titter, he deliberately stared down into its black gulf. He referred back and back, as far as his mind would take him, and knowledge did not come to him so much as it physically seized him. The brush of the long ass's ears around his own cheeks. The plucking up of his whole spine into a rich, red comb, topped with bells. The whirligig of his coat plaids turning to lozenges. His grip on the whip thinning, loosening to a fragile, foolish hold upon the stick of a marotte. One foot jingled beneath him, and quite suddenly he could feel just where the whip was going to cut.

He did the one thing possible in the moment left before the black gulf itself turned over and sat upon his head for a cap. He jumped into it at last.

"Stay!" he shouted to the Fool. "Stay right here! Right by my side! Right here with me!"

Then he whirled around and doubled over in laughter, jeering widely at the suddenly defeated jangling thing in the chair.

"Right?" he whispered. "Right, right?"

The Fool's vaacnt stare was afire like a bone pit, but his marotte nodded its eternal grin.

V

He was still laughing when the knock came at his door. Very cautiously he judged his surprise at it. No, it was no longer an interruption of his solitude. It was an intrusion upon their intimacy. The Fool shook both fists as if beating back at the door, letting loose a rage of bells.

"Who is it?" he asked, smiling at the angry Fool.

"Nelson, sir. Are you all right?"

He and the Fool shrugged at each other, both repressing laughter this time. He was still a little bit in awe of his own triumph, the confidence they had so suddenly found in each other. But then why, he wondered, had it taken so long to see what the Fool was there for?

"Sir?"

Young Nelson was anxious. He chortled to himself. The Fool immediately understood him and giggled into his two ass's ears which he had crossed gleefully over his mouth.

"I heard—well, laughing, sir. I just wondered if everything's all right. I thought I heard. . . ." Nelson left off.

He hesitated because he wanted to savor this moment, the superb jest it had finally turned out to be. With this to top if off.

"No, I'm perfectly fine. Excellent fettle." He winked at the Fool. "Come in, if you've a moment."

The door eased open, just far enough for Nelson to squirm around it, braving everything with his shadow first. He nodded from it, smiling, while his eyes flicked nervously around the room. His stare scurried into every corner, and then he flushed, realizing he had absolutely no excuse.

"No, really. Sit down, sit down."

Nelson gratefully moved over to the chair and plumped down in it. The Fool bounced up just in time. He shook his bells angrily, and scowled. The old man chuckled good-naturedly. Nelson joined him in chuckling, out of deference.

"I'm really sorry, sir." He shifted once, twice in the chair. "Honestly, it sounded like you were in here laughing yourself silly."

"No, no. I was just—" How to put it, how to put it? "I've just finished up my work on *Lear,* you see, and I was having a good laugh over it."

Nelson grew terribly puzzled, but only above the eyebrows. The Fool caught it, and took off this sedate puzzlement with a mock petite frown of his own. An irresistible bit of fleering. Again the old man chuckled, worrying Nelson into joining him again. The frown looked even more ridiculous over the polite chuckle.

"Oh, I must fill you in," he said. "It's just that this whole business with *Lear* has turned out to be, after all—well, a pretty big joke."

"I'm sorry about that," Nelson said elaborately. "Really very sorry."

He looked at the young instructor sharply. He'd caught something, just for a second. Nelson *was* sorry for him, of course. Flamboyantly sorry. Poor old codger. But there was something more, edging in, smacking distinctly of derring-do. He glanced at the Fool, who was leaning with both elbows on the back of Nelson's chair. The Fool poked two saucy fingers up for ears behind Nelson's head, and blew his lips flatulently.

"But I can see how it might come out that way," Nelson went on. "*Lear* is such a difficult play—and . . . *disappointing,* don't you think?"

Had he jumped? He felt sure the Fool had. But the skittishness was not so much in them, he sensed, as in Nelson. Was he about to skip and run for it on his own?

"Perhaps you've found—" Nelson paused at a near stutter and then hurdled. "what *I've* always found." The Fool stared, and then lifted himself on the chair back, kicking his bells together at the heels in muffled joy. "In the end, it really all comes to nothing, doesn't it? Dr. Johnson may have been right."

"Then you *have* been. . . ."

He saw instantly that Nelson was going to misinterpret him. There would now be a painstaking mending of fences, he could tell, which would only delay the real point. **Only the Fool** had the patience for it. His greedy eyes puddled, and that same inane grin sank down once more into the vapid face like water crumbling sand.

"No, no," said Nelson, starting in on his fences. "I honestly haven't. I was leaving that all to you. I touch on the play, yes, but only with reference to some work I'm trying to do on the older play. *Leir.*" He leaned forward, and for an awful moment the old man thought that from the undermining of the grin, the Fool's face had at last caved in entirely and fallen upon Nelson's own. But then he saw it was only a great, watery leer. "But if you *are* giving up on your own work—I mean, if you're leaving the field free again—and that's the only way I'd want to have it, frankly—I think I might try to treat the two plays together."

"What *exactly* is it you're going to show?" Besides this abruptness, this, this. . . .

"It'll be tough sledding, but I'm pretty clear now that *Leir* is infinitely the better play. At least, in my own mind. You see, sir. . . ."

Then the flights and dips and swoops and long drifts of a young, excited mind swept over him. A swift, ignorant, sweet bird beating its new wings in the heart of an old storm. He listened as carefully as he could, and tried not to look at the Fool. He was afraid that if he hid, he would not be able to account for his tears. Why was it so irretrievably sad? All that he heard was challenging and clever and zealous. But it depended upon so many certainties that weren't really there. The dimness, the vagueness, the lack of distinction that blurred every final thought, every last, best guess—he saw that the young man did not even feel their menace. Perhaps, on some midnight balance of his secret fears, Nelson allowed himself to know he might be wrong, but did he ever allow himself to know he might not even be that?

The old man's gaze drifted in mute appeal to the Fool. Then it simply drifted, caught up in the aimless wandering of the Fool's vacuous stare. Just in time, he saw his mistake. He looked quickly away before the Fool had a chance to throw his own lugubriousness back at him, and pulled himself together, alert to danger. He cursed his own stupidity. How very much, he realized bitterly, my very own.

He was losing his Fool.

"Nelson." He said it for once affectionately, as a first name, not a last. "How sure are you of all these things?" He meant the question to be only cautionary, but he could see it had gone hopelessly wrong. Nelson's face hardened a bit, and the gleeful Fool twirled the marotte over Nelson's head, badgering the old man for—what?—simply an old man, what more. He tried to think of a way to make his words less discouraging, less cantankerous. "I mean, it all sounds very wonderful, but is this to be a whole-hearted plunge into—" Into what? He knew the word he wanted to use, but also what irreparable damage it would do his little contact with the young man. And whose fault is it, he asked himself, the contact is so little? How very much, he thought bitterly again, my very own.

"A plunge into what, sir?"

A plunge into Folly. That's what he wanted to say. There was the Fool behind the chair, with as large a charter as the wind, to blow on whom he pleased. No man could hold him back. *Numerus stultorum est infinitus.*

"Let me put it this way, Nelson. I can't tell you how to do your work. Nobody can." He stopped helplessly. The Fool had turned and lifted one fat buttock at him, dropping the marotte down between his motley legs. The tiny head wigwagged at him like a phallus with an obscene, upsidedown grin. He forced himself ahead. "Do you have any idea what it's really like to work your way to the limits of something?" Limits? Limits of what? "I don't mean just setting out to settle a moot point. I mean plunging in so far that you can't—can never succeed—succeed in getting out again."

He pressed his hands together for steadiness. He saw the Fool imitate him, turning it into a silly prayerful gesture.

"You're alone. But accompanied. It's funny, but your companions are all there to help you feel alone. Because you don't, you mustn't admit they're there." He smiled. "That's the funny part about it. Once you admit—"

The Fool shook like a Sunday morning of church bells.

"Once you admit—" He looked hard at Nelson. There was nothing in his face but sufferance. Deferential sufferance. "Think of Lear of the heath, Nelson Who are his companions? Who? The boundaries of his loneliness, really. Aren't they?"

He waited now. The burden was on the other.

"I'm pretty sure of my ground, I think, sir. Others have had the same idea about *Leir,* I'm sure you're aware. Tolstoi, for instance, gave it my interpretation. What I should say is, I'm taking up *his.*"

So the harlequinade will go on, he thought helplessly. He did not even look about for his Fool. He tried to keep his weak eyes fixed on a single, groomed tuft of Nelson's beard.

"I appreciate all your advice, and I'd like to come to you for some help, if that's all right with you. But for the moment. . . ."

He didn't hear the rest. They said things near the door, but to him, it was an absolutely wordless parting. He could not be sure, but he thought that something scuttled hastily between his knees as he shut himself in.

He stepped over to his window. It was still snowing, as if forever. Across the flurry he could see Nelson trudging away. A shadow—only a shadow—scurried and scraped about him in the storm with grotesque, unhallowed gestures. With great pain, he admitted they were gestures of fondness. Finally he thought he saw it leap up on the man's back, like a loving thing, and that bowed his own head to the cold window pane.

He knew. Deserted now, even by his own measure of solitude, he knew what he would never know again. Any boundary to his own loneliness. He supposed, since he was still alive, that he must take this to be wisdom.

1967

TV

It's been going on a long time.
For instance, these two guys, not saying much, who slog
Through sun and sand, fleeing the scene of their crime,
Till one turns, without a word, and smacks
His buddy flat with the flat of an axe,
Which cuts down on the dialogue
Some, but is viewed rather as normal than sad
By me, as I wait for the next ad.

It seems to me it's been quite a while
Since the last vision of blonde loveliness
Vanished, her shampoo and shower and general style
Replaced by this lean young lunk—
Head parading along with a gun in his back to confess
How yestereve, being drunk
And in a state of existential despair,
He beat up his grandma and pawned her invalid chair.

But here at last is a pale beauty
Smoking a filter beside a mountain stream,
Brief interlude, before the conflict of love and duty
Gets moving again, as sheriff and posse expound,
Between jail and saloon, the American Dream
Where Justice, after considerable horsing around,
Turns out to be Mercy; and where the villain was knocked off,
A kindly uncle offers syrup for my cough.

And now these clean cut American types
In global hats are having a nervous debate
As they stand between their individual rocket ships
Which have landed, appropriately, on some rocks
Somewhere in Space, in an atmosphere of hate
Where one tells the other to pull up his socks
And get going, he doesn't say where; they fade,
And an angel food cake flutters in the void.

I used to leave now and again,
No more. A lot of violence in American life
These days, mobsters and cops all over the scene.
Still there's a lot of love, too, mixed with the strife,
And kitchen-kindness, like a bedtime story
With rich food and a more kissable depilatory.
But I keep my weapons handy, sitting here
Smoking and shaving and drinking the dry beer.

AARON SISKIND. (*TQ* #8)

1967

81

Two essays

E. M. CIORAN

Thinking against oneself

ALMOST ALL OUR DISCOVERIES are due to our violences, to the exacerbation of our instability. Even God, insofar as He interests us—it is not in our innermost selves that we discern God, but at the extreme limits of our fever, at the very point where, our rage confronting His, a shock results, an encounter as ruinous for Him as for us. Blasted by the curse attached to acts, the man of violence forces his nature, rises above himself only to relapse, an aggressor, followed by his enterprises, which come to punish him for having instigated them. Every work turns against its author: the poem will crush the poet, the system the philosopher, the event the man of action. Destruction awaits anyone who, answering to his vocation and fulfilling it, exerts himself within history; only the man who sacrifices every gift and talent escapes: released from his humanity, he may lodge himself in Being. If I aspire to a metaphysical career, I cannot, at any price, retain my identity: whatever residue I retain must be liquidated; if, on the contrary, I assume a historical role, it is my responsibility to exasperate my faculties until I explode along with them. One always perishes by the self one assumes: to bear a name is to claim an exact mode of collapse.

Faithful to his appearances, the man of violence is not discouraged, he starts all over again, and persists, since he cannot exempt himself from suffering. His occasional efforts to destroy others are merely a roundabout route to his own destruction. Beneath his self-confidence, his *braggadocio,* lurks a fanatic of disaster. Hence it is among the violent that we meet the enemies of themselves. And we are all violent—men of anger who, having lost the key of quietude, now have access only to the secrets of laceration.

Instead of letting it erode us gradually, we decided to go time one better, to add to its moments *our own*. This new time grafted onto the old one, this time elaborated and projected, soon revealed its virulence: objectivized, it became history, a monster we have called up against ourselves, a fatality we cannot escape, even by recourse to the formulas of passivity, the recipes of wisdom.

Try as we will to take the "cure" of ineffectuality; to meditate on the Taoist fathers' doctrine of submission, of withdrawal, of a sovereign absence; to follow, like them, the course of consciousness once it ceases to be at grips with the world and weds the form of things as water does, their favorite element—we shall never succeed. They scorn both our curiosity and our thirst for suffering; in which they differ from the mystics, and especially from the medieval ones, so apt to recommend the virtues of the hair shirt, the scourge, insomnia, inanition and lament.

"A life of intensity is contrary to the Tao," teaches Lao Tse, a normal man if ever there was one. But the Christian virus torments us: heirs of the flagellants, it is by refining our excruciations that we become conscious of ourselves. Is religion declining? We perpetuate its extravagances, as we perpetuate the macerations and the cell-shrieks of old, our will to suffer equalling that of the monasteries in their heyday. If the Church no longer enjoys a monopoly on hell, it has nonetheless riveted us to a chain of sighs, to the cult of the ordeal, of blasted joys and jubilant despair.

The mind, as well as the body, pays for "a life of intensity". Masters in the art of thinking against oneself, Nietzsche, Baudelaire and Dostoievsky have taught us to side with our dangers, to broaden the sphere of our diseases, to acquire existence by division from Being. And what for the Great Chinaman was a symbol of failure, a proof of imperfection, constitutes for us the sole mode of possessing, of making contact with ourselves.

"If a man loves nothing, he will be invulnerable" (Chuang Tse). A maxim as profound as it is invalid. The apogee of indifference—how attain it, when our very apathy is tension, conflict, aggression? No sage among *our* ancestors, but malcontents, triflers, fanatics whose disappointments or excesses we must continue.

According to our Chinese again, only the detached mind penetrates the essence of the Tao; the man of passion perceives only its effects: the descent to the depths demands silence, the suspension of our vibrations, indeed of our faculties. But is it not revealing that our aspiration to the absolute is expressed in terms of activity, of combat, that a Kierkegaard calls himself a "knight of Faith" and that a Pascal is nothing but a pamphleteer? We attack and we struggle; therefore we know only the effects of the Tao. Further, the failure of Quietism, that European equivalent of Taoism, tells the story of our possibilities, our prospects.

The apprenticeship to passivity—I know nothing more contrary to our habits. (The modern age begins with two hysterics: Don Quixote and Luther.) If we *make time,* produce and elaborate it, we do so out of our repugnance to the hegemony of essence and to the contemplative submission it presupposes. Taoism seems to me wisdom's first and last word: yet I resist it, my instincts reject it, as they refuse to *endure* anything—the heredity of revolt is too much for us. Our disease? Centuries of attention to time, the idolatry of becoming. What recourse to China or India will heal us?

1967

There are certain forms of wisdom and deliverance which we can neither grasp from within nor transform into our daily substance, nor even frame in a theory. Deliverance, if we insist upon it, must proceed from ourselves: no use seeking it elsewhere, in a ready-made system or in some Oriental doctrine. Yet this is often what happens in many a mind avid, as we say, for an absolute. But such wisdom is fraudulent, such deliverance merely dupery. I am indicting not only theosophy and its adepts, but all those who adopt truths incompatible with their nature. More than one such man has an Instant India and supposes he has plumbed its secrets, when nothing—neither his character nor his training nor his anxieties—prepares him for any such thing. What a swarm of the pseudo-"delivered" stares down at us from the pinnacle of their salvation! Their conscience is clear—do they not claim to locate themselves *above* their actions? An intolerable swindle. They aim, further, so high that any conventional religion seems to them a family prejudice by which their "metaphysical mind" cannot be satisfied. To convert to *India,* doubtless that is more satisfying. But they forget that India postulates the agreement of idea and act, the identity of salvation and renunciation. When one possesses a "metaphysical mind," such trifles are scarcely worth one's concern.

After so much imposture, so much fraud, it is comforting to contemplate a beggar. He, at least, neither lies nor lies to himself: his doctrine, if he has one, he embodies; work he dislikes, and he proves it; wanting to possess nothing, he cultivates his impoverishment, the condition of his freedom. His thought is resolved into his being and his being into his thought. He *has* nothing, he *is* himself, he endures: to live on a footing with eternity is to live from day to day, from hand to mouth. Thus for him, other men are imprisoned in illusion. If he depends on them, he takes his revenge by studying them, a specialist in the underbelly of "noble" sentiments. His sloth, of a very rare quality, truly "delivers" him from a world of fools and dupes. About renunciation he knows more than many of your esoteric works. To be convinced of this, you need only walk out into the street. . . . But you prefer the texts that teach mendicancy. Since no practical consequence accompanies your meditations, it will not be surprising that the merest bum is worth more than you. . . . Can we conceive a Buddha faithful to his truths *and* to his palace? One is not "delivered-alive" and still a landowner. I reject the generalization of the lie, I repudiate those who exhibit their so-called "salvation" and prop it with a doctrine which does not emanate from themselves. To unmask them, to knock them off the pedestal they have hoisted themselves on, to hold them up to scorn is a campaign no one should remain indifferent to. For at any price we must keep those who have too clear a conscience from living and dying in peace.

*

When at every turn you confront us with "the absolute," you affect a profound, inaccessible little ogle, as if you were at grips with a remote world, in a light, a darkness all your own, masters of a realm to which nothing outside of yourselves can gain access. You grant us other mortals a few scraps of the

84

great discoveries you have just made, a few vestiges of your prospecting. But all your labors result in no more than this: you murmer one poor word, the fruit of your reading, of your learned frivolity, of your bookish void, your borrowed anguish.

The Absolute—all our efforts come down to undermining the sensibility which leads to the absolute. Our wisdom (or rather our unwisdom) repudiates it; relativists, we look for our equilibrium not in eternity but in time. The *evolving absolute,* Hegel's heresy, has become our dogma, our tragic orthodoxy, the philosophy of our *reflexes.* Anyone who supposes he can avoid it is either boasting or blind. Stuck with appearances, we keep espousing an incomplete wisdom, half-fantasy and half-foolishness. If India, to quote Hegel again, represents "the dream of infinite mind," the turn of our intellect, as of our sensibility, obliges us to conceive of *incarnate* mind, limited to historical processes, embracing not the world but the world's *moments,* a faceted time which we escape only by fits and starts, and only when we betray our appearances.

The sphere of consciousness shrinks in action; no one who acts can lay claim to the universal, for to act is to cling to the properties of being at the expense of being itself, to a form of reality to reality's detriment. The degree of our liberation is measured by the quantity of undertakings from which we are emancipated, as by our capacity to convert any object into a non-object. But it is meaningless to speak of liberation apropos of a hurried humanity which has forgotten that we cannot reconquer life nor revel in it without having first abolished it.

We breathe too fast to be able to grasp things in themselves or to expose their fragility. Our panting postulates and distorts them, creates and disfigures them, and binds us to them. I bestir myself, therefore I emit a world as suspect as my speculation which justifies it; I espouse movement, which changes me into a generator of being, into an artisan of fictions, while my cosmogonic verve makes me forget that, led on by the whirlwind of *acts,* I am nothing but an acolyte of time, an agent of decrepit universes.

Gorged on sensations and on their corollary—becoming, we are "undelivered" by inclination and by principle, sentenced by choice, stricken by the fever of the visible, rumaging in surface enigmas of a piece with our bewilderment and our trepidation.

If we would regain our freedom, we must shake off the burden of sensation, no longer react to the world by our senses, break our bonds. For all sensation is a bond, pleasure as much as pain, joy as much as misery. The only free mind is the one that, pure of all intimacy with beings or objects, plies its own vacuity.

To resist happiness—the majority manages that; suffering is much more insidious. Have you ever tasted it? You will never be sated once you have, you will pursue it greedily and preferably where it does not exist, you will project it there since without it everything seems futile to you, drab. Wherever there is suffering, it exhausts mystery or renders it luminous. The savor and solution of things, accidents and obsession, caprice and necessity—suffering will make you love *appearance* in whatever is most powerful, most lasting, and truest, and will tie you to itself forever, for "intense" by nature, it is, like any "intensity," a servitude, a subjection. The soul unfettered, the soul indifferent and void—how *in the world* can we achieve that? How conquer absence, the freedom of absence? Such freedom will never figure among our *mores,* any more than "the dream of infinite mind."

To identify oneself with an alien doctrine, one must adopt it without restrictions: what is the use of acknowledging the truths of Buddhism and of rejecting transmigration, the very basis of the idea of renunciation? Of assenting to the Vedanta, of accepting the Unreality of matter and then behaving as if matter existed? An inconsistency inevitable for any mind raised in the cult of phenomena. For it must be admitted: we have *the phenomenon* in our blood. We may scorn it, abhor it, it is nonetheless our patrimony, our capital of agonies, the symbol of our sentence here on earth. A race of convulsionaries, at the center of a cosmic farce, we have imprinted on the universe the stigmata of our history and shall never be capable of that illumination which lets us die in peace. It is by our works, not by our silences, that we have chosen to disappear: our future may be read in our features, in the grimaces of agonized and busy prophets. The smile of the Buddha, that smile which overhangs the world, does not elucidate our faces. At best, we conceive happiness; never felicity, prerogative of civilizations based on the idea of salvation, on the refusal to savor one's sufferings, to revel in them; but, sybarites of suffering, scions of a masochistic tradition, which of us would hesitate between the Benares sermon and Baudelaire's *Heautontimoroumenos*? "I am both wound and knife"—that is our absolute, our eternity.

As for our redeemers, come among us for our greater harm, we love the noxiousness of their hopes and their remedies, their eagerness to favor and exalt our ills, the venom that infuses their "lifegiving" words. To them we owe our expertise in a suffering that has no exit. To what temptations, to what extremities does lucidity lead! Shall we desert it now to take refuge in unconsciousness? Anyone can escape into sleep, we are all geniuses when we dream, the butcher the poet's equal there. But our perspicacity cannot bear that such a marvel should endure, nor that inspiration should be brought within everyone's grasp; daylight strips us of the night's gifts. Only the madman enjoys the privilege of passing smoothly from a nocturnal to a daylight existence: no distinction between his dreams and his waking. He has renounced our reason, as the beggar has renounced our belongings. Both have found a way that leads beyond suffering and solved all our problems; hence they remain examples we cannot follow, saviors without adepts.

Even as we ransack our own diseases, those of other people regard us no less. In an age of biographies, no one bandages his wounds without our attempting to lay them bare, to expose them to broad daylight; if we fail, we turn away, disappointed. And even he who ended on the cross—it is not because he suffered *for us* that he still counts for something in our eyes, but because he *suffered* and uttered several lamentations as profound as they were gratuitous. For what we venerate in our gods are our own defeats *en beau*.

*

Doomed to corrupted forms of wisdom, invalids of duration, victims of time, that weakness which appals as much as it appeals to us, we are constituted of elements that all unite to make us rebels divided between a mystic summons which has no link with history and a bloodthirsty dream which is history's symbol and numbus. If we had a world all our own, it would matter little whether it was a world of piety or derision! We shall never have it, our position in existence lying at the intersection of our supplications and our sarcasms, a zone of impurity where sighs and provocations combine. The man too lucid to worship will also be too lucid to wreck, or will wreck only his . . . rebellions; for what is the use of rebelling only to discover, afterwards, a universe *intact?* A paltry monologue. We revolt against justice and injustice, against peace and war, against men and against the gods. Then we come around to thinking the worst old dotard may be wiser than Prometheus. Yet we do manage to smother a scream of insurrection and continue fuming over everything and nothing: a pathetic automatism which explains why we are all statistical Lucifers.

Contaminated by the superstition of action, we believe that our ideas must *come to something.* What could be more contrary to the passive consideration of the world? But such is our fate: to be incurables who *protest,* pamphleteers on a pallet.

Our knowledge, like our experience, should paralyze us and make us indulgent to tyranny itself, once it represents a constant. We are sufficiently clear-sighted to be tempted to lay down our arms; yet the reflex of rebellion triumphs over our doubts; and though we might have made accomplished Stoics, the anarchist keeps watch within us and opposes our resignations.

"We shall never accept history": that, it seems to me, is the adage of our incapacity to be true sages, true madmen. Are we then no more than the ham actors of wisdom and of madness? Whatever we do, with regard to our acts we are subject to a profound insincerity.

From all evidence, a believer identifies himself up to a certain point with what he does and with what he believes; there is no significant gap between his lucidity, on the one hand, and his thoughts and actions on the other. This gap widens excessively in the *false believer,* the man who parades convictions without adhering to them. The object of his faith is a succedaneum. Bluntly: my rebellion is a faith to which I subscribe without believing in it. But I cannot *not* subscribe to it. We can never ponder enough Kirilov's description of Stavrogin: "When he believes, he doesn't believe he believes; and when he doesn't believe, he doesn't believe he doesn't believe."

*

Even more than the style, the very rhythm of our life is based on the *good standing* of rebellion. Loath to admit a universal identity, we posit individuation, heterogeneity as a primordial phenomenon. Now, to revolt is to postulate this heterogeneity, to conceive it as somehow anterior to the advent of beings and objects. If I oppose the sole truth of Unity by a necessarily deceptive Multiplicity—if, in other words, I identify the *other* with a phantom—my rebellion is meaningless, since to exist it must start from the irreducibility of individuals, from their condition as monads, circumscribed essences. Every act institutes and rehabilitates plurality, and, conferring reality and autonomy upon *the person,* implicity recognizes the degradation, the parcelling-out of *the absolute.* And it is from the act, and from the cult attached to it, that the tension of our minds proceeds, the need to explode and to destroy ourselves *at the heart of duration.* Modern philosophy, by establishing the superstition of the Ego, has made it the mainspring of our dramas and the pivot of our anxieties. To regret the repose of indistinction, the neutral dream of an existence without qualities, is pointless; we have chosen to be *subjects,* and every subject is a break with the quietude of Unity. Whoever takes it upon himself to attenuate our solitude or our lacerations acts against our interests, against our vocation. We measure an individual's value by the sum of his disagreements with things, by his incapacity to be indifferent, by his refusal as a subject to tend toward the object. Whence the obsolescence of the idea of Good; whence the vogue of the Devil.

As long as we lived amid elegant terrors, we accommodated ourselves quite well to God. When others—more sordid because more profound—took us in charge, we required another system of references, another *boss.* The Devil was the ideal figure. Everything in him agrees with the nature of the events of which he is the agent, the regulating principle: *his attributes coincide with those of time.* Let us pray to him, then, since far from being a product of our subjectivity, a creation of our need for blasphemy or solitude, he is the master of our questionings and of our panics, the instigator of our deviations. His protests, his violences have their own ambiguity: this "Great Melancholic" is a *rebel who doubts.* If he were simple, all of a piece, he would not touch us at all; but his paradoxes, his contradictions are our own: he amasses our impossibilities, serves as a model for our rebellions against ourselves, our self-hatred. The recipe for hell? It is in this form of revolt and hatred that it must be sought, in the torment of inverted pride, in this sensation of being a *terrible* negligible quantity, in the pangs of the "I", that "I" by which our end begins. . . .

Of all fictions, that of the golden age confounds us most: How could it have grazed our imaginations? It is in order to expose it, to denounce it, that history, *man's aggression against himself,* has taken its flight and form; so that to dedicate oneself to history is to learn to rebel, to imitate the Devil. We never imitate him so well as when, at the expense of our being, we emit time, project it outside ourselves and allow it to be converted into events. "Henceforth, there will be no more time," announces that impromptu metaphysician who is the Angel of the Apocalypse, and thereby announces the end of the Devil, the end of history. Thus the mystics are right to seek God in themselves, or elsewhere, anywhere but in *this world* of which they make a *tabula rasa,* without for all that stooping to rebellion. They leap outside the age: a madness to which the rest of us, captives of duration, are rarely susceptible. If only we were as worthy of the

Devil as they are of God!

*

To be convinced that rebellion enjoys an undue privilege among us, we need merely reflect on the manner in which we describe minds unfit for it. We call them insipid. It is virtually certain that we are closed to any form of wisdom because we see in it a tranfigured insipidity. However unjust such a reaction may be, I cannot help experiencing it—to Taoism itself. Even knowing that it recommends effacement and abandonment in the name of the absolute, not of cowardice, I reject it at the very moment I suppose I have adopted it; and if I acknowledge Lao Tse's victory a thousand times over, I still understand a murderer better. Between serenity and blood, it is toward blood one finds it natural to incline. Murder supposes and crowns revolt: the man who is ignorant of the desire to kill may profess all the subversive opinions he likes, he will never be anything but a conformist.

Wisdom and Revolt: two poisons. Unfit to assimilate them naively, we find neither one a formula for salvation. The fact remains that in the Satanic adventure we have acquired a mastery we shall never possess in wisdom. For us, even *perception* is an upheaval, the beginning of a trance or an apoplexy. A loss of energy, a will to erode our available assets. Perpetual revolt involves an irreverence toward ourselves, toward our powers. How can we find in it the wherewithal for contemplation, that *static* expenditure, that concentration in immobility? To leave things as they are, to regard without trying to regulate the world, to perceive essences—nothing is more hostile to the conduct of our thought; we aspire, rather, to manipulate things, to torture them, to attribute to them our own rages. It must be so: idolators of the gesture, of the wager and of delirium, we love the dare-devil, the stake-all, the desperado, as much in poetry as in philosophy. The *Tao Te Ching* goes further than *Une Saison En Enfer* or *Ecce Homo*. But Lao Tse has no delirium to propose, whereas Rimbaud and Nietzsche, acrobats straining at the extreme limits of themselves, engage us in their dangers. The only minds which seduce us are the minds which have destroyed themselves trying to give life a meaning.

*

No way out for a man who both transcends time and is bogged down in it, who accedes by fits and starts to his last solitude and nonetheless sinks into appearances. Wavering, agonized, he will drag out his days as an invalid of duration, exposed at once to the lure of becoming and of eternity. If, according to Meister Eckhart, there is an "odor" of time, there must with all the more reason be an odor of history. How can we remain insensitive to it? On a more immediate level, I distinguish the illusion, the nullity, the rottenness of "civilization"; yet I feel I belong to this rottenness: *I am the lover of carrion.* I cannot forgive our age for having subjugated us to the point of haunting us even when we detach ourselves from it. Nothing viable can emerge from a meditation on circumstances, from a reflection on the event. In other, happier times, the mind could *unreason* freely, as if it belonged to no age, emancipated as it was from the terror of chronology, engulfed in a moment of the world which it identified with the world itself. Without concern for the relativity of its work, the mind dedicated itself to that work entirely. Inspired stupidity, gone forever! Fruitful exaltation, never compromised by a consciousness drawn and quartered! Still to divine the timeless and to know nonetheless that we *are* time, that we produce time, to conceive the notion of eternity and to cherish our nothingness; an absurdity responsible for both our rebellions and the doubts we entertain about them.

To seek out suffering in order to avoid redemption, to follow in reverse the path of deliverance, such is our contribution in the matter of religion: belious *illuminati,* Buddhas and Christs hostile to salvation, preaching to the wretched the charm of their distress. A superficial race, if you like. The fact still remains that our first ancestor left us, for our entire legacy, only the horror of paradise. By giving names to things, he prepared his own Fall and ours. And if we seek a remedy, we must begin by debaptizing the universe, by removing the label which, assigned to each appearance, isolates it and lends it a simulacrum of meaning. Meanwhile, down to our nerve cells, everything in us resists paradise. *To suffer:* sole modality of acquiring the sensation of existence; *to exist:* unique means of safeguarding our destruction. It was ever thus, and will be, so long as a cure-by-eternity has not disintoxicated us from becoming, from duration, so long as we have not approached the state in which, according to a Chinese Buddhist, "a single moment is worth ten thousand years".

*

Then since the Absolute corresponds to a meaning we have not been able to cultivate, let us surrender to all rebellions: they will end by turning against themselves, against us. . . . Perhaps *then* we shall regain our supremacy over time; unless, the other way round, struggling to escape the calamity of consciousness, we rejoin animals, plants, things, return to that primordial stupidity of which, through the fault of history, we have lost even the memory.

Advantages of Exile

IT IS A MISTAKE to think of the expatriate as someone who abdicates, who withdraws and humbles himself, resigned to his miseries, his outcast state. On a closer look, he turns out to be ambitious, aggressive in his disappointments, his very acrimony qualified by his belligerence. The more we are dispossessed, the more intense our appetites and our illusions become. I even discern some relation between misfortune and megalomania. The man who has lost everything preserves as a last resort the hope of glory, or of literary scandal. He consents to abandon everything, except his *name.* But how will he impose his name when he writes in a language of which the cultivated are either ignorant or contemptuous?

Will he venture into another idiom? It will not be easy for him to renounce the words on which his past hinges. A man who repudiates his language for another changes his identity, even his disappointments. Heroic apostate, he breaks with his memories and, to a certain point, with himself.

*

Let us say a man writes a novel which makes him, overnight, a celebrity. In it he recounts his sufferings. His compatriots, in exile, envy him: they too have suffered, perhaps more. And the man without a country becomes—or aspires to become—a novelist. The consequence: an accumulation of confusions, an inflation of horrors, of *frissons* that *date*. One cannot keen renewing Hell, whose very characteristic is monotony, or the face of Exile either. Nothing in literature exasperates a reader so much as The Terrible; in life, it is too tainted with the obvious to give us pause. But our author persists; for the time being he buries his novel in a drawer and awaits his hour. The illusion of a surprise, of a renown which eludes his grasp but which he discounts, sustains him; he lives on unreality. Such, however, is the power of this illusion that if, for instance, he works in some factory, it is with the notion of being freed from it one day or another by a fame as sudden as it is inconceivable.

*

Equally tragic is the case of the poet. Walled up in his own language, he writes for his friends—for ten, for twenty persons at the most. His longing to be read is no less imperious than that of the improvised novelist. At least he has the advantage over the latter of being able to get his verses published in the little *émigré* reviews which appear at the cost of almost indecent sacrifices and renunciations. Let us say such a man becomes—transforms himself into—an editor of such a review; to keep his publication alive he risks hunger, abstains from women, buries himself in a windowless room, imposes privations which confound and appal. Tuberculosis and masturbation, that is his fate.

No matter how scanty the number of *émigrés,* they form groups, not to protect their interests but to get up subscriptions, to bleed each other white in order to publish their regrets, their cries, their echoless appeals. One cannot conceive of a more heart-rending form of the gratuitous.

That they are as good poets as they are bad prose-writers can be accounted for readily enough. Consider the literary production of any "minor" nation which has not been so childish as to make up a past for itself: the abundance of poetry is its most striking characteristic. Prose requires, for its development, a certain rigor, a differentiated social status, and a tradition: it is deliberate, constructed; poetry *wells up*: it is direct or else totally fabricated; the prerogative of cave-men or aesthetes, it flourishes only on the near or far side of civilization, never at the center. Whereas prose demands a premeditated genius and a crystallized language, poetry is perfectly compatible with a barbarous genius and a formless language. To create a *literature* is to create a prose.

*

What could be more natural than that so many possess no other mode of expression than poetry? Even those who are not particularly gifted draw, in their uprooted state, upon the automatism of their exclusion, that bonus talent they would never have found in a normal existence.

Whatever the form it happens to take, and whatever its cause, exile—at its start—is an academy of intoxication. And it is not given to everyone to be a drunkard. It is a limit-situation, and resembles the extremity of the poetic state. Is it not a *favor* to be transported to that state straight off, without the detours of a discipline, by no more than the benevolence of fatality? Think of Rilke, that expatriate *de luxe,* and of the number of solitudes he had to accumulate in order to liquidate his connections, in order to establish a foothold in the non-existent. It is not easy to be *nowhere* when no external condition obliges you to do so. Even the mystic attains his ascesis only at the cost of monstrous efforts. To extricate oneself from the world—what a labor of abolition! This exile achieves it without turning a hair, by the cooperation—*i.e.,* the hostility—of history. No torments, no vigils in order for him to strip himself of everything; events compel him. In a sense, he is like the invalid who also installs himself in metaphysics or in poetry without personal merit, by the force of circumstances, by the good offices of disease. A trumpery absolute? Perhaps, though it is not proved that the results acquired by effort exceed in value those which derive from a surrender to the inescapable.

*

One danger threatens the exiled poet: that of adapting himself to his fate, of no longer suffering from it, of enjoying himself because of it. No one can save youth from its griefs; they wear themselves out. The same is true of homesicknesses, of any nostalgia. Regrets lose their luster, use themselves up by their own momentum, and after the fashion of the elegy, quickly fall into desuetude. What then is more natural than to establish oneself in exile, the Nowhere City, a *patrie* in reverse? To the degree that he revels in it, the poet erodes the substance of his emotions, the resources of his misery, as well as his dreams of glory. The curse from which he drew pride and profit no longer afflicting him, he loses, along with it, both the energy of his exceptional status and the reasons for his solitude. Rejected by Hell, he will try in vain to reinstate himself there, to regain his infernal temper: his sufferings, too mild now, will make him forever unworthy of it. The cries of which he was only yesterday still proud have become bitterness, and bitterness does not become verse: it will lead him beyond poetry. No more songs, no more excesses. His wounds healed, there is no use pointing to them in order to extract certain accents: at best he will be the epigone of his pains. An honorable downfall awaits him. Lacking diversity, original anxieties, his inspiration dries up. Soon, resigned to anonymity and even intrigued by his mediocrity, he will assume the mask of a bourgeois from *nowhere in particular.* Thus he reaches the term of his lyrical career, the most stable point of his degeneration.

*

"Shelved", established in the comfort of his fall, what will he do next? He will have the choice between two forms of salvation: faith and humor. If he drags along some vestiges of anxiety, he will gradually liquidate them by means of a thousand prayers; unless he consoles himself with a reassuring metaphysic, pastime of exhausted versifiers. And if, on the contrary, he is inclined to mockery, he will minimize his defeats to the point of rejoicing in them. According to his temperament, he will therefore sacrifice to piety or to sarcasm. In either case, he will have triumphed over his ambitions, as over his misfortunes, in order to achieve a higher goal, in order to become a decent victim, a respectable outcast.

translated by **Richard Howard**

DANIEL MROZ. (*TQ* #9)

The Fly

She sat on a willow-trunk
watching
part of the battle of Crécy,
the shouts,
the gasps,
the groans,
the tramping and the tumbling.

During the fourteenth charge
of the French cavalry
she mated
with a brown-eyed male fly
from Vadincourt.

She rubbed her legs together
as she sat on a disembowelled horse
meditating
on the immortality of flies.

With relief she alighted
on the blue tongue
of the Duke of Clervaux.

When silence settled
and only the whisper of decay
softly circled the bodies

and only
a few arms and legs
still twitched jerkily under the trees,

she began to lay her eggs
on the single eye
of Johann Uhr,
the Royal Armourer.

1967

And thus it was
that she was eaten by a swift
fleeing
from the fires of Estrées.

translated by George Theiner

ADOLPH HACHMEISTER. *PORTRAIT OF KAFKA*. (*TQ #9*)

The Burning Hands

Two burning hands are sinking
In the depths of heaven

They do not grasp at the star
That floats around them
And twinkles and crosses itself

They are saying something with their fingers
Who can guess
The tongue of fingers in the flame

Solemnly they put their palms together
To signify a peak

Are they talking of an old house
That they left burnt down
Or perhaps of a new one
That they are just thinking of building

The Homeless Head

A severed head
A head with a flower in its teeth
Wandering circles the earth

The sun meets it
It bows to him
And goes on its way

The moon meets it
To him it smiles
And does not stop in its way

Why does it growl at the earth
Can't it return
Or go off for good

**translated by
Anne Pennington**

Ask its lips when the flower comes out

1967

ALEKSANDER WAT

translated by Czeslaw Milosz

A damned man

First in my dream appeared a coffee mill.
Most ordinary. The oldfashioned kind. A coffee-brown color.
(As a child, I liked to slide open the lid, peek in and instantly
snap it shut. With fear and trembling! So that my teeth chattered from terror!
It was as if I myself were being ground up in there! I always knew
I would come to a bad end!)
So first there was a coffee mill.
Or perhaps it only seemed so, because a moment later a windmill stood there.
And that windmill stood on the sea, on the horizon's line, in its very center.
Its four wings turned creaking and cracking. They probably were grinding
up somebody.

And at the tip of every one of them
an equilibrist in white
revolved to the melody of "The Merry Widow",
supported by his left hand resting on the wing he floated, fiery, fluid, fleeting,
a silver flame fluttering his feet in the ether.
Then he waned. And so one after the other. It would have been dark if not for a
Oh, where did they come from? Equestriennes?! My marvellous equestriennes!
Lightly on heavy but swift percherons they gallop one after another, I see crowds,
crowds of them—some in ruffles of tulle, others naked, stark naked in black
silk stockings,
still others in beads—golden, turquoise, black and iridescent,
and their thighs white like sugar! Like teeth! And strong, o mighty God, how
strong!
(As a young boy I dreamed : an equestrienne—only an equestrienne!
will saddle the great love in my life! Well, I've never met one.
And it's probably better that way, for what a couple we would have made;
an equestrienne and a bookkeeper in a nationalized funeral parlor.)
Well, nothing lasts forever. Since a moment later
instead of equestriennes, Sabines were parading, armored women much more
vulgar after all
(eleven years ago I fell in love with a certain Sabina,
a divorcee, alas without reciprocity).

Thus the Sabines
not ravished but, let me concede, ravishing. Taking me where?
Where? How can I know where?
In any case—towards annihilation.
I woke up. I always knew I would come to a bad end.

1967   97

From the wave

It mounts at sea, a concave wall
    Down-ribbed with shine,
And pushes forward, building tall
    Its steep incline.
Then from their hiding rise to sight
    Black shapes on boards
Bearing before the fringe of white
    It mottles towards.

Their pale feet curl, they poise their weight
    With a learned skill.
It is the wave they imitate
    Keeps them so still.

The marbling bodies have become
    Half wave, half men,
Grafted it seems by feet of foam
    Some seconds, then,

Late as they can, they slice the face
    In timed procession:
Balance is triumph in this place,
    Triumph possession.

The mindless heave of which they rode
    A fluid shelf
Breaks as they leave it, falls and, slowed,
    Loses itself.

Clear, the sheathed bodies slick as seals
    Loosen and tingle;
And by the board the bare foot feels
    The suck of shingle.

They paddle in the shallows still;
Two splash each other;
Then all swim out to wait until
The right waves gather.

JOHN CRAIG. ETCHING. (*TQ* #10)

Meeting Hall of the
Sociedad Anarquista, 1952

The rough wooden floor impedes the dancers,
Who, unable to glide, move by steps,
And, warmed by Gallo wine, gain speed, their pleasure
Neither false nor excessive, though uncertain.
Too sparse for the loft, the rest, making many,
Crowd the phonograph and wine jug on the table.

Folded chairs convene against the walls;
On the shelves, piles of rebellious pamphlets,
Absolute with ardor and fraternity, receive
New York's ubiquitous indifferent soil,
Dust where a few Spaniards with weakened eyes
Withdraw in the long fadeout of history.

Tonight, under convenient anonymity,
Toneless lamp of familiar guises, young friends
Have organized to welcome a friend,
A woman fiery-looking, childless, and stubborn
Who, embarrassed by gloom, sits on the floor
And smiles her description of famine in Italy.

These two who dance have met since parting, yet,
Because she has come alone, because he, too, is,
Like one recently divorced, freshly marketable,
Novel with the glamor of commodity,
A vividness revises his elder desire,
Selects her cropped hair with loving recurrence.

Her response is rare volubility,
Her conversation challenging, obscene,
Embittered or descends to jokes or glorifies
Giving, pictures Nietzsche dying for want of love.
It is quite certain she does not like him; certain,
She wishes to please. Her caricature boringly enacts

A passion genuine and chaotic. Wearing red,
At twenty-four having desired, having failed
To be reborn a negro, Israeli, gypsy;
Devastated by freedom, her uncompleted soul
Retains its contact with psychosis, and with
The incredible softness of a woman.

Her manic vehemence drops. Dances off, gazes,
And says he looks sad, and to restore his spirits
Offers the nursery of this body she
Exhibits and detests; her pity and her guilt,
Like children deprivation has misled,
Hold hands tenderly, without affection.

Before night ends, forgotten at two by a mad
Mother, dragged along by her father, lodged
With orphans, she jumps, denuded, gleaming,
Nervous, from the bed, and producing
Her repertoire of wifeliness,
Asks would he like a book to read.

JOHN FREDERICK NIMS

Few things to say

It's true, we write so little. Years between
Words in this, that, or the other magazine.
Few things to say—two maybe. Girls, know why?
You craze the air with pleasure. And you die.

C. P. CAVAFY

The town

You said, "I'm leaving for another town, another sea.
Surely there must be a better town than this one.
All that I attempt here is foredoomed.
My heart is like a corpse,
How long must my mind decay here, rotting?
Whenever I look I see only
My life's black ruins in this place
Where I have stayed, corrupted, wrecked."

You will not find new lands, new seas.
The town will follow you, the same.
You will wander the same old streets,
In these habitual quarters you'll grow old,
Always returning to this town.
Don't hope for other places—
There is no ship for you, no open road.
The way in which your life is ruined here
In this small corner
Is how it's ruined everywhere.

translated by Stephen Spender and Nikos Stangos

ILLUSTRATION BY ZBIGNIEW JASTREBSKI. (*TQ* #12)

1968

Tuesday siesta

GABRIEL GARCÍA MÁRQUEZ

The train emerged from the quivering tunnel of sandy rocks, began to cross the symmetrical, interminable banana plantations, and the air became humid and they couldn't feel the sea breeze any more. A stifling blast of smoke came in the car window. On the narrow road parallel to the railway there were oxcarts loaded with green bunches of bananas. Beyond the road, in odd, uncultivated spaces, there were offices with electric fans, red brick buildings, and residences with chairs and little white tables on the terraces among dusty palm trees and rosebushes. It was eleven in the morning, and the heat had not yet begun.

"You'd better close the window," the woman said. "Your hair will get full of soot."

The girl tried to, but the shade wouldn't move because of the rust.

They were the only passengers in the lone third-class car. Since the smoke of the locomotive kept coming through the window, the girl left her seat and put down the only things they had with them: a plastic sack with some things to eat and a bouquet of flowers wrapped in newspaper. She sat on the opposite seat, away from the window, facing her mother. They were both in severe and poor mourning clothes.

The girl was twelve years old, and it was the first time she'd ever been on a train. The woman seemed too old to be her mother, because of the blue veins on her eyelids and her small, soft, and shapeless body, in a dress cut like a cassock. She was riding with her spinal column braced firmly against the back of the seat, and held a peeling patent-leather portfolio in her lap with both hands. She bore the conscientious serenity of someone accustomed to poverty.

By twelve the heat had begun. The train stopped for ten minutes to take on water at a station where there was no town. Outside, in the mysterious silence of the plantations, the shadows seemed clean. But the still air inside the car smelled like untanned leather. The train did not pick up speed. It stopped at two identical towns with wooden houses painted bright colors. The woman's head nodded and she sank into sleep. The girl took off her shoes. Then she went to the washroom to put the bouquet of flowers in some water.

When she came back to her seat, her mother was waiting to eat. She gave her a piece of cheese, half a cornmeal pancake, and a cookie, and took an equal portion out of the plastic sack for herself. While they ate, the train crossed an iron bridge very slowly and passed a town just like the ones before, except that in this one there was a crowd in the plaza. A band was playing a lively tune under the oppressive sun. At the other side of town the plantations ended in a plain which was cracked from the drought.

The woman stopped eating.

"Put on your shoes," she said.

The girl looked outside. She saw nothing but the deserted plain, where the train began to pick up speed again, but she put the last piece of cookie into the sack and quickly put on her shoes. The woman gave her a comb.

"Comb your hair," she said.

The train whistle began to blow while the girl was combing her hair. The woman dried the sweat from her neck and wiped the oil from her face with her fingers. When the girl stopped combing, the train was passing the outlying houses of a town larger but sadder than the earlier ones.

"If you feel like doing anything, do it now," said the woman. "Later, don't take a drink anywhere even if you're dying of thirst. Above all, no crying."

The girl nodded her head. A dry, burning wind came in the window, together with the locomotive's whistle and the clatter of the old cars. The woman wrapped up the pancake with the rest of the food and put it in the portfolio. For a moment a complete picture of the town, on that bright August Tuesday, shone in the window. The girl wrapped the flowers in the soaking-wet newspapers, moved a little farther away from the window, and stared at her mother. She received a pleasant expression in return. The train began to whistle and slowed down. A moment later it stopped.

There was no one at the station. On the other side of the street, on the sidewalk shaded by the almond trees, only the pool hall was open. The town was floating in the heat. The woman and the girl got off the train and crossed the abandoned station—the tiles split apart by the grass growing up between—and the street to the shady sidewalk.

It was almost two. At that hour, weighted down by drowsiness, the town was taking a siesta. The stores, the town offices, the public school were closed at eleven, and didn't reopen until a little before four, when the train went back. Only the hotel across from the station, with its bar and pool hall, and the telegraph office at one side of the plaza stayed open. The houses, most of them built on the banana company's model, had their doors locked from inside and their blinds drawn. In some of them it was so hot that the residents ate lunch in the patio. Others leaned a chair against the wall, in the shade of the almond trees, and took their siesta right out in the street.

Keeping to the protective shade of the almond trees, the woman and the girl entered the town without disturbing the siesta. They went directly to the priest's house. The woman scratched the metal grating on the door with her fingernail, waited a moment, and scratched again. An electric fan was humming inside. They did not hear the steps. They hardly heard the slight creaking of a door, and immediately a cautious voice, right next to the metal grating: "Who is it?" The woman tried to see through the grating.

"I need the Father," she said.

"He's sleeping now."

"It's an emergency," the woman insisted.

Her voice showed a calm determination.

The door was opened a little way, noiselessly, and a plump, older woman appeared, with very pale skin and hair the color of iron. Her eyes seemed too small behind her thick eyeglasses.

"Come in," she said, and opened the door all the way.

They entered a room permeated with an old smell of flowers. The woman of the house led them to a wooden bench and signaled them to sit down. The girl did so, but her mother remained standing, absent-mindedly, with both hands clutching the portfolio. No noise could be heard above the electric fan.

The woman of the house reappeared at the door at the far end of the room. "He says you should come back after three," she said in a very low voice. "He just lay down five minutes ago."

"The train leaves at three-thirty," said the woman.

It was a brief and self-assured reply, but her voice remained pleasant, full of undertones. The woman of the house smiled for the first time.

"All right," she said.

When the far door closed again, the woman sat down next to her daughter. The narrow waiting room was poor, neat, and clean. On the other side of the wooden railing which divided the room, there was a worktable, a plain one with an oilcloth cover, and on top of the table a primitive typewriter next to a vase of flowers. The parish records were beyond. You could see that it was an office kept in order by a spinster.

The far door opened and this time the priest appeared, cleaning his glasses with a handkerchief. Only when he put them on was it evident that he was the brother of the woman who had opened the door.

"How can I help you?" he asked.

"The keys to the cemetery," said the woman.

The girl was seated with the flowers in her lap and her feet crossed under the bench. The priest looked at her, then looked at the woman, and then through the wire mesh of the window at the bright, cloudless sky.

"In this heat," he said. "You could have waited until the sun went down."

The woman moved her head silently. The priest crossed to the other side of the railing, took out of the cabinet a notebook covered in oilcloth, a wooden penholder, and an inkwell, and sat down at the table. There was more than enough hair on his hands to account for what was missing on his head.

"Which grave are you going to visit?" he asked.

1969

107

"Carlos Centeno's," said the woman.

"Who?"

"Carlos Centeno," the woman repeated.

The priest still did not understand.

"He's the thief who was killed here last week," said the woman in the same tone of voice. "I am his mother."

The priest scrutinized her. She stared at him with quiet self-control, and the Father blushed. He lowered his head and began to write. As he filled the page, he asked the woman to identify herself, and she replied unhesitatingly, with precise details, as if she were reading them. The Father began to sweat. The girl unhooked the buckle of her left shoe, slipped her heel out of it, and rested it on the bench rail. She did the same with the right one.

It had all started the Monday of the previous week, at three in the morning, a few blocks from there. Rebecca, a lonely widow who lived in a house full of odds and ends, heard above the sound of the drizzling rain someone trying to force the front door from outside. She got up, rummaged around in her closet for an ancient revolver that no one had fired since the days of Colonel Aureliano Buendia, and went into the living room without turning on the lights. Orienting herself not so much by the noise at the lock as by a terror developed in her by twenty-eight years of loneliness, she fixed in her imagination not only the spot where the door was but also the exact height of the lock. She clutched the weapon with both hands, closed her eyes, and squeezed the trigger. It was the first time in her life that she had fired a gun. Immediately after the explosion, she could hear nothing except the murmur of the drizzle on the galvanized roof. Then she heard a little metallic bump on the cement porch, and a very low voice, pleasant but terribly exhausted: "Ah, Mother." The man they found dead in front of the house in the morning, his nose blown to bits, wore a flannel shirt with colored stripes, everyday pants with a rope for a belt, and was barefoot. No one in town knew him.

"So his name was Carlos Centeno," murmured the Father when he finished writing.

"Centeno Ayala," said the woman. "He was my only boy."

The priest went back to the cabinet. Two big rusty keys hung on the inside of the door; the girl imagined, as her mother had when she was a girl and as the priest himself must have imagined at some time, that they were Saint Peter's keys. He took them down, put them on the open notebook on the railing, and pointed with his forefinger to a place on the page he had just written, looking at the woman.

"Sign here."

The woman scribbled her name, holding the portfolio under her arm. The girl picked up the flowers, came to the railing shuffling her feet, and watched her mother attentively.

The priest sighed.

"Didn't you ever try to get him on the right track?"

The woman answered when she finished signing.

"He was a very good man."

The priest looked first at the woman and then at the girl, and realized with a kind of pious amazement that they were not about to cry. The woman continued in the same tone:

"I told him never to steal anything that anyone needed to eat, and he minded me. On the other hand, before, when he used to box, he used to spend three days in bed, exhausted from being punched."

"All his teeth had to be pulled out," interrupted the girl.

"That's right," the woman agreed. "Every mouthful I ate those days tasted of the beatings my son got on Saturday nights."

"God's will is inscrutable," said the Father.

But he said it without much conviction, partly because experience had made him a little skeptical and partly because of the heat. He suggested that they cover their heads to guard against sunstroke. Yawning, and now almost completely asleep, he gave them instructions about how to find Carlos Centeno's grave. When they came back, they didn't have to knock. They should put the key under the door; and in the same place, if they could, they should put an offering for the Church. The woman listened to his directions with great attention, but thanked him without smiling.

The Father had noticed that there was someone looking inside, his nose pressed against the metal grating, even before he opened the door to the street. Outside was a group of children. When the door was opened wide, the children scattered. Ordinarily, at that hour there was no one in the street. Now there were not only children. There were groups of people under the almond trees. The Father scanned the street swimming in the heat and then he understood. Softly, he closed the door again.

1969

"Wait a moment," he said without looking at the woman.

His sister appeared at the far door with a black jacket over her nightshirt and her hair down over her shoulders. She looked silently at the Father.

"What was it?" he asked.

"The people have noticed," murmured his sister.

"You'd better go out by the door to the patio," said the Father.

"It's the same there," said his sister. "Everybody is at the windows."

The woman seemed not to have understood until then. She tried to look into the street through the metal grating. Then she took the bouquet of flowers from the girl and began to move toward the door. The girl followed her.

"Wait until the sun goes down," said the Father.

"You'll melt," said his sister, motionless at the back of the room. "Wait and I'll lend you a parasol."

"Thank you," replied the woman. "We're all right this way."

She took the girl by the hand and went into the street.

translated by J. S. Bernstein

JORGE DE LA VEGA. INK DRAWING. (*TQ* #13–14)

The sea

Before our human dream (or terror) wove
Mythologies, cosmogonies, and love,
Before time coined its substance into days,
The sea, the always sea, existed: was.
Who is the sea? Who is that violent being,
Violent and ancient, who gnaws the foundations
Of earth? He is both one and many oceans;
He is abyss and splendor, chance and wind.
Who looks on the sea, sees it the first time,
Every time, with the wonder distilled
From elementary things—from beautiful
Evenings, the moon, the leap of a bonfire.
Who is the sea, and who am I? The day
That follows my last agony shall say.

translated by John Updike

because her running stirred up the air; the little girl shedding tears of pleasure. Amilamia sitting under the eucalyptus trees, pretending to cry so that I'd go up to her. Amilamia lying face down with a flower in her hands: the petals of a cattail that—I discovered later—didn't grow in this garden but somewhere else, perhaps in the garden at her house, because the only pocket in her blue-checked apron was often full of those white flowers. Amilamia watching me read, standing with both hands on the bars of that green bench, inquiring with her gray eyes; I remember that she never asked me what I was reading, as if she could discover in my eyes the images born from the pages of the book. Amilamia laughing with pleasure when I picked her up by the waist and made her spin around my head and she seeming to find a new perspective on the world in that slow flight. Amilamia turning her back and saying good-bye with her arm raised and her fingers waving. And Amilamia in the hundreds of poses she used to take around my bench: hanging from her head with her legs in the air and her bloomers puffed out; sitting on the gravel with her legs crossed and her chin resting on the palm of her hand; lying on the grass, her navel bared to the sun; weaving together branches from the trees; drawing animals in the mud with a stick; licking the bars of the bench; hiding under the seat; silently breaking off stray growths from aged trunks; looking fixedly at the horizon over the hill; humming with her eyes closed; imitating the sounds of birds, dogs, cats, hens, horses. All for me, and yet it was nothing. It was her way of being with me, all this that I remember, but it was also her way of being alone in the park. Yes; perhaps I remember her fragmentarily because I alternated between my reading and contemplating the plump-faced little girl with the straight hair whose color changed with the light: now straw-colored, now burnt chestnut. And only now does it occur to me that at the time, Amilamia established the other reference point in my life, the one that created a tension between my own unresolved childhood and the open world, the promised land that was beginning to be mine through books.

Not then. Then I dreamed of the women in my books, the females —the word disturbed me—who disguised themselves as the Queen so as to buy a necklace incognito; the mythological creations—part recognizable beings, part salamanders, white-breasted and damp-wombed—who awaited monarchs in their beds. And thus, imperceptibly, I moved from an indifference toward my infantile company to an acceptance of the little girl's grace and seriousness, and from there to an unexpected rejection of that useless presence. It was finally irritating to me—me, already a fourteen year old, to be around that seven year old girl who wasn't, then, a memory and nostalgia of it, but the past and its actuality. I had given in to a weakness. We had run together, hand in hand, over the meadow. We had shaken the pines together and gathered the cones, which Amilamia put eagerly into her apron pocket. We had made paper sailboats together and followed them overjoyed along the edge of the drain. And that afternoon, when we rolled down the hill together, amidst cries of happiness, and fell down together at the bottom, Amilamia on my chest, the little girl's hair in my lips, and when I felt her panting in my ear and her little arms sticky with candy around my neck, I pushed away her arms angrily and let her fall. Amilamia cried, stroking her wounded elbow and knee, and I went back to my bench. Then Amilamia left and the next day returned and without a word, she gave me the piece of paper and disappeared humming into the forest. I couldn't decide whether to tear up the card or keep it between the pages of the book: *Afternoons on the Farm*. Being around Amilamia had even made my reading become childish. She did not come back to the park. After a few days, I left for vacation, and when I came back, it was to the duties of a first year baccalaureate student. I never saw her again.

II

And now, almost rejecting the image which without being fantastic is unusual, and in being real is more painful, I am going back to that forgotten park, and now, standing in front of the pine grove and eucalyptus trees, I realize how small the foresty spot is, how my memory has insisted on drawing things large enough to permit my imagination to flood it with its waves. For it was here that Strogoff and Huckleberry Finn, Milady de Winter and Geneviève de Brabante were born, talked and died; in this little garden enclosed by rusty lattices, planted scantily with old unkempt trees, hardly decorated by the cement bench, an imitation of a wooden bench, which makes me wonder whether my beautiful forged iron bench, painted green, ever existed, or whether it was part of my orderly retrospective delirium. And the hill . . . how could I believe that this was it, the promontory that Amilamia ran down and climbed up on her daily walks, the steep slope we rolled down together? Barely a mound of fodder, with no more relief than what my memory insists on giving it.

"Look for me here where the pichure shows." This meant that I had to cross the garden, leave the forest behind, go down the mound in three strides, cross that small orchard of hazelnut trees—it was undoubtedly here that the little girl gathered those white petals—, open the creaky park gate and suddenly remember, know, find myself in the street, realize that all those afternoons of my adolescence, as if by a miracle, had managed to make the surrounding city stop beating, do away with that din of horns blowing, bells ringing, shouting, moaning, motors running, radios, cursing . . . Which was the real magnet, the quiet garden or the feverish city? I wait for the light to change and cross the street without taking my eyes from the red light which is keeping the traffic in check. I consult Amilamia's paper. In the last analysis, this rudimentary map is the real magnet of the moment I am living, and just to think of it startles me. My life after those lost afternoons I spent when I was fourteen was obliged to follow a disciplined course and now, at twenty-nine, duly graduated, the head of an office, assured of a reasonable income, still single, having no family to support, mildly bored by going to bed with secretaries, scarcely excited by some eventual trip to the country or the beach. I lacked a main interest like the ones I had earlier, in my books, my park and Amilamia. I head through the street of this flat, gray suburb. One-story houses succeed each other monotonously with their elongated grilled windows and their big front doors, the paint peeling off. The buzzing of various tasks being done hardly breaks the monotony. The screeching of a knife-sharpener here, the hammering of a shoemaker there. In the side passages, the neighborhood children play. The music of an organ reaches my ears mixed with the children's singing. I stop a minute to look at them, with the fleeting impression that Amilamia may perhaps be among those groups of children, showing her flowered bloomers with impunity, hanging by her legs from a balcony, addicted as usual to her acrobatic extravagances, with her apron pocket full of white petals. I smile, and for the first time I want to envision the twenty-two year old miss who, if she still lives at the address jotted down, will laugh at my memories or perhaps will have forgotten the afternoons spent in the garden.

The house is exactly like the others. The big door, two grilled windows with the shutters closed. One story only, crowned with a fake Neo-Classic balustrade, most likely disguising the functions of the rooftop: clothes hung out, troughs of water, the servants' room, the poultry yard. Before ringing the doorbell, I want to rid myself of any illusions. Amilamia doesn't live here anymore. Why should she have stayed in the same house for fifteen years? Besides, in spite of her premature independence and solitude, she seemed to be a well-bred little girl, well dressed, and this neighborhood is no longer elegant; Amilamia's parents have no doubt moved. But perhaps the new residents know where they are.

I ring the doorbell and wait. I ring again. That's another possibility; there may be no one here. Will I feel the need to look for my little friend again? No, because it will no longer be possible to open a book from my adolescence and happen to come across Amilamia's card. I would go back to my routine, I would forget the moment which had been important only because of its fleeting surprise.

I ring again. I put my ear to the door and am surprised: hoarse and irregular breathing coming from the other side; a heavy panting accompanied by the disagreeable smell of rancid tobacco filters through the cracked boards.

"Good afternoon. Could you please tell me . . .?"

Upon hearing my voice, the person withdraws with heavy, uncertain steps. I ring the bell again, this time shouting:

"Hello! Open up! What's wrong? Can't you hear me?"

I receive no reply. I keep ringing the bell, but with no results. I withdraw from the door without shifting my eyes from the thin slits in the door, as if distance could give me perspective and even the ability to penetrate. Concentrating fixedly on the cursed door, I keep walking backwards, cross the street; a sharp cry saves me in time, followed by a horn blown hard and long, while I confusedly look for the person whose voice has just saved me; all I see is the car going down the street and I embrace a lamp post, a handhold which, more than security, offers me a place to lean on as my icy blood rushes into my burning skin and I sweat. I look at the house that was, had been, must have been, Amilamia's. Behind the balustrade, just as I had guessed, there are clothes waving. I don't know what the rest is: slips, pajamas, blouses, I don't know; I see that little blue-checked apron, stiff, clothes-pinned onto the long line that is swaying between an iron bar and a nail in the white wall of the rooftop.

1969

III

At the City Clerk's Office of Deeds they told me that the property was in the name of a Mr. R. Valdivia who rents the house. To whom? That they wouldn't know. Who is Valdivia? He states that he's a businessman. Where does he live? Who are you?, the young lady asks me with haughty curiosity. I didn't know how to be calm and sure of myself. Sleep hadn't relieved my nervous fatigue. Valdivia. I leave the Clerk's Office; the sun offends me. I associate the repugnance which the foggy sun sieved by low clouds—and therefore more intense—provokes in me with the desire to return to the damp and shady park. No, all it is, is my desire to know whether Amilamia lives in that house and why I'm not admitted there. But what I should reject, and the sooner the better, is the absurd idea that didn't let me get a wink of sleep last night. To have seen the apron drying on the roof, the same one in whose pocket she kept the flowers, and to think because of this that a seven year old girl whom I knew fourteen or fifteen years ago still lived in the house. . . . She might have a little daughter. Yes. Amilamia, at twenty-two, was the mother of a little girl who perhaps dressed the same way, looked like her, repeated the same games, who knows?, went to the same park. And musing on this I again arrive at the front door of the house. I ring the bell and wait for the hard breathing from the other side of the door. I was wrong. The door is opened by a woman who must not be over fifty. But wrapped in a shawl, dressed in black, and in low-heeled shoes, no make-up, her hair pulled back to the nape of her neck, graying, she seems to have given up any illusion or pretext of youth and she observes me with eyes that are almost cruel, they're so indifferent.

"You wished?"

"Mr. Valdivia sent me." I cough and run my hand through my hair. I should have picked up my briefcase at the office. I realize that without it I won't play the role well.

"Valdivia?" the woman asks me with neither alarm nor interest.

"Yes. The owner of the house."

One thing is clear: the woman won't let anything show in her face. She looks at me fearlessly.

"Oh yes. The owner of the house."

"May I? . . ."

In bad plays I think the traveling salesman sticks his foot in the door to keep them from shutting it in his face. I do this, but the lady steps aside and with a gesture of her hand invites me to come in to what must have been a place to keep the car. To one side is a glass door in a peeling wooden frame. I walk toward it, over the yellow tiles of the entrance patio, and ask again, facing the lady, who is following me in tiny steps: "This way?"

She assents, and for the first time I notice that in her hands she has a three decade rosary which she doesn't cease to play with. I haven't seen those old rosaries since my childhood and I'd like to remark on it, but the brusque and decided manner in which the lady opens the door impedes any gratuitous conversation. We enter a long and narrow room. The lady hastens to open the shutters but the room is still darkened by four perennial plants growing in porcelain and encrusted glass flowerpots. The only thing there is in the living room is an old, high-backed wicker sofa and a rocking chair. But it's not the scarcity of furniture or the plants which draw my attention. The lady asks me if I would like to sit down on the sofa before she herself sits in the rocking chair.

At my side, on the wicker sofa, there is an open magazine.

"Mr. Valdivia apologizes for not having come himself."

The lady rocks back and forth without blinking. I look out of the corner of my eye at that comic book.

"He sends his greetings and . . ."

I hesitate, hoping for a reaction from the woman. She keeps rocking. The comic book has been scrawled on with a red crayon.

". . . and he has asked me to inform you that he will have to disturb you for a few days . . ."

My eyes search quickly.

". . . The house has to be re-assessed for the cadastre. It seems that it hasn't been done since . . . You've been living here for how many years? . . ."

Yes; that red lipstick is under the chair. And if the lady smiles she does so with her slow hands which caress the rosary beads; for a minute I feel there's a joke on me which doesn't quite upset her features. She doesn't answer me this time either.

". . . for fifteen years at least, haven't you . . . ?"

She does not affirm. She does not deny. And on her pale thin lips there isn't the slightest trace of lipstick . . .

". . . you, your husband and . . . ?"

She looks at me fixedly, without varying her expression, almost defying me to continue. We stay silent for a moment, she playing with the rosary, I bent forward with my hands on my knees. I get up.

"So I'll be back this afternoon with the papers . . ."

The lady assents as she silently picks up the lipstick and the comic book and hides them in the folds of her shawl.

IV

The scene hasn't changed. This afternoon, as I take down imaginary numbers in a notebook and pretend to be interested in establishing the quality of the floorboards and the dimensions of the room, the lady rocks back and forth, rubbing the three decades of her rosary with the cushions of her fingers. I sigh as I finish the supposed inventory of the living room and ask her if we might go to other parts of the house. The lady sits up, bracing her long black arms on the seat of the rocking chair and adjusting her shawl on her narrow and bony shoulders.

She opens the opaque glass door and we enter a dining room that is hardly more furnished. But the table with round, metallic legs, accompanied by four vinyl-covered chairs in nickel frames, doesn't offer even the hint of distinction which the living room furniture had. The other grilled window, with the shutters closed, must at certain times illuminate this bare-walled dining room without a buffet nor a mantel. All there is on the table is a plastic bowl of fruit with a cluster of black grapes, two peaches and a buzzing crown of flies. With her arms crossed and her face inexpressive, the lady stands behind me. I dare to disrupt the order: it is evident that the family rooms will tell me nothing about what I want to know.

"Couldn't we go up to the roof?" I ask. "I think it's the best way to cover the total surface."

The lady looks at me with a spark in her eyes which is sharp, perhaps because it contrasts with the shadows in the dining room.

"What for?" she says finally. "Mr. . . . . Valdivia . . . knows very well what the dimensions of the house are."

And those pauses, one before and one after the owner's name, are the first signs that there is something which is disturbing the lady and making her resort to irony out of self-defense.

"I don't know," I make an effort to smile. "Perhaps I would prefer to start at the top and not . . ." —my false smile is slowly dissolving— ". . . from the bottom."

"You'll do as I say," the lady says with her hands joined over the silver cross hanging on her dark stomach.

Before smiling weakly, I force myself to think that my gestures are useless in the shadows; they're not even symbolic . . . The binding creaks as I open the notebook and continue noting down, with as much speed as possible, without shifting my glance, the numbers and estimates of this job whose fictitious nature—the mild blush on my cheeks, the definite dryness of my tongue—isn't fooling anyone. And as I fill the graphed page with absurd signs, square roots and algebraic formulas, I ask myself what it is that keeps me from going to the heart of the matter, from asking about Amilamia and leaving with a satisfactory answer. No. And yet I feel sure that even though I would obtain a reply if I took this approach, I wouldn't discover the truth. My thin and silent companion has a silhouette I wouldn't stop to notice in the street. but in this house of coarse furniture and absent inhabitants, it ceases to be an anonymous face in the city and becomes a stereotype of mystery. This is the paradox, and if my memories of Amilamia have once again awakened my craving to imagine things, I will follow the rules of the game, I will wear out appearances and I won't rest until I have found the answer—perhaps a simple and obvious one—behind the unexpected veils the lady drops along the way. Am I attributing some gratuitous strangeness to my reluctant hostess? If I am, I will enjoy my labyrinthical invention more. And the flies buzz around the bowl of fruit, but they light on that damaged spot of the peach, that nibbled out chunk—I approach it, using my notes as an excuse—, where there is an imprint of tiny teeth in the velvety skin and ochre flesh. I don't look toward where the lady is. I pretend that I'm still taking notes. The fruit seems to have been bitten into but not touched. I crouch to get a better look at it, I lean my hands on the table, I pucker my lips as if I wanted to repeat the act of biting it without touching it. I lower my eyes and I see another trace of something next to my feet: it is of two tires which seem to have been bicycle tires, two rubber marks stamped on the faded wooden floor; they go as far as the edge of the table and then head back, more and more faintly, across the floor to where the lady is . . .

I close my notebook.

"Let's continue, madam."

When I turn toward her I find her standing with her hands on the back of a chair. Seated, in front of her, is a heavy-shouldered man with an invisible expression in his eyes, coughing from the smoke of his cigarette: his eyes are hidden by his wrinkled, swollen, thick eyelids, similar to the neck of an old turtle, yet nevertheless they seem to follow my movements. The badly shaved cheeks, cracked by hundreds of gray lines, hang from his prominent cheek-bones, and his greenish hands are hidden under his armpits. He is wearing a coarse blue shirt, and his curly hair, mussed up, looks like the bottom of a boat covered with barnacles. He doesn't move and the real sign that he's alive is that hard breathing (as if his breathing had to get through a series of locks made of phlegm, irritation, worn out organs) which I had already heard between the cracks of the front door.

Ridiculously, I murmur: "Good afternoon . . ." —and I'm ready to forget the whole thing: the mystery, Amilamia, the assessment, the clues. The sight of this asthmatic wolf justifies a quick escape. I repeat "Good afternoon," this time in a tone of farewell. The turtle's mask opens up into an atrocious smile: every pore of that flesh seems to have been made of breakable rubber, rotten oilcloth. He puts out his arm and stops me.

"Valdivia died four years ago," the man says in that suffocated, remote voice, located in his entrails and not in his larynx: a weak, treble voice.

Arrested by that strong, almost painful claw, I tell myself that it's useless to pretend. The wax and rubber faces observing me say nothing and because of it I can, in spite of everything, pretend for the last time, make believe that I'm talking to myself when I say:

"Amilamia . . ."

Yes: the pretending is over for all of us. The fist that pressed against my arm affirms its strength only for a moment; then it relaxes and finally it falls, weak and shaky, before he raises it and takes the wax hand that was on his shoulder; perplexed for the first time, the lady looks at me with eyes that seem to be a wounded bird's, and she cries, and it is a dry moan that doesn't alter the rigid disturbance in her features. The ogres of my mind are suddenly two lonely old peo-

1969

mouth, and the little frightened hands drop the comic book on the wet flagstones.

translated by Agnes Moncy

ERNESTO DEIRA. INK DRAWING. GALERIA BONINO, NEW YORK. (*TQ* #13–14)

from
Unusual occupations
JULIO CORTÁZAR

SIMULACRA

We are an uncommon family. In this country where things are done only to boast of them or from a sense of obligation, we like independent occupations, jobs that exist just because, simulacra which are completely useless.

We have one failing: we lack originality. Nearly everything we decide to do is inspired by—let's speak frankly, is copied from—celebrated examples. If we manage to contribute any innovation whatsoever, it always proves to have been inevitable: anachronisms, or surprises, or scandals. My elder uncle says that we're like carbon copies, identical with the original except another color, another paper, another end-product. My third youngest sister compares herself to Andersen's mechanical nightingale. Her romanticizing is disgusting.

There are a lot of us and we live in Humboldt Street.

We do things, but it's difficult to tell about it because the most important elements are missing: the anxiety and the expectation of doing the things, the surprises so much more important than the results, the calamities and abortive undertakings where the whole family collapses like a card-castle and for whole days you don't hear anything but wailing and peals of laughter. Telling what we do is hardly a way of filling in the inevitable gaps, because sometimes we're poor or in jail or sick, sometimes somebody dies or (it hurts me to mention it) someone goes straight, finks out, renounces us, or heads in the UNPOSITIVE DIRECTION. But there's no reason to conclude from this that things are terrible with us or that we're incurably unhappy. We live in this lower middle class neighborhood called the *barrio Pacifico,* and we do things every chance we get. There are a lot of us who come up with ideas and manage to put them into action. The gallows, for instance: up till now, no one's agreed on how the idea got started; my fifth sister asserts that it was one of my first cousins, who were very much philosophers, but my elder uncle insists that it occurred to him after reading a cloak-and-dagger novel. Basically, it's not very important to us, the only thing that counts is to do things, and that's why I tell it, unwillingly almost, only so as to not feel so close the emptiness of this rainy afternoon.

The house has a garden in front of it, an uncommon thing in Humboldt Street. It's not much bigger than a patio, but it's three steps higher than the sidewalk, which gives it the fine aspect of a platform, the ideal site for a gallows. As it has a high railing of ironwork and masonry, one can work without the passers-by being, as one might say, installed in the house itself; they can station themselves at the railings and hang around there for hours, which doesn't bother us. "We shall begin at the full moon," my father ruled. By day we went to find lengths of wood and iron in the warehouses in the Avenida Juan B. Justo, but my sisters stayed home in the parlor practicing the wolf howl, after my youngest aunt maintained that gallows-trees draw wolves and move them to howl at the moon. The responsibility of acquiring a supply of nails and other hardware fell to my cousins; my elder uncle made a sketch of the plans, and discussed with my mother and my other uncle the variety and quality of the various instruments of torture. I remember the end of that discussion: they decided austerely on a reasonably high platform upon which would be constructed the gibbet and a rack-and-wheel, with an open space which could be used for torture or beheading, depending upon the case. It seemed to my elder uncle a rather poor and meeching construction compared with his original idea, but the size of the front garden and the cost of construction materials are always restricting the family's ambitions.

We began the construction work on a Sunday afternoon after the raviolis. Although we had never concerned ourselves with what the neighbors might think, it was clear that the few onlookers thought we were adding one or two floors to enlarge the house. The first to be astonished was Don Cresta, the little old man in the house across from us, and he came over to inquire why we were putting up a platform like that. My sisters were gathered in one corner of the garden and were letting loose with a few wolf howls. A goodly group of people gathered, but we went on working until nightfall and got the platform finished and the two little sets of stairs (for the priest and the condemned man, who ought not to go up together). Monday one part of the family went to its respective employments and occupations—after all, you have to live somehow—and the rest of us began to put up the gibbet while my elder uncle consulted ancient engravings to find a model for the rack-and-wheel. His idea was to set the wheel as high as possible upon a slightly irregular pole, for example a well-trimmed poplar trunk. To humor him, my second oldest brother and my first cousins went off with the pickup truck to find a poplar; my elder uncle and my mother, meanwhile, were fitting the spokes of the wheel into the hub and I was getting an iron collar ready. In those moments we amused ourselves enormously because you could hear hammering on all sides, my sisters howling in the parlor, the neighbors crowding against the iron railings exchanging impressions, and the silhouette of the gibbet rose between the rosaniline bed and the evening mallows and you could see my younger uncle astride the crosspiece driving in the hook and fixing the running knot for the noose.

At this stage of things the people in the street could not help realizing what it was we were building, and a chorus of threats and protests was an agreeable encouragement to put the final stroke to the day's labor by erecting the wheel. Several disorderly types had made an effort to keep my second-oldest brother and my cousins from conveying into the house the magnificent poplar trunk which they'd fetched in the pickup truck. An attempt at harassment in the form of a tug-of-war was won easily by the family in full force tugging at the trunk in a disciplined way, and we set it down in the garden along with a very young child trapped in the roots. My father personally returned the child to its exasperated parents, putting it genteelly through the railings, and while attention was concentrated on these sentimental alternatives, my elder uncle, aided by my first cousins, fitted the wheel onto one end of the trunk and proceeded to raise it. The family was congregated on the platform at the moment the police arrived and commented favorably on how well the gallows looked. My third sister had stationed herself alone by the gate, so the dialogue with the deputy commissioner himself was left up to her; it was not difficult for her to persuade him that we were laboring within the precincts of our own property upon a project only the use of which could vest it with an illegal character, and that the complaints of the neighborhood were the products of animosity and the result of envy. Nightfall saved us from losing any more time.

We took supper on the platform by the light of a carbide lamp, spied upon by a crowd of around a hundred spiteful neighbors; never had the roast suckling pig tasted more exquisite, or the chianti been blacker and sweeter. A breeze from the north swung the gallows rope gently back and forth; the wheel of the rack creaked once or twice, as though the crows had already come to rest there and eat. The spectators began to go off, muttering vague threats; some twenty or thirty stayed on, hanging around the iron railing; they seemed to be waiting for something. After coffee we put out the lamp so that we could see the moon which was rising over the balustrades of the terrace, my sisters howled and my cousins and uncles loped slowly back and forth across the platform, their steps making the foundation shake underfoot. In the subsequent silence the moonlight came to fall at the height of the noose, and a cloud with silver borders seemed to stretch across the wheel. We looked at it all, so happy it was a pleasure, but the neighbors were murmuring at the railings as if they were disappointed or something. They were lighting cigarettes or were wandering off, some in pajamas and others more slowly. Only the street remained, the sound of the cop's nightstick on pavement in the distance, and the 108 bus which passed every once in a while; as for us, we had already gone to sleep, and were dreaming of fiestas, elephants, and silk suits.

POSTAL & TELEGRAPH SERVICE

One time a very distant relative of ours managed to get to be a minister and we fixed it so that a large part of the family received appointments in the postoffice substation in the Calle de Serrano. It didn't last long, that's for sure. Of the three days we were there, two of them we spent attending to the needs of the public with astounding celerity, which served us well on a surprise visit by an inspector from the Central Postoffice and earned us a laudatory squib in the *Civil Service Leader.* We were certain of our popularity by the third day, for people were already coming in from other sections of the city to send off their correspondence and to make out money orders to Purmamarca and other equally absurd places. Then my elder uncle gave us free rein and the family really began handling things, adapting procedures to their principles and predilections. At the stamp window, my second youngest sister was giving away a colored balloon to everyone who bought stamps. The first recipient of a balloon was a stout housewife, who stood there as if she'd been nailed to the floor, balloon in one hand, in the other a one-peso stamp, already licked, which was already curling up on her finger little by little. A youth with long hair flatly refused to accept his balloon, and my sister admonished him severely, while contrary opinions began to be raised in the line behind him. At the next window, divers provincials stupidly engaged in remitting part of their salaries to their distant relatives were somewhat astonished to receive small shots of vodka and every once in a while a breaded veal cutlet; all this my father took charge of, and to top it off he recited the old gaucho Vizcacha's better maxims at the top of his lungs. My brothers in the meantime, in charge of the parcel post counter, smeared the packages with tar and were dunking them in a bucket filled with feathers. They presented them later to the thunderstruck truckman, pointing out the happiness with which such improved packages would be received. "No string showing," they said. "Without all that vulgar sealing-wax, and with the name of the addressee that looks like it's been printed under a swan's wing, you notice?" Not everyone proved to be enchanted, one has to be truthful about it.

When the bystanders and the police invaded the premises, my mother closed the act with a beautiful gesture: she flew many paper airplanes over the heads of the assembled public, all different colors, made from telegrams, forms for postal money-orders and for registered letters. We sang the national anthem and retired in good order; I saw a little girl, third in line at the stamp window, crying, when she realized it was already too late for them to give her a balloon.

THE TIGER LODGERS

Long before bringing our idea to the level of actual practice, we knew that the lodging of tigers presented a double problem, sentimental and moral. The first aspect is not so much related to the lodging as to the tiger himself, inasmuch as it is not particularly agreeable for these felines to be lodged and they summon all their energies, which are enormous, to resist being lodged. Is it fitting under those circumstances to defy the idiosyncrasy of the abovementioned animals? But this question leads us directly to the moral level where any act can be the cause, or the effect, splendid or ignominious. At night, in our little house in Humboldt Street, we meditated over our bowls of rice and milk, forgetting to sprinkle the cinnamon and sugar on them. We were not really sure of our ability to lodge a tiger, and it was depressing.

It was decided finally that we would lodge just one for the sole purpose of seeing the mechanism at work in all its complexity; we could always evaluate the results later. I shall not speak here of the problem of coming by the first tiger: a delicate and troublesome job, a race past consulates, drugstores, a complex chain of tickets, airmail letters, and work with the dictionary. One night my cousins came back covered with tincture of iodine: success. We drank so much Chianti that my younger sister ended up having to clear the table with a rake. We were much younger in those days. Now that the experiment has yielded known results, I can supply the details of the lodging. The most difficult perhaps would be to describe everything related to the environment, since it requires a room with a minimum of furniture, a thing rather difficult to find in Humboldt Street. The layout is arranged in the center: two crossed planks, a complex of flexible withes, and several earthenware bowls filled with milk and water. To lodge a tiger is really not too difficult; the operation can miscarry, however, and you've got everything to do over again. The real difficulty begins when, already lodged, the tiger recovers his liberty and chooses—in one of the many manners possible—to exercise it. At that stage, known as the intermediate stage, my family's reactions are pretty basic; everything depends on how my sisters behave, on the smartness with which my father manages to get the tiger lodged again, utilizing the natural propensities of the tiger to the maximum. The slightest mistake would be a catastrophe, the fuses burned out, the milk on the floor, the horror of those phosphorescent eyes shining through the utter darkness, warm spurts with every thud of the paw; I resist imagining what would follow since, up till now, we've managed to lodge a tiger without dangerous consequences. The layout, as well as the varying duties all of us must perforce perform, from the tiger down to my second cousins, are seemingly efficient and articulate harmoniously. The fact of lodging a tiger is not in itself important to us, rather that the ceremony be completed to the very end without a mistake. Either the tiger agrees to be lodged, or must be lodged in such a way that its acceptance or refusal is of no consequence. At these moments which one is tempted to call crucial—perhaps because of the two planks, perhaps because it's a mere commonplace expression—the family feels itself possessed by an extraordinary exaltation; my mother does not hide her tears, and my first cousins knit and unknit their fingers convulsively. Lodging a tiger has something of the total encounter, lining oneself up against an absolute; the balance depends upon so little and we pay so high a price that these brief moments which follow the lodging and which confirm its perfection sweep us away from ourselves, annihilating both tigerness and humanity in a single motionless movement which is a dizziness, respite and arrival. There's no tiger, no family, no lodging. Impossible to know what there is: a trembling that is not of this flesh, a centered time, a column of contact. And later we all go out to the covered patio, and our aunts bring out the soup as though something were singing or as if we were all at a baptism.

translated by Paul Blackburn

Montesano unvisited

With houses hung that slanted and remote
the road that goes there if you found it
would be dangerous and dirt. Dust would cake
the ox you drive by and you couldn't meet
the peasant stare that drills you black. Birds
might be at home but rain would feel rejected
in the rapid drain and wind would bank off
fast without a friend to stars. Inside
the convent they must really mean those prayers.

You never find the road. You pass the cemetery,
military, British, World War Two and huge.
Maybe your car will die and the garage
you go to will be out of parts. The hotel
you have to stay in may have postcard shots,
deep focus stuff, of graves close up
and far off, just as clear, the bright town
that is someone's grave. Towns are bad things happening,
a spear elected mayor, a whip ordained.
You know in that town there's a beautiful girl
you'd rescue if your horse could run.

When your car is fixed you head on north
sticking with the highway, telling yourself
if you'd gone it would have been no fun.
Mountain towns are lovely, hung way away
like that, throbbing in light. But stay in one
two hours. You pat your car and say
let's go, friend. You drive off never hearing
the bruised girl in the convent screaming
take me with you. I am not a nun.

RICHARD HUGO

A. R. AMMONS

Possibility
along a line of difference

At the crustal
discontinuity
I went down and
walked
on the gravel bottom,
head below gully rims

tufted with
clumpgrass and
through-free roots:
prairie flatness crazed
by that difference,
I grew

excited with
the stream's image left
in dust
and farther down
in confined rambling
I

found a puddle
green, iridescent
with a visitation of daub-singing wasps,
sat down and watched
tilted shadow untilting
fill the trough,

1969

imagined cloudbursts
and
scattered pillars of rain,
buffalo at night routed
by lightning
leaping,

falling back,
wobble-kneed calves
tumbling, gully-caught;
coyote, crisp-footed
on the gravel,
loping up the difference.

JEAN FOLLAIN

Life

A child is born
in a vast landscape
half a century later
he is simply a dead soldier
and that was the man
whom one saw appear
and set down on the ground a whole
heavy sack of apples
two or three of which rolled
a sound among the sounds of a world
where the bird sang
on the stone of the door-sill.

translated by W. S. Merwin

1969

Footprints on the glacier

Where the wind
year round out of the gap
polishes everything
here this day are footprints like my own
the first ever
frozen
pointing up into the cold

and last night someone
marched and marched on the candle flame
hurrying
a painful road
and I heard the echo a long time afterwards
gone and some connection of mine

I scan the high slopes for a dark speck
that was lately here
I pass my hands
over the melted wax
like a blind man
they are all
moving into their seasons at last
my bones face each other trying
to remember a question

nothing moves while I watch
but here the black trees
are the cemetery of a great battle
and behind me as I turn
I hear names leaving the bark
in growing numbers and flying north

The eagle exterminating company

There are birds larger than us, I know that.
There is a bird in the bedroom much larger than the bed.
There is a photograph of a dead bird somewhere, I can't remember.
There is a wingspan that would put us all in the shadows.

There is the birdcall I must anticipate each night.
There are feathers everywhere.
Everywhere you walk there are feathers, you can try
to hop over and between them but then
you look like a bird. You are too small to be one.

You look like a tiny one-winged bird.
If you are your mother will come and kill you.
If you are not you will probably beat yourself to death.

But what matters is that every room in the house is filled,
is filled with the cry of the eagle.
Exterminating the eagles is now all but impossible
for the house would fall down without them.

There is a photograph of a dead bird somewhere.
Everywhere you walk there are feathers.
You look like a tiny one-winged bird.
There is the birdcall. There is the wingspan.

1969   139

The double dream of spring

for Gerrit Henry

Mixed days, the mindless years, perceived
With half-parted lips
The way the breath of spring creeps up on you and floors you.
I had thought of all this years before
But now it was making no sense. And the song had finished:
This was the story.

Just as you find men with yellow hair and blue eyes
Among certain islands
The design is complete
And one keeps walking down to the shore
Footsteps searching it that way
Yet they can't have it can't not have the tune that way
And we keep stepping . . . down . . .
The rowboat rocked as you stepped into it. How flat its bottom
The little poles pushed away from the small waves in the water
And so outward. Yet we turn dolefully
To examine each other in the dream. Was it fine sap
Coursing in the tree
That made the buds stand out, each with a peculiar coherency?
For certainly the sidewalk led
To a point somewhere beyond itself
Caught, lost in millions of tree-analogies
Being the furthest step one might find.

And now amid the churring of locomotives
Moving on the land the grass lies over passive
Beetling its "end of the journey" mentality into your forehead
Like so much blond hair awash
Sick starlight on the night
That is readying its defenses again
As day comes up

1969

Toward a new program for the university
CHRISTOPHER LASCH

In advanced capitalist society the university performs three functions.

(1) It provides the members of the ruling class with a broad and general culture that enables them to look after the general affairs of society and also helps to legitimize the existence of the ruling class by identifying it with the highest human aspiration, the search for order and meaning. This was the original function of the university in the West, to which was later added the training of lawyers and other professionals needed to run an increasingly complicated system of production. Throughout most of its history, however, the university has trained not specialists but men of general culture who govern society not through the application of specialized skills to the solution of technical problems, but through the elaboration of a unified world-view that makes sense of experience and to which all activities can be related. Thus the highly practical business of law could be regarded until recently as a branch of ethics, for which one prepared not merely by mastering a body of specialized technique but through the study of history, philosophy, and even theology. Nor was science conceived as specialized problem-solving, a sort of higher technology,

as it is considered today; it too was regarded as a special form of general knowledge, the pursuit of which was intended to lead to synthesis and the discovery of unifying principles.

Since these principles remained, for the most part, the monopoly of the ruling class, the university throughout most of its history was an instrument of ruling-class domination. At the same time, the search for a unified world-view demanded in the university an atmosphere of unrestricted inquiry and freedom from outside interference. The universities early achieved a high degree of autonomy relative to most other institutions of ruling-class control. This permitted them, on occasion, even to become centers of opposition to the ruling class. General culture has always been potentially subversive of elitist pre-rogatives, as the bourgeoisie demonstrated during its long struggle against the feudal nobility; for by identifying itself with the universal needs and hopes of mankind, the ruling class provides the cultural values by which its own hegemony can be called into question.

One of the most important facts about modern society is that the bourgeoisie has largely outgrown its dependence on general culture and now requires, for the maintenance and growth of its institutions, a quite different kind of culture—instrumentalized knowledge, knowl-edge as problem-solving. Pragmatism and behaviorism provide the philosophical (or anti-philosophical) rationale for this new culture or anti-culture, which increasingly expresses itself in non-verbal sym-bols instead of words. The decline of general culture is closely related to the decline of the universities as centers of independent and creative thought. The pursuit of humane learning, once the central purpose of the university, has become peripheral, and the humanistic concep-tion of education now serves merely as window-dressing for a factory-like operation to which such learning is increasingly irrelevant, or as a means of training sophisticated consumers (particularly in the case of women) with expensive tastes and habits. The idea of the univer-sity as a place of general learning survives mostly as an ideal to which educators pay lip service but in which few of them believe.

(2) This does not mean that the university no longer trains mem-bers of the governing elite; only that the kind of training the ruling class requires has changed. Formerly the university provided the ruling class with general culture; now it provides advanced training in the new mathematical and computerized culture on which an ad-vanced economy more and more depends. The "hard sciences"—those in which data can be easily quantified and expressed in sym-

bols—have established themselves as the only legitimate means of apprehending objective reality, while everything else is relegated to the sphere of esthetics and "value judgments" that are supposed to be subjective by definition and therefore irrelevant to the search for truth. The new ruling class, still bourgeois in the sense that its interests are bound up with the survival of capitalism, no longer consists of men broadly trained in law, philosophy, and the classics; it consists of managerial types who speak a symbolic language as incomprehensible to the masses as Latin was incomprehensible to the medieval multitude. It is the business of the university to provide advanced training in this new language, and also to carry on governmentally financed research that will be directly useful to the corporations and to government, particularly the military. Because this research is directly financed by the corporations and the state, the university no longer enjoys the relative autonomy it formerly enjoyed. Moreover, the new symbolic culture, though it demands a certain degree of intellectual freedom in the university, no longer necessarily implies, as the old humanistic culture implied, the freedom to raise philosophical questions about the very premises of the society it serves. Those premises now tend to be taken for granted by the scientific elite. Hence there is no longer any reason that the university should be open to dangerous ideas, except that to suppress them would violate the traditions of the university, which retain some lingering force.

(3) So far we have considered the university as a ruling-class institution pure and simple. In the last twenty-five years, however, the university has also become, in a special sense of the term, a working-class institution. It trains people, in large numbers, who can only be described as intellectual and technical workers—people with the special skills needed to run the industrial and governmental bureaucracies and to carry out all the commands of the managerial elite. Advanced society, as is well known, tends to replace manual work with brain work and thus to create what has variously been described as a new middle class and a new working class. The brain workers are middle-class in income and life-style but working-class in the sense that they are salaried servants of the ruling class who have little to say about the general conditions of their work or the social purposes it serves. The demand for such workers is insatiable; hence the unprecedented expansion of higher education.

The training of intellectual workers—bureaucrats, technicians, engineers, researchers, teachers—has become the most important reason for the university to exist, especially the mass universities that have proliferated so rapidly in the last three decades. The first of the functions of the university—promotion of general culture—has become peripheral. The second—training the new scientific elite and doing scientific research for the corporations and the state—can be performed elsewhere almost as easily as it can be performed in the university. This last is a point that is not clearly understood by those who would ban military research from the university. There are good grounds for getting rid of this kind of activity, for its undermines the autonomy of the university. But many of those who seek to banish war- and production-oriented research do so under the illusion that purifying the university of these influences will at the same time deal a fatal blow to American imperialism. They see the university as the weak link in the institutional structure of imperialism, and they hope that by destroying its capacity to serve the corporations and the military they will thereby bring down the whole system. Nothing could be more naive. The university, as we have seen, is already obsolete as a ruling-class institution in its traditional sense. (For this reason the attack on ROTC is an attack on an anachronism; ROTC is the last survival of the archaic concept of the officer-gentleman.) And it is rapidly becoming obsolete as a ruling-class institution in the new sense of training a scientific elite and carrying out war research. Those activities do have to go forward (whereas humanistic learning can be dispensed with entirely); that is, they are necessary to the survival of advanced capitalism. But there is no pressing reason why they should be associated with the university. In fact they are not really compatible with the third function of the university, to train a new type of worker. The latter demands that higher education become universal and that the universities become, in effect, trade schools. It also gives rise, unavoidably, to student discontent which (for reasons analyzed below) will probably become chronic, unless it becomes too threatening and has to be bloodily suppressed. For these reasons, high-level researchers may find it convenient to remove themselves and their most faithful apprentices to the student-less peace and security of the advanced research institute. Indeed this development is already taking place. From the point of view of the ruling class it is not altogether a desirable development, because it deprives the new mathematical anti-culture of the prestige bestowed by proximity to the old humanist culture (however attenuated). An academic environment, moreover, affords a few concrete advantages that may be hard to duplicate in a research institute. Nevertheless it has been apparent for some time that "teaching" and "research" are splitting apart in the university itself, and the logical result of this process is for the split to become formalized in completely separate institutions. Attacks on military research, therefore, although they may help to improve the university itself, will not bring down the "power structure." Unless they are combined with a much broader strategy of university reform, they will only hasten the conversion of the university into a trade school.

For the trade-school function is the one function that cannot be performed by some other institution—not without changing our entire social system. The ruling class no longer needs the university to train its own intellectual elite; that can now be done elsewhere. It does need the university, however, to train the working force. That fact underlies all the nonsense, preached by the most prominent educators and incongruously echoed by the left itself, about the universal "right" to higher education. What the "right" to higher education means is that in order to qualify for admission to the new working force of brain workers, the prospective worker has to undergo compulsory training that will equip him with a specialty while at the same time systematically depriving him of any critical points of view that might enable him to understand the meaning of his work, its relation to other work, or the general social purposes it serves. University students, it is true, are ritually exposed to the "humanities" as part of their "general education," but the content of general education has become demonstrably so thin that it has fallen into complete discredit. The general tendency is toward early and narrow specialization. Mere exposure to the humanities, in any case, does not make the engineering or science or sociology major automatically into a well-rounded man of letters. Since most teachers in the humanities and "soft sciences" implicitly accept the judgment of the "hard sciences" that these fields have no relation to objective reality and deal only in judgments, exposure to the humanities may only reinforce the contempt with which most students already regard them.

If one considers the universities principally as trade schools, as a new form of industrial apprenticeship, the proper goals of university reform appear to be quite different from those to which the student left has given most of its efforts. The attempt to disrupt and paralyze the university not only reflects the naive theory of state power already criticized, it also runs directly counter to the interests of the workers in the name of which the new left claims to speak. The student left hopes to use confrontations within the university to "radicalize" other students, but its conception of radicals as people who have opted out of the system reflects the movement's elitism, its preoccupation with the spiritual turmoil of those who are bored or sickened by affluence, and its essential indifference to the needs of people who cannot afford the luxury of dropping out. These people, whether they come from the ghetto, from the white working class, or from the middle class itself, are determined to get what they consider to be an education, and they (together with the communities from which they come) are therefore determined that the universities shall remain open. They know—what affluent dropouts from suburbia can afford to overlook —that higher education represents their only chance to acquire the skills that lead in turn to economic security. What they do not know is that the same system that provides them with those skills also serves to make them into passive and easily manipulatable workers, at once highly trained and intellectually docile, proficient in specialized skills but incapable of questioning the underlying conditions of their existence.

This presents the left with the opportunity to make the reform of the university into a wider issue capable of speaking to the needs of working people in general. Calls for the disruption of the university, for student power, or even for an end to military research do not speak to those needs—a fact that incidentally explains why SDS has scored its few successes at elite universities like Harvard, Cornell, and Columbia. In order to win the support of the new technical and intellectual workers and of the working classes generally, the left would have to put forward a very different kind of program for the university, the main elements of which can be characterized as follows:

(i) *An end to violence and terror on the campus.*

(ii) *An end to demonstrations that disrupt academic work, as opposed to demonstrations that merely disrupt the administrative routine.*

The left cannot afford to deprive itself of forceful methods of making its influence felt, by falling in with the official civil libertarian position that disruptions and strikes of any kind have no place in the university and that those who oppose the existing system should confine their opposition to speech.

But radicals do not have the right to interfere with the free speech of others, to shut down the classes of professors with whom they do not happen to agree, or to prevent the majority of students (whose patience in any case has begun to wear somewhat thin) from proceeding with the terms of their apprenticeship.

(iii) *An end to military research and other ties with government and the corporations that undermine the autonomy of the university.*

As already explained, elimination of these functions will hardly revolutionize American society. Nevertheless it is a necessary condition of any real reform of the university, for the general objective of reform should be to defend the existing autonomy of the university and steadily and systematically to expand it.

(iv) *Humanization of the conditions of industrial apprenticeship.* Having recognized that apprenticeship, disguised as liberal education, has become the principal function of the university, the left should proceed to organize a broad coalition of forces within the university community (and eventually in American society in general) for the purpose of providing students with the means of becoming not merely intellectual workers but workers who can think and question and thereby defend their own class interests against those who would keep them docile and passive. This emphatically does not mean providing students with courses in guerrilla warfare or the crimes of American imperialism. It implies something far more serious than that—restoration of the unity of learning. Science must become once again a branch of philosophy, a means not simply of solving predefined problems but of raising questions about the ends and means of human existence. The arts and humanities must be rescued from their present degraded, diffuse, essentially ornamental position and established on an equal footing with science, as studies that make their own indispensable contribution to the understanding of the objective world. Unless these things are done, the working class—broadly defined to include the intellectual and technical strata—will have no defense against a technological anti-culture that incinerates its enemies abroad and increasingly reduces its own citizens to a state of general insecurity, while trying to buy them off with a great plenty of consumer goods.

What is required, therefore, is not more curricular reforms designed to provide a sugar coating of the humanities and "general education" for industrial apprenticeship, but a fundamental reform of apprenticeship itself in the form of a general attack on the instrumental conception of culture that has become so pervasive. The issue, reduced to its simplest terms, is the issue between an enlightened and a degraded working class; but bound up in that issue is the very survival of all that is best in Western culture.

Indeed the fact that the ruling class in advanced countries now tramples on that culture, which it claims to defend against the infidels without, is the best reason for overthrowing it and replacing it with a genuinely democratic regime.

(v) *Creation of a new system of secondary education.* The last stage of a radical program for the universities—one that can be reached only after the others have been at least partially accomplished, but which should be borne in mind throughout—is to remove the trade-school function altogether and embody it in a new system of secondary schools. So far I have considered the problems of the university without any reference to the problems of youth. I have considered students chiefly as prospective (intellectual and technical) workers; but they must also be regarded in their capacity as young people subjected in great numbers to an entirely novel experience, namely the prolongation of adolescence well into the twenties. Advanced capitalism requires that masses of young people be kept off the labor market and maintained in a subordinate and dependent status at a time when they are mature and formerly would have qualified for adult status.

These changes, superimposed on an already existing tendency to make the school into a total educational environment (a tendency that goes back as far as the seventeenth century, and was based on a new sensitivity to the needs of children and adolescents), spelled the final death of the medieval concept of education, which left the pupil free of supervision outside school hours. In the twentieth century the older concept, already extinct in the secondary schools, has disappeared even from higher education and is replaced by the phenomenon of the university *in loco parentis*: the residential college with its close supervision of all aspects of students' lives. The university, like the high school, becomes among other things a place of detention and custody.

These conditions underlie the generational character of the student revolt and are reflected in some of its demands. The demand for "relevance" and the demand that the university involve itself more directly in life reflect the highly artificial isolation of young people who are forced to extend their years of preparation for life far beyond what was demanded by any previous society. To make matters worse, many students are doubly victimized by the national cult of youth (largely the creation of Madison Avenue) and hence do not really want the adult status they claim to be demanding. Perhaps because they believe their position to be essentially helpless, they prefer to insist on the special virtue and wisdom peculiar to youth.

Universal higher education is a cruel fraud; it does a direct disservice to the people whom it is supposed to benefit, namely the young. Ostensibly an unmitigated blessing and "opportunity," it in fact is a manifestation of society's refusal to provide young people with a training that would enable them to qualify for employment at eighteen or nineteen instead of at twenty-two, twenty-three, or even twenty-six or -seven. The effort to humanize technical education in the university, therefore, should be seen merely as the first step toward the creation of an entirely new system of higher and secondary education designed to destroy the custodial function of schools; to dissociate education from the process of qualification for work, so far as that is possible, and where it is not, to recognize more frankly the character of education as apprenticeship and to provide institutions appropriate to that purpose; and finally, to provide unstigmatized alternatives to formal schooling, both for young people and for adults. This last is an essential part of any such reform, but requires detailed treatment in its own right and will have to be passed over here.

Another essential part of a new educational system is a new kind of secondary school, the technical school or college of science, graduation from which (at eighteen or nineteen) would not necessarily mean the end of a person's education but would qualify him for most work now open only to holders of a college degree. The technical college would abandon the pretense of educating scholars in the old-fashioned sense and would concentrate instead on a rigorous program in science, aimed at training skilled workers with a broad understanding of science in its many forms. It would train people without many of the accomplishments and refinements traditionally associated with liberal scholarship and high social status, but who, unlike the present college graduate, would be capable of critical thought on a variety of subjects, particularly on the social consequences of applied science. By sacrificing its pretensions to a classical education—and these now survive only as pretensions in the university itself—the college of science would be in a better position than the university to capitalize on students' hunger for "relevance" by emphasizing, for instance, the scientific understanding of society and the relation of scientific research to social decisions, instead of burdening students with required courses in the humanities that seem "irrelevant" for various good and bad reasons.

The college of science, in other words, would abandon the claim —which in any case has become very hollow—to offer a rounded, liberal education. It would also retreat from the present swollen conception of the school as the *only* education, the sum total of a person's intellectual training. In the existing universities, and even more in the high schools, this conception is a necessary counterpart of the custodial function of the school; the school becomes the only educational agency (even to the exclusion of the family) because the students are expected to spend all their time there. In the technical college, by contrast, young people from twelve or thirteen to eighteen or nineteen would be required to spend only part of their time in classes, thus leaving time for games and jobs (is it necessary to insist that these too are educational?), putting an end to the absurd regime of a five-day school week, breaking down the enforced separation between learning and "life," and in general breaking down the segregation of the young.

A parallel system of secondary schools, also for students between twelve and nineteen, would offer a six-year program of studies in the arts—not, again, as preparation for university work (although it might serve as such) but as a complete course in its own right. It might be objected that separate systems of secondary schools, one for the arts and one for science, merely reinforce the division between science and the humanities. This objection disappears, however, when science itself is defined, not as a collection of discrete fields of specialization, but as a branch of philosophy which aims, like the humanities, to give order and meaning to human life. Parallel systems of secondary schools, one for the arts and one for science (both broadly defined), imply, not a radical divorce between the two (with the consequent trivialization of the humanities as essentially ornamental and oriented to the consumption of culture), but recognition of the practical difficulty that a full synthesis of the two can take place only in the university, at the highest level of academic thought, and that students meanwhile have to make decisions (not necessarily irrevocable, as they tend to be today) that force them to emphasize certain kinds of studies over others. We have already seen that in the existing university the humanities have largely become a mere appendix to technical training, and it should be obvious that the attempt to gather all learning together in one institution does not at all guarantee a synthesis. That ideal can be realized only in a true university where scholars pursue advanced studies for their own sake; a university, in other words, shorn of the extraneous functions it now exercises and restored to its original purpose of disinterested inquiry—without the elitist view of society with which that purpose was formerly associated.

This hasty survey necessarily simplifies a complex subject and leaves large parts of the argument unelaborated. The decline of general culture, for instance, cannot be understood solely as a result of changing modes of production. It has to be seen, more broadly, as a manifestation of the collapse of a unified view of the world and of the entire rationalist tradition. The attempt to reestablish general culture in the university, while at the same time providing a new system of industrial apprenticeship, cannot, therefore, be seen as a matter that concerns educational reformers alone.

I have already tried to show that educational reform concerns the working class as a whole—particularly its technical and intellectual elements—and will not be achieved until it becomes part of a general social program embodied in a new mass political movement. But such a movement will itself come to nothing unless it has as its overriding objective nothing less than a new cultural synthesis, based on the rationalist tradition but transcending its narrow elitism and its traditional disregard of the social consequences of individual achievements. Without such a synthesis, industrial civilization—capitalist or socialist—will become increasingly brutal and meaningless.

ON FOLLOWING PAGES: PHOTOGRAPHS BY
JENNIFER BRADY, KAREN SAVAGE,
JENNIFER BRADY. (*TQ* #16)

Three meetings

STANLEY ELKIN

I met him, of all places, in western Kentucky in the, of all seasons, summer of, of all times, 1941. I was curator of a highway
zoo and snake show gasoline station complex on U.S. Bypass 97
eleven miles west of Humphries. I don't flatter myself that Vladi
stopped because of the wonders collected there. There was a gas
war and Dmitri had to use the Men's. (Nor am I showing off
when I use the pet name. A gracious and democratic man, Vladi
instructed me to call him thus not five minutes after we had
met.)

You know how it is with these highway zoos. The specimens
are scrawny and seem somehow *sideshow,* freakish reductions,
bestial lemons teetering on the brink of some evolutionary mis-
step. Well there's good reason, but it isn't what you think. You
mustn't be too hasty to blame the curator. Nobby understood
this. (Never a formal man, he instructed me to call him thus

This piece was Elkin's contribution to *TQ*'s special issue entitled *Nabokov* (*TQ* #17).

not ten minutes after we had met.) He knew the debilitating effect of the tourists on the fauna. It is the stare they bring, a glazed gaze between boredom and boldness on them like pollen, like the greasy dust of the last state line, like fruitflies and parasites on the oranges and plants between Arizona and California. What can you do? You can't have them wash their faces first. It's a ruinous hypnotism, this wear and tear of the eyes. With their fixed look they can intimidate even the healthiest animal, and over the course of a season actually impoverish it. (I've seen the rich oriental rug of a snake's second skin turn to a moldy scab under this gaze.)

I accompanied Boko through the menagerie—not one to stand on ceremonies, he ordered me call him after this fashion not seventeen minutes after we met—and watched as he grew sad contemplating my failing beasts. Every so often he would shake his head and punctuate his unhappiness with lush Cyrillic *tch tch's* which would have been beautiful had I not guessed at the torment behind them. When we had toured all the corrals and pens he looked significantly toward a woman tourist with New Hampshire plates who was depressing my porcupine.

"There's your trouble," he said.

"I know, but what can I do? It can't be helped."

"Have them wash their faces first," he said gently.

"That's brilliant. It just might work, Boko."

"More rasp on the *k* sound. It takes a strong *h*."

Struck by the incisiveness of his recommendation, I serendipitously offered to show him my butterfly cases. (I did not know who he was at this time, but there is something in a curator's temperament or even in a caretaker's or guard's which makes him always keep something special in reserve which the ordinary public never sees. This is universally true. Remember it the next time you visit the top of the Empire State Building or go out to see the Statue of Liberty. We don't necessarily do it for the tip, mind.) It was a standard collection made somewhat exceptional by the inclusion of two rare specimens—the Bangelor Butterfly and the highly prized Lightly Salted Butterfly.

I could see that Boko was very excited. "Where did you come upon this?" he asked animatedly, and pointing with a shaking finger to the Lightly Salted Butterfly. "I have searched in Pakistan and sought in Tartary. I've been up the slopes of Muz Tagh Ata and down Soputan's cone. I have stood beneath Kile's waterfall and along the shores of Van. I must know. Where?"

"In the meadow."

He revealed who he was and gave me his card and said that if there was ever anything he could ever do for me I should look him up.

And that was the first meeting.

I saw him a second time in Venezuela after the war. We had met in Cair at a boatel, or marina, where we had both gone independently to be outfitted for an expedition up the Orinoco in search of the most fabulous and legendary creature in the entire species—the Great Bull Butterfly. (The highway zoo had failed due to the construction of a new interstate and a settlement of the gas war. With the acceleration of construction on the Federal Highway System many small curators were out of a job in those days. There is no more room for the little man, it seems. Many former highway zookeepers—those who have not been absorbed by larger institutions—have been driven by their love of display and the diminished outlet for their talents to exhibitionism and been arrested.) We decided to join forces. It was Uncle Volodya who suggested it. (Never an uncompassionate man, he had seen that the rasping *kh* sound was giving me the sore throat and permitted me to call him thus.) By now I knew his reputation and his great work in lepidopterology and would have been too shy to put forth the idea myself. I was sitting in the boatel sipping an Orinoco-Cola and reading.

"What are you reading?" Uncle asked. I hadn't noticed him, but recognized him at once. I didn't know if he would remember me, however, and so did not presume to remind him of our first meeting.

"Oh," I said, "it's a birthday card. Today is my birthday. Have you ever noticed how a birthday card always arrives on your birthday? Never a day early, never a day late. My people are in far-off Kentucky, yet the card was in this morning's mail." It was the longest speech I had yet made to him. He was clearly moved, and I have reason to believe that it was on the strength of this insight that he asked me to accompany him on the Great Bull Butterfly hunt.

We set out next morning and for the next five weeks assiduously traveled downstream, searching along the banks by day and camping by night. We encountered many strange and rare larval and pupal forms, together with some lovely eggal forms I had never before seen, but nothing approaching the mature imago we sought. Perhaps the natives were mistaken in their descriptions, I thought, never daring to voice my suspicions aloud of course. Or perhaps, I thought racistically, they lied. Maybe the Great Bull Butterfly was a Wild Goose Chase. As I say, I never said this, but one night I was sitting glumly in front of the campfire. He noticed that I was not playing my saxophone.

"You're not playing tonight, Shmoolka. Why?"

"It's the reeds, Uncle," I lied. "I've worn out the last reed."

"That's not it. What? Tell."

"Well, if you must know, I think the expedition will fail. I think it's a cruel hoax."

"A hoax, Shmoolko?"

"We've been searching five weeks, and if you can't find a diurnal creature in broad daylight in five weeks—"

"*Diurnal be damned,*" he shouted suddenly, falling unconsciously into his fabled alliteration. "You've given me an idea. What if—what if the Great Bull Butterfly is *nocturnal*? If he were, then of course we wouldn't have found him. Shmuel, I think that's the solution, I think that's it." Before I could even reply, he was on his feet and off into the jungle. He darted heedlessly across the path of a black cat and gave it bad luck. I followed breathlessly. We found it that night.

But, alas, we had been gone longer than we had expected. The bearers had run off. We were low on supplies. The trip back to Cair was upstream against a heavy current made more dangerous by the torrential rains. We had no more food. We had eaten my last saxophone reed the day before. I don't think we could have lasted another twenty-four hours, but we were found at the eleventh hour by natives—Uncle puts it at the eleventh hour; I don't think it could have been past ten-thirty—who fed us and promised to conduct us back to Cair the next morning. They knew a shortcut.

"Why are you so hung up on butterflies, Nuncle?" I asked at campfire that night after marshmallows.

"Shmuel, that's because they're a metaphor is why."

"A meadow flower?"

"A metaphormorphosis."

"I met a fire more for us? A meaty forest?"

"Call me Steve."

"But why *butterflies*, Steve?"

"Lepidopterology—don't you hear that word leper in there? They're the outcasts, you know. They're exiles. Like me. Anyway it wasn't always butterflies; for a time it used to be squirrels and swordfish. Then for a while it was pinto ponies. But I've been east and I've been west, and I think butterflies is best."

"Could you speak about them?"

In the glow of the fire his face seemed serene and very sad.

"Like ur-airplanes they are," he spoke suddenly. "Lopsided glider things riding turbulence like the snowflakes. Heroic, heraldic. Bug pennants, bucking, choppy flags of the forest."

"That's beautiful," I told him.

"Also, if you keep one in your pocket it's good luck."

"Call me Ishmuel."

And that was the second meeting.

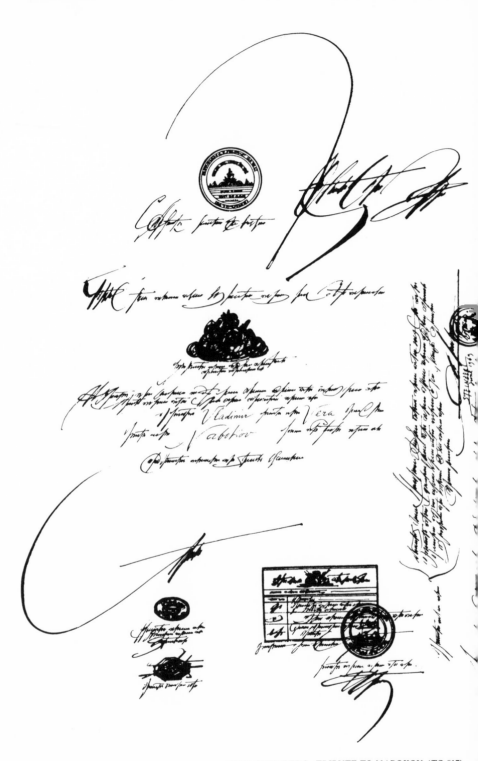

SAUL STEINBERG. *TRIBUTE TO NABOKOV.* (*TQ* #17)

THREE BY W. S. MERWIN

WITHIN THE WARDROBES

No one who was not born and brought up in them really knows of the life in the clothing drawers, and very few of those who did grow up there are willing to divulge any details of that ancient existence so close to our own, or as we like to say within our own, and yet so unfamiliar. No, they answer, everything has been taken from us from the beginning and you have given us only what you chose to, with no concern for us. What essentials remain to us, the secrets of our life, we will keep to ourselves. If our way of life is doomed as a result of yours, its secrets will die with it, and its meaning. We will not lend those to you for your masquerades.

By now scholars have tried everything to bring those secrets to the light of present-day reality, and with almost no success. Devices for opening the drawers suddenly have revealed nothing but the contents lying like the dead whom the light suddenly surprises. Cameras with flash-bulbs, left in the drawers in houses where no one was staying, and timed to go off during the darkest and most silent hours, have disclosed still more eerie vistas of inert recumbency; always the life has remained cloaked in the motionless forms. Electronic recording devices rigged in the same manner have picked up nothing but the gradual sinking into sleep of consciousness after consciousness in the house, until at last only one alien witness remained awake: the recorder was registering its own unrewarding vigil. It has been claimed that these last results, nevertheless, represent a step forward. If not a record of the life itself, at least they supply a record of the outer world from that life's point of view.

As might have been expected, most of the few sources of information on this life so turned away from our own have come from milieus in which neglect in one form or another has already advanced its work. Loose garments, tossed in unfolded, perhaps uncleaned, long ago, and abandoned to their own shapes, have not always been able to conceal the evidences of a life to which they were born and which they had almost forgotten the need to hide. A darkness from their own world, and an odor of it, clings to them here and there when they are too abruptly hauled into ours. Others that once existed as pairs and have lost their consorts, stray buttons, fragments of ornamentation, demoralized and with a weakened sense of the future, also betray at times the existence of other mores, other values, other hopes, if not those things themselves. These are not ideal witnesses, perhaps, but is there any such thing?

At any rate it is hard to sort out probability from sectarian wishful thinking, in the scant testimony thus gathered. The witnesses suggest that their own order of things, its darkness, its anticipation in which time plays no part, its community without sound, its dances, its dances, whatever they may be, are part of an order that is older than the cupboards and will survive them. They also infer quite calmly that the world of uses, for which they were fashioned and in which they are worn, knows almost nothing of reality.

THE BASILICA OF THE SCALES

There is disagreement about the dates of each phase of the present edifice. No one can establish incontrovertibly when the first primitive chapel was constructed on this site. Parts of the crypt survive from that earliest place of worship. Massive squat squared pillars of gray stone. Medals and military decorations of a later day have been affixed to them on all sides like cloaks, and glitter in the light of the votive candles. The church has been rebuilt at least three times, incorporating the designs and proportions of successive ages. Each time it has been considerably enlarged. The facade has moved west. It is from there that we enter. From farther away. The transept has broadened like the canyon of a gray river flowing between us and the chancel. Most important of all, each time the ceiling, the ceiling has risen.

It cannot be seen. Not from anywhere in the basilica. All that meets the eye when one looks up, wherever one is, are the scales. Like leaves they hang everywhere above the worshippers and the curious. They are suspended at all heights, from those that can barely be descried through the pans and chains of others lower down, to a few which seem to be almost within reach—an illusion caused by some trick of perspective, as one discovers if one finds oneself near them. They are of all sizes, from delicate brass instruments such as apothecaries still use, to vast measures with pans that a heavy man could stand in, beams thicker than an arm and longer, and chains in proportion. And they too are of all ages. Some of them, it is said, are older, much older, than the first building itself. They were brought from far away and their origins are legendary like that of the grail. But none of them belong to our accounts any longer. No one climbs to examine them.

And it would be unthinkable to take one down. In the course of the many centuries since the last building was finished, two or three have fallen. One can imagine the terror that swept through the devout who were present when one of the silent measures suspended above them suddenly detached itself, with a sound of metal snapping and groaning, from what had seemed its everlasting equilibrium, and had crashed down through the lower choirs of chains and hammered pans, setting up a clangor of cymbals, a rocking and lamentation that left the farthest scales in the remote ceiling swinging and vibrating with dying songs. The fallen measures lay like dead supplicants on the granite floor. No one touched them. No one was sure what they meant. No one knelt to pray near them on the bare stone unless the crowd of worshippers pressed them closer than they would have chosen to be. In time iron railings were erected around the collapsed measures where they lay. Black cloth was draped from the rail and removed only between the evening of Good Friday and Easter morning. Candles—not votive lights but thick columns of wax the color of the faces of the dead—flickered perpetually at the corners of the enclosures.

As for the scales suspended above, it would be hard to say at a glance whether they are still or moving. A distant quiet hangs in the pans like dust. And yet the eye that remains fixed upon them for some time detects, or seems to detect, a scarcely perceptible motion, such as we think we see if we stare for long at the faces of the dead. And in fact the scales are at all times in motion. Often it is so slight that the unaided eye could not discern it at all if it were not that the thousands of minute swayings all cast shadows into the thickets of chains, beams, pans, and the shadows magnify the movements, giving that impression of a breathing lost in itself. Occasionally a single balance will forsake its equilibrium, without apparent warning, and one of its pans will slowly sink farther and farther as the other rises, then even more slowly right itself. The phenomenon has fostered various explanations. Some say it is due to a death. Some ascribe it to a peculiar fervor of prayer. Others declare that it is the dove descending. Or a wind. Past, present, or to come.

THE DACHAU SHOE

My cousin Gene (he's really only a second cousin) has a shoe he picked up at Dachau. It's a pretty worn-out shoe. It wasn't top quality in the first place, he explained. The sole is cracked clear across and has pulled loose from the upper on both sides, and the upper is split at the ball of the foot. There's no lace and there's no heel.

He explained he didn't steal it because it must have belonged to a Jew who was dead. He explained that he wanted some little thing. He explained that the Russians looted everything. They just took anything. He explained that it wasn't top quality to begin with. He explained that the guards or the kapos would have taken it if it had been any good. He explained that he was lucky to have got anything. He explained that it wasn't wrong because the Germans were defeated. He explained that everybody was picking up something. A lot of guys wanted flags or daggers or medals or things like that, but that kind of thing didn't appeal to him so much. He kept it on the mantelpiece for a while but he explained that it wasn't a trophy.

He explained that it's no use being vindictive. He explained that he wasn't. Nobody's perfect. Actually we share a German grandfather. But he explained that this was the reason why we had to fight that war. What happened at Dachau was a crime that could not be allowed to pass. But he explained that we could not really do anything to stop it while the war was going on because we had to win the war first. He explained that we couldn't always do just what we would have liked to do. He explained that the Russians killed a lot of Jews too. After a couple of years he put the shoe away in a drawer. He explained that the dust collected in it.

Now he has it down in the cellar in a box. He explains that the central heating makes it crack worse. He'll show it to you, though, any time you ask. He explains how it looks. He explains how it's hard to take it in, even for him. He explains how it was raining, and there weren't many things left when he got there. He explains how there wasn't anything of value and you didn't want to get caught taking anything of that kind, even if there had been. He explains how everything inside smelled. He explains how it was just lying out in the mud, probably right where it had come off. He explains that he ought to keep it. A thing like that.

You really ought to go and see it. He'll show it to you. All you have to do is ask. It's not that it's really a very interesting shoe when you come right down to it but you learn a lot from his explanations.

Pain

The lore of it is something they keep from you.
As with sex, the mechanics are little rehearsed.
Not even among grown men and women the specifics—
yes he unbuttoned her, yes she was a good lay
but how? and in exactly what circumstance?

The nurses will not tell you. They baste and simmer
tools in the autoclave. The doctors whisper
Demerol into their stethoscopes. And the interns,
that volleyball team still challenging its acne,
can only pump up the bag full of blood pressure.

Meanwhile pain comes in dressed up like a spy.
A bearded spy wearing sneakers and murmuring eat!
Eat my quick poison. And of course I nibble the edges.
I eat my way to the center of his stem
because something inside it is secret.

At night rowing out to sea on drugs, rowing out
on my little oars, those carefully deployed spoons,
sometimes I think I catch a glimpse of that body
of knowledge. It is the fin of a flying fish.
It is a scrap of phosphorescent plankton
I would take hold of crying, wait!
Thinking, tell me.

Understand that by this time the man next door
is calling *police police police*—his pain
burgles him. *Police,* that kind of father.
Understand that on the other side an old lady
in the thin voice of a music teacher is calling
yoo-hoo, help me, am I alone in this house?
She is dying with the shades pulled in a deserted villa.

1970

Meanwhile I continue putting out to sea
on my little wooden ice cream spoons.
Although I am not a Catholic, the priest has laid
his hands upon me. He has put God into my pain.
Somewhere in my pineal gland He sits and gloats.

As for the lore, I have learned nothing to hand on.
I go out nightly past these particular needles
and these knives.

ROLAND TOPOR. (*TQ* #18)

1970

167

What's that you say, Cesar?

To Cesar Ortiz-Tinoco

The poet—a political animal?
Yes! Yes!
The way you said that phrase undressed me completely.
There I was naked in a painting of Orozco
holding up a torch which was my own
arm burning above the elbow.
And you yourself were Father Hidalgo
tolling the church-bell of Dolores,
pulling yourself straight up into the air
with your own emotion.
At a moment like that, who would not agree?
yes—yes—a poet is a political animal.

But he is as many other kinds of animal as possible too.
A suffering animal—delegated
to take on the madness and feckless atrocity of us all,
and of everything.
A hungry animal.
Everything at which he looks with passion
he desires to eat.

A living animal—almost so much more alive
than he or anyone else can have the patience to endure.
A traveling animal, emitting and transmitting
Marquesas and Popocatepetls like bubbles in his afterglow.
A fighting animal. He is always down
at the back fence gathering handfuls of ass-manure.
He is able to throw three hundred yards
and strike his enemy in the eye without fail.
A capricious animal.
Here he is sniffing at the holes of bad fortune
and good fortune,
he is trying to decide which will taste better
and is worth digging out of the ground.

A lustful animal.
See how everything he looks at makes him either angry
or in love?
He is always down by the docks helping Venus
out of the sea to be raped.
He is always avenging her rape in a vertigo of righteous rage.

Backs and buttocks and breasts—
he is thrown into spells of deep breathing
and scalded imagination by backs and buttocks and breasts.
By the *idea* of backs and buttocks and breasts!
(male or female)
He falls away constantly
into snatches of mating dances and fertility incantations.

Well then, of course—
when he has been all these kinds of animal,
what you say, too.
Certainly he is in love with the idea of kings and queens,
also presidents, secretaries, first commissars,
leaders of communes, oligarchists and prime ministers.
He does not disdain dictators.
He has been one, he expects to be one again,
at the first overturning of the state.
Do you see that creature crawling below
about the ballot boxes, snuffling?
It is he.
Also that one standing on the balcony
eating up the cheers.
If anyone loves justice, he is there.
If anyone loves injustice,
he is there also.
He is in the place where anyone lives or no-one.
Whatever made you think he was some person in particular?
He was meant to be you.

ABOVE AND FACING PAGE: ROLAND TOPOR. (*TQ* #18)

Enigma for an angel

Dreams rock the blanket-universe.
But someone strains to see the ocean;
it looms in the black night, sliced off
by sharp knives of the window casing.
The shrubs have trapped a moon-balloon.
Rowboats are sunk in conversation.
The shoes that glitter in this room
will not oppress the oyster nation.

A hand that holds a pillow fast
is creeping down a polished bedpost,
making its way to a cloud breast
by this inept and tongue-tied gesture.
A sock, torn on a jagged rock,
twists in the dark; its curve is swan-like.
Its funnel mouth is all agog;
it stares up like a blackened fishnet.

The wall helps us to have two seas
(perhaps we're helped by hazy thinking),
divided up in such a way
that two dark nets, which still hang empty
at depths that must be measureless,
wait to be surfaced, and to follow
twin lines lashed to the Northern Cross
that sparkles in the open window.

1970

A star glows yellow on the waves;
the rowboats loom, bereft of motion.
The Cross alone moves, and its shape
recalls some swan on urgent mission.[1]
The two nets move at steady pace
from empty depths to the bright surface;
they hope that the revolving Cross
will pull them in and cast them elsewhere.

All this takes place quite silently.
The empty window still is hopeful,
despite its immobility,
that the next cast will bring a netful.
The window in this dark night sees [2]
(the moon has made its whole world brighter)
how flower beds roll in like waves,
and front-yard shrubs crash down like breakers.

The house is motionless, the fence
dives in the dark, with all its cork floats;
a hatchet stuck in the front steps
keeps its sharp eye on the wet dock-posts.
A clock is chattering. Far off
the grumbling of a speedboat's motor
drowns out the crunch of oyster shells
heel-trodden by a fleshless stroller.

Two eyes emit a piercing scream.
The eyelids close, with a vague rustle,
like oyster shells curved, in the gloom,
to cover and protect the pupil.
How long until this pain is drowned,
swamped by the talk of outboard motors,
to break out then in smallpox sores
on the warm whiteness of a forearm?

1. The Northern Cross is also known as Cygnus, the Swan.
2. In Russian the connection between "window" (*okno*) and "eye" (*oko* in Old Slavic) is somewhat more evident than in English.

1970

How long? Till morning? Can it be?
The wind tugs at the cobwebs, slipping
their home-spun veils from twisted twigs.
The moon-balloon's great eye is drooping.
The nets are all hauled in. A screech
piped by a hoopoe-bird has headed
off would-be thieves. On the dark beach
the stroller, wordless still, has faded.

1964

translated by George L. Kline

ROLAND TOPOR. (*TQ* #18)

Two poems

OSIP MANDELSTAM

Night outside. An uppercrust lie.
After me—the flood. Who cares?
And what then? Citizen snores
And the crush in cloakrooms.

Masquerade ball. Wolfhound century.
So get this straight:
Cap in hand, clear out now,
And God protect and keep you.

April 1931

My age, my animal . . . who'll be able
To look into your eyes
And glue together with his blood
Two centuries' vertebrae?
Blood the builder gushes
Through the throat from earthly things,
The hanger-on is only trembling
On the sill of modern times.

Blood the builder gushes
Through the throat from earthly things,
And like a burning fish it throws
Warm sea-cartilage on the shore
And from the high birdnet pours,
From the moist azure blocks,
Pours, pours indifferently
On your fatal wound.

To liberate the age from jail,
To start a new world,
The passages of knotted days
Must be connected by a flute.
It's the age that rocks the wave
With the sadness of mankind,
And in the grass an adder breathes
To the age's golden beat.

And the buds will go on swelling
And the sprint of green will burst,
But your backbone has been shattered,
My splendid, wretched age.
Cruel and weak, you'll look back
With an idiotic smile
Like an animal, supple once,
On the tracks of your own paws.

1923–3 February 1936

translated by Clarence Brown

JACK KEROUAC: *To Edward Dahlberg*

Don't use the telephone.
People are never ready to answer it.
Use poetry.

1970

EDWARD DAHLBERG: *Confessions*

> *But Age, allas! that al wole envenyme,*
> *Hath me biraft my beautee and my pith.*
> —Chaucer

So much of me has departed. Long ago I left massy tufts of my
hair in boxcars, and in cheap, venereal hotel rooms in the Mexican
quarter of Los Angeles, and all for a pence of a thought. How hard
and usurious is the Muse, exacting the cruelest payment for the
mite she gives.

My youth is clean gone, and for a cock of prose thin and dwarfed
as the lichen in the Barren Grounds. I sigh for vision, and know
not what shirt I wore that day. I examine my hands and wonder
whose they are; my nose is a stranger to my face. When I think I
know, I do not know. If I am quiet, impatience were better; if
choleric, it is a dudgeon day. That's how it is with me.

I've got no theories to peddle, for I hawk parables, or chew my
mouldy weather, and that's good too. That's how it is with me.

I swallow people's scoffs, and that's not a dirty meal either; in
the long run, I like that I've got to bolt down. That's how it is
with me.

When I don't tremble, I am full of multitude. Would you be
prophetic or sink into the dotage of the Many? Touch me, and
you'll be soothsayers. You don't think so, I do. That's how it is
with me.

O hungry ones, I am starved, and I drink the rains and the
heavens. When I'm empty, and there are freezing steppes in my

This extract includes the 28th and 40th (and final) sections of Edward Dahlberg's *Confessions*, published by George Braziller, Inc., in 1970. — *Ed.*

spirit, I disgorge my Muse, the Void. What a constellation is Nothing. Still what have I gotten out of it? But everything matters. That's how it is with me.

Wherever I am I wish to be elsewhere. I leave my unfriended steps in last year's snow, and give my confidence to a sharper in today's rain. That's how it is with me.

I try to mend my lot, though I am my portion. I endeavor to pick myself up when I fall, but it is better there. Truth has given me nothing, yet that nothing I require. That's how it is with me.

As I write this I'm seated at a kitchen table in Geneva, in a pinched bald room of an old manor house where Voltaire once lived and wrote. My bones shake, and my pulses scarce murmur, yet I hope, poor fool that I am, to get off a line that flames like tow. And after that, what? I wait for the morrow, another guillotine morning. That's how it is with me.

But it is better to gnaw my secondhand sour sighs, and eat old groans, and suck up the foul drizzle of hackneyed disappointments —better to be pinheaded François Villon, with his long-knived nose, and chew my days that are bread "black as a maulkin" than to nuzzle at the slops of other people's opinions. The real sacrilege is the low farce, everyday life. That's how it is with me.

Jesus was a nervous man and just as unsure of himself as I am, and though nothing can be proved I have all the evidence in my vest pocket. Who understands the divine man who begged the world to smite him on the other cheek? Long ago I found out that only he who requires love most of all is absolutely crestfallen when nobody even bothers to do him the slightest mischief.

The poor holy ghost appeared before the disciples, and although he had been absent for the shortest while, they didn't know him. They had eaten together day after day, gone on foot to Capernaum, walked about the Sea of Galilee together and discussed various stiff-necked infidel towns yet the twelve looked at him without a tithe of recognition. He had to tell them to handle him and *see*. Be plain, is there any other way of seeing except by touching? I am that sort of specter and, though profane, a distant kin of his; for every friend I ever had has been a blundering stranger who did not know me. How many times they cogged me, or stabbed me with a simper; just a passing leer grieves my entrails. Still, if I were sharp as they it would be bad for me. That's how it is with me.

When someone strokes my shoulder or caresses my coat lapel, I'm lost. Once a rogue grinned at me, and though I don't care for a smile that is no more than cosmetics on the mouth, could I turn my back on him and step on his feelings? I admit it: Christ is my sort of poet. Once you decline to turn the other cheek you're ignominious. So while I bent my neck toward him he picked my purse. Suppose I had ignored him, I would have been spiteful, and malice is lust. Of course my wallet sorrowed for many weeks and even now it hasn't gotten over that wicked experience. But if I hadn't been deceived could I possess what belongs to me?

Then a former convict came to my apartment. I knew he was a confidence man, and he realized right away I could be taken. But didn't he know me? And is that evil? When he asked me for twenty-five dollars could I refuse him? He said he had a ring at the pawnbroker's which he would redeem and would return the money the next day. I knew he would not come back. That was his greatest unkindness, for we could have talked some more and exchanged the cruelties in our lives. I never saw him again. Yet why should he imagine I would not receive or embrace him? I always forgive my enemies; they're so close to me. That's how it is with me.

How hard it is to know what to do with one's self. The shoe knows it must be worn; otherwise it's been abandoned. A button understands that it hangs by a thread to a coat. A rock knows what to do in the fog or a long mean rain. A headland is just as calm in foul weather as it is in a mild sun. The shingle at Tierra del Fuego doesn't show any disgust with carrion whale washed up on it. A pebble knows how to handle a pack of wolvish winds that beat it all day long. But I'm thrown down by a trifling slight. I offer affection to people who mean nothing to me, and am courteous to one who has done his best to hinder me; shrewd as he is he doesn't know that's my lot and he's served me. A passerby roughly jostles me, and though I beg his pardon for doing it his silence cuts me. That's how it is with me.

What bothers me more than anything else is a day of zero. When nothing happens I cry out for an event, an unlooked-for pain, a stitch in my side, or I moan for long-standing scums of water; I boil over everything. Aristotle says worms are born in snow. Would that I were a frosty maggot, but that would be bad for my nature. That's how it is with me.

Suppose Christ had not drunk his cup of affliction, or that the cruel Roman Titus had not slaughtered a million Jews in ancient Jerusalem, what could I now do with a so-called life that had not made everyone suffer? That's how it is with me.

> *The whole of this material universe of*
> *ours, with all its suns and its milky*
> *ways—is nothing.*—Tolstoy

I had fled from the universal theology of lucre but could not avoid the snare of politics. I had reached the end, which is another path to perception. My skies were sackcloth, my distempered lakes were dried up, my body a dead gully. The abyss is no-feeling, that is the ultimate despondency. When I'm cauterized, flea'd or bled, I want to feel it.

The first intimation of my condition came not from my intellect but from my foot. Ill luck had been settling in my joints and un-singing knees; worst of all, my feet were forceless sinking shadows. When the feet despair the mind is a Tartarus of black humors. The neck, the arms, the elbows, and especially the feet know what is going on long before the head has intelligence of it. One thing I want to make plain is that the mind is the most ignorant part of the body. Could I only forget my old footsteps I might cure a jot of my nature.

Realizing I could cony-catch myself better than any enemy, I came to another indecision. I resolved to make the journey alone, with nothing to guide me except the oar of the prophet Tiresias, also blind, which Odysseus had gotten. I saw it was either the Many or the Socratic hemlock of ostracism—a ticklish choice, but life took care of that.

I dimly understood I would never be out of the forest, so deep and wild was the dusky foliage of Nodh in my breast. As a writer I had not even begun my apprenticeship. It took more than the strength of the phoenix for me to raise my maimed pinions from the ashes of my brute scrawl.

Wherever I went I was the victim of a doltish Communist Ajax ready to slay me with his dullness. Everything got worse though nothing was ever any good. Unable to escape my persecutors I brooded over the disappearing American earth; as Péguy said, the world had become a people-less land. The machine had displaced human beings.

What was my Atlean heresy? Gibbeted because I had a great dislike for the coarse gallows scribblings of Hemingway and Caldwell, I was the meal and booty of the rapacious salt tooth of Rumor. The Stalinist myrmidons spread the report I was an informer. Would to heaven I could spy upon my own feelings. I could not eschew their fangs of malice: "Thy reason, dear venom, give thy reason," laments Shakespeare, and Ben Jonson asserts: "I am beholden to calumny."

The Stalinist book slayers were stationed on almost every paper and magazine that claimed importance. What wolves were the Communist lambs who spoiled the vines of any writer who abhorred the banner of homogeneity. They pretended my volumes did not exist, and cast them into Tophet without a reviewer's obituary notice. "As good almost kill a man as kill a good book," it is written in Milton's *Areopagitica*. Whether I was in New York, Los Angeles, or San Francisco, I was pursued by the beagles, the Stalinists and FBI agents.

Man covers the planet with gore for justice, but where is it? Tamburlaine spilled far less blood than Stalin. Can anybody imagine that Breznev, the czarist clerk garbed in the drab vestments and chasuble, the double-breasted suit of the assassin businessman, who impudently intones "Holy Russia" and "Our Mother Land," is a Lycurgus or an Agesilaus? Little wonder that Leopardi saw the world as a vast league of criminals ruthlessly warring against a few virtuous madmen. The soul pants for the tender frolicking hills, the small meditative brooks, the miracle of human warmth, and an apocryphal Eden. In the Jewish legends it is said that dying Adam asked Seth his son to fetch oil from the Tree of Knowledge, but Paradise had vanished.

I fell into hourless Orcus, and the leaden fog on the rigging of my soul was frozen hard. I saw that the Barren Grounds is not the coldest region on the earth: it is the human heart. I stuffed my ribs and naked moaned: "My name, my name, thou hast been besmirched, every rogue has bayed thee. Be quiet, poor flensed waif, and sit in the dusty dry corner of thy self." I shrouded myself in seven syllables of silence, in seven leaves of years, within seven Ephesian graves.

Would I ever find a northwest passage to the Moluccas? That could not be. I've always been a helpless ninny, an inexplicable ludicrous one. Imagine I sought affection from people I never needed; they were senseless and droll enough to suppose I required them. That was the only hoax I was ever able to impose upon these average unfeeling noddles. Naturally I gather together a few persons now and then to decoy me. A man has to provide himself with a covey of Judases; that's what is called life.

Then I wrote books, a useless occupation, and I would have done something else had I thought of it. Seneca advises his readers that a man must do something though it be to no purpose. Besides, I got into a squabble with myself about truth and justice. Am I really serious about this? How should I know? All I can say is though I am no astute worldly Pontius Pilate I ask what is truth since no one lives by it. " 'And there is some good in the world,' replied Candide. 'Maybe so,' said Martin, 'but it has escaped my knowledge.' "

No matter how often I studied Homer I could not be sane about the vain and imbecile pursuit of wisdom. The Sirens endeavor to tempt Odysseus to approach the perfidious rocks by offering him what no mortal can attain, knowledge.

Then I fell into another predicament: what mite of consciousness could ever be mine? The more I am on guard against my emptiness and fatuity the more obtuse I am. How can one be vigilant twenty-four hours of the day? Not even the disciples could remain awake long enough for the vigil. I am sure they were automatic. Did they walk to Capernaum? I doubt it; they thought they did. They never lived; nobody has. No, I am not quibbling: I do not believe I exist. Suppose I'm wrong, it won't be momentous anyway. The universe is a slumbering animal that has visions. "I think the world's asleep," says Lear.

Descartes was sure of his paltry dictum: "I think, therefore I am." But I think and am not. I grant either way there is no evidence. Our short pilgrimage is obviously one of renunciations. At first we trust what we are sure we see, but this is a seminal delusion. Then little by little, as our rude and coarse physical forces dwindle, we become extremely suspicious, and begin to assume the earth's a ruse and that we have been taken in all the while. What are these things since everyone perceives them differently? I came to feel that space is a void and time the flux and ebb of a dying dream.

When people die we very soon forget how they looked. Did they ever exist is our unrelieved groan. It never occurred to me that I would regard trees, the ground, a shingle, the sea as God's baubles. Heraclitus states: "All things we see when awake are death." One can go on and on.

Meanwhile I have accumulated a pile of wrinkles which are basely attributed to time by toad-spotted heads. Once in a while I regard a new crease around my mouth as a frightful defeat and my downfall. I have another fear which contradicts whatever I have said. Although I have confessed I don't care a tittle for my intelligence, what will happen if my faculties begin to flag? Lucretius revealed that "when Democritus was warned by his ripe old age that the memory-bringing motions of his mind were languishing, he spontaneously offered his head to death."

What has the Worm taught me? I believe that Shakespeare's hundred and fifty-four sonnets were a hundred and fifty-four Gethsemane nights. Is that all? Is there nothing else? I pity the squalid drabs of the bribed Muses and pickthank feelings who've never been ripened by shame, mire, the ditch of humiliation. Not one author has sung the song of the dying swan, what Socrates referred to as the thinker's last senilia. They linger on, their wings shriveled, dissipated echoes of their youthful dotages. "Many a one, alas, waxeth too old for his truths," said Nietzsche. Would that I weren't a writer; since I am, I'd like to produce one page that is a replica of the handkerchief of St. Veronica upon which was impressed the divine and tragic features of Jesus.

I have another pelting vexation. Suppose there is a Creator, or a Demiurge who framed day and night, will it make any difference? Won't I arise in the morning petulant because there is rime on the windowsill, a cramp in the small part of my back, acid mildew in my lungs, or my head is clogged with fenny yesterdays? And if there is no God, will it not be the same? I'll die anyway.

Would I had a dram of calm. Will the grave provide it? Is death total cessation, or may it not be a wailing and gnashing of the grieving bones? There might be a grain of truth in this, for the body is no liar. Let me taste the constellations when I go my way unhindered to the great Worm, enjoy one infinite second of quiet.

Since there's no solution I stalk the stage in buskins though I speak in my comic socks, and I dismiss the immense self-delusion, life, and bid farewell to the world with: "Sir, money is a whore."

This is not all. Another small matter frets me: why am I obscure to myself? Could I understand my experience, I would annihilate myself. However, as nature will do it for me, I sha'n't bother. It just occurred to me: Is God acquainted with Himself? All He can utter is: I am that I am. Is that a great revelation? Shakespeare, a better poet than God, is as vague; he merely mimicks the Lord and says: I am that I am.

That cutpurse I venerate, François Villon, palmed off this mournful stave: "I know the doublet by its collar; I know the monk by his habit; I know the master by his servant; I know the nun by her veil; I know the sharper by his jargon; I know fools fed on creams; I know wine by its barrel; I know all, except myself."

What else? I'm as lost as I was. Nobody has ever found himself. What I am searching for is a man with an unbearable void within him. I am seeking myself.

I confess I do not know my own bounds. Be done, ye caitiff cowards who announce your limits. I need stellar aetiologies.

No secular person, I am the small gleanings of many devout sages. This book has been hanging over my head like the rock of Tantalus. I have battered mountains, torn up seas as elephants in rage break grass by the roots, for a metaphor.

This is a song of no-knowledge, a chant of shame. What else can a memoir be but an enchiridion of chagrins? If I have not divulged all, it is that life is illicit. St. Paul saw in a vision things "unlawful to utter." I walk upon my hurts which readers entitle my books. Sunset writes for me, and rain scribbles my woes. Forgive me, dear unknown readers, for I cannot pardon myself nor life.

Before it's all over with me I am going out into the world to swear at the most depraved and cunning of all harlots, Reason. Ye who demand evidence are the culprits, for I am the proof. When I am clean out of reason I am out of guile. Have you not learned that a logician will cut your heart into a thousand gammons and languorously champ it? Does this make me a weeping trunk of dust? Only a rationalist would so affront me.

In one respect I am resigned to be the staunch companion of Alone. A writer is a banished man. Euripides died in Macedonia; Thucydides wrote his history of the war between the Athenians and the Peloponnesians near the forest Scapte; Herodotus migrated to Thurii. While the "fishes are quivering on the horizon, and all the Wain lies over Taurus," I sacrifice reverently to the shade of holy outcast Spinoza.

In bringing this trembling exile book to a close, I pray it is the clay that smells of the flesh from which Prometheus moulded man. My own darkness, my wilderness, and the black Cain leaves crying in my breast are Odysseus' apostrophe to his own nature: "Endure, my soul, endure."

New York, Dublin, Barcelona, Tel Aviv, Geneva, New York, 1966–1970

from "The tunnel": Why windows are important to me

WILLIAM H. GASS

From this window I can see our garden's stubbled face beneath the snow, and beyond that, through a leafless hedge, the frozen lowness of the meadow where my children sometimes skate; then at quite a distance, like a gray haze, trees. We live a long way from the river. There are miles of cornfield between us and the Wabash, which is hard as a piece of slate this time of year, its muddy banks congealed and stony, the peeled trunks of the sycamores gleaming like licked bones. Around them, weed-stalks, stiff and brittle, un-cared for as a corpse's beard, collect in thickets now so cold as often to be birdless. I never go there. I've two eyes, and walk; yet it's always a window which lets me see. Windows, therefore, are important to me. My university has granted me a large one, high up and at the corner of the campus where winter's stilled the swings in the public park and the grass in summertime is sandy. These are the porches of appearance. Through them move the only uncoded messages which I receive. We've no sinking land to raise up moun-tains here, no silhouettes of giant hills. The horizon's clear except for that occasional gray frieze, and soon a crowd of starlings will waddle over the crusted snow after last year's seeds. A bookish man, I make a count of bodies. Symbols lie in state around me, or they wait a wedding, christening, Second Coming—I don't know. I wish I had a vase for flowers, or on the sill outside a temperature gauge. The pond smokes sometimes in the morning. Perhaps the roses *will* freeze. Where I am there's Goethe, Dante, wisdom in brutality, blood in the peaceful page.

How many books are worth a window? This half-closed eye I have here, or my wide one at the office, they let in whatever chooses them, and not at any shout of mine will they behave. Their scenes move on as surely as the thread-line of my watch. For picture after picture they provide the frame, proscenium to stage, and everything is altered in them into art . . . or into history . . . which seems, in circumstances of my kind, the same.

¿Qué hicisteis vosotros gidistas,
intelectualistas, rilkistas . . . ?

So I'm here, am I? That's what *she* thinks: that I am here, washing my hands in this light, preparing for bed but not for her, because, as I've said, she's too fat and I love another. Nothing in this little room is mine—this study where I lead my life, in Mad Meg's chair, which I had shipped from Germany. He nearly died in it, my teacher, teaching still. Covered, they carried him off on a tray to the hospital . . . like those sterile instruments whose appetite is operation. He grew even thinner there, even paler; shook so much they took his teeth. My son, he said, my son . . . but I was no one's son; spores in the air begot me; I was cultured in this country—a common, inexplicable disease. Instead of Mad Meg now I've Herschel, Culp, and Planmantee for colleagues. Herschel is a sad man, tired; he has a tired gray moustache; he slumps in his suit, its shoulders powdered with gray ash from his barely burning head. The folds of his face droop, his smile is tentative and thin; he apologizes for his every thought: I'm sorry, he begins. Pardon me, he says. Excuse . . . I could lay my head on Herschel. Sleep. Ohio sleeps on the Ohio. Sleep the sleep light sleeps within a window. Herschel. Humble man and comfort pillow. Whose heels hurt Herschel as they tread him down, so full of feathers, fickle as a sneezing nose? He'll smooth one dent to take another, receive each head that's lowered onto him as graciously as whores at spreadleg swallow any vintage and never, unkindly, send back the bad bottle.

187

I hide in Herschel as he hides in me. Cocked, I look through Herschel where his hairs cross. Pow!

When I woke, my face in the keys again, a wheelchair padded with red plastic sat in front of the building, its chrome intensely flashing as a ship might, signaling at sea. There were dents in my lip and cheeks, and crease sleep made across my forehead, but below me I could see a lemon yellow sweater trimmed in green, gray hair like a cloth cap, and a coarse gray lap robe at whose knotty bottom edge two scraps of green slack showed, while store-new yellow canvas shoes dangled from each trouser-end. From my perspective they seemed spilled: hair, robe, sweater, canvas shoes, as though discarded by a rider who had taken up his legs, perhaps, and walked, his hands remaining on the robe like mislaid gloves. I didn't remember them. Or the glint of glasses. It's a woman. Her hair coasts slowly crabwise and a pale hand flutters up to rest the head. Earlier on this same cool sunny Sunday afternoon two girls in frosted hair like hers had wandered by the building, impishly waving when I looked down, both with light cosmetic faces, both wearing large soft buttocks in their trousers—the best thing about them—from which their straight and skinny trunks pushed up like impoverished trees, as if, despite anatomy, they were victims of overcrowding. The minutes pass, both hers and mine. She is so patient. O my mute invalid and chastened body . . . lady . . .

C'est avec nous que tout vivra

And now her hands will rise to ennecklace her neck, though her gaze is still spilling from her face to fill her lap. I play my type-writer for her. Out the open window I send her her description. Is there any singing in her as I finger the keys which dented me, or does she only hear the groaning of her body? I play a romantic ballad:

**This is my love, a cripple abandoned;
roll her beside me on big wheels of chrome.
Fishing for souls, you can see what I've landed:
2 boots and a tire,
3 jews still on fire,
my cock in the crack of this crone.**

Here come children. We are surrounded.

Lou's love-nest for that other summer had a single second-story window. We could see the middle trunk and branches of the spruces close at hand, together like a clump of temples, a whole band of them, far away from Indiana . . . across the ocean maybe . . . I imagine—in Japan. The light passing through became magical. Though first a pale green which frequent rains had, where it entered, leached to yellow, it deepened in a net of twigs and secondary branches, growing heavier until it seemed to sink like sap along the gray and furrowed trunks, leaving lines like tidal water lipped around the dry old scars of the spruce, dark as arm-holes, wounds from many amputated sleeves. Now and then, still affixed or borne up by the living, a dead bough bloomed defiantly, its needles the color of thick rust; and through the interstices of all these—needles, twigs, and limbs—a pale blue sky would lie in burning patches like a distant lake—peaceful and lovely beyond endurance—while chickadees rode the gentle fanning branches with all the calm and arrogance of gulls.

Look there, Herschel . . . how she is so patient. The sun is harmless, falling softly everywhere, though in the distance clouds are coming on like floes. Her head is up, unsteady on its stem, perhaps to watch the children running. Minutes pass, and there she sits, as I sit, in this cool day, among this beauty, rubber-wheeled as I am castered, listening possibly to my machine as it performs a piece of her life, and also, of course, a piece of mine. We'd make fine mates—a perfect pair. The muscles in my back are tight from tension, the tension of long sitting and hard work, of life in a swivel. What was she doing beneath my window in her red-armed chair? old cripple left outside to melt in a shumble of clothing, those canvas shoes kept stout with a shoe-tree—and a wooden one, clearly. How did this happen? Who brought her here? Did her life last no longer than opened soda, thus to silently vanish in a magician's thin air? But now a young man in shades and sport shirt appears. Without a word the woman releases the brake—she has a puffy lined soft mushroom-pale face like my mother—and without a word he trundles her bumpily into the grass. Go, I say—go! for who wants a love like this crippled gray-capped drooping patient lady, held in stainless steel like a brace, and now going tippity-bippity over the lawn, even if she is lately warm from the sun and new clothing, even if her chair is red-armed, wheeled and gleaming?

With the window open a wasp has flown in, and out of old habit I quickly put a match to his abdomen.

Thus this day passes as all the others: a few small thoughts, some meager visions, a half-a-dozen actions, each equally insignificant, the normal number of observations, none of them striking, the usual cigarettes and meals and useless erections, a few hours of work at the office, a few hours at home, one class, one student with a stupid question (but Professor Kohler, do you believe that Bismarck was . . . Bismarck *was,* young man, that's what you must remember), four chapters of a brash new book on the Weimar Republic which I'm to review (I've that wise bird by the balls, which is at least something), one trivial conversation—no, by god, *three*—about what, I've already forgotten, uncounted cups of tepid coffee, a glimpse in the hall of dark hair like Lou's —almost growing—which made my farmer's heart turn over, Planmantee at a distance (but seen plainly in my mind's eye, teeth fleeing from his mouth), a little painful urination, Culp with verses written on his tongue unrolling like a bandarole, a feeling or two spread over the day like a small pat of butter—in short, the banal contents of a banal life; and then I take up my pen and fill more paper with these stiff Germanic figures of mine in order to say that this day has passed as others have, although darkness has fallen and I've neglected to turn on a light.

Maybe . . . Perhaps . . . Just possibly . . . Herschel: you're my muse. And here is Culp, the motor man, who's always zizzing. Maybe . . . Herschel sends his claims of ignorance ahead, a scouting party; he's ready in an instant to withdraw. I'm not up on this, he says. I sometimes think . . . Have a heart, Herschel, and tow away your rhyming friend. But he begins: I sometimes think . . . How he dares to think at all I've never understood; still Herschel has a deferential charm, and when excited he will pinch his neck, as if to slow himself down—from what high speed I've yet to calculate. Nevertheless he's definite about one thing: the meek will never inherit the earth. He repeats this often, often out of any context which would lend it sense, and never in any which would remove it from cliché; he states it quietly, but with a conviction unusual for him, as if it were the single shamanism in his life he's learned—his lonely truth—and I can believe it—for he is one of them, the meek, and he'll inherit nothing. He lives his gray life out of common view, uncared for, quite alone. He is a nebbish—Herschel: one one kicks.

On tiptoe, Culp, his arms outspread, jubilantly comes to a decision:

> **If I could choose another life,**
> **I'd be a dog or American wife . . .**

Where is my disintegrator ray, my camps, my ovens? Black doubts seize Culp suddenly:

> **or maybe in that other dawn,**
> **I'd rather be a suburb lawn.**
> **It's hard to say which would be better:**
> **manicured girl, or grass, or setter.**

RE ONCE WAS THERE ONCE WAS THERE ONCE WAS THERE ONCE WAS THERE ONCE WAS THE
)UNG MAN FROM NILES, A YOUNG MAN FROM ERIE, A YOUNG MAN FROM CANTON, A YOUNG

Culp, head bowed, hands humbly clasped, confesses with noticeable contrition:

> **I once went to bed with a nun**
> **who didn't know how it was done.**
> **She thought that my handle**
> **was an offering candle,**
> **and lit me before I could run.**

It's a noyade I've planned for you, Culp, as in the Reign of Terror.

> **I once went to bed with a nun**
> **who put her hair up in a bun;**
> **not on her head—no—**
> **she shaved that all off so**
> **dee dum dee dee dum dee dee dum.**

A five dollar bill for any last line that beats mine, Culp crows.

N FROM AKRON A YOUNG MAN FROM YOUNGSTOWN A YOUNG MAN FROM WARREN A YOUNG MAN
WHO'LL BE THE JUDGE?   I, SAID THE

I worked through sunset into silence.
Chapter on ideology. Funny cartoons from Der Stürmer.
Fascinating remarks by Mr. Rosenberg. Free silver. The spread
of the pox. Shirer's curious reading of Mein Kampf. *Racism as*
a Hebrew notion. Political motives of the Emancipation
Proclamation. Fascinating remarks by Mr. Rosenberg.
Chamberlain, Nordau, and Gobineau. The Red revolt in the armies.
Hitler's philosophical genius. Mutterrecht. *Cézanne's little*
sensation. Fascinating remarks by Mr. Rosenberg. The birch in
English education. Lou Andreas Salomé's not sleeping with
Andreas. The à trois *trip to Russia. Fascinating remarks by Mr.*
Rosenberg. Lenin at Yasnaya Polyana where Rilke meets Tolstoy
and Prussian militarism is overstated. Fascinating remarks by

Mr. Rosenberg. Fantasia of the Unconscious. *Wilson's women.*
Degas and Céline. Spengler as a secret optimist. Hesse again
anticipates the Führer. *Fascinating remarks by Mr. Rosenberg.*
Hygiene. The shock of circumcision. Rosa's monument. Harding's
weakness. The Dawes Plan. Jung's defection. Fascinating
remarks by Mr. Rosenberg. Fichte, Schelling, and Heidegger.
Kristallnacht. *Lou Salomé's not sleeping with Nietzsche. Not*
sleeping with Freud either. Fascinating remarks by Mr.
Rosenberg. Chesterton's degeneracy. Schopenhauer on silence.
Riots at the first performance of The Wasteland. Wozzeck.
Fascinating account by Mr. Rosenberg. The Chevalier Raoul.
Rousseau. Several shades of shirt. Kant's clock. The covert
fascism of the Webbs. Irish marching songs. Giovanni Gentile
and Social Credit. Cunnilingus. *The Vienna Circle. Fagin.*
Fascinating remarks by Mr. Rosenberg. Roosevelt not the God
of the Jews as sometimes alleged. Fellatio. *Hugo's huge ego.*
Archbishop Laud. The Wreck of the Deutschland. *Patriotism of*
De Sade. Last chance to unify Europe lost. Lincoln as leader.
Zola's murder. The French overrun Paris. Culp the metermaid.
Herschel as history. Fascinating remarks by Mr. Rosenberg.

Culp, forefinger up, has an important announcement to make
concerning his limerickal history of the human race, that is to
say, the triumphant completion of Chapter MDCCCLXIV: The
Geneva Convention.

> **The heads of all the great powers,**
> **after talking for hours and hours,**
> **were finally able,**
> **their guns on the table,**
> **to reach an agreement**
> **on prisoner treatment,**
> **and the cost of small funeral flowers.**

How quiet. The lights have left the buildings—as I should leave
—and the corridors will echo with me. Rug-smothered stairs are
also silent. I open my door and listen in the hallway. Brick, glass,
plaster . . . the tunnel's unbreathing. I hold my own to hear its
heart thud. When large sounds are gone the small ones swell up.
Like those undernourished girls, so sweetly bunned. My blotter
is also a cushion. Fanless air and cunts are quiet. Through pipes
someplace a vein of water must be moving. On the window . . .
nada—thickly brushed. Like coffee steaming from its cup, light
streams from the punctured ceiling while I hang on for dear life,
riding a spider who's suspended down-side up. I've closed the case

on my typewriter; there are no children noisily dreaming; my wife floats wildly in her anger somewhere like a slowly exploding pillow. The fog's hush is mostly propaganda, but drapes do muffle. There's soft wool and pewter, blood flooding my penis, swans swimming on eraser rubber, ashes and velvet. Stuffed chairs are quieter than skinny ones, and books dampen sound like the ground in a drizzle. My head expands and I hear my own voices, for when large cocks are absent, the small ones will cack-a-daddle.

Some years ago in a similar silence, though in another office of this building, I unscrewed with a dime a metal plate fastened low on the wall (it was like opening a tomb through the plaque of its monument), and entered a passage filled with cobweb and pipe.

> . . . she auctioned her quim
> one day on a whim . . .

On edge I inched along. I was in one of the maintenance tunnels. Tales are told of them on every campus now: of students who lived in the tunnels all winter, for example, frying eggs on steam tubes and boiling coffee, or how an enterprising fraternity man stole final exams from the mimeo room and thus, by the end of his senior year, had founded his future fortune, or how a group of solicitous girls, where a passage widened nicely like a thigh, established a profitable brothel (boys eagerly entering while propped on wrapped pipes, or on conduits crammed with impulsive wires and other things electrical). In one house I lived in as a child (and I lived in many), there was a long narrow arm of closet off my rooms which bent around a central chimney. Unless you pushed your way through my kiddie clothing, hanging like beaded strings to ward off flies, you couldn't know that it went out of sight like an elbow. There on the arm where the fist would be I often hid, as I also sometimes did in the lollipop maples that lined our street—made chunky by the telephone company which was always topping them. I lived in the limbs more like a coiled snake than a bird; I was a boa constrictor or a Bengal tiger; and I showed my evil teeth, or I wickedly leered, as people passed unwittingly under me. I may have been physically confined in that closet, and certainly the maples didn't permit much movement if you wanted to remain hidden by the leaves, but I was totally free in the realm of spirit. I was, as I should say now, a true self-by-itself, and so a self-inside-itself like Kant's unknowable noumenal knower, when I crouched in the backside of my parents' bedroom ingle; yet I was every bit an untrammeled and fountainous will too—a pure gust of forthcoming, as Rilke might have written—a perception, a presence, a force. To enter yourself so completely that you're like a peeled-off glove; to become to the world invisible, entirely out of touch, no longer defined by the eyes of others, unanswering to anyone; to go away with such utterness behind a curtain or beneath a tented table, in the unfamiliar angles of an attic or the menace of a basement; to be swallowed by a chest or hamper as the whale-god swallowed Jonah, and then to find yourself alive, and even well, in the belly of your own being—in a barn loft, under a porch, anywhere out of the mob's middle distance like a Stuart Little, a Tom Thumb, or a Tinker Bell—unnoticed and therefore all the more noticing beneath the thick hooping skirts of a bush or the beard of a fir tree; to go so supremely away like this was to re-enter through another atmosphere, and to experience, perhaps for the first time, a wholly unpressured seeing; it was bliss; and I remember the killdeer running across a wet meadow, his own strident cries of joy and exultation taking him aloft as easily as the wind lifts the seeds of the maples, though even more wildly, so steep are the slopes of his rising; and if this is what the Marquis had in mind when he spent himself; if he thought this the god in his overworkéd phallus, he was on the right track though he took the wrong train, for he did want his partners to sink into the sleep of objects, their cries of pain and pleasure to take place, like bullets kissing in their ricochets (any agitation of things: the hum of wires, or the whine of machinery), as if neither the prick nor the aim of its pricking were in any human presence. For me it was not quite the same. When I played Satan in the tree, or rode the New York subway later, I was not an animal in anybody's little cage of vision, but they were surely caught in mine. Your mother, the doctor wondered, does she tend to play the passive role in your parents' marriage? Ah, *ja* . . . yes *und* never . . . *nein* . . . Is she the rolled and folded, strangled, beaten dough? No no . . . Yes. No. Oh how often could I have killed him for it! I'd have gladly put on a *Jugend* shirt and shorts in order to denounce him. Yet Dante could not have punished him with better justice than he has been. Calcified.

Any roofed-over hole could give the same confort, and my friends and I dug some, covering them with cardboard, and once we buried a refrigerator box, cleverly placing its entrance in a thicket. How stupid adults were, we thought; they'd never guess that if we wished and if they continued to hound us, we could go to ground like the fox, hide out in a moment. I made elaborate bed tents too, stretching blankets from the headboard which I pressed against the wall to hold them. Under that canopy I would lie hidden for hours, my penis like a baby chick I tenderly warmed with my hand. The love I lavished on myself then, later only Lou received, or ever gave . . . the nubbled wool, the eventually exasperated nerves . . . the sky-blue blanket like a sky-blue sky . . . the wholly imaginary breeze . . . unwetting rain. Such shelters from the world really widen the vision: how much we took in, yet how far we also went with our inventions. St. Anthony saw monsters, shapely women, too. It was in one of those early hideaways (they were trenches, castles, dugouts, outposts, graves) that I accomplished my second seduction. My first was a cousin, tall as a column, whom I ravished from a distance. She loved to finger the lobes of my ears while my swollen eyes entered her. The second was a neighbor, round as a hug. Both grew up and haired themselves over, I imagine, but then it was only their twots which were naked, smiles without lips like the Mona Lisa's; yet bringing that girl underground as I did, and stretching her out for exploration— O my newfound mistress, neighbor, Culp and Herschel, my vast middle of the West!—was a violation of that sacred space, and earned the vengeful anger of its gods. The reality of dreams was what you were intended to perceive there, not the dreamy unreality of underclothes, or between pale skinny thighs that little pouty container. And the silly thing kept saying: why do you do that? why do you want to touch me there? Well, why do I want to wade in mountain water? rub my penis on the cartilage of Lou's ear? Desire is epidemic, though we are given shots when young to ward it off, and at a later age wear charms like chips of holy bones around our necks against it. So your father was the active partner then? What, you ass, that pusillanimous bastard, that bantam rooster and twice-a-life cripple in his wheel-side highchair? yes, he was active, ran the dash, and thrashed his legs the whole length of the long jump, except that he landed in pain, not in sand or sawdust, moistened clay, or the soft marsh of my mother, and his bones blew up. When my unsmiling mother—my sweet mummum —then young and heart-faced in a way I never knew her—hauled me like a wagon from my schooling and sat me in a corner of the kitchen the remainder of the morning where, while she quietly ironed, I silently dunced, it never occurred to me to think we hadn't hidden our hole well; and though I knew she believed I'd been bad with my neighbor, it never occurred to me, either, that our investigations, as completely removed from the world as we were when we undertook them, weren't entirely secret. No, I knew my mother— soft guiltless being. I knew she didn't know a thing. And the charge against me was no more honest than the one which poisoned Socrates: I had taken off the sweater I'd been told to wrap the wind with. Her rayon pants had made a red crease like a thin red worm across her belly. Therefore I had sinned. So I built buildings full of hidden hallways with my blocks—secret stairs and unreachable rooms. Played spy. With pencil and paper drew mazes of brightly tangled hair you couldn't find your way through. And reread the designs in our rugs as maps of unscalable mountains or impenetrable forests, sheer cliffs and fast rapids, lands gone without anyone's caring from all human view: swamps infested with moccasins, deserts where the wind blew solid sheets of sand in your eyes and lead soldiers wandered in circles till they tipped over on their backs and died, oceans in perpetual states of storm, whirlpools and murderous shoals, ice floes which crumpled ships like paper in an angry fist, quicksand and volcanoes, canyons, treacherous arroyos, waterfalls which disappeared in their own mists, and endless stretches of emptiness and cold—snowfields cut with crevices abruptly opening under you and closing slowly as you fell like some huge child's indifferent mouth upon a piece of sucking candy. There were islands which sank or exploded, seas which grew so calm a rock could not have rippled them—out of sight of land, marooning you in birdless water; there were bewildering fogs and circular winds, tidal waves, areas where landslides were endemic, where blizzards were continuous and earthquakes habitual: hills bursting, lengths of earth slipping like crocodiles into the ocean, lakes spilled, their basins broken, entire regions split like logs or covered with lava like syrup on a sundae, while everywhere droughts, fires, floods, and famines were as frequent and inescapable as drawing breath. I've lived in the landscape of that carpet ever since, beset but protected, swept by silent gales and mute contractions, guided by designs which others see as merely decorative and meaningless. I also hid things under stones, behind pipes and baseboards, in rafters, lofts, on cornices, in jars and jugs, beneath bark, in every cranny I could find—so often and so well that like a squirrel I sometimes lost them—pennies, matches, candy, gum, documents in codes I had constructed or messages in milk or lemon juice and later semen (the chief ingredient in a formula I never found effective), and then eventually two blurry photographs which showed a pair of hairless nude Chinese, in postures both unnecessary and impossible, engaged in acts for which I had no name. I also carefully nested boxes (never quite so well as my aunt would learn to), told an endless string of inconsequential lies, and publicly maintained a whole set of beliefs I privately put no stock in, among them: Santa Claus and Shirley Temple, the fun of birthday parties, scouting, ferris wheels, and baseball, the uncertainty of future happiness, all honesty, the therapy of work, what a pleasure it was to give or how nice it would be to have a sister, the peacefulness of Sundays, roller skating, the perils of chewing gum, the prize in Cracker Jack, anything at all three miles from me, each of those rules my father described as summing up common sense or Herbert Hoover, and every one of the so-called laws of God, Man, Nature, and the State. The older I got the oftener I disappeared down trapdoors which looked deceptively like squares of sidewalk or seemed to be post boxes or had the modest, servile air of back steps—never through anything so obvious as a manhole—and once I'd gone "in," I might travel to a cupboard in a blink, appear behind a sofa or a chair, a closet or a locker, from whence, with mousy caution, I'd emerge to live a little where the clock ticks; to dwell "out there," as I contemptuously referred to it, and condescend to be in common view and touch again, the world's awareness eroding me like rain; but as an ordinary mortal, with a merely mortal presence, mortal powers, not a soul suspected I was dangerous, so it was one more sort of smooth disguise. Then in another house (for we moved, and moved, and moved), I was able to drop from my bedroom window, always with the softness of a pillow, to the roof of the back porch—it had an easy slope—and I would make my way from there, when the garage door was open, across its thin, wobbly, wooden edge—an intrepid, a beautiful, balancer—to the garage roof next, with its far more radical pitch. Here I took a tree, and then, quite easily, another—a moving miracle of a man, a drifting wraith (I was never a boy—*I was never!*)—moving, drifting, as I consider it now, perhaps fifty or sixty dangerous, dizzy feet across our lot and maybe a bit beyond it, where I swung down from a limb and touched my toes to a garbage lid. Playing hide and seek, I could disappear in a twinkling, and whenever I tired of the game I would float through the trees and pass over buildings to my window. Below me, *out there,* for many minutes sometimes, the befooled would continue calling and pursuing. Yet no one guessed my divinity. No one knew me. Even though my family often moved, I felt secure, although they drifted. There'd always be forgotten places, wide-eyed windows which imprisoned their perceptions; everywhere some cubbyhole or spy-tree grew unwitnessed. In any neighborhood there'd surely be paths of concealment crisscrossing it, and those virginal countries with their small bald vaginas too, where I could go as sudden as surprise into retirement —into my secret company, my private childhood, and my conspiracies. You can lose yourself in a book (as I was more and more frequently to do—it was a disaster), but this was a gain, not a loss; I did not trade myself for any other; and I understood at once why Alice went after the rabbit or melted in her mirror; the tunnel was more attractive than the rabbit was. That's why windows are important to me, and I suppose why I continued to crawl behind my office wall like a worm in the building until I found myself caught in the passage, unable to back or turn, and frightened of going on. Now I know how it feels to be lodged in a throat. Whether I really hid behind my hangered clothing, in a hole felt the funny folds of girlies, or as pure spirit passed through walls, or sank like dust into the carpet and became its implacable climate and ferocious geography, scarcely mattered: I went away every time with the same result: that powerful out of the world feeling; and like the killdeer, less than weightless, propelled by outcry, by the sheer force of my freedom, would see my soul expelled from its body, and with a following sigh, my pistoned penis spit its seed. Beneath me, in the sullen darkness, rows of wheelchairs like parked cars attend this show of silence. The maimed march in robust lines through the stadium, handfuls of gravel strike the drums; the mad, the sane, the sober and the drunk, cry out. Flags snap and flutter in the general shout as the yellow polished brasses bellow. My study smokes. My office door is shut. Rockets for the Fourth fly up. Perhaps the frost will draw roses. It is warm in the tunnel, and not as dusty as you might think, remote as an intestine in its fatty coat, safe from the haze of human shuffle. My father was the active partner—yes . . . my mother melting jello, pudding pulp. He ended up in chains, his royalty around his wrists and ankles, while she, long past Ophelia's pearly beauty, drowned herself in drink . . . was twenty years in dying, the life-span of the poplar. Look at the precision of the rows, the helmets growing like a formal garden. O the multitudes were massed, flagged, and belted bands brought from every corner of the Reich, each throat a trumpet. What a sight! And their yells sailed up with a dry whistle and then blew to starry pieces all July, all August, all repose. Look! Look at the precision of the rows! My life as turbulent as grocery string, I wrap these bundles. A sleeve had caught me, and a button. I tore both crawling out. I could not hold the dime still when I screwed the entrance back, and the plate kept slipping out of alinement. How quiet. How soundlessly the light beats on my books. See how it leaps from metal to metal like a percussionist. My father grew his bones together. They swelled like tubers at the joints. My mother merely . . . wept and shook crossing Canada one day when we'd run out of liquor. Hard are the hardships of the traveler in a foreign country. Down on you, you merely giggled, then asked me coldly how you tasted. Why should another's body be so beautiful its absence is as painful as the presence of your own? I bit my thumb enough it bled. You taste like the Third Reich, I said, blood-salt on my lips, and you were offended. You were offended, yet I would never love my wife again. A cunt that's so indifferent to the tongue cannot be trusted. Look at the lines: foot, boot, bootlace, trouser and rifle, arranged like music over Europe, the Reich and its leader, dancing their limerickal dance.

> They discovered in one of the camps
> how to make Jews into lamps;
> but whenever they lit them,
> the dirty kikes bit them . . .

Mad Meg stirs his pots. I fight shy of women, leave the companionship of the front line to other men. How quiet. Quiet. One can feel the lawns lying in darkness like the pelt on a beast; there's the scent of red pencils, the hum of distant energies, ranks of closed doors at attention. Did I hear the scream then, then the groan— one or the other?

> so, their jaws held with wires,
> with a fine pair of pliers,
> they extracted their teeth in advance.

When I was a kid I used to be returned to Grand sometimes to spend the summer. The attic was full of Henty and Horatio Alger books. At the bottom of the back stair hung my grandfather's pistol in a polished holster, looking so lethal I used to tiptoe past it. My grandfather was chief of the Volunteer Fire Department, and therefore merited a pistol—to shoot looters, I suppose—though I never saw him wear it. Then just above a pair of boots, huge enough, it seemed to me, to hide in, a sort of loose slicker dangled too—the emptied skin of a nigger. Once in a while the fire bell would ring in the ears of the church, and grandfather would appear clothed like a god, a great bright-bladed ax across his shoulders. Every child in town would run pell-mell after the firemen who were easy to catch and even pass because they were usually pulling a two-wheeled cart whose axle-drum had hoses coiled like jungle snakes around it, or a pumper worked by hand like a see-saw which was used to suck up dousing water from close wells. I particularly recall a fire which occurred in a small shoe repair store one misty morning. The bells rang, we kids flung ourselves like stones into the street, the firemen ran like horses, and the small store smoked like a pile of damp leaves. I was disappointed not to see flames, and I can remember watching, both bewildered and amazed, while my grandfather chopped holes in the roof, other men smashed the doors and windows, and still others wet everything and everyone, their hoses pissing languidly in realistic starts and stops, until the whole shop sagged and finally folded in upon itself as though it had been made of slotted cardboard. Of the actual fire, I never saw a lick. It was too elusive and escaped their Homeric whacks. Morning fires never seemed real after that . . . an Indian signal sent up in a fog. These amateurs, these volunteers didn't comprehend combustion, I thought. I felt someone should explain to them that flames weren't like the limbs of trees to be lopped off from their origins with an ax, however sharp the blade or strenuously swung, but of course I was far too shy; I was awed by the mysteries of the grown-up world at that age, and kept my peace. So after an hour or two of heavy labor, when a pile of shattered boards half smothered in smoke lay charring weakly along the sidewalk, my grandfather announced the fire's official finish, and then we all stood around a while wishing for something really incendiary—for more than smoke to mix in the mist—before letting go our hopes and going home. I knew the owner slightly. Czech, he was the only Jew in town. The creek, though, was as slow and glassy as Grand itself was, and only when you put your hand in, or if you tossed a leaf upon the water, could you tell it was moving. Sometimes dust would shade it, and then the surface seemed a kind of skin, covered with tiny webs and puckers, passing along like an unrolling roll of soiled wallpaper. Not even an occasional waterbug could change your feeling that the bottom was imprisoned. The grocery store smelled of pickles, cheese, and open crackers; the creamery only of cream and churning butter and blue milk, though there were rows of gray-white eggs on which you should have sniffed the sea; the butcher shop of blood and sausage spices, the bakery of yeast and warm bread and wax paper, the blacksmith shop of horses, leather, shade, and metal-sizzled water. I should have expected, from that burned-out store, the reek of thongs and rubber, a smoke black as polish, the acetylene hiss of volatile oils; but it was all low and gray-headed—the smoke— carrying, as far as I could tell, only the odor of pissed-on paper. Later I rescued a thin-headed hammer with blackened handle from the ruins, and I used it the remainder of that summer to set off giant caps, aiming blows which left red paper sticking to the sidewalk as though each bang had bled.

Bill, he begins. (What a Billywilliam I've become to Herschel; what a fall from William Frederick Kohler, Herr Professor, Man of Note.) I hope you will, he says, in that big new book of yours . . . Herschel smiles like a thirty-watt bulb; he has no book, not even a little one; he has a wee MA from a weer school; the pity of others has tenured him, and he holds on by relaxing every grip, assistant professor forever, teaching courses of the lowest number, shallow surveys of Western Civ—history as photo'd from the moon. The world is full of Herschels: little sparse-haired gray-eyed men who never make the news, even as a mole-cule in a mob. They pass through history like water through a comb. Literally, nothing is known of them. Bill, he begins. In your long one, Bill, I hope you will consider giving . . . How right he is, from Mad Meg's point of view, for it is the historian who gives—who takes and gives—while history itself just suffers and receives. As all my memories. Bill, he begins. Bill, I'm sure it'll be—ah—great as it is large (yes, he's smiling shyly, holding me by my name, as Tabor did, lest I get away). Could you consider giving . . . giving the big men more weight—I mean more attention, you know—than you did in your first. I felt . . . (Herschel feels! It's indecent—undressing in my presence.) I felt you were a trifle inclined then, though I may be wrong—yes, I probably am—but didn't you stress the common man a bit more than perhaps he . . . His voice goes out like a blown match. Poor Herschel—*pauvre, pòvero, pobre* . . . Even in my books he hopes he and his friends will remain unremarked and unremembered, that no one will rec-ognize or record them, and it brings him to the fearful edge of criticism. He's a can of Dr. Scholl's . . . *dieser armer Mann.* I shall sprinkle him out. Little? small? common?—like Culp, the zizzler? So he ends. Piff-poof. Herschel ends, ends Herschel.

> **A sensitive Nazi at Auschwitz**
> **was annoyed by rabbinical outfits.**
> **These habits retard**
> **the processing of lard,**
> **which is the reason for being of Auschwitz.**

In the park a grove of oaks and beeches with a bandstand; in the parlor a piano with a lidded bench containing sheets of music (*Cathleen, Song of India,* others); in the living room long foaming sofas and a minuscule TV. I think I see black shapes on that glass ground. I give the screw a final twist and the dime flips from my hand, skips away, rolls away, ringing like my nerves. My wife will think a student's torn my shirt in her passion. They all have a passion for fat these days and want a man with a girlish bosom, nipples they can gnaw on, a belly they can pound and knead—was your mother the passive partner in your parents' marriage?—and the fat man's small cock hidden out of sight in his thighs like the lady from Ghent who revealed when she bent; oh, they want a weight to ride on, haw and gee, god damn them, and you too, Lou, you bitch, you bawd, you dehomered Helen, you soft stuffed toy (who rules more sternly than the teddy bear?), ahead of me in every feeling, wiser, dark and fair as a forest on a sunlit evening (what is all this shit about leaves and light?), innocent as a hankie, honest as Christmas wrapping, female faggot, fanny fucker, whore, nag, bore, bawd, bitch, Lou, you too, love—you! and in the park a simple ceremony of maples, a single elm in the center like a fountain, and the lady-fingers snapping rapidly—acciaccatura— against the whootling of my father's cornet in Findley's Kilty Band, as later, in Ohio, he bugled for the Legion. I cannot breathe. It is too quiet. Then the scream, the groan—which was it? I listened as I listened in the tunnel. No mistaking . . . a groan, a scream, a moan below me somewhere down the empty steps lit by their own laziness for safety, the rails precipitous, walls slick, paths of crushed rock trailing through the trees, a speech by the mayor about America, polite applause amid the cannon crackers, and the young girls with their asses on casters, boy-bottomed, bodies I was mostly indifferent to, and unringing red bells in the ice cream, bells the flavor of strawberry, the size on slot-machines, I carefully spooned around, I liberated, freeing them forever from vanilla, and young girls with cherry bombs between the tines of their thighs, and in their fists small flags fluttering down the steps to the floor below me, the building a riddle of worm halls, and the young girls with their crisp dresses dragging, and packs of dogs we scattered with grenades, girls flaunting their naked clothing—how silent the skin is, the flesh is, growing—popcorn, banners, parades be- low me, someone is groaning, is unmistakably pained, and I listen to the oratory, I strain toward the sound, and send tin cans from the muzzle of my mortar, tilt the halls toward heaven like a battery of barrels: pow! pow! pow! remember the glow and the smell of punk? the satisfying fizzle of the fuse? the stunned air after? there is no question but those noises changed its color, shook it so it rained. My grandfather met the trains. The station smelled of creosote and timbers, and the rails were radiant all summer. On the bed of his truck he hauled away huge crates made of fragrant soft cream-colored fuzzy wood as nude as you were as you calmly lay across the spread awaiting me and yet were moist and ready when I reached you; so I've seen some paintings of a beauty so supreme they drew the fingers to the pigments, not to touch their surface, but to sink inside them, and had Christ walked *within* the water I'd believe, nor is there any better symbol for the single longing of my life than the penetration which your body begged and I supplied that single summer, and afterward remember how I trembled . . . trembled . . . for I knew . . . I knew I could go on no longer, could not continue, could not . . . could not like a pond its water hold these feelings as the light was held by the pines in our window, their arms around the aether—for me, for Newton—proof . . . proof there was another medium through which at any time, if we were physical enough to be a spirit, we could feel, could enter, Lou-like, free as a strawberry bell from vanilla forever. And on that night of breaking glass in Germany, when the windows of the Jews were being smashed; when I was caught up in the excitement, infected by the frenzy too, by the joyous running through the streets, until my arm was lifted and I hurled a brick myself; I thought of the flash of my grandfather's ax, shattering the shingles of that poor Czech's roof, although my brick sailed through a jagged hole and fell somewhere in the store without a sound—in fact with so much silence that, despite the hubbub in the neighborhood, I heard no groaning, heard no screams from any of my other selves as, after the girls with their heavenly haunches had stirred me, or that woman on wheels had, after all that labor on my work had worn me out, I heard them just below me in the building. I sat on the edge of the bed . . . yes, trembling, you remember. My belly sagged pathetically, and the rag rug rested my stupid feet. *I* remember. And I've thin arms despite my weight. How could I believe in happiness? How could I, who loved you physically, believe in your love? Those perfect hands enclosing my imperfect penis, those slender fingers, pale tapered nails; they had to be the tools of a professional, a bawd; those moist eyes and parted lips were lies. Lou, weren't you supposed to be a bed-tent, too? where I could hide as I hide in Herschel? How could I believe that if I squeezed it evenly our new-laid love, like the egg, would demonstrate its strength? with thighs which widened when I sat like soft tires? No. It was simply too good to *be,* as the old saw says. Happiness has no friend in time, in history; it has no friend in me. Some prisoners cannot bear release, Lou; they've lived too long in climates of concrete; they know that happiness is just a priest who reads us words of consolation while we walk up the steps to the hangman. Yet we'd be suicides without that low intoning, without the sunlight raining in the forest; we'd swing in our cells without silly things like flowers, sentimental hand clasps, helpless babies, the bodies which charm us. We are used to these, we demand them, as we expect foolery from a clown or deception from a magician. Would the condemned man know he was going if they came with whips? if they left behind, in the office of the executioner, the grave faces of the witnesses, the pleasantries of prayers, the dark dress, the black book, beads? and so the Jews, who knew they were destined for death—death could scarcely have surprised them—could not believe in their own murders when managed in this manner, for such ceremony as they had come to count on was removed; it was so open, more matter-of-fact than even brutal, so fearless, honest, unemotional—so *sincere*—like spraying for mosquitoes; it so clearly transcended all excuse, it did away with reasons. On that splendid disdain for subterfuge, they flew—the Nazis; (O hear me, Herschel!) they rose as gods from the graves of their middle-class lives; anointed, they left their little businesses behind, the normal world with all its petty laws, for sainthood. These laws, these rules, these lies which lips at least for centuries had served—they did not need them; they were so self-contained, so internally secure, they were above even the ancient hypocrisies of heaven; and they lived in the realm of the spirit, of *der Heilige Geist,* as they'd been taught by their religions and philosophies; what were bodies? meat and bones to be disposed of: new grinders and new ovens, new gases and mass graves (as large as lakes, as long as rivers), a raw material calling for a new technology, new plants and processes, a fresh imagination, fresh inventions; what were bodies compared to principles, and what were principles compared to destiny, the Reich's will, and history's aim? More theoretical, therefore, than most men, they did not dream, they saw, *foresaw;* they left the dreaming to the Jews, who did—they dreamed—like drummers marching at a cannon. The one-thousand-year Reich was a State to be constructed, just like happiness, out of time, like the millennium of the Marxist. No angels from on high or demons from below with fiery swords or flaming forks came to balk them. Nature punishes gluttony, not avarice or hate. To Nature it's most important that you get a good night's sleep. No. Only further murders—theirs—prevented them from murdering further, as we flew bombers to Japan and powdered them to peace . . . god willing. I am sloppy, pudgy, like someone who has stuffed himself with sweets—a child, preserved in ice, the years blue-streaked and gleaming coldly. Thus when I heard the groans below me (screams, groans, which?), I quickly left my office and the building, fluttered like a moth down the stairwell, so slippery with light, and drove out of their hearing in my Chevvy.

THERE ONCE WAS THERE ONCE WAS THERE ONCE WAS THERE ONCE WAS THERE ONCE WAS A YOUNG MAN FROM CRESTLINE A YOUNG MAN FROM CLEVELAND A YOUNG MAN FROM BRY

When I hear the bursting of the rockets, my hearing makes no noise; when I see the sky, my seeing's silent; consciousness, just like the dead, is also quiet. So quiet. Am I any less indifferent and a coward if the voice I failed—the moan I ran from—was a phantom . . . was my own? My brick passed through that window like a ghost. I never heard it land. I was simply never fated to break glass. That's why, Lou, I couldn't continue us. And that's why windows are important to me.

J. KEARNS. (*TQ* #19)

The wheel

The wheel is not only the most beautiful discovery of mankind
    but the only one as well
there is the sun which turns
there is the earth which turns
there is your face which rolls back and forth around the axis
    of your neck when you weep
so how about you minutes of all time won't you coil yourself
    around this take-up reel of life
like lapped-up blood
the art of suffering sharpened like the stumps of trees against
    the knives of winter
the deer drunken with thirst
which balances me on the sudden unexpected edge of your face
    like a storm-struck schooner
your face
like an entire village asleep at the bottom of a lake
but which is reborn again during the days of rising grass and
    the season for flowering

translated by Michael Benedikt

FRANZ MON. *ABSTRAKTION* (1963). (*TQ* #20)

A tale from *Lailonia*

LESZEK KOLAKOWSKI

The humps

When Ajio, the stonemason who worked for the highway department, suddenly contracted an illness in his back, four doctors held
a consultation. One should not suppose that in Lailonia any time a
stonemason has a backache four doctors are immediately in attendance. Most of the time there is not even one. This time there
were four of them; not because Ajio was sick, and most certainly
not because he was a stonemason. It was simply because Ajio's
illness was very strange and doctors are eager to examine unusual
sicknesses, not unlike ordinary people. The strangeness of the
illness did not depend on the hump, since a hump is not strange
at all, but quite common. It depended on the fact that it
was not an ordinary hump, but an eccentric hump, a peculiar
hump, a hump-which-only-happens-once-every-one-hundred-and-
eight-years-in-the-kingdom-of-Lailonia-(if-it-happens-that-often).

The hump, as it grew wider and larger, began to assume all
sorts of extraordinary shapes. As time went by these shapes began
to resemble parts of the human body—arms, legs, a head, neck,
stomach, and a behind. (We shall mention here that the hump was
classified as a cryptogenic hump; that is, that its peculiar property
was that no doctor could explain its appearance.)

The doctors gathered for a consultation to determine whether or not they could cure Ajio of his hump. They met in a special office reserved for consultations, where Ajio, of course, could not be admitted. The oldest doctor spoke first:

"Gentlemen, let's admit honestly and without delay that medicine is helpless in this case. A hundred and eight years ago, our colleague, Surgeon Braindigent, described a similar case, which he was unable to cure. And since this kind of thing could not be cured 108 years ago, we most certainly won't be able to cure it today. A century ago, as we all know, people were scientifically more advanced than we are today."

"But what are we to do, then?" a young doctor asked. "We must do something or else they will call us a bunch of fools."

"How can you ask?" the old doctor seemed very surprised. "We must treat the sick man!"

"But you just said that there could be no cure . . ."

"To treat a sick man, dear friend, has nothing whatever to do with finding a cure," the old doctor said gently. "This is the basic principle of our profession. The job of a doctor is to give treatment, just as the aim of a singer is to sing, the job of a player is to play."

"I suggest that we might be able to partially cure the patient," said the third doctor. "We might not be able to eliminate the hump, but we might be able to prevent its further growth. To achieve this we should encase it in plaster of Paris. This will prevent the hump from enlarging. And as for people being more advanced scientifically a hundred years ago—that is a still unproven theory."

"I find this highly unethical," the fourth doctor shouted. "Since we cannot cure the hump, we most certainly should not treat it."

"But why?"

"That should be self-evident! Because we cannot cure it!"

"Completely, no, but partially, yes."

"We shall fail no matter how we look at it. The hump will still remain, and therefore we should have no illusions about its cure."

The doctors debated this point for a long time. Meanwhile the hump grew and grew with an increasing rapidity. The various parts which branched out from it became more recognizable. The hump's head began to sprout hair, eyes appeared, a nose, ears, and a mouth. The arms lengthened and the legs almost touched the ground. As if overnight the hump became a complete human figure. This figure was actually another Ajio, his spitting image. He was connected to the first Ajio by his back, but besides that, he looked exactly like him. And from the start he talked.

The first Ajio, the real one, from the very beginning was most concerned about his illness. But when he saw that his back had given birth to his identical twin, Ajio was terrified and didn't know what he should do.

Ajio was an honest and a solid citizen, a conscientious worker. He was liked and respected by everyone. Now, since he had grown a double, people could not tell the first Ajio from the one who had evolved from the hump. What was worse, though the twins were so identical Ajio's own wife could not tell them apart—they were identical as far as physical appearance was concerned—the character and the personality of the second Ajio were totally different from the character and personality of the first Ajio. His very first words were not spoken but shouted; he was irritable about everything, and hateful toward everyone, especially toward the first Ajio. Moreover, he refused to work, offended everyone, and continually complained that the first Ajio forbade him to walk. This was true only in so far as, being connected by the back, each faced in the opposite direction. When one walked ahead, the other had to back up, which was tremendously uncomfortable.

But worst of all was the fact that the second Ajio, after he had grown to such an extraordinary duplication of the first, began to announce that he was the real Ajio, and the other was merely a hump that had never been a human being.

"Cut off that damned hump!" he would shout angrily to the doctors or to anyone who would listen. "Why should I have to bear on my back this horrid growth? What ignorant people those doctors are! They know nothing at all about surgery."

Friends who saw Ajio were very surprised at the change in his personality.

"Is it really you, Ajio?" they would ask the hump and the hump would shout as loudly as he could:

"Of course, it's me! Who else should I be? Have you gone blind? Can't you see it's me, Ajio, whom you've known for years? That thing behind me is the hump I grew. Oh, what misery!"

To make doubly sure the friends would ask the first, the real, Ajio:

"And you, who are you?"

"I'm Ajio," the other would answer, but quietly, since he was a timid and a modest man.

When the other Ajio would hear this he would burst out laughing unpleasantly and shout: "Look at it! The hump wants to be a man! Isn't that a laugh! I've never heard anything more ridiculous in my entire life. That shameless hump wants to convince people that he is not a hump! And what else are you, you leather bag? This is fantastic, a hump claiming to be Ajio! I can't bear it any longer! Cut off that horrid hump or I shall die of indignation. Shut up, you scabby growth! Dear friends, don't listen to that horror."

And each time Ajio would timidly claim he was the real one, the hump would burst out with such vehement denials and such swearing that finally the people, the doctors, his friends, and even Ajio's wife stopped being surprised and came to believe that the man who shouted was the real Ajio.

Meanwhile the real Ajio, more and more desperate and intimidated, more and more uncertain of himself, spoke ever more softly and infrequently and when he did speak stammered so foolishly that people didn't even want to listen to him. Of course, all the while the new Ajio was even more insolent, even louder, even more argumentative than before.

"Oh, but Ajio has changed," the friends would say sadly. "It's hard to recognize him. He used to be so kind, so gentle. We all liked him, now no one can stand him."

"What do you expect?" replied the others. "He got a hump. Misfortunes make people change."

Then the conversation would turn to other people who were visited by misfortune, made bitter by sickness or bad luck, and they would forget about Ajio.

However, all through this time, the doctors continued to work on a treatment. They worked hard, day and night; they researched and they diagnosed, and finally, after many months, they invented a medicine for the hump. This was a powder, to be taken internally, three times a day after meals. They hoped that the powder would shrink the hump into oblivion within a few days.

The taste of the powder was bitter, but that could hardly matter if it were successful in curing the hump. The doctors experimented on several humpbacks, with ordinary humps, and found the results highly satisfactory. People lost their humps and praised the new medicine.

Finally the doctors were ready to administer their new medical discovery to Ajio. When they arrived at his house, Ajio, not the real one but the hump, began, as always, to scream his loud complaints about how it was impossible for him to go on and demanded that they cure him on the spot. The doctors calmed him by telling him that indeed that was what they had come for, that they had invented a most excellent treatment for his hump. The first Ajio, the real one, began to cry softly, whispering that he was the man, and the other merely his sickness. No one paid him much attention since the second Ajio silenced him by loud name-calling. Ajio's small son was the only one who cried loudly, trying to tell the doctors that the gentle one was his father and the loud one was a stranger. The grownups ignored him, since small children have not judgment enough to know better than adults.

The doctors, after a short consultation, administered the powder to the second Ajio, to the hump. The second Ajio eagerly swallowed it. As soon as he tasted its bitterness he began to revile the doctors for their stupidity in not inventing a sweet-tasting medicine, or possibly one with an artificial orange flavor.

And what happened was to be expected. Once the second Ajio started to take the powder, the first, the real Ajio began to shrink quite rapidly until he became just an ordinary hump on the second Ajio's back.

Since the powder was still effective, the ordinary hump, the real Ajio, soon started to shrink, until the second Ajio, the one who once was but a hump, stood up straight and happy, with nothing at all on his back. There was not a trace of the first Ajio to be found anywhere.

The doctors and all of Ajio's friends, even his wife, were convinced that the one who had disappeared must really have been the hump. Only Ajio's little son cried bitterly and accused them all of having taken his daddy away from him. The new Ajio promptly hit him with a leather strap and shouted at him to stop his blubbering.

Afterwards Ajio became a famous man, for how many such men were there? People did not like him, for he was mean and destructive, but they feared him. And for the same reasons.

But Ajio was not satisfied with his victory. He began to behave very strangely. Whenever he met an acquaintance he would ask suddenly:

"When are you going to get rid of your hump? After all, the doctors did invent a most excellent cure. There is no reason at all for you to carry that thing around. Why don't you see your doctor?"

"But I haven't got a hump," the man would protest.

Ajio would burst out laughing.

"*You* don't have a hump!?" he would shout. "It might seem to you you don't! Everyone has a hump. Can't you see that? Everyone does! With one exception. I'm the exception. Only I am without a hump. I used to have one, but I don't now. But the others! They've all got horrible humps and it's only their stupidity that prevents them from being cured."

And Ajio would tell everyone in town the same thing. Soon a terrible fear spread among the people. They would look at themselves in their mirrors to make sure that they did not see a growth on their backs. Even when they did not see anything they continued worrying and would look again and again. Soon no one knew for certain whether he was hump-backed or not. The fear was general. People now avoided each other, sneaking around corners, walking silently along the walls of the houses, and continually passing store windows to see their own reflections and make sure that they had not suddenly sprouted a hump. Only Ajio walked around straight, proud and unafraid, like a peacock, repeating over and over, without a pause:

"You're all hump-backed! Every one of you has a most horrible hump. How can it be that you can't see it? Have you also gone blind?"

After a while Ajio changed his tactics. He began to tell people that it didn't matter that they had humps. What did matter was that they had become humps. Their humps, having for some time now been their twins, and not having been cured, had simply devoured the human beings and taken over. Now, with him as the single exception, the entire world was inhabited by humps and not real human beings.

"You're a hump," he would hiss at every passing person. "Do you understand? You're a hump and not a human being. You pretend to be a man but you can't fool me. You've devoured the real man and you're nothing but a hump. I alone am a human being."

He shouted so much, he hissed so much, he repeated it so often, he was so persuasive, he grew so angry, and he announced so convincingly that he was the only survivor of the human race that finally people believed him. They were convinced that they were humps and that they should, without further delay, do something about returning to their original, humpless, human selves. They were now also terribly ashamed of themselves and sorry for having done such injury.

At last the majority decided that since Ajio had been so successful in getting rid of his hump, they should try the powder themselves and maybe something would happen. They began to buy the miraculous medicine and swallowed eagerly even more than was prescribed as a sufficient dose. Even those among the townspeople who once had been humpbacks and been cured took to the powder.

But since not one of these people had a hump to start with it was quite impossible for them to get rid of something that wasn't there. Instead, shortly after they took the powder, they all noticed, with great unease, that something quite opposite in effect was happening to them. Everyone began to grow a hump. The humps widened and lengthened, and as once in Ajio's case, they sprouted limbs and soon looked identical to the people who carried them on their backs.

It was evident that the same powder which was so effective in shrinking the humps into oblivion now induced the growth on humpless people. When people noticed this effect, it was too late. Everyone already possessed a twin attached to his back. And immediately, as in Ajio's case, the humps began to shout that they were real people, and the others merely their humps.

Ajio was radiant. He had a multitude of friends, just like him, although still attached to the backs of the people. All of the humps were exactly the same as Ajio in character. They all argued, shamelessly and loudly, that they wanted to rid themselves of their horrid growths—that is, the real people, whom they declared were humps.

Among themselves the humps were friendly, and when meeting each other on the streets they would make merciless fun of people, whom they now carried on their backs as if they were humps.

Finally all the humps declared that they had had enough, that they would no longer tolerate being hump-backed and began to swallow the miraculous powder.

That is the reason why in the kingdom of Lailonia there is a town of humps where there is not a single humpback. No one has recorded any further the history of that particular town. As far as anyone knows, it still exists. It is only known that Ajio's small son, in spite of threats, refused to be fed the powder. He escaped from the town, promising to return and take care of the humps, and as he was leaving, the story goes, he broke into tears.

translated by Maia Rodman

Men fought
JORGE LUIS BORGES

This is the story of how Northside and Southside put their bravery to the test in matters of the knife. I speak of a time when the straggling outskirts of the city, with their rose-hued walls, were also lit up by the flash of steel; of when challenging *milongas* hoisted the names of certain neighborhoods on a knife point; of when these little countries were a cult. I speak of 1896 or '97, and time is a hard road along which to backtrack.

Nobody used the word "outskirts" in those days. The zone of poverty that was not downtown was the *"orillas,"* the city's outer edges—a term more derogatory than topographically precise. From this outer edge, then, from the edge of the Southside, came El Chileno. Well known around the Stockyards as a knife fighter, a master of arrogance and of intricate tango steps, a bully who'd make his way into a saloon or into a row behind a torrent of foul-mouthed insults aimed at no one in particular and everyone in general—he was, in short, the pride of his fellows at the slaughterhouse. Having heard that in Palermo there was a real man, someone called—after his renown—El Mentao, he decided to look him up and fight him. Rowdies from the precinct known as the "Solid Twelfth" went with him.

He came from the other end of the damp night. Crossing the railroad tracks in Centro América, he found himself in a land of unlit streets. He kept to the sidewalk. An abject moon roamed an empty lot; decent houses were asleep for the night. He walked for blocks and blocks. Chained barking rushed out to keep him back from gardens. He turned north. Occasional unseen whistles made the rounds of darkened walls. On he went, treading brick and mud, skirting the sad-walled Penitentiary. A hundred cocky-walking steps more and he reached a street corner alive with toughs, its saloon lit up as if the entrance were ablaze. It was the corner of Cabello and Coronel Diaz—a low wall, a willow with its Argentine despondency, in the back alley the wind holding sway.

He walked in straight to the bar, coming face to face with the Northside gang, only holding back his insults. He was not out for them. He was out for Pedro—El Mentao—a big, burly man, who sat eyeing the three closely-held cards of his *truco* hand.

With the shyness of a stranger and plenty of "sirring" left and right, El Chileno asked for someone half yellow or yellow all over who played at being brave—God knows with whom!—and whose nickname was El Mentao. The man holding the cards stood up, quick to say, "If you want, we might go look for him out in the street." The two swaggered out, knowing all eyes were on them.

The pack of hardened toughs saw them fight. (There was a dangerous politeness between the men of Palermo and the men of the Southside—a silence in which insults lurked.) The stars went their eternal course, and a poor tired moon tugged at the sky. Below, the **knives** sought paths to death. A lunge, and El Chileno's face was slashed by a chopping blow; another blow sent death into his chest. On the dirt of the alley, soft as the sky, his blood ran out.

He died unpitied. "Good for nothing but gathering flies," said someone at the end, picking him clean. He died gratuitously, and guitars all along the Palermo riverfront were exultant.

Such was the meeting of a knife from the North and a knife from the South. God knows what justifies it; when the Judgment resounds from the trumpets, we shall hear.

translated by Norman Thomas di Giovanni
in collaboration with the author (1927)

Meredith Dawe
JOYCE CAROL OATES

(*from a novel in progress*)

MEREDITH DAWE
Number: 0187425   Michigan State Prison

August 17, 1972

Your Honor:

It has taken me many weeks to draft this document, owing to physical
infirmities and a general depression of the spirit. But I have come to
realize that only a direct and forthright appeal, based upon sound legal
principles, will make any impression upon you and the world you
represent. Am I correct? I am also sending carbon copies of this letter
and its accompanying memoranda to a trusted friend on the outside,
for safekeeping. I realize now that such caution is necessary in order
to prevent men like yourself from misusing their authority.

Judge Couteau, I am speaking for the record not only of the State of
Michigan but of the Supreme Court of the United States, which I
am confident will eventually hear my appeal, and find in my favor, and
also of the entire world. I am speaking for the record of your conscience, as a private, humane individual, and I hope you will give
me your fullest attention.

I will outline to you the series of actions I am going to take:

My first petition is a plea for the bench to re-examine every detail
of the transcript of my trial. This must be done immediately, and by
an objective, just man, who is not connected in any way with the
Court of the State of Michigan. I request that Your Honor assign a
non-partisan observer for this purpose. This observer will surely come

to the conclusion that the Assistant Prosecuting Attorney made many statements and accusations about me that were allowed to pass and to be heard by the jury, without the right for him to do so, in that his hatred of me surpassed all legal evidence and was a constant source of bewilderment and chagrin to me. Not only this, again and again the transcript notes objections made by my counsel, Mr. John Morrissey, of Detroit, Michigan, which Your Honor chose to ignore. An impartial observer must come to the conclusion that I did not receive a fair trial before you and that the entire conviction must therefore be reversed.

My second act is to give notice to you that I am filing suit against you personally, in your position as a judge, and against the Police Commissioner of the City of Detroit, for a nonpartisan referee to enforce the above-mentioned petition.

My third act is to give notice to you by this communication that I am filing suit against you in the Federal Court in Detroit for a sum no less than $1 million, in that my constitutional rights and my civil rights have been grossly violated by your action in handing down to me, Meredith Dawe, a sentence of 8 to 10 years in the penal system of the State of Michigan. This sentence, delivered by Your Honor, Judge Carl Couteau, sitting in Recorder's Court in the City of Detroit, on Monday 5 June 1972, does restrict my freedom of speech, my freedom to move to and from any fixed point, and curtails in general the civil rights guaranteed to all citizens of the United States under our Constitution. In addition, I want to inform you that this sentence constitutes cruel and unusual punishment, since I am at present a prisoner not only in prison but in a hospital ward, and my spirit is seriously depressed by the misery all around me and by my own occasional infirmity. I note in myself flashes of fear, concerning my immediate future (I am undergoing another spinal operation shortly) and the future of my adulthood, as well as the future of this sorrowful, doomed nation.

In addition, I am preparing a lengthy writ of *habeas corpus* to the effect that I was not truly represented by counsel during my trial and during the many weeks preceding my trial. Though this will be difficult to prove, I am undertaking the task confidently, and I am only puzzled at present how to begin. I believe I will frame the writ in the shape of an autobiographical work. Your Honor will appreciate the fact (though this is not a threat against Your Honor) that such a writ, made public, will sway to my side vast segments of the American people, who will clamor for justice. At present, I am awaiting important documents concerning my family history, which are essential for any reader to comprehend the nucleus of my writ of *habeas corpus,* which, as I understand must be no more than two or three pages long, must be framed by an exhaustive introduction and as many appendices and indices as are necessary. The "Autobiography of Meredith Dawe" may perhaps be cast in the form of a novel, since no other form of communication (that is not tactile) can approach the terrifying density, the overwhelming weight, of a novel. My autobiography, properly studied, will illuminate not only a single act of savage misjustice (committed by a jury of 12 representative but tragically prejudiced citizens and compounded by Your Honor in his punitive zeal in excess of all charges) but an entire nation, a despoiled and vandalized Garden of North America, which begs us to purify it and restore it to its original innocence. How long must we await the resanctification of our gardens?

In support of this writ, and closely allied with my suit against Your Honor (for violating my rights as a citizen), I want to state for the record that Your Honor's refusal to allow me to dismiss my attorney and to act in my own defense, on the fourth day of my trial, was perhaps the most grievous single curtailment of my freedom. Considering this fact and also the fact that my attorney, Mr. John Morrissey of Detroit, Michigan, was in no way sympathetic with my basic beliefs and my personality, and approached the entire case simply as a professional challenge, any fair-minded person will see that I did not have an attorney at all. I really did not have an attorney to defend me. My own role in this confusion was a slowness to perceive what other people evidently recognized at once, and tried to communicate to me, that the attorney who was defending me was not defending "me" but an abstract principle. However competent Mr. Morrissey may be as an officer of the court, he did not comprehend my state of mind at the time of the alleged crime, the time of my arrest, at any time during the weeks leading up to and including my trial, and he did not then, in fact, represent *Meredith Dawe*. Thus, the basis for my writ, which will admittedly involve many weeks of preparation. (I will state here, purely for Your Honor's information, that I am also filing suit against my ex-attorney, for a sum of $500,000, for the above-mentioned reasons, and that I will include a carbon copy of this document for your perusal.)

I give notice to Your Honor, to the Court of Appeals, and to all relevant courts, that I, Meredith Dawe, insist most bitterly that in all further litigation I will act as my own counsel. I absolutely deny the right of the Court to appoint any counsel in Mr. Morrissey's place. I deny the right of anyone to speak for me and to interpret any actions or words of mine. As may be evident from this document, I have begun a study of the Law myself, using the books available in the library here. I am not going to be silenced.

In addition, Your Honor, I want to state for the record that I am bringing a civil suit against the police witness and informer Joseph Langley, in that he betrayed not only my spiritual bond with him (which I realize now cannot be proven in court) but any possibility of my exercising my constitutional and civil rights during the terms of my sentence. Your Honor was very wrong to listen so closely to him! He lied on the witness stand, as did the other prosecution witnesses, concerning the direction in which the marijuana cigarette was travelling (it travelled *from* Shirley Klein and *to* Mr. Langley, because he requested it, and not *from* Mr. Langley *to* Miss Klein) and also about whether the cigarette was burning or not. I maintain that it had *gone out* at the time I touched it and handed it to Mr. Langley. This renders it less dangerous and would impress any impartial observer as an important piece of evidence. . . . I am going to attach to this document several pages of analysis of the harmless effects of marijuana as a drug, reported by a federal committee, in the hope that Your Honor, not moved by such evidence at the trial, will re-examine it now quietly, away from the anger and confusion of the courtroom. This information, supplemented by many more research findings, will make up one of the indices of my writ of *habeas corpus*. But I can't hope to have that document ready for many months.

In addition, I hereby give notice that I am bringing civil suits against the People of the State of Michigan and in particular Assistant District Attorney Eliot Tyburn, for violating my privacy and my right to speak freely without fear of harassment, and for the public showing of certain films of my lectures, during the trial, to upset the jurors and make them hate me. All these will be listed in a separate memorandum. At the time of my trial I publicly stated (in defiance of my attorney, I admit) that I acknowledged all these words, thoughts, and intentions, and that I would gladly stand by them, but subsequent to the jury's verdict and Your Honor's harsh sentencing I wish to advise you that I deny not the words, thoughts, and intentions of those lectures in their original form, but I do deny (1) the right of the prosecution to show them in public and for their own advancement (I will investigate copyright law and see if a separate suit cannot be filed on this count, for I surely did not assign copyright in any formal way to the prosecution for their use of these original lectures) and (2) the right of the prosecution to edit them. I am at the present time preparing a petition in which I make clear how my First Amendment rights were violated by this illegal action of the prosecution. I am also preparing a separate petition in which I argue that the public showing of these films in which I expound my personal philosophy (viciously edited and re-arranged so as to seem insane) constitutes a violation of my right under the Constitution not to speak in incrimination of myself, which I believe goes back all the way to the 18th century, in English Common Law, and prevents the police from torturing us according to their wishes. There are many forms of torture, Your Honor.

Also, I might mention here, pursuant to the above, that I am contemplating a suit against my ex-attorney, Mr. Morrissey, in that he attempted to litigate the entire case for the defense on the issue of police entrapment, and that, failing to convince the jurors of Mr. Langley's obvious treachery and his violation of a law (why has no one arrested him? why may he touch a marijuana cigarette, lit or burnt-out, with such impunity?), failing to overcome the natural prejudice of the jurors *for* the police and *against* a defendant as innocent as myself (though everyone in the courtroom and in the entire world knew that entrapment obviously occurred), he nevertheless attempted (in private) to dissuade me from seizing upon my legal rights in testifying in my own defense, in order to explain to the Court the intricacies of my philosophy, so as to powerfully counteract the prosecution's claims and innuendos that I was, in fact and potentially, a public enemy (advocating the overthrow of all laws, etc.) whether or not I did, in fact, ever touch a marijuana cigarette (at which point I could not restrain myself from laughter!—which so angered Your Honor, who surely misunderstood), lit or unlit, travelling in any direction (right to left, or left to right) past me; and, having failed in this attempt to make a purely legal point supersede my own testimony, to deny my existence, as it were, Mr. Morrissey did then, when I was on the witness stand and at last able to speak directly to the world, by his very narrow questions and his strategy of interrupting me so frequently, attempt to curtail my freedom of speech, in order (as he said) that I should not offend the sensibilities of the jurors and the Court, and thereby cause prejudice against my case (which he saw as *his* case). Though he was correct about this, this does not lessen his moral guilt, and I am suing him as well under a separate claim for malpractice, since his questions and interruptions and attempts to restrain me might have indicated that he lacked proper faith in his own client, which you, as an experienced judge, might have noticed. Allied with this was Mr. Morrissey's technique of repeatedly interrupting the cross-examination, and even the interruption of certain of my replies, so as to give the impression that there were things in my personal life that the prosecution had no right to inquire about. This made everyone think I had something to hide. This obviously inspired prejudice and disgust not only in the jury, but in Your Honor. There was no moral reason why my attorney should have objected to my being questioned in open court and in any manner desired by the prosecution, since an innocent man may surely speak his heart.

An innocent man may surely speak his heart.

Your Honor, why do you hate me?
Why wish me so much evil? I lie here trying to get my mind clear from
the drugs and the stiffness and the awful memory of my trial and I
think of you, your hatred of me, kept so hidden. But why? Why?
When I first walked into your courtroom I believed what the plaque
said on the wall—JUSTICE IS THE GUARANTEE OF LIBERTY—and
I was prepared to love you and work for your conversion (as I am
dedicated to the conversion of men like yourself), but not violently
and not through hate. Never would I have consented to your
imprisonment . . . for any crime at all, anything at all, but especially
not for your private beliefs. And yet you must have hated me so
much that your hatred overcame your natural instinct toward justice.
Why is this? Until the very end, until your charge to the jury, my
attorney and I and many others truly believed that even though the
jury might be against me Your Honor was impartial, unbiased, and
sympathetic, and would rule on my innocence or guilt (for I suppose
I was "guilty" of a legal lapse, if not a conscious crime—and my
admission of this point should not have been used so repeatedly against
me by both the prosecution and Your Honor) of the crime I was
charged with in the indictment, and not on any personal philosophy
of mine or on my soul, though I am still confused about why anything
I say or do or my entire personality should be assumed to be "in
violation of all community standards of decency."

Why?

In conclusion, I submit also to Your Honor that the publicity surrounding the case all along (to which I inadvertently contributed,
believing always in the good-will of the various reporters and interview-
ers who approached me) made a fair trial impossible. If a suit can be
initiated for an after-the-fact crime, I would like to sue a local
newspaper for its editorial entitled "A Victory for Decency" and I
would like to bring an injunction against the press and the communications media to prevent any further such libels, in that an appeal,
if and when I am granted an appeal, will be influenced also negatively.
All this, I submit, represents a conspiracy to thwart my receiving
justice, on the part of people I have never met, and it is all in
tragic excess of any charges originally brought against me in the
indictment, which I hereby restate for Your Honor's information:

> The Grand Jury of the County of Wayne, Michigan, by this
> Indictment accuses Meredith Dawe of the crime of violation of
> Public Health Law with respect to Narcotic Drugs, a Felony,
> committed as follows:

The Defendant, on or about the 5th day of December, 1970, in the City of Detroit, County of Wayne and State of Michigan, unlawfully and in violation of Public Health Law, had in his possession and under his control one quarter of an ounce of a preparation, compound, mixture and substance containing cannabis.

Must I be destroyed because of ¼ ounces of marijuana . . . ?

Very sincerely yours,

Meredith Dawe

August 18, 1972

Your Honor:

In the event that you might misread and misinterpret my letter of August 17 (yesterday), written under much distress here in the prison hospital (my writ will go into the humiliating detail of what all the prisoners are suffering here, in addition to their illnesses) I am writing another communication which Your Honor is respectfully requested to file for the record.

My previous letter ended wih the question, *Must I be destroyed because of ¼ ounces of marijuana . . . ?* I request that this question be stricken from the record. I request most urgently that Your Honor not interpret that question to mean that I am accusing him of wanting to destroy (i.e., commit a crime) me or anyone. I have suffered many hours of anxiety since writing my letter of August 17, in which my emotions sometimes overcame my legal arguments, and I hope that Your Honor will not see fit to instigate any suit against me for slander or (in the event my letter is somehow published) libel.

Please understand that it was not my intention to accuse Your Honor of acting with the premeditated intention of committing any illegal act or with any premeditation at all . . . in the sense of being pre-judiced (prejudicial) . . . or . . . meditational in any illegal sense of the word.

Sincerely,

Meredith Dawe

August 21, 1972

Your Honor:

Since having written to you last week (August 17 and August 18, to be exact) I have waited for your response patiently. But, receiving no letter from you, and in the event that such a letter was in fact sent to me and was not received (for the record I will state that *no letter was received* even if Your Honor's letter was sent by way of ordinary mail and not as a registered letter (which I would suggest for the protection of all concerned)), I see fit to inform Your Honor that I am now preparing a brief which will petition for the appointment of an impartial observer (this petition will, of course, supersede the petition outlined in paragraph 4 of my letter of August 17 (paragraph beginning "My first petition . . .")), who is a non-native-born person of demonstrated intelligence, literacy, and human sympathy, but who is *not* conversant in any way with the English language. This observer will then function as referee, and his duty would be to carefully examine the lectures and public addresses and various interviews of mine, all the tapes, films, and transcripts used by the prosecution to argue its case against me (as an advocate of "anarchy through drugs"), this to be effected in two stages: (1) their original shape, (2) the edited, distorted, abbreviated shape used by the prosecution in order to poison the jurors' minds and bring about a verdict of Guilty. The foreign-born referee will then make a detailed report to Your Honor concerning the degree of editing, on a statistical basis entirely (since the referee would not know English, two very significant results would be achieved: (1) he could not be prejudiced against me, (2) the Court would be forced to assume the truly objective nature of his report).

I will be awaiting your response and I suggest that for the protection of all concerned this above-mentioned referee be appointed within one week of this notice sent to the Honorable Carl Couteau, Judge, District Court of Detroit, 21 August 1972.

Sincerely,

Meredith Dawe

August 29, 1972

Your Honor:

I have uncovered new evidence which requires automatic reversal of the verdict against me, since it refutes the basic wording of the indictment originally handed down. I am basing my accusation on a statute of 1927 which states that such indictments must be filed within a certain amount of time of the offense allegedly committed. I believe that it is not demonstrable by any known scientific method that certain deeds have or have not occurred, since all witnesses and all alleged violators of civil and criminal laws have evolved since the historical time at which the "crime" allegedly took place, and in no way can their testimony be accepted as scientific evidence. If Your Honor doubts the validity of these statements, I will remind him that my original training was in the sciences, especially physics, and that it is a matter of public record (or could very easily become a matter of public record, since my academic transcripts are on file at the following accredited universities: Harvard University (1962–1963); the University of Michigan (1963–1967); the University of Chicago (1967–1968); Stanford University (Fall, 1968–approximately February 1969) and that my training includes a wide variety of subjects in both the scientific and the humanistic fields, especially physics.)

I submit to Your Honor that my findings entirely refute the prosecution's arguments (further weakened by the prosecution's failure to present a single scientist as a witness against me), my own attorney's procedure of defense, the jurors' probable deliberations and consequently their verdict, Your Honor's sentencing, and, in point of fact (cancelling each of the above), the original indictment, which I am enclosing with this letter so that Your Honor can familiarize himself with it if he has forgotten certain key phrases.

Sincerely,

Meredith Dawe

(indictment enclosed)

September 8, 1972

Your Honor:

Your Honor will be pleased to be informed of my completion of the series of spinal operations performed by the following neurosurgeons: Dr. Monroe Baskin, Dr. Felix Quigley, and Dr. Raymond Doyle. If there is any conspiracy to render me impotent it will be medically evident upon examination by any physicians exclusive of the above, but note that I am not accusing said surgeons or the State of Michigan or (least of all) Your Honor of any conspiracy whatsoever.

The purpose of this communication (sent in a moral vacuum since I despair of its being answered) is also to inform Your Honor that, contrary perhaps to the tone of my earlier letters, I am considering the possibility of Your Honor's being innocent of any prejudicial hatred of me, which may inspire Your Honor to reply to some if not all of my letters. I am certain that a letter from a Detroit judge would be delivered to me here, quite immune from censorship (if Your Honor would indicate somehow that it is *not* to be opened by the prison authorities: he might simply write, in his own handwriting, such a request, signed with his initials, the envelope to be an official one with the return address clearly stating Your Honor's position and address) but, if such an act is actually committed, either party (correspondent or receiver) might then instigate suit against this invasion of privacy as well as a file for an injunction against its occurring again in the future so that, if this very document which I am now preparing, this very letter I am composing to you, is intercepted, and these very words are, in fact, studied by the prison censor, they might in themselves constitute prior warning (though I am somewhat shaky on the law concerning this point since the books available to me here stop at 1968).

The reason for my consideration of this alteration of blame (which did in fact never take the form of any accusation) is that, in the last several days, I have been hearing again the words of Assistant District Attorney Eliot Tyburn, sometimes as he sums up the case against me to the jury (in which he made cruel and unusual use of my own phrase, "lapse of legality," in order to poison the jurors' minds against me) but more often as he argued to Your Honor, at the sentencing of 5 June 1972. That I am not interfering with Mr. Tyburn's privacy or autonomy in any way may be underscored by the fact that *I would rather hear* the plea made by my attorney, Mr. Morrissey, on that very same day (but, unfortunately, I can remember only snatches of Mr. Morrissey's argument . . . which was as close to being a human, passionate, loving speech as Mr. Morrissey could perhaps make, being himself a most limited and unloving man, though perhaps not incapable of *being loved* and, as a consequence, himself *loving,* were he able to recreate his soul to that extent; I remember only the phrases ". . . pure, self-determined . . . make kind of mistakes others . . . cowardly . . . we are frightened and demand revenge . . . he . . . they . . . he is not . . . he is . . . I plead for a . . . young man of . . . not a criminal . . . I plead for a suspended sentence . . .") but as if it were somehow part of the invisible tortures planned for me by the State, Mr. Morrissey's argument to You is continually outshouted and overcome by Mr. Tyburn's argument though, in fact, as I recall, neither man raised his voice. Therefore, helpless as I have been during the past several days (unless time has lapsed longer than I know, and the date is actually not 8 Sept. 1972 but some other date, unimaginable to me) I have continually heard Mr. Tyburn's voice, but not willfully or intentionally, and, inadvertently hearing this voice (of a private individual *but* in his role as public prosecutor), I have come to the conclusion that this powerful, deathly, terrifying voice may have had the effect, on the morning of 5 June 1972, of influencing Your Honor unduly, in his sentencing of me; and that this re-consideration would seriously re-cast the entire event, absolving Your Honor entirely of blame. I know the words so well now that I may include them here without the slightest fear of misquotation (though this is *not* an official document, but simply a personal letter to you, between two parties who share a mutual concern over the tragedies of injustice sometimes committed by well-meaning people). Study this speech carefully, Your Honor, and see whether it does not attempt to influence the listener (You), and to sway him against any human act of mercy:

> I ask on behalf of the People of this County that the defendant Meredith Dawe's sentence be one of the maximum imprisonment under the Law of the State of Michigan . . . and in support of that request I would like to state, if it please the court, that the defendant has not, prior to the trial, during the period of the trial, and since the trial, suggested in public or in private that he has felt any remorse for his criminal act, that he does not totally countenance in others the wholesale repetitions of that act (and others contrary to the legal and moral code), and that, by his unique influence as a local public figure (whose talent for publicity may indeed transform him into a national public figure if he remains free) . . . he has in effect encouraged among young people the use of narcotics. He has shown no remorse at all. He has shown no remorse at all . . . no remorse at all . . . no remorse. . . .

Now, Your Honor, leaving aside for the moment the mind-shattering riddle of how I can show remorse if *I am innocent,* let us consider this: You, Judge Carl Couteau, had perhaps formed a certain sympathy with me, during the course of the trial, such sympathy being, of course, not demonstrated by any facial signs or, certainly, uttered words, directed toward either my attorney or myself, and, perhaps inclined to believe me innocent, accepted the jurors' verdict as a commonplace miscarriage of justice perpetrated by frightened and angry citizens to whom the notion of "love" must be obscene (especially as underscored and exaggerated by prosecution witnesses who lied, under oath, about observing me in various postures and behaviors offensive to community standards—though it is debatable, in my mind, as to whether a "community" exists at all, being the legal definition of a political entity, or rather *not* being, so far as I know, any legal definition of anything, but simply a poetic expression of an indefinable mood), but intended, quite autonomously, to rectify this verdict by a wise, humane, and very generous atonement (i.e., a suspended sentence); such intention then being savagely mutilated by Mr. Tyburn's words, and totally obliterated, due to the confusion of the moment and the fact (which Mr. Morrissey informed me of, and I have no reason to suspect that he would lie on this issue) that the most important words to be said to the Judge at the time of sentencing are *those of the Prosecution,* it seems to me likely that Judge Couteau, either overwhelmed by the prosecution's demands or for reasons of his/Your own not listening closely to Mr. Morrissey's plea, was influenced.

Therefore, I ask you, Your Honor, to re-examine your mind before the day of sentencing, to re-experience the vicious argument against me, and to inform me as soon as possible whether, in fact, this argument did sway you. I hope I will hear from you at your earliest convenience, since it is possible (indeed, probable) that the words of Mr. Tyburn are such a din in my head *because* they are meant to inform me of Your actual innocence. This would mean so much to me. . . .

They have said that the operations are concluded, and yet certain humiliating and very painful examinations continue (involving surgical needles at least 12″ in length which I would not look at, to lessen my terror, but which I feel I must see in order to note any possible prior staining, rusting, or evidence of filth) at all hours of the day and night, often when I am deep in meditation, so far from the externalities of my body that my body is defenseless. It is becoming clear that the original operations were not successful, and that more operations are being planned, though the Director denies this, no doubt in order to protect the surgeons responsible for these errors from charges of malpractice, such charges not contemplated *at present* because the information I would require concerning medical malpractice suits is mysteriously missing from the book it should be in (one-third of the book's pages have been torn out) and, yesterday, the book itself was not where I hid it, but vanished. If it turns out, as I think it might, that Your Honor did feel this prior sympathy to me, You might also be moved enough by my sufferings here to make a quick telephone call (it would probably have to be in person—I doubt that your secretary's voice would be sufficient) to forbid any further mutilation of my body, especially when I am not sufficiently conscious to defend it.

Thank you very much.

Sincerely,

Meredith Dawe

Morning—Unnumbered Day

Your Honor:

Is it possible that a well-intentioned action of Your own has resulted in an evil? I refer to the request made to you in a direct communication

sent some days ago (my records state 8 Sept. 1972 but it is possible
that one of the prison officials has altered the notation, imitating my
handwriting)—that you simply telephone the Director of the
hospital here and state your preference that I, Meredith Dawe, not be
subjected to any further medical actions (whether "for reasons of
health" or for reasons of torture (unstated)). Assuming that, at least,
you were moved and disturbed by my helplessness (I am confined
in a kind of circular bed, a device that must be rotated every two
hours in order to allow for (according to the torturers) maximum
circulation and utilization of nerves and the expenditure of muscles
that would otherwise atrophy and, most significantly, for distribution
of weight-pressure on the damaged vertebrae; as Your Honor might
well imagine, my condition has deteriorated seriously), and perhaps
influenced by petitions from citizens of Michigan, or, if such petitions
do not exist, the possibility of such petitions when the *Autobiography
of Meredith Dawe* is made public, and the well-intentioned voters
and taxpayers of the State realize what a miscarriage of justice
has been perpetrated in their name (I cringed every time Mr. Tyburn
uttered the words "The People of the State of Michigan" as if the
People, and not Mr. Tyburn himself (and the police) wanted my
destruction), such miscarriage made more pathetic by the senseless
and unprovoked beating I suffered prior to the trial and subsequent
to the issuing of the indictment, by a man whose name I will not
mention here, in the company of other like-minded individuals who,
acting murderously in order to defend, as they stated, the United
States against a "traitor" (choosing to isolate my pronouncements on
the War in Vietnam, as if I did not clearly state, in all my lectures,
that the present War is but one symptom of the total rottenness, decay,
despoilization, vandalization, and doom of the Empire represented
by the United States of America and that, of course, all young men
are morally bound to oppose it and to refuse induction) . . . assuming
this, that your crisis of conscience did result in a telephone call, it may
well have been resented by the medical staff here, especially the
Director (a long-faced, bony, slow-speaking man, obviously an
enemy of the Body though he imagines himself a skillful physician),
in that, and I speak cautiously here, and wish that I retained more
of my Latin so that I could switch into a language that Your Honor
might read that would be protected from the eyes of prison officials,
spies, and other tax-supported creatures of the State, one professional
man might be angered that another professional man would see fit to
interfere with his actions. In other words, may a man of the Law,
however legally sound his actions are, have the slightest influence
whatsoever over a man of Medicine? It occurred to me, Your Honor,
almost as soon as I mailed that perhaps fateful letter, that I had
made a blunder and that the very effectiveness of my arguments to

You (urging you to intercede here in my behalf) would work against me. . . . The scalpel of the surgeon is perhaps more deadly than the sword of Justice.

Your Honor, the next morning they started on me again.

Your Honor, there is a paradox operating here: if you feel pain, you are dehumanized. If they do not allow you to feel pain (by way of drugs—medically-sanctioned non-pleasure drugs), you are dehumanized because you are not in control of yourself. Doped-up, drowsy, slow-moving and slow-thinking, a spiritual and physical cripple . . . all this results from that beating, in which my entirely non-political lecture ("Light and Heavy Love") was interrupted by men somehow sworn to destroy me, but against whom I had no ill-wishes (refusing, as Your Honor must know, to press charges against them). If you telephoned the hospital and spoke to the Director, perhaps you antagonized him (secretly—he would not have hinted anything to you) and the result was, contrary to Your Honor's wishes, further neurological torture of me. I do not know.

Might I request that you undo the damage by another telephone call? Based upon the perhaps erroneous (but probably valid) assumption that you *did* call to forbid them their tortures, might you now call to say you have experienced a change of heart, and that further spinal examinations and even operations are permissible? This may have the anxiously-awaited effect of their reversing their procedure, and allowing me to return to my cell, my reading, and my preparation of the lengthy writ (now my main reason for existing). . . . Your Honor, my very soul is in your trust.

Sincerely,

Meredith Dawe

Morning—Unnumbered
Day

Your Honor:

I realize that You are not my father, since my father does physically exist (though he has not communicated with me since 1968, at which time he ordered me out of his home under threat of police violence) but, in my dreams, it has become clear that You are designated as my spiritual father. I am not your son and yet I am willing to be your son, if you will have me. Why must there be only formal relationships, based entirely upon biology tempered by Law (only "legitimate" heirs recognized)? What is the Law, that it renders us into totally separate beings?

When you asked me, staring down at me from your bench, if there was any reason why sentence should not be imposed at that time, I am sure you understood my staring back at you mutely and then my smiling at you, my need to communicate spiritually with you though my attorney had told me I should answer "No" and nothing more. I based my appeal on human sympathy and not on the sterile logic of the law (needle-sterile logic of the Law), and also on the fact that human contact of souls is sacred *whether it is loving or destructive* and that I, loving, might well absorb Your un-loving.

I dream of you often, and I wish myself into Your dreams, so that you will understand our relationship. Nothing is accidental in the universe—this is one of my Laws of Physics—except the entire universe itself, which is Pure Accident, pure divinity. So it cannot be an accident that I think of you so constantly.

Sincerely,

Meredith Dawe

Winter morning XXX yr.

Your Honor:

I request a reversal of all prior communications sent to you, and in their place file this single brief:

My failure in my single experience with the Law derives solely from the fact that I attempted to absorb into myself the hatreds of a great body of spectators (not simply those crowded into the courtroom, but the entire world) and that this did, in fact, distract me from Your Honor and His importance in that courtroom. This might in itself constitute an illegal action or a sin.

I request forgiveness for the above-mentioned error.

Being that there seemed to be, at that time, a physical essence to Your Honor, I was perhaps doubly distracted, by the evidence of (1) my senses, (2) yours. The senses are something which must be overcome. In my former life I often utilized a saying from Confucius: *The way out is via the door. Why is it that no one will use this method?* To achieve the door one must obliterate his senses and, at the time of my trial, I had failed to do so. This may well constitute the sin Your Honor noted in me.

However, there being no verifiable physical essence to Your Honor (except through the senses) it is evident that my love for You is transcendent and sacred in itself, immune to any object. To have termed You my "father" is surely a gross blasphemy for which I beg forgiveness, noting, however, that I was at a crude stage in my development at that time. You will have patience with me.

Am I sullying You just by this communication? Is Your name perhaps too holy to be uttered?

In my past life I sometimes gave a lecture in which I utilized the expression "Nécessité fait loi," which in my profanity I interpreted as "Necessity knows no law." I tried to influence my audiences accordingly, not knowing of my own ignorance. Now I have come to see that "Nécessité fait loi" does in literal fact mean that Necessity Makes Law and that, conversely, Law Makes Necessity.

Law Makes Necessity.

And so in Your Law, or in You, as the highest emblem of the Law, I have the possibility of being fulfilled. A necessary unit in the accidental universe is, in itself, *necessary* (i.e., loved). Therefore I am partly and, I hope, will be someday totally fulfilled in Your judgment and annihilated in my own profane being. I will say goodbye to You.

In one of the sacred books of the Buddha there is a parable of the necessity of this fulfillment (i.e. annihilation) but to my shame I did not understand it at the time, though I imagined I did. Now it is constantly with me, in Your words and with Your (visible) face:

> The Zen Master holds a stick over the pupil's head and says to him, fiercely, "If you say this stick is real, I will strike you with it. If you say this stick is not real, I will strike you with it. If you say nothing, I will strike you with it."

Meredith Dawe

from
Ninety-two in the shade
THOMAS McGUANE

"Ma'am, you want to hand me that lunch so I can stow it?" Skelton took the wicker basket from Missus Rudleigh; and then the Thermos she handed him. "I've got plenty of water," he said.

"That's not water."

"What is it?"

"Gibsons."

"Let me put them in the cooler for you then—"

"We put them in the Thermos," said Rudleigh, "so we don't have to put them in the cooler. We like them where we can get at them. In case we need them, you know, real snappy."

Tom Skelton looked up at him. Most people when they smile expose a cross-section of their upper teeth; when Rudleigh smiled, he exposed his lower teeth.

"Hold the Thermos in your lap," Skelton said. "If that starts rolling around the skiff while I'm running these banks I'll throw it overboard."

"An ecologist," said Missus Rudleigh.

"Are you sure Nichol cannot appeal his sentence, Captain?" asked Rudleigh.

"I'm sure," said Skelton.

Missus Rudleigh reached out one hand and bent it backwards so her fingernails were all in display; she was thinking of a killer line but it wouldn't come; so she didn't speak.

1973

Skelton felt sick. What a beginning. He knew from other guides he could not let the clients run the boat for him; but he had never expected to have to rebuff such bids; now all three of them were glancing past one another with metallic eyes.

Missus Rudleigh came and Skelton put her in the forward chair. Rudleigh followed in squeaking bright deck shoes and sat aft swiveling about in the chair with an executive's preoccupation.

"Captain," Rudleigh began. Men like Rudleigh believed in giving credit to the qualified. If an eight year old were running the skiff, Rudleigh would call him "Captain" without irony; it was a credit to his class. "Captain, are we going to bonefish?" Missus Rudleigh was putting zinc oxide on her thin nose and on the actual edges of her precise cheekbones. She was a thin pretty woman of forty who you could see had a proclivity for hysterics, slow burns and slapping.

"We have a good tide for bonefish."

"Well, Missus Rudleigh and I have had a good deal of bonefishing in Yucatan and we were wondering if it mightn't be an awfully long shot to fish for permit . . ."

Skelton knew it was being put to him; finding permit—big pompano—was a guide's hallmark and he didn't particularly have a permit tide. "I can find permit," he said though, finishing a sequence Rudleigh started with the word "Captain."

Carter strolled up. He knew the Rudleighs and they greeted each other. "You're in good hands," he said to them, tilting his head toward Skelton. "Boy's a regular fish hawk." He returned his head to the perpendicular.

"Where are your people, Cart?" Skelton asked to change the subject.

"They been partying, I guess. Man said he'd be late. It only shortens my day."

Skelton choked the engine and started it. He let it idle for a few minutes and then freed up his lines. The canal leading away from the dock wandered around lazily, a lead green gloss like pavement.

"Ought to find some bonefish in the Snipes on this incoming water," Carter said. Skelton looked at him a moment.

"We're uh permit fishing, Cart."

"Oh, really. Why permit, huh."

"What do you think? Boca Chica beach?"

"Your guess is as good as mine. But yeah okay, Boca Chica."

Skelton idled on the green tidal gloss of the canal until he cleared the entrance, then ran it up to five thousand r.p.m. and slacked off to an easy plane in the light chop. He leaned back over his shoulder to talk to Rudleigh. "We're going to Boca Chica beach. I think it's our best bet for permit on this tide."

"Fine, fine."

"I hate to take you there, a little bit, because it's in the landing pattern."

"I don't mind if the fish don't mind."

Skelton swung in around by Cow Key Channel, past the Navy hospital, under the bridge where boys were getting in some snapper fishing before it would be time for the military hospitals; then out the channel along the mangroves with the great white wing of the drive-in theater to their left with an unattended meadow of loudspeaker stanchions; and abruptly around the corner to an expanse of blue Atlantic. Skelton ran tight to the beach, inside the boat-wrecking niggerheads; he watched for sunken ice cans and made the run to Boca Chica, stopping short.

The day was clear and bright except for one squall to the west, black with etched rain lines connecting it to sea; the great reciprocating engine of earth, thought Skelton, looks like a jellyfish.

"Go ahead and get ready, Mr. Rudleigh, I'm going to pole us along the rocky edge and see what we can see." Skelton pulled the pushpole out of its chocks and got up in the bow; Rudleigh was ready in the stern behind the tilted engine. It took two or three leaning thrusts to get the skiff underway, and then they were gliding over the sand, coral, sea fans, staghorn and lawns of turtle grass. Small cowfish, sprats and fry of one description or another scattered before them and vanished in the glare. Stonecrabs backed away in bellicose, pentagonian idiocy in the face of the boat's progress. Skelton held the boat into the tide at the breaking edge of the flat and looked for moving fish.

A few small sharks came early on the flood and passed downlight, yellow-eyed and sweeping back and forth schematically for something in trouble. After the sharks, the first of the military aircraft came in overhead, terrifyingly low; a great delta winged machine with howling, vulvate exhausts and nervous quick moving control flaps; so close were they that the bright hydraulic shafts behind the flaps glittered; small rockets were laid up thickly under the wings like insect eggs. The plane approached, banked subtly and the pilot glanced out at the skiff; his head looking no larger than a cocktail onion. A moment after the plane passed, its shock wave swept toward them and the crystal perfect world of the flat paled and vanished; not appearing until some minutes later and slowly. The draconic roar of the engines diminished and the twin blossoms of flame shrank away toward the airfield.

"It must take a smart cookie," said Missus Rudleigh, "to make one of those do what it is supposed to."

"It takes balls for brains," said Rudleigh.

"That's even better," she smiled.

"Only that's what any mule has," Rudleigh added.

Missus Rudleigh threw something at her husband who remained in the stern, modeling for a clipper ship bowsprit, rigid as a gun carriage.

Skelton was so determined that this first day of his professional guiding be a success that he felt with some agony the ugliness of the aircraft that came in now at shorter and shorter intervals, thundering with their mists of unspent fuel drifting over the sea meadow.

The Rudleighs had opened the Thermos and were consuming its contents exactly as the heat of the day began to spread. Skelton was now poling down-light, flushing small fish; then two schools of bonefish, not tailing but pushing wakes in their hurry; Rudleigh saw them late and bungled the cast, looking significantly at Missus Rudleigh after each failure.

"You've got to bear down," she said.

"I'm bearing down."

"Bear down harder, honey."

"I said: I'm bearing down."

Now the wading birds that were on the flat in the early tide were flooded out and flew Northwest to catch the Gulf of Mexico tide. Skelton knew they had about lost their water.

"It's kind of slow, Captain," said Rudleigh.

"I've been thinking the same thing," Skelton said, his heart chilling within him. "I'm going to pole this out and make a move."

A minute later, he was running to Saddlebunch and got there

in time to catch the incoming water across the big sand spot; he hardly had a moment to stake the skiff when the bonefish started crossing the sand. Now Missus Rudleigh was casting, driving the fish away. Rudleigh snatched the rod from her after her second failure.

"Sit down!"

The contents of the Thermos may have had something to do with it. Rudleigh was rigidly prepared for the next fish. Skelton would have helped him but knew in advance it would make things worse.

"You hawse's oss," said Missus Rudleigh to her husband. He seemed not to have heard. He was in the vague crouch of lumbar distress.

"I can fish circles around you, queen bee," he said after a bit. "Always could."

"What about Peru? What about Cabo Blanco?"

"You're always throwing Cabo Blanco in my face without ever, repeat, ever a word about Tierra del Fuego."

"What about Piñas Bay, Panama?"

"Shut up."

"Seems to me," she said, "that Raúl commented that the señora had a way of making the señor look real bum."

A small single bonefish passed the skiff. Rudleigh flushed it by casting right into its face. *"Cocksucker."*

"That's just the way you handled striped marlin. Right there is about what you did with those stripes at Rancho Buena Vista."

Rudleigh whirled around and held the point of his rod under Missus Rudleigh's throat. "I'm warning you."

"He had a tantrum at the Pez Maya Club in Yucatan," Missus Rudleigh told Skelton.

"Yes, ma'am. I see."

"Uh, Captain—"

"I'm right here, Mister Rudleigh."

"I thought this was a permit deal."

"I'm looking for permit on this tide. I told you they were a long shot."

"Captain, I know about permit. I have seen permit in the Bahamas, Yucatan, Costa Rica and at the great Belize camps in British Honduras. I know they are a long shot."

Skelton said, "Maybe your terrific familiarity with places to fish will tell us where we ought to be right now."

"Captain, I wouldn't presume."

A skiff was running just off the reef, making sheets of bright water against the sun.

"Do you know what today's tides are?" Skelton asked.

"No."

"Which way is the Gulf of Mexico?"

Rudleigh pointed all wrong. Skelton wanted to be home reading Kierkegaard, studying the winos or copulating.

"Is that a permit?" Missus Rudleigh asked. The black fork of a large permit surfaced just out of casting range. Rudleigh stampeded back into position. Skelton slipped the pole out of the sand and began to ghost quietly toward the fish and stopped. Nothing visible. A long moment passed. Again, the black fork appeared.

"Cast."

Rudleigh threw forty feet beyond the permit. There was no hope of retrieving and casting again. Then out of totally undeserved luck, the fish began to change course toward Rudleigh's bait. Rudleigh and Missus Rudleigh exchanged glances. "Please keep your eye on the fish," Skelton pleaded; he was overwhelmed by the entirely undeserved nature of what was transpiring. In a moment, the big fish was tailing again.

"Strike him."

Rudleigh lifted the rod and the fish was on. Skelton poled hard following the fish, now streaking against the drag for deep water. The same skiff that passed earlier appeared running in the other direction; and Skelton wondered who it could be.

"God, Captain, will I be able to cope with this at all? I mean, this is power! I knew the fish was strong. But honest to God, this is a nigger with a hot foot."

"I'm still admiring your cast, darling."

Skelton followed watching the drawn bow the rod had become, the line shearing water with precision.

"What a marvellously smooth drag this reel has! A hundred smackers seemed steep at the time, but when you're in the breach, as I am now, a drag like this is the last nickel bargain in America!"

Skelton was poling after the fish with precisely everything he had. And it was difficult on the packed bottom with the pole inclining to slip out from under him.

His feeling of hope for a successful first day guiding was considerably modified by Rudleigh's largely undeserved hooking of the fish. And now the nobility of the fish's fight was further eroding Skelton's pleasure.

When they crossed the edge of the flat, the permit raced down the reef line in sharp powerful curves, dragging the line across the coral. "Gawd, gawd, gawd," Rudleigh said, "this cookie is stronger than I am!" Skelton poled harder and at one point overtook the fish as it desperately rubbed the hook on the coral bottom; seeing the boat, it flushed once more in terror, making a single long howl pour from the reel. A fish that was exactly noble, thought Skelton, who began to imagine the permit coming out of a deep water wreck by the pull of moon and tide, riding the invisible crest of the incoming water, feeding and moving by force of blood, only to run afoul of an asshole from Connecticut.

The fight continued without much change for another hour, mainly outside the reef line in the green water over a sand bottom: a safe place to fight the fish. Rudleigh had soaked through his khaki safari clothes; and from time to time, Missus Rudleigh advised him to "bear down." When Missus Rudleigh told him this, he would turn to look at her, his neck muscles standing out like cords and his eyes acquiring broad white perimeters. Skelton ached from pursuing the fish with the pole; he might have started the engine outside the reef line, but he feared Rudleigh getting his line in the propellor; and he had found in the past that a large fish was held away from the boat by the sound of a running engine.

As soon as the fish began to show signs of tiring, Skelton asked Missus Rudleigh to take a seat; then he brought the big net up on the deck beside him. He hoped he would be able to get Rudleigh to release this hugely undeserved fish—though not on that basis but because the fish had fought so very bravely. No, he admitted to himself, Rudleigh would never let the fish go.

By now the fish should have been on its side. It began another long and accelerating run, the pale sheet of water traveling higher up the line, the fish swerving somewhat inshore again; and to his terror, Skelton found himself poling after the fish through the shallows, now and then leaning over to free the line from a sea fan. They glided among the little hammocks and mangrove keys of Saddlebunch in increasing vegetated congestion, in a narrowing tidal creek that closed around and over them with guano covered mangroves and finally prevented the boat from following another foot. Nevertheless, line continued to pour off the reel.

"Captain, consider it absolutely necessary that I kill this fish."

Skelton did not reply; he watched the line slow its passage from the reel, winding out into the shadowy creek, then stop. He knew there was a good chance the desperate animal had reached a dead-end.

"Stay here," he said to Rudleigh. He glanced over at Missus Rudleigh who stared at him ambiguously and held his glance and confusion a moment more.

Skelton climbed out of the boat and, running the line through his fingers lightly, began to wade the tidal creek. The mosquitoes found him quickly and held in a pale globe around his head. He waded steadily, flushing herons out of the mangroves over his head. At one point he passed a tiny side channel blocking the exit of a blue heron that raised its stiff wings very slightly away from its body and glared at him.

He stopped a moment to look at the bird. All he could hear was the slow musical passage of tide in the mangrove roots and the low pattern of bird sounds more liquid than the sea itself in these shallows. He moved away from the side channel, still following the line. Occasionally, he felt some small movement of life in it; but he was certain now the permit could go no farther. He had another thirty yards to go, if he had guessed right looking at Rudleigh's partially emptied spool.

Wading along, he felt he was descending into the permit's world; in knee-deep water, the small mangrove snappers, angelfish and baby barracudas scattered before him. The brilliant blue sky was reduced to a narrow ragged band quite high overhead now, and the light wavered more with the color of the sea and of estuarine shadow than that of vulgar sky. Skelton stopped and his eye followed the line back toward the direction he had come. The Rudleighs were at its other end, infinitely far away.

Skelton was trying to keep his mind on the job he had set out to do. The problem was, he told himself, to go from Point A to Point B; but every breath of humid air, half sea, and the steady tidal drain through root and elliptical shadow in his ears and eyes, diffused his attention. Each heron that leaped like an arrow out of his narrow slot, spiraling invisibly into the sky, separated him from the job.

Very close now. He released the line so that if his appearance at the dead-end terrified the permit there would not be sufficient tension for the line to break. The sides of the mangrove slot began to yield. Skelton stopped. An embowered, crystalline tidal pool: the fish lay exhausted in its still water, lolling slightly and unable to right itself. It cast a delicate circular shadow on the sand bottom. Skelton moved in and the permit made no effort to rescue itself; instead, it lay nearly on its side and watched Skelton approach with a steady following eye that was, for Skelton, the last straw.

He took the permit firmly by the base of its tail and turned it gently upright in the water. He reached into its mouth and removed the hook from the cartilaginous periculum. He noticed that the suddenly loosened line was not retrieved: Rudleigh hadn't even the sense to keep tension on the line.

By holding one hand under the permit's pectoral fins and the other around the base of its tail, Skelton was able to move the fish back and forth in the water to revive it. When he first tentatively released it, it teetered over on its side again, its wandering eye still fixed upon him. He righted the fish again and continued to move it gently back and forth in the water; and this time when he released the permit it stayed upright, steadying itself in equipoise, mirror sides once again purely reflecting the bottom. Skelton watched a long while until some regularity returned to the movement of its gills.

Then he cautiously—for fear of startling the fish—backed once more into the green tidal slot and turned to head back for the skiff. Rudleigh had lost his permit.

Torpid smoke
VLADIMIR NABOKOV

Foreword

Tyazhyolïy dïm *appeared in the daily* Posledniya Novosti, *Paris, March 3, 1935, and was reprinted in my collection of short stories* Vesna v Fialte *by Chekhov Publishing House (New York, 1956). It has now been translated by my son and me into English with particular care. In two or three passages, brief phrases have been introduced to elucidate points of habitus and locale, unfamiliar today not only to foreign readers but to the incurious grandchildren of the Russians who fled to Western Europe in the first three or four years after the Bolshevist Revolution. Otherwise the translation is acrobatically faithful—beginning with the title, which in a coarse lexical rendering that did not take familiar associations into account would read "Heavy Smoke."*

The story belongs to that portion of my short fiction which refers to émigré life in Berlin between 1920 and the late thirties. Seekers of biographical tidbits should be warned that my main delight in composing those things was to invent ruthlessly assortments of exiles who in character, class, exterior features, and so forth were utterly unlike any of the Nabokovs. The only two affinities here between author and hero are that both wrote Russian verse and that I had lived at one time or another in the same kind

of lugubrious Berlin apartment as he. Only very poor readers (or perhaps some exceptionally good ones) will scold me for not letting them into its parlor.
Montreux, March 8, 1971

When the streetlamps hanging in the dusk came on, practically in unison, all the way to Bayerischer Platz, every object in the unlit room shifted slightly under the influence of the outdoor rays which started by taking a picture of the lace curtain's design. He had been lying supine (a long-limbed, flat-chested youth with a pince-nez glimmering in the semiobscurity) for about three hours, apart from a brief interval for supper, which had passed in merciful silence: his father and sister, after yet another quarrel, had kept reading at table. Drugged by the oppressive, protracted feeling so familiar to him, he lay and looked through his lashes, and every line, every rim, or shadow of a rim turned into a sea horizon or a strip of distant land. As soon as his eye got used to the mechanics of these metamorphoses, they began to occur of their own accord (thus small stones continue to come alive, quite uselessly, behind the wizard's back), and now, in this or that place of the room's cosmos, an illusionary perspective was formed, a remote mirage enchanting in its graphic transparency and isolation: a stretch of water, say, and a black promontory with the minuscule silhouette of an araucaria.

At intervals scraps of indistinct, laconic speech came from the adjacent parlor (the cavernal centerpiece of one of those bourgeois flats which Russian *émigré* families used to rent in Berlin at the time), separated from his room by sliding doors, through whose ripply mat glass the tall lamp beyond shone yellow, whilst lower down there showed through, as if in deep water, the fuzzy dark back of a chair placed in that position to foil the propensity of the door-leaves to crawl apart in a series of jerks. In that parlor (probably on the divan at its farthest end) his sister sat with her boy friend; and, to judge by the mysterious pauses, resolving at last in a slight cough or a tender questioning laugh, the two were kissing. Other sounds could be heard from the street: the noise of a car would curl up like a wispy column to be capitaled by a honk at the crossing; or, vice versa, the honk would come first, followed by an approaching rumble in which the shudder of the door-leaves participated as best it could.

And in the same way as the luminosity of the water and its every throb pass through a medusa, so everything traversed his inner being, and that sense of fluidity became transfigured into something like second sight. As he lay flat on his couch, he felt carried sideways by the flow of shadows, and, simultaneously, he escorted distant foot-passengers, and visualized now the sidewalk's surface right under his eyes (with the exhaustive accuracy of a dog's sight), now the design of bare branches against a sky still retaining some color, or else the alternation of shop windows: a hairdresser's dummy, hardly surpassing the queen of hearts in anatomic development; a picture framer's display, with purple heathscapes and the inevitable *Inconnue de la Seine,* so popular in the Reich, among numerous portraits of President Hindenburg; and then a lampshade shop with all bulbs aglow, so that one could not help wondering which of them was the workaday lamp belonging to the shop itself.

All at once it occurred to him, as he reclined mummy-like in the dark, that it was all rather awkward—his sister might think that he was not at home, or that he was eavesdropping. To move was, however, incredibly difficult; difficult because the very form of his being had now lost all distinctive marks, all fixed boundaries. For example, the lane on the other side of the house might be his own arm, whilst the long skeletal cloud that stretched across the whole sky with a chill of stars in the east might be his backbone. Neither the striped obscurity in his room, nor the glass of the parlor door which was transmuted into nighttime seas shining with golden undulations, offered him a dependable method of measuring and marking himself off; only then did he find that method when in a burst of agility the tactile tip of his tongue, performing a sudden twist in his mouth (as if dashing to check, half-awake, if all was well), palpated and started to worry a bit of soft foreign matter, a shred of boiled beef firmly lodged in his teeth; whereupon he reflected how many times, in some nineteen years, it had changed, that invisible but tangible householdry of teeth, which the tongue would get used to until a filling came out, leaving a great pit that presently would be refurnished.

He was now prompted to move, not so much by the shamelessly frank silence behind the door as by the urge to seek out a nice, pointed little tool, to aid the solitary blind toiler. He stretched, raised his head, and switched on the light near his couch, thus entirely restoring his corporeal image. He perceived himself (the pince-nez, the thin, dark mustache, the bad skin on his forehead) with that utter revulsion he always experienced on coming back to his body out of the languorous mist, promising—what? What shape would the force oppressing and teasing his spirit finally take? Where did it originate, this thing growing in me? Most of my day had been the same as usual—university, public library—but later, when I had to trudge to the Osipovs on Father's errand, there was that wet roof of some pub on the edge of a vacant lot, and the chimney smoke hugged the roof, creeping low, heavy with damp, sated with it, sleepy, refusing to rise, refusing to detach itself from beloved decay, and right then came that thrill—right then.

Under the table lamp gleamed an oilcloth-bound exercise book, and next to it, on the ink-mottled blotter, lay a razor blade, its apertures encircled with rust. The light also fell on a safety pin. He unbent it, and following his tongue's rather fussy directions, removed the mote of meat, swallowed it—better than any dainties; after which the contented organ calmed down.

Suddenly a mermaid's hand was applied from the outside to the ripply glass of the door; then the leaves parted spasmodically and his sister thrust in her shaggy head.

"Grisha dear," she said, "be an angel. Do get some cigarettes from Father."

He did not respond, and the bright slits of her furry eyes narrowed (she saw very poorly without her horn-rimmed glasses), as she tried to make out whether or not he was asleep on the couch.

"Get them for me, Grishenka," she repeated, still more entreatingly. "Oh, please! I don't want to go to him after what happened yesterday."

"Maybe I don't want to either," he said.

"Hurry, hurry," tenderly uttered his sister. "Come on, Grisha dear!"

"All right, lay off," he said at last, and, carefully reuniting the two halves of the door, she dissolved in the glass.

He examined again his lamp-lit island, remembering hopefully that he had put somewhere a pack of cigarettes which one evening a friend had happened to leave behind. The shiny safety pin had disappeared, whilst the exercise book now lay otherwise and was half open (as a person changes position in sleep). Perhaps, between my books. The light just reached their spines on the shelves above the desk. Here were haphazard trash (predominantly) and manuals of political economy (I wanted something quite different, but Father won out); there were also some favorite books that at one time or another had done his heart good: Gumilyov's collection of poems *Shatyor* (tent), Pasternak's *Sestra moya Zhizn'* (life, my sister), Gazdanov's *Vecher u Kler* (evening at Claire's), Radiguet's *Le Bal du Comte d'Orgel,* Sirin's *Zashchita Luzhina* (Lushin's defense), Ilf and Petrov's *Dvenadtsat' Stul'ev* (twelve chairs), Hoffmann, Hölderlin, Baratīnski, and an old Russian guidebook. Again that gentle, mysterious shock. He listened. Would the thrill be repeated? His mind was in a state of extreme tension, logical thought was eclipsed, and when he came out of his trance, it took him some time to recall why he was standing near the shelves and fingering books. The blue-and-white package that he had stuck between Professor Sombart and Dostoevski proved to be empty. Well, it had to be done, no getting out of it. There was, however, another possibility.

In worn bedroom slippers and sagging pants, listlessly, almost noiselessly, dragging his feet, he passed from his room to the hallway and groped for the switch. On the console under the looking glass, next to the guest's smart beige cap, there remained a crumpled piece of soft paper: the wrappings of liberated roses. He rummaged in his father's overcoat, penetrating with squeamish fingers into the insensate world of a strange pocket, but did not find there the spare pack he had hoped to obtain, knowing, as he did, his father's heavyish providence. Nothing to be done, I must go to him.

Here, that is at some indeterminate point in his somnambulic itinerary, he again stepped into a zone of mist, and this time the renewed vibration within him possessed such power, and especially was so much more vivid than all external perceptions, that he did not immediately identify, as his proper confines and countenance, the stoop-shouldered youth, with the pale, unshaven cheek and the red ear, who glided soundlessly by in the mirror. He overtook his own self and entered the dining room.

There, at the table which long since, before going to bed, the maid had laid for late-evening tea, sat his father: one finger was grating in his black, gray-streaked beard; between the finger and thumb of his other hand he held aloft a pince-nez by its springy clips; he sat studying a large plan of Berlin badly worn at the folds. A few days ago, at the house of some friends, there had been a passionate, Russian-style argument as to which was the shortest way to walk from a certain street to another, neither of which, incidentally, did any of the arguers ever frequent; and now, to judge by the expression of displeased astonishment on his father's inclined face, with those two pink figure eights on the sides of his nose, the old man had turned out to be wrong.

"What is it?" he asked, glancing up at his son (with the secret hope, perhaps, that I would sit down, divest the teapot of its cosey, pour a cup for him, for myself). "Cigarettes?" he went on in the same interrogatory tone, having noticed the direction in which his son gazed. The latter had started to go behind his father's back to reach for the box, which stood on the far side of the table, but his father was already handing it across, so that there ensued a moment of muddle.

"Is he gone?" came the third question.

"No," said the son, taking a silky handful of cigarettes.

On his way out of the dining room, he noticed his father turn his whole torso in his chair to face the wall clock as if it had said something, and then begin turning back—but here the door I was closing closed, and I did not see that bit to the end. I did not see it to the end, I had other things on my mind, yet that, too, and the distant seas of a moment ago, and my sister's flushed little face, and the indistinct rumble on the circular rim of the transparent night—everything, somehow or other, helped to form what now had at last taken shape. With terrifying clarity, as if my soul were lit up by a noiseless explosion, I glimpsed a future recollection; it dawned upon me that exactly as I recalled such images of the past as the way my dead mother had of making a weepy face and clutching her temples when mealtime squabbles became too loud, so one day I would have to recall, with merciless, irreparable sharpness, the hurt look of my father's shoulders as he leaned over that torn map, morose, wearing his warm indoor jacket powdered with ashes and dandruff; and all this mingled creatively with the recent vision of blue smoke clinging to dead leaves on a wet roof.

Through a chink between the door-leaves, unseen, avid fingers took away what he held, and now he was lying again on his couch, but the former languor had vanished. Enormous, alive, a metrical line extended and bent; at the bend a rhyme was coming deliciously and hotly alight, and as it glowed forth, there appeared, like a shadow on the wall when you climb upstairs with a candle, the mobile silhouette of another verse.

Drunk with the italianate music of Russian alliteration, with the longing to live, with the new temptation of obsolete words (modern *bereg* reverting to *breg,* a farther "shore," *holod* to *hlad,* a more classic "chill," *veter* to *vetr,* a better Boreas), puerile, perishable poems, which, by the time the next were printed, would have been certain to wither as had withered, one after the other, all the previous ones written down in the black exercise book; but no matter: at this moment I trust the ravishing promises of the still breathing, still revolving verse; my face is wet with tears, my heart is bursting with happiness, and I know that this happiness is the greatest thing existing on earth.

Berlin, early 1935
Montreux, early 1971 (trans.)

translated from the Russian by Dmitri Nabokov
in collaboration with the author

My encounters with Chekhov
KONSTANTIN KOROVIN

1

It all took place, if I'm not mistaken, in 1883.

On the corner of Dyakovskaya and Sadovaya Streets in Moscow there was a hotel called Oriental Rooms, though no one knew what was Oriental about it. It had very shabby furnished rooms. Three bricks hanging on a rope were attached to the front door to help it close more securely.

Anton Pavlovich Chekhov lived on the first floor, Isaak Levitan —who was at the time still a student at the School of Painting, Sculpture, and Architecture—lived on the second.

It was spring. Levitan and I were on the way home from our school on Myasnitskaya Street after our final painting exam. We had both received silver medals—I for drawing, he for painting.

As we went into the hotel, Levitan said to me, "Let's stop in at Antosha's [i.e. Chekhov's]."

Anton Pavlovich's room was filled with smoke. There was a samovar on the table, surrounded by bread, sausages, and beer. The couch was strewn with papers and lecture notebooks: Anton Pavlovich was preparing for the final examinations at the university, after which he would become a doctor.

He was sitting on the edge of the couch wearing a gray jacket of the type many students wore at the time. Some young men whom we didn't know were in the room with him. They were university students.

The students were talking heatedly—there was an argument going on—drinking tea and beer, and eating sausage. Anton Pavlovich sat quietly, only occasionally answering the questions put to him.

He was extremely handsome. He had a large, open face with kind, laughing eyes. When talking with someone, he would sometimes fix his eyes on him for a moment, only to lower them immediately and smile his own special shy smile. His whole appearance—his open face, his broad chest—inspired in people a special sort of confidence. It was as if he emanated waves of warmth and protection. Despite his youth, despite his adolescent appearance, he even then made you think of a kind old man whom you could approach and ask about the meaning of life, tell of your sorrows, and confess something very important, the kind of secret everyone has somewhere down deep. Anton Pavlovich was simple and natural; he was unpretentious and lacked the least bit of affectation or self-admiration. Innate modesty, his own special sense of measure, even timidity were always a part of his character.

It was a sunny spring day. Levitan and I asked Anton Pavlovich to come to Sokolniki Park with us.

We told him about the medals we had received. One of the students present asked, "Well, are you going to wear them around your neck the way doormen do?"

It was Levitan who answered. "No, they're not meant to be worn. They aren't used for anything. They're awarded at graduation as a sign of distinction."

"Like the ribbons dogs get at dog shows," added another student.

The students were different from Anton Pavlovich. They loved to argue, and they were in some peculiar way opposed to just about everything.

"If you have no convictions," said one student turning to Chekhov, "you can't be a writer."

"No one can say, 'I have no convictions,' " said another. "I can't understand how anyone could not have convictions."

"I have no convictions," replied Chekhov.

"You claim to be a man without convictions, but how can you

write a work of literature without any ideology? Don't you have an ideology?"

"I have no ideology and no convictions," answered Chekhov.

These students had an odd way of arguing. They were apparently displeased with Anton Pavlovich. It was clear that they could not fit him into the didactic turn of their outlook or into their moralizing ideology. They wanted to guide, to instruct, to lead, and to influence. They knew everything. They understood everything. And Anton Pavlovich was plainly bored by it all.

"Who needs your stories? Where do they lead? They don't oppose anything. They contain no ideas. The *Russian Bulletin,* say, would have no use for you. Your stories are entertaining and nothing else."

"Nothing else," answered Anton Pavlovich.

"And why, may I ask, do you sign your stories Chekhonte? What's the point of such an outlandish pen name?"

Chekhov laughed.

"And when you get to be a doctor," the student added, "you'll be ashamed of having written without ideology or protest."

"You're right," answered Chekhov, still laughing. Then he added, "Let's go to Sokolniki. It's a beautiful day. The violets will be in bloom by now. We can breathe fresh air and enjoy spring."

So off we went to Sokolniki.

At Red Gate we took a horse-drawn omnibus and rode past the train stations, past Red Pond and all the wooden houses with green and red iron roofs, out along the outskirts of Moscow.

On the way, Levitan continued the interrupted conversation. "What do you think?" he asked. "Take me, now. You see, I too have no ideology whatsoever. May I or may I not be an artist?"

"Impossible," the student replied. "A man cannot exist without ideology."

"What a crocodile you are," Levitan said to the student. "What am I supposed to do now? Give up painting?"

"Yes, give it up."

Anton Pavlovich entered the conversation with a laugh. "How can he give up painting? No! Isaak's a sly one. He won't give it up. After all, he's got a medal around his neck. Now he's on his way to a Stanislaus, and a Stanislaus isn't that easy to come by.

That's what they say: I've got a Stanislaus, so don't punch me in the nose."

We laughed. The students were angry.

"What sort of ideology is it if I feel like painting pine trees in the sun or a spring landscape?"

"Allow me, but your pine tree is a product, see? A building product, you see? Timber belongs to the people. It's something nature creates for the people—you see?" The student was wrought up. "For the people!"

"But it makes me sick to see a tree being chopped down. Trees are every bit as alive as we are, and birds sing in them. They—those birds—are better than we are. When I paint, I don't think of trees as timber. I can't think that. You really are a crocodile!" said Levitan.

"And why are singing birds better than us, pray tell?" asked the student indignantly.

"Yes, this offends me too," said Anton Pavlovich. "Isaak, you must prove why."

"Be so kind as to prove why," insisted the student seriously, looking at Levitan with his piercing eyes and with an air of extreme importance.

Anton Pavlovich laughed.

"This is all so stupid," snapped Levitan.

"We'll be at Sokolniki soon. We're getting close."

A lower class woman who was sitting next to Levitan held out a red Easter egg to him, saying, "You're a handsome boy. [Levitan was very handsome.] Eat this egg. My father died forty days ago. Pray for him."

Levitan and Chekhov burst out laughing. Levitan took the egg and asked what her father's name was so he would know for whom to pray.

"Are you a priest, son? Is that what you are?"

The woman had had a few too many. "They are students, that's what they are. What a bunch. A book under their arm and that's all they own. I declare . . ."

We arrived at Sokolniki Circle.

Getting out of the omnibus, the woman who was sitting next to us turned to Levitan and said in farewell: "Pray for my father. His name was Nikita Nikitich. And when you graduate from the seminary, you will have beautiful hair. Come to Pechatniki. Everybody knows Anfisa Nikitishna. I'll give you a good meal. Even though you're scholars, you don't seem to get much to eat."

Anton Pavlovich laughed. The students were serious; they seemed depressed. It was as if Old Woman Woe were trailing at their heels. They were full of obsessive ideas. Something heavy and contrived was weighing down on them like some compulsory duty that had fettered their youth. They lacked simplicity and the ability to yield simply to life's moments. And that spring was so beautiful! Yet when Levitan referred to the beauty of the forest —"Look, how beautiful"—one of the students responded, "Nothing special. Nothing exciting. A forest, so what? What's so beautiful about it?"

"What would you know about it, you dodo!" Levitan replied.

We walked along a path.

The forest was mysteriously beautiful. Highlighted by the rays of the vernal sun, the tops of the pine trees glittered with reddish sparks against the deep, dark blue sky. There was a constant whistling of thrushes and in the distance the cuckoos were mysteriously reckoning how many years each of us has left on this enigmatic earth of ours.

The students, with lap rugs around their shoulders, also became more lively and began singing:

> **Raise your glasses to the one**
> **Who wrote "What Is to Be Done."** [1]
> **Drink a toast to him and to his great ideal . . .**

Anton Pavlovich and Levitan walked side by side; the students were up ahead. At a distance their long hair—long hair was stylish at the time—was plainly visible against the background of the lap rugs.

"What's that flying over there?" one of them cried out, turning to Levitan.

"It's probably a falcon," answered Anton Pavlovich jokingly.

Actually it was a crow.

"I doubt that Sokolniki has any more falcons," added Chekhov. "I've never seen a falcon.[2] Oh, my fair falcon! What are you thinking of, my falcons? Falcons and falcon hunts must have been popular throughout medieval Russia."

By this time we had come to the edge of the forest. There was a path for the railroad tracks in front of us, and some tables covered with tablecloths soon came into view. A large number of people were drinking tea, their samovars steaming. We too sat down at one of the tables. Drinking tea was the thing to do at Sokolniki. The hawkers came up to us immediately.

Their trays were covered with rolls, biscuits, sturgeon fillets, and smoked sausage.

"Take your pick, good people."

A group of extremely drunk merchants—they looked as if they came from the Okhotnyi Riad Market—had taken seats around a nearby table and were looking us over in a most unfriendly manner.

"You're students," said one of them who was very drunk, turning in our direction. "You're the ones who . . . and if you dare . . ." And he showed us his fist.

Another tried to convince him not to bother us.

"Don't pick on them. What do you want? Maybe they're not even students. What do you want?"

"The servant serves; the loafer loafs," said the glassy-eyed drunk in our direction.

It was clear they had no love for us. Their puzzling enmity toward us "students" was breaking through to the surface.

Anton Pavlovich took out a small notebook and quickly noted something in it.

I remember his telling me on the way back: "Spring has a kind of yearning to it. Deep yearning and anxiety. Everything is alive, but there is an incomprehensible sadness in all nature, despite her new life."

And after we had said good-bye to the students, he said to Levitan and me, smiling, "Those students will make excellent doctors. They are lovely people, and I envy them having their heads full of ideas."

2

Much time had passed since our Sokolniki walk. It was the spring of 1904, and shortly after I arrived in the Crimea, in Yalta, I went to see Anton Pavlovich Chekhov at his home in Upper Autka. When I went through the gate, what did I see in front of me, in the front yard, sticking out his neck, standing on one foot, but a live crane! When he saw me, he spread his wings and began hopping around, dancing an animated dance as if to show off all the fancy steps he could do.

I found Anton Pavlovich in his room. He was sitting by the window reading a newspaper, *New Times.*

"What a nice crane you have," I said to Anton Pavlovich. "He does such an amusing dance."

"Yes, he's a most remarkable and most kindly creature. He loves us all," said Anton Pavlovich. "You know, he flew back to us this spring. He flew off for the winter to find other, well, different climes, off to the hippopotami, but he's come back for a visit. We love him so, Masha and I. Isn't it strange and mysterious—flying away and flying back again? I don't think it's only for the frogs he's always killing here in the garden. No, he's proud, and besides he's happy to be asked to dance. He's an artist, and he loves to hear us laugh at his amusing dances. Artists like to play in different places and then they fly off. My wife, for instance, has flown away to Moscow, to the Art Theater."

Anton Pavlovich picked up from the table a piece of paper rolled into a short tube, had a fit of coughing, spit into it, and threw it into a jar filled with solution.

Everything was neat, clean, bright, and simple in Anton Pavlovich's room; it looked somewhat like a sickroom and smelled of creosote. On the table were a calendar and many photographs inserted fanlike into a special stand—portraits of actors and acquaintances. The walls were also adorned with photographs—once again portraits, but this time people like Tolstoy, Mikhailovsky,[3] Suvorin, Potapenko, Levitan, and others.

Maria Pavlovna came into the room to say that the cook had fallen ill and was in bed with a bad headache. At first Anton Pavlovich paid no attention, but then all of a sudden he stood up and said, "Oh, I'd forgotten. I'm a doctor, aren't I? Of course I am. Let me go see what is the matter with her."

And he went into the kitchen to have a look at the patient. As I followed him, I remember noticing how stooped his frame had become under the impact of the illness; he was thin and his sharply protruding shoulders bore witness to the grave ailment undermining his strength.

The kitchen was off to one side of the house. I stayed outside with the crane. He had begun to dance again and enjoyed hopping up and down so much that he spread his wings, flew up and around the garden, and landed again in front of me. "Craney, craney," I called, and he came right up to me and looked at me from the side with his penetrating eye, probably expecting a reward for his art. I offered him my empty hand. He looked at it and screamed something. What? "Cheat!" probably, or something worse. After all, I hadn't paid him for his performance.

Later I showed Anton Pavlovich some new work I had recently done in the Crimea, hoping to entertain him a bit—pictures of large ships asleep in the night. He asked me to leave them with him. "Leave them. I want to look at them again alone," he said.

Anton Pavlovich was planning to go to Moscow. I advised him against it; he looked very ill and had a husky cough. At dinner he asked me, "Why don't you drink wine? I would if I were healthy. I do so love wine."

Everything about him bore the stamp of illness and distress.

I told him I wanted to buy a small plot of land in the Crimea and build myself a studio on it. Not in Yalta, though somewhere in the vicinity.

"Masha," he said to his sister, "how about giving him our plot? Would you like a plot in Gurzuf right by the cliffs? I lived there for two years, right by the sea. Listen, Masha, why don't I give the land to Konstantin Alexeyevich? Would you like it? The only problem is that the sea is eternally roaring there. Would you like it? There's a cottage there. I'd be happy to have you take it."

I thanked Anton Pavlovich, but I too would have been unable to live right by the sea. I can't sleep so near the sea; it gives me palpitations.

That was the last time I saw Anton Pavlovich Chekhov.

Later I did live in Gurzuf; I built myself a studio there. And from my window I could see the cottage by the cliff where Anton Pavlovich had once lived. I often painted that scene: roses . . . and Anton Pavlovich's cottage standing out cozily against the seascape. It conveyed the mood of a far-off land, and the sea roared near the poor little cottage where the soul of a great writer had dwelt, a man who had been poorly understood in his time.

More than once Anton Pavlovich had said to me, "Women don't like me, you know. Everyone thinks I'm a scoffer, a comic writer, but they're wrong. . . ."

translated by Tatiana Kusubova

Notes

1. I.E. Nikolai Chernyshevsky, the radical critic and novelist of the 1860's, framed and sent to Siberia by the tsarist government.

2. The name of Sokolniki Park is derived from the Russian word for "falcon." Chekhov quotes several traditional formulas associated with falcons in Russian folktales and folksongs.

3. Probably the minor novelist Nikolai Garin-Mikhailovsky, with whom Chekhov was friendly at the end of his life, rather than the famous and powerful Populist critic of that name who repeatedly tried to discredit Chekhov with liberal readers and to wreck his literary career.

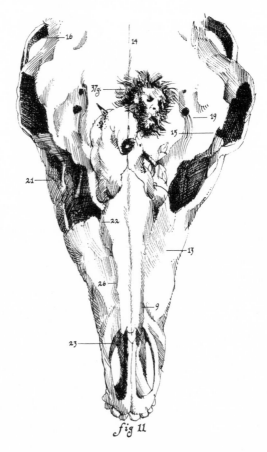

fig 11

ABOVE AND FACING PAGE: DRAWINGS BY ELWOOD H. SMITH. (*TQ* #29)

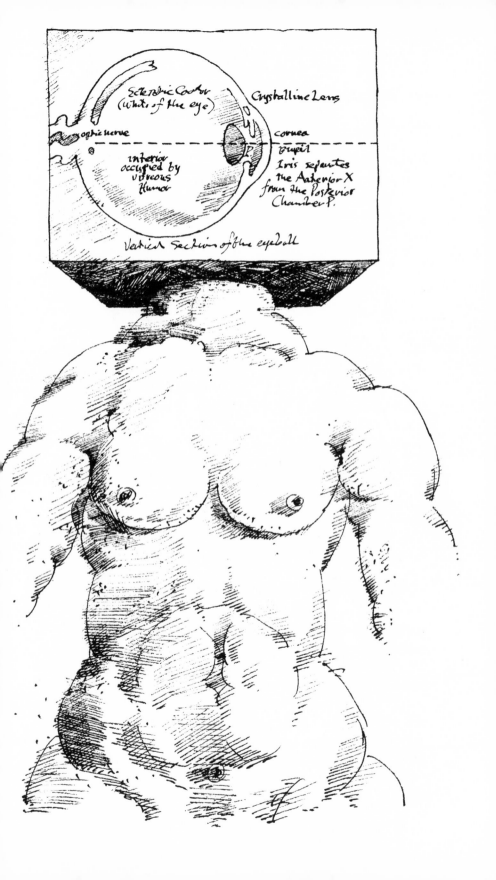

Commitment without empathy:
a writer's notes on politics, theatre and the novel
DAVID CAUTE

In the realm of truth, too, familiarity breeds contempt. Yet it remains the case today, as yesterday, that our world is blotched and distorted by exploitation, oppression and wanton massacre. If we face this fact we cannot really argue—even putting Marx, Bakunin and Guevara in parentheses—that this abominable and humiliating state of affairs is inseparable from the human condition. We do possess, after all, a fund of inherited criticism which enables us to discern the causes of social disease and to glimpse, at the very least, the remedies. But can it be maintained that this whole central province of concern is germane only to our identity as citizens, but never to our calling as writers, as poets, novelists and playwrights? Is art so holy?

For some years past, it has been fashionable to say so. On the great stock exchanges of literary appreciation, the shares marked "commitment" have hovered near the floor, bereft of buyers and depressed by the insistence of the leading brokers that the company is virtually bankrupt. Political passion and partisan polemic, we are constantly reminded, enter through the gates of literature as Trojan Horses. "Literature," Robbe-

Grillet has explained, "is not a means which the writer puts at the service of some cause . . . the novel is not a tool. . . . The writer by definition does not know where he is going." In other words, the only valid commitment for the writer is to the act and art of writing itself. An English critic disparages the "ghastly critical naïvete of the so-called committed writer", and reminds us that our polemical intentions will always be thwarted by the "genius" of our native language. And here, for good measure, is an American view:

The *problem* of commitment arises when the artist is committed to values or actions extrinsic to the immediate concerns of his art, when the moral urgency of outside imperatives forces him into non-aesthetic areas of consideration.

So: periodically Dame Literature, so often laid and mislaid, smooths down her skirts and announces her scorn for the coarse blandishments of polemicists thirsting to inseminate her. That she feels compelled to put on this act periodically should alert us to the provocations and insults she suffers at the hands of agit-prop ideologues, those politically infatuated rogues who cannot distinguish a harlot from a lady of somewhat elastic virtue.

Nevertheless, whenever she wends her way to church and bends her knee at the altar of art for art's sake, we do well to sniff the incense. It is never very pure or consistent in texture. And the high priests of formalist criticism, too, beneath their cassocks of white, have not washed themselves with care. Pay attention to their sermons: the denunciation of Sartre followed by a pretty tribute to Camus; a swipe at Sholokhov followed by a message of comfort to Solzhenitsyn. Certainly Sartre, at a certain moment of time, gave his blood to the idea of *une littérature engagée*; but why is Camus, whose novels and plays so often represent a systematic transcription of a political and philosophical standpoint into fictional terms, hailed as a pure artist? Juxtapose, for example, his essays, *Lettres á un Ami allemand,* with his novel, *The Plague;* or trace the central notions of *The Rebel* to that highly didactic play, *The Just.* Could it be that Sartre was chosen as the whipping-boy not because his novels and plays were politically committed, but, on the contrary, because they were committed in an uncomfortable direction? As for Solzhenitsyn, which contemporary novelist can match him for sustained and passionate—even obsessive—political commitment?

One senses the objection to this argument, but the objection is a trap. Both Camus and Solzhenitsyn, it might be argued, and Orwell too, raised their voices *against* the devastating effects of dogmatic ideologies; their plea and call is to give man, the individual, a little breathing space, the chance to be true to himself. But such an attitude, given its particular frame of reference, is also an ideological one. It is a common fallacy, notably among conservative literary critics, to equate ideology as such with "extremism" or radicalism, whether of Right or Left, and to imagine that the peaceful pastures of the central status quo are irrigated by common sense. The reason for this error is not obscure: movements calling for social change, for a disruption of continuities, are compelled both to fashion coherent theories and to emphasise the distinctive identity of the class or group demanding the change. The possessing or conservative classes, on the other hand, make their first line of defence a pretended community of interest within society, at the same time insisting that certain moral and rational values are relevant and available to all men, regardless of wealth or station. Thus, the French bourgeoisie, in its moment of revolutionary pugnacity, was pleased to trumpet the rights of the Third Estate; but soon afterwards, threatened from below, by the *sans-culottes,* this same bourgeoisie shed its particularist identity and equated itself, simply, with Man (The Rights of Man, etc.).

These reflections are not intended to disparage Orwell, Camus or Solzhenitsyn, to challenge their radicalism, or to characterise them as servants of the status quo. But it is useful, at the outset, to demonstrate that a good many apparently aesthetic objections to committed writing, socialist realism and utilitarian art, are in fact prompted less by absolute literary principle than by ordinary ideological prejudice. In our own century, a recurring theme of conservative ideology has been the assault on ideology as such, combined with the elevation of philosophy—conceived as a force altogether more disinterested, universal and noble—as the proper source of literary inspiration. Normally, religion is accorded an equal indulgence.

It is not, however, my purpose here to embark on a backs-to-the-wall, fundamentalist defence of social/socialist realism in an age which, for reasons I hope to explore, can no longer accommodate it. If, as is the case, the political and artistic avant-gardes have for many decades regarded one another with suspicion, and even enmity, the fault lies partly with the dogged aesthetic conservatism so prevalent within the Old Left —I mean the socialist and communist generations whose style of thought and expression was programed in the late nineteenth century. In these circles, one still encounters a faith in a type of literary realism which aspires to representational mimesis and to the creation of a self-sufficient fictional universe, a canvas on which no brush strokes are visible. The reader is invited to suspend all disbelief and, by way of empathy, to surrender completely to an illusion. While this mode of writing may have represented a vanguard stance a century ago, I do not believe that socialist writers living in the electronic age can afford any longer to rely on an *Anschauung* evolved in the age of the steam engine. A dead voice produces a dead song.

Of course, we must not deny the Roundheads their due. In so far as naturalism and realism are relatively comprehensible literary modes, and accordingly more accessible to the ordinary reader, our desire to communicate with that wider audience which must of necessity be the agency of social change will keep us working within certain naturalistic boundaries. Nor is the distrust felt by the Old Left for that elitist, masturbatory art, which has remained *haute culture,* altogether to be despised. Nevertheless the general suspicion of Modernism which prevailed among political radicals prior to the emergence of the New Left was sustained at too high a price, involving as it did a rejection of a crucial and authentic contemporary sensibility: self-consciousness and self-doubt. When the Soviet critic demands: ''Write the unvarnished truth'', we are bound to reflect that all writing is a kind of varnish. The emerging certainties of the nineteenth century had been anticipated during the Renaissance: we can admire both epochs, but we cannot follow. ''That painting is most praiseworthy which is most like the thing represented," noted Leonardo da Vinci. Over three hundred years later, the Russian materialist and political radical Chernyshevsky reiterated this point of view: "Thus, the first purpose of art is to reproduce nature and life, and this applies to all works of art without exception." Gorky added: "Literature must attain to the level of real life. That is the point." Some years later, a French Marxist critic, Jean Fréville, put it as follows: "Realism demands that nothing be interposed between the world and its literary representation." In all these statements the central thread is mimesis. The naturalist philosophy took root in an age when progressive, rationalist opinion was inclined, broadly, to accept the claims of Saint-Simon, Comte and Durkheim that ultimately sociology and even politics could be understood on a basis no less scientific or "positive" (to quote Comte) than physics and chemistry. Zola drew the simple conclusion that literature, too, could and must achieve the status of a science. "What we need," said Zola, "is detailed reproduction." Everything within the pages of a book must be "lifelike"; everything must march "in step along the great naturalistic road." The incidents portrayed in a novel or play should be "absolutely typical" of both the social cycle and the life cycle. Engels was of the same opinion, calling as he did for "the truthful representation of typical characters under typical circumstances."

But our own epistemology is and has to be rather different. We no longer believe that language, correctly conceived and accurately deployed, constitutes part of a mental superstructure which reflects a socio-economic infrastructure; that concepts derive from reality and are then mirrored faithfully in words; or that it is possible to eliminate the hiatus between the signifier and what he signifies. The partial dualism of language and the world confronts us whether we like it or not, and so, unless we play the ostrich, or simply continue to spin exciting yarns without regard to the shape of the web, we are bound to confront a number of related dialectical processes:

language-perception-language
structure-reality-structure
literature-writer-literature

subject-form-content
action-description-action

These, I admit, are steep slopes. And maybe the writer's fate, on such gradients, will inevitably resemble that of Sisyphus; but, unless one continues to push, to climb, one may as well fall asleep in a library of old books on a hot afternoon (which, I again admit, is pleasant enough).

There exist, in addition, pragmatic considerations. The committed writer joins battle within the broad arena of communications. That is to say, he is no longer merely engaged in a debate with other, competing voices, as in the Oxford Union; he is also placed in the role of the opera singer undergoing an audition to prove that his voice is not only strong but also authentic. The struggle for men's minds and allegiances is today waged within a network of proliferating signals, images and hypnotic affects, a syndrome of calculated distortions and manipulations patronised by vested interests which, almost by definition, are dedicated to the defence of the status quo. False consciousness and systematic cretinization are big business, yielding dividends which outstrip the immediate financial returns. Therefore, we have become increasingly aware that the first confrontation for radicals is not *what* is said, but *how* it is said (since the "what" is so subtly enslaved by the "how"). Compare, for example, a change of substance or subject, on the one hand, with a change of content induced by a shift of form, on the other:

A. Negroes rioted today.
   Whites rioted today.
B. Negroes rioted today.
   Blacks rioted today.

Quite obviously, a literature which aspires to combat false consciousness in its audience must first attempt to excise its own; for example, when I begin, drifting with the Good People, to substitute the word "black" for "Negro", I must admit to myself, and my readers, why. Yet the old naturalist-realist technique, even when used by writers of exemplary socialist vision, was in effect substituting one mystique, one illusion, and one attempt at hidden persuasion for another.

Although commitment is traditionally regarded as antithetical to doubt, I am sure that a literature prepared to probe the ambiguities surrounding social behaviour cannot afford to trade in certainties or to present itself as a precision instrument. If, as novelist or playwright, I attempt to smooth over the artifices and disguises endemic to my art, then the world I depict emerges crippled by innocence. John Berger has put the case very well:

> The new totality which reality represents is by its nature ambiguous. These ambiguities must be allowed in long-term art. The purpose of such art is not to iron out the ambiguities, but to contain and define the totality in which they exist. In this way art becomes an aid to increasing self-consciousness instead of an immediate guide to direct action.

Now it is certainly the case that there have been instances when a novel or play, avowedly didactic and agitational, has exercised a remarkable influence on public opinion, precipitating healthy reforms. Upton Sinclair's *The Jungle* apparently speeded the passage of the pure food laws through Congress (though it is worth noting that both public opinion and Congress were more recalcitrant about legislating socialism, which I take to be the real, normative demand of the novel). Galsworthy's play, *Justice,* is said to have provoked a reform of British strike law, and not long ago a British television play, *Cathy, Come Home,* generated a popular outcry about housing conditions which no documentary could have provoked. But such examples merely remind us that cartoons are not paintings, and that short-term agitational writing provokes a favourable and tangible response only where it appeals to values already widely accepted. The real problem lies elsewhere: to convince people with a highly developed sense of artistic appreciation that political commitment need not impurify art itself. In this respect, serious works of literature are subject to a law of re-entry precisely the opposite of the one governing the safe return of spacecraft through the earth's atmosphere: entering too narrow a funnel at too precise an angle, they burn up. The brief flare brings light only to the already converted. And indeed the flaw in so much committed writing is that it is confirmatory (or celebratory) rather than exploratory, a kind of mass rally wedged between paper covers.

My line of reasoning here forces me to link the concept of

'art' to a certain level of achievement, to a value judgment. If one accepts this premise, one notices that the higher art rarely thrives in a social inferno. The novelists we tend to admire usually take evasive action when the guns are actually firing or —to revert to the point made in the preceding paragraph— when they themselves intend to fire guns on the printed page. Either they side-step immediate actuality by resorting to allegory, utopia, dystopia or an historical setting, or, alternatively, they lay aside fictional invention altogether in favour of direct reportage and didactic exposition. The American writer who reached Hiroshima within days of the bomb was unlikely to write a novel about it. Confronted by Nazism, by a reality so overwhelming and menacing, the German democratic writers turned to history for perspectives and solutions. Both Malraux and Sartre abandoned fiction when they advanced from the speculative politics of theatre to the more urgent and consuming theatre of politics. One also notices that America produced a brilliant galaxy of Negro novels in the years when America had merely a Negro "question" or "problem"; but when, abruptly (or so it seemed), the Negro became the black and threatened to consume the whole social fabric in flame and thunder, then the Negro novelist virtually disappeared, giving way to the black reporter, polemicist and literary agitator. And why? Because for both writer and reader alike, the practice and enjoyment of art, fantasy and imagination are luxuries to the extent that they require a modicum of withdrawal, relaxation and detachment. Presumably, even the men of the Iron Age painted their caves only after dinner; when the wild bull is charging, you don't attempt to capture his likeness on the wall; on the contrary, you shout, "Bull", and that shout is not art. Nevertheless, it is the first seed in the family tree of agit-prop.

We live in an age of radical epistemological doubt. And if we are hesitant about knowing, we must inevitably be hesitant about what we know. The committed realist novelist who blandly conceals that his own work is an artifact, and therefore artificial, will with a crippling innocence "iron out" the ambiguities to which Berger refers. Nor will our disbelief be suspended by the realist whose very didacticism and partisan commitment to a renovated society dynamites his claim to be holding a camera with a flawless lens up to the lives of men. When Lukács speaks of "the timeless rules of epic narration", he gives the game away. The nineteenth-century *Bildungsroman*, which Lukács so admired, offers a certain shape, a chronological, consequential, unfolding shape, to the notion that "no man is an island". However, life itself is not a *Bildungsroman*, any more than it is a sonnet, an elegiac couplet or a stream of consciousness. The lens is merely the view. Neither my life nor yours is punctuated by chapters, paragraphs or semicolons, and it is obvious that a novelist's search for what is socially typical is fairly different from a sociologist's.

One sees why Marxists and radical writers in general have been governed by the naturalist-realist heritage, by Jamesian illusionism, by the literary equivalent of the conjuror's proud boast: "Look, no hands!" Marxism trades in certainties; it proclaims itself a science; it means what it says and it says what it means. Generally, Marxist dialecticians have contrived to ignore the dialectic of language itself, leaving the (ever) declining bourgeoisie to fester in their morbid doubts about words and meanings, about authorial interventions and manipulations. At the same time—until the 1960's brought on a rush of self-awareness, a kind of cultural Treaty of Brest-Litovsk—they resolved the old problem of form and content with equally emphatic simplicity. Content (society) was accorded primacy, and form was regarded as a kind of conveyor belt running from an initial truth to the reader's eye. Admittedly, there have been more (Ernst Fischer, for example) or less (Ralph Fox, for example) sophisticated variations on this theme, but the essential argument remained the same.

Now let me turn my attention for a moment in the opposite direction, towards those who not only argue that art and commitment are incompatible, but make a fetish of art as an absolute *en-soi*, insisting that form alone governs the meaning of a work of literature. This kind of criticism talks of autonomous internal codes, synchronic systems, and structures explicable by a purely interior analysis. Northrop Frye once wrote that "the work of art must be its own object: it cannot be ultimately descriptive of something, and can never be ultimately related to any other system of phenomena, standards, values or final causes." Robbe-Grillet has told us that "content resides in form", and that a true writer "has nothing to say, only a manner of saying it." According to Roland Barthes, "the word [*la parole*] is neither an instrument nor a vehicle, it is a structure." A proper reading of language thus becomes strictly symbolic, and language assumes a notational nature as strict as that of music.

Common sense surely refutes so extreme a view. Certainly the two sentences, "she is here" and "here she is", achieve a shift of meaning by means of a purely structural alteration. But, "there she is" involves a *significative* modification. It seems to me that, during the long argument about form and content, both the dogged realists and the more fashionable structuralists or formalists have confused "content" with "subject" or "theme", thereby forgetting that the content of a book or play is in fact the subject mediating and mediated by the form employed. A writer aware of this triadic process, and honest enough to acknowledge it, will attempt to show how what he writes about affects and is affected by how he writes about it, the result being what he says; or what is said. Such a programme, of course, is equally relevant to the "private" or politically unconcerned type of writer, but in such circles it is more readily adopted than among those legionnaires of the pen who fear that the slightest tremor of literary self-consciousness will blur the message, demoralise the potential militants, and so perpetuate the reign of darkness. However, serious literature should not and cannot, contrary to what Clifford Odets once cockily asserted, shoot like bullets. A typewriter is not any kind of barricade; nor is a theatre. Acceptance of this (perhaps chastening) fact might purge the scene of much superficial posturing and noisy rhetoric.

Which words carry me to a brief consideration of the cultural style now associated with—very loosely defined—the New Left and the Underground (whatever that is!). Obviously this anti-culture provides no solution at all, though it apparently generates a lot of Fun, and though it could be construed as an attempt to marry socio-political commitment with an adventurous approach to artistic form. In the "third theatre" one encounters not only illiteracy but anti-literacy, a distrust of coherence and a concomitant appetite for the fairground swirl of loud sounds and strong sensations, the cult of spontaneity and improvisation (more often than not carefully planned) which really capitulates to the commercial inebriation it affects to fight. A throw-away art will not persuade audiences to reach and see beyond surface kaleidoscopes, to think as well as feel, to judge as well as react. In the productions of, for example, The Living Theatre, I find that sincerity or dedication fails to atone for stereotyped political protest, wild caricature, glibness, simplistic nihilism, raw, uncooked emotionalism, meaningless sexuality, and a cult of violence which shamelessly presents itself as the enemy of violence. Witch-doctors also share the pathetic belief that the enemy can be exposed and so destroyed by mere mimicry and parody. The attempts of such theatre companies to disintegrate the distinction between the cast and the audience is either a charade or a rather nasty form of dishonesty—test, as a member of the audience, the limits of your initiative, and you'll find yourself handcuffed or beaten to death. Behind the cult of manic participation there lurks a distinctly totalitarian mood.

The key, or first principle, of a truly dialectical and critical literature or theatre lies in the principle of alienation (as in the German word *Verfremdung*). This means above all else recognising things for what they are: a play is a play, a performance a performance, just as a novel is a novel. An audience walks in out of the cold, off the street, unrehearsed: it remains an audience. A theatrical event is always a performance, by some for others. Any attempt to integrate or immerse that audience in what follows is merely to vary the old, tired strategy practised by practitioners of the illusionist novel or the 'well-made' play; in the one case, the actors invade the auditorium, in the other case, the spectators are asked to live inside Pinero's stage drawing room as if it were real. Though the style is very different, it would not be pressing a paradox too far to argue that traditional, empathetic realist theatre represents a kind of continual Happening. For what happens? The audience is encouraged to lose itself, its own identity, and therefore its own critical faculty. But the silliest thing about the modern

Underground theatre is its childish desire to have an id without a superego.

This demi-culture falls headlong into the trap presented by the permissive society which, neither an accident of Supreme Court decisions nor a symptom of Rome's waning influence, is precisely the logical field of energies evolved by a highly profit- and consumer-oriented capitalist system. Being free to say *anything,* the writer traps himself by doing so, like an infant offered a big bag of candies; he thereby assumes both the license and the ineffectuality of the court jester or fool. As soon as the artist's role is socially typified as one of scurrilous iconoclasm, no one takes him seriously. He squats on the boulevard making rude gestures at the passers-by; sometimes they drop a penny into his lap and give him an answering wink. "Real life" grinds on all around him, but he is not part of it, though he is probably congratulating himself on his fearless honesty. The day comes when he reads enviously of censorship and even imprisonment imposed on his colleagues in the Popular Democracies; suppression is at least a sign of some respect. Long ago, Marcuse made the point that art tends to win its freedom from the reality principle in proportion to its irrelevance to the reality principle. In the long run, there is one thing that THEY up there fear we might do, en masse: think for ourselves. Art, naturally, is not purely a cerebral or conceptual affair, but all the feeling and emotion involved, all the appeals to beauty, rhythm and subconscious transport, must ultimately converge and coalesce in the notion of criticism. The man who is aware is the ultimate subversive, not in isolation, but in massive fraternity with others who aspire to see things as they are. That may be impossible; we may all, artists and audiences alike, be thrusting up the same slope as Sisyphus; but the motion, the journey, is the only conceivable undertaking.

Yet we cannot begin to see things as they are until we see how we see.

Any mundane historian or sociologist or economist knows that. He supports assertion with evidence: en route to his conclusions, he lays bare his process of deduction. In other words, he shows the works, the engine beneath the polished hood. Why should art be subject to an altogether different law

—pretence, hypnotism, cosmetics and (one has to say it) bad faith? Art is not a deep dark forest of voodoo and black magic inhabited by faith healers. It might be tedious to publish our novels complete with the original notes, deletions and insertions, but that in a sense is what we have to do if the product is to be understood as a process, the "finished" work as simply a moment, more or less arbitary, in which the motion is frozen, offered, retailed.

I am well aware that what I am proposing cannot really be done. When the Brechtian actor declares, "Look, I'm only an actor, I'm only pretending to play Galileo", or when the novelist inserts a footnote to the effect that the chapter originally had a different conclusion, when such "confessions" are made we continue to reside within the orbit of cunning and artifice. Similarly, the partial dualism of words and things, of literary structures and the reality they try to portray, cannot be eradicated, but they can indeed be depicted both as an active space and as a span of tension. The writer adopting the dialectical approach will certainly renounce all claims to mimesis, acknowledging his ambivalent role as both the master and servant of the medium in which he works. And if, as is inevitable, the writer cannot completely jettison the weapons of mimesis and empathy, if the invitation to suspend disbelief must occasionally be extended to the reader, then these pretences are adopted only to be unmasked.

Unfortunately, any politically committed writer who subscribes to any of the self-scrutinising techniques associated—broadly—with the modernist movement must undertake the onerous task of liberating those techniques from the pessimistic and obscurantist attitudes towards the human condition which have been so characteristic of modernist writing and theatre. I mean the derisive dismissal of all knowledge as mere subjectivity, the view of history as chaotic and arbitrary, a cycle of animal spasms. According to this *Weltanschauung,* with its great debt to the philosophers of the late nineteenth-century anti-Enlightenment, man is never more free than a slave crawling east along the deck of a boat travelling west. Alienation is explained as strictly ontological, as rooted in the human condition, and therefore as incurable. Ever since the revolutions of 1848 and the Paris Commune of 1871, an influential group within the artistic avant-garde has turned its fastidious back on the popular masses, at best a passive herd, at worst a vile, iconoclastic mob of philistines. Chronological time has been dissolved and with it the concept of personal identity. Who am I?—"*Je est un autre.*" With pronounced *Schadenfreude,* this elite has celebrated the helplessness of man.

As a result, we are bound to revere the efforts of those writers who have tried to marry genuine social commitment with a genuinely modern approach to writing. Yet their fate has not been encouraging: the brilliant Russian avant-garde of the post-Revolutionary years was soon shown the door by a regime devoted to literary realism; the French surrealists were hounded out of the Communist Party, Mayakovsky committed suicide, and Brecht survived only by cunning, compromise and good luck.

The techniques employed by Brecht in his pursuit of a genuinely dialectical theatre, together with the theories expounded in his notebooks, are by now so well known that it would be superfluous to recapitulate them here. Nevertheless, one must emphasise that Brecht remains for the committed playwright a giant of inspiration in whose shadows we can comfortably linger. One must also emphasise a point picked up by Brecht—that a rupture with the conventions of nineteenth-century realism, far from amounting to a defiance of timeless laws of art, signifies instead a return to honoured traditions of honest self-awareness. The medieval Corpus Christi cycle, though models of passionate commitment, scorned total illusion and mimesis. The actors portrayed not the complete character of God (admittedly some task), but merely a selection of His actions. No actor attempted to perform the entire role of any single character—a blow to mimesis. In the streets and open spaces of the medieval town, the spectators crowded round to witness a *performance,* and no attempt was made to hypnotise them into a trance of absolute empathy. And if we move a little closer in time, we find that Shakespeare, Calderón, and other playwrights of the early modern age relished a theatrical self-consciousness which was rejected as naive or clumsy in the age of Ibsen. Listen to Shakespeare's Cleopatra:

and I shall see
Some squeaking Cleopatra boy my greatness
I' th' posture of a whore.

Let us look briefly at Genet, who wanted *The Maids* to be portrayed by male actors, this portrayal to be an ostensible metaphor for what is portrayed. In Genet's work, the essential alienation is conveyed by and through the ritual, symbolic and allegorical resources of the theatre. The world, the writer, his beliefs, dreams and art, the play itself, are all wrapped round each other; and yet Genet's plays are authentically political, obsessed as they are with a fundamental theme, the relationship of the rulers to the ruled. The two maids, the clients of the brothel in *The Balcony,* the blacks in *The Blacks*, all *perform,* acting out their lives in a conscious acknowledgment of the circumstance of their own incarnation, which is theatre. Thus they are both the subject and the object of art; art comes back at them, helping them (not always conclusively) to bridge the gap between their predicament and their aspirations.

In *The Blacks,* Genet sets up two complementary structures: (a) "actors" and "audience" *within The Blacks;* (b) actors and audience *of The Blacks.* A shift in the racial composition of any one of these four elements automatically generates a modification of total meaning for the real audience. Genet, therefore, provides us not only with multiple reinsurance against illusion and empathy, but also with a delicate commentary on the interplay of art and reality, on how content emerges from the dialogue between subject and form. He uses myth, symbol, ritual and allegory to delineate the levels of consciousness and political aspiration operating in the world outside the theatre. In a less elaborate manner, Brecht had already achieved the same effect in *Arturo Ui*, a play which achieves its political impact by a central device of displacement (the Chicago waterfront, not Berlin), in itself an important form of alienation, whether realised in terms of time *(We, Brave New World, 1984)* or place *(Penguin Island, Animal Farm).* Brecht does not attempt to mirror the real Hitler; instead he offers us a theatrical image as a means of persuading us to get away from Hitler in order to see him the more clearly. However, it should be noted that displacement is only one contributing element to dialectical writing or theatre, and can

276   1974

be somewhat neutralised—as in some of the novels mentioned above—by the author's insistence that we fully empathise with the artificial scenario he has created.

In this context I would like to mention one other play, Barbara Garson's *MacBird!*, which, largely because it attracted so much attention at the time of its first production, is now no doubt dismissed as an ephemeral period-piece. But it is worth remembering. Garson offered, and then juxtaposed, two myths: the mode of Shakespearian political sentiment and the mode of American machine politics. Cutting across both was the cult of hero and villain. From the moment that a middle-aged man wearing a business suit and carrying a sword declared, "Oh for a fireless muse, that could descend ... ", Garson sustained a truly penetrating alienation-effect. However passionate the author's rejection of the Vietnam war, American imperialism, racism and cynical political maneuver, she attained a higher level of political consciousness by divorcing the chosen subject from its most obvious form of expression, thereby achieving a content, a critical awareness, capable of raising the audience's general political sensibility.

MacBird! is more than just an amusing satire, and so indeed is Brecht's *A Man's a Man*. Both make the central "as if" of artistic representation a focal point of the representation. (Picasso draws a distorted nose to persuade us to see what real noses look like.) This fond caressing of the "as if" is also crucial to the work of such great exponents of political mime as Chaplin and Fialka, who make a deliberately extended theatricality into an aid to vision, a means of seeing rather than just looking. The adult puppet theatre carries the same potential. For children, puppets pose the (unconscious) question: how close can art approach to life? For adults the question is, or should be, reversed: how close does life approach to a mocking art? In the Japanese Bunraku theatre—a form with immense political potential—the puppeteers, much larger than their puppets, make no attempt to conceal themselves. Thus, the illusion (the actions of the puppets), and the counter-illusion (the visible presence of the puppeteers) both foster and explode empathy in a continual interaction. The effect is reinforced by the Joruri singer, highly emotional in his tone, pitch and tempo, yet alienating on account of his physical detachment from the action, his aloof role as chorus. I should add that what little I have been able to see of the New York Bread and Puppet Theatre confirmed my belief in the political potential of this kind of theatre.

I turn now to the question of the novel. Needless to emphasise, I regard the illusionist manicure so dear to Henry James as both dishonest and unsustainable. (Unsustainable if only because one reads on the second page of "Washington Square", "It will be seen that I am describing a clever man . . ." Later one is pulled up short by this: "I doubt, however, whether Catherine was irritated, though she broke into a vehement protest." The dangerous word here is not "I", since the authorial presence can claim omniscience and so admit its existence, but the "doubt", which makes us sceptical about all the certainties hitherto offered.) In fact, the naturalist and realist novelists have always slipped on the banana skins presented by the desire to supply information, or to convey a heavier message than the narrative itself can bear. Dreiser, for example, was capable of hurling his reader right out of nineteenth-century Philadelphia with some such observation as, "the telephone had not yet been invented." Upton Sinclair and Louis Aragon, groaning to discharge The Message, were apt to abandon the illusionist mode in the last chapter, ushering in the Coming Day by means of long climactic sermons. Alternatively, when Richard Wright, in *Native Son,* wished to impart his own thoughts without revealing his own authorial presence, he was compelled to stuff those same thoughts into the head of simple Bigger Thomas, and then to excuse the whole trick improbably with the explanation, "In a sullen way Bigger was conscious of this."

It is curious, looking back from the prevailing realist assumptions, to recall that *Don Quixote,* widely regarded as the foundation stone of the modern novel, positively celebrates its own nature as a contrivance. "Notice that this second part of *Don Quixote,* which I place before you, is cut by the same craftsmen from the same cloth as the first . . . " Where Richard Wright tries to hide the authorial voice under a stone, Cervantes mocks any such attempt: "When the translator of this history comes to write this fifth chapter, he declares that he considers it apocryphal, because in it Sancho's style is much superior to what one would expect of his limited understanding . . . '' Brecht pointed out that epic structures convey alienation effects more easily than dramatic ones. In *Don Quixote,* there is certainly a discernible sequence of events, one thing leading to another, but the structure is sufficiently episodic to permit a reshuffling of the chapters. Most important, Cervantes emphasised that literature to a large extent creates what it expresses. In the second part of the novel, the knight learns that he is *already* the subject of a book by Cide Hamete Benegali! How could this be true, he wonders, if the blood of his slain enemies was scarcely dry on his sword blade? Well, if it is so, he will henceforward have to justify and exceed his own literary image.

Cervantes turned the assumptions of the Renaissance upside down, just as we, in a sense, have to repudiate the cultural assumptions of the age of Darwin. In Cervantes' work, writing refuses to posture as the mirror-image of a coherent world, and words do not pretend to be immanent to things. He appreciated that the relationship of words to things must be understood as a code of signs and analogies. What at first sight appeared to be a case of madness (the knight's loss of contact with reality) is ultimately interpreted analogically in terms of literature's own internal contradictions. On his death bed, Don Quixote repents of having given the author the occasion to publish ''so many gross absurdities.'' *Don Quixote* was published in 1604. One hundred and fifty years later, Sterne still wrote under its shadow, rejecting the hidden god and insisting on the nature of art as artifice. But with Fielding we find a writer with a foot in two centuries, gradually surrendering authorial honesty to the growing demand of the bourgeoisie for a literature which would reflect its own comfortable certainties.

Paradoxically, the anti-bourgeois socialist movement altered the certainties but retained the demand for comfort. The rebellion in our own century has, unfortunately, been spearheaded not by politically committed novelists (though Zamyatin provided an isolated inspiration) but, rather, by essentially ''private'' writers such as Gide, Moravia and Butor. In short, the novel lacks its Mayakovsky or Brecht. Nevertheless, most readers can, I expect, think of one or two talented novelists who, if not yet figures of universal stature, have successfully adopted a dialectical approach to creative writing, thereby fostering the sense of freedom through a freeing of the senses.* Brecht remarked: "What the spectator, anyway the experienced spectator, enjoys about art is the making of art, the active creative element." Brecht perhaps mistook the wish for the reality, and the statement, in any case, does not cover the whole experience. But the direction is right. As writers, particularly as committed ones, we can help to coax those "experienced spectators" (and perhaps swell their number) towards the attitude of expecting and demanding greater honesty of the author. To do this, we must cease to hurl at them messages as unequivocal as a gust of wind in a language as self-assured as machine-gun fire. A good novel or play should not be, and cannot be, merely an extended slogan.

---

*Dos Passos' *USA* constitutes a half-buried metropolis worth limitless excavation. Of more recent fiction, I would particularly draw attention to Alberto Moravia's *The Lie*, the work of Günter Grass and Michel Butor, and John Fowles's *The French Lieutenant's Woman* (although the orientation of these writers is not ostensibly political); to Uwe Johnson's *Two Views* and Mailer's *Why Are We in Vietnam?*; to passages or tendencies within Sol Yurick's *The Bag* and E. L. Doctorow's *The Book of Daniel*; and, perhaps most stimulating of all, to John Berger's recent novel, *G*.

ELWOOD H. SMITH. (*TQ* #29)

Agnes Denes

Human dust

He was an artist. He died of a heart attack. He was born fifty years ago, which means he lived half a century, or appr. ⅔ of his expected life span. His father was a tailor and his mother a housewife. He had 4 brothers and 1 sister. He was in love 3 times, married once, fathered 2 human beings, thus beginning a chain of 60 or more human beings added to the world population within 4 generations (counting up to 2000 A.D.). Taking genetic and environmental factors into consideration, 4 of these will be doctors, 2 will write, 34 will bear children, 6 will be engineers or teachers, 1 will have an unusual talent, 1 will be a politician, 1 will collect garbage, 8 will be unskilled laborers, 1 will go to jail and 2 are uncertain. During his lifetime he visited 18 countries and spoke 2 languages. He traveled 55,000 miles not including commuting and read 4,100 books. He attended college for one year. His aspirations were to be a great writer or a great artist. He wrote about ½ million words and painted 48 paintings, all told. In his lifetime he earned $160,000.00, was fired three times and held 17 positions after maturity. He was unhappy and lonely more often than not, achieved 1/10,000 of his dreams, managed to get his opinions across 184 times and was misunderstood 3,800 times when it mattered. He believed in a god, was fairly religious at the beginning and toward the end of his life and could be considered superstitious. During his lifetime he consumed 4,800 lbs. of bread, 3,000 gallons of water, 140 gallons of wine and 360 quarts of whiskey. He ate 56,000 meals, slept 146,850 hours and moved his bowels 18,548 times. He was sick 23 times, caught 31 colds, pneumonia once, had 7 virus infections and broke his leg falling off a chair while hanging one of his paintings. He served in the marines, was shot at several times but never wounded. He had relations with 27 women in his lifetime and ejaculated 3,858 times. He voted in 24 elections and knew his opinions changed nothing. He was not a popular man—he had honest but uneven beliefs. His work was good but not great, and the last 10 years of his life he resigned himself to this fact. He had 4 friends at various times in his life and was loved by 17 people, including his parents. He was liked by 312. His brain contained 10^{10} neurons and it received 10^9 electrical impulses from his own sense organs, to each of which he responded. He smoked 210,000 cigarettes and tried drugs twice. 34 people remembered him or spoke of him after his death and his remains shown here represent $1/85$ of his entire body.

AGNES DENES. (*TQ* #32)

Max Apple: Heart attack

My sickness bothers me, though I persist in denying it. It is
indigestion I think and eat no onions; gout and I order no liver
or goose. The possibility of nervous exhaustion keeps me abed
for three days, breathing deeply. I do yoga for anxiety. But, finally,
here I am amid magazines awaiting, naked to the waist, cough
at the balls, needle in the vein. From my viral pneumonia days,
I remember his Sheaffers desk set and the 14kt gold point. It
writes prescriptions without a scratch. In the time of the bad
sunburn my damaged eyes scanned the walls reading degrees and
being jealous of the good-looking woman, the three boys, the
weeping willow in the back yard.

   I have a choice of *Sports Illustrated, Time, Boy's World,* others.
As if by design, I choose the free pamphlet on the wall. Fleisch-
mann's Margarine gives me some straight talk about cholesterol.
I remember the ten thousand eggs of my youth, those miracles
of protein that have perhaps made my interior an artgum eraser.
Two over easy in the morning, a hard one every night, poached,
sometimes eviscerated by mayonnaise. In many ways I have
been an egg man. The pamphlet shows my heart, a small pump
the size of my fist. I make a fist and stare at knuckles, white as
the eggshells I wish I had eaten instead. Where did I learn that
your penis is the size of your middle finger plus the distance that
finger can reach down your arm. Mine cannot make it to the
wrist. My heart too must be a pea in this flimsy, hairless chest.

   From a door marked PRIVATE a nurse, all in white, comes to
me. She sits very close on the couch and looks down at my
pamphlet. She takes my damp hand in hers and tickles my palm.

Her soft lips against my ear whisper musically, "Every cloud has a silver lining. . . ."

"But arteries," I respond, "my arteries are caked with the mistakes of my youth."

She points to the pamphlet. "Arteries should be lined only with their moist little selves. Be good to your arteries, be kind to your heart. It's the only one you'll ever have." She puts her tongue in my ear, and one arm reaches under my shirt. She sings, "A fella needs a girl. . . ."

"I need a doctor . . . my arteries."

She points again to the pamphlet and reads, "Arteries, though similar to, are more important than girls in several ways. Look at this one pink and flexible as a Speidel band. Over there threatens cholesterol, dark as motor oil, thick as birthday cake. Cholesterol is the bully of the body. It picks on blood, good honest blood who bothers no one and goes happily between the races, creeds, and colors."

"I have pains," I tell her, "pains in my chest and my tongue feels fat and moss grows in my joints."

She unbuttons my shirt slowly. Her long cool fingers cup me as if I were all breasts. Her clever right hand is at my back counting vertebrae. She takes off the stiff nurse's cap and nuzzles my solar plexus. Into my middle she hums, "I'm as corny as Kansas in August . . ." The vibrations go deep. She responds to me. "There," I gasp, "right there." I am overcome as if by Valium. As I moan she moves me down on the cracking vinyl couch. Her lips, teeth, and tongue fire between my ribs. She hums Muzak and the room spins until I sight the pamphlet clinging to a bobby pin. In my ecstasy, I see the diagram of cholesterol, in peaks and valleys, nipping at blood which makes its way, like a hero, through the narrow places.

When she lets me up, I am bruised but feeling wonderful. Her lips are colorless from the pressure she has exerted upon me. I start to take off my trousers. She stays my hand at the belt buckle, kisses me long. "The oath," she whispers.

"I'm cured," I say. "Forget him. Forget the urine and the blood. Look." I beat my chest like Tarzan, I spit across the room into a tiny bronze ashtray.

"I'll pack," she says. She goes into PRIVATE while I pick out a few *Reader's Digests* for the road, *Today's Health* for the bathroom. She returns carrying a centrifuge and a rack of test tubes.

We embrace, then I bend to help with her things.

"Don't be cruel," she whispers, "to a heart that's true . . ."

On the way out we throw a kiss to the pharmacist and my blood slips through.

WILLIAM E. BIDERBOST. (*TQ* #33)

David Wagoner: The return of Icarus

He showed up decades later, crook-necked and hip-sprung,
Not looking for work but cadging food and wine as artfully
As a king, while our dogs barked themselves inside out
At the sight of his hump and a whiff of his goatskin.

We told him Daedalus was dead, worn out with honors
(Some of them fabulous), but especially for making
Wings for the two of them and getting them off the ground.
He said he remembered that time, but being too young a mooncalf,

He hadn't cared about those labyrinthine double-dealings
Except for the scary parts, the snorting and bellowing.
He'd simply let the wax be smeared over his arms
And suffered handfuls of half-stuck secondhand chicken feathers

And flapped and flapped, getting the heft of them, and taken
Off (to both their amazements), listening for his father's
Endless, garbled, and finally inaudible instructions
From further and further below, and then swooping

And banking and trying to hover without a tail and stalling
While the old man, a slow learner, got the hang of it.
At last, with the weight of his years and his genius,
Daedalus thrashed aloft and was gawkily airborne.

And they went zigzagging crosswind and downwind over the water,
Half-baked by the sirocco, with Daedalus explaining
Everything now: which way was up, how to keep your mouth
Shut for the purpose of breathing and listening,

How to fly low (having no choice himself) in case of Harpies,
And how to keep Helios beaming at a comfortable distance
By going no higher than the absolute dangling minimum
To avoid kicking Poseidon, the old salt, square in the froth.

1976

But Icarus saw the wax at his skinny quill-tips sagging,
And he couldn't get a word in edgewise or otherwise,
So he strained even higher, searching for ships or landfalls
While he still had time to enjoy his share of the view,

And in the bright, high-spirited silence, he took comfort
From his father's lack of advice, and Helios turned
Cool, not hot as Icarus rose, joining a wedge of geese
For an embarrassing, exhilarating moment northward,

And then grew cold till the wax turned brittle as marble,
Stiffening his elbows and suddenly breaking
Away, leaving him wingless, clawing at nothing, then falling
Headfirst with a panoramic, panchromatic vista

Of the indifferent sun, the indifferent ocean, and a familiar
Father passing sideways, still chugging and flailing away
With rows of eagle feathers. When Icarus hit the water,
He took its salt as deeply as his own.

He didn't tell us how he'd paddled ashore or where
He'd been keeping himself or what in the world he'd been doing
For a living, yet he didn't seem bitter. "Too bad
You weren't around," we said, "there'd have been something in it

For you, probably—an apartment straddling an aqueduct,
Orchards, invitations, hecatombs of women."
"No hard feelings," he said. "Wings weren't *my* idea."
And he told odd crooked stories to children for hours

About what lived under water, what lived under the earth,
And what still lived in the air, and why. A few days later
He slouched off on his game leg and didn't come back.
He didn't steal any chickens or girls' hearts

Or ask after his father's grave or his father's money
Or even kick the dogs. But he showed us calluses
Thicker than hooves on his soles and palms, and told us
That's how he'd stay in touch, keeping his feet on the ground.

With Uncle Sam at Burning Tree

Robert Coover

I was sitting on the floor of my inner office, surrounded by every
scrap of information I could find on the Rosenberg case, feeling
scruffy and tired, dejected, lost in a surfeit of detail, and further
from a final position on the issue than ever, when the bell on my
clock rang twice for a quorum call. It was late, goddamn late. I
thought Lyndon Johnson had long since given up. I desperately
wanted to get rid of this atom spy affair and go home. If I left
the damned thing now, I'd just have to come back, and then where
would it end? Why the devil had Uncle Sam got me into this silly
business? Just to convince me of the enormity of their crime?
But I was already convinced. How many Americans had died
and would die because of what they had done? Would the Reds
have dared invade South Korea, rape Czechoslovakia, support the
Vietminh and Malayan guerrillas, suppress the freedom-hungry
East German workers if the Rosenbergs had not given them the
bomb? We were headed, truly, into a new Era of Peace after
World War II, our possession of the ultimate weapon and our
traditional American gift for self-sacrifice would have ensured that—
and we might even have helped our friend Chiang return to the
Chinese mainland where he belonged, loosened things up a little
inside Russia to boot—but the Rosenbergs upset all that. When
the Russians tested their first A-bomb in 1949, I was one of
the first to hit at Truman's failure to act against Red spies in the
United States. "I feel the American people are entitled to know the
facts about the espionage ring which was responsible for turning
over information on the atom bomb to agents of the Russian
government," I'd said then, even though no one knew at the time

whether such a spy ring existed or not. It was just a hunch I'd had, based on the conviction that Communist science was too mired in ideology ever to keep up with the Free World, and as it turned out, I'd been right. Of course, I admit, I'd got a little hint from J. Edgar Hoover, who was fast becoming a useful pal of mine, and Father Cronin had pirated some pretty sinister-looking material out of the FBI files for me, but none of it really hung together to make a convincing case, and I don't think Edgar himself knew very much at the time either. And then when they got Fuchs in England in 1950, I called for a full congressional investigation of atomic espionage to find out who might have worked with Fuchs in this country. I moved quickly, caught most congressmen napping, got most of the headlines. And deserved them. No, Dick Nixon knew what was going on, all right, and was quick to say so; that's how I beat that fancy-pants movie star for senator that year, and even though finally I didn't have all that much to do with the Rosenberg case itself, I always felt that—indirectly anyway— it was my baby.

All the more so when you considered that it was my successful pursuit of Alger Hiss which had given courage and incentive to the entire nation, made communism a real issue, restored the dignity and prestige of HUAC and the Early Warning Sentinels, changed the very course of America and the Free World, and ultimately had made these electrocutions possible. In Whittaker Chambers' new best-seller, *Witness,* he wrote: "On a scale personal enough to be felt by all, but big enough to be symbolic, the two irreconcilable faiths of our time—Communism and Freedom—came to grips in the persons of two conscious and resolute men. . . . Both knew, almost from the beginning, that the Great Case could end only in the destruction of one or both of the contending figures, just as the history of our times . . . can end only in the destruction of one or both of the contending forces!" And hadn't I been the catalyst that gave Whittaker and the Free World victory? I'll never forget the day that Hiss, beaten, walked over to the old davenport in Room 1400 of the Commodore Hotel in New York to examine Chambers' molars: "Would you mind opening your mouth wider? I said, would you open your mouth!" What pathos! If these two were indeed, as Whittaker had so brilliantly and profoundly suggested, the momentary Incarnations of the contending forces of the universe, there was something deeply ironic about the Force of Darkness and Evil poking petulantly but almost tearfully among the dental ruins in the soft but firm jowls of the

Force of Goodness and Light. I think he hoped that Whittaker would bite him so that he could cry from pain rather than humiliation. I finally had to ask him, "Excuse me, before we leave the teeth, Mr. Hiss, do you feel that you, uh, would have to have the dentist tell you just what he did to the teeth before you could tell anything about this man?" From that moment on, Hiss was finished; like that snake that eats its own tail, he just couldn't keep his foot out of his mouth after that. It was maybe the most fun I ever had in politics, outside of elections, and when it was over, I felt like one chosen. Like Whittaker said: "I do not know any way to explain why God's grace touches a man who seems unworthy of it. But neither do I know any other way to explain how a man like myself . . . could prevail so far against the powers of the world arrayed almost solidly against him, to destroy him and defeat his truth." Which was even more true of me, who unlike Chambers must struggle for a lifetime. Not that I'm unworthy. No, that's just it, the powers arrayed against the good man are formidable and indefatigable, there are few who can stay the course. Defeat and disappointment dog every footstep. If old Hiss hadn't been a liar, for example—and an eager one at that!—I might have been destroyed before I could ever get started. So thank **God** at least for that: it gave me the power to prevail, it was a milestone in human history, and marked me once and for all as the greatest of the Early Warning Sentinels.

In short, my conscience was clean—so why had Uncle Sam brought this Rosenberg case up, especially so late in the ball game? Of course, he'd only mentioned it in passing while washing his balls on the seventh tee, but I had long since learned that with Uncle Sam nothing was mere happenstance, you had to listen to him with every hole in your body. The case itself seemed cut and dried: a routine FBI investigation, a sequence of confessions from Fuchs to Gold to Greenglass, leading directly to Julius and Ethel Rosenberg. They denied all accusations, but then so did Hiss—in fact, their reactions were very similar, very high and mighty, very hurt and offended. And they had a much more telling witness against them than a fat spooky slob like Whittaker Chambers. David Greenglass was also something of a fat slob, true, and a bit spooky as well, but he was more than that: he was also Ethel's own brother. His story of his recruitment by Julie and Ethel, how he drew up the lens mold sketches and lists of personnel, passed them on to Harry Gold, how he discussed these things with the Rosenbergs, with little details of family life mixed in, how Julie tried to help him escape—it was all very convincing. The only question remaining really was, Who else was in the spy ring besides the Rosenbergs, Greenglasses, Gold, and the Russian Yakovlev? Uncle Sam had wanted maximum pressure to be applied to the Rosenbergs to get them to talk, which was the reason Judge Kaufman had given them the death penalty, with a hint that confessions might soften his heart. He'd come to Washington before passing sentence to talk with Attorney General McGrath, and apparently those were the instructions he'd got. There had been a lot of evidence brought forward over the past two years to support some of the Rosenbergs' minor testimony and try to destroy David's credibility as a witness and, having studied the case, I could perceive a lot of backstage scene-rigging and testimony-shaping by the prosecuting team that deprived the courtroom performances of some of their authenticity and power, but there was no shaking off the general conviction: the Rosenbergs were as guilty as hell. So why—?

The "Yeas and Nays" bell rang. I leaped to my feet, hauled on my jacket, and dashed out the door. I took the subway car over to the Capitol, arriving breathlessly in the middle of the roll call. "Jesus, Dick, where the goddamn hell ya been?" whined Knowland through clenched teeth. I rushed forward to relieve Purtell and count the vote: it was another tie, this time 41 to 41. Once again I cast the tie-breaker, but then into the Chamber came Dennis Chavez, Democrat from New Mexico: "Mr. President, ah, due to unavoidable circumstances . . ." That did it. All this effort for nothing, I thought. I felt weak from the run over, sweaty—I realized I'd forgotten to have lunch; mustn't let supper go by, I could make myself sick. A. Willis Robertson, yellow dog Democrat from Virginia, announced flatly, almost sadly, that he wished to speak for three minutes on the dubious merits of the issue, and then he would call for a vote on the conference report and have it simply voted up, eh, or down . . . that is, unless the distinguished Senator from California wished to postpone a vote on the report until 3 P.M. on Monday, as the Democrats had originally requested.

I watched the collapse set in on Knowland's big florid face, it was like an old fortress turning to putty. Ah shit, I could hear him console himself, it's time to go have a fucking drink. He rose slowly, heavily, like a tired old walrus, and made one last stand: all right, goddamn it, not till Monday then—but 2 P.M., not 3 P.M. Knowland probably thought the Democrats would let him have that point to save his pride, but he was wrong. A prolonged argument ensued. I sighed impatiently. I appreciated Knowland's plight, but I was growing weary of all the pettifogging bloviating. I wanted to get back to my office and get some of my thoughts down on index cards before I forgot them—not just about the Rosenbergs and their goddamn fourteenth wedding anniversary, either. I remembered that I'd had an important thought about the 1954 campaign tactics that had already slipped my mind, and another about the Dark Ages. Monday afternoon, whatever the hour, seemed light years away. And the mess: above all, I had to clean up that goddamned mess! I like a clean room. My desk is always clean. You can't let your mind get cluttered. I believe that you have to live like a Spartan, spare and clean, be at your best at all times, be physically and mentally disciplined to make decisions in a balanced way, and people who have messes around them all the time also have messy minds. I have a note to myself somewhere on the subject. But right now, I knew, my office was a disaster area, the Rosenberg letters strewn everywhere, the trial transcripts, secret FBI reports, my notes, books on the floor—if anybody who knew me well should see it, they'd think old Dick Nixon was losing his mind. Or else that somebody hostile to me, malicious, vindictive, had got in while I was out. As I watched Knowland crashing to complete defeat, I remembered Uncle Sam had asked me about Julius' talmudic code name—it was Jonah, and that was how I felt right now: trapped and drowning in the goddamn whale's belly! Had Uncle Sam foreseen all these consonances? Hell, what did he *not* foresee, being Uncle Sam? And then, as I banged the ivory gavel down, terminating the exercise and giving the Democrats their victory, it suddenly occurred to me that . . . ivory was the traditional gift for fourteenth wedding anniversaries!

I took the elevator down to the subway, jammed in with others on their way to their offices and home, but once below I decided against riding the subway car—it was crowded and I saw I might have to sit facing the rear of the car, something I always hated to do. It even made me motion-sick sometimes, as short a ride as it was. Also, they were squeezing as many as sixteen to eighteen on the damned thing, and I hated to sit that close to anybody, especially perspiring as I was now, so I set out on foot on the walkway beside the monorail. It was windy down here, it was always windy in this tunnel, but it seemed windier than usual today, threatening, almost as bad as it was out at Burning Tree Sunday. The Burning Tree Golf Club was also known on Capitol

Hill as the Smoldering Stump, but I now thought of it as the Burning Bush, because it was there, during the past few months, where Uncle Sam had most often dropped his mask and talked with me directly about such things as statecraft and incarnation theory, rules for the Community of God, the meaning of the sacred in modern society and the source of the Phantom's magical strength, the uses of rhetoric and ritual, and the hierology of free enterprise, football, revival meetings, five-card stud, motion pictures, war, and the sales pitch. And it was there last Sunday, in the comparative seclusion of the seventh tee, that he slipped out of his duffer's disguise, hit a hole in one, and, on the way over to rinse off his balls, asked me what I thought about the Rosenberg case.

In the aftershock of Uncle Sam's transmutation, it is difficult even to hear a question, much less to grasp or answer it. One is struck by a kind of inner thunder, a loss not so much of vision as of the coordinates of vision, and a loosening of all the limbs as though in sympathy with the dissolution of the features of Uncle Sam's current Incarnation. I say he went over to rinse off his balls and asked me about the Rosenbergs—but perhaps he had asked me long before, while watching his drive arc distantly toward the flag on the sixth green, for example, or even during the backswing, somewhere in that timeless era between the first snap and crackle of metamorphosis, Ike's blue eyes flashing me a glance full of fear and trembling as the moment grew in him, and my own slow recovery from the awesome dazzle of this miraculous transubstantiation. My senses only began to pull together and function again, as it happened, while watching his large pale freckled hands plucking the little white balls, gleaming wet, out of the suds and popping them into the gray folds of the towel; at that moment it came to me that Uncle Sam, freshly shazammed out of the fretful old general, had just whipped out a five-iron, smacked the ball four hundred yards to the green, vacated the tee like a priest his altar, and somewhere along the way, asked me my opinion on the atom spies.

I realized he was putting me on the spot, testing me, and I didn't know quite what to answer. Did it have something to do with Korea? Stalin? My Checkers speech? American jurisprudence? Alger Hiss? I raked my mind for some clue to his drift. He was leaning against a bench, tossing the shiny white balls up in the air, juggling them two, three, seven . . . thirteen at a time. His white cuffs flashed in the sunlight like signal flags. Of course, I expected to be tested like this, expected it and welcomed it, knew it to be part of the sacred life, something Uncle Sam had to do to protect his powers. And I trusted him—he'd never used kid gloves on me, but he'd never been unkind to me either, I was pretty sure he liked me—I trusted him and was eager to please him. Maybe he only wants to be reassured, I thought.

I was glad about the way the case turned out, of course, but he knew this already. After all, having gone out on a limb about it back in '49, I couldn't help being flattered when J. Edgar Hoover actually found a spy ring and busted it. But past that, I had to admit, I didn't know too much about the case. The trouble was, by the time it came up in '51, I had begun to catch glimpses of Uncle Sam's blue coattails and was pretty busy chasing them, and so, except for a glance at the odd headline and a few peculiar vibrations of guilt and intimacy I had felt for being of the same generation as the principals, I had pretty much stayed out of Hoover's and Irving Saypol's way. Oh, I knew well enough what the Big Issue was, my whole political career had been built on it. And I knew of course that the Rosenbergs were part of it, an important part: Edgar had called it "the crime of the century," and I'd gone along with that, even if I did think he should have given equal billing to the perjury of Alger Hiss. And even though I didn't follow the details—about all I knew for sure was that Fuchs had led the FBI to his American courier Harry Gold who had led them to Ethel Rosenberg's brother David Greenglass who subsequently had turned state's evidence against the Rosenbergs (Morton Sobell fitted in there somewhere—maybe he was the one who tore the Jello box)—I did admire Irving Saypol's dynamic, intransigently hostile prosecution of the case, applauded the breadth of Judge Kaufman's vision and courage, and was properly relieved when the Supreme Court, still dangerously New Deal-tainted, refused to review the case. On the other hand, let me say—and I don't mind being controversial on this subject—I was a little sorry that two people, a father and mother of two little boys, had to die. I'm always sorry when people have to die, my mother taught me this. Especially women and children. But how much of the world's sadness can any one man handle, no matter how sensitive he is? I had troubles of my own, and I knew that Uncle Sam would do what was right and necessary; just stay on the reservation, keep the faith, do your own job well, get your rhetoric ready, and don't ask too many irrelevant questions: that seemed the best policy.

But maybe it was not. Maybe I had not done enough. I fussed

about, choosing a ball for teeing up, worried about this. Everything was remarkably green, the sky was deep blue, the balls a blinding white; my senses were still on edge from the transmutation. Uncle Sam was now balancing a putter on his sharp thin nose while juggling the golf balls. The empty tee awaited me: the novice called upon to show what he knows. I'd built my reputation on the thoroughness with which I'd pursued the Hiss case, after all, and maybe I'd gone soft on this one, lost some of my fabled diligence and so part of my image as well, perhaps this was the thrust of Uncle Sam's question now. He somehow had his old plug hat up on top of the putter and was twirling it around. His playfulness could be deceptive. I wasn't sure whether or not the actual conspiracy charge had been proven, but let's be frank about it, it was just a technicality anyway—mainly because of the statute of limitation, I supposed, and the fact that in these espionage cases there were rarely two witnesses to anything. They were being tried in fact for treason, never mind what the Constitution might say, which was anyway written a long time ago—and on that charge J. Edgar Hoover's word was as good as a conviction.

"Well," I said finally, poking around bravely in my golf bag, "well, I believe they're, uh, probably guilty."

Uncle Sam blinked in amazement, gathering in the balls with one big hand, catching the putter and hat as they fell with the other. *"Guilty!"* he roared, his chin whiskers bristling. I realized, glancing away, pretending to study the distant green, that Abraham Lincoln, whom I'd always admired, was probably the most terrifying man of his age. "Well, hell, *yes,* they're guilty!"

I knew by his reaction I must be miles off the mark, but my answer still made sense to me and I resented what seemed like some kind of entrapment. Instinctively, I counterattacked: "Well, naturally I haven't had ample opportunity to study the transcripts carefully, but I, uh, from what I've seen of them, the case has not been proven—"

"The case!" he snorted incredulously. "Proven! Gawdamighty, you do take the rag off the bush, boy!"

I stared miserably into my golf bag while he railed at me. Not only was I giving all the wrong goddam answers, I was also having trouble with my drives. I do not believe that some men are just naturally cool, courageous, and decisive in handling crisis situations, while others are not. I chose a number-two wood for a change. I knew this was a mistake and put it back. "There . . . there was no hard evidence," I said, pressing on desperately. "And since the

Rosenbergs refused to cooperate, all we had left really was the brother's story!" I wasn't sure this was true. I'd read it somewhere. I thought: there is less than a 50 percent chance that what I'm doing will help me. "And to get *that,* we'd had to make this deal with him and his wife which—"

"So all that courtroom splutteration was a frame-up," he blustered—he was in a ferocious state, "what trial isn't?"

"Wait, that's not what I meant!" I protested. "Irving Saypol's a fine trial lawyer!" I wished I could keep my mouth shut. But I'd always admired Saypol since he prosecuted Hiss for me and got him sent up, and he'd been the one to nail the Communist party leaders, too, though I knew he was mean and ornery with a mind about as broad as a two-by-four, and a Tammany Democrat to boot. I pulled out my driver, swished it around a little. My hands were so sweaty, it nearly slipped right out. "I don't think he or Roy Cohn would ever—"

"Rig a prosecution?" laughed Uncle Sam sourly. I knew better, of course, I was being a fool. "Hell, *all* courtroom testimony about the past is ipso facto and teetotaciously a baldface lie, ain't that so? Moonshine! Chicanery! The ole gum game! Like history itself—all more or less bunk, as Henry Ford liked to say, as saintly and wise a pup as this nation's seen since the Gold Rush— the fatal slantindicular futility of Fact! Appearances, my boy, appearances! Practical politics consists in ignorin' facts! *Opinion* ultimately governs the world!"

"Yes, but . . . I thought—"

"You *thought!* Cry-eye, look out when the great God lets loose a thinker on this planet, we're all in for it! I'm telling you, son, the past is a bucket of cold ashes: rake through it and all you'll get is dirty! A lousy situation, but dese, as the man says, *are de conditions dat prevail!*"

I felt my neck flush, so to cover up, I stooped and concentrated on teeing up my golf ball, grunting to kill time. My hand was shaking and the ball kept falling off. I seemed to see my father down in the front row at a school debate, flushing with rage as I disgraced myself with a weak rebuttal.

"And so a trial in the midst of all this flux and a slippery past is just one set of sophistries agin another—or call 'em mettyfours if you like, approximations, all the same humbuggery—and God shine his everlastin' light on the prettiest ringtailed roarer in the courtroom! Am I right? You remember that Ayn Rand play you were in years ago: a game for actors!"

I didn't know he knew about that. If he knew that, what didn't he know? How could I compete? I felt like a fighter wearing sixteen-ounce gloves and bound by the Marquis of Queensberry rules, up against a bare-knuckle slugger who gouged, kneed, and kicked. But life for everyone is a series of crises, I cautioned myself, it's not just you, and with that I finally got the ball on the tee. I stood, gazed off toward the seventh green, trying to see the flag there. It was red, I knew. I was on to what this golf game was all about, all right, but I still hadn't figured out what Uncle Sam was up to. Did he mean the Rosenbergs might be innocent? Or their crime insignificant? I addressed the ball. I remembered my opening line from that Ayn Rand play: *Gentlemen of the jury—on the sixteenth of January—near midnight—the body of a man came hurtling through space, and crashed—a disfigured mass—at the foot of the Faulkner Building.* That was just how I felt. "But you said—I mean, President Eisenhower said, and J. Edgar Hoover, Judge Kaufman, everybody: a crime that has endangered the lives of millions, maybe even the whole planet—!"

"Damn right!—and much of Madness to boot, and more of Sin, and Horror the soul of the plot, but we're not just talkin' about that little piece of technological cattle-rustlin'! Even though that's more than enough to scrag a man all right—like Sweet Andy Carnegie used to say: upon the sacredness of property civilization itself depends—but still, we all know how he got his: no, a little healthy thievin' never hurt anybody. But real guilt, real evil— listen, son, get that right hand around there on that club, like you're shakin' hands with it, not jerkin' it off!"

I twisted my hand around on the club: the toe turned in and tapped the ball accidentally, knocking it off the tee again.

"God may forgive sins," Uncle Sam observed grimly, "but awkwardness has not forgiveness in heaven or earth—that'll cost you a stroke." He could be as cold as a New England parson sometimes. "No, guilt, real guilt, is like grace: some people got it, some don't. These people got it. Down deep. They wear it like a coyote wears its lonesomeness or a persimmon its pucker. They are suffused with the stuff, it's in their bones, their very acids, it's no doubt a gift of the promptuary, even their organs are guilty, their feet are guilty, their ears and noses—"

"You mean, because . . . because they're Jews?"

"Jews! What in Sam Hill has *that* got to do with it?" I'd missed again. I was completely lost. I couldn't even find my goddamn tee. "Irving Kaufman's a Jew, isn't he? Is he guilty? Is Irving

Saypol guilty? Roy Cohn? Hell, I got a touch of kike in me myself, son, not much, just enough for a little color and wile and to whet my appetite for delicatessen—shoot, I might even incarnate myself into one of 'em some day. . . ."

I glanced up. He was as stern as ever, but there was a malicious twinkle in his eye. My mind raced uneasily over the possibilities. I felt sure I had a good head start on all of them. I knew, too, it would help a helluva lot if I hit a decent tee shot for a change. If I could find my tee. "It's under your right foot," Uncle Sam said flatly.

"No, bein' a Jew ain't it, though it probably didn't help them none either. Their kind of depravity is something deeper even than that, something worse. You don't see it so much in the shape of their noses as in the way they twitch and blow them. You see it in how they shuffle and squat, how they bend, snort, and grimace. You see it in their children, their greasy flat, their friends—even their crockery betrays them, their lawyer, their pajamas, their diseases. It's no accident, son, that they've been nailed with such things as Jello boxes, console tables, and brown paper wrappers—and it coulda just as easily been the studio couch they slept on, their record-player, medicine chest, or underwear— they stink with it, boy, it's on everything they touch!"

I knew now what he meant. It was the feeling I'd had about Alger Hiss. Others, less perceptive, had had that feeling about Whittaker Chambers. In our case, it had been pumpkins, carpets, typewriters, and teeth. Whittaker, who had smelled a little unhealthy himself for a while, had emerged aromatic as a saint. "Perjury wasn't Hiss's crime either," I said. I'd been talking more or less to myself, but as soon as I said it, I knew I was on the right track at last.

"No," Uncle Sam agreed. "That's right." I glanced up. He was watching me closely, fierce as a tiger and cool as a cucumber, as the Gospel says, rolling the balls around in his mighty fist as though he were peddling them to me, a gesture of such iconic depth that I felt suddenly elevated past myself.

"It wasn't . . . it wasn't even espionage or double-dealing!" I was nearly there. . . . "Uh . . ."

"They have walked in the path of the spirit of perversity," whispered Uncle Sam hoarsely, leaning toward me like an eager schoolmaster, urging me on, "violators of the Covenant, defilers of the sanctuary . . ."

"*Sons of Darkness!*" I cried.

Uncle Sam leaned back and smiled, not a smile of self-content-
ment or amusement, but a smile of blessing, the smile of a life
insurance salesman who has just successfully put your affairs in
order, or of a parent who has come to see you graduate from
Duke Law School—or any law school, for that matter—and he set
his plug hat back on his head. I knew I'd turned the corner. I
began to feel I might actually hit a decent drive after all. "And
what's the reward for all them what walk in such ways?" He tossed
one of the golf balls up in the air and smashed it, baseball
fashion, out of sight. "A multitude of afflictions at the hands of all
the angels of destruction!" *Whack!* "Everlastin' perdition through
the angry wrath of an avengin' god!" *Swat!* "Etarnal horror and
perpetual *re*-proach!" *Smack!* "Darkness throughout the vicis-
sissitudes of life in ever' generation, doleful sorrow, boils on the ass,
contumely in the opinions of Christian men, bitter misfortune and
darklin' ruin!" *Slam!* "And the disgrace of final annihilation in
the . . . ," *splat!* ". . . fire!"

He was something to watch, all right—he had a lot of style. A
lot of styles, I should say: now that of Larry Doby, next Country
Slaughter, then Mel Ott, Hank Greenberg, Johnny Mize, Luke
Appling—but though he'd organized baseball's liturgy and had
governed its episcopacy (to be sure, there was more of Judge
Kenesaw Mountain Landis in his briary nineteenth-century features
than of, say, Bill Harding or Herbert Hoover), he'd never actually
played it. Golf was his game, the first he'd come to, back in the
capacious days of William Howard Taft, and it was still the only
one he played regularly. Before that, he'd pretty much limited
himself to hunting and fishing, riding, swimming, war, billiards,
and the odd cockfight—indeed, the very idea of Uncle Sam wasting
his time playing idle games would have been unthinkable fifty
years ago. But such was the character of our twentieth-century
revolution: games-playing was now the very pulse and purpose of
the nation. It was Taft's successor, Woody Wilson, who gave it its
fateful turn: he was sometimes out on the course as early as
five in the morning, even played the game in the dead of winter,
using black golf balls to find them in the snow, until that awful
day when the transmutation did not quite come off and left only
half of Wilson still working. Now golf was part of the presidential
discipline—indeed, why else would I be out here?—and every
time Uncle Sam eagled out or blasted his way mightily from a
sand trap to the pin, somewhere the Phantom cringed.

I dug up my tee and set my ball on it, took a practice cut at a dandelion. "But how can you, uh, tell for sure?" I asked, and—*whick!*—took the head off the dandelion. Why couldn't I hit a golf ball like that? "I mean, even Foster Dulles trusted Hiss. . . ."

"Ah, well, the pact with the Phantom is no less consecratin' in its dire way than gettin' graced by Yours Truly," said Uncle Sam, and, imitating Stan Musial's quirky stance, smacked another golf ball out over the horizon. "Ask that mackerel-snapper Joe McCarthy about the Grace su'ject!" He tossed up his last ball and belted it high in the air—in fact, I lost sight of it completely. I wondered, if it got up high enough, would it just stay there? Where does gravity run out? But finally it did come down, about fifty feet from the seventh green, and lodged in the roots of a tree. I supposed he wanted to keep his hand in on approach shots. Or got a kick out of blasting trees—Burning Tree indeed! you'd think it was Ben Franklin's private lightning lab to see the way Uncle Sam's left the vegetation out here. Now he tucked his putter under one arm and withdrew his corncob pipe, knocked it out on the heel of one boot. "The impure, through their presumptulous contact with the sacred, are momentaneously as lit up with this force as are the pure, and it's easy for folks to confound the two," he said, leaning back against the bench, "as much, I might add, to the unwarranted sufferin' of the holy as to the ephemeral quickenin' of the nasty . . ." He gazed at me meaningfully . . . aha! so *that* was why I had been accused of the secret slush fund! why, in spite of everything, I was still so distrusted many people said they wouldn't even buy a used car from me! The Philistines wouldn't have bought a used car from Jesus either, right? Things were becoming clear now. I concentrated on the ball, sitting firm on the tee like truth itself, and took a practice back stroke, trying to keep my elbow straight. "You're gonna top the ball, son," Uncle Sam said gloomily.

I did. I tried my damndest to lift the ball and I swung so hard I splintered the tee, but the ball only plopped about six feet ahead. Judas, I thought, I really hate this fucking game.

"Ya know, you're about as handy with that durn stick," muttered Uncle Sam irritably, tucking the pipe in his mouth, "as Adlai Stevenson is with a set of dumbbells!"

I was badly stung by this. I would be a good golfer if I had the time to play regularly, but a man can't give himself to everything on this earth. And the innuendos worried me: Stevenson was a loser. I realized it was still touch and go. . . .

1976   301

Uncle Sam sucked on his empty pipe a couple of times, then blew it out, reached into his pantaloon pockets for tobacco. "There's one thing about criminals and kings, priests and pariahs," he said. He packed the tobacco into his pipe with one long bony finger, peering at me as though over spectacles. "They may be as unalike as a eagle to a rattlesnake, but they both got a piece a that dreadful mysterious power that generates the universe!" As he said this, he whipped a long wooden match out from behind his ear. "The difference," he went on, "is what happens when they try to use it. The ones with the real stuff, the good guys, they achieve peace and prosperity with it—these are . . ." he scratched the head of the match with his thumbnail and it popped ablaze: ". . . the Sons of Light!" He cupped it over the pipe bowl and continued: "The other geezers, the (*puff!*) Phantom's boys, well, if you (*puff! puff!*) don't watch out, they can haul off and (*puff!*) exfluncticate the . . ." he looked up and held the match out, still burning, then crushed it in his fist: "*whole durn shootin' match!*"

It's true, I thought, he's not exaggerating, the Rosenbergs no longer belonged to the ordinary world of men, that was obvious, you could see the sort of energy they now possessed, even though stuffed away in Sing Sing prison, in the rising fervor of world dissent—in France the whole damned government was being shaken. I walked up to my ball, teed it up on a little hump of grass. I felt a little shaky myself. "You mean, we're not executing them . . . just because . . .?" I poked my toe about, looking for firm footing.

"We ain't goin' up to Times Square just to fulfill the statutorial law, if that's what you mean," Uncle Sam said. He blew a smoke ring, then another and another, each inside the other, ending with a little puff of smoke for the center. "This is to be a consecration, a new charter of the moral and social order of the Western world, the precedint on which the future is to be constructified to ensure peace in our time!" He hacked up a gob and spit into his smoke rings, hitting the bull's eye. . . . "We're goin' up there to *wash our feet, son!*" A miniature mushroom cloud welled up from the center, and the concentric rings flattened out and spread like shock waves.

Ha. I understood his question now. I turned back to my ball, dug my feet firmly into the turf. Times Square, the carnival atmosphere, the special ceremonies: form, *form,* that's what it always comes down to! In statesmanship get the formalities right, never mind about the moralities—why did I keep forgetting that? I smiled. "Then, wouldn't it have been better to burn them on the Fourth of July?" I commenced my back swing, shifting my weight confidently onto my right foot.

"Well now," said Uncle Sam, plainly pleased, "that's what I said to young Judge Kaufman, but he favored the summer solstice and the anniversary angle—"

"Eh—?" I was so startled my knees buckled, and I sliced the ball out of bounds. "The—*what?*"

"Thunder and tarnation, boy! That's four strokes already, and you ain't even off the damn tee yet!" cried Uncle Sam.

"I . . . I'm sorry! I, uh, thought you said . . ."

"The solstice and the anniversary, soap out your ears, son!" he repeated irascibly. "Yep, sometimes I suspect all judges of bein' cabalists at heart."

"Cabalists? Anni . . . versary?" My God, why didn't he just come out and tell me? I could hardly make my limbs work, my head think. I'd been right all along! They're after my whole generation! I fumbled for a new ball. They all seemed to have big gashes in them. I was pale and trembling, I knew, so I kept my back turned, hoping he wouldn't notice, a trick I learned early in coping with my old man.

"Yes, it's their fourteenth wedding anniversary—now, come on, son, get a leg on! Pick up a ball and throw it, if you have to!"

I turned around to face him. He had blown a smoke ring shaped like an outline map of the United States and, as it expanded, was trying to fill in the several states. "*Their*—?" I squeaked.

"The Rosenbergs'. The eighteenth of June," he muttered around puffs and rings. He was trying to squeeze the District of Columbia into his map, but it was getting very cluttered in that area. He seemed about to lose his patience. "I thought you knew that!"

So! It was also the Rosenbergs' anniversary! I'd thought all along he'd been referring to *my* wedding anniversary! When Kaufman had set the date finally for the week of June 15, I had seen that it could fall on Pat's and my anniversary—our *thirteenth*!—on June 21. And I'd seen that summer solstice angle, too: after all, we hadn't married on the twenty-first for nothing. It was the climax to our "Beauty and the Beast" game, time of the roar of Behemoth and all that. Then, when I learned that this year it was also Father's Day, it had suddenly looked like a sure thing. I'd said nothing to anyone about this, but it had worried me for days: if it was intentional, were they doing it as a favor, giving Pat and me something extra to commemorate? or was somebody out to get me? I'd feared the latter, usually the safest of the two assumptions when you're in politics. But then the marshal had scheduled it officially for the eighteenth, and I'd forgotten about it . . . until now. I teed the new ball up, twitching my shoulders and wrists, trying to loosen up. I had a better understanding of things now, but it didn't make me feel any easier. Their fourteenth! And what were *we* doing here on the seventh tee? "I . . . I guess I missed that," I admitted frankly.

"It seems to me you missed just about everything!" snapped Uncle Sam. "You don't know no more about this case than a goose knows about rib stockings!" He had given up on the map and with a flick of his finger had drawn the Canadian border up to a straight perpendicular line, the Great Lakes clustering like a knot, turning the whole thing into a kind of gigantic hangman's noose. "Do you know what law the Rosenbergs were actually convicted under? Do you know who the Clark House Players were? Sarah O'Ken? Helen Rosenberg? Catharine Slip? Do you know why they called David Greenglass 'Little Doovey' or what Julius Rosenberg's secret talmudic name was? Why was Julius born in Harlem? How is it that Roy Cohn was working for Irving Saypol? What were the Rosenbergs doing in Peekskill in 1943, or Irving Kaufman in Washington in 1948? Eh? Did you even know that Ethel Rosenberg played the Major Bowes talent rackets? that Julius read Horatio Alger and Tom Swift and took to the stumps against the National Biscuit Company? or that Emanuel Bloch's marriage is on the rocks? And who's that screamer workin' for anyway?"

"I thought you . . . you said the past was a pot of lies. . . ."

"We ain't talking about trials now, boy, stay awake, *we're talkin' about the sacraments!*"

"I . . . I'm sorry," I said and stepped up to the ball. I felt like I'd been stepping up to this goddamn ball all afternoon. Roy Cohn once mentioned that Irving Saypol used to be a really rotten golfer himself, but that he read almost every book ever written on the subject, and it improved his game immeasurably. Maybe that was what I ought to do.

Uncle Sam raved on and on about the case; most of the time I had no idea what he was talking about. I tried to pay attention, I knew it was important, but the coincidence of anniversaries and my own stupid panic about it when he brought it up were still troubling me. "And what about the CCNY class of '39? Why was J. Parnell Thomas sent to the same jail as Ring Lardner, Jr., of the Hollywood Ten? What the hell's a proximity fuse? Should we feed 'em on cheese and barley cakes and beat 'em with fig branches? Why does that Russian astronomer now say that the vegetation on Mars is blue? Eh? Eh?" Of course, June—a lot of people get married that month. Eisenhower's own anniversary was just another ten days away, wasn't it? It wasn't all that improbable. But it was all tied up somehow with those generational vibrations which were exercising such a grip on me these days—how many other parallels might there be? I was afraid to find out. Maybe it was because I'd just passed forty, things like this happened to people when they reached forty, I supposed. Uncle Sam was trying to explain why it was the Rosenbergs, why the Lower East Side, the Foley Square courthouse (another link to the Hiss case! my subcommittee *met* there, it was just before I finally nailed the bastard!), Sing Sing, and now Times Square, why Nelson Eddy and Bernard Baruch had to be there, Arthur Godfrey and Dr. Kinsey, why an electric chair instead of sending them out to sea in a leaking boat as in the old days, and why just now, this week . . . "I mean, McCarthy's got such a cactus up his corn hole, he's bound to blow it soon, and now that we've laid the threat of a A-bomb attack on them heathen Chinks, they gotta fold their hand any day now, and what with Stalin dead the whole goddamn mood could change—this may be our last chance to kill these people! And what if he squeezes an extra day out somewhere? Have you thought about that? The Phantom's known to have a lotta contacts in the jew-dishiary—then what? If we had to go through the Fourth without them atom spies burnt or burning, the whole shebang could come unhinged like a hog shed in a Okie twister!"

"That's . . . that's true," I agreed, vaguely aware of the wind commencing to blow across Burning Tree, but unaware at the time how prophetic he'd been—or had he been telling me something I should have picked up on? Should I have got Edgar to put a watch on Douglas right then? I was too distracted to think about it—a few days to play with, a couple days' delay: then Pat and I could *still* get hit with it! "Uh, Judge Black's especially unreliable," I offered. "He's voted against us nearly every time." I wasn't certain of this, but supposed it was probably true.

"Yeah, well, I got a hunch Judge Black's gonna get sick and go to the hospital," grumped Uncle Sam, cocking one eyebrow.

"Mmm, yes," I said, getting a grip on myself and my club, "better to play it safe." I didn't, though. I swung too hard again, and again topped the ball, sent it skittering this time into the rough about a hundred yards away.

"Damn it all, boy!" thundered Uncle Sam, rearing up off the bench, brandishing his putter like a saber, and stomping forward like Ulysses Grant debouching from his field tent. "The brave man inattentive to his duty and who don't keep his eye on the ball is worth little more to his country than the coward who deserts her in the hour of danger! Life is real! Life is earnest! You gotta get on top of this thing! You gotta get your ass in gear!"

"I'm sorry . . . I just can't seem to get the hang—"

"That's just it! We *gotta* get the hang! We gotta exsect these vinimous critters this week or our name is shit with a capital mud! This ain't just another ball game, johnny, we are gonna have to fight for the reestablishment of our national *character,* and we shall nobly save or meanly lose the last best hope of earth—namely, *me!*"

"*You*—?" I croaked. "But you . . . you're . . . you can't—!"

"Die? Oh, I ain't immortal, son, I'd hate to think I was. Nothin' goes on forever, Amber, not even History itself, so why should I? Sooner or later, the Phantom gets us all!"

I was truly shaken. I caught myself staring at him the way I used to stare at my mother when I first realized that she had to die. Suddenly everything seemed very fragile and tenuous. Brittle. "But you're so . . . so strong—!"

"Remember the old kings, boy, the times don't change: I'm the force what'll raise up the whole sin-besotten world, see if I don't . . . but I'll get et by it, too!"

"I . . . I don't understand . . . ?"

"I would not live alway, I ask not to stay, loveliest of lovely things are they, on earth what soonest pass away, so long as you get your kicks in in the passin'! That's poetry, boy! Xerxes the Great did die; and so must you and I!"

Yes, I was shaken, but oddly I also felt like I was very near the center of things. There's been a point to all this, after all, I thought. I felt closer to Uncle Sam than I'd ever felt before.

"Oh, probably, after it was over, like Christ, I could come back some day. . . ." He sighed wistfully, puffed on his pipe, blew a plume of smoke shaped like a bird—an eagle. "But it wouldn't be the same. . . ." He added wings and it flapped off into the sun: I was blinded by the light but as far as I could see it simply disappeared. When I looked back at Uncle Sam, he was staring at me very strangely, his blue eyes glowing as though lit from behind. "Sometimes," he said softly, "sometimes I almost *want* to die. . . ."

A cold chill rattled through me. My sense of Uncle Sam's presence in front of me dipped briefly, almost imperceptibly, as a candle will gutter in a faint draft—and for that fraction of a second, I seemed to have an intuitive awareness of everything happening in Uncle Sam's head. And then, as quickly, it passed.

My head ached slightly and I felt a momentary emptiness down in the marrow of my bones. Then that, too, filled up.

"Don't worry," Uncle Sam laughed, "it ain't such a grave matter, if you'll pardon the pun, son—in fact, it's a lot more fun this way." He put his arm around me and led me down the fairway toward my ball. He seemed to have shrunk some in the last few minutes. "It's like old Tom Paine useter say, panics in some cases got their uses— we ain't had a party good as this one's gonna be since you were just a little tyke sayin' your breakfast prayers back home on Santa Gertrudes!" I felt swarmed about with fears and absences. Paradox. But I felt protected at the same time. I had a feeling that every- thing in America was coming together for the first time: an emergence into Destiny. . . . "Oh, I don't reckon we could live like this all year round," he said, "we'd only expunctify ourselves. But we do need us an occasional peak of disorder and danger to keep things from just peterin' out, don't we?" I nodded, remembering my own peaks—the Hiss case and the Checkers speech, and before that my school highs, debate wins, romances with Ola and Pat, the war, even my brothers' deaths—and I knew how they could light things up, make everything new again: after all, that was what light and darkness, the sacred and the diabolic, death and regener- ation were all about! "Well, then," said Uncle Sam, pocketing his corncob pipe and clapping me on the shoulder, "let us, then, be up and doin', with a heart for any fate; still achievin', still pursuin', and though hard be the task, keep a stiff upper lip!"

"Oh, yes!" I said, flushing with pride and joy and eager to begin, for he'd just singled me out among all men: that echo from the past was a piece of Longfellow's "Psalm of Life," which Grandma Milhous penned by hand under a photo of Abe Lincoln she gave me on my thirteenth—*thirteenth!*—birthday—I kept it on the wall above my bed all through high school and college! *Learn to labor and to wait!* "I will!"

"Good boy!" he said. "I press thee to my heart as Duty's faithful childering! Be prepared for anything, for this is one a them hard contests where men must win at the hazard of their lives and at the risk of all they hold, dear! But be brave, and whatever happens, just remember the words a that other Poor Richard long ago: 'Fools make feasts, my boy . . . *and wise men eat 'em!*' So whet up that appetite!" He hugged me, then gave me his club to swing with, saying: "Now, listen here, a golf ball is propelled forward by the verlocity imparted to it by a club head, see—this is physics, now, my boy—and it's kept aloft by under-rotation or backspin, which producifies a cushion of air, and this is what gives the ball lift. To get this backspin, the club head's gotta travel *downward,* right swat whippety-snap through the *center* of the ball, and this is where you been goin' wrong. You think you gotta lift the ball up, and this is makin' you pull your swing . . ."

"Ah . . ."

"Actually the uplift is projectorated by the spin, and the spin is got by hittin' *down* and *through,* you got it? Now, another problem is movin' your maximum verlocity back to six inches . . ."

Down and through, got it. I took a practice swing, keeping my shoulder down, my eye on the ball—then, because when I looked up I realized that people were staring at me (got to watch it, can't let my guard down like that), swung on up into a friendly wave at a carload of senators disembarking from the subway car. "See ya, Dick!" "Don't miss the show!" "Not for the world!" "Take it easy!" Down and through. And out and up, back to the office, get rid of this goddamn thing. With maximum verlocity.

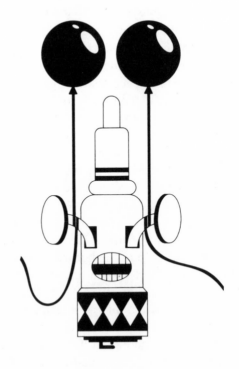

WILLIAM E. BIDERBOST. (*TQ* #34)

Gala

Paul West

Ultrafondness: love of the distant, of the distant child, that's for
me—not an astronomer-royal but an astronomer-ordinary, looking
out at the constellation into which pain, or mortality, fits without
fuss; into the jazz of cosmic chemistry. At least it might make this
abiding headache go away as if winked at, even if it soon returns
recharged, more elaborately nagging, all the way from brainpan to
Adam's apple.

Unkindly kind, the situation is that visits are allowed, she to me,
I to her, as if either of us were in the lockup, some Lubianka of the
kinship state. Prisoner of February 23 awaits arrival of prisoner
of October 18, as simply as that—except of course that she, being
what's politely called "exceptional," has to be fetched, like a baby
giraffe or a box of new-cut lilies. No matter how big she looks at
fourteen, on womanhood's edge (on a bigger nothing's margin),
she entails preparations, logistics, goods, befitting one who steers
toward the Magellanic Clouds, as if her own planet were hostile
to the very life form she represents, as it almost is. What a commotion, what a marathon of getting ready. Tickets, schedules,
emergency numbers and remedies, calendrical affidavits—all I
haven't consulted being the sundial, the almanac, the *I Ching*.
Were she slinking out from behind the Iron Curtain, it would seem
easier, except that we don't need guns or darkness. A bit of a
gauntlet to run, all the same, what with time zones, jet lag, international variations in fodder, lefthand drive for right (I can see her
now, scowling because the driver's on the wrong side), ninety
degrees in the shade for sixty-five among the dogs and the mad

English, and her own private metabolic clock, working as usual on sidereal time, though that isn't the only reason I call her Milk.

As for the conventions of her two-week visit, they're few and far between, more like an armistice or an amnesty than like rules of procedure. We'll build things, maybe even wreck a few, but descend to neither enueg (long medieval bleat) nor a put-up job (such as staging the Week of the Creation twice over in six rooms). It's going to be more like my eavesdroppings on our behalf, on what we might have said had things been otherwise. And this will survive, a lexical echo of where she was, and what.

As I read through, even so early, I find every C and G, A and U a textural obbligato to what went wrong at her vagitus, or even before, as many as nine months earlier—when, as the books tell us, the DNA of the sperm unites with that of the ovum and that is that, beyond revision. Occasionally, nature makes a mistake and binds the wrong molecule into the chain, the result being that, when splitting occurs, the two molecules that form won't be identical, and, as the books calmly enough point out, there will be corresponding changes in the code of instructions and the individual will deviate from the original pattern. Clinical horror story I know by heart. If she could understand that explanation, she might not need it. So let me pay my dues again and again to C, G, A, and U, the gods of the copybook: to cytosine, that sounds close to trigonometry; guanine, evocative of bird droppings; adenine, almost a girl's name; and uracil, which might almost be the magical toothpaste of the year. Grand committee of teleological agents, they'll never be far from mind, heading each thought, steering each fit. I'll stop, and then on.

Graffias in Scorpio, Cheleb in Ophiuchus, Unukalhai in Serpens, Almaak in Andromeda: uncouth-sounding stars which, in no special order, keep coming to mind and hinting at unmentionable teratologies as I pore over the grease-thumbed tar black of the star charts lined in Euclidean white. No matter: with each paragraph I lose a little of me to chemistry; a little of chemistry becomes my own. Win a few, lose . . .

Uncanny that tomorrow's the day, confirmed expensively by telephone, and all I need to do, having readied the house and vowed to change my sleeping habits, is to clean up the strategies of this the intended remnant after she's come and gone like a nova that bursts forth and fades, even if to erupt again years later, like RS Ophiuchus, 1898, 1933, 1958, 1967. Here's hoping, I tell

myself (there is hoping here indeed), it won't ever be that long
for Milk and me, who have never been able to exchange letters,
what with her being incommunicado (unlettered and unphonable)
as well as in a nonstop category called constant supervision. No
postscripts to her presence, then, not from her anyway; hence my
need for verbal spoor, something beyond the school's guarded
reports (she is making progress and learning to recognize coins).
That when she was twelve. And now that tomorrow has come, I
see myself setting out full of giddy foreboding. An arch, as Leonardo said, is only a strength caused by two weaknesses. Draw
strength from that thought, I tell myself. Draw from it now.

Abbreviating chores, I'll record only that I'm driven to one
airport, where the handwritten country menu reads "Doughnought"
with an "Oops!" above it and a line through the second *ught,* then
fly to another that has a long arcade of display cases crammed
with trash, then cross several thousands of miles, in the course of
which a homebound Englishman reading a journal about metals
spills whiskey on my shoe and I decline to dab it or kick aside the
fallen ice. I avert my clogged gaze from a South African film about
a patrician former Olympic gold medalist who wants his son to win
a local marathon, and instead, while music, on channels (or canals)
obedient to a rotating wheel under my left thumb, flows into the
stethoscope I rent for the price of a paperback, I observe the dawn's
vertical spectrum as it fattens behind my plexiglas porthole.

Approaching her at over five hundred miles an hour, though
much slower than Earth spins, I divide the sleepless hours between
Classics in Stereo (2) and the Jazz File (9), which is to say
between hosts Carmen Dragon and Leonard Feather, unlikely-
sounding watchmen whom I splice back to back, Cain and Abel
of the ether, in the violet night sky. Here is how the menu of the
earphone reads: two movements from Tchaikovsky's Suite Number
One, music of soul vermilion, while the horizon flickers (what on
earth the time is, I have no idea, but I'm sure *she* isn't watching
the dawn); then Mozart's Serenade Number Six in D Major, in
which a chamber group seems to be counterpointing a full ensemble.
What appetizing euphoria as the east blisters white.

About the time that Ellington's *Johnnie Come Lately* thumps
forth with flaunting fused brass, the dawn is a visual scald, the
pastel spectrum has almost gone.

Go Back Home, a raucous percussion from the Don Ellis orches-
tra, comes almost as a hint while I tug down the plastic shade

over a window brimming with eye-wounding silver. But I've seen the day come up like thunder, Rudyard Kipling's fetish; I've scanned Earth's drowsing meniscus; I've felt like a returning astronaut aloof behind the heat shield. Leonard Feather says goodbye, "Take care of yourselves and of each other," which sounds like an intrusive rebuke. Or was that Carmen Dragon? I don't care as I sip the orange juice an alert hostess delivers. Air maid, I think; she's an *airmaid*.

Already past more time zones than birds allow themselves in one go, I walk down the steps from the jet in clubfooted reverie and show a passport in a country other than the country of origin (as the inside cover of my ticket says in a tart addendum concerning the Treaty of Warsaw). I was born here in a season of fogs. All I have to do now is wait an hour or two, shave because I won't have chance to do so later on, come round enough to collect one tall girl infatuated still with planes, and (if not in this order, at least in this approximate dimension) lunch awkwardly as part of a disbanded trio at the airport restaurant, check documents and cabin supplies, and hope to board at the 1300-hour departure without too much fuss, streak back along the great circle route before local time takes hold, yet not before general fatigue sets in. I'll be setting a retarded child five hours further back, a grimmish thought on which I cannot linger.

An impossible enterprise? Of course. Akin to recovering a space capsule? Nearly. There yesterday, here today, there today, and gone tomorrow. Not quite, but close enough to it. Where, I'll be asking, did the day get lost? Arrive there at 1530, which is 2230 here, and settle down to five hours by car. The logistics are special, are they not? More like logarithms. She cannot, ever, travel alone, even with a label around her neck like the schoolchildren whom the hostesses, airmaids, ply with tiny pilot's badges, flight logbooks scaled down, coloring blocks, soft drinks, and daintily wrapped candy. And you can't drive alone with her because she might leap out or seize the wheel on a turnpike at seventy miles an hour. But at least we two get to board first, along with the elderly and parents with toddlers. My twitching mind strays to the Epstein bronze marooned behind the terminal's giant picture window; commemorating Brabazon, patron of aviators, it's like a lava flow frozen in mid-air over its pedestal. Supposedly Icarus, or the spirit of flight, it appears to unfurl untidily above the passengers' and watchers' heads. My mind makes common cause with it and goes null, hovering.

Uh-huh, the bar is closed, but what care I, having no need of it, as for several years now. A bar to moan at, however, might be something worthwhile. The restaurant is stalled between the end of breakfast and the start of lunch. I exchange a few Washington-headed dollars for the Queen-embossed pounds that seem smaller yearly and a handful of outsize Britannic coins that buy too little considering their weight. A telephone call later, the experiment is on, and this piece of its raw material is already wincing at the prospect. I lap up the phenomena of disorientation: coffee tasting of cocoa, Muzak from the sixties, flight announcements in an accent so fastidiously muted it might be a laryngitic sloth, an aroma of cut roses from the flower stall, one of leather from the gift boutique, a gust of hops as the bar seems to open and close again like a bloom of evil, a reek of kerosene from the runways, even a whiff of vomit from under the seat. Somnambulistically patrolling the imitation marble floor, which makes each footstep glide a fraction as if I'm walking gingerly without meaning to, I buy English and French newspapers, note the headlines, fold the stack double into my bruise-black flight bag, and go to eat haddock with an egg, refusing the always-offered french-fried potatoes. This country's future will be found to have been long behind it, spurned in the 1890s when it showed its face. Unfair? I know it is, but this morning I'm hardly capable of balanced thought.

Communiqué: the pair of them, it seems, will take their lunch at home, not ten miles away as the swallow flies. An elegiac repast. So be it: I'm guaranteed a minimum of unrelished contact; I'll have time to brood on the status of this reverie, the thing which is assembling itself within the cerebral illusion I've made. I can only call it the prewritten enactment of what hindsight knows took place today in Utopia, meaning Nowhere. It's the past written in the present prophetic tense, as befits. I plan. I go. I claim my Perdita at this distant terminal, whiz her away, will have to ferry her back again, after which . . . there is a metal fatigue of the mind: a wing falls off, the nose splits, the tail crumples up. I do these words to draw my line through time, across the Mercator quadrants, to prove it all happened, was capable of happening, and so can go on happening. Saying it, I do it. Saying I do it, I'm planning it. Planning it, I do it. Having done it, I keep it in the present tense to make it last. I know that to write in the past tense confers an illusion of command and fixedness, but the future tense is just as final. For instance: *I bought her a doll,* a second ago, and now the sentence is cold. *I buy her a doll,* am buying it now, and already the act is over as the hasty, never-quite-simultaneous sentence that almost sheathes it dies. *I will buy her a doll,* and the act is over before begun. Something always keeps the rhetoric from coming true. Something always keeps the truth from being rhetorical. Better, perhaps, to kiss events without thinking at all.

Clearly there are subtler ways of living than writing things down, *whenever.*

Aramaic? No. Oggam script? Never. Linear B? Hardly. Then what? Just allowing the electrical scribble of cognition to fizz and fade out.

Going to hell on an abacus, mouthing prayers in code: that might describe me.

Urging on my mind's eye without looking at the outside world.

Careful now, I instruct myself. Be tactful. You'll soon be high over the ocean again, watching Milk grin at the cloud floor.

Arrange, arrange, arrange. Reconfirm pre-reconfirmed reservations.

Calmly take over when that ironclad umbilical has to stretch, and reassure the girl as best you can. That she'll get her mother back in fourteen sleeps. *Vordeen zleep.*

Get her aboard fast, beguile her with aeronautics, the upness of the plane she has always called *abbala,* stress on the first syllable, please.

Check that her two hearing aids aren't on the blink (and abstain from awful metaphors). Then let her shed them for the trip, if she so wants, what with her lipreading so demonically accurate. See all, hear nothing. What else? Tranquilizer at the ready, one she won't reject.

All ballpoints, fiberpoints, puzzles, crayons, in the status astronauts call GO.

Get mentally ready for custodianship, and urge whatever beneficence warms the cosmos not to make her run amok, ripping out the flotation cushions, fisting loaded plastic trays of near-computerized food, clamoring for snow, or TV, or a ride on her swing, a slide on her slide, a sleep in her very own bed. All that up there, among the invisible stars.

Going westward in daylight (which precedes going west and gone west), we won't see Jupiter, as I did while coming, but we'll certainly be flying to an intenser summer than this gusty carbon copy, copyright by the temperate zone. In her lingo, summer is *when the moon is hot,* season in which she likes to ford rivers, romp in her plastic pool outside on the lawn that I no longer tread. She still has no word for sun.

Count out the time for her, I remind myself, and mark her face when, after two mealtimes, she arrives almost at the hour she took off. Where, I wonder, will she think the time went, she having no abstractions. Entering into the anomie of travel, she may well laugh, loving an uncontaminated surd; or, aghast, she'll rip the cabin apart, given chance, as her true old circadian rhythms tell her she's been betrayed, it isn't 1530 body-time at all, it's half past ten, two hours after she goes to sleep.

Going to sleep on board, though, she'd come to life at midnight Eastern Standard Time, just when she should be dropping off, as I. Helpless, I leave it to nature, which . . .

A lottery, as everyone has told me. Play by ear and expect a crisis somewhere along the line of flight. I'm just tempted to fly back empty-handed, having anticipated enough in the past hour to fuel a month; but no, I'll go according to plan, hoping hard she's been as fully briefed as possible about the day's and the next two weeks' events. As it is, she'll have more sense of going from than of going toward, more of being severed than of being reattached. Surely thought has now canceled itself right out?

Greenwich time is creeping up to embarkation time. My head fills with bags for motion sickness, glibly dubbed. My sinuses hold isinglass, dark and cold. My third coffee sets up an old familiar tremor in my wrists, and, just as I light up a cigarillo in the shadow of Epstein's Icarus, I see them across the hall at the head of the escalator, loaded with bags. Why did they come upstairs? Rendez-vous was ground-floor, at the check-in point, and not for another fifteen minutes. Now we'll have to go down again.

At an enormous distance I hear my friends' voices, expostulating, analyzing, adding diffident riders. Pi: Is it worth all the emotional turmoil? Won't it upset her more than it's worth? And you? (She is usually right in her levelheaded acuity, born under Libra, like Milk herself, like my mother.) And Chad: Leave well alone, my friend; distance is the healer. Out of sight, out of trouble. Absence makes the heart grow stronger. (Facetious-sounding, especially when I try out on him prospective titles for some new stars, he's at core serious, a postgraduate in both marital and cardiac attrition.) The legal opinion, as so often, leaves it up to me, cautioning me, however, that what one is legally entitled to isn't always a joy. Why, then, am I committed to this high-wire act, this emotional binge, when the reward is only scars made wounds again, the final catch an exhausted goodbye at this very airport? Pride, paternity, curiosity, masochism, involuntary defiance—my hand includes at least these cards, as well as one that lengthily reads: Addiction to ontological ground-floors, *nostalgie de deinosis,* which last was Tacitus' word for the presentation of things in their most horrible aspect. At bottom, I find a passion for disharmony, because harmony there is none, and anyone who thinks there is has another think coming. All that hubris in a dunce's cone upon my head, and then some.

Consider, though, her accreted beauty, which exists, is just now a few yards from my suntanned hand. A Nordic elf, brunette where she once was flaxen, but with the same wide, pale blue-green eyes. Pubescent, long, and given to agitated skips while her head rakes sideways in bursts of eager curiosity. My long-distant, heavy-featured face she knows; this extended smile is no pretense after diligent briefing. She *has* no pretenses: she knows what she knows, knows not what she doesn't. *Yah,* she says loudly, meaning not *ja* but me, and with her usual ritualized protocol asks for a present, an *oo-ba,* as of old, ostentatiously shielding one eye with a cupped hand. *Soon,* I mouth, exaggerating the vowel to her, front-face (I'm saving the doll for the crisis). Does she know she, and she only, will soon be in the *abbala* with me, up high, fourteen sleeps, water, swim, where the moon is hot? Then home again? I ask, and she gives an affirmative, impatient nod. This has never happened before, not to her, so let there be light and sweetness indeed. Once upon a time, to all such novelty, or to an unknown person, she would say her imperious, conclusive no, followed by her bye-bye-bye. Now, though, she awaits the next step, grinning almost slyly, all mercenary sheen. Encased in the strictest of demeanors, her mother gets the show on the road, anxious for the anesthetic to be given, the first incision made, and aching already to come-to in the recovery room in a fortnight's time.

Check in, show documents as if in iron mask; people stare at this girl, and not always unkindly. She spellbinds with her looks, her bravura symmetries. Too soon to board, so helplessly I agree to coffee, more of it. *Beebee,* says Milk, meaning she's lip-read that much and wants some too, using her generic word for anything to drink, anxious never to be left out. For no solid reason, an ad comes to mind: "Any fluid you can find in nature, we can deliver by flask or trailer, plus an almost infinite number of mixtures." One day I may need them, royal plural and near-infinity and all, even if only for something to metabolize while being nervous.

Grope up the escalator again, which Milk adores, has always called *bo*.

God (that clutch of ions or steam), the goodbyes have been said, and I escort my backward-frowning child through the door to motherless limbo. From now on, screams or fits or mayhem notwithstanding, I have to see her through. *Eureka,* I have found it. Found what? The daring to go on. Oddly, she faces front, a little as if I am going to back her to the wall while the firing squad waits to one side (an image *she*'d never supply), and we arrive at the duty-free shop, which has an oddly liberated sound. I buy her some toilet water, resisting the connotation, and a blue silk scarf on which dragons are evanescing, and (since she hasn't one, is bound for the country where every second counts) an inexpensive watch. Erratically I read the signs behind the counter, marveling at one bit of irrelevant pageantry saying, beside a scarlet flag imprinted with crescent moon and a star, both white, "Turkish currency is *not* accepted." Had such currency *ever* been proffered here, at this secondary although international airport? Milk's big teenage hand is a vise for mine. I walk her to the toilet, just in case, then realize I've taken her to MEN. There is no one to embarrass, or incite, my young and busty Viking with her two microphones against her canary-yellow jumper and her sizzling earpieces tuned in to phenomena she likes to do without. A bud of euphoria starts to peel open, but I nip it: we're not even on the way. No tears, though, no frenzy. After all, she is fourteen. I remember her first pun, akin to an esoteric allusion to Galileo from an Easter Islander, calling her then thirty-four-year-old mother *dirty-fork*. To the lip-reader the sounds look alike, but Milk relished the difference. An inborn wit among the garbled engrams painted that distant day in gold.

Conversation piece while waiting: *Abbala,* I say (it is blue and white out there, all its refueling done, its tailfin high as a tree; I've already spent half a dozen hours in it today). She utters nothing, but hungrily points, eyes nacreous with the old aerial craving. She thinks she's going, but isn't sure even now. "Michaela up?" Fanning her fingers at me, she again checks that figure of fourteen sleeps that will restore her to mother, and I confirm. If an expression can be of disgruntled complacency, she has one, wears it with potent will. Off soon, we're travelers from an antique land setting out for a peak in Darien, hands linked in First Class (an innovative extravagance), with nothing to declare except each the other. Mickel, she calls herself, never Michaela, and never knowingly Milk, which is my own private tag for good and sentimental and almost religious reasons. Perhaps Milt would have been as good. No. If parents knew beforehand that their child would be damaged, they'd perhaps choose more suitable names, easier ones at any rate, like Beau (easy for the child to say) or Bab (almost as easy); but if they knew beforehand, they'd probably get as far as passive euthanasia. Christ's blood clots in the firmament. Gynecology in the stirrups howls. And these are not thoughts to fly around with.

Untold prevarications dog me now I've thought that. I wish, I wish, I wish.

Calmer, just a bit calmer.

Good going, I've cheered up again; I'm on my way to a classical reunion. I'm nearly *there*.

At long last we obey the manicured glottals directing us to gate something-or-other, the ramp, the steps, the ribbed platform at the oval door into Kubla Khan's anteroom, a-sprinkle with a new batch of white-gloved debutantes in freshly sprayed aromas. Two of them coax her into the broad window seat, exclaiming and cooing while she scans the tarmac for mother. I, Deulius, feel like a rejected sponsor, or a used-up battery, or a flipped-off seat belt. The air in the cabin is crisp and even, has just been beautifully manufactured; and how coolly the airmaids bow, unfurl their apple-firm arms, pirouette, adjust, succor, calm. We have been taken in by a hospice of the sky. We are almost home, in this six-hundred-mile-an-hour living room. Milk is entranced, kneading a royal blue cushion while I, I'm unwinding so fast I almost fall asleep. As a turbine faintly revolves into life, she unplugs her hearing aids, unbuckles their harness and hands it over, microphones and all, like so much bungled knitting. I transfer it to an airmaid, who pretends to put it on, causing Milk to laugh aloud at one so hindered. Tribute to this airline, its light militia has cool; but, then, they can take almost anything for seven hours and a half; and for the nigh-mythic price I've paid I can tap their spines as well. I wonderingly await catastrophe as we taxi out, strapped in.

Alert to the straight-line takeoff (an obsessed-feeling trundle that might prove Einstein's propositions about rectilinear speed), Milk smirks like a maenad, giving herself over to upholstered vibration and the back-thrust phases of landscape. Her lifelong love of violent motion—being swung around by the shoulders, being carried upside down, or of handstanding herself against any available wall—takes over; this best roller coaster of all drives her into a broad uncaptious grin that lasts until we leave the ground. That abrupt shift to smoothness piques her at first, but the thump of upfolded wheels renews the grin. If only, I think, we could cross the ocean at takeoff speed on terra firma all the way, or on ice, stampeding past polar bears and earthbound whales, careening past bergs and frozen waterspouts, while the tremor in our feet goes on and on. If only Hendrik Hudson and his crew would keep on creating the special thunder of playing bowls, then she, the Rip Van Winkle of *paideia,* would never sleep again. Clearly, though, we have taken off right on time, which she at once, with newly developed skill, tells me as I adjust her new wristwatch. One and a half, she mouths, juicily oblivious of Earth's rotation and west-east headwinds at bitter altitudes.

After that, the cornucopia of executive luxury (doesn't the *consultative* echelon ever fly?) breaks open and a menthol-fresh airmaid, facially not unlike her, plies us with carbonated drinks while another, dusky with romany curls, demonstrates the ocher life jackets, a charade which Milk enjoys, chortles at around her two barber's-pole straws, as if the airmaid in question is a hopelessly discombobulated goon, victim of her own truss. Quizzical, Milk looks around for hers, to don and then top-up by blowing through the mouthpiece. Again I thank the deity of ions for not allowing oxygen masks to flop down before us from the overhead compartments. When they do, we'll need them; until then, if you please, no circus rehearsals.

Comes a headset each. What a lark. To Milk this is like shelling peas. On goes hers, like a parody of what she wears daily, except this doesn't prod deep, in toward the drum. After a sly frown at the headbrace, she plugs into the chair-arm socket and happily spins to maximum volume the wheel I show her, getting 110 decibels with luck. Spinning the channels as I too listen, I see one of her biggest smiles, even a tiny flush, as big-band swing slams out, Count Basie to be sure. This is Leonard Feather's Channel 9, where I came in, and I time-travel back to my own teenage record collection, which included such other samples of Basie's raucous ping as *Basie Boogie, Pound Cake, The 9:20 Special, Clap Hands Here Comes Charlie,* and *It's Square but It Rocks.* Briefly I yearn for the amplified farts of Gene Krupa's *Tuxedo Junction,* the demure stomp of Goodman's *Jumping at the Woodside,* the motoric jam of Herman's *Perdido,* and other rhythmic gems. My teens are meeting hers; she has just heard, says Leonard Feather, *Everday,* from Basie and Joe Williams, and the critic's voice goes on within the vacuum fastness, invulnerable to the roar and cold of half a thousand miles an hour as we go on climbing over Ireland. She pouts questioningly, can hear nothing now, until Miles Davis' rendition of *It Never Entered My Mind,* and I dumbly applaud the abstract quality of music which, titled something like that, or *Copenhagen,* or *Mission to Moscow,* makes the maximum style out of a minimal allusion, whereas words, my own congeners, need to tell so much. And while Milk attends to music (that notorious stimulant to the brain's subdominant hemisphere) with befuddled-looking calm, not tapping her foot of course (her only rhythms are her own), I let my mind roam as it wants, gratefully marking the aroma of lunch from the microwave ovens, wondering madly if scraping potatoes makes the airmaids cough, and thanking more than a few of my lucky stars.

A nothing, like that which reasserts itself through contrast after words have been used, now includes us, unlikely-looking pair of fellow travelers, though with the same nose, mouth, and shape of eye. Chances are she'll listen to the one channel all the way, her tastes favoring sameness, patterns, constants, each time finding Basie, Davis, or the Don Ellis ensemble not so much new as still at a distance, unappraisable as time itself, a camel through a microscope, or blood spilled on a galaxy. Divided-up noise, *that* she hears, however, and relishes the bombardment next to her stirrup and cochlea, making something fidget in her middle brain, her teeth tingle, maybe, her head at length, as almost always, ache with an ache she's learned to confide about: *Ah, sore!,* indicating temple or scalp in its bush of tropical-thick hair.

Aspirin is easily procured in this high-altitude cul-de-sac, where we shirk the natural context of ice, hydrogen, and sun, that much nearer the neutrinos raining through us every second like mortality itself. I light another cigarillo (cigar privilege denied you in Tourist Class), and Milk poufs the match as an airmaid with wings and patented smile hands me a handful of book matches that image Africa, Singapore, Rome: inflammatory tabloids with which to undermine the domain of Uncle Sam. For some reason Channels 7 and 3 are blank and I shake my First Class head at the technical explanation I'm given. Damn the Norns of audio. Damn the Norns of ciné—man who make round trip, same day on same plane, see same movie. But no: not again the marathon about the South African Olympic medalist patrician feuding with his sons, but *The Way We Were,* picturesque at least, a campus abscess lanced. Milk will yawn, of course, but might even pick up Barbra Streisand at her plangentest, in which event she will flick an eye sideways like one discovering an elephant's tusk in her ice cream. Is this OK? says the look. Is it often thus? Is this how *you* hear things? One of her least respectable habits is to leer in ridicule at her handicapped compatriots, caricaturing the spastics and the truncated-fin rhetoric of the thalidomides, all the time asking in dumbshow what the hell is *she* doing among schoolmates this ungainly. Why, look at them, there's something wrong; whereas . . . She evokes that old chestnut of the philosophers, the class of all classes that are not members of themselves, and she will probably find Streisand just as impeded, stunted, halt, victim of macrorhiny or whatever nose-blight's called.

A cruel pair, we'll wound even the caviar, the plaice, the tournedos, the Roquefort fresh from this morning's Paris plane. As for the wines, so help me, I'll curb her: the girl's a compulsive bibber, forever in those old days hunting the key to the liquor cupboard in order to settle down to a good long splash with the rest of us. And what am I going to tell her, I whom she'd ply back then with Dry Sack, when I show my nondrinking colors, intact these last three years? Will she force feed me from a bottle or, like a mother penguin, squirt into my mouth what she's squooshed around in hers?

Unabashed in the toilet, she helps herself like a Hottentot to all the cosmetics Elizabeth Arden's powder cottage has provided. She insists. We emerge reeking of ambergris or civet, but my main thought just now is that, when I pee, I'll do it alone. Her predatory curiosity, fanned by immodest boys at that superb school, is worse than ever; she'll try to seize and tug until life is over. Foul and feral games we may have played in an almost mythical past, when she was a hooligan child, but now she'd better turn on some decorum. Some, at least. Now she gets a cabin bag, the sac of status complete with the airline's acronym, and she jubilantly finds within it more toiletries, akin to those in the pure-pure rear cubicle we've just left. Again she makes up her face, again a shade tartish, but with exemplary finesse; the motions are deft, the results loud. *Yah?* she suggests. Not today, I inform her. *Ankew no?* she snaps, to confirm my aberrant refusal, and she echoes the negative, her headset on, blotting out whatever is playing with an exquisitely tapered diphthong, an orchestration all her own of the rounded vowel, that makes everyone look, even the intensely preoccupied carnation-sporting VIP with his thirty-seven global newspapers. Sir Fitzcontumely Rex-Relish, was it? (What did the fawning senior airmaid say?) He looks as if he has just seen an engine rip away from under a wing, but then he recognizes it was only one of the semiaphasic unmentionables next to an unkempt barbarian oaf with a suntan and glazed eyes. Back to his *Paris-Match* he turns with an Etonian grunt, while Milk ransacks the bag for something that isn't there, then pitches it beneath her, as if into the cloud clumps themselves.

Champagne has me saying oh-to-hell-with-it, I'll drink. We'll arrive looped and be taken away in cuffs to Ryker's Island or wherever the sauce-afflicted go. Sipping, with a fistful of smoked salmon, Milk looks suave and wise, for once in a world (other than school) where earpieces are worn in autistic raptness. She lip-reads the cabin staff, who clearly are used to being read thus by sybarites aloft, not only in sky but in an enclosed continuum of private sound comparable to her own nonstop tinnitus of seashell surf. She has more in common with them than she knows, as if the Monte Cristo chocolate tart had made the Many into One. Plied, we take. Half-tipsy, we tremble with expensive mirth—not least, in our very different perspectives, at the noncommunication for years (no letter comes; one cannot phone) right next to this Lucullan reunion in a zooming tube. Vicissitude undoes me quite, and I release a long-saved tear that Milk espies, deplores with a vehemence befitting an aunt, and blots with tissue. Under control again, I let her puff my cigarillo once, which cures her for hours, and blithely take aboard another thousand calories with the fish, a sauce like almond-streaked cirrostratus. Among these colors, in this cabin dedicated to Joseph's coat, the gray line is the present (as it said under some cosmogonical diagram I somewhere saw), and the present is at the moment hard to see. Refraction through a small tear. We're living in animated suspension in a churn of cream embedded in royal-blue velvet, and I half-ban the future, near and distant: if this be altitude euphoria, let it never end. All I'll ask is a little sleep, like Milk, who's succumbed to Mumm's, alcoholic strength by volume 12 percent. Good night, imminent lady, you've almost gone a thousand miles, with only headwinds retarding us.

Much honorable sleeplessness has gone into whatever thoughts

I have on all of this, forever envisioning myself next to Milk, whom the universe bungled into an unselfconscious oddity, and wondering how much accommodation a mind can make. For instance, saying: she belongs more to the universe than to me, has more in common with the hydrogen flowing *back* from the Clouds of Magellan to the Milky Way than with me, for all my own bizarre metabolism. For instance, saying: there are miracle cures, or even miracles, but these will take a half-century to come, and I contrast her fate with that of the latest maltreated famous Russian, his balalaika on fire, asking myself what is remediable faster *en bloc,* brain damage or totalitarianism. The former, I imagine, because the second isn't remediable at all: the brain damaged are retarded, the commissars are not. One day we shall all grow up, when the hippic and the reptilian brains have withered away, then solve everything with nothing but the fairly recent neocortex. I can't finish the thought. Nothing, I begin dimly to see, corresponds to my not knowing what part of nature to blame for making her the way she is, or just recognizing one can't bring a case for damages against the internal compulsions of the DNA chain. Paired base and triple coding: what kind of a scapegoat's that?

Canted sideways, her broad but fragile-skinned face has the flush of winy slumber. I guess at dreams I'll never hear about: a candy-stripe avalanche or obsidian blank. And it becomes easier to possess her mind on her own behalf, in default of discursive conversations, than to stomach just the minimum she cerebrates. Hence, then, galas that implode: silver charms (Lisbon *Fado* Singer, Atlanta Cotton Bale), the penny gumball machine that doubles as a lamp with bright-checked gingham shade, the kaleido-go-round clock of pastel-colored discs, all culled from the in-flight gift catalogue. Or others, verbal mainly, from sickening pun (the Cyclops' favorite musical note is middle C) to pyrotechnics, of which I find no sample currently available, as if coincidence or wit gave us a contributing editorship to the tears of things. There's the absurd you find, and the absurd you invent to hurl at it in therapeutic feud.

Unless you just stand still. Umpteen miles high, seven of air, above the mid-Atlantic trench, in the pell-mell capsule of this maniac's haven, I'd freeze this expedition, halt us here for ever, given enough sandwiches, toys, and toilet tissue, until it all came right, and, imagining we were en route to Alpha Centauri, four and a half light years away, yellow and red, age not a jot during the sixty-two-billion-mile trip. Our cosmic Lourdes. A hyperbolical way of putting it, of course, but nowhere near as frightening, in the spectrum of outlandish wants, as the sentence in which you express your feeling so well you feel it no longer. Better, perhaps, never to say it thus palpably perfect, with always new reaches of the lexical superb to aim for; better to hold tight her hand, dab her sweating hair, and choose a fresh channel to listen to after switching hers off while leaving her headset in place. I do, and hit on what I discover was *Gimme a Pigfoot and a Bottle of Beer,* hardly First Class, but of the Earth earthy, and pertinent when I recall how this child used to eat, more grossly than any wild child of legend, her feet a-wave over her naked belly, a hambone or drumstick in her paw.

Good: there is a high-wire act of trying to keep our every minute together from becoming a high-wire act. We ate lunch absent-mindedly, right on top of one she'd only just had, oblivious of such shudders as the plane gave. Like a team chosen for difficult assignments. Shoulder to shoulder, we fueled up, and now I have the stretched-tight cobweb in the head that comes from no sleep at all while she, frayed with too much emotion and not enough understanding (a blend of parcel, waif, and heiress), grows little blebs of tissue over the splintery nerve ends, perhaps to storm furious or jolly among us while the most elaborate afternoon tea in the world is served by the same, but even fresher-smelling, girls. My mind, on strike, knits a puzzle that unravels thus: *gala*—a holiday with sports or festivities; *gala—galaktos,* Greek for milk, hence *galaktikos,* whence galaxy; Galatea?—statue whom or which Pygmalion brought to life. Am I engaged in some unwitting triple play that converts bringing this girl to life into a galactic holiday? Taking my own hints like one obsessed? Perhaps not, but that is much how it would feel. In a blue reefer, she. Jaw, chalcedony-cool. A fleck of mustard at her mouth corner. Book open on her knees. Albatrosses flying through the cabin. Heavy squawks. Followed by a glazier, bearing a sheet of glass five feet square. Now she reads out, not end-stopping the lines, Shelley's *Ozymandias:* "I met a traveller from an antique land / Who said: 'Two vast and trunkless legs of stone / Stand in the desert. . . .'" Then says, "A bit grandiose, isn't it? The poem that poetry-haters love." Thus the dream within the dream.

Undying afternoon light over mid-Atlantic is the slaty blue of the Siberian cat, or the blue-bonnet salmon in its first few months. Reflying back into morning (an abstract one to be sure), we're only just a bit more ourselves than we aren't. A flat-out Vikingess tests the webbing of her safety belt, flicks an athlete's shoulder as she moves against the buckle, blinks, blinks, blinks. My headache's gone.

Unnumbered minutes later, the wheels go thump in the day above the Eastern seaboard. I haven't even bothered to crane out over Labrador or the Hudson Valley. A refreshed but bewilderingly peaceful Milk has stuffed herself with tea and buttered scones, fruit cake and Danish pastries. We have accomplished our toilet together without mishap or insult, lurching and laughing. She has proudly unearthed her supply of sanitary napkins right there in the cabin, setting one muslin-wrapped wad alongside an outsize eclair. I have taught her how to play ticktacktoe and, in trying on the quiet to lose, have mostly won. Stomach-twisting anticlimax sets in as we lose height, until I think: this is where the trouble starts, pax's tail in uproar's mouth, but all she does, for now, is beam condescendingly at the drab, hot terra cotta as it soars out of storage. Our cards and customs forms are ready for the groinch-groinch of the inspectors' stamps. Her hearing aids she's rejected, maybe anxious to make an unencumbered entrance into the New World. I feel as if, all night, I've been squinting into my telescope, foolishly neglecting to use both eyes and staring, as one should not, into the moon at full. I'm amazed; she's not. We're there. We're here. The one country has become the other. All is ground.

Grounded, out into 85 degrees Fahrenheit, and then inside to a frosty 60 that sets her shivering at once, we call at the toilet in limbo, a *Damas* without a suffixed *cus,* between gate and immigration, where she deposits a first Columbian trickle. I'd like to patent whatever's kept things going this smoothly: no scenes, no incontinence, no demands for what's nearly four thousand miles ago. For one panicky moment I think she's decided she's back where she began, after a lavish circular trip. Then she asks, with bright candor, *Where?* and includes in a festive hand-sweep the terminal, the state, the nation. *Meriga!* she hoots, in frisky postscript to Vespucci; and where I had expected bureaucratic obtuseness at the entry counter, a man in a pale blue shirt decaled with his chore looks hard at her when she says her new word for the dozenth time, and sternly answers, "It sure is." We are through. Customs here is more wearing than in that other country, where, if you've nothing to declare, you follow the green signs, otherwise the red. But even this costive local apparatus spews us out and free after fifteen minutes. When we are met, Milk sees an ebullient woman with black waist-length hair (such hair a fetish with Milk since childhood), who confronts her with her first pair of polaroid sunglasses. In my pocket I press the tube of sun-screen balm she has to wear. I remember the doll, forgotten. Five minutes later, we follow a redcap's trolley out into the hot air of the first day.

MICHAEL VOLLAN. FROM *GOING TO HEAVEN*, A PHOTO-NARRATIVE. (*TQ* #37)

The Sewing Harems

Cynthia Ozick

It was for a time the fashion on the planet Acirema for the more sophisticated females to form themselves into Sewing Harems. Each Sewing Harem would present itself for limited rental, in a body, to a rich businessman capable of housing it in a suitably gracious mansion or tasteful duplex apartment or roomy ranch or luxurious penthouse. Prices ran high. The typical Sewing Harem could be had for a little over $75,000, but hiring one of these groups was splendidly prestigious, and was worth sacrificing foreign travel, a new car, or even college for one's children.

What the Sewing Harems sewed was obvious. Do not visualize quilting bees, samplers, national flags.

What I have failed to mention so far is that the atmosphere of this planet contained a profusion of imperva molecules, which had the property of interacting with hormonal chemistry in such a way as to allow the women of that place to sew their own bodies with no anguish whatsoever. Imperva molecules had been present only since the last ice age, and their inherent volatility offered no guarantee that they could withstand the temperature assaults of the next ice age; but since no one was predicting a new ice age, and since the last one had been over for at least a hundred million years, no immediate atmospheric peril was anticipated.

Once rented, the Sewing Harem would incarcerate itself in comfortable chambers, feast abundantly but privately, and rest prodigiously. After a day or so of hungerless inactivity, the sewing would begin.

There was considerable virtuosity in the style of stitches, but the

ON FOLLOWING PAGE: PHOTOGRAPHY BY RISA GOLDMAN. (*TQ* #40)

most reliable, though not the most aesthetic, was the backstitch, which consists of two, sometimes three, running stitches, the final one repeated over upon itself. One woman would sew another, with the most cooperative cheerfulness imaginable, though occasionally an agile woman—an athlete or acrobat or dancer—managed, with fastidious poise, in exquisite position, to sew herself.

There was, as I have explained, no anguish in the flesh. Still, there was the conventional bleeding while the needle penetrated again and again, and the thread, whatever color was used, had to be tugged along swollen by wet blood, so that the whole length of it was finally dyed dark red. Healing took the usual week or so, and then the man who had leased the Sewing Harem was admitted to try whatever licentious pleasure his fancy and theirs could invent— except, of course, bodily entry. Inaccessibility increased wit, discrimination, maneuverability, and intellectuality on both sides.

The terms of the rental did not allow for snipping open stitches.

At the close of the rental period (between three and six months), a not insignificant number of the women would have become pregnant. How this could have happened I leave to the reader's nimble imagination, but surely in several instances stitches had been opened in defiance of contractual obligations, and perhaps even with the complicity and connivance of the women in question.

The terms of rental further stipulated that, should any children be born to any of the women as consequence of the activity of the leasing period, said children would be held in common by all the women: each one, equal with every other, would be designated as mother.

Now it should be immediately evident that all of this was far, far less than ordinary custom. The lighthearted hiring of Sewing Harems was practiced in a number of the great cities of that planet, but could be found hardly at all in the underdeveloped countries. The formation of Sewing Harems—or so it was charged by the Left and the Right—was the fad of the self-indulgent and the irrepressibly reckless. Yet not altogether so, since after the period of the lease expired, the members of each Sewing Harem, in their capacity as equal mothers, often attempted to remain together and to continue as a serious social body, in order to raise its children intelligently.

Given the usual temperamental difficulties, the peregrinations of restless individuals, the nomadic habits of the group as a whole, and the general playfulness (their own word being the more ironic "frivolousness") of the membership, a Sewing Harem was frequently known to disband not many years after the nearly simultaneous birth of its children.

But the chief reason for the dissolution of a Sewing Harem was jealousy over the children. The children were few, the mothers many. Each child was everyone's child in the mind of the community, but by no means in the mind of the child. At first the babies were kept together in a compound, and all the mothers had equal access to them for dandling, rocking, and fondling. But of course only the mothers who could breast-feed were at all popular with the babies, since the theorists of these societies, who had a strong and authoritative caucus, frowned on bottles. Consequently, the mothers who had not experienced parturition, and who had no breast milk, were avoided by the babies, and soon the community of mothers began to be divided into those the babies preferred and those the babies shunned; or, into milkers and nonmilkers; or, into elite mothers and second-class mothers.

Somehow, even after the children were weaned, the original classifications persisted, causing depression among the second-class mothers.

As the children grew older, moreover, it was discovered that they *interrupted*. By now, several of the second-class mothers, feeling disappointed, had gone off to join other Sewing Harems just then in the process of putting themselves out for rental. And only these defeated mothers, by virtue of being no longer on the scene, were not interrupted. All the rest were. It was found that the children interrupted careers, journeys, appointments, games, telephone calls, self-development, education, meditation, sexual activity, and other enlightened, useful, and joyous pursuits. But since the children were all being brought up with the highest self-expectations, they believed themselves to be ("as indeed you are," the mothers told them) in every way central to the community.

They believed this in spite of their understanding that, morally and philosophically, they had no right to exist. Morally, each one had been conceived by breach of contract. Philosophically, each one had been born to a mother theoretically committed to the closure of the passage leading to the womb. In brief, the children knew that they were the consequence of unpredictable deviations from a metaphysical position; or, to state it still more succinctly, the fruit of snipped stitches.

That the children interrupted the personal development of the mothers was difficulty enough. In a less dialectical community there might have been a drive toward comfortable if imperfect solutions. But these were (as it ought by now to be radiantly clear) no ordinary women. Ordinary women might have taken turns in caring for the children, or hired men and other women for this purpose, or experimented with humane custodial alternatives. A Sewing Harem, however, was a community of philosophers. And just as bottle-feeding had been condemned as an inferior compromise, so now were the various permutations of day-care proposals scorned. Each child was regarded as the offspring not simply of a single philosopher, but of a community of philosophers; hence not to be subjected to rearing by hirelings, or by any arrangement inferior to the loftiest visions of communal good.

As for taking turns, though it might be fair, it was inconceivable: just as each child was entitled to the highest self-expectation without compromise, so was each philosopher entitled to the highest self-development without compromise or interruption.

The children, as they grew, not only interrupted the mothers; they interfered with the mothers' most profound ideals. The blatant fact of the birth of a large group of children hindered ecological reform, promoted pollution, and frustrated every dramatic hope of rational population reduction. In short, the presence of the children was antiprogressive. And since not only joy and self-development, but also friendship and truth, were the dearest doctrines of a Sewing Harem, the children were made to understand that, in spite of their deserving the highest self-expectations, they represented nevertheless the most regressive forces on the planet.

It is hardly necessary to note, given the short life of any novelty, that by the time the children became adults, the fad of the Sewing Harems had virtually died out (excepting, now and then, an occasional nostalgic revival). Not surprisingly, the term "Harem" itself was by now universally repudiated as regressive and repugnant, despite the spirited voluntarism and economic self-sufficiency of the original societies. But the historic influence of those early societies was felt throughout the planet.

Everywhere, including the most backward areas, women were organizing themselves for sewing—with the result, of course, that there were fewer and fewer natural mothers and more and more adoptive mothers. The elitist distinctions observed by the founding groups no longer pertained, and were, in fact, reversed by the overwhelming vote of the underdeveloped countries. Devotion to egalitarian principles put the sewn majority in the saddle; and since the majority were adoptive mothers, or women whose lives were peripheral to children, or women who had nothing to do with children at all, natural motherhood (though it continued to be practiced, with restraint, in all circles except the very literary) was little noticed and less remarked on, neither as neurosis nor as necessity. It was neither patronized nor demeaned, and it was certainly not persecuted. It was not much on anyone's mind.

It goes without saying that society at large instantly improved. The planet took on a tidier appearance: more room for gardens and trees, a diminution of garbage and poverty, fewer smoky factories, highways decently uncrowded for a holiday drive. In the international sphere, matters were somewhat less satisfactory, at least in the view of the men and women who ran the planet. Though the wicked remained dominant, as always, it was not much worthwhile making wars any more, since in any conflict it is preferable that vast and vaster quantities of lives be butchered, and the numbers of young soldiers available for losing the bottom halves of their torsos went on diminishing.

To put it as briefly and delightfully as possible: the good (those self-respecting individuals who did not intend to waste their years) had greater opportunities to add to their goodness via self-improvement and self-development, the wicked were thwarted, and the planet began to look and smell nicer than anyone had ever expected.

And all this was the legacy of a handful of Sewing Harems which had once been dismissed as a self-indulgent ideological fad.

Meanwhile, something rather sad had happened, though it applied only to a nearly imperceptible minority and seldom drew anyone's constructive attention.

The children of the Sewing Harems had become pariahs. How this occurred is not of much interest. Whether they were regarded as a laughingstock anachronism, the spawn of geishas, scions of an antiquated and surely comical social contrivance the very reminder of which was an embarrassment to the modern temper; whether they were taken as the last shameful relic of an aggressively greedy entrepreneurial movement; whether they were scorned as personalities mercilessly repressed by the barbaric extremes of the communal impulse; whether they were damned as the offspring of the pornographic imagination; whether they were jeered at as the deformed cubs of puritanical bluestockings; whether all of these or none, no one can rightly say.

Sociologists with enough curiosity to look into the origins of the sect pointed, predictably, to their upbringing: they were taught that they were at the root of the planet's woes, and yet they were taught that they had earned not one, but many, mothers. As a consequence of the first teaching, they fulfilled themselves as irrational demons and turned themselves into outcasts. As a consequence of the second teaching, they idolized motherhood.

You will have noticed that I have referred to these unfortunates as a sect. This is exactly true. They were content to marry only one another, or perhaps no one else was content to marry any of *them*. Since some of them had the same father, or the same natural mother, or both, they were already afflicted with the multitudinous ills of inbreeding, and their fierce adherence to endogamy compounded these misfortunes. They had harelips, limps, twisted jaws and teeth, short arms, diseases of the blood, hereditary psychoses; some were wretchedly strabismic, others blind or deaf. They were an ugly, anxious, stern-minded crew, continually reproducing themselves.

Any woman of the sect who sewed herself they would kill; but this was generally unheard of among them, since sewing was their most ferocious taboo. Male babies born in any way sexually deformed were admitted to early surgery, but female babies born with unusually small or sealed vaginas were fed cyanide. The only remaining resemblance to the gaily lucid and civilizing Sewing Harems from which these savages derived was their prohibition of bottle-feeding.

They were organized into strong family units, and emphasized family orderliness and conventionality. All this was within the tribe. Otherwise they were likely to be criminals—members of the sect were frequently convicted of having murdered sewn women. If they had any gift at all, it was for indulgence in unusual art forms. They had a notorious talent for obscene stonecutting.

Worst of all was their religious passion. They had invented a superior goddess. A single unimaginative and brutish syllable of three letters, two of them identical, formed her name—ingenious nonetheless, since it was a palindrome, pronounced identically whether chanted forward or backward. The goddess was conceived as utterly carnal, with no role other than to nurture the urge to spawn; under her base auspices the tribe spewed forth dozens of newborn savages in a single day.

In addition to murdering sewn women, the descendants of the Sewing Harems were guilty of erecting religious statuary on highways in the dead of night. These appeared in the likenesses of immense round gate pillars, which, looming without warning in the blaze of day where there had been nothing the evening before, were the cause of multiple bloody traffic accidents. The best were carved out of enormous rocks quarried no one knew where, hauled on trucks, and set in place by cranes. The cheapest were made of concrete, mixed on the spot and left to dry behind sawhorses hung with bright rags. In police reports these structures were usually described as mammary replicas; in actuality they had the shapes of huge vulvae. Sometimes the corpse of a sewn woman, stinking of some foul incense, a shiny magazine picture of an infant nailed into her thigh, would be found between the high walls of the two horrendous labia.

I have already remarked that these primitives did not number significantly in the general population (though they were disproportionately present in the prison population). They were pests rather than a pestilence, and their impact on the planet would without doubt have continued negligible had the imperva molecules not suddenly begun first to deteriorate in the skies and then to disintegrate entirely. All this was inexplicable; until now every firm scientific expectation was that no such dissolution could occur except under the climatic threat of a new ice age. Such a comment was always taken for a joke. In point of fact it remained a joke. There were no extraordinary atmospheric upheavals; the normal temperature of the planet was undisturbed.

But it became, of course, impossible for women to sew themselves as casually, uncomplicatedly, and joyfully as they had been capable of doing for immemorial generations—ever since, in fact, that planet's version of Eden: a humane Eden, incidentally, which had passed on no unkindnesses or encumbrances, whether to women or to men.

And because of irresistible advances in technology, the vulval thread had been so improved (composed of woven particles of infertels encased in plastic, it could now withstand blood dye) that the stitches could not be undone except by the most difficult and dangerous surgery, which the majority eschewed because of the side effects of reversed infertels when they are burst. The treacherous stitch snipping of the Sewing Harems, so long a subject of mockery and infamy among those who admired both progress and honest commitment, was all at once seen to be a lost treasure of the race.

1977

Nearly all of the sewn women remained sewn until their deaths.

And the pariahs, the only source of mothers, bred like monkeys in their triumph, until the great stone vulvae covered the planet from end to end, and the frivolous memory of the Sewing Harems was rubbed away, down to the faintest smear of legend.

ABOVE: BRAD HOLLAND, *THE OVERSEER*, FOLLOWED BY *THEY DON'T KNOW WHEN* AND *NIGHT WATCH* (*TQ* #42) AND PHOTOGRAPHS BY JIM MATUSIK. (*TQ* #44)

Two shoes for one foot

John Hawkes

In a small mill city in Bavaria there lived some children who were afraid of a one-legged man called the Kommandant. He lived within walking distance of the shops and houses, so near that with the help of his crutch he often swung in the direction of their cobbled streets and little blackened windows and smoking chimneys. The Kommandant frightened the boys, of course, because he had only one leg; yet it was just for this, for their dreams of fleeing the single foot, that they talked of surprising him with their bravery and cleverness and skill. But they had no Teutonic helmets, no wooden swords; to the boys it would be nothing less than an exchange of heart for heart.

One evening while it was still light and before the frost became hard, they approached the Kommandant, stared at the straight trouser leg and at the folded trouser leg, and made him an offer. He heard them silently, then followed them, and they were careful not to walk too quickly. They took him by back streets and through an unproductive orchard to the house of the oldest boy, Heinrich; they led him directly inside where he stood wearing his Kommandant's cap and leaning on his crutch. He looked closely at what the boys were offering for sale, at what they dared offer no one but himself. The smallest of the boys darted forward suddenly and pulled the coverlet from the bed. The Kommandant stepped near the bed which filled nearly the whole of the room. Through the narrow single window the sunset was cold and red, a brutal light on the still figure now stretched before them.

KINUKO CRAFT. (*TQ* #46)

"He is ours," whispered Heinrich, and the boys' eyes were the eyes one sees at dusk under the roots of a tree, five pairs or more, in winter, staring up to the surface of the earth with that animal curiosity which shines from the pitiless lair. In this room only the bed, the Kommandant, the boys: and the boys stood there like brothers, each as familiar as Heinrich himself with the chipped walls, the hole in the floor, the place where he hung his jacket and put his shoes; all of them ragged and expectant in the intimacy of boys together.

"Come look, mein Herr," Heinrich whispered and his companions also pressed closer. They tried not to touch the Kommandant's crutch. The boys waited for the bargain to be sealed as if they felt that no one else would come here or become aware in any way, ever, of what was happening in Heinrich's room while the sun set.

Upon the bed lay a man, heavy and fully dressed in a shirt and black suit of a good cut but tight across the chest, a man who appeared to be neither asleep nor dead though the cloth and the hair were wet with the rains so frequent in this country.

"He is complete. He is not damaged, not at all damaged, Herr Kommandant," whispered Heinrich, and the eyes of his companions were the eyes of moles. "He is all here," Heinrich told him again in his soft, decisive voice.

"But look," said the Kommandant. "Look at his feet, boys. Where are the shoes?"

Heinrich smiled and went to the wooden rack where he kept his own worn pairs of boots. "On the rack, mein Herr. They were soiled, you can see for yourself; they were covered with blood. So I removed them. But they belong with him and they shall go with him." Without hesitating he returned to the bed and placed the great swollen shoes on the coverlet next to the feet, exactly as if he had tipped the scales from a crafty, childish generosity.

"Good," said the Kommandant.

The sun fell sharply through the window and lit the buttons on the dead man's coat. The eyeglasses began to shine, but for a moment only. Following some curious law of growth, some urge dictated by its sap and fibers, the lowest branch of one of the few trees in the orchard, a tree planted too near the house, had reached to the window and pressed its crowded shape to the panes. Now, like an arm twisted in some invisible grip, it moved as much as it could and scratched painfully on the glass. The sun came into the room through the window and between the gray twigs of the branch that struggled and obscured the view. Beyond a few dead leaves and the dusty glass could be seen a layer of smoke from the mills, and farther yet, under the red streaks of the sun, the gathering of the night itself.

"Good," murmured the Kommandant again and frowned, considering the man on the bed. The eyeglasses were cracked and twisted, but they had been readjusted on the bridge of the nose. Though not expertly, the hair had been brushed into place.

"And, Herr Kommandant," said the oldest boy, "he has papers also." Heinrich unfastened the top button, drew away the coat, and pointed. The papers protruded thick and white from the inside pocket until quickly Heinrich hid them away again and smoothed the lapel.

"He is cold," Heinrich said, peering up, smiling, indicating the heavy breast of the man. He continued to watch the Kommandant for some change in his face.

"Herr Herzenbrecher!" the smallest boy shouted. "He is Herr Herzenbrecher!"

The sun passed away, the orchard became dark; the boys shifted, and one of them held the smallest idly by his hand. They could hear the sounds of all the things that woke Heinrich in the night. Now the buttons no longer flashed on the coat, the lifelike expression was shadowed on the dead man's face, his black waistcoat was tight and fastened awry over the belly still filled with air. Dusk in this city, despite the wireless and industry, was the time when the inhabitants feared to see the dead taking to the open roofs.

"But your bed? You bring him to your own bed?" asked the Kommandant.

"Oh," said Heinrich quickly, "it's all right. I slept on the floor. But of course I covered him each night with the blanket until the sun rose." Then by a slight gesture, a movement of his finger, calling attention to the watch chain and to the belt buckle which must have been loosened after the last meal, all the while staring at the Kommandant, Heinrich pursed his lips and asked, "Well? What do you think of him?"

A shrill whistle, like the furious sound that regulates life in prisons, came from far off in the direction of the mills, and the iron machines began scraping in that distant end of the city. Heinrich waited. Suddenly the smallest boy snatched up the bloodied shoes and ran with them into the orchard. "Look," he cried, "I have stolen his shoes! Look here, I have stolen Herr Herzenbrecher's shoes!" He ran under the trees, to and fro, laughing, fat, and his childish and impetuous and uneven flat steps came boldly back from the earth out there. He wet his stockings in the leaves. He hugged the shoes. "Two shoes for one foot!" he shouted under the withered apple tree. "Two shoes for one foot!" He was wrapped in the mist and bare armed, hurrying between the hanging trees, squatting and hiding himself at every twisted trunk. "Two shoes . . ." he tried to shout again, but the boys caught him and stopped his shrill humor with their white hands. He began to sniffle as they led him inside the house.

"If you are not good," said Heinrich, "he will blow his breath on you. Now mein Herr," he said, forgetting to smile, forgetting to change the sternness in his voice, "what of our business?"

The Kommandant nodded and leaned closer, as if to sit on the edge of the bed. It was so dark now that the boys' heads were little skulls in the shadows, featureless except for the large dark charcoal smears of eyes and mouths. The body was larger in the darkness.

"We have washed him. Have we not done well, mein Herr?"

The Kommandant could hear the beating of the children's hearts. He tried to see what he could of the room; he smelled the coverlet and the leaves and the wet paper wadded under the coat. "Yes," he answered at last.

The smallest boy began to cry and struggled to run, knocking against his comrades, weeping and laughing at the same time. "Herr Herzenbrecher is bad, Heinrich. He is going to blow his breath on Heinrich."

"Hush," said Heinrich. "But would you care to look in his pockets, Herr Kommandant? Perhaps if you glance in one pocket anyway . . ."

It started to rain. The rain filled the orchard with droplets that did not stream slantwise down the window but clouded it, dulling it with the harmless but telltale puffing of a dead storm—the kind of rain which, if it is a dark night and the sun has been red, drenches the coat of fur noiselessly and in a moment, before the dog can take cover. Such rain did not help the apple trees to grow.

Heinrich lit a candle and tilted it so that not a line in Herr Herzenbrecher's face could be missed. He noticed a clot of dirt on the trousers and brushed it off. For a long moment he admired Herr Herzenbrecher. Then he smiled and all the boys around the bed smiled also. "No one has ever found anything like Herr Herzenbrecher," he whispered. "Herr Herzenbrecher looks like my father. He looks like Hansel's father also. He is not a plaything,

Kommandant, you can be sure."

The room was small for the Kommandant, and in it his crutch cast a dark shadow. The room so belonged to a child that it was hardly part of the house—but dusty, slowly sinking off its plumb, empty except for the boy living within and except for his friends who appeared out of the orchard, knowing so well the weather-beaten paths to it. The room itself, the wind, the boys. And now Herr Herzenbrecher. And now the Kommandant. The boys held each other by the hands, the limb of the apple tree moved against the window.

"But what of marks on his person?" asked the Kommandant. "Nothing of violence?"

"Oh yes," answered Heinrich shortly, "you will see." Heinrich put his fingers lightly on the dead man's shoulder. "However, they are not noticeable, mein Herr, and we covered them. Perhaps you will not even find them."

"Heinrich," asked the Kommandant slowly, "do you know how long the man has been dead?"

Heinrich stared and moved as if to blow out the candle; he hugged the smallest boy and pulled on his stockings; his face was whiter than ever.

"For as long as my Papa has been dead," answered Heinrich at last.

"But you have not thought of telling anyone about this man?"

"No, mein Herr."

"Nor of summoning the police?"

"No, mein Herr."

"But now you want to give him up," said the Kommandant.

"Mein Herr. We are only *offering* you Herr Herzenbrecher. He is ours. We found him. He has a gold watch. He is with us, and now we are all men."

"But this man is dead!"

"Comrades," whispered Heinrich, "assure the Kommandant that we know that Herr Herzenbrecher is dead."

"Mamma, Mamma, Mamma," cried the smallest boy until Heinrich picked him up and still holding him, and perspiring, spoke again to the one-legged man: "Are you thinking of his murderer, mein Herr?"

At that moment the window smashed and the branch, at last finding entrance through the broken glass, intruded, nodding and twisting as if it had finally penetrated a wall of stone.

"Tell me," said the Kommandant, speaking as plainly and softly as he could, "do you know how Herr Herzenbrecher died?"

Heinrich's face shone like gold and became thin and bright with pleasure. But he remained silent.

"Well, do you know?" repeated the Kommandant.

"Yes. Of course. Mein Herr," Heinrich whispered then, staring at the window, "he died fighting, throwing himself upon a great animal armed with scales. Bravely."

The Kommandant frowned and leaned on his crutch. He stopped himself from speaking.

The mill whistle blew again beyond the orchard, beyond the electric cables tapping in the mist. There came a slight odor of apples through the rain. In the forward part of the house a bell tinkled sharply. Immediately Heinrich stepped away from the corpse, laughed awkwardly, and bowed before the officer.

"Pardon, mein Herr Kommandant. My grandmother is calling me to our supper. I must be with her. We eat together. But will you take him, Your Honor?"

The Kommandant waited and then nodded and then from his heavy leather purse he gave each boy a few marks and a few pfennigs.

Then Heinrich signaled. They scurried about and produced a long umbrella, a bundle containing a flattened hat and handwoven shawl, and a piece of cord with which they securely tied the shoes. All this they thrust upon the Kommmandant.

The smallest boy pulled Heinrich to the door and shouted after the Kommandant, who was laboriously pushing his wooden cart into the darkness and rain: "Live well, Herr Herzenbrecher, live well!"

KINUKO CRAFT. (*TQ* #46)

Coyote holds a full house in his hand

Leslie Marmon Silko

He wasn't getting any place with Mrs. Sekakaku. He could see that. She was warming up leftover chili beans for lunch, and when her niece came over, they left him alone on the red plastic sofa and talked at the kitchen table. Aunt Mamie was still sick, her niece was telling her, and they were all so worried because the doctors at Keams Canyon said they'd tried everything already and old man Ko'ite had come over from Oraibi and still Aunt Mamie was having dizzy spells and couldn't get out of bed. He was looking at the same *Life* magazine he'd already looked at before, and it didn't have any pictures of high school girls twirling batons, or plane crashes, or anything he wanted to look at more than twice, but he didn't want to listen to them because then he'd know just what kind of gossip Mrs. Sekakaku found more important than him and his visit.

He set the magazine down on his lap and traced his finger over the horse's head embossed on the plastic cushion. It was always like that. When he didn't expect it, it always came to him, but when he wanted something to happen, like with Mrs. Sekakaku, then it shied away.

Mrs. Sekakaku's letters had made the corner of the trading post where the mailboxes were smell like the perfume counter at Woolworth's. The Mexican woman with the fat arms was the postmaster and ran the trading post. She didn't approve of perfumed letters and she used to pretend the letters weren't there, even when he could smell them and see their pastel edges

1980

sticking out of the pile in the general delivery slot. The Mexican woman thought Pueblo men were great lovers. He knew this because he heard her say so to another Mexican woman one day while he was finishing his strawberry soda on the other side of the dry-goods section. In the summer he spent a good number of hours there watching her because she wore sleeveless blouses that revealed her fat upper arms, full and round, and the tender underarm creases curving to her breasts. They had not noticed he was still there, leaning on the counter behind a pile of overalls. " . . . The size of a horse" was all that he had heard, but he knew what she was talking about. They were all like that, those Mexican women. That was all they talked about when they were alone. "As big as a horse"—he knew that much Spanish and more too, but she had never treated him nice, not even when he brought her the heart-shaped box of candy, having carried it on the bus all the way from Albuquerque. He didn't think it was his being older than her; she was over thirty herself. It was because she didn't approve of men who drank. That was the last thing he did before he left town; he did it because he had to. Liquor was illegal on the reservation, so the last thing he did was have a few drinks to carry home with him, the same way other people stocked up on lamb nipples or extra matches. She must have smelled it on his breath when he handed her the candy because she didn't say anything and she left the box under the counter by the old newspapers and balls of string. The cellophane was never opened, and the fine gray dust that covered everything in the store finally settled on the pink satin bow. The postmaster was jealous of the letters that were coming, but she was the one who had sent him into the arms of Mrs. Sekakaku.

In her last two letters Mrs. Sekakaku had been hinting around for him to come see her at Bean Dance time. That was after Christmas when he had sent a big poinsettia plant all the way to Second Mesa on the mail bus. Up until then she had never answered the parts in his letters where he said he wished he could see the beautiful Hopi mesas with snow on them. But that had been the first time a potted plant ever rode into Hopi on the mail bus, and Mrs. Sekakaku finally realized the kind of man he was. All along, that had been the trouble at Laguna: nobody understood just what kind of man he was. They thought he was sort of good-for-nothing, he knew that, but for a long time he kept telling himself to keep on trying and trying.

But it seemed like people would never forget the time the whole village was called out to clean up for feast day and he sent his mother to tell them he was sick with liver trouble. He was still hurt because they didn't understand that with liver trouble you can walk around and sometimes even ride the bus to Albuquerque. Everyone was jealous of him and they didn't stop to think how much it meant to his mother to have someone living with her in her old age. All they could talk about was the big COD that came to the post office in his name and she cashed her pension check to pay for it. But she was the one who had told him, "Sonny Boy, if you want that jacket, you go ahead and order it." It was made out of brown vinyl, resembling leather, and he still wore it whenever he went to town. Even on the day she had the last stroke, his two older brothers had been telling her to quit paying his bills for him and to make him get out and live on his own. But she always stood up for him in front of the others, even if she did complain privately at times to her nieces, who then scolded him about the bills from the record club and the correspondence school. He always knew he could be a lawyer; he had listened to the lawyers in the courtrooms of the Federal Building on those hot summer afternoons when he needed a cool place to sit while he waited for the bus to Laguna. He listened and he knew he could be a lawyer because he was so good at making up stories to justify why things happened the way they did. He thought correspondence school would be different from Indian school, which had given him stomachaches and made him run away all through his seventh-grade year. Right after that he had cut his foot pretty bad, chopping wood for his older brother's wife—the one who kept brushing her arms across his shoulders whenever she poured coffee at the supper table. The foot had taken so long to heal that his mother agreed he shouldn't go back to Indian school or chop wood any more. A few months after that, they were all swimming at the river and he hurt his back in a dive off the old wooden bridge, so it was no wonder he couldn't do the same work as the other young men.

When Mildred told him she was marrying that Hopi, he didn't try to stop her, although she stood there for a long time like she was waiting for him to say something. He liked things just the way they were down along the river after dark. Her mother and aunts owned so many fields they expected a husband to hoe them, and he had already promised his mother he wouldn't leave her alone in her old age. He thought it would be easier this way, but after Mildred's wedding, people who had seen him and Mildred together started joking about how he had lost out to a Hopi.

Hopi men were famous for their fast hands and the way they could go on all night. But some of the jokes hinted that he himself was as lazy at lovemaking as he was with his shovel during spring ditch cleaning, and that he would take a girlfriend to the deep sand along the river so he could lie on the bottom while she worked on top. Later on, some of the old men took him aside and said he shouldn't feel bad about Mildred, and told him about women they'd lost to Hopis when they were all working on the railroad together in Winslow. Women believed the stories about Hopi men, they told him, because women liked the sound of those stories, and the women didn't care if it was the Hopi men who were making up the stories in the first place. So when he finally found himself riding the Greyhound bus into Winslow on his way to see Mrs. Sekakaku and the Bean Dance he got to thinking about those stories about Hopi men. It had been years since Mildred had married that Hopi, and her aunts and her mother kept the man working in their fields all year round. Even Laguna people said "Poor thing" whenever they saw the Hopi man walking past with a shovel on his shoulder. So he knew he wasn't going because of that—he was going because of Mrs. Sekakaku's letters and because it was lonely living in a place where no one appreciates you even when you keep trying and trying. At Hopi he could get a fresh start; he could tell people about himself while they looked at the photos in the plastic pages of his wallet.

He waited for the mail bus and drank a cup of coffee in the cafe across the street from the pink stucco motel with a cowboy on its neon sign. He had a feeling that something was about to change because of his trip, but he didn't know if it would be good for him or bad. Sometimes he was able to look at what he was doing and to see himself clearly two or three weeks into the future. But this time when he looked, he only saw himself getting off the bus on the sandy shoulder of the highway below Second Mesa. He stared up at the Hopi town on the sand rock and thought that probably he'd get married.

1980

The last hundred feet up the wagon trail seemed the greatest distance to him and he felt an unaccustomed tightness in his lungs. He knew it wasn't old age—it was something—something that wanted him to work for it. A short distance past the outside toilets at the edge of the mesa top, he got his breath back and their familiar thick odor reassured him. He saw that one of the old toilets had tipped over and rolled down the side of the mesa to the piles of stove ashes, broken bottles, and corn shucks on the slope below. He'd get along all right. Like a lot of people, at one time he believed Hopi magic could outdo all the other Pueblos, but now he saw that it was all the same from time to time and place to place. When Hopi men got tired of telling stories about all-nighters in Winslow motels, then probably the old men brought it around to magic and how they rigged the Navajo tribal elections one year just by hiding some little painted sticks over near Window Rock. Whatever it was he was ready for it.

He checked his reflection in the window glass of Mrs. Sekakaku's front door before he knocked. Gray hair made him look dignified; that was what she had written after he sent her the photographs. He believed in photographs, to show to people as you were telling them about yourself and the things you'd done and the places you'd been. He always carried a pocket camera and asked people passing by to snap him outside the fancy bars and restaurants in the Heights, where he walked after he had had a few drinks in the Indian bars downtown. He didn't tell her he'd never been inside those places, that he didn't think Indians were welcome there. Behind him he could hear a dog barking. It sounded like a small dog but it also sounded very upset and little dogs were the first ones to bite. So he turned, and at first he thought it was a big rat crawling out the door of Mrs. Sekakaku's bread oven, but it was a small, gray wirehaired dog that wouldn't step out any farther. It must have known it was about to be replaced because it almost choked on its own barking. Only lonely widows let their dogs sleep in the bread oven, although they always pretended otherwise and scolded their little dogs whenever relatives or guests came. "Not much longer, little doggy," he was saying softly while he knocked on the door. He was beginning to wonder if she had forgotten he was coming, and he could feel his confidence lose its footing just a little. She walked up from behind while he was knocking; that was something he always dreaded because it made the person knocking look so foolish—knocking and waiting while the one you wanted wasn't inside the house at all but was standing right behind you. The way the little dog was barking, probably all the neighbors had seen him and were laughing. He managed to smile and would have shaken hands, but she was bending over petting the little dog running around and around her ankles. "I hope you haven't been waiting too long! My poor Aunt Mamie had one of her dizzy spells and I was over helping." She was still looking down at the dog while she said this and he noticed she wasn't wearing her perfume. At first he thought his understanding of the English language must be failing—that she had really only invited him over to the Bean Dance, that he had misread her letters when she said that a big house like hers was lonely and that she did not like walking home alone in the evenings from the water faucet outside the village. Maybe all this had only meant she was afraid a bunch of Navajos might jump out from the shadows of the mesa rocks to take turns on top of her. But when she warmed up the leftover chili beans and went on talking to her niece about the dizzy spells, he began to suspect what was going on. She was one of those women who wore Evening in Paris to Laguna feast and sprinkled it on letters, but back at Hopi she pretended she was somebody else. She had lured him into sending his letters and snapshots and the big poinsettia plant to show off to her sisters and aunts—and now his visit, so she could pretend he had come uninvited, overcome with desire for her. He should have seen it all along, but the first time he met her at Laguna feast, a gust of wind had showed him the little roll of fat above her garter and left him dreaming of a plunge deep into the crease at the edge of the silk stocking. The old auntie and the dizzy spells gave her the perfect excuse and a story to protect her respectability. It was only two-thirty, but already she was folding a flannel nightgown while she talked to her niece. And here the whole bus ride from Laguna he had been imagining the night together—fingering the creases and folds and the little rolls while she squeezed him with both hands. He felt it lift off and up like a butterfly moving away from him, and the breathlessness he had felt coming up the mesa returned. He was feeling bitter—that if that's all it took, then he'd find a way to get that old woman out of bed.

He said it without thinking—the words just found his mouth

and he said, "Excuse me, ladies," straightening his belt buckle as he walked across the room, "but it sounds to me like your poor auntie is in bad shape." Mrs. Sekakaku's niece looked at him for the first time all afternoon. "Is he a medicine man?" she asked her aunt, and for an instant he could see Mrs. Sekakaku hesitate and he knew he had to say, "Yes, it's something I don't usually mention myself. Too many of those guys just talk about it to attract women. But this is a serious case." It was sounding so good that he was afraid he would start thinking again about the space between the cheeks of the niece's ass and be unable to go on. But the next thing he said was they had a cure that they did at Laguna for dizzy spells like Aunt Mamie was having. He could feel a momentum somewhere inside himself. It wasn't hope because he knew Mrs. Sekakaku had tricked him, but whatever it was, it was going for broke. He imagined the feel of grabbing hold of the tops of the niece's thighs, which were almost as fat and would feel almost as good as the tops of Mrs. Sekakaku's thighs. "There would be no charge; this is something I want to do especially for you." That was all it took because these Hopi ladies were like all the other Pueblo women he ever knew—always worrying about saving money, and nothing made them enemies for longer than selling them the melon or mutton leg they felt they should get for free as a love gift because all of them, even the thin ones and the old ones, believed he was after them. "Oh, that would be so kind of you! We are so worried about her!" "Well, not so fast," he said, even though his heart was racing. "It won't work unless everything is just so. All her clans-women must come to her house, but there can't be any men there, not even outside." He paused. He knew exactly what to say. "This is very important. Otherwise the cure won't work." Mrs. Sekakaku let out her breath suddenly and tightened her lips, and he knew that any men or boys not in the kivas preparing for Bean Dance would be sent far away from Aunt Mamie's house. He looked over at the big loaf of fresh oven bread the niece had brought when she came; they hadn't offered him any before, but now, after she served him a big bowl of chili beans, she cut him a thick slice. It was all coming back to him now, about how good medicine men get treated, and he wasn't surprised at himself any more. Once he got started he knew just how it should go. It was just getting it started that gave him trouble sometimes.

Mrs. Sekakaku and her niece hurried out to contact all the women of the Snow Clan to bring them to Aunt Mamie's for the cure. There were so many of them sitting in rows facing the sick bed—on folding chairs and little canvas stools they'd brought just like they did for a kiva ceremony or a summer dance. He had never stopped to think how many Snow Clan women there might be, and as he walked across the room he wondered if he should have made some kind of age limit. Some of the women sitting there were pretty old and bony, but then there were all those little girls; one squatted down in front of him to play jacks and he could see the creases and dimples of her legs below her panties. The initiated girls and the women sat serious and quiet with the ceremonial presence the Hopis are famous for. Their eyes were full of the power the clanswomen shared whenever they gathered together. He saw it clearly and he never doubted its strength. Whatever he took, he'd have to run with it, but the women would come out on top like they usually did.

He sat on the floor by the fireplace and asked them to line up. He reached into the cold, white juniper ashes and took a handful, and told the woman standing in front of him to raise her skirt above her knees. The ashes were slippery and they carried his hands up and around each curve, each fold, each roll of flesh on her thighs. He reached high, but his fingers never strayed above the edge of the panty leg. They stepped in front of him one after the other, and he worked painstakingly with each one, the silvery white ashes billowing up like clouds above the skin they dusted like early snow on brown hills— and he lost all track of time. He closed his eyes so he could feel them better—the folds of skin and flesh, the little crevices and creases—as a hawk must feel canyons and arroyos while he is soaring. Some thighs he gripped as if they were something wild and fleet like antelope and rabbits, and the women never flinched or hesitated because they believed the recovery of their clan sister depended on them. The dimple and pucker at the edge of the garter and silk stocking brought him back and he gave special attention to Mrs. Sekakaku, the last one before Aunt Mamie. He traced the ledges and slopes with all his fingers pressing in the ashes. He was out of breath and he knew he could not stand up to get to Aunt Mamie's bed; so he bowed his head and pretended he was praying. "I feel better already. I'm not dizzy," the old woman said, not letting anyone help her out of bed or walk with her to the fireplace. He rubbed her thighs as carefully as he had the rest, and he could tell by the feel that she'd probably live a long time.

The sun was low in the sky and the bus would be stopping for the outgoing mail pretty soon. He was quitting while he was ahead, while the Hopi men were still in the kivas for the Bean Dance. He graciously declined any payment, but the women insisted they wanted to do something, so he unzipped his jacket pocket and brought out his little pocket camera and a flash cube. As many as could squeeze together stood with him in front of the fireplace and someone snapped the picture. By the time he left Aunt Mamie's house he had two shopping bags full of pies and piki bread.

Mrs. Sekakaku was acting very different now: when they got back to her house she kicked the little gray dog and blocked up the oven hole with an orange crate. But he told her he had to get back to Laguna right away because he had something important to tell the old men. It was something they'd been trying and trying to do for a long time. At sundown the mail bus pulled onto the highway below Second Mesa, but he was tasting one of the pumpkin pies and forgot to look back. He set aside a fine-looking cherry pie to give to the postmaster. Now that they were even again with the Hopi men, maybe this Laguna luck would hold out a little while longer.

Dillinger in Hollywood

John Sayles

You know how they get after New Year's when the visits dry up and the TV is bust and there's steamed chicken for lunch three days in a row? It was one of those weeks, and Spurs Tatum starts in after rec therapy, before we could wheel them all out of the day room.

"Hoot Gibson held my horse," says Spurs. "I took falls for Randolph Scott. I hung from a wing in *The Perils of Pauline*. And Mr. Ford," he says, "Mr. Ford he always hired me on. You see a redskin blasted off a horse in one of Mr. Ford's pictures, like as not it's me. One-Take Tatum they called me, before the 'Spurs' thing took."

We'd heard it all before, every time there was a western or a combat picture on the TV, every time a patient come in with a broken hip or a busted rib, all through the last days when the Duke was dying in the news. Heard how Spurs had thought up most of the riding stunts they use today, how he'd been D. W. Griffith's drinking buddy, how he saved Tom Mix's life on the Sacramento River. It was hot and one of those weeks and we'd heard it all before so I don't know if it was that or the beating he'd just taken at Parcheesi that made old Casey up and say how he used to be John Dillinger.

His chart said that Casey had been a driver on the Fox lot long enough to qualify for the Industry fund. I told him I hadn't realized he'd done any stand-in work.

"The bird who done the stand-in work," says Casey, "is the one they potted at the Biograph Theater. I used to be Johnnie

Dillinger. In the flesh.''

He said the name with a hard g, like in "finger," and didn't so much as blink.

Now we've had our delusions at the Home, your standard fading would-of-been actresses expecting their call from Mr. De Mille, a Tarzan whoop now and then during the full moon, and one old gent who goes around mouthing words without sound and overacting like he's on the silent picture screen. Generally it's some glorified notion of who they used to be. Up to this point Casey's only brag was he drove Joe DiMaggio to the airport when the Clipper was hitched to Monroe.

"If I remember right," says Spurs, giving me an eye that meant he thought the poor fella had slipped his tracks, "if I'm not too fuzzy on it, I believe that Mr. Dillinger, Public Enemy Number One, departed from our midst in the summer of '34."

"You should live so long," says Casey.

Now I try to give a man the benefit of a doubt. With Spurs I can tell there's a grain of fact to his brags because I was in the wrangler game myself. I was riding broncs in Santa Barbara for their Old Spanish Days and this fella hires me to stunt for some rodeo picture with Gig Young in it. He says I take a nice fall.

The pay was greener than what I saw on the circuit, so I stuck in Hollywood. See, I could always *ride* the sumbitches, my problem came when it was time to get *off*. What I had was a new approach to tumbling from a horse. Whereas most folks out here bust their ass to get *in*to pictures, I busted mine to get *out*. Some big damn gelding bucked me before I'd dug in and I landed smack on my tailbone. The doctor says to me—I'm laying on my stomach trying to remember my middle name— the doctor comes in with the X rays and he says, "I don't know how to tell you this, Son, but you're gonna have to learn to shit standing up."

If they'd known who I was *Variety* would of headlined "Son Bishop Swaps Bridle for Bedpan." Horses and hospitals were all I knew. Over the years I'd spent more time in emergency rooms than Dr. Kildare. So it was hospitals, and pretty soon I drifted into the geriatric game. Your geriatrics and horses hold a lot in common—they're high-strung, they bite and kick sometimes, and they're none of them too big on bowel control. Course if a geriatric steps on your foot it don't take a wood chisel to peel it off the floor.

It's a living.

So Spurs I can back sometimes, though I'm sure he didn't play such a starring role in the invention of the saddle. With Casey I had to bring it up at report.

"He thinks he's a dead gangster?" says Mrs. Goorwitz, who was the charge nurse that night.

"No, he thinks he's an old man in a Hollywood nursing home. He says he *used* to be John Dillinger."

"In another life?"

"Nope," I answered her, "in this one."

We had this reincarnated character in here once, claimed to have been all the even-numbered King Louies of France from the second right up to Louie the Sixteen. I asked how he ended up an assistant prop man at Warners and he said after all that commotion his spirit must of needed the rest.

"I thought he was shot," says Mrs. Goorwitz.

"At point-blank range," I tell her. "They couldn't of missed."

Mrs. Goorwitz was a bit untracked by the news. She hates anything out of its place, hates waves, and many's the geriatric she's hounded to death for holding a book overdue from the Home library. She pulled Casey's chart and studied it. "It says here his name is Casey Mullins."

"Well that's that, isn't it?"

"Confused behavior," says Mrs. Goorwitz as she writes it into the report. "Inappropriate response. Watch carefully."

The only thing that gets watched carefully in this joint is the time-punch at two minutes till shift change, but I figured I might save Casey some headache.

"Maybe he's just lying," I tell her. "To work up a little attention."

"Did he say anything else?"

She was on the scent now and threatening to go practice medicine on somebody any minute.

"Not a whole lot," I tell her. "But if we breathe a word to the Feds he claims they'll find us off Santa Monica Pier with our little toes curled up."

"This bird Jimmy Lawrence, a very small-time character," says Casey, "he had this bum ticker. A rheumatic heart condition, congenital since birth. We dated the same girl once is how I got to know him. People start coming up to say, 'Jeez, you're the spittin' image of Johnnie Dillinger, you know that?' and this girl, this mutual friend, tells me and I get the idea.''

After he let the Dillinger thing out Casey got very talkative, like he had it stewing in him a long time and finally it blows out all at once. I'd be in his room tapping the catheter bags on these two vegematics, Kantor and Wise, and it would be just me and this fella Roscoe Baggs who was a midget listening. Roscoe had been in *The Wizard of Oz* as a Munchkin and was a very deep thinker. He reads the kind of science-fiction books that don't have girls in loincloths on the cover.

"This girl has still got the yen for me,'' says Casey, "so she steers Lawrence to a doctor connection who tells him two months, maybe three, and it's the last roundup. The guy is demolished. So I make him this offer—I supply the dough to live it up his final days and he supplies a body to throw to the authorities. You could buy Chicago cops by the job lot back then so it was no big deal arranging the details. Hard times. Only two or three people had to know I was involved.

"Well the poor chump didn't even know how to paint the town right. And he kept moaning that he wanted us to hold off till after the Series, onnaconna he followed the Cardinals. That was the year Ripper Collins and the Dean brothers tore up the league.''

"Just like Spangler,'' says Roscoe. "Remember, he wanted to see a man walk on the moon? Held off his cancer till he saw it on television and the next day he went downstairs.''

Downstairs is where the morgue and the kitchen are located.

"One step for mankind,'' says Roscoe, "and check-out time for Spangler. You got to admire that kind of control.''

"Another hoax,'' says Casey. "They staged the whole thing in a little studio up the coast. I know a guy in video.''

I told Casey I'd read where Dillinger started to run when he saw the cops outside the picture show. And how his sister had identified the remains the next day.

"He turned chickenshit on me, Son. We hadn't told him the exact date, and there he is, coming out from the movies with a broad on each arm and all of a sudden the party's over. What would you do, you were him? And as for Sis,'' says Casey, "she always done what she could to help me out.

"The day after the planting we send in a truck, dig the coffin out, pour in concrete and lay it back in. Anybody wants another peek at the stiff they got to drill a mine shaft.''

It sounded reasonable, sort of. And when the shrink who comes through twice a year stopped to ask about his Dillinger fixation Casey just told him to scram. Said if he wanted his brains scrambled he'd stick his head in the microwave.

I did some reading and everything he said checked out pretty close. Only I couldn't connect Casey with a guy who'd pull a stunt like that on the Lawrence fella. He was one of the nice ones, Casey—never bitched much even with his diabetes and his infected feet and his rotting kidneys and his finger curling up. A stand-up character.

The finger was curling up independent from the others on his right hand. His trigger finger, bent like he was about to squeeze off a round.

"It's like the *Tell-Tale Heart*," says Roscoe one day. I'm picking up dinner trays in the rooms and Roscoe is working on four chocolate puddings. They had put one on Casey's tray by mistake and I didn't have the time to spoon the other two down Kantor and Wise.

"The what?" asks Casey.

"It's a story. This guy kills an old man and stuffs him under the floorboards. When the police come to investigate he thinks he hears the old man's heart beating under the boards and he cracks and gives himself away."

"So what's that got to do with my finger?"

"Maybe your finger is trying to blow the whistle on your life of crime. Psychosomatic."

"Oh." Casey mauled it over in his mind for a minute. "I get it. We had a guy in the can, kilt his wife. Poisoned her. At first everybody figured she'd just got sick and died, happened all the time in those days. But then he starts complaining to the cops about the neighborhood kids—says they're writing nasty stuff on the sidewalk in front of his place: 'Old Man Walsh croaked his wife with rat bait,' stuff like that. So the cops send a guy to check it out on his night rounds. The cop's passing by and out comes Walsh, sleepwalking, with a piece of chalk in his hand. Wrote his own ticket to the slammer, right there on the sidewalk, onnaconna he had a leaky conscience."

It had been bothering me so I took the opening to ask. "Do you ever feel bad? About things you done back then?"

Casey shrugged and looked away from me and then looked back. "Nah," he says, "What am I, mental? This guy Walsh, he was AWOL."

AWOL is what we call the senile ones. Off base and not coming back.

"Hey Roscoe," says Casey, "why'd this telltale character kill the old man in the first place?"

"Because this old man had a big eye. He wanted to kill the big eye."

Just then Spurs wheels in looking to vulture a loose dessert.

"I wonder," says Casey, "what he would of done to a fat head?"

It seemed to make him feel better, talking about his life as Dillinger. Kept him up and alert even when his health took a big slide.

"Only reason I'm still percolating," he'd say, "is I still got my pride. They beat that into me my first stretch."

I told him I'd never heard of beating pride into somebody.

"They beat on you one way or the other," he says. "The pride comes in how you stand up to it."

I went on the graveyard shift and after two o'clock check I'd go down to chew the fat with Casey. Roscoe slept like the dead and the two veggies were on automatic pilot so it didn't make any difference how loud we were. Casey was a hurtin cowboy and his meds weren't up to knocking him out at night. We'd play cards by the light from the corridor sometimes or sometimes he'd cut up old scores for me. He told me about one where their advance man posed as a Hollywood location scout for a gangster movie. When they come out of the bank holding hostages the next day, sniping at the local shields, the townspeople just smiled and looked around for cameras.

He didn't have much to say on his years driving for Fox. He only hung on because of what he called the "fringe benefits," which mostly had to do with women.

"Used to be a disease with me," he'd say. "I'd go two days without a tumble and my eyeballs would start to swoll up, my brains would start pushing out my ears. Shut me out for three days and I'd hump anything, just anything. Like some dope fiend."

When I asked how he'd dealt with that while he was in the slammer he clammed up.

He was still able to wheel himself around a bit when Norma took up with him. Norma had bad veins and was in a chair herself. She'd been in the silents in her teens, getting rescued from fates worse than death. Her mother was ninety and shared a room with her. The old vulture just sat, deaf as a post, glaring at Norma for not being Mary Pickford. Norma had been one of the backgammon crowd till word spread that Casey thought he was John Dillinger. She studied him for a week, keeping her distance, eavesdropping on his sparring matches with Spurs Tatum, watching how he moved and how he talked. Then one day as the singalong is breaking up she wheels up beside him. Norma's voice had gone deeper and deeper with the years and she filled in at bass on "What a Friend We Have in Jesus."

"All I do is dream of you," she sings to Casey, "the whole night through."

"That used to be my favorite song," he says.

"I know," says Norma.

It give me the fantods sometimes, the way they'd look at each other like they known one another forever. Norma had been one of those caught up by the press on Dillinger when he had his year in the headlines. A woman near thirty years old keeping a scrapbook. She had picked up some work as an extra after her silent days were over, but it never came to much. She still had a shoe box full of the postcards her mother had sent out every year to agents and flacks and producers—a grainy blowup of Norma in a toga or a buckskin shift or a French peasant outfit. Norma Nader in *Cimarron*. Norma Nader in *The Pride and the Passion*. Norma Nader in *The Greatest Story Ever Told*. They were the only credits she got in the talkies, those postcards, but her mother kept the heat on. I'd find Norma out in the corridor at night, wheels locked, watching the light coming out from her room.

"Is she in bed yet?" she'd ask, and I'd go down and peek in on Old Lady Nader.

"She's still awake, Norma."

"She always stood up till I come home, no matter what hour. I come in the door and it's not 'Where you been?' or 'Who'd you see?' but 'Any work today?' She had spies at all the studios so I could never lie about making rounds. Once I had an offer for a secretary job, good pay, steady, and I had to tell them sorry, I got to be an actress."

Casey had his Dillinger routine down pretty well, but with Norma along he was unstoppable.

"Johnnie," she'd say, "you member that time in St. Paul they caught you in the alleyway?" or "Johnnie, remember how

Nelson and Van Meter were always at each other's throats?"
—just like she'd been there. And Casey he'd nod and say he
remembered or correct some little detail, reminding her like
any old couple sharing memories.

I'd come on at eleven and they'd be in the day room with
only the TV for light, Casey squirming in his chair, hurting, and
Norma waiting for her mother to go to sleep, holding Casey's
hand against the pain. We had another old pair like them, a
couple old bachelors were crazy for chess. One game could
take them two, three days. Personally I'd rather watch paint
dry.

Usually some time around one o'clock Norma would call and
we'd wheel them back to their rooms. I'd park Casey by the
window so he could watch the traffic on Cahuenga.

By the time I got back on day shift Casey needed a push
when he wanted to get anywhere. He could still feed himself
and hit the pee-jug nine times out of ten, though we were
checking his output to see what was left of his kidneys. This
one morning we had square egg for breakfast, which is the
powdered variety cooked up in cake pans and cut in little bars
like brownies. If they don't get the coloring just right they'll
come up greenish and they wiggle on your fork just like jello.
Even the blind patients won't touch them. Usually our only
taker is this character Mao, who we call after his resemblance
to the late Chinese head Red. Mao is a mongoloid in his
mid-thirties whose favorite dishes are square egg and ther-
mometers. Already that morning a new candy striper had given
him an oral instead of a rectal and he'd chomped it clear in half.
Now she was fluttering around looking for Mr. Hellman's other
slipper.

"I looked in his stand and under his bed," she says to me,
"and all I could find is the right one."

"He doesn't have a left one," I tell her.

"Why not?"

"He doesn't have a left leg."

"Oh." The candy stripers are good for morale but they take a
lot of looking after.

"Next time peek under the covers first."

"Well I started to," she says, "but he was flipping his—you
know—his *thing* at me."

"Don't you worry, honey," says Spurs Tatum. "Worst
comes to worst I'd lay odds you could outrun the old goat."

"When they give us this shit in the state pen," says Casey so's everybody in the day room could hear him, "we'd plaster the walls with it."

The candy striper waggles her finger at him. "If you don't care for your breakfast, Mr. Mullins, I'm sure somebody else would appreciate it."

"No dice," says Casey. "I want to see it put down the trash barrel where it can't do no harm. And the name's Dillinger."

"I'm sure you don't mind if somebody shares what you don't want. I mean what are we here for?" Lately we've been getting candy stripers with a more Christian outlook.

"What we're *here* for," says Casey, "is to die. To die. And some of us," he says looking to Spurs, "aren't doing much of a job of it."

Casey was on the rag that morning, with a bad case of the runs his new meds give him and a wobbling pile of square egg staring up at him. So when the candy striper reaches to give his portion over to Mao, Casey pushes his tray over onto the floor.

"You birds keep swallowin this shit," he calls out to the others, "they'll keep sending it up."

Mao was well known for his oatmeal tossing. You'd get two spoonfuls down him and he'd decide to chuck the whole bowl acrost the room. Or wing it straight up so big globs stuck to the ceiling. The old-timers liked to sit against the back wall of the day room afternoons and bet on which glob would loosen and fall first. So when Mao picked up on Casey and made like a catapult with his plate there was chunks sent scattering clear to the bingo tables.

"Food riot!" yells Roscoe, flicking egg off his fork, aiming for old oatmeal stains on the ceiling. "Every man for himself!" he yells and then goes into "Ding-Dong the Witch Is Dead."

I didn't think the old farts had it in them. It was like being inside a popcorn popper, yellow hunks of egg flying every whichway, squishing, bouncing, coffee sloshing, toast frisbee-ing, plates smashing, orange juice showering while Mrs. Sha-piro, stone blind and AWOL for years is yelling "Boys, don't fight! Don't fight, your father will get crazy!"

The rec therapist is a togetherness freak. They sing together, they make place mats together, they have oral history sessions together. So somebody starts throwing food the rest of them are bound to pitch in. When there was nothing left to toss they calmed down. We decided to wheel them all back to their rooms before we cleaned out the day room.

"I'm hungry," says Spurs. "Crazy sumbitch made me lose my breakfast. Senile bastard."

"Shove it, cowboy," says Casey. "In my day we'd of used you for a toothpick."

"In *my* day we'd of stuck you in the bughouse. Dillinger my ass."

Casey didn't say a thing but Norma wheeled up between them, a big smear of grape jelly on her cheek.

"John Dillinger," she said, "was the only one in the whole lousy country was his own man, the only one that told them all to go hang and went his own way. Have some respect."

I never learned if she really thought he was Dillinger or if they just shared the same interest like the chess players or the crowd that still reads the trade papers together. When Norma went AWOL it was like her mother called her in from the playground. She left us quick, fading in and out for two weeks till she give up all the way and just sat in her chair in her room, staring back at her mother.

"I'm sorry," she'd say from time to time. No word on why or what for, just stare at Old Lady Nader and say, "I'm sorry."

Casey tried to pull her out of it at first. But it's like when we have a cardiac arrest and we pull the curtain around the bed—even if you're right in the room you can't see through to know what's happening.

"You remember me?" he'd say. "You remember about Johnnie Dillinger?"

Usually she'd just look at him blank. One time she said, "I seen a movie about him once."

For a while Casey would have us wheel him into Norma's room and he'd talk at her some but she didn't know who he was. Finally it made him so low he stopped visiting. Acted like she'd gone downstairs.

"You lose your mind," he'd say, "the rest of you ain't worth spit."

Mrs. Goorwitz got on his case then and tried to locate relatives. None to be found. What with the way people move around out here that's not so unusual. Casey's chart was nothing but a medical record starting in 1937. Next Mrs. Goorwitz loosed the social worker on him, Friendly Phil, who ought to be selling health food or real estate somewhere. Casey wasn't buying any.

"So what if I am crazy?" he'd say to Phil. "Delusional, schizo, whatever you wanna call it. I can't do squat one way or the other. What difference does it make if I was Dillinger or Norma was Pearl White or Roscoe was the King of Poland? You're all just a bag a bones in the end."

He went into a funk, Casey, after Norma faded—went into a silence that lasted a good month. Not even Spurs could get his goat enough to argue. He spent a good part of the day trying to keep himself clean.

"I'm on the cycle," he whispered to me one day. "I'm riding the down side."

The geriatric racket is a collection of cycles. Linen goes on beds, gets dirtied, down the chute, washed, dried and back onto the beds. Patients are checked in downstairs, up to the beds, maintained a while and then down to the slabs with them. Casey even found a new cycle, a thing in the paper about scientists who had learned how to make cow flops back into cow food.

"I don't want to make accusations here," says Casey one day, pointing to his lunch, "but what does *that* look like to you?"

The day came when Casey lost his control, racked up six incontinents on the report in one week. His health was shot but I tried to talk Mrs. Goorwitz out of it when she handed me the kit. He had a thing about it, Casey.

"A man that can't control his bowels," he'd say, "is not a man."

He knew what was up when I started to draw the curtain. Roscoe scowled at me from across the room and rolled over to face the wall. Kantor and Wise lay there like house plants. It was midnight and they'd given Casey some heavy meds with his dinner. He looked at me like I come to snuff him with a pillow over the face. He was too weak to raise his arms so I didn't have to put the restraints on.

"It has to be, Casey," I told him. "Or else you'll be wettin all over yourself."

I washed my hands with the soap from the kit.

"If they ask why I done it, the banks and all," he whispers, "tell them I was just bored. Just bored crapless."

I took the gloves out of their cellophane and managed to wriggle into them without touching my fingers to their outside. I washed Casey and laid the fenestrated sheet over so only his thing stuck through. If the stories about Dillinger's size are true, Casey was qualified. The girls on the evening shift called it "The Snake." I swabbed the tip of it, unwrapped the catheter tube, and coated it with K-Y.

"You been white to me, Son," says Casey. "I don't put no blame on you."

"I'm sorry."

"Don't ever say that," says Casey. "Don't ever say you're sorry. Do it or don't do it but don't apologize."

I pushed the catheter tube down till it blocked at his sphincter, wiggled it and it slipped past. It was the narrowest gauge but still it's a surprise that you can fit one into a man. I stuck the syringe into the irrigation branch and shot the saline up till the bulb was inflated in his bladder. I gave a tug to see if it was anchored. Casey was crying, looking away from me. His eyes had gone fuzzy, the way fish eyes do after you beach them. I hooked the plastic tubing and the piss-bag to the catheter.

"I used to be somebody," said Casey.

I had a long weekend, and when I came back on I didn't get a chance to talk with him. Mrs. Goorwitz said in report how he'd been moved to Intensive Care. On my first check I found him looking like the pictures of the Biograph shooting—blood everywhere, hard yellow light. Something had popped inside and he'd bled out the mouth. He had pulled the catheter out, bulb and all, and he was bleeding down there. We put sheets on the floor and rolled him sideways across the bed on his belly so he drained out onto them. It takes a half hour or so.

I traced him back through the medical plan at Fox and ran into nothing but dead ends. Usually I forget about them once they go downstairs but Casey had gotten his hooks in. There at Fox I found an old fella in custodial who remembered him.

"Always taking the limos for joyrides," he said. "It's a wonder he didn't get his ass fired."

I brought the subject up at the nurses' station one night— how maybe he could of been—and they asked me how much sleep I'd been getting. So I don't know one way or the other. Roscoe, he's sure, he's positive, but Roscoe also thinks our every move is being watched by aliens with oversized IQs. I figure if they're so smart they got better things to occupy their time.

One day I'm tube-feeding some vegomatic when out in the corridor I hear Spurs Tatum giving his brag to a couple recent admissions that come in with their feet falling off.

"Hoot Gibson held my horse," says Spurs. "I took falls for Randy Scott. John Wayne blew me off a stagecoach. And once," he says, "I played Parcheesi with John Herbert Dillinger."

KINUKO CRAFT. (*TQ* #46)

Walking out

David Quammen

As the train rocked dead at Livingston he saw the man, in a worn khaki shirt with button flaps buttoned, arms crossed. The boy's hand sprang up by reflex, and his face broke into a smile. The man smiled back gravely, and nodded. He did not otherwise move. The boy turned from the window and, with the awesome deliberateness of a fat child harboring reluctance, began struggling to pull down his bag. His father would wait on the platform. First sight of him had reminded the boy that nothing was simple enough now for hurrying.

They drove in the old open Willys toward the cabin beyond town. The windshield of the Willys was up, but the fine cold sharp rain came into their faces, and the boy could not raise his eyes to look at the road. He wore a rain parka his father had handed him at the station. The man, protected by only the khaki, held his lips strung in a firm silent line that seemed more grin than wince. Riding through town in the cold rain, open topped and jaunty, getting drenched as though by necessity, was—the boy understood vaguely—somehow in the spirit of this season.

"We have a moose tag," his father shouted.

The boy said nothing. He refused to care what it meant, that they had a moose tag.

"I've got one picked out. A bull. I've stalked him for two weeks. Up in the Crazies. When we get to the cabin, we'll build a good roaring fire." With only the charade of a pause, he added, "Your mother." It was said like a question. The boy waited. "How is she?"

"All right, I guess." Over the jeep's howl, with the wind stealing his voice, the boy too had to shout.

"Are you friends with her?"

"I guess so."

"Is she still a beautiful lady?"

"I don't know. I guess so. I don't know that."

"You must know that. Is she starting to get wrinkled like me? Does she seem worried and sad? Or is she just still a fine beautiful lady? You must know that."

"She's still a beautiful lady, I guess."

"Did she tell you any messages for me?"

"She said . . . she said I should give you her love," the boy lied, impulsively and clumsily. He was at once embarrassed that he had done it.

"Oh," his father said. "Thank you, David."

They reached the cabin on a mile of dirt road winding through meadow to a spruce grove. Inside, the boy was enwrapped in the strong syncretic smell of all seasonal mountain cabins: pine resin and insect repellent and a mustiness suggesting damp bathing trunks stored in a drawer. There were yellow pine floors and rope-work throw rugs and a bead curtain to the bedroom and a cast-iron cook stove with none of the lids or handles missing and a pump in the kitchen sink and old issues of *Field and Stream,* and on the mantel above where a fire now finally burned was a picture of the boy's grandfather, the railroad telegrapher, who had once owned the cabin. The boy's father cooked a dinner of fried ham, and though the boy did not like ham he had expected his father to cook canned stew or Spam, so he said nothing. His father asked him about school and the boy talked and his father seemed to be interested. Warm and dry, the boy began to feel safe from his own anguish. Then his father said:

"We'll leave tomorrow around ten."

Last year on the boy's visit they had hunted birds. They had lived in the cabin for six nights, and each day they had hunted pheasant in the wheat stubble, or blue grouse in the woods, or ducks along the irrigation slews. The boy had been wet and cold and miserable at times, but each evening they returned to the cabin and to the boy's suitcase of dry clothes. They had eaten hot food cooked on a stove, and had smelled the cabin smell, and had slept together in a bed. In six days of hunting, the boy had not managed to kill a single bird. Yet last year he had known that, at least once a day, he would be comfortable, if not happy. This year his father planned that he should not even be comfortable. He had said in his last letter to Evergreen Park, before the boy left Chicago but when it was too late for him not to leave, that he would take the boy camping in the mountains, after big game. He had pretended to believe that the boy would be glad.

The Willys was loaded and moving by ten minutes to ten. For three hours they drove, through Big Timber, and then north on the highway, and then back west again on a logging road that took them winding and bouncing higher into the mountains. Thick cottony streaks of white cloud hung in among the mountaintop trees, light and dense dollops against the bulking sharp dark olive, as though in a black-and-white photograph. They followed the gravel road for an hour, and the boy thought they would soon have a flat tire or break an axle. If they had a flat, the boy knew, his father would only change it and drive on until they had the second, farther from the highway. Finally they crossed a creek and his father plunged the Willys off into a bed of weeds.

His father said, "Here."

The boy said, "Where?"

"Up that little drainage. At the head of the creek."

"How far is it?"

"Two or three miles."

"Is that where you saw the moose?"

"No. That's where I saw the sheepman's hut. The moose is farther. On top."

"Are we going to sleep in a hut? I thought we were going to sleep in a tent."

"No. Why should we carry a tent up there when we have a perfectly good hut?"

The boy couldn't answer that question. He thought now that this might be the time when he would cry. He had known it was coming.

"I don't much want to sleep in a hut," he said, and his voice broke with the simple honesty of it, and his eyes glazed. He held his mouth tight against the trembling.

As though something had broken in him too, the boy's father

laid his forehead down on the steering wheel, against his knuckles. For a moment he remained bowed, breathing exhaustedly. But he looked up again before speaking.

"Well, we don't have to, David."

The boy said nothing.

"It's an old sheepman's hut made of logs, and it's near where we're going to hunt, and we can fix it dry and good. I thought you might like that. I thought it might be more fun than a tent. But we don't have to do it. We can drive back to Big Timber and buy a tent, or we can drive back to the cabin and hunt birds, like last year. Whatever you want to do. You have to forgive me the kind of ideas I get. I hope you will. We don't have to do anything that you don't want to do."

"No," the boy said. "I want to."

"Are you sure?"

"No," the boy said. "But I just want to."

They bushwhacked along the creek, treading a thick soft mixture of moss and humus and needles, climbing upward through brush. Then the brush thinned and they were ascending an open creek bottom, thirty yards wide, darkened by fir and cedar. Farther, and they struck a trail, which led them upward along the creek. Farther still, and the trail received a branch, then another, then forked.

"Who made this trail? Did the sheepman?"

"No," his father said. "Deer and elk."

Gradually the creek's little canyon narrowed, steep wooded shoulders funneling closer on each side. For a while the game trails forked and converged like a maze, but soon again there were only two branches, and finally one, heavily worn. It dodged through alder and willow, skirting tangles of browned raspberry, so that the boy and his father could never see more than twenty feet ahead. When they stopped to rest, the boy's father unstrapped the .270 from his pack and loaded it.

"We have to be careful now," he explained. "We may surprise a bear."

Under the cedars, the creek bottom held a cool dampness that seemed to be stored from one winter to the next. The boy began at once to feel chilled. He put on his jacket, and they continued climbing. Soon he was sweating again in the cold.

On a small flat where the alder drew back from the creek, the hut was built into one bank of the canyon, with the sod of the hillside lapping out over its roof. The door was a low dark opening. Forty or fifty years ago, the boy's father explained, this hut had been built and used by a Basque shepherd. At that time there had been many Basques in Montana, and they had run sheep all across this ridge of the Crazies. His father forgot to explain what a Basque was, and the boy didn't remind him.

They built a fire. His father had brought sirloin steaks and an onion for dinner, and the boy was happy with him about that. As they ate, it grew dark, but the boy and his father had stocked a large comforting pile of naked deadfall. In the darkness, by firelight, his father made chocolate pudding. The pudding had been his father's surprise. The boy sat on a piece of canvas and added logs to the fire while his father drank coffee. Sparks rose on the heat and the boy watched them climb toward the cedar limbs and the black pools of sky. The pudding did not set.

"Do you remember your grandfather, David?"

"Yes," the boy said, and wished it were true. He remembered a funeral when he was three.

"Your grandfather brought me up on this mountain when I was seventeen. That was the last year he hunted." The boy knew what sort of thoughts his father was having. But he knew also that his own home was in Evergreen Park, and that he was another man's boy now, with another man's name, though this indeed was his father. "Your grandfather was fifty years older than me."

The boy said nothing.

"And I'm thirty-four years older than you."

"And I'm only eleven," the boy cautioned him.

"Yes," said his father. "And someday you'll have a son and you'll be forty years older than him, and you'll want so badly for him to know who you are that you could cry."

The boy was embarrassed.

"And that's called the cycle of life's infinite wisdom," his father said, and laughed at himself unpleasantly.

"What did he die of?" the boy asked, desperate to escape the focus of his father's rumination.

"He was eighty-seven then. Christ. He was tired." The boy's father went silent. Then he shook his head, and poured himself the remaining coffee.

Through that night the boy was never quite warm. He slept on his side with his knees drawn up, and this was uncomfortable but his body seemed to demand it for warmth. The hard cold mountain earth pressed upward through the mat of fir boughs his father had laid, and drew heat from the boy's body like a pallet of leeches. He clutched the bedroll around his neck and folded the empty part at the bottom back under his legs. Once he woke to a noise. Though his father was sleeping between him and the door of the hut, for a while the boy lay awake, listening worriedly, and then woke again on his back to realize time had passed. He heard droplets begin to hit the canvas his father had spread over the sod roof of the hut. But he remained dry.

He rose to the smell of a fire. The tarp was rigid with sleet and frost. The firewood and the knapsacks were frosted. It was that gray time of dawn before any blue and, through the branches above, the boy was unable to tell whether the sky was murky or clear. Delicate sheet ice hung on everything, but there was no wetness. The rain seemed to have been hushed by the cold.

"What time is it?"

"Early yet."

"How early?" The boy was thinking about the cold at home as he waited outside on 96th Street for his school bus. That was the cruelest moment of his day, but it seemed a benign and familiar part of him compared to this.

"Early. I don't have a watch. What difference does it make, David?"

"Not any."

After breakfast they began walking up the valley. His father had the .270, and the boy carried an old Winchester .30–30, with open sights. The walking was not hard, and with this gentle exercise in the cold morning the boy soon felt fresh and fine. Now I'm hunting for moose with my father, he told himself. That's just what I'm doing. Few boys in Evergreen Park had ever been moose hunting with their fathers in Montana, he knew. I'm doing it now, the boy told himself.

Reaching the lip of a high meadow, a mile above the shepherd's hut, they had not seen so much as a magpie.

Before them, across hundreds of yards, opened a smooth lake of tall lifeless grass, browned by September drought and killed by the frosts and beginning to rot with November's rain. The creek was here a deep quiet channel of smooth curves overhung by the grass, with a dark surface like heavy oil. When they had come fifty yards into the meadow, his father turned and pointed out to the boy a large ponderosa pine with a forked crown that marked the head of their creek valley. He showed the boy a small aspen grove midway across the meadow, toward which they were aligning themselves.

"Near the far woods is a beaver pond. The moose waters there. We can wait in the aspens and watch the whole meadow without being seen. If he doesn't come, we'll go up another canyon, and check again on the way back."

For an hour, and another, they waited. The boy sat with his hands in his jacket pockets, bunching the jacket tighter around him, and his buttocks drew cold moisture from the ground. His father squatted on his heels like a country man, rising periodically to inspect the meadow in all directions. Finally he stood up; he fixed his stare on the distant fringe of woods and, like a retriever, did not move. He said, "David."

The boy stood beside him. His father placed a hand on the boy's shoulder. The boy saw a large dark form rolling toward them like a great slug in the grass.

"Is it the moose?"

"No," said his father. "That is a grizzly bear, David. An old male grizzly."

The boy was impressed. He sensed an aura of power and terror and authority about the husky shape, even at two hundred yards.

"Are we going to shoot him?"

"No."

"Why not?"

"We don't have a permit," his father whispered. "And because we don't want to."

The bear plowed on toward the beaver pond for a while, then stopped. It froze in the grass and seemed to be listening. The boy's father added: "That's not hunting for the meat. That's hunting for the fear. I don't need the fear. I've got enough in my life already."

The bear turned and moiled off quickly through the grass. It disappeared back into the far woods.

"He heard us."

"Maybe," the boy's father said. "Let's go have a look at that beaver pond."

A sleek furred carcass lay low in the water, swollen grotesquely with putrescence and coated with glistening blowflies. Four days, the boy's father guessed. The moose had been shot at least eighteen times with a .22 pistol. One of its eyes had been shot out; it had been shot twice in the jaw; and both quarters on the side that lay upward were ruined with shots. Standing up to his knees in the sump, the boy's father took the trouble of counting the holes, and probing one of the slugs out with his knife. That only made him angrier. He flung the lead away.

For the next three hours, with his father withdrawn into a solitary and characteristic bitterness, the boy felt abandoned. He did not understand why a moose would be slaughtered with a light pistol and left to rot. His father did not bother to explain; like the bear, he seemed to understand it as well as he needed to. They walked on, but they did not really hunt.

They left the meadow for more pine, and now tamarack, naked tamarack, the yellow needles nearly all down and going ginger where they coated the trail. The boy and his father hiked along a level path into another canyon, this one vast at the mouth and narrowing between high ridges of bare rock. They crossed and recrossed the shepherd's creek, which in this canyon was a tumbling free-stone brook. Following five yards behind his father, watching the cold, unapproachable rage that shaped the line of the man's shoulders, the boy was miserably uneasy because his father had grown so distant and quiet. They climbed over deadfalls blocking the trail, skirted one boulder large as a cabin, and blundered into a garden of nettles that stung them fiercely through their trousers. They saw fresh elk scat, and they saw bear, diarrhetic with late berries. The boy's father eventually grew bored with brooding, and showed the boy how to stalk. Before dusk that day they had shot an elk.

An open and gently sloped hillside, almost a meadow, ran for a quarter mile in quaking aspen, none over fifteen feet tall. The elk was above. The boy's father had the boy brace his gun in the notch of an aspen and take the first shot. The boy missed. The elk reeled and bolted down and his father killed it before it made cover. It was a five-point bull. They dressed the elk out and dragged it down to the cover of large pines, near the stream, where they would quarter it tomorrow, and then they returned under twilight to the hut.

That night even the fetal position could not keep the boy warm. He shivered wakefully for hours. He was glad that the following day, though full of walking and butchery and oppressive burdens, would be their last in the woods. He heard nothing. When he woke, through the door of the hut he saw whiteness like bone.

Six inches had fallen, and it was still snowing. The boy stood about in the campsite, amazed. When it snowed three inches in Evergreen Park, the boy would wake before dawn to the hiss of sand trucks and the ratchet of chains. Here there had been no warning. The boy was not much colder than he had been yesterday, and the transformation of the woods seemed mysterious and benign and somehow comic. He thought of Christmas. Then his father barked at him.

His father's mood had also changed, but in a different way; he seemed serious and hurried. As he wiped the breakfast pots clean with snow, he gave the boy orders for other chores. They left camp with two empty pack frames, both rifles, and a handsaw and rope. The boy soon understood why his father felt pressure of time: it took them an hour to climb the mile to the meadow. The snow continued. They did not rest until they reached the aspens.

"I had half a mind at breakfast to let the bull lie and pack us straight down out of here," his father admitted. "Probably smarter and less trouble in the long run. I could have come back on snowshoes next week. But by then it might be three feet deep and starting to drift. We can get two quarters out today. That will make it easier for me later." The boy was surprised by two things: that his father would be so wary in the face of a gentle snowfall and that he himself would have felt disappointed to be taken out of the woods that morning. The air of the meadow teemed with white.

"If it stops soon, we're fine," said his father.

It continued.

The path up the far canyon was hard climbing in eight inches of snow. The boy fell once, filling his collar and sleeves, and the gun-sight put a small gouge in his chin. But he was not discouraged. That night they would be warm and dry at the cabin. A half mile on and he came up beside his father, who had stopped to stare down at dark splashes of blood.

Heavy tracks and a dragging belly mark led up to the scramble of deepening red, and away. The tracks were nine inches long and showed claws. The boy's father knelt. As the boy watched, one shining maroon splotch the size of a saucer sank slowly beyond sight into the snow. The blood was warm.

Inspecting the tracks carefully, his father said, "She's got a cub with her."

"What happened?"

"Just a kill. Seems to have been a bird. That's too much blood for a grouse, but I don't see signs of any four-footed creature. Maybe a turkey." He frowned thoughtfully. "A turkey without feathers. I don't know. What I dislike is coming up on her with a cub." He drove a round into the chamber of the .270.

Trailing red smears, the tracks preceded them. Within fifty feet they found the body. It was half-buried. The top of its head had been shorn away, and the cub's brains had been licked out.

His father said "Christ," and plunged off the trail. He snapped at the boy to follow closely.

They made a wide crescent through brush and struck back after a quarter mile. His father slogged ahead in the snow, stopping often to stand holding his gun ready and glancing around while the boy caught up and passed him. The boy was confused. He knew his father was worried, but he did not feel any danger himself. They met the trail again, and went on to the aspen hillside before his father allowed them to rest. The boy spat on the snow. His lungs ached badly.

"Why did she do that?"

"She didn't. Another bear got her cub. A male. Maybe the one we saw yesterday. Then she fought him for the body, and she won. We didn't miss them by much. She may even have been watching. Nothing could put her in a worse frame of mind."

He added: "If we so much as see her, I want you to pick the nearest big tree and start climbing. Don't stop till you're twenty feet off the ground. I'll stay down and decide whether we have to shoot her. Is your rifle cocked?"

"No."

"Cock it, and put on the safety. She may be a black bear and black bears can climb. If she comes up after you, lean down and stick your gun in her mouth and fire. You can't miss."

He cocked the Winchester, as his father had said.

They angled downhill to the stream, and on to the mound of their dead elk. Snow filtered down steadily in purposeful silence. The boy was thirsty. It could not be much below freezing, he was aware, because with the exercise his bare hands were comfortable, even sweating between the fingers.

"Can I get a drink?"

"Yes. Be careful you don't wet your feet. And don't wander anywhere. We're going to get this done quickly."

He walked the few yards, ducked through the brush at streamside, and knelt in the snow to drink. The water was painful to his sinuses and bitterly cold on his hands. Standing again, he noticed an animal body ahead near the stream bank. For a moment he felt sure it was another dead cub. During that moment his father called:

"David! Get up here right now!"

The boy meant to call back. First he stepped closer to turn the cub with his foot. The touch brought it alive. It rose suddenly with a high squealing growl and whirled its head like a snake and snapped. The boy shrieked. The cub had his right hand in its jaws. It would not release.

It thrashed senselessly, working its teeth deeper and tearing flesh with each movement. The boy felt no pain. He knew his hand was being damaged and that realization terrified him and he was desperate to get the hand back before it was ruined. But he was helpless. He sensed the same furious terror racking the cub that he felt in himself, and he screamed at the cub almost reasoningly to let him go. His screams scared the cub more. Its head snatched back and forth. The boy did not think to shout for his father. He did not see him or hear him coming.

His father moved at full stride in a slowed laboring run through the snow, saying nothing and holding the rifle he did not use, crossed the last six feet still gathering speed, and brought his right boot up into the cub's belly. That kick seemed to lift the cub clear of the snow. It opened its jaws to another shrill piggish squeal, and the boy felt dull relief on his hand, as though his father had pressed open the blades of a spring trap with his foot. The cub tumbled once and disappeared over the stream bank, then surfaced downstream, squalling and paddling. The boy looked at his hand and was horrified. He still had no pain, but the hand was unrecognizable. His fingers had been peeled down through the palm like flaps on a banana. Glands at the sides of his jaw threatened that he would vomit, and he might have stood stupidly watching the hand bleed if his father had not grabbed him.

He snatched the boy by the arm and dragged him toward a tree without even looking at the boy's hand. The boy jerked back in angry resistance as though he had been struck. He screamed at his father. He screamed that his hand was cut, believing his father did not know, and as he screamed he began to cry. He began to feel hot throbbing pain. He began to worry about the blood he was losing. He could imagine his blood melting red holes in the snow behind him and he did not want to look. He did not want to do anything until he had taken care of his hand. At that instant he hated his father. But his father was stronger. He all but carried the boy to a tree.

He lifted the boy. In a voice that was quiet and hurried and very unlike the harsh grip with which he had taken the boy's arm, he said:

"Grab hold and climb up a few branches as best you can. Sit on a limb and hold tight and clamp the hand under your other armpit, if you can do that. I'll be right back to you. Hold tight because you're going to get dizzy." The boy groped desperately for a branch. His father supported him from beneath, and waited. The boy clambered. His feet scraped at the trunk. Then he was in the tree. Bark flakes and resin were stuck to the raw naked meat of his right hand. His father said:

"Now here, take this. Hurry."

The boy never knew whether his father himself had been frightened enough to forget for that moment about the boy's hand, or whether his father was still thinking quite clearly. His father may have expected that much. By the merciless clarity of his own standards, he may have expected that the boy should be able to hold onto a tree, and a wound, and a rifle, all with one hand. He extended the stock of the Winchester toward the boy.

The boy wanted to say something, but his tears and his fright would not let him gather a breath. He shuddered, and could not speak. "David," his father urged. The boy reached for the stock and faltered and clutched at the trunk with his good arm. He was crying and gasping, and he wanted to speak. He was afraid he would fall out of the tree. He released his grip once again, and felt himself tip. His father extended the gun higher, holding the barrel. The boy swung out his injured hand, spraying his father's face with blood. He reached and he tried to close torn dangling fingers around the stock and he pulled the trigger.

The bullet entered low on his father's thigh and shattered the knee and traveled down the shin bone and into the ground through his father's heel.

His father fell, and the rifle fell with him. He lay in the snow without moving. The boy thought he was dead. Then the boy saw him grope for the rifle. He found it and rolled onto his stomach, taking aim at the sow grizzly. Forty feet up the hill, towering on hind legs, she canted her head to one side, indecisive. When the cub pulled itself up a snowbank from the stream, she coughed at it sternly. The cub trotted straight to her with its head low. She knocked it off its feet with a huge paw, and it yelped. Then she turned quickly. The cub followed.

The woods were silent. The gunshot still echoed awesomely back to the boy but it was an echo of memory, not sound. He felt nothing. He saw his father's body stretched on the snow and he did not really believe he was where he was. He did not want to move: he wanted to wake. He sat in the tree and waited. The snow fell as gracefully as before.

His father rolled onto his back. The boy saw him raise himself to a sitting position and look down at the leg and betray no expression, and then slump back. He blinked slowly and lifted his eyes to meet the boy's eyes. The boy waited. He expected his father to speak. He expected his father to say *Shinny down using your elbows and knees and get the first-aid kit and boil water and phone the doctor. The number is taped to the dial.* His father stared. The boy could see the flicker of thoughts behind his father's eyes. His father said nothing. He raised his arms slowly and crossed them over his face, as though to nap in the sun.

The boy jumped. He landed hard on his feet and fell onto his back. He stood over his father. His hand dripped quietly onto the snow. He was afraid that his father was deciding to die. He wanted to beg him to reconsider. The boy had never before seen his father hopeless. He was afraid.

But he was no longer afraid of his father.

Then his father uncovered his face and said, "Let me see it."

They bandaged the boy's hand with a sleeve cut from the other arm of his shirt. His father wrapped the hand firmly and split the sleeve end with his deer knife and tied it neatly in two places. The boy now felt searing pain in his torn palm, and his stomach lifted when he thought of the damage, but at least he did not have to look at it. Quickly the plaid flannel bandage began to soak through maroon. They cut a sleeve from his father's shirt to tie over the wound in his thigh. They raised the trouser leg to see the long swelling bruise down the calf where he was hemorrhaging into the bullet's tunnel. Only then did his father realize that he was bleeding also from the heel. The boy took off his father's boot and placed a half-clean handkerchief on the insole where the bullet had exited, as his father instructed him. Then his father laced the boot on again tightly. The boy helped his father to stand. His father tried a step, then collapsed in the snow with a blasphemous howl of pain. They had not known that the knee was shattered.

The boy watched his father's chest heave with the forced sighs of suffocating frustration, and heard the air wheeze through his nostrils. His father relaxed himself with the breathing, and seemed to be thinking. He said,

"You can find your way back to the hut."

The boy held his own breath and did not move.

"You can, can't you?"

"But I'm not. I'm not going alone. I'm only going with you."

"All right, David, listen carefully," his father said. "We don't have to worry about freezing. I'm not worried about either of us freezing to death. No one is going to freeze in the woods in November, if he looks after himself. Not even in Montana. It just isn't that cold. I have matches and I have a fresh elk. And I don't think this weather is going to get any worse. It may be raining again by morning. What I'm concerned about is the bleeding. If I spend too much time and effort trying to walk out of here, I could bleed to death.

"I think your hand is going to be all right. It's a bad wound, but the doctors will be able to fix it as good as new. I can see that. I promise you that. You'll be bleeding some too, but if you take care of that hand it won't bleed any more walking than if you were standing still. Then you'll be at the doctor's tonight. But if I try to walk out on this leg it's going to bleed and keep bleeding and I'll lose too much blood. So I'm staying here and bundling up warm and you're walking out to get help. I'm sorry about this. It's what we have to do.

"You can't possibly get lost. You'll just follow this trail straight down the canyon the way we came up, and then you'll come to the meadow. Point yourself toward the big pine tree with the forked crown. When you get to that tree you'll find the creek again. You may not be able to see it, but make yourself quiet and listen for it. You'll hear it. Follow that down off the mountain and past the hut till you get to the jeep."

He struggled a hand into his pocket. "You've never driven a car, have you?"

The boy's lips were pinched. Muscles in his cheeks ached from clenching his jaws. He shook his head.

"You can do it. It isn't difficult." His father held up a single key and began telling the boy how to start the jeep, how to work the clutch, how to find reverse and then first and then second. As his father described the positions on the floor shift the boy raised his swaddled right hand. His father stopped. He rubbed at his eye sockets, like a man waking.

"Of course," he said. "All right. You'll have to help me."

Using the saw with his left hand, the boy cut a small forked aspen. His father showed the boy where to trim it so that the fork would reach just to his armpit. Then they lifted him to his feet. But the crutch was useless on a steep hillside of deep grass and snow. His father leaned over the boy's shoulders and they fought the slope for an hour.

When the boy stepped in a hole and they fell, his father made no exclamation of pain. The boy wondered whether his father's knee hurt as badly as his own hand. He suspected it hurt worse. He said nothing about his hand, though several times in their climb it was twisted or crushed. They reached the trail. The snow had not stopped, and their tracks were veiled. His father said:

"We need one of the guns. I forgot. It's my fault. But you'll have to go back down and get it."

The boy could not find the tree against which his father said he had leaned the .270, so he went toward the stream and looked for blood. He saw none. The imprint of his father's body was already softened beneath an inch of fresh silence. He scooped his good hand through the snowy depression and was startled by cool slimy blood, smearing his fingers like phlegm. Nearby he found the Winchester.

"The lucky one," his father said, "That's all right. Here." He snapped open the breach and a shell flew and he caught it in the air. He glanced dourly at the casing, then cast it aside in the snow. He held the gun out for the boy to see, and with his thumb let the hammer down one notch.

"Remember?" he said. "The safety."

The boy knew he was supposed to feel great shame, but he felt little. His father could no longer hurt him as he once could, because the boy was coming to understand him. His father could not help himself. He did not want the boy to feel contemptible, but he needed him to, because of the loneliness and the bitterness and the boy's mother; and he could not help himself.

After another hour they had barely traversed the aspen hillside. Pushing the crutch away in angry frustration, his father sat in the snow. The boy did not know whether he was thinking carefully of how they might get him out, or still laboring with the choice against despair. The light had wilted to something more like moonlight than afternoon. The sweep of snow had gone gray, depthless, flat, and the sky warned sullenly of night. The boy grew restless. Then it was decided. His father hung himself piggyback over the boy's shoulders, holding the rifle. The boy supported him with elbows crooked under his father's knees. The boy was tall for eleven years old, and heavy. The boy's father weighed 164 pounds.

The boy walked.

He moved as slowly as drifting snow: a step, then time, then another step. The burden at first seemed to him overwhelming. He did not think he would be able to carry his father far.

He took the first few paces expecting to fall. He did not fall, so he kept walking. His arms and shoulders were not exhausted as quickly as he had thought they would be, so he kept walking. Shuffling ahead in the deep powder was like carrying one end of an oak bureau up stairs. But for a surprisingly long time the burden did not grow any worse. He found balance. He found rhythm. He was moving.

Dark blurred the woods, but the snow was luminous. He could see the trail well. He walked.

"How are you, David? How are you holding up?"

"All right."

"We'll stop for a while and let you rest. You can set me down here." The boy kept walking. He moved so ponderously, it seemed after each step that he had stopped. But he kept walking.

"You can set me down. Don't you want to rest?"

The boy did not answer. He wished that his father would not make him talk. At the start he had gulped for air. Now he was breathing low and regularly. He was watching his thighs slice through the snow. He did not want to be disturbed. After a moment he said, "No."

He walked. He came to the cub, shrouded beneath new

snow, and did not see it, and fell over it. His face was smashed deep into the snow by his father's weight. He could not move. But he could breathe. He rested. When he felt his father's thigh roll across his right hand, he remembered the wound. He was lucky his arms had been pinned to his sides, or the hand might have taken the force of their fall. As he waited for his father to roll himself clear, the boy noticed the change in temperature. His sweat chilled him quickly. He began shivering.

His father had again fallen in silence. The boy knew that he would not call out or even mention the pain in his leg. The boy realized that he did not want to mention his hand. The blood soaking the outside of his flannel bandage had grown sticky. He did not want to think of the alien tangle of flesh and tendons and bones wrapped inside. There was pain, but he kept the pain at a distance. It was not *his* hand any more. He was not counting on ever having it back. If he was resolved about that, then the pain was not his either. It was merely pain of which he was aware. His good hand was numb.

"We'll rest now."

"I'm not tired," the boy said. "I'm just getting cold."

"We'll rest," said his father. "I'm tired."

Under his father's knee, the boy noticed, was a cavity in the snow, already melted away by fresh blood. The dark flannel around his father's thigh did not appear sticky. It gleamed.

His father instructed the boy how to open the cub with the deer knife. His father stood on one leg against a deadfall, holding the Winchester ready, and glanced around on all sides as he spoke. The boy used his left hand and both his knees. He punctured the cub low in the belly, to a soft squirting sound, and sliced upward easily. He did not gut the cub. He merely cut out a large square of belly meat. He handed it to his father, in exchange for the rifle.

His father peeled off the hide and left the fat. He sawed the meat in half. One piece he rolled up and put in his jacket pocket. The other he divided again. He gave the boy a square thick with glistening raw fat.

"Eat it. The fat too. Especially the fat. We'll cook the rest farther on. I don't want to build a fire here and taunt Momma."

The meat was chewy. The boy did not find it disgusting. He was hungry.

His father sat back on the ground and unlaced the boot from

his good foot. Before the boy understood what he was doing, he had relaced the boot. He was holding a damp wool sock.

"Give me your left hand." The boy held out his good hand, and his father pulled the sock down over it. "It's getting a lot colder. And we need that hand."

"What about yours? We need your hands too. I'll give you my—"

"No, you won't. We need your feet more than anything. It's all right. I'll put mine inside your shirt."

He lifted his father, and they went on. The boy walked.

He moved steadily through cold darkness. Soon he was sweating again, down his ribs and inside his boots. Only his hands and ears felt as though crushed in a cold metal vise. But his father was shuddering. The boy stopped.

His father did not put down his legs. The boy stood on the trail and waited. Slowly he released his wrist holds. His father's thighs slumped. The boy was careful about the wounded leg. His father's grip over the boy's neck did not loosen. His fingers were cold against the boy's bare skin.

"Are we at the hut?"

"No. We're not even to the meadow."

"Why did you stop?" his father asked.

"It's so cold. You're shivering. Can we build a fire?"

"Yes," his father said hazily. "We'll rest. What time is it?"

"We don't know," the boy said. "We don't have a watch."

The boy gathered small deadwood. His father used the Winchester stock to scoop snow away from a boulder, and they placed the fire at the boulder's base. His father broke up pine twigs and fumbled dry toilet paper from his breast pocket and arranged the wood, but by then his fingers were shaking too badly to strike a match. The boy lit the fire. The boy stamped down the snow, as his father instructed, to make a small ovenlike recess before the fire boulder. He cut fir boughs to floor the recess. He added more deadwood. Beyond the invisible clouds there seemed to be part of a moon.

"It stopped snowing," the boy said.

"Why?"

The boy did not speak. His father's voice had sounded unnatural. After a moment his father said:

"Yes, indeed. It stopped."

They roasted pieces of cub meat skewered on a green stick. Dripping fat made the fire spatter and flare. The meat was scorched on the outside and raw within. It tasted as good as any meat the boy had ever eaten. They burned their palates on hot fat. The second stick smoldered through before they had noticed, and that batch of meat fell in the fire. The boy's father cursed once and reached into the flame for it and dropped it and clawed it out, and then put his hand in the snow. He did not look at the blistered fingers. They ate. The boy saw that both his father's hands had gone clumsy and almost useless.

The boy went for more wood. He found a bleached deadfall not far off the trail, but with one arm he could only break up and carry small loads. They lay down in the recess together like spoons, the boy nearer the fire. They pulled fir boughs into place above them, resting across the snow. They pressed close together. The boy's father was shivering spastically now, and he clenched the boy in a fierce hug. The boy put his father's hands back inside his own shirt. The boy slept. He woke when the fire faded and added more wood and slept. He woke again and tended the fire and changed places with his father and slept. He slept less soundly with his father between him and the fire. He woke again when his father began to vomit.

The boy was terrified. His father wrenched with sudden vomiting that brought up cub meat and yellow liquid and blood and sprayed them across the snow by the grayish-red glow of the fire and emptied his stomach dry and then would not release him. He heaved on pathetically. The boy pleaded to be told what was wrong. His father could not or would not answer. The spasms seized him at the stomach and twisted the rest of his body taut in ugly jerks. Between the attacks he breathed with a wet rumbling sound deep in his chest, and did not speak. When the vomiting subsided, his breathing stretched itself out into long bubbling sighs, then shallow gasps, then more liquidy sighs. His breath caught and froth rose in his throat and into his mouth and he gagged on it and began vomiting again. The boy thought his father would choke. He knelt beside him and held him and cried. He could not see his father's face well and he did not want to look closely while the sounds that were coming from inside his father's body seemed so unhuman. The boy had never been more frightened. He wept for himself, and for his father. He knew from the noises and movements that his father must die. He did not think his father could ever be human again.

When his father was quiet, he went for more wood. He broke

limbs from the deadfall with fanatic persistence and brought them back in bundles and built the fire up bigger. He nestled his father close to it and held him from behind. He did not sleep, though he was not awake. He waited. Finally he opened his eyes on the beginnings of dawn. His father sat up and began to spit.

"One more load of wood and you keep me warm from behind and then we'll go."

The boy obeyed. He was surprised that his father could speak. He thought it strange now that his father was so concerned for himself and so little concerned for the boy. His father had not even asked how he was.

The boy lifted his father, and walked.

Sometime while dawn was completing itself, the snow had resumed. It did not filter down soundlessly. It came on a slight wind at the boy's back, blowing down the canyon. He felt as though he were tumbling forward with the snow into a long vertical shaft. He tumbled slowly. His father's body protected the boy's back from being chilled by the wind. They were both soaked through their clothes. His father was soon shuddering again.

The boy walked. Muscles down the back of his neck were sore from yesterday. His arms ached, and his shoulders and thighs, but his neck hurt him most. He bent his head forward against the weight and the pain, and he watched his legs surge through the snow. At his stomach he felt the dull ache of hunger, not as an appetite but as an affliction. He thought of the jeep. He walked.

He recognized the edge of the meadow but through the snow-laden wind he could not see the cluster of aspens. The snow became deeper where he left the wooded trail. The direction of the wind was now variable, sometimes driving snow into his face, sometimes whipping across him from the right. The grass and snow dragged at his thighs, and he moved by stumbling forward and then catching himself back. Twice he stepped into small overhung fingerlets of the stream, and fell violently, shocking the air from his lungs and once nearly spraining an ankle. Farther out into the meadow, he saw the aspens. They were a hundred yards off to his right. He did not turn directly toward them. He was afraid of crossing more hidden creeks on the intervening ground. He was not certain now whether the main channel was between him and the aspen grove or behind him to the left. He tried to project from the canyon trail to the aspens and on to the forked pine on the far side of the meadow, along what he remembered as almost a straight line. He pointed himself toward the far edge, where the pine should have been. He could not see a forked crown. He could not even see trees. He could see only a vague darker corona above the curve of white. He walked.

He passed the aspens and left them behind. He stopped several times with the wind rasping against him in the open meadow, and rested. He did not set his father down. His father was trembling uncontrollably. He had not spoken for a long time. The boy wanted badly to reach the far side of the meadow. His socks were soaked and his boots and cuffs were glazed with ice. The wind was chafing his face and making him dizzy. His thighs felt as if they had been bruised with a club. The boy wanted to give up and set his father down and whimper that this had gotten to be very unfair; and he wanted to reach the far trees. He did not doubt which he would do. He walked.

He saw trees. Raising his head painfully, he squinted against the rushing flakes. He did not see the forked crown. He went on, and stopped again, and craned his neck, and squinted. He scanned a wide angle of pines, back and forth. He did not see it. He turned his body and his burden to look back. The snow blew across the meadow and seemed, whichever way he turned, to be streaking into his face. He pinched his eyes tighter. He could still see the aspens. But he could not judge where the canyon trail met the meadow. He did not know from just where he had come. He looked again at the aspens, and then ahead to the pines. He considered the problem carefully. He was irritated that the forked ponderosa did not show itself yet, but not worried. He was forced to estimate. He estimated, and went on in that direction.

When he saw a forked pine it was far off to the left of his course. He turned and marched toward it gratefully. As he came nearer, he bent his head up to look. He stopped. The boy was not sure that this was the right tree. Nothing about it looked different, except the thick cakes of snow weighting its limbs, and nothing about it looked especially familiar. He had seen thousands of pine trees in the last few days. This was one like the others. It definitely had a forked crown. He entered the woods at its base.

He had vaguely expected to join a trail. There was no trail. After two hundred yards he was still picking his way among trees and deadfalls and brush. He remembered the shepherd's creek that fell off the lip of the meadow and led down the first canyon. He turned and retraced his tracks to the forked pine.

He looked for the creek. He did not see it anywhere near the tree. He made himself quiet, and listened. He heard nothing but wind, and his father's tremulous breathing.

"Where is the creek?"

His father did not respond. The boy bounced gently up and down, hoping to jar him alert.

"Where is the creek? I can't find it."

"What?"

"We crossed the meadow and I found the tree but I can't find the creek. I need you to help."

"The compass is in my pocket," his father said.

He lowered his father into the snow. He found the compass in his father's breast pocket, and opened the flap, and held it level. The boy noticed with a flinch that his right thigh was smeared with fresh blood. For an instant he thought he had a new wound. Then he realized that the blood was his father's. The compass needle quieted.

"What do I do?"

His father did not respond. The boy asked again. His father said nothing. He sat in the snow and shivered.

The boy left his father and made random arcs within sight of the forked tree until he found a creek. They followed it onward along the flat and then where it gradually began sloping away. The boy did not see what else he could do. He knew that this was the wrong creek. He hoped that it would flow into the shepherd's creek, or at least bring them out on the same road where they had left the jeep. He was very tired. He did not want to stop. He did not care any more about being warm. He wanted only to reach the jeep, and to save his father's life.

He wondered whether his father would love him more generously for having done it. He wondered whether his father would ever forgive him for having done it.

If he failed, his father could never again make him feel shame, the boy thought naively. So he did not worry about failing. He did not worry about dying. His hand was not bleeding, and he felt strong. The creek swung off and down to the left. He followed it, knowing that he was lost. He did not want to reverse himself. He knew that turning back would make him feel confused and desperate and frightened. As long as he was following some pathway, walking, going down, he felt strong.

That afternoon he killed a grouse. He knocked it off a low branch with a heavy short stick that he threw like a boomerang. The grouse fell in the snow and floundered and the boy ran up and plunged on it. He felt it thrashing against his chest. He reached in and it nipped him and he caught it by the neck and squeezed and wrenched mercilessly until long after it stopped writhing. He cleaned it as he had seen his father clean grouse and built a small fire with matches from his father's breast pocket and seared the grouse on a stick. He fed his father. His father could not chew. The boy chewed mouthfuls of grouse, and took the chewed gobbets in his hand, and put them into his father's mouth. His father could swallow. His father could no longer speak.

The boy walked. He thought of his mother in Evergreen Park, and at once he felt queasy and weak. He thought of his mother's face and her voice as she was told that her son was lost in the woods in Montana with a damaged hand that would never be right, and with his father, who had been shot and was unconscious and dying. He pictured his mother receiving the news that her son might die himself, unless he could carry his father out of the woods and find his way to the jeep. He saw her face change. He heard her voice. The boy had to stop. He was crying. He could not control the shape of his mouth. He was not crying with true sorrow, as he had in the night when he held his father and thought his father would die; he was crying in sentimental self-pity. He sensed the difference. Still he cried.

He must not think of his mother, the boy realized. Thinking of her could only weaken him. If she knew where he was, what he had to do, she could only make it impossible for him to do it. He was lucky that she knew nothing, the boy thought.

No one knew what the boy was doing, or what he had yet to do. Even the boy's father no longer knew. The boy was lucky. No one was watching, no one knew, and he was free to be capable.

The boy imagined himself alone at his father's grave. The grave was open. His father's casket had already been lowered. The boy stood at the foot in his black Christmas suit, and his hands were crossed at his groin, and he was not crying. Men with shovels stood back from the grave, waiting for the boy's order for them to begin filling it. The boy felt a horrible swelling sense of joy. The men watched him, and he stared down into the hole. He knew it was a lie. If his father died, the boy's mother would rush out to Livingston and have him buried and stand at the grave in a black dress and veil squeezing the boy to her side like he was a child. There was nothing the boy could do about that. All the more reason he must keep walking.

Then she would tow the boy back with her to Evergreen Park. And he would be standing on 96th Street in the morning dark before his father's cold body had even begun to grow alien and decayed in the buried box. She would drag him back, and there would be nothing the boy could do. And he realized that if he returned with his mother after the burial, he would never again see the cabin outside Livingston. He would have no more summers and no more Novembers anywhere but in Evergreen Park.

The cabin now seemed to be at the center of the boy's life. It seemed to stand halfway between this snowbound creek valley and the train station in Chicago. It would be his cabin soon.

The boy knew nothing about his father's will, and he had never been told that legal ownership of the cabin was destined for him. Legal ownership did not matter. The cabin might be owned by his mother, or sold to pay his father's debts, or taken away by the state, but it would still be the boy's cabin. It could only forever belong to him. His father had been telling him *Here, this is yours. Prepare to receive it.* The boy had sensed that much. But he had been threatened, and unwilling. The boy realized now that he might be resting warm in the cabin in a matter of hours, or he might never see it again. He could appreciate the justice of that. He walked.

He thought of his father as though his father were far away from him. He saw himself in the black suit at the grave, and he heard his father speak to him from aside: *That's good. Now raise your eyes and tell them in a man's voice to begin shoveling. Then turn away and walk slowly back down the hill. Be sure you don't cry. That's good.* The boy stopped. He felt his glands quiver, full of new tears. He knew that it was a lie. His father would never be there to congratulate him. His father would never know how well the boy had done.

He took deep breaths. He settled himself. Yes, his father would know somehow, the boy believed. His father had known all along. His father knew.

He built the recess just as they had the night before, except this time he found flat space between a stone bank and a large fallen cottonwood trunk. He scooped out the snow, he laid boughs, and he made a fire against each reflector. At first the bed was quite warm. Then the melt from the fires began to run down and collect in the middle, forming a puddle of wet boughs under them. The boy got up and carved runnels across the packed snow to drain the fires. He went back to sleep and slept warm, holding his father. He rose again each half hour to feed the fires.

The snow stopped in the night, and did not resume. The woods seemed to grow quieter, settling, sighing beneath the new weight. What was going to come had come.

The boy grew tired of breaking deadwood and began walking again before dawn and walked for five more hours. He did not try to kill the grouse that he saw because he did not want to spend time cleaning and cooking it. He was hurrying now. He drank from the creek. At one point he found small black insects like winged ants crawling in great numbers across the snow near the creek. He stopped to pinch up and eat thirty or forty of them. They were tasteless. He did not bother to feed any to his father. He felt he had come a long way down the mountain. He thought he was reaching the level now where there might be roads. He followed the creek, which had received other branches and grown to a stream. The ground was flattening again and the drainage was widening, opening to daylight. As he carried his father, his head ached. He had stopped noticing most of his other pains. About noon of that day he came to the fence.

It startled him. He glanced around, his pulse drumming suddenly, preparing himself at once to see the long empty sweep of snow and broken fence posts and thinking of Basque shepherds fifty years gone. He saw the cabin and the smoke. He relaxed, trembling helplessly into laughter. He relaxed, and was unable to move. Then he cried, still laughing. He cried shamelessly with relief and dull joy and wonder, for as long as he wanted. He held his father, and cried. But he set his father down and washed his own face with snow before he went to the door.

He crossed the lot walking slowly, carrying his father. He did not now feel tired.

The young woman's face was drawn down in shock and revealed at first nothing of friendliness.

"We had a jeep parked somewhere, but I can't find it," the boy said. "This is my father."

They would not talk to him. They stripped him and put him before the fire wrapped in blankets and started tea and made him wait. He wanted to talk. He wished they would ask him a lot of questions. But they went about quickly and quietly, making things warm. His father was in the bedroom.

The man with the face full of dark beard had telephoned for a doctor. He went back into the bedroom with more blankets, and stayed. His wife went from room to room with hot tea. She rubbed the boy's naked shoulders through the blanket, and held a cup to his mouth, but she would not talk to him. He did not know what to say to her, and he could not move his lips very well. But he wished she would ask him some questions. He was restless, thawing in silence before the hearth.

He thought about going back to their own cabin soon. In his mind he gave the bearded man directions to take him and his father home. It wasn't far. It would not require much of the man's time. They would thank him, and give him an elk steak. Later he and his father would come back for the jeep. He could keep his father warm at the cabin as well as they were doing here, the boy knew.

While the woman was in the bedroom , the boy overheard the bearded man raise his voice:

"He what?"

"He carried him out," the woman whispered.

"What do you mean, carried him?"

"Carried him. On his back. I saw."

"Carried him from where?"

"Where it happened. Somewhere on Sheep Creek, maybe."

"Eight miles?"

"I know."

"*Eight miles?* How could he do that?"

"I don't know. I suppose he couldn't. But he did."

The doctor arrived in half an hour, as the boy was just starting to shiver. The doctor went into the bedroom and stayed five minutes. The woman poured the boy more tea and knelt beside him and hugged him around the shoulders.

When the doctor came out, he examined the boy without

speaking. The boy wished the doctor would ask him some questions, but he was afraid he might be shivering too hard to answer in a man's voice. While the doctor touched him and probed him and took his temperature, the boy looked the doctor directly in the eye, as though to show him he was really all right.

The doctor said:

"David, your father is dead. He has been dead for a long time. Probably since yesterday."

"I know that," the boy said.

KINUKO CRAFT. (*TQ* #46)

Where is everyone?

Raymond Carver

I've seen some things. I was going over to my mother's to stay a few nights, but just as I came to the top of the stairs I looked and she was on the sofa kissing a man. It was summer, the door was open, and the color TV was playing.

My mother is sixty-five and lonely. She belongs to a singles club. But even so, knowing all this, it was hard. I stood at the top of the stairs with my hand on the railing and watched as the man pulled her deeper into the kiss. She was kissing back, and the TV was going on the other side of the room. It was Sunday, about five in the afternoon. People from the apartment house were down below in the pool. I went back down the stairs and out to my car.

A lot has happened since that afternoon, and on the whole things are better now. But during those days, when my mother was putting out to men she'd just met, I was out of work, drinking, and crazy. My kids were crazy, and my wife was crazy and having a "thing" with an unemployed aerospace engineer she'd met at AA. He was crazy too. His name was Ross and he had five or six kids. He walked with a limp from a gunshot wound his first wife had given him. He didn't have a wife now; he wanted my wife. I don't know what we were all thinking of in those days. The second wife had come and gone, but it was his first wife who had shot him in the thigh some years back, giving him the limp, and who now had him in and out of court, or in jail, every six months or so for not meeting his support payments. I wish him well now. But it was different then. More than once in those days I mentioned weapons. I'd say to my wife, I'd shout it, "I'm going to kill him!" But nothing ever happened. Things lurched on. I never met the man, though we talked on the phone a few times. I did find a couple of pictures of him once when I was going through my wife's purse. He was a little guy, not too little, and he had a mustache and was wearing a striped jersey, waiting for a kid to come down the slide. In the other picture he was standing against a house—my house? I couldn't tell—with his arms crossed, dressed up, wearing a tie. Ross, you son of a bitch, I hope you're okay now. I hope things are better for you too.

The last time he'd been jailed, a month before that Sunday, I found out from my daughter that her mother had gone bail for him. Daughter Kate, who was fifteen, didn't take to this any better than I did. It wasn't that she had any loyalty to me in this—she had no loyalties to me or her mother in anything and was only too willing to sell either one of us down the river. No, it was that there was a serious cash-flow problem in the house and if money went to Ross, there'd be that much less for what she needed. So Ross was on her list now. Also, she didn't like his kids, she'd said, but she'd told me once before that in general Ross was all right, even funny and interesting when he wasn't drinking. He'd even told her fortune.

He spent his time repairing things, now that he could no longer hold a job in the aerospace industry. But I'd seen his house from the outside; and the place looked like a dumping ground, with all kinds and makes of old appliances and equipment that would never wash or cook or play again—all of it just standing in his open garage and on his drive and in the front yard. He also kept some broken-down cars around that he liked to tinker on. In the first stages of their affair my wife had told me he "collected antique cars." Those were her words. I'd seen some of his cars parked in front of his house when I'd driven by there trying to see what I could see. Old 1950s and 1960s, dented cars with torn seat covers. They were junkers, that's all. I knew. I had his number. We had things in common, more than just driving old cars and trying to hold on for dear life to the same woman. Still, handyman or not, he couldn't manage to tune my wife's car properly or fix our TV set when it broke down and we lost the picture. We had volume, but no picture. If we wanted to get the news, we'd have to sit around the screen at night and listen to the set. I'd drink and make some crack to my kids about Mr. Fixit. Even now I don't know if my wife believed that stuff or not, about antique cars and such. But she cared for him, she loved him even; that's pretty clear now.

They'd met when Cynthia was trying to stay sober and was going to meetings three or four times a week. I had been in and out of AA for several months, though when Cynthia met Ross I was out and drinking a fifth a day of anything I could get my hands on. But as I heard Cynthia say to someone over the phone about me, I'd had the exposure to AA and knew where to go when I really wanted help. Ross had been in AA and then had gone back to drinking again. Cynthia felt, I think, that maybe there was more hope for him than for me and tried to help him and so went to the meetings to keep herself sober, then went over to cook for him or clean his house. His kids were no help to him in this regard. Nobody lifted a hand around his house except Cynthia when she was there. But the less his kids pitched in, the more he loved them. It was strange. It was the opposite with me. I hated my kids during this time. I'd be on the sofa with a glass of vodka and grapefruit juice when one of them would come in from school and slam the door. One afternoon I screamed and got into a scuffle with my son. Cynthia had to break it up when I threatened to knock him to pieces. I said I would kill him. I said, "I gave you life and I can take it away."

Madness.

The kids, Katy and Mike, were only too happy to take advantage of this crumbling situation. They seemed to thrive on the threats and bullying they inflicted on each other and on us—the violence and dismay, the general bedlam. Right now, thinking about it even from this distance, it makes me set my heart against them. I remember years before, before I turned to drinking full time, reading an extraordinary scene in a novel by an Italian named Italo Svevo. The narrator's father was dying and the family had gathered around the bed, weeping and waiting for the old man to expire, when he opened his eyes to look at each of them for a last time. When his gaze fell on the narrator he suddenly stirred and something came into his eyes; and with his last burst of strength he raised up, flung himself across the bed, and slapped the face of his son as hard as he could. Then he fell back onto the bed and died. I often imagined my own deathbed scene in those days, and I saw myself doing the same thing, only I would hope to have the strength to slap each of my kids and my last words for them would be what only a dying man would have the courage to utter.

But they saw craziness on every side, and it suited their purpose, I was convinced. They fattened on it. They liked being able to call the shots, having the upper hand, while we bungled along letting them work on our guilt. They might have been inconvenienced from time to time, but they ran things their way. They weren't embarrassed or put out by any of the activities that went on in our house either. To the contrary. It gave them something to talk about with their friends. I've heard them regaling their pals with the most frightful stories, howling with laughter as they spilled out the lurid details of what was happening to me and their mother. Except for being financially dependent on Cynthia, who still somehow had a teaching job and a monthly paycheck, they flat-out ran the show. And that's what it was too, a show.

Once Mike locked his mother out of the house after she'd stayed overnight at Ross's house. . . . I don't know where I was that night, probably at my mother's. I'd sleep over there sometimes. I'd eat supper with her and she'd tell me how she worried about all of us; then we'd watch TV and try to talk about something else, try to hold a normal conversation about something other than my family situation. She'd make a bed for me on her sofa—the same sofa she used to make love on, I supposed, but I'd sleep there anyway and be grateful. Cynthia came home at seven o'clock one morning to get dressed for school and found that Mike had locked all the doors and windows and wouldn't let her in the house. She stood outside his window and begged him to let her in—please, please, so she could dress and go to school, for if she lost her job what then? Where would he be? Where would any of us be then? He said, "You don't live here any more. Why should I let you in?" That's what he said to her, standing behind his window, his face all stopped up with rage. (She told me this later when she was drunk and I was sober and holding her hands and letting her talk.) "You don't live here," he said.

"Please, please, please, Mike," she pleaded. "Let me in."

He let her in and she swore at him. Like that, he punched her hard on the shoulders several times—whop, whop, whop—then hit her on top of the head and generally worked her over. Finally she was able to change clothes, fix her face, and rush off to school.

All this happened not too long ago, three years about. It was something in those days.

I left my mother with the man on her sofa and drove around for a while, not wanting to go home and not wanting to sit in a bar that day either.

Sometimes Cynthia and I would talk about things—"reviewing the situation," we'd call it. But now and then on rare occasions we'd talk a little about things that bore no relation to the situation. One afternoon we were in the living room and she said, "When I was pregnant with Mike you carried me to the bathroom when I was so sick and pregnant I couldn't get out of bed. You carried me. No one else will ever do that, no one else could ever love me in that way, that much. We have that, no matter what. We've loved each other like nobody else could or ever will love the other again."

We looked at each other. Maybe we touched hands, I don't recall. Then I remembered the half-pint of whisky or vodka or gin or Scotch or tequila that I had hidden under the very sofa cushion we were sitting on (oh, happy days!) and I began to hope she might soon have to get up and move around—go to the kitchen, the bathroom, out to clean the garage.

"Maybe you could make us some coffee," I said. "A pot of coffee might be nice."

"Would you eat something? I can fix some soup."

"Maybe I could eat something, but I'll for sure drink a cup of coffee."

She went out to the kitchen. I waited until I heard her begin to run water. Then I reached under the cushion for the bottle, unscrewed the lid, and drank.

I never told these things at AA. I never said much at the meetings. I'd "pass" as they called it: when it came your turn to speak and you didn't say anything except "I'll pass tonight, thanks." But I would listen and shake my head and laugh in recognition at the awful stories I heard. Usually I was drunk when I went to those first meetings. You're scared and you need something more than cookies and instant coffee.

But those conversations touching on love or the past were rare. If we talked, we talked about business, survival, the bottom line of things. Money. Where is the money going to come from? The telephone was on the way out, the lights and gas threatened. What about Katy? She needs clothes. Her grades. That boyfriend of hers is a biker. Mike. What's going to happen to Mike? What's going to happen to us all? "My God," she'd say. But God wasn't having any of it. He'd washed his hands of us.

I wanted Mike to join the army, navy, or the coast guard. He was impossible. A dangerous character. Even Ross felt the army would be good for him, Cynthia had told me, and she hadn't liked him telling her that a bit. But I was pleased to hear this and to find out that Ross and I were in agreement on the matter. Ross went up a peg in my estimation. But it angered Cynthia because, miserable as Mike was to have around, despite his violent streak, she thought it was just a phase that would soon pass. She didn't want him in the army. But Ross told Cynthia that Mike belonged in the army where he'd learn respect and manners. He told her this after there'd been a pushing and shoving match out in his drive in the early morning hours when Mike had thrown him down on the pavement.

Ross loved Cynthia, but he also had a twenty-two-year-old girl named Beverly who was pregnant with his baby, though Ross assured Cynthia he loved her, not Beverly. They didn't even sleep together any longer, he told Cynthia, but Beverly was carrying his baby and he loved all his children, even the unborn, and he couldn't just give her the boot, could he? He wept when he told all this to Cynthia. He was drunk. (Someone was always drunk in those days.) I can imagine the scene.

Ross had graduated from California Polytechnic Institute and gone right to work at the NASA operation in Mountain View. He worked there for ten years, until it all fell in on him. I never met him, as I said, but we talked on the phone several times, about one thing and another. I called him once when I was drunk and Cynthia and I were debating some sad point or another. One of his children answered the phone and when Ross came on the line I asked him whether, if I pulled out (I had no intention of pulling out, of course; it was just harassment), he intended to support Cynthia and our kids. He said he was carving a roast, that's what he said, and they were just going to sit down and eat their dinner, he and his children. Could he call me back? I hung up. When he called, after an hour or so, I'd forgotten about the earlier call. Cynthia answered the phone and said "Yes" and then "Yes" again, and I knew it was Ross and that he was asking if I was drunk. I grabbed the phone. "Well, are you going to support them or not?" He said he was sorry for his part in all of this but, no, he guessed he couldn't support them. "So it's no, you can't support them," I said, and looked at Cynthia as if this should settle everything. He said, "Yes, it's no." But Cynthia didn't bat an eye. I figured later they'd already talked that situation over thoroughly, so it was no surprise. She already knew.

He was in his mid-thirties when he went under. I used to make fun of him when I had the chance. I called him "the weasel," after his photograph. "That's what your mother's boyfriend looks like," I'd say to my kids if they were around and we were talking, "like a weasel." We'd laugh. Or else "Mr. Fixit." That was my favorite name for him. God bless and keep you, Ross. I don't hold anything against you now. But in those days when I called him the weasel or Mr. Fixit and threatened his life, he was something of a fallen hero to my kids and to Cynthia too, I suppose, because he'd helped put men on the moon. He'd worked, I was told time and again, on the moon project shots, and he was close friends with Buzz Aldren and Neal Armstrong. He'd told Cynthia, and Cynthia had told the kids, who'd told me, that when the astronauts came to town he was going to introduce them. But they never came to town, or if they did they forgot to contact Ross. Soon after the moon probes, fortune's wheel turned and Ross's drinking increased. He began missing work. Sometime then the troubles with his first wife started. Toward the end he began taking the drink to work with him in a thermos. It's a modern operation out there, I've seen it—cafeteria lines, executive dining rooms, and the like, Mr. Coffee's in every office. But he brought his own thermos to work, and after a while people began to know and to talk. He was laid off, or else he quit—nobody could ever give me a straight answer when I asked. He kept drinking, of course. You do that. Then he commenced working on ruined appliances and doing TV repair work and fixing cars. He was interested in astrology, auras, I Ching—that business. I don't doubt that he was bright enough and interesting and quirky, like most of our ex-friends. I told Cynthia I was sure she wouldn't care for him (I couldn't yet bring myself to use the word "love" about that relationship) if he wasn't, basically, a good man. "One of *us*," was how I put it, trying to be large about it. He wasn't a bad or an evil man, Ross. "No one's evil," I said once to Cynthia when we were discussing my own affair.

My dad died in his sleep, drunk, eight years ago. It was a Friday night and he was fifty-four years old. He came home from work at the sawmill, took some sausage out of the freezer for his breakfast the next morning, and sat down at the kitchen table, where he opened a quart of Four Roses. He was in good enough spirits in those days, glad to be back on a job after being out of work for three or four years with blood poisoning and then something that caused him to have shock treatments. (I was married and living in another town during that time. I had the kids and a job, enough troubles of my own, so I couldn't follow his too closely.) That night he moved into the living room with his bottle, a bowl of ice cubes and a glass, and drank and watched TV until my mother came in from work at the coffee shop.

They had a few words about the whiskey, as they always did. She didn't drink much herself. When I was grown, I only saw her drink at Thanksgiving, Christmas, and New Year's—eggnog or buttered rums, and then never too many. The one time she had had too much to drink, years before (I heard this from my dad who laughed about it when he told it), they'd gone to a little place outside Eureka and she'd had a great many whiskey sours. Just as they got into the car to leave, she started to get sick and had to open the door. Somehow her false teeth came out, the car moved forward a little, and a tire passed over her dentures. After that she never drank except on holidays and then never to excess.

My dad kept on drinking that Friday night and tried to ignore my mother, who sat out in the kitchen and smoked and tried to write a letter to her sister in Little Rock. Finally he got up and went to bed. My mother went to bed not long after, when she was sure he was asleep. She said later she noticed nothing out of the ordinary except maybe his snoring seemed heavier and deeper and she couldn't get him to turn on his side. But she went to sleep. She woke up when my dad's sphincter muscles and bladder let go. It was just sunrise. Birds were singing. My dad was still on his back, eyes closed and mouth open. My mother looked at him and cried his name.

I kept driving around. It was dark by now. I drove by my house, every light ablaze, but Cynthia's car wasn't in the drive. I went to a bar where I sometimes drank and called home. Katy answered and said her mother wasn't there, and where was I? She needed five dollars. I shouted something and hung up. Then I called collect to a woman six hundred miles away whom I hadn't seen in months, a good woman who, the last time I'd seen her, had said she would pray for me.

She accepted the charges. She asked where I was calling from. She asked how I was. "Are you all right?" she said.

We talked. I asked about her husband. He'd been a friend of mine and was now living away from her and the children.

"He's still in Richland," she said. "How did all this happen to us?" she asked. "We started out good people." We talked a while longer; then she said she still loved me and that she would continue to pray for me.

"Pray for me," I said. "Yes." Then we said good-bye and hung up.

Later I called home again, but this time no one answered. I dialed my mother's number. She picked up the phone on the first ring, her voice cautious, as if expecting trouble.

"It's me," I said. "I'm sorry to be calling."

"No, no, honey, I was up," she said. "Where are you? Is anything the matter? I thought you were coming over today. I looked for you. Are you calling from home?"

"I'm not at home," I said. "I don't know where everyone is at home. I just called there."

"Old Ken was over here today," she went on, "that old bastard. He came over this afternoon. I haven't seen him in a month and he just shows up, the old thing. I don't like him. All he wants to do is talk about himself and brag on himself and how he lived on Guam and had three girlfriends at the same time and how he's traveled to this place and that place. He's just an old braggart, that's all he is. I met him at that dance I told you about, but I don't like him."

"Is it all right if I come over?" I said.

"Honey, why don't you? I'll fix us something to eat. I'm hungry myself. I haven't eaten anything since this afternoon. Old Ken brought some Colonel Sanders over this afternoon. Come over and I'll fix us some scrambled eggs. Do you want me to come get you? Honey, are you all right?"

I drove over. She kissed me when I came in the door. I turned my face. I hated for her to smell the vodka. The TV was on.

"Wash your hands," she said as she studied me. "It's ready."

1980   405

Later she made a bed for me on the sofa. I went into the bathroom. She kept a pair of my dad's pajamas in there. I took them out of the drawer, looked at them, and began undressing. When I came out she was in the kitchen. I fixed the pillow and lay down. She finished with what she was doing, turned off the kitchen light, and sat down at the end of the sofa.

"Honey, I don't want to be the one to tell you this," she said. "It hurts me to tell you, but even the kids know it and they've told me. We've talked about it. But Cynthia is seeing another man."

"That's okay," I said. "I know that," I said and looked at the TV. "His name is Ross and he's an alcoholic. He's like me."

"Honey, you're going to have to do something for yourself," she said.

"I know it," I said. I kept looking at the TV.

She leaned over and hugged me. She held me a minute. Then she let go and wiped her eyes. "I'll get you up in the morning," she said.

"I don't have much to do tomorrow. I might sleep in a while after you go." I thought: after you get up, after you've gone to the bathroom and gotten dressed, then I'll get into your bed and lie there and doze and listen to your radio out in the kitchen giving the news and weather.

"Honey, I'm so worried about you."

"Don't worry," I said. I shook my head.

"You get some rest now," she said. "You need to sleep."

"I'll sleep. I'm very sleepy."

"Watch television as long as you want," she said.

I nodded.

She bent and kissed me. Her lips seemed bruised and swollen. She drew the blanket over me. Then she went into her bedroom. She left the door open, and in a minute I could hear her snoring.

I lay there staring at the TV. There were images of uniformed men on the screen, a low murmur, then tanks and a man using a flamethrower. I couldn't hear it, but I didn't want to get up. I kept staring until I felt my eyes close. But I woke up with a start, the pajamas damp with sweat. A snowy light filled the room. There was a roaring coming at me. The room clamored. I lay there. I didn't move.

1980

Hunters in the snow

Tobias Wolff

Tub had been waiting for an hour in the falling snow. He paced the sidewalk to keep warm and stuck his head out over the curb whenever he saw lights approaching. One driver stopped for him, but before Tub could wave the man on he saw the rifle on Tub's back and hit the gas. The tires spun on the ice.

The fall of snow thickened. Tub stood below the overhang of a building. Across the road the clouds whitened just above the rooftops, and the streetlights went out. He shifted the rifle strap to his other shoulder. The whiteness seeped up the sky.

A truck slid around the corner, horn blaring, rear end sashaying. Tub moved to the sidewalk and held up his hand. The truck jumped the curb and kept coming, half on the street and half on the sidewalk. It wasn't slowing down at all. Tub stood for a moment, still holding up his hand, then jumped back. His rifle slipped off his shoulder and clattered on the ice; a sandwich fell out of his pocket. He ran for the steps of the building. Another sandwich and a package of cookies tumbled onto the new snow. He made the steps and looked back.

The truck had stopped several feet beyond where Tub had been standing. He picked up his sandwiches and his cookies and slung the rifle and went up to the driver's window. The driver was bent against the steering wheel, slapping his knees and drumming his feet on the floorboards. He looked like a cartoon of a person laughing, except that his eyes watched the man on the seat beside him.

"You ought to see yourself," said the driver. "He looks just like a beach ball with a hat on, doesn't he? Doesn't he, Frank?"

The man beside him smiled and looked off.

"You almost ran me down," said Tub. "You could've killed me."

"Come on, Tub," said the man beside the driver. "Be mellow. Kenny was just messing around." He opened the door and slid over to the middle of the seat.

Tub took the bolt out of his rifle and climbed in beside him. "I waited an hour," he said. "If you meant ten o'clock, why didn't you say ten o'clock?"

"Tub, you haven't done anything but complain since we got here," said the man in the middle. "If you want to piss and moan all day you might as well go home and bitch at your kids. Take your pick." When Tub didn't say anything, he turned to the driver. "Okay, Kenny, let's hit the road."

Some juvenile delinquents had heaved a brick through the windshield on the driver's side, so the cold and snow tunneled right into the cab. The heater didn't work. They covered themselves with a couple of blankets Kenny had brought along and pulled down the muffs on their caps. Tub tried to keep his hands warm by rubbing them under the blanket, but Frank made him stop.

They left Spokane and drove deep into the country, running along black lines of fences. The snow let up, but still there was no edge to the land where it met the sky. Nothing moved in the chalky fields. The cold bleached their faces and made the stubble stand out on their cheeks and along their upper lips. They had to stop and have coffee several times before they got to the woods where Kenny wanted to hunt.

Tub was for trying some place different; two years in a row they'd been up and down this land and hadn't seen a thing. Frank didn't care one way or the other; he just wanted to get out of the goddamned truck. "Feel that," Frank said. He spread his feet and closed his eyes and leaned his head way back and breathed deeply. "Tune in on that energy."

"Another thing,"said Kenny. "This is open land. Most of the land around here is posted."

Frank breathed out. "Stop bitching, Tub. Get centered."

"I wasn't bitching."

"Centered," said Kenny. "Next thing you'll be wearing a nightgown, Frank. Selling flowers out at the airport."

"Kenny," said Frank. "You talk too much."

"OK" said Kenny. "I won't say a word. Like I won't say anything about a certain baby-sitter."

"What baby-sitter?" asked Tub.

"That's between us," said Frank, looking at Kenny. "That's confidential. You keep your mouth shut."

Kenny laughed.

"You're asking for it," said Frank.

"Asking for what?"

"You'll see."

"Hey," said Tub. "Are we hunting or what?"

Frank just smiled.

They started off across the field. Tub had trouble getting through the fences. Frank and Kenny could have helped him; they could have lifted up on the top wire and stepped on the bottom wire, but they didn't. They stood and watched him. There were a lot of fences and Tub was puffing when they reached the woods.

They hunted for over two hours and saw no deer, no tracks, no sign. Finally they stopped by the creek to eat. Kenny had several slices of pizza and a couple of candy bars; Frank had a sandwich, an apple, two carrots, and a square of chocolate; Tub put out one hard-boiled egg and a stick of celery.

"You ask me how I want to die today," said Kenny. "I'll tell you, burn me at the stake." He turned to Tub. "You still on that diet?" He winked at Frank.

"What do you think? You think I like hard-boiled eggs?"

"All I can say is, it's the first diet I ever heard of where you gained weight from it."

"Who said I gained weight?"

"Oh, pardon me. I take it back. You're just wasting away before my very eyes. Isn't he, Frank?"

Frank had his fingers fanned out, tips against the bark of the stump where he'd laid his food. His knuckles were hairy. He wore a heavy wedding band, and on his right pinky was another gold ring with a flat face and "F" printed out in what looked like diamonds. He turned it this way and that. "Tub," he said, "you haven't seen your own balls in ten years."

Kenny doubled over laughing. He took off his hat and slapped his leg with it.

"What am I supposed to do?" said Tub. "It's my glands."

They left the woods and hunted along the creek. Frank and Kenny worked one bank and Tub worked the other, moving upstream. The snow was light, but the drifts were deep and hard to move through. Wherever Tub looked, the surface was smooth, undisturbed, and after a time he lost interest. He stopped looking for tracks and just tried to keep up with Frank and Kenny on the other side. A moment came when he realized he hadn't seen them in a long time. The breeze was moving from him to them; when it stilled he could sometimes hear them arguing but that was all. He quickened his pace, breasting hard into the drifts, fighting the snow away with his knees and elbows. He heard his heart and felt the flush on his face, but he never once stopped.

Tub caught up with Frank and Kenny at a bend in the creek. They were standing on a log that stretched from their bank to his. Ice had backed up behind the log. Frozen reeds stuck out, barely nodding when the air moved.

"See anything?" asked Frank.

Tub shook his head.

There wasn't much daylight left, and they decided to head back toward the road. Frank and Kenny crossed the log and started downstream, using the trail Tub had broken. Before they had gone very far, Kenny stopped. "Look at that," he said, and pointed to some tracks going from the creek back into the woods. Tub's footprints crossed right over them. There on the bank, plain as day, were several mounds of deer sign. "What do you think that is, Tub?" Kenny kicked at it. "Walnuts on vanilla icing?"

"I guess I didn't notice."

Kenny looked at Frank.

"I was lost."

"You were lost. Big deal."

They followed the tracks into the woods. The deer had gone over a fence half buried in drifting snow. A no-hunting sign was nailed to the top of one of the posts. Frank laughed and said the son of a bitch could read. Kenny wanted to go after him, but Frank said no way—the people out here didn't mess around. He thought maybe the farmer who owned the land would let them use it if they asked, though Kenny wasn't so sure. Anyway, he figured that by the time they walked to the truck and drove up the road and doubled back it would be almost dark.

"Relax," said Frank. "You can't hurry nature. If we're

meant to get that deer, we'll get it. If we're not, we won't."

They started back toward the truck. This part of the woods was mainly pine. The snow was shaded and had a glaze on it. It held up Kenny and Frank, but Tub kept falling through. As he kicked forward, the edge of the crust bruised his shins. Kenny and Frank pulled ahead of him, to where he couldn't even hear their voices any more. He sat down on a stump and wiped his face. He ate both the sandwiches and half the cookies, taking his own sweet time. It was dead quiet.

When Tub crossed the last fence into the road, the truck started moving. Tub had to run for it and just managed to grab hold of the tailgate and hoist himself into the bed. He lay there panting. Kenny looked out the rear window and grinned. Tub crawled into the lee of the cab to get out of the freezing wind. He pulled his earflaps low and pushed his chin into the collar of his coat. Someone rapped on the window, but Tub would not turn around.

He and Frank waited outside while Kenny went into the farmhouse to ask permission. The house was old, and paint was curling off the sides. The smoke streamed westward off the top of the chimney, fanning away into a thin gray plume. Above the ridge of the hills another ridge of blue clouds was rising.

"You've got a short memory," said Tub.

"What?" said Frank. He had been staring off.

"I used to stick up for you."

"Okay, so you used to stick up for me. What's eating you?"

"You shouldn't have just left me back there like that."

"You're a grown-up, Tub. You can take care of yourself. Anyway, if you think you're the only person with problems, I can tell you that you're not."

"Is something bothering you, Frank?"

Frank kicked at a branch poking out of the snow. "Never mind," he said.

"What did Kenny mean about the baby-sitter?"

"Kenny talks too much," said Frank. "You just mind your own business."

Kenny came out of the farmhouse and gave the thumbs up, and they began walking back toward the woods. As they passed the barn, a large black hound with a grizzled snout ran out and barked at them. Every time he barked he slid backward a bit, like a cannon going off. Kenny got down on all fours and snarled and barked back at him, and the dog slunk away into the barn, looking over his shoulder and peeing a little as he went.

"That's an old-timer," said Frank. "A real graybeard. Fifteen years, if he's a day."

"Too old," said Kenny.

Past the barn they cut off through the fields. The land was unfenced, and the crust was freezing up thick, and they made good time. They kept to the edge of the field until they picked up the tracks again and followed them into the woods, farther and farther back toward the hills. The trees started to blur with the shadows, and the wind rose and needled their faces with the crystals it swept off the glaze. Finally they lost the tracks.

Kenny swore and threw down his hat. "This is the worst day of hunting I ever had, bar none." He picked up his hat and brushed off the snow. "This will be the first season since I was fifteen that I haven't got my deer."

"It isn't the deer," said Frank. "It's the hunting. There are all these forces out here and you just have to go with them."

"You go with them," said Kenny. "I came out here to get me a deer, not listen to a bunch of hippie bullshit. And if it hadn't been for Dimples here, I would have, too."

"That's enough," said Frank.

"And you . . . you're so busy thinking about that little jailbait of yours, you wouldn't know a deer if you saw one."

"I'm warning you," said Frank.

Kenny laughed. "I think maybe I'll have me a talk with a certain jailbait's father," he said. "Then you can warn him, too."

"Drop dead," said Frank and turned away.

Kenny and Tub followed him back across the fields. When they were coming up to the barn, Kenny stopped and pointed. "I hate that post," he said. He raised his rifle and fired. It sounded like a dry branch cracking. The post splintered along its right side, up toward the top.

"There," said Kenny. "It's dead."

"Knock it off," said Frank, walking ahead.

Kenny looked at Tub and smiled. "I hate that tree," he said, and fired again. Tub hurried to catch up with Frank. He started to speak, but just then the dog ran out of the barn and barked at them. "Easy, boy," said Frank.

"I hate that dog." Kenny was behind them.

"That's enough," said Frank. "You put that gun down."

Kenny fired. The bullet went in between the dog's eyes. He sank right down into the snow, his legs splayed out on each side, his yellow eyes open and staring. Except for the blood, he looked like a small bearskin rug. The blood ran down the dog's muzzle into the snow.

They all looked at the dog lying there.

"What did he ever do to you?" asked Tub. "He was just barking."

Kenny turned to Tub. "I hate you."

Tub shot from the waist. Kenny jerked backward against the fence and buckled to his knees. He folded his hands across his stomach. "Look," he said. His hands were covered with blood. In the dusk his blood was more blue than red. It seemed to belong to the shadows. It didn't seem out of place. Kenny eased himself onto his back. He sighed several times, deeply. "You shot me," he said.

"I had to," said Tub. He knelt beside Kenny. "Oh, God," he said. "Frank. Frank."

Frank hadn't moved since Kenny killed the dog.

"Frank!" Tub shouted.

"I was just kidding around," said Kenny. "It was a joke. Oh!" he said, and arched his back suddenly. "Oh!" he said again, and dug his heels into the snow and pushed himself along on his head for several feet. Then he stopped and lay there, rocking back and forth on his heels and head like a wrestler doing warm-up exercises.

Frank roused himself. "Kenny," he said. He bent down and put his gloved hand on Kenny's brow. "You shot him," he said to Tub.

"He made me," said Tub.

"No, no, no," said Kenny.

Tub was weeping from the eyes and nostrils. His whole face was wet. Frank closed his eyes, then looked down at Kenny again. "Where does it hurt?"

"Everywhere," said Kenny. "Just everywhere."

"Oh, God," said Tub.

"I mean where did it go in?" said Frank.

"Here." Kenny pointed at the wound in his stomach. It was welling slowly with blood.

"You're lucky," said Frank. "It's on the left side. It missed your appendix. If it had hit your appendix, you'd really be in the soup." He turned and threw up onto the snow, holding his sides as if to keep warm.

"Are you all right?" asked Tub.

"There's some aspirin in the truck," said Kenny.

"I'm all right," said Frank.

"We'd better call an ambulance," said Tub.

"Jesus," said Frank, "what are we going to say?"

"Exactly what happened," said Tub. "He was going to shoot me but I shot him first."

"No, sir!" said Kenny. "I wasn't either!"

Frank patted Kenny on the arm. "Easy does it, partner." He stood. "Let's go."

Tub picked up Kenny's rifle as they walked down toward the farmhouse. "No sense leaving this around," he said. "Kenny might get ideas."

"I can tell you one thing," said Frank. "You've really done it this time. This definitely takes the cake."

They had to knock on the door twice before it was opened by a thin man with lank hair. The room behind him was filled with smoke. He squinted at them. "You get anything?" he asked.

"No," said Frank.

"I knew you wouldn't. That's what I told the other fellow."

"We've had an accident."

The man looked past Frank and Tub into the gloom. "Shoot your friend, did you?"

Frank nodded.

"I did," said Tub.

"I suppose you want to use the phone."

"If it's okay."

The man in the door looked behind him, then stepped back. Frank and Tub followed him into the house. There was a woman sitting by the stove in the middle of the room. The stove was smoking badly. She looked up and then down again at the child asleep in her lap. Her face was white and damp; strands of hair were pasted across her forehead. Tub warmed his hands over the stove while Frank went into the kitchen to call. The man who had let them in stood at the window, his hands in his pockets.

"My partner shot your dog," said Tub.

The man nodded without turning around. "I should have done it myself. I just couldn't."

"He loved that dog so much," the woman said. The child

squirmed and she rocked it.

"You asked him to?" said Tub. "You asked him to shoot your dog?"

"He was old and sick. Couldn't chew his food any more. I would have done it myself but I don't have a gun."

"You couldn't have anyway," said the woman. "Never in a million years."

The man shrugged.

Frank came out of the kitchen. "We'll have to take him ourselves. The nearest hospital is fifty miles from here and all their ambulances are out anyway."

The woman knew a shortcut, but the directions were complicated and Tub had to write them down. The man told where they could find some boards to carry Kenny on. He didn't have a flashlight, but he said he would leave the porch light on.

It was dark outside. The clouds were low and heavy-looking, and the wind blew in shrill gusts. There was a screen loose on the house, and it banged slowly and then quickly as the wind rose again. They could hear it all the way to the barn. Frank went for the boards while Tub looked for Kenny, who was not where they had left him. Tub found him farther up the drive, lying on his stomach. "You okay?" said Tub.

"It hurts."

"Frank says it missed your appendix."

"I already had my appendix out."

"All right," said Frank, coming up to them. "We'll have you in a nice warm bed before you can say Jack Robinson." He put the two boards on Kenny's right side.

"Just as long as I don't have one of those male nurses," said Kenny.

"Ha ha," said Frank. "That's the spirit. Get ready, set, over you go," and he rolled Kenny onto the boards. Kenny screamed and kicked his legs in the air. When he quieted down, Frank and Tub lifted the boards and carried him down the drive. Tub had the back end, and with the snow blowing into his face he had trouble with his footing. Also he was tired and the man inside had forgotten to turn the porch light on. Just past the house Tub slipped and threw out his hands to catch himself. The boards fell and Kenny tumbled out and rolled to the bottom of the drive, yelling all the way. He came to rest against the right front wheel of the truck.

"You fat moron," said Frank. "You aren't good for diddly."

Tub grabbed Frank by the collar and backed him hard up against the fence. Frank tried to pull his hands away, but Tub shook him and snapped his head back and forth and finally Frank gave up.

"What do you know about fat?" said Tub. "What do you know about glands?" As he spoke, he kept shaking Frank. "What do you know about me?"

"All right," said Frank.

"No more," said Tub.

"All right."

"No more talking to me like that. No more watching. No more laughing."

"OK, Tub. I promise."

Tub let go of Frank and leaned his forehead against the fence. His arms hung straight at his sides.

"I'm sorry, Tub." Frank touched him on the shoulder. "I'll be down at the truck."

Tub stood by the fence for a while and then got the rifles off the porch. Frank had rolled Kenny back onto the boards and they lifted him into the bed of the truck. Frank spread the seat blankets over him. "Warm enough?" he asked.

Kenny nodded.

"Okay. Now how does reverse work on this thing?"

"All the way to the left and up." Kenny sat up as Frank started forward to the cab. "Frank!"

"What?"

"If it sticks, don't force it."

The truck started right away. "One thing," said Frank, "you've got to hand it to the Japanese. A very ancient, very spiritual culture and they can still make a hell of a truck." He glanced over at Tub. "Look, I'm sorry. I didn't know you felt that way, honest to God, I didn't. You should have said something."

"I did."

"When? Name one time."

"A couple of hours ago."

"I guess I wasn't paying attention."

"That's true, Frank," said Tub. "You don't pay attention very much."

"Tub," said Frank, "what happened back there—I should have been more sympathetic. I realize that. You were going

416

through a lot. I just want you to know it wasn't your fault. He was asking for it."

"You think so?"

"Absolutely. I would have done the same thing in your shoes, no question."

The wind was blowing into their faces. The snow was a moving white wall in front of their lights; it swirled into the cab through the hole in the windshield and settled on them. Tub clapped his hands and shifted around to stay warm, but it didn't work.

"I'm going to have to stop," said Frank. "I can't feel my fingers."

Up ahead they saw some lights off the road. It was a tavern. Outside in the parking lot were several jeeps and trucks. A couple of them had deer strapped across their hoods. Frank parked and they went back to Kenny. "How you doing, partner?" said Frank.

"I'm cold."

"Well, don't feel like the Lone Ranger. It's worse inside, take my word for it. You should get that windshield fixed."

"Look," said Tub, "he threw the blankets off." They were lying in a heap against the tailgate.

"Now look, Kenny," said Frank, "it's no use whining about being cold if you're not going to try and keep warm. You've got to do your share." He spread the blankets over Kenny and tucked them in at the corners.

"They blew off."

"Hold on to them then."

"Why are we stopping, Frank?"

"Because if me and Tub don't get warmed up we're going to freeze solid and then where will you be?" He punched Kenny lightly in the arm. "So just hold your horses."

The bar was full of men in colored jackets, mostly orange. The waitress brought coffee. "Just what the doctor ordered," said Frank, cradling the steaming cup in his hand. His skin was bone white. "Tub, I've been thinking. What you said about me not paying attention, that's true."

"It's OK."

"No. I really had that coming. I guess I've just been a little too interested in old number one. I've had a lot on my mind— not that that's any excuse."

"Forget it, Frank. I sort of lost my temper back there. I

guess we're all a little on edge."

Frank shook his head. "It isn't just that."

"You want to talk about it?"

"Just between us, Tub?"

"Sure, Frank. Just between us."

"Tub, I think I'm going to be leaving Nancy."

"Oh, Frank. Oh, Frank." Tub sat back. "What's the problem? Has she been seeing someone?"

"No. I wish she was, Tub. I wish to God she was." He reached out and laid his hand on Tub's arm. "Tub, have you ever been really in love?"

"Well . . ."

"I mean *really* in love." He squeezed Tub's wrist. "With your whole being."

"I don't know. When you put it like that."

"You haven't, then. Nothing against you, but you'd know it if you had." Frank let go of Tub's arm. "Nancy hasn't been running around, Tub. I have."

"Oh, Frank."

"Running around's not the right word for it. It isn't like that. She's not just some bit of fluff."

"Who is she, Frank?"

Frank paused. He looked into his empty cup. "Roxanne Brewer."

"Cliff Brewer's kid? The baby-sitter?"

"You can't just put people into categories like that, Tub. That's why the whole system is wrong. And that's why this country is going to hell in a rowboat."

"But she can't be more than . . ." Tub shook his head.

"Fifteen. She'll be sixteen in May." Frank smiled. "May fourth, three twenty-seven P.M. Hell, Tub, a hundred years ago she'd have been an old maid by that age. Juliet was only thirteen."

"Juliet? Juliet Miller? Jesus, Frank, she doesn't even have breasts. She doesn't even wear a top to her bathing suit. She's still collecting frogs."

"Not Juliet Miller—the real Juliet. Tub, don't you see how you're dividing people up into categories? He's an executive, she's a secretary, he's a truck driver, she's fifteen years old. Tub, this so-called baby-sitter, this so-called fifteen-year-old has more in her little finger than most of us have in our entire bodies. I can tell you this little lady is something special."

Tub nodded. "I know the kids like her."

"She's opened up whole worlds to me that I never knew were there."

"What does Nancy think about all of this?"

"Nothing, Tub. She doesn't know."

"You haven't told her?"

"Not yet. It's not so easy. She's been damned good to me all these years. Then there's the kids to consider." The brightness in Frank's eyes trembled and he wiped quickly at them with the back of his hand. "I guess you think I'm a complete bastard."

"No, Frank. I don't think that."

"Well, you *ought* to."

"Frank, when you've got a friend it means you've always got someone on your side, no matter what. That's how I feel about it anyway."

"You mean that, Tub?"

"Sure I do."

Frank smiled. "You don't know how good it feels to hear you say that."

Kenny had tried to get out of the truck but he hadn't made it. He was jackknifed over the tailgate, his head hanging above the bumper. They lifted him back into the bed and covered him again. He was sweating and his teeth chattered. "It hurts, Frank."

"It wouldn't hurt so much if you just stayed put. Now we're going to the hospital. Got that? Say it: I'm going to the hospital."

"I'm going to the hospital."

"Again."

"I'm going to the hospital."

"Now just keep saying that to yourself and before you know it we'll be there."

After they had gone a few miles, Tub turned to Frank. "I just pulled a real boner," he said.

"What's that?"

"I left the directions on the table back there."

"That's okay. I remember them pretty well."

The snowfall lightened and the clouds began to roll back off the fields, but it was no warmer and after a time both Frank and Tub were bitten through and shaking. Frank almost didn't make it around a curve, and they decided to stop at the next roadhouse.

There was an automatic hand dryer in the bathroom and they took turns standing in front of it, opening their jackets and shirts and letting the jet of hot air breathe across their faces and chests.

"You know," said Tub, "what you told me back there, I appreciate it. Trusting me."

Frank opened and closed his fingers in front of the nozzle. "The way I look at it, Tub, no man is an island. You've got to trust someone."

"Frank . . ."

Frank waited.

"When I said that about my glands, that wasn't true. The truth is I just shovel it in."

"Well, Tub . . ."

"Day and night, Frank. In the shower. On the freeway." He turned and let the air play over his back. "I've even got stuff in the paper towel machine at work."

"There's nothing wrong with your glands at all?" Frank had taken his boots and socks off. He held first his right, then his left foot up to the nozzle.

"No. There never was."

"Does Alice know?" The machine went off and Frank started lacing up his boots.

"Nobody knows. That's the worst of it, Frank, not the being fat—I never got any big kick out of being thin—but the lying. Having to lead a double life like a spy or a hit man. This sounds strange but I feel sorry for those guys, I really do. I know what they go through. Always having to think about what you say and do. Always feeling like people are watching you, trying to catch you at something. Never able to just be yourself. Like when I make a big deal about only having an orange for breakfast and then scarf all the way to work. Oreos, Mars bars, Twinkies, Sugar Babies, Snickers." Tub glanced at Frank and looked quickly away. "Pretty disgusting, isn't it?"

"Tub. Tub." Frank shook his head. "Come on." He took Tub's arm and led him into the restaurant half of the bar. "My friend is hungry," he told the waitress. "Bring four orders of pancakes, plenty of butter and syrup."

"Frank . . ."

"Sit down."

When the dishes came, Frank carved out slabs of butter and just laid them on the pancakes. Then he emptied the bottle of syrup, moving it back and forth over the plates. He leaned forward on his elbows and rested his chin in one hand. "Go on, Tub."

Tub ate several mouthfuls, then started to wipe his lips. Frank took the napkin away from him. "No wiping," he said. Tub kept at it. The syrup covered his chin; it dripped to a point like a goatee. "Weigh in, Tub," said Frank, pushing another fork across the table. "Get down to business." Tub took the fork in his left hand and lowered his head and started really chowing down. "Clean your plate," said Frank when the pancakes were gone, and Tub lifted each of the four plates and licked it clean. He sat back, trying to catch his breath.

"Beautiful," said Frank. "Are you full?"

"I'm full," said Tub. "I've never been so full."

Kenny's blankets were bunched up against the tailgate again.

"They must have blown off," said Tub.

"They're not doing him any good," said Frank. "We might as well get some use out of them."

Kenny mumbled. Tub bent over him. "What? Speak up."

"I'm going to the hospital," said Kenny.

"Attaboy," said Frank.

The blankets helped. The wind still got their faces and Frank's hands but it was much better. The fresh snow on the road and the trees sparkled under the beam of the headlight. Squares of light from farmhouse windows fell onto the blue snow in the fields.

"Frank," said Tub after a time, "you know that farmer? He told Kenny to kill the dog."

"You're kidding!" Frank leaned forward, considering. "That Kenny. What a card." He laughed and so did Tub. Tub smiled out the back window. Kenny lay with his arms folded over his stomach, moving his lips at the stars. Right overhead was the Big Dipper, and behind, hanging between Kenny's toes in the direction of the hospital, was the North Star, pole star, help to sailors. As the truck twisted through the gentle hills, the star went back and forth between Kenny's boots, staying always in his sight. "I'm going to the hospital," said Kenny, but he was wrong. They had taken a different turn a long way back.

from A flag for sunrise

Robert Stone

"Well," Sister Mary Joseph said, "I don't believe for a minute that it all ends in the old grave."

She and Sister Justin Feeney were sitting in the shade on the mission veranda drinking iced tea. Sister Justin frowned at the sunlit ocean. Mary Joe's Bronxy certainties drove her to fury.

"Let's not talk theology," she said.

"Who's talking theology?"

"You," Sister Justin said. "Pie in the sky."

Sister Mary Joseph had come down from the mountains around Lake Tapa to talk sense to Justin. Her own situation was very different; her order was strong and adaptable, and her dispensary could measure its effectiveness in lives preserved. Arriving at French Harbor, she had quickly surmised that the local people were staying away, that something was seriously wrong with Father Charlie Egan, and that the stories she had heard about the state of the Devotionists on the coast were at least partly true.

"You gotta have an element of pie in the sky, kiddo," she told Sister Justin. "That's part of the basics."

Justin shaded her pale blue eyes from the glare of sky and ocean and leaned her chin on her fist.

Sister Mary Joe stood up and took their tea glasses.

"You want to talk pragmatism—okay, we'll do that." Holding

the glasses between her thumb and fingers she waved them before Justin's averted face. "You're accomplishing nothing. You're not needed. Am I reaching you now?"

These were words as hard as Mary Joe commanded, and the satisfaction with which she flung them at poor Justin caused her immediate remorse.

She was rinsing the glasses in the kitchen when Father Egan came in, shuffling toward the icebox, holding a fly swatter absently in his right hand.

"How's things, Father?" Sister Mary asked, looking him up and down.

"My dear Joe," Egan said, "things are rich." He fixed himself a glass of water and gave her a vague smile. "How nice of you to come and visit us."

"Beats working," she told him. "Still going over your book?"

"Scribble, scribble, scribble," the priest said and retreated back to his room.

Mary Joe wiped the glasses and went to the refectory to get a stethoscope from her black bag. Then she rapped once on Father Egan's door and let herself in.

She found him sitting by his window, the shutters thrown open to the green hillside below, a working bottle of Flor de Cana at his feet. Outside, chickens picked among the morning-glory vines; an old woman chopped at a stand of plantain with her machete.

Sister Mary settled her thick body on the window rail.

"We're old friends, aren't we, Father? We can speak plainly to each other."

"Yes," Egan said, "we're old pals, Joe." His smile faded, and he turned his head to look over his shoulder. "And I won't have her tyrannizing you. You don't have to listen to her."

"C'mon," Mary Joseph said," Justin's okay. She's a good kid." She opened one of the buttons of his white cotton shirt and pressed the scope over his breastbone. "Let's talk about you."

The beat was feathery and irregular. Egan was in his late fifties, but to Mary Joe his heart sounded as though it should belong to a very old man.

"So how about laying off the sauce?"

"Ah," Father Egan said. "You have me there."

"Yeah, I got you there, Charlie. And from where I'm standing you look a little portly to me, and what do you bet your liver's enlarged? The right bug would knock you flat on your back."

She bent down, picked up the rum, and set it down on Egan's desk beside the crucifix.

"You need to go home, Father. This kind of life—keep it up and it'll be curtains."

Father Egan scratched his ear and looked out of the window.

"I mean, what are you guys doing here anyway?" Sister Mary demanded. "Your instructions are to close this joint. This is the religion where people do what they're told, right?"

"Yes, well," Father Egan said, "you see I thought I'd finish the book before we struck the flag."

"Boo for that idea," the nun said. "Because if you want to finish that book you better strike your flag or whatever—quick."

"Look," she told him. "I'll leave some pills with Justin for you. Take one every four hours instead of the joy juice. But don't take them both or you're dead."

"Bless you, Joe," Father Egan said. He said it in a far-off manner that Mary Joe found alarming.

"God bless you, Charlie," she said. "Pray for me."

She went back to the refectory, put the stethoscope away, and carried her bag out to the veranda. Sister Justin was still in her chair, staring sadly out to sea, and Mary Joseph suspected she had been crying. Mary Joseph was not very sympathetic.

From time to time, up at Lake Tapa, Sister Mary had found herself with the obligation to comfort some of the younger and tenderer agents of the Peace Corps. She forgave them their tears. Tecan was a hard place and they were young and American. First time away from their skateboards, she liked to say.

But the sight of a nursing nun in tears made her feel ashamed and angry. Tears were for the Tecanecan women, who always had plenty to cry about.

"Great day in the morning," she declared, forgetting that she had repented her earlier hardness, "if I lived around here and I needed help I sure wouldn't try to get if from this balled-up operation. I'd go right straight to the Seventh Day Adventists, or the LSA's, or to somebody who knows what the heck they're doing."

"The LSA's," Justin said savagely, "the LSA's are a bunch of right-wing, psalm-singing sons of bitches. They've got a picture of the president on their wall, they suck ass with the Guardia, and they fink for the CIA."

In spite of herself, Mary Joseph blushed.

"You got a lot of nerve," she said, "to talk like that."

Justin looked down at the veranda deck and shielded her eyes. Mary Joe waited for her to calm down and then sat beside her.

"Look, Justin. The very fact that you have the leisure to sit around and brood should tell you that you're not doing your job. I mean great guns, kid—it's no time or place for ego trips."

"Am I ego tripping?" Justin asked. "Isn't it supposed to bother me that people starve so America can have Playboy clubs and bottomless dancing."

Sister Mary snickered. "Aw, c'mon," she said.

"Maybe I'm putting it stupidly. Doesn't it bother you?"

"If it's true, it bothers me. But what do I know? I'm just a pill pusher. So are you. Nobody elected us.

"You know," she told Justin, "in many ways you're a typical Devotionist. You all tend to be very bright and high-strung and short on horse sense."

Sister Justin brushed the windblown hair under her checkered bandana.

"I've had it with the order and I've had it with my sister of mercy number."

"Then it's time you went home," Sister Mary said. Justin's words made her shudder. "Justin—something special is happening now. The church is really turning back to Jesus. It's gonna be great, and it would be a shame to miss out on it."

Justin put her hand across her eyes.

"If I told you," Sister Mary went on, "that you need to pray— that you need to ask God's help—would you say I was talking pie in the sky again?"

Sister Justin had turned her face away and was pursing her lips to make her tears stop. Mary Joseph watched her young friend cry; she no longer felt it in her to be outraged.

"Doesn't it mean anything to you any more?"

Justin only shook her head.

She was a real beauty, Mary Joseph thought, the genuine article. In her own order they would never have let someone so pretty and headstrong take final vows. But it was hindsight: Justin had soldiered on for twelve years, cheerful and strong, the wisest of catechists, a cool and competent nurse. A little too good to be true in the end.

"This is no place for a personal crisis," Mary told her.

"I know," Justin said. She patted her cheek with a folded handkerchief. "On the practical level—the fruit company repurchased the property. You can't stall them forever. And there's really a lot of negative talk. The archbishop is starting to get upset."

"That old creep," Justin said. "He's not even a Christian. He's a cross between a Grand Inquisitor and an Olmec priest."

Sister Mary sat stiffly for a moment and then dissolved in guilty laughter.

"Justin—you're such a smart aleck."

Even Justin distraught could not help smiling back at her.

"Well, he ain't Bing Crosby," Sister Mary said in a low comedy mutter. "But he represents the church here and that means plenty. And, believe it or not, he's protecting you from a government investigation."

Justin Feeney rose from her chair and walked to the edge of the veranda.

"Give me a few days before you speak to anyone. I have to make some plans of my own."

Mary Joseph frowned. She did not believe that one could plan in idleness.

"Now, I want to hear from you in a week and I want to hear a date of departure. If you need extra help, maybe I can sneak you some Peace Corps kiddos to pull and tote."

"Thanks, Joe. Thanks for giving a damn."

Mary Joseph picked up her black bag and went to the top of the steps. She had mastered an impulse to touch Justin on the cheek or to give her a hug. Such demonstrations were contrary to her training.

"Hey, listen. You did an A-1 job here for a long time. Don't go feeling like a complete flop. Don't let yourself get morbid. Just get busy and pack up."

Justin nodded briskly.

"God loves you, Justin. You're his special lady. He'll help you."

"Okay, Joe."

On the first step down, Sister Mary Joseph was smitten with dread. In Justin's impatient good-bye smile she read the word *lost*—and the word sounded in her scrubbed soldierly soul with a grim resonance.

"Hey," she said, turning around, "I got a thing for Charlie Egan, know what I mean? I really want to see him get home alive. Can you take care of it for me?"

"You bet," Justin said.

Walking to her jeep, Sister Mary caught sight of another vehicle rounding the palm grove between Freddy's Chicken Shack and the water's edge. It was a four-wheel-drive Toyota jeep and the driver she recognized as Father Godoy, a Tecanecan priest from Puerto Alvarado. She waited beside her Willys as he pulled up.

Father Godoy wore creased chino pants, a blue plaid shirt, and expensive sunglasses. He was out of his Toyota shaking her hand and breathing English pleasantries before she could utter a greeting.

His long face lengthened further in a bony, yellow smile; he was tall and angular, a tragical Spaniard of a man.

"Well, it's going great, Father," Sister Mary heard herself declare. "We have an OB now, and some new hardware and, God willing, we're going to have a real good year."

He bobbed his head before her in agreement with everything in sight. Very sexy, she thought. She distrusted intellectual priests, and the native clergy she generally regarded as soft, spoiled, and unprogressive.

"Terrific," he was saying, in the racy stateside which he affected for people of her sort. "Really great! What would they do without you up there?"

"Looking in on our friends here, Father?"

"Right, right," he said, as though he had not understood her question.

"Well, so long," Sister Mary said, climbing in her jeep and turning the key.

"All the best," Godoy called to her. "All the best to everybody."

When she had driven as far as the palm grove, she stopped the jeep with the engine idling and bent into the lee of the dashboard to light a cigarette. Inhaling, she glanced over her shoulder and saw Godoy at the top of the steps beside Sister Justin. Both of them were looking out to sea.

"Oh, boy," she said to herself as she put the jeep in gear, "a couple of stars."

Father Godoy was complimenting Sister Justin on the beauty of the ocean and her good fortune in living beside it. His doing so made her feel guilty.

"Would you like some tea?" she asked.

"No, no, please." He looked about him cheerfully, further embarrassing Justin with the station's lack of activity.

"How's himself?" Godoy asked in a low voice.

She smiled at the missionary Irishism.

"Not well, I'm afraid. He's rather crushed and not always rational. A while ago he had the boat out in the middle of the night. I can't imagine why."

"Strange," the priest said. "A little worrying, eh?"

"Please have some tea."

"I have to go. It's the day of the procession in town."

"Oh, drat," Justin said. "It just got away from me. I haven't missed it once since I've been here and today I forgot." She shrugged sadly.

"I can take you in tonight," he said. "For the festival afterward. You see, I'm coming back to take some children from the company school. So we'll stop for you if you like."

"That'd be great. Would you?"

"Yes, of course. Of course. In fact I came now to ask you."

"Well," Justin said, laughing, "yes, please."

"Great," the priest said. "I'll go now and then after six we'll pick you up."

"Wonderful."

"Well, until then," he said and went down the steps, leaving the image of his shy smile behind him.

"Wonderful," she said.

Wonderful. "Wonderful wonderful," she repeated dully under her breath. "Goddamn it, what a fool I'm becoming."

As she watched Godoy get into his jeep, she felt mortified and panic-stricken. She hurried from the veranda before he could turn and see her.

For a while she busied herself with sweeping out the empty dispensary, spraying the stacked linens for mildew, poking in the corners for centipedes or scorpions. Within the hour a man came from the village with a red snapper and a basket of shrimp; Justin went down the steps to pay him. The man brought a message from the Herreras, a mother and daughter who did cooking and cleaning for the station, that they would not be coming for several days. They had not come for some time before—nor had the young women who worked as nurse's aides, two girls from the offshore islands whom Justin herself had taught to read and write, her barefoot doctors. It was just as well, since there was no work for them.

Somewhat later, Lieutenant Campos drove by to give Sister Justin a quick glimpse of herself in his silvered sunglasses.

She cleaned and scaled the snapper, washed the shrimp, and showered in her own quarters. Changing, she put on a cool khaki skirt, a red-checked shirt, an engineer's red scarf over her hair. When she went back into the kitchen, she found Father Egan mixing cold well-water into his rum.

"Are we friends today?" she asked him.

"There's a level, Justin, on which we're always friends. Then there's a level on which we can't be."

Justin received this response in silence. Mystical as ever, she thought. She picked up the cleaned fish, stood holding it for a few moments, then set it down again.

"Sister Mary Joseph is after us to close. You probably know that."

"Yes," the priest said. "Of course it's up to you."

"Why is everything up to me?" she asked, wiping her hands on a towel. "I mean, what's happening with you? It's very worrying."

"Don't reproach me." Father Egan said. "I'm reinforcing this mutiny with my frail presence. It's up to you because you're a sensible girl."

"Must you keep drinking?"

"Never mind that," Father Egan said.

She walked over to the kitchen table and leaned on her fist, watching him.

"You've been so darn irrational I can't cope. And I know you've been worse since that night you had the boat out. I wish I knew what *that* was about."

"Under the seal," Egan said. "The rest is silence."

Sister Justin shook her head to clear it of his madness.

"I don't feel very sensible now," she said. "I feel like a complete idiot."

"Not at all," Egan said. "Do you want to know what I think?"

"Yes, please."

"I think you're very intelligent and moral and all good nunnish things. You had an attack of self-righteousness and you decided to try the impossible. Nothing wrong with that, Justin. Fine tradition behind it."

"You encouraged me."

"Yes. Well, I wanted to stay too. And I respect you, you see. Believe it or not."

"I thought I could pull it off."

"Because you were always made much of by the order. They want to keep you. You've had things your own way. You've been spoiled, dear."

"Oh, Lord," Justin said, "spoiled, hell." She folded her arms angrily and went to stand in the doorway with her back to him. "I've been on my hands and knees since college. I mean—I work for a living. I wouldn't call this a cloistered life, would you?"

She heard his dry, sickly laughter and turned.

"Is what I'm saying ridiculous?"

"You've been morally spoiled. There's always been someone around to take your good intentions seriously—and if that isn't being spoiled I don't know what is." He sniffed at his rum and sniffed it. "Religious women are always a good deal younger than their ages. Mary Joe's an example. Religious men are worse that way. One's always a kid. The life is childish." He shrugged. "Believing *at all* is childish, isn't it?"

Justin looked at him, surprised. Perhaps, she thought, he was snapping a paradox. They were all great Chestertonians in his generation.

"You haven't been saying your office," she said, realizing it for the first time. "You haven't said it for ages."

"I consider it wrongly written down."

She smiled, watching him polish off the rum.

"Are you serious?"

"I will—if called upon—say Mass. I will administer the sacraments. But my office is strictly between me and God, and I won't say it their way. It's all wrong, you know," he said, fixing her with an unsettling stare. "They have it all wrong. The whole thing."

"I give up," Justin said.

"Interesting my orthodoxy should make any difference to you. Surely you don't believe?"

"I can't answer that question."

"Well," Egan said, "you're supposed to answer it every day."

At the kitchen counter she took up the fish again. The right thing would be to broil it, to make a sauce with peppers and onions and greens. But he would be more likely to eat it if she simply shredded it into the soup with some shrimp. It was such a shame. Red snapper.

It went into the soup, and Egan faded back toward his quarters.

Justin found herself on the veranda again. Her hands were clenched on the rail as she leaned out toward the ocean, the ebbing tide. The sea's surface was soft blue; the sun had withdrawn beyond the green saw-toothed hills above the station.

Utter total foolishness, she repeated silently.

Her soul extended along this meditation as it might in prayer. There was nothing. Only the sea. Her heart beat quietly alone, its panicked quickening like a signal to the void, unanswered, uncomforted. It beat only for her, to no larger measure, a futile rounding of blood. The desire for death made her dizzy; it felt almost like joy.

She was still leaning over the rail, half stunned with despair, when she saw a young man walking along the beach from the direction of the village. He was barefoot and full bearded, extraordinarily blond; he wore a white shirt, of the sort that required a detachable collar, and faded bib overalls. When he drew closer she could see the filthy condition of his shirt and the dirt and dried blood that soiled his hands. His appearance bespoke need, and for this reason she was vaguely glad to see him there. She assumed he was one of the North American kids who drifted up and down the isthmus following the beach, and that, like some of them, he was far gone with dope or alcohol. Her ready impulse was to have him come in and see if there was anything that might be done—before Campos and his men or the local ratones caught scent of him.

Justin had gone as far as the top step when the odd cut of his hair registered on her. It was a crude cropping that one did not see on even the weirdest passing gringos—almost medieval, monkish. As she started down to the beach, he turned toward her and his face stopped her cold.

Although the man's walk and carriage were youthful, his face was like an old man's, the skin not tanned but reddened and weathered, deeply seamed around the features. The massiveness of his brows and cheekbones made his upper face as square as a box; his nose was long, thin, and altogether outsized, upturned toward the tip. Elfin, she thought staring at him, gnomish—but suggestive of carving, like some sort of puppet, a malignant Pinocchio.

Two things about his small blue eyes impressed her: one was that they were not, she was sure, the eyes of an English-speaker, the other that they were the most hating eyes she had ever seen.

Justin had to remind herself that she was in lay clothes. But even people who thought nuns bad luck had never looked at her so.

Fascinated, she watched the man's mouth open, and braced herself for a threat or an obscenity. His shout, though when it came it contorted his face, was absolutely silent.

It seemed that one of the words he mouthed at her was *Schwein*—the bared teeth savaging the lower lip. There were other words. *Du* was one. She had known German only as a tourist in Austria, but she felt certain that German was his language: *Schwein, du.*

"Beast" was the word that came to her. She was quite frightened.

Then the youth walked on, toward Puerto Alvarado. He was very big. His shoulders under the stained white shirt looked broad as an ox yoke.

She went back into the kitchen, lifted the pot lid, and stirred her red snapper and vegetable soup. The young man, she realized, must be a Mennonite; there were a few of their settlements in the south, inland. They were not numerous in Tecan, and years ago she had seen a band of them in the capital, in the central bus station there. They had seemed shy, cheerful people, very clean and friendly.

It was the time of late afternoon when the color drained out of the day. Sky and ocean gentled to temperate pastels and the jungle on the hillsides was a paler green. Wandering to the doorway, she savored the breeze.

Along the beach, from the grove at Freddy's to the point southward, there was no one to be seen. Vanished, the passing youth seemed to be a creature compounded of her fears; the hatred, the German-ness were the stuff of nightmare and bad history. Somehow her despair had summoned him.

When Godoy and his jeep load of small boys pulled up at the foot of the station steps, she ran down gratefully to join them. The boys were black Caribs, and there were six of them crowded into the jeep, some with the Indian cast of eye or the shock of coarse straight hair that marked the Caribs among the black people of the coast.

"Buenas," she called to them and to Godoy.

"Buenas," the boys said and made room for her. Some of the younger boys smiled; the two oldest ogled her with grim elaborateness. She sat down next to the priest.

"We're off," he declared.

"Right on," Sister Justin said gaily.

Along the roadside, plantation hands walked homeward, cradling their machetes against their shoulders; children struggled along under loads of firewood for the evening meal. At every fresh creek there were women gathering up laundry from the rocks on which it had been drying in the last of the daylight, and other women hurrying along balancing ochre jugs on their heads, filled with cooking water from the public well. But most of the people on the road were walking toward Puerto Alvarado and what remained of the day's fiesta.

Each time they passed a settlement of sticks and palm thatch, Godoy would sound his horn, a child would wave, and the boys in the jeep would display their privilege as passengers in a private vehicle.

The road led them inland through banana and then pineapple, to the top of Pico Hill, where they could see the ocean again and the wharves of the distant port; then down again past acres of yellow-painted, numbered company houses; finally to the tin and crate-wood shacks on the edge of town. From the town center they could hear the report of exploding firecrackers and the blare of the sound truck the Syrian storekeeper had hired to publicize his holiday specials.

There was a block of paved street where the houses had carports and painted fences, then the Gran Hotel, the Texaco station—and they turned into the crowded plaza. Godoy eased the jeep through the crowds and parked against the church wall, behind a barrier of bicycle stands. As soon as the jeep was stopped, the six Carib boys leaped out and disappeared into the crowd.

Godoy watched them go and looked at his watch.

"Now," he told Justin with a sad smile, "the trick will be to get them back."

The two of them went past a line of helmeted Guardia and along the edge of the church steps.

In the center of the square, a ceiba tree had been hung with paper garlands and an elderly band in black uniform was ranged beneath its branches. There were Japanese lanterns strung between trees at two sides of the plaza, and the square itself was jammed with people. Men of property stood with transistor radios pressed against their ears, teenage parents in cheap cotton dress-up clothes clung to their several tiny children—and lone children by the hundreds puzzled their way through the legs of the crowd. The shoe-shine boys had given over their space by the fountain and sat together with their boxes at the park edge, watching for flung cigarette butts, fallen change, loose wallets.

The sailors' girls had marched uptown from the waterfront brothels and occupied their own space on one lawn, where they sat on open newspapers, singing along to the music of the nearest radio and trading comic books with each other.

Along the fountain there were teenagers, arranged according to social class—the boys watching the prostitutes and the girls, more or less demurely, watching the boys.

There were girls in hip huggers and Kiss Me Stupid T-shirts and girls whose fancy dress was their school uniform. There were nearly-white boys who wore Italian-style print shirts and looked bored; stiff, self-conscious mestizos in starchy white sport shirts; blacks who broke their Spanish phrases with *mon* and *bruddah,* practiced karate moves, danced with themselves in a flurry of loose wrists, flashing palms, and swaying knees. Across the street, at the gate of Municipalidad, a few Guardia leaned against the pillars and watched the crowd. They were given all the space they might require.

In the street at the foot of the church steps, a squad of local technicians were struggling with an enormous anti-aircraft searchlight, adjusting the dogs and swivels, playing out the wire that led up the steps and into the church interior. Nearby were men and boys in the purple hoods and cassocks of the Holy Brotherhood, those who had carried the images in the afternoon's procession.

Justin and Father Godoy stood together near the ceiba tree, facing the church. The air smelled of frangipani, of perfume and hair oil, above all of the raw cane liquor, barely rum, that was being passed in coke bottles among the sports in the crowd.

At the stroke of darkness, the band broke into a reedy pasodoble and the great searchlight sent forth an overpowering light. The light broke up the foremost ranks of the crowd, sending the people reeling back, forcing them to turn away, hands to their eyes. Then it swept around the square, ascending until the beam was pointed straight upward—a pillar of white fire heavenward. A great gasp of joy broke from the crowd.

Spinning again, the column of light descended on the plaza, catching each second a dozen transfixed faces; dazzled the old men in their wicker chairs in the Syrian's shop, and the lounging Guardia; electrified the posters of *Death Wish* in front of the cinema. It made the whores' beads sparkle, shone on the balloons and patent leather shoes of the better off children and on the slick flesh of the banana plants. As it whirled, the crowd screamed and applauded. Justin and Father Godoy exchanged smiles.

The beam came finally to rest on the steps of the church, centering on a glass and mahogany coffin which four men in the purple robes of the Brotherhood had carried out during the display. Prone in the coffin was the figure of Christ, which was the occasion of Puerto Alvarado's rejoicing.

Christ wore a burial shift of waxy linen and worn lace; his

hands, clutching a lily, were folded across his chest. Around his brow was a crown of thorns, and his long hair was matted with blood. Both the hair and the blood had the appearance of reality, and Sister Justin, who had seen the figure many times before, had always wondered about them. The eyelids were also quite authentic; one felt they might be pulled back to show dark, dead eyes beneath.

A hush settled as the light fell on the dead Christ—but only for a moment. As the plaza beheld its murdered Redeemer, a murmur rose from the crowd that grew louder until it drowned out the dirge of the band, swelled into moans and the cries of women, hoarse *Viva el Cristo*'s, drunken whoops of devotion.

As Christ lay under the light in his glass box, he looked for all the world as though he had died the same day, in Tecan: of meningitis like the overseer's daughter who went at Christmas, or of an infected scorpion bite, of undulant fever, of a knife on the docks. So the crowd began to cheer: the children of the early dead, the parents of perished angelitos, secure in their own and their children's resurrection—cheering the sharer and comforter of death.

Around Justin there were people on their knees. Some steps away, a woman holding a balloon in one hand and her infant daughter's hand in the other was weeping for the deceased—out of courtesy, perhaps, or habit.

Justin turned to Godoy and in the shadowy light saw a look of patient detachment on his face. When he realized that she was looking at him, he said: "See? It's all done with light. Like the movies."

She thought that it was something very like what she might say, although what she felt at the moment was very different. It made her wonder whether he said it only for her benefit, from embarrassment for his country.

After a few minutes the searchlight was turned off, and the encoffined Saviour carried inside and placed at the side altar, where he always reposed except during procession days and Holy Week. A number of people stood chatting in the church doorway, and among them Justin recognized Father Schleicher, an Oblate missionary from the middle west. The other clerics there were two Tecanecans, or rather Spaniards—one the vicar of the cathedral and the other a monsignor from the capital, a representative of the Archbishop.

"We should go up there," Father Godoy said when they had

done a round of the square. "I have to, at least."

Together they climbed the church steps, and while Godoy made his obeisances to the senior clergy, Justin endeavored to converse with Schleicher and a young Tecanecan woman who was with him.

Father Schleicher was young and was said to be politically engaged. Sister Justin had heard also that he had unofficially purchased a colonial press edition of the *Quixote* from a clerk at the Catholic university in the capital, and that he paid plantation workers to bring him such pre-Columbian artifacts as they might find. Although none of this was quite illegal, although it was practically innocent hobbyism and a mark of his cultivation, Justin held what she heard against Schleicher's account. She disliked him; he was chubby and blond, and it seemed to her that his face was set continually in an expression of thick-lipped self-satisfaction. A creep was what she called him.

They talked for a while about American politics, and Schleicher introduced the girl with him as a community planner. When the conversation ran thin, they all turned toward the interior of the church to look for more to talk about.

Inside, a great many people were crowded in a semicircle around the dead Cristo, kneeling on the floor.

"It's an incredible statue," Justin said. "Isn't it strange to see him presented like that—I mean *laid out*?"

"When I first saw it," Schleicher said, "it reminded me of Che. You know the picture taken after he was killed? It still makes me think of him."

The Tecanecan girl smiled slightly and nodded.

"I wonder what it's made of," Justin said.

The Tecanecan girl laughed, a bit too merrily for Justin, and turned to Schleicher.

"It's such a North American question," the girl said. "'What's it made of?'"

Schleicher laughed as though he too thought it was such a North American question.

"I'm like that," Sister Justin said. "When I saw Notre Dame cathedral, I wondered what it weighed. We're all like that where I come from."

The girl's laughter was a little less assured. Father Schleicher hastened to ask her where it was that she came from, but Justin ignored him. She had told him often enough before.

"Did you study in the States?" Justin asked the Tecanecan girl.

"Yes. Yes, in New Orleans. At Loyola."

"That must have been fun," Justin said. "Community planning."

"Yes," the girl said warily.

Godoy disengaged himself from the old Spaniards and joined them for a moment's stiff exchange of pleasantries. Then he and Justin said their goodbyes and went back down the steps to the square. Justin found herself wondering whether the hip Father Schleicher might be sleeping with his young community planner. She sighed, despising her own petty malice. That night she was against anyone with a purpose to declare, anyone less lonely and beaten than herself.

The plaza was emptying as she and Godoy walked across it. Men approached them in the shadow of the trees, begging, calling for a blessing against bad visions from the cane alcohol. A youth warbled a birdcall after them, and a woman laughed.

The crowds, the lights, and the music were on the other side of the church now, where they had set up a market and a fun fair for the children. The trees had been stripped of garlands and lanterns by the crowd, and the central street ran deserted toward the harsh bright lights of the company piers.

"Hungry?" Godoy asked.

Justin was not at all hungry, but she supposed that he must be. She nodded pleasantly.

"We'll give the kids some time at the games," the priest said, "before we go and arrest them. Now we can go to the Chino's if you like."

The Chino's was a restaurant that called itself the Gran Mura de China. It had a small balcony section with two tables that overlooked the harbor.

The lower floor of the Gran Mura de China was empty when they arrived; the Chino's wife and daughter sat at a table stringing firecrackers. Justin and Godoy smiled at them and went upstairs to the balcony. They sat down and Godoy lighted a Winston.

"Do you know what Father Schleicher said about the image?" Justin asked Godoy. "He said he thought it looked liked Che."

Godoy looked at her evenly, unsmiling.

"Father Schleicher said that? Was he joking?"

"Not exactly joking. I think he had a point to make."

"Iconography," Godoy said vaguely, tapping his ash and looking out over the pier lights at the dark ocean.

After a minute the Chino's daughter came up to serve them.

Under her apron the child wore a white party dress; she had been up to the plaza.

Godoy asked for shrimp and rice, Justin for a bottle of Germania.

"You may have heard about our troubles," Justin said, when they had ordered. She found Godoy's puzzled look disingenuous. It was impossible, she thought, that he had not heard.

"I'm going to close us down and go home. I'm tired of arguing with the order, and I don't believe we're getting anything done."

"It's a shame you had no support. It must be difficult."

"Yes, it's difficult to make a fool of yourself to no good purpose. But of course it's a lesson." She was beginning to grow quite irritated with Godoy. "Yet another goddamn valuable lesson."

"I have to tell you," the priest said as he watched the little girl serve his dinner and their beer, "that I'm very sorry to hear that you're closing."

"Really?" Justin said impatiently. "Why, thank you."

He's downright superserviceable, she thought.

"Please excuse me," Godoy said. "I haven't yet eaten today."

"Please go ahead," Justin said. She decided that he was dandified and vain. Frightened of, and therefore hostile to, women. For a long time it had seemed to her that Godoy had a difficulty in comprehending plain English that went beyond any unfamiliarity with the language.

"You know," Godoy said, tasting delicately of his shrimp, "I think you stayed this long because I wanted you to."

"Are you kidding?" Justin demanded.

"Just a superstition of mine."

"If you wanted us to stay you were very subtle."

"It wasn't only because I like you," the priest said. "And not because I thought you were the very model of a Yankee missionary. Obviously you are not that."

The bluntness of his language startled her. "Then why?" she asked.

"Because I know how you think. I know your attitudes. I even know the books you own."

Justin watched him delicately take his shrimp.

"Then everyone must," she said. "So I'm probably in trouble."

He shrugged.

"You are North American, and that protects you. The Archbishop in his way protects you."

"Campos," she said.

438   1981

"Don't worry about Campos for now." He kept his eyes on his plate as he said it.

"Really," Justin said, "it was stupid of me to try to keep the station open."

Godoy gave her a quick, amused glance.

"I don't know what you were thinking of. But I admire you for it. And I sympathize."

"I was being naive as usual."

He looked up from his plate again and held her with the look.

"You were never as naive as I was," he said, "and I was born here. You think you've failed? Of course you failed. There's nothing but failure here. The country is a failure. A disaster of history."

"That's very hopeless talk," Justin said.

"It's where we begin," Godoy said. "We start from this assumption."

His meal finished, the priest took a sip of beer and lit another Winston. The beer seemed to bring a faint rosiness to his pale, pitted cheek.

"When I was in the Jesuit College here I wrote a letter of which I was very proud. I wrote to your President Eisenhower."

"Good Lord," Justin said. "To dear old Ike."

"Yes, to Ike himself. And I sent the same letter to the leader of our opposition; his name was Enrique Matos of the great Liberal party. In this letter—which I covered with tears—I told them that if the free world was to conquer communism it must not follow the way of greed and narrow self-interest but the way of the Great Redemptor, He whom we saw dead tonight."

Godoy crushed his Winston out in an ashtray and put another in his mouth.

"I told Ike and Matos—I was only a kid, you understand—that their leadership must be spiritual. Also that they were overlooking the evils of our country, that we were suffering because of the government and the rich and the North American attitude.

"In the same week my father disappeared. Not for long, and he came back alive. You see he was a watchmaker in the capital, an immigrant from Spain. He wasn't hurt badly, but he was very frightened. He told me not to write any more letters.

"A little later there arrived a message from the White House in Washington. I can tell you that it was an occasion of terror in my house. My parents were quite unsophisticated in some ways. It was a perfectly amiable letter. It thanked me. It was signed by an assistant. A typical letter."

"A form letter," Justin corrected him.

"Yes, a form letter." He lit his Winston and blew the smoke upward. "Under that government, people often disappeared. When our great hope, Matos, became president it was the same. It's the same now. When Matos was president there was a man from your country in the capital. He was the head of your intelligence here and Matos's great friend. Last year his name was in the papers a little because of the scandals in Washington. We believe now that he knew a great deal about who disappeared and why. It was strange to read about him in the newspapers. He seemed a foolish, trivial man, almost likable."

Justin said nothing.

"I'll call you Justin," Godoy said.

"It's been my name so long," she said, "I guess it's my name."

"If you tell your superiors that you agree to leave—how long can you keep the mission station?"

"Well," Justin said, "it's company property to start with and they'll take it right back. There are medicines there and furniture, so I guess they'll reoccupy it and we can be out in a week."

Godoy shook his head in exasperation.

"No good," he said. Before she could ask what he meant, he asked her, "What will you do in the States?"

"I don't know. I'm going to laicize anyway. I suppose I'll look for a job." She touched her hair, confused. "I'm afraid to think about it."

"I want you to keep the station open. For a month anyway. You can stall. Say that Father Egan is too ill to travel."

"Father Egan will die if he stays."

"All right, then, send Egan back. But keep open any way you can. I'll help you to keep open."

"But why?" she asked him.

"Because," Godoy said, "I have friends who are doing illegal work. They are going to make a foco in the mountains. They need a place on the coast for a while."

"They're going to fight?"

"Not here. But not so far away. You see, for years it's all been smoke." He permitted himself a quick smile. "But it's time now."

"Oh, my gosh," Justin said. Her heart soared.

"So we need you if you can help us. If you want to."

"Thank you for asking me," Justin said. "For trusting me."

"I have good reasons to trust you," Godoy said, "and it's easy to ask." He watched her, and she knew that he was measuring her hesitation.

"It's not only for the use of the station. We need you too, if you think you can help. If you feel you can't—well, I understand."

"I will," Justin heard herself say. "I'll help you any way I can. Not only with the station. There's nothing I want more."

"I don't try to seduce you in this," Godoy said. "You have to make your own decision."

"I have no family," Justin told him, smiling. "No special home. Where people need me that's where I go. See, I'm lucky that way."

She could not read his look. Suddenly she wanted him to reach out and touch her in some way, clap her on the shoulder, shake her hand, give some human token of what they had entered into. But he did not move and neither did she.

"This is work of armed struggle, so people may get killed. I won't deceive you."

"I don't come from a pacifist tradition," she said. Immediately it struck her as a cold and pedantic thing to say. She kept wondering how she must appear to him. That he would ask, that he would say she herself could help—it meant he must esteem her. Surely, she thought, he must.

Godoy looked at his watch.

"We'll go," he said.

She walked beside him toward the dark square; somewhere beyond it there was music, uncertainly amplified, and the noise of a crowd.

"Maybe," he said as they walked, "we can arrange your status within the church if you stay. It would be better."

"Whatever you think."

"We won't talk about it any more now. During the week we can meet and talk further."

Justin nodded. She felt lonely again, and frightened.

As they started across the plaza, Godoy stopped and turned to her.

"In the work we're doing," he said, "one has to change a little. You develop and you become a slightly different person. It's hard on the ego, but it's for the best."

"I understand," she said. She understood thoroughly. His message was the one she had been receiving all her adult life, the one she had always lived by.

I'll be right at home in this outfit, she thought. It would have cheered her up to have said it aloud to him, but she did not—

because it would be boastful and presumptuous and because he would not have understood her. As far as she could tell, he was without humor.

Immediately she reproached herself for reflecting on his lack of humor. It was judgmental and perhaps a little racist. Look to your own seriousness, she told herself.

They found the little fun fair on the far side of the church, behind the ruined eighteenth-century wall. In the space between the old church wall and the river a traveling carnival from the capital had parked its bright machines. There were two carousels, a small loop-the-loop with pink and purple cockpits, and a whirly ride called the Carretera de Fortuna. Two ice-cream sellers had brought their wagons up from the square. There was a man with balloons, a man with a fortune-telling parrot, and an Oriental in a kimono demonstrating karate strokes to an audience of teenagers and cane cutters. A stand sold soda and beer and black or white rum.

The Syrian's sound truck was parked beside a mobile generator with its sale signs still aloft, but it was empty and silent. The carnival machines made their own music as they turned—music as peeled and rusted at the seams as the machines themselves. The fairground was surrounded by colored lights, and around each bulb was a little cloud of insects drawn from the river.

As Justin and Godoy walked toward the fair, beggars crept out of the shadow of the church wall to intercept them. In the darkness they were tiny, barely human figures, small wads of cloth appended to upturned palms, uttering soft wails. Justin handed out some ten- and twenty-centavo pieces. Father Godoy gave them nothing.

One of the machines played "The Merry Widow Waltz" as the two of them strolled out on the little midway. The light there was fantastical, compounded of rainbow colors. Children's faces were unearthly shades; the grass underfoot looked painted.

The men in the crowd were drunk and somber, but there were mainly women and children about. A few groups of teenagers huddled beyond the light like predators around a camp, some of them smoking marijuana. In the darkness by the river, a drunk or a madman was screaming, but his cries were drowned by the music.

People greeted Father Godoy as he passed among them. Stony Indian faces softened toward him; there was some quick whisking off and clutching of straw sombreros. Both he and Justin towered over the crowds.

"A fair was a great thing once," Godoy said. "There were a great many tents and tricks. Today it's not so much because the movies come here now."

"It's still a great thing," Justin said.

Four of Godoy's schoolboys were waiting in line by the larger carousel. Justin watched him apprehend them and show them his watch. The boys waved little red ticket stubs up at him. He shrugged and then stood looking about him over the heads of the crowd. Justin thought of having a beer but decided it would not be right for her to approach the stand and the drunken men there.

"I'm missing two," Godoy said to her. "It's a nuisance."

"It's fine," Justin said. "I'll wait by the merry-go-round."

While Godoy combed the shadows, Justin found herself some space by the rail to watch the carousel. Around her were women whose children rode and women who stood with their children around them, watching the others.

He sees me as a fool, Justin thought fearfully. He sees my foolishness.

Under the lights, her faced fixed on the whirl before her, she contemplated her inward place. It was a foolish place, of course, but orderly. Like a corridor in some worthwhile institution, the walls and floors all scrubbed, the suffering and the flesh behind white screens. A virgin's place, a bit of a whited sepulcher.

It was dim and Lenten, its saints were shrouded, and if it held any tabernacles they were open and empty. It was very far away.

The notion frightened her. Far, she thought—far from where?

It was fearful and a prison and so was the world. She looked at the crowd across the lights from where she stood; she and they were separated by miles.

But she had been in prison before and she had been afraid. Marched through the cicada din of a Mississippi night to a place where the cotton fields were ringed with hooded watch lights and barbed wire under a million stars, to a blockhouse smelling of drains and urine. And then they turned out the lights in the block and the matron came out to tell ghost stories in the dark. It was the torment reserved for outside agitators that night, the treatment the guards had smirked about all the way to Parchman. No prods, no bucket across the skull, not that night, but darkness and ghost stories.

Somebody said, "Boy, if Folkways Records was here." They were in a black block because the white girls would kill them. In the dorm outside their jammed segregation cell, the black girls laughed or moaned and cried; some of them were sisterly, some insane and armed with razors.

The matron's dusty little voice demanded, "Who Got Mah Golden Ahm?"

The jughead innocence had its own horror. And nuns were bad luck there.

Goddamn it, Justin said to herself, I'm not a fool. He must know that.

She had seen the guns and the dogs; she knew well enough the difference between real wounds and painted martyrdoms. She had courage—her parents had it and she had it from them. All her life she had worked and soldiered with the best; wherever work and soldiering were required she could pay her way. We are not afraid today, she thought. What am I getting myself into? She shivered.

Then she looked up and saw that Father Godoy had taken a place opposite her along the carousel rail and, with the lights behind her, she felt that she could look at him unembarrassed. The two older boys whom he had sought stood, looking annoyed and drunk, behind him. Godoy was watching the children on the carousel.

The machine was playing a march from an old operetta. The children, with their eyes full of light, were reaching out to snatch the brass ring that was suspended by a strap from a stanchion beside where Godoy stood. They circled past his gaze—undersized, rickettsial, plenty of them dwarfed or scabrous, the 65 percent, the survivors of birth and infancy in Tecan—on their painted horses. He looked at them as no father she had ever seen had looked at his own children. His grey eyes shone like theirs, with such fierce love that she trembled to see him.

She felt then that all the companionship, all the moral recognition she had ever required from the universe reposed in the eyes of this priest. Between them the children went round and round, children of the campesinos, rojos, jibaros—the wretched, the pobrecitos. She could not take her eyes from his face as he watched them.

Embryology
Magdalena Abakanowicz

1 IN THE PAST
I was very little. Crouching over the edge of a marshy pond, I observed tadpoles. Enormous, about to be transformed into frogs. They were swarming by the bank. Through the fine membranes covering their distended stomachs one could clearly see the tangle of their guts. They were replete with the process of transformation, sluggish. They were tempting you to reach out for them. When they were pulled out with a stick onto the bank or inadvertently touched, their bulging bellies split and the contents leaked out in a confusion of knots. In a minute flies fell upon them. My heart was beating fast. I sat there shaken by what was happening. The destruction of soft matter and the boundless mystery of softness. It was not unlike looking at a broken stalk from which the sap brought forth by an indecipherable internal process, a force only imprecisely known, was flowing out. The mystery of never completely explored interior, soft, perishable.

Many years later, I began to work in a material that was soft, with a complicated tissue. It gives me a feeling of kinship and affinity with a world that I don't wish to explore other than by touch, apprehending it and connecting with parts of me that lie deepest.

CREATION
There is no intermediary of tools between the material that I mould and myself. I select it with my hands. I shape it with my hands. My energy is transmitted to it by my hands. Translating the intention into shape, my hands pass on to it something that eludes conceptualization. They reveal what is unconscious.

INTERIOR
The shapes that I design are soft. They conceal in their interiors the origin of softness. They conceal everything that I leave to the imagination. Unexplained by the eye, the skin of the finger that probes or the palm that informs the brain about the questioning sensations. The interior is as important as the outer sheath. Formed again and again as a consequence of the exterior or

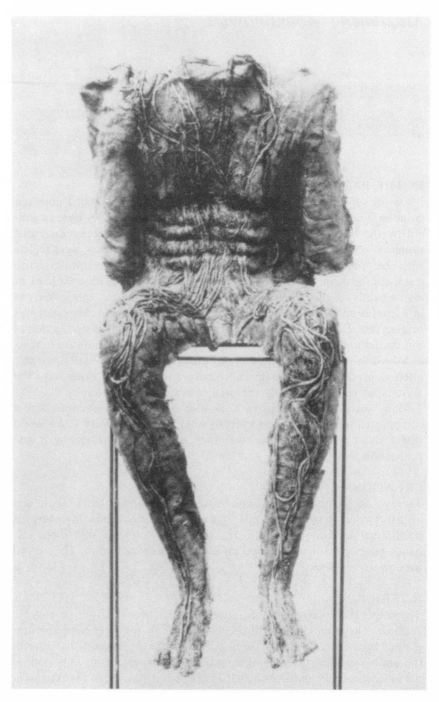

MAGDALENA ABAKANOWICZ. *SEATED FIGURE* (1974–75). (*TQ* #53)

externalized as the consequence of the interior—only in conjunction do they become a whole. The invisible center that can be divined is equally important as if it were open to anyone and permitting a physical penetration.

MEDITATION
Creating something that is more lasting than myself would multiply the imperishable dustheaps of human ambitions crowding the environment. If my thoughts and imaginings as well as the shapes that I create turn, like myself, into dust, this will be a good thing. There is so little room.

2 COEXISTENCE
My forms are like so many skins that I shed, marking the stages of my progress. They belong to me as intimately as I belong to them so that we cannot be apart. I watch over their existence. Soft, they contain an infinite variety of possible shapes from which one only is selected by me as the right, meaningful form.

In exhibition halls I create for them space in which they spread the radiation of the energy that I have bestowed upon them. They exist with me, dependent on me, and I depending on them. Co-existing, we mutually create each other. Veiling my face, they are my face. Without me, like severed parts of a body separated from the trunk—they make no sense.

DISCLOSURE
Impermanence is the inescapable necessity of everything that is alive: it is a truth contained in an organism that is soft. How to protest about the defect inherent in life other than by transforming a lasting thought into a perishable material? Thought is a monument. Thought is a bastion against disappearance. Thought is timeless. The perverse product of soft tissue that will disintegrate, and one day cease to connect. Expressed in a material of which the durability is akin to that of the being that had bred it, it begins really to live—it becomes mortal.

COMMUNION
I touch and learn the temperature. I learn smoothness and roughness. Is the object dry or moist? Moist from warmth or from cold? Pulsating or relaxed? Does it give under one's finger? Does its surface resist? What is its reality? Not having touched, I don't know.

EMBRYOLOGY
Forms ripen when carried a long time in the imagination. When the time comes to externalize them, by the tension of my whole body I become at one with the object created. My body turns ugly, mortified by bringing forth an image. It gets rid of something that had been its part, that began with an idea and ended with the skin. In getting rid of it, it becomes ugly from the effort.

My womb has never produced the germ of another life. My hands are shaping forms in quantity and seek affirmation in each exemplar. As if it were a herd where each individual is subordinate or one of the leaves that a tree brings forth.

REMINISCENCE

Yet at the very beginning, when I began to weave and use a material that was soft, it was from a need to protest. I wished to upset all rules and habits connected with this material. Softness is comfortable and useful. It is luxuriant. The material that wraps our bodies is obedient; it dampens the sound of footsteps. It covers the walls decoratively and warmingly. It gladdens the eyes. It serves usefully. By progressing with our civilization from its beginnings, it has acquired a role, a definable range of tasks regulated by our needs and habits.

This is why the fight against acquired habits struck me as so fascinating. Fascinating was the disclosure and unveiling of what is organic in fabrics, their softness. Showing the qualities unnoticed by the blindness of usage. The autonomous attributes. Showing everything that this material might become as a liberated carrier of its organic world.

And, later, the showing of objects, things that negate the former functions of this material and extend man's consciousness of the matter that surrounds him, of the objects he lives with, of his environment.

3   SOFTNESS

I touch my body. It still obeys me. It fulfils my instructions efficaciously, without resistance. The muscles move cleverly. When I will it, they lift my hand, move my fingers. When I want to, I can close and open my eyes. Turn my tongue. Under my skin, the flesh is formed with precision. Springy. Everywhere, in the wholly enclosed porous container encased in skin—pulsations. Everything heated uniformly, saturated with moisture that is thick, a red juice, white mucus, jelly-like secretions. Everything stretched on bones. Inside the bones, channels filled with nets, threads of what is soft and friable. Hot, greasy.

It belongs to me. It is me. It creates me.

Translated by Celina Wieniewska

Going to the dogs

Richard Ford

My wife had just gone out West with a groom from the local dog track, and I was waiting around the house for things to clear up, thinking about catching the train to Florida to change my luck. I already had my ticket. It was on the dinette, in my wallet.

It was the day before Thanksgiving, and all week long there had been hunters parked down at the gate: pickups and a couple of old Chevys sitting empty all day—mostly with out-of-state tags—occasionally, two men standing beside their car doors drinking coffee and talking. I hadn't given them any thought. Gainsborough—who I was thinking at that time of stiffing for the rent—had said not to antagonize them and let them hunt unless they shot near the house, and then to call the state police and let them handle it. No one had shot near the house, though I had heard shooting back in the woods and had seen one of the Chevys drive off fast with a deer on top, but I didn't think there would be any trouble.

I wanted to get out before it began to snow and before the electricity bills started coming, and since my wife had sold our car before she left, getting my business settled wasn't easy, and I hadn't had time to pay much attention.

Just after ten o'clock in the morning there was a knock on the front door. Standing out in the frozen grass were two fat women with a dead deer.

"Where's Gainsborough?" the one fat woman said. They were both dressed like hunters: one had on a red plaid lumberjack's jacket and the other a greenish camouflage suit. Both of them had the little orange cushions that hang from your back belt loops and get hot when you sit on them. Both of them had guns.

"He's not here," I said. "He's gone back to England. Some trouble with the government. I don't know about it."

Both fat women were staring at me as if they were trying to get me in better focus. They had green and black camouflage paste on their faces and looked like they had something on their minds. I still had on my bathrobe.

"We wanted to give Gainsborough a deer steak," the one who had spoken first said and turned and looked at the dead deer, whose tongue was out the side of his mouth and whose eyes looked like a stuffed deer's eyes. "He lets us hunt and we wanted to thank him in that way," she said.

"You could give me a deer steak," I said. "I could keep it for him."

"I suppose we could do that," the one who was doing all the talking said. But the other one, who was wearing the camouflage suit, gave her a look that said she knew Gainsborough would never see the steak if it got in my hands.

"Why don't you come in," I said. "I'll make some coffee and you can warm up."

"We *are* pretty cold," the one in the lumberjack's jacket said and patted her hands together. "If Phyllis wouldn't mind."

Phyllis said she didn't mind at all, though it was clear that accepting an invitation to have coffee had nothing to do with giving away a deer steak.

"Phyllis is the one who actually brought him down," the pleasant fat woman said when they had their coffees and were holding their mugs cupped between their fat hands, sitting on the davenport. She said her name was Bonny and that they were from across the state line. They were big women in their forties with fat faces, and their clothes made them look like all their parts were sized too big. Both of them were jolly, though—even Phyllis when she forgot about the deer steaks and got some color back in her fat cheeks. They seemed to fill up the house and make it feel jolly. "He ran sixty yards after she hit him and went down when he jumped the fence," Bonny said authoritatively. "It was a heart shot, and sometimes those take time to have effect."

"Ran like a scalded dog," Phyllis said, "and dropped like a load of shit." Phyllis had short blond hair and a hard mouth that seemed to want to say hard things.

"We saw a wounded doe, too," Bonny said and looked aggravated about it. "That really makes you mad."

"The man may have tracked it, though," I said. "It may have been a mistake. You can't tell about those things."

"That's true enough," Bonny said and looked at Phyllis hopefully, but Phyllis didn't look up. I tried to imagine the two of them dragging a dead deer out of the woods and it was easy.

I went out to the kitchen to get a honey pull-apart I had put in the oven, and they were whispering to each other when I came back in. The whispering, though, seemed good-natured, and I gave them the honey pull-apart without mentioning it. I was happy they were here. My wife is a slender, petite woman who bought all her clothes in the children's sections of department stores and said they were the best clothes you could buy because they were made for hard wearing. But she didn't have much presence in the house; there just wasn't enough of her to occupy the space—not that the house was so big, in fact it was very small—a prefab Gainsborough had had pulled in on a trailer. But these women seemed to fill up everything and to make it seem like Thanksgiving was already here. Being that big never seemed to have a good side before. But now it did.

"Do you ever go to the dogs?" Phyllis asked with part of her pull-apart in her mouth and part floating in her mug.

"I do," I said. "How did you know?"

"Phyllis says she thinks she's seen you at the dogs a few times," Bonny said and smiled.

"I just bet the quinellas," Phyllis said. "But Bon will bet anything, won't you, Bon? Trifectas, daily doubles, anything at all. She doesn't care."

"I sure will," Bon said and smiled again and moved her orange hot-seat cushion from under her seat so that it was on top of the davenport arm. "Phyllis said she thought she saw you with a woman there once, a little, tiny woman who was pretty."

"Could be," I said.

"Who was she?" Phyllis said gruffly.

"My wife," I said.

"Is she here now?" Bon asked, looking pleasantly around the room as if someone were hiding behind a chair.

"No," I said. "She's on a trip. She's gone out West."

"What happened," said Phyllis in an unfriendly way. "Did you blow all your money on the dogs and have her bolt off?"

"No." I didn't like Phyllis nearly as well as Bon, though in a way Phyllis seemed more reliable if it ever came to that, and I didn't think it ever could. But I didn't like it that Phyllis knew so much, even if the particulars were not right on the money. We had, my wife and I, moved up from the city. I had some ideas about selling advertising for the dog track in the local restaurants and gas stations and arranging coupon discounts for evenings out at the dogs that would make everybody some money. I had spent a lot of time, used up my capital. And now I had a basement full of coupon boxes that nobody wanted, and they weren't paid for. My wife came in laughing one day and said my ideas wouldn't make a Coke fizz in Denver, and the next day she left in the car and didn't come back. Later a fellow had called to ask if I had the service records on the car—which I didn't—and that's how I knew it was sold, and who she'd left with.

Phyllis took a little plastic flask out from under her camouflage coat, unscrewed the top, and handed it across the coffee table to me. It was early in the day, but I thought what the hell. Thanksgiving was the next day. I was alone and about to jump the lease on Gainsborough. It wouldn't make any difference.

"This place is a mess," Phyllis said and took back the flask and looked at how much I'd had of it. "It looks like an animal starved in here."

"It needs a woman's touch," Bon said and winked at me. She was not bad-looking, even though she was a little heavy. The camouflage paste on her face made her look a little like a clown, but you could tell she had a nice face.

"I'm just about to leave," I said and reached for the flask, but Phyllis put it back in her hunting jacket. "I'm just getting things organized back in the back."

"Do you have a car?" Phyllis asked.

"I'm getting antifreeze put in it," I said. "It's down at the BP. It's a blue Camaro. You probably passed it. Are you girls married?" I asked. I was happy to steer away from my troubles.

Bon and Phyllis exchanged a look of annoyance, and it disappointed me. I was disappointed to see any kind of displeasure cloud up on Bon's nice, round features.

"We're married to a couple of rubber band salesmen down in Petersburg. That's across the state line," Phyllis said. "A real pair of monkeys, if you know what I mean."

I tried to imagine Bonny's and Phyllis's husbands. I pictured two skinny men wearing nylon jackets, shaking hands in the dark parking lot of a shopping mall in front of a bowling alley bar. I couldn't imagine anything else. "What do you think about Gainsborough?" Phyllis asked. Bon was just smiling at me now.

"I don't know him very well," I said. "He told me he was a direct descendant of the English painter. But I don't believe it."

"Neither do I," said Bonny and gave me another wink.

"He's farting through silk," Phyllis said.

"He has two children who come snooping around here sometime," I said. "One's a dancer in the city. And one's a computer repairman. I think they want to get in the house and live in it. But I've got the lease."

"Are you going to stiff him?" Phyllis said.

"No," I said. "I wouldn't do that. He's been fair to me, even if he lies sometimes."

"He's farting through silk," Phyllis said. "Just like Commander McCann."

Phyllis and Bonny gave each other a knowing look. Out the little picture window I saw it had begun to snow, just a mist, but unmistakable.

"You act to me like you could use a good snuggle," Bon said, and she broke a big smile at me so I could see her teeth. They were all there and white and small. Phyllis looked at Bonny without any expression, as if she'd heard the words before. "What do you think about that?" Bonny said and sat forward over her big knees.

At first I didn't know what to think about it. And then I thought it sounded pretty good, even if Bonny was a little heavy. I told her it sounded all right with me.

"I don't even know your name," Bonny said and stood up and looked around the sad, little room for the door to the back.

"Henderson," I lied. "Lloyd Henderson is my name. I've lived here six months." I stood up.

"I don't like Lloyd," Bonny said and looked at me up and down now that I was up, in my bathrobe. "I think I'll call you Curly, because you've got curly hair. As curly as a Negro's," she said and laughed so that she shook under her clothes.

"You can call me anything you want," I said, and felt good.

"If you two are going into the other room, I think I'm going to clean some things up around here," Phyllis said. She let her big hand fall on the davenport arm as if she thought dust would puff out. "You don't care if I do that, do you, Lloyd?"

"Curly," said Bonny, "say Curly."

"No, I certainly don't," I said and looked out the window at the snow as it began to sift over the field down the hill. It looked like a Christmas card.

"Then don't mind a little noise," she said and began collecting the cups and plates on the coffee table.

Without her clothes on Bonny wasn't all that bad-looking. It was just as though there were a lot of heavy layers of her, but at the middle of all those layers you knew she was generous and loving and as nice as anybody you'd ever meet. She was just fat, though probably not as fat as Phyllis if you'd put them side by side.

There were a lot of clothes on my bed and I put them all on the floor, but when Bon sat on the cover she sat on a metal tie tack and some pieces of loose change and she yelled and laughed, and we both laughed. I felt good.

"This is what we always hope we'll find out in the woods," Bonny said and giggled. "Somebody like you."

"Same here," I said. It wasn't at all bad to touch her, just soft everywhere. I've often thought that fat women might be better because they don't get to do it so much and have more time to sit around and think about it and get ready to do it right.

"Do you know a lot of funny stories about fatties?" Bonny said.

"A few," I said. "I used to know a lot more, though." I could hear Phyllis out in the kitchen, running water and shuffling dishes around in the sink.

"My favorite is the one about driving the truck," Bonny said.

I didn't know that one. "I don't know that one," I said.

"You don't know the one about driving the truck?" she said, surprised and astonished.

"I'm sorry," I said.

"Maybe I'll tell you sometime, Curly," she said. "You'd get a big kick out of it."

I thought about the two men in nylon jackets shaking hands in the dark parking lot, and I decided they wouldn't care if I was doing it to Bonny or to Phyllis, or if they did they wouldn't find out until I was in Florida and had a car. And then Gainsborough could explain it to them, along with why he hadn't gotten his rent or his utilities. And maybe they'd rough him up before they went home.

"You're a nice-looking man," Bonny said. "A lot of men are fat, but you're not. You've got arms like a wheelchair athlete."

I liked that. It made me feel good. It made me feel reckless, as if I had killed a deer myself and had a lot of ideas to show to the world.

"I broke one dish," Phyllis said when Bonny and I were back in the living room. "You probably heard me break it. I found some Magic Glue in the drawer though, and it's better than ever now. Gainsborough'll never know."

While we were gone, Phyllis had cleaned up almost everything and put away all the dishes.

She had on her camouflage coat now and looked like she was ready to leave. We were all standing in the little living room, filling it, it seemed to me, right up to the walls. I had on my bathrobe and felt like asking them to stay over. I felt like I could grow to like Phyllis better in a matter of time, and maybe we could eat some of the deer for Thanksgiving. Outside, snow was all over everything. It was too early for snow. It felt like the beginning of a bad winter.

"Can't I get you girls to stay over tonight?" I said and smiled hopefully.

"No can do, Curly," Phyllis said. They were at the door. Through the three glass portals, I could see the buck lying outside in the grass with snow melting in his insides. Bonny and Phyllis had their guns back over their shoulders. Bonny seemed genuinely sorry to be leaving.

"You should see his arms," she was saying and gave me a wink. She had on her lumberjack's jacket again and her orange cushion was fastened to her belt loops. "He doesn't look strong. But he is strong. Oh my God! You should see his arms," she said.

I stood in the door and watched them. They had the deer by the horns and were pulling him off down the road toward their car.

"You be careful, Lloyd," Phyllis said. Bonny smiled over her shoulder.

"I certainly will," I said. "You can count on me."

I closed the door.

I stood in the little picture window and watched them walk down the road to the fence, sledding the deer through the snow, making a swath behind them. I watched them laugh when they stood by the car, watched them drag the deer under Gainsborough's fence and haul it up into the trunk and tie down the lid with string. The deer's head stuck out the crack to pass inspection. Then they stood up and looked at me in the window and waved, each of them, big wide waves. Phyllis in her camouflage and Bonny in her lumberjack's jacket. And I waved back from inside. Then they got in their car, a new blue Pontiac, and drove away.

I stayed around in the living room most of the afternoon, wishing I had a TV, watching it snow, and being glad that Phyllis had cleaned up everything so that when I cleared out I wouldn't have to do that myself. I thought about how much I would've liked one of those deer steaks.

It began to seem after a while like a wonderful idea to leave, just call a town cab, take it all the way in to the train station, get on for Florida, and forget about everything, about Tina on her way to Phoenix with a guy who only knew about greyhounds and nothing else.

But when I went to the dinette to have a look at my ticket in my wallet, there was nothing on the dinette but some change and some matches, and I realized it was only the beginning of bad luck.

Editorial

We debate the future of fiction and poetry a great deal in literary magazines, in classrooms and bars, at meetings like the American Writers' Congress. If what worries us is the continuation of imaginative writing, then it seems obvious that there will always be those who write, even if it is only for a few hours a week between household chores and child-raising responsibilities, or on scraps of cigarette paper in prison cells. But if we mean, as most of the debaters do, that it is not clear how this work will survive and who will read it, then there are two related questions.

Do we have doubts because much poetry and fiction seems undistinguished? Or is it because the reading audience also fails to distinguish itself and does not often honor the work that is most substantial, that speaks to us with the greatest emotional power, quickest sense of the complexity of life, and beauty?

We can reassure ourselves there will always be some readers who cherish imaginative accomplishment, even if they are to be found only among the ranks of fellow writers. But we must also see, each day, that writers need a larger audience, and that the larger audience needs imaginative accomplishments to feed on. Why then is the imagination so often crowded out of our attention?

Loves and births; crimes and outrages; terrors and inhuman force wielded against both innocent and guilty; the triumphs against such force; the pain of divided allegiances in families, courtrooms, nations; any profundity of understanding of our everyday actions: buying a toy, stealing a car, leaving home, loving or hating or hurting or hearing music or frying eggs—all of this should be the province of imaginative endeavor, which is simply a part of our way of understanding how we are formed as persons, and what sense our actions may have, what effect they produce on ourselves and on others. But all this is precisely what seems so complicated and almost removed from us at times by the drive in our culture to make all of us into creatures whose lives are defined by *quantities* and ruled by distant and incomprehensible sources of power. We are left little time by jobs and the media for reflection; and little energy to spare for thinking, even for feeling. As readers most of us are often tired and as undistinguished as the work we read, and this is so partly because of the demands clamoring around us.

I don't mean only the demands of family and work, that must be honored and if we are lucky can be lovingly answered. But so many impersonal, deceitful and alien voices cajole, browbeat, lie, tease, politick, lobby, coax, threaten and flirt around us, at us, with us, that we often find it difficult to give concentrated attention to a story, a drawing or a photograph, a poem, a piece of music. And the newer the imaginative work is, the more it has its own roots in these very same clamoring voices that we want to shut off, and many would rather read Hardy or Keats or listen to Mozart or Brahms (though in their own day they, too, had to fight for the attention of *their* contemporaries). And, after all, shouldn't we all be glad that *anyone* wants to read Hardy or listen to Mozart?

What do writers think of this state of affairs? Just "get it into print," a novelist friend told me, when I asked him what was most important to him. "*However* you can," he said. "I've been lucky, my publishers have always published my work when it was ready, even if the editions were very small." But is this enough, mere preservation for anonymous future readers?

In his Nobel lecture, Czeslaw Milosz spoke of a crisis of memory, a kind of cultural amnesia that cheapens our ability to act responsibly by keeping from us the knowledge of what has gone before; thus our responses as readers are cheapened as well. For without a sense of the history of men and their works, we are prey to both political and artistic manipulation. Milan Kundera's *Book of Laughter and Forgetting* presents us with a parable of the same crisis, in which an abolished party member, removed by political surgery from Czech history, can be inferred only from the presence of his hat on another man's head in an official photograph. If knowledge of the past is what feeds a writer's sense of his own work, helping him to see what must be done now, out of what has been done before (whether he is concerned with the rhythms in a single line of a poem or the canvas against which he wants to place figures in a war), then a knowledge of the history of imaginative accomplishment gives a *reader* a place to stand in drawing sustenance from imaginative works, in judging them. We become laughable when our daily lives declare that we don't think there is much at all in the accumulated artistic accomplishment of man that could please us or instruct us. Remembering is a task, a responsibility, as much as it is a pleasure; for many it just takes too much time and trouble.

Our responsibility as readers is clear: diligent attention to new writing, as much of it as we can get hold of, and generous help, when we can give it, and however, to the best work we can find. And there is enormous pleasure in reading good new work, and that is what sustains good readers through the lifelong and wearisome task of keeping up, a task that is the literary editor's consuming responsibility.

"Perhaps the greatest misfortune for a man of letters is not in being the object of his brethren's jealousy, or the victim of conspiracies, or held in contempt by the mighty of this world; but in being judged by idiots." That caution is not recent, but came from Voltaire, and the warning is as clear now as then, to an editor, to dispose of biases and peeves as much as possible, to read with eyes and ears open, with expectations that are high but not categorical. After only a few months as editor of *TriQuarterly*, I have been chastened already by the way practical realities, too—schedules and money and correspondence with writers, some of them still my friends—erode principles and plans. I have asked myself not only what I hope to publish in *TriQuarterly*, but also what responsibility it is that *TriQuarterly* or any small literary magazine should bear, in this welter of voices, vices, arguments and despairing cries in which the good works provide a miraculous exhilaration.

If *TriQuarterly* has a recognizable identity, it arises out of its energy and its range, it seems to me. Its readers respect its devotion to short fiction (a devotion that will remain unchanged), its seriousness (and sometimes its frivolousness), its heft, its handsomeness, and what one would have to call its tone of voice—by turns straightforward, edgy, flashy, testing, theoretical, encyclopedic, heavy, campy, once in a while avant-gardish, scholarly, esoteric. The magazine has been lucky to have the support of Northwestern University, without which it might not have survived (the twentieth anniversary is coming soon). It has won prizes for what it has published and for the way it has presented itself. Its special issues have often been reprinted as hardback books by other publishers. This special and recognizable identity will continue to draw readers, I hope, and more and more writers will send to *TriQuarterly* the best work they have to offer, as many have done in the past.

The most important work, the best, cannot be categorized or described in advance by anyone. But I think it will often look to the world outside the writer, to the culture swirling around his or her solitary labor. Narrow, self-regarding, clever work always has some appeal to the small reader in us, that imp of a reader who doesn't wish to be led out of himself toward others, toward the world, or even toward deeper pleasure or understanding. But there is a larger reader in us, too, who responds to work that is free of self-indulgence; that goes beyond a trivial occasion; that will break, when it needs to, all formal expectations; that has emotional and even philosophical weight; that binds us to others rather than asserting that our solitariness is an interesting state of mind. Or, when we must face our essential solitariness, as the writer does when he or she is writing, then such work explores that state with passion as well as anger, with vision as well as accomplishment and cleverness. The *material* of such work is anywhere and everywhere, in bedrooms and newscasts and at racetracks and wakes, and in imaginative flights beyond what is familiar. A fundamental attitude of wonder and delight in seeing what is there—that's the mark that Conrad and Welty and Milosz and many others have found in good writing. It is wonder I find put down this way in a story of William Goyen, "Old Wildwood": "There was so much more to it all, to the life of men and women, than he had known before he came to Galveston just to fish with his grandfather, so much in just a man barefooted on a rock and drinking whiskey in the sun, silent and dangerous and kin to him." And in this sentence, from Goyen's "The White Rooster": "He had a face which, although mischievous lines were scratched upon it and gave it a kind of devilish look, showed that somewhere there was abundant untouched kindness in him, a life which his life had never been able to use."

In short, *TriQuarterly* will look for a special sort of engagement arising out of the largest view of the individual life (which is the irreducible material of fiction and poetry) and out of that craftsmanlike and loving awareness of predecessors that both instructs and challenges good writers. Out of that engagement, that intimacy, that remembering, comes the work that is most innovative, that binds us fiercely to others, that lays down a path for future rememberers to trace. These are my preoccupations and hopes as editor. My greatest hope is that *TriQuarterly*'s readers will return to the magazine again and again, to see what new voice has for a moment entered the forum, asking to be heard.—*Reginald Gibbons*

Dear Lydia E. Pinkham

Pamela White Hadas

"I am always dying and it makes no difference."—E. B. Browning

for Robert Pack

10 West Fourteenth Street
New York City
1 April, 1897

Mrs. Lydia E. Pinkham
Lydia E. Pinkham Medicine Co.
Lynn, Massachusetts

Dear Mrs. Pinkham: I hesitate to take
my pen in hand, or waste your time with this,
but I'd like a woman's ear, one hundreds have
confided in, if one can trust the papers.
(I do not find the ads for Lydia E.
Pinkham's Vegetable Compound "obscene
and titillating," as my husband does).
My maid seems healthy, and the cook tells me
she's been drinking Pinkham's every day
for the last month. (The cook won't touch it though,
because of the alcohol.) My husband's friend,
Dr. Thorstein Fallis, famous young
gynecologist, has treated me
for years. He blames my "naughty ovaries"
for all: the fits and faints, the weeping laughter. . .

Ever since my honeymoon (five years)
I've suffered cravings, backache, nausea,
suppression of the "turns"—would you agree
it's from the ovaries? Those sweet pink hearts?
And that's not all. He says my womb's inspired
inconsequent behavior, petulance,
caprice and lying artfulness, plus tense
lassitude. And last, not least—I'm told—
"the solitary vice." I have been warned
insanity is but a step from this.
It may be crazy to sing to your ovaries;
still, I do, as I don't have a child.
In the dark, my dark, I see pale fists
of unborn faces, turned up toward my heart,
plump fruits, my wanderlusts. Till now I fear
I have been too content to be no more
than an invalid, achieving neither cure
nor death. I move in neurasthenic circles
descanting symptoms with even sicklier women
(thus being indisposed does pass the time).
I've tried warm baths and cold baths, abstinence
from spicy food. I've tried electrical,
mesmeric, hydropathic, chemical
fads and fashions, from plugs to pessaries. . .

But what I really want to ask I fear
is something I can't mention to my friends.
It's when my doctor starts his "medical
manipulations" testing for those known
unnatural responses that imply
derangement of the female organs. When
he strokes here, then there, inserting his
new-fangled slowly sliding speculum,
I jerk and weep. "Aha!" says he, "don't be
afraid. I am an expert with the knife.
The operation is quite simple, Dear."
It's called "female castration," and if I don't
improve by fall, he says, we'll have to try it.
Is this what you call "belly-ripping" or
is Dr. Fallis right, that it will help

1982   459

clear and elevate my moral sense,
save me from gluttony and just cussedness?
(I feel a pressure on the little cup
of my collarbone and my heart begins to beat
in every organ, every fingertip,
when Thorstein Fallis treads my stair and knocks.
The walls tilt in, and the objects in my room begin
to leer—ebony looms and ormolu
clock, woolwork portraits, gas jets, polished grates—
accuse, accuse, creep closer, sneer like nurses.)
I itch. And yet I fear the knife, the "death
of Woman in the woman," death in life.
I quiver and toss; my womb is all a-prance.
Is there any feeling in a female frame
that cannot be or signify an illness?

It is not ladylike to be in love.
I hope I'm not, but when that doctor comes,
whose hands have been beneath my petticoats,
I must tear my hair, contort my limbs and howl. . .

Once I bit dear Thorstein's hand. It bled.
But he's bled me! When the curse it pleased the Lord
to grant to Woman ceased in me that man
stuck his leeches to those . . . lips; they sucked
down there until I swooned. It didn't help.

I try to be a perfect blend of puppy
and princess, frail, yet built for childbirth, dumb,
just hopelessly flawed, meant "ceaselessly to suffer
from love's eternal wound" as I make tea
and knit. Hired for the price of a ring: I do
nothing, and I do it splendidly. . .

Malingering is "one expensive hobby,"
as Charles would have it, who used to love my pallor—
so spiritual, so beautiful, but now
he wants a son, he wants a wife who meets
her "marital appointment" more than seldom.
I've seen his eyes go straying toward my maid.

(Why are the females of the lower classes
so healthy?) Take Dorcas now: she's just eighteen
of course, the type they call a "buxom lass,"
straight from the country, milk-fed, brash.
At first I didn't think she had a nerve
in her body, but the New York pace
may have infected even her. (Else why
is she using Pinkham's every day?)
I've wondered if she might not be in love—
the vulgar blushes, the silly songs she hums
or whistles thoughtlessly all day. I think
robust vitality is crude somehow.

I wouldn't want to die in perfect health,
but how long can I balance on this edge?
As if I didn't have enough to see to,
Dorcas sometimes sulks—but only till
Charles comes home. Oh—then she is on top
of the world and saying how very good I look,
don't I? At times I am perturbed by this:
I dream she's coupling in my bed, and with
my husband. Winking from the dark skylight,
I feel my fingers chill and chill creeps up
my arms and when it hits my heart I start
to laugh, and then I sink away. It seems
my arousal is my fall. Forgive me, dear
Mrs. Pinkham, for running on. It does
relieve my mind to write, but just so long
as Dr. Fallis don't find out. The world
is nervous and my skin is thin. Do tell
me if the Pinkham brew will fix me up.
"A Baby in Every Bottle," is what you say.
Could you be clear just how this works?
With what I've told you, can you recommend
a course of treatment, or is my case past hope?
Looking to your answer, I remain
Your supplicant, Triphena Twitchell-Rush.

*   *   *

1982   461

10 West 14th St.
Apr. 1, 1897

Dear Lydia E. Pinkham, I haven't got
no friends to turn to. I just come to town
not but four months since. My father passed
away from his heart, my mother from her womb.
We was always poor. Now I have trouble
with both my heart and womb. The place I got
is with this fancy doctor's family, but
seeing as how his wife is always sickly
and doctors coming here like fruitflies round
a rotten peach, I don't think it does
no good to ask a doctor. She ain't better.
(Sometimes with all their help I figure she's worse.)
I hope I haven't caught what ails the Mrs.
from the windows always being closed in there
and listening all day long to this and that
complaint. And then I overhear the doctor
say that reading novels is a cause
of uterine decay and lesions with
The Castle of Otranto right there by
her sofa, and me reading it to her
a week now. Could that cause "congestion of
the ovaries," like I seen in the letters
to you in the paper, I've got dragging down
and filled up feelings and the returns has stopped
for near on three months now, from almost when
I come to this place. So I want to ask
will your tonic that dissolves and throws out
tumors and brings on the monthly flow
(I think there's something in me sucking all
my strength) restore me? I've been using it
a month or so and so far I'm the same.

And maybe you could give an opinion on
my mistress, she is one of those high-strung
types, real pale, and even sipping tea
seems to fatigue her, but, oh, she's beautiful
as some fairy princess, golden hair and hands

the light goes trembling through, but then she faints.
(She never goes too far from something soft
to fall on.) The other day she flipped and flopped
herself around like a hooked fish and screamed
what I daren't write. And then the doctor said,
"We'll have to shave her head," and so she stopped.
Then he whispered to me and the master, "Fear
is a sedative." I wonder. I toss all night
till the bed is all of a topsyturvydom,
and after those nights I can't keep down no food.
It's dreams: in one I saw a "female organ"
blown up like a balloon and rising right
into the sky; and the doctor comes with one
of them pointed poles for picking up stray trash
and stabs it, and gray worms rain down on me.

It's been three months since all of this began.
I'd ask the master, seeing how he is
a doctor, but (I don't know if I should
say this part) I am afraid of him
since almost the first night that I was here
and he came by my room, asking for pity
and I was helpless. . . Well, that is enough.
A poor girl just can't ask that class of man
even if . . . and I don't know, this thing. . .

What I only have to know is does your tonic
clean out the womb, eventually, and soon?
Should I use the Sanitive Wash and Syringe?
Do you think I will "go smiling through"?
I anxiously await your answer. I
remain, Your Humble Servant, Dorcas Flowers.

                    *   *   *

10 West Fourteenth Street
New York City
4 July, 1897

Dear Mrs. Pinkham: Here am I again.
If I'm not cured, I don't know what I am.

So here's my testimonial. I've heard
that every woman who's dissatisfied
with her lot is sick—well, they just haven't tried
to liquidate that lot with Mrs. Pinkham's
Vegetable Compound. And thank you for
the little book. I used to hate descriptions
of anatomy. (I blushed to mention
even a table's *leg*.) Now I am full
as a Chinese toy shop, caught in my own web
of defects, and I love them when I've had
my daily dose, I dare my Charles to peek
at "Teeny Pheeny" (Sshhh—it's my pet name)
and I don't care when he storms out to his club.
I don't mind that Dorcas is blowing up
under her apron, for I knew she took
a good deal of your recipe, and I
need only wait and meanwhile lull myself
with nothings tra la la la la la la. . .

My brain feels polished, put up on a shelf,
while my womb is fortified with your
magic potion, does my thinking for me.
(Dr. Fallis would say that this is health.)

Idleness is an art; the uterus is
a sewer, tra la. I dreamt I heard a door
forced below so I went down to. . . He
Himself, as big as death. (I recognized
his cuff links, though he wore a mask.) He bore
a satchel, stuffing it with all I would
not sacrifice. ("You're ill to the degree
you own yourself!") I see a trail of blood,
its source between his legs. He said, "It's not
my body but my heart," so I say, "Good,
we'll cut it out." And then he died, tra la.

1982

Sometimes I think that Charles has married Dorcas.
Sometimes I think perhaps she has my child
in her oven, or I'm their child. When Charles comes home,
he always wants to know why why why why . . .
he finds me singing softly in the closet
behind the row of boots (well, that is where
I keep you, Mrs. Pinkham, darling, cases).

The dark gets full of swirling colors; they
take shape in a fine ballet of oozing cells;
I tell myself these are the true untried
ovarian forms of thought, the nerves in air
ramified by my relationship
to my "mother's milk." I haven't given up
my life of symptomania (where is
the poet of pathology? oh, yes:
Mrs. Browning, healthy compared to me)
nor animal economy, the commotions of
my tender tubings, oval agents, woe
manifold, nor infinite Fallopian. . .
O my. O you, in your black silk and white
fichu, they say you are a table-rapper
and a quack, those doctors! pooh! with their heroic
gulping purges, blisters, laudable pus. . .

So I am a riddle, Terra Incognita,
as far as Charles is concerned, queen of the clumsy
tangle, a house within a house, an engine
within an engine. La! It takes just three
bottles a day to keep me going. I
used to be afraid of the chloral faces
in window curtains, I'd whimper down the dark
keyhole, cave. . . Now each day "Pinkham's lark"
(that's what I call the winglike sweep
across my brain when I'm behind the boots)
brings me to my mission, to be happy
with my lot. I sit and concentrate
on moon and tides. My mind's a Pandora's box.
Hope's the only evil left in it.

It's Independence Day, and Dorcas cares
for me. Let's all be free with love and all
things out of our control. I'll take as much
of the doctor's nostrum as Dorcas measures out.
More than one life is in the willing hands
I will to her. Mrs. Pinkham, I am
so happily sorry for the length of this.
I might have been a writer, but a woman
must write with blood, and I'm too weak to spare
blood, even with your tonic in my veins.
But I'm mostly cured. I don't care what I'm not.
With blessings on you, Mrs. Pinkham, I
remain myself, Triphena Twitchell-Rush.

Song of napalm

Bruce Weigl

for my wife

After the storm, after the rain stopped pounding,
We stood in the doorway watching horses
Walk off lazily across the pasture's hill.
We stared through the black screen,
Our vision altered by the distance
So I thought I saw a mist
Kicked up around their hooves when they faded
Like cut-out horses
Away from us.
The grass was never more blue in that light, more
Scarlet; beyond the pasture
Trees scraped their voices into the wind; branches
Crisscrossed the sky like barbed wire
But you said they were only branches.

Okay. The storm stopped pounding.
I am trying to say this straight: for once
I was sane enough to pause and breathe
Outside my wild plans and after the hard rain
I turned my back on the old curses. I believed
They swung finally away from me. . .

But still the branches are wire
And thunder is the pounding mortar;
Still I close my eyes and see the girl
Running from her village, napalm
Stuck to her dress like jelly,
Her hands reaching for the no one
Who waits in waves of heat before her.

So I can keep on living,
So I can stay here beside you,

1982

467

I try to imagine she runs down the road and wings
Beat inside her until she rises
Above the stinking jungle and her pain
Eases, and your pain, and mine.
But the lie swings back again.
The lie works only as long as it takes to speak
And the girl runs only as far
As the napalm allows
Until her burning tendons and crackling
Muscles draw her up
Into that final position
Burning bodies so perfectly assume. Nothing
Can change that; she is burned behind my eyes
And not your good love, and not the rain-swept air
And not the jungle green
Pasture unfolding before us can deny it.

MAGDALENA ABAKANOWICZ. *SEATED FIGURES* (1974–75). (*TQ* #53)

Three prose pieces

Stephen Berg

IN A NEW LEAF

Three weeks before he died, my father acted as an extra in A *New Leaf*, a movie about an alcoholic, her lover, and a stranger who showed up and would, as it happened, try to save her. Cassavetes and May were making the film in Philly on 13th Street, using a defunct hotel, renamed The Royal, for the battles between the fucked-up couple. Night after night the crew would take their places—at the camera, yelling directions, searching for extras in the crowds that lined up six deep around the roped-off set and watched Peter Falk (the stranger) fifty times do a scene in which he's passing The Royal on his way somewhere and a whiskey bottle flies out a window and hits the ground at his feet and he looks up, sees someone (the woman, I think) in the window and dashes (there's a scream) into the dark building. It seems the woman and her lover (Cassavetes) are holed-up there, planning a robbery. Falk is tanned, dressed in a custom-cut Navy-blue silk suit and delicate black shoes, Italian style, the kind tap dancers use because of their flexibility, their near-weightlessness. In and out, in and out he goes, bottle after bottle arcing from the window, the pieces swept away each time by one of the crew, and none of the fans and gawkers really knows what's up with the three characters. It was like watching real life, it doesn't matter whose life, with one big difference: that scene lost all meaning because it was repeated so many times. We watched for hours this same scene being reshot, in early June. It was beginning to get hot the way it does in Philly—thick heavy humidity blanking your mind, hanging on for days so every little thing feels difficult, so everything looks like it has dirt on it. My father had had a massive, fifth heart attack and when we picked him up at his house he was wearing a raincoat with a full button-in camel's-hair liner, and under it a suit, tie and scarf. A gray felt hat and gray doeskin gloves lent the finishing touches. His face was the color of those gloves, but with a dull shine like solder or like those skies you get in Philly before a rain when blossoming puffs of air cool your face but it stays hot and the sun has disappeared and everything is drained of strong color.

Well, he walked shuffling one foot at a time very very slowly, stopping between each step, as if on a tightrope, almost floating, with great caution and weakness and fear, to the car. Settled in the front seat, he barely spoke. We heard the movie was being made, thought it would be fun to watch the production, a rare distraction from all he had gone through. We drove the few blocks to the place, parked, walked over to the people at the ropes circling The Royal, and faded into the crowd. My Dad, for some reason of his own, drifted to another side of the crowd and stood there. Everything on the street was blue-white under the lights; the mist of humidity in the glare made everything look as if a fine pearly veil hung between you and whatever you saw. Once in a while I'd glance over to see how he was. Inch by inch he had slipped back from the back of the mob until now he was standing right up front pressing against the waist-high rope. He was all gray: raincoat, gloves, hat, face. Except for his Watch-plaid cashmere scarf. He looked like an ailing Mafia don: expressionless terrified mask of a face, a man with secrets and power who refused the world any hint of emotion that might reveal who he was. Was his mind silent as he stood there or did he hear one of those primitive, sourceless, pure, self-defining voices that haunt us, left over from the gods, telling him not to smile, not to speak, not to show anything to the enemy world, telling him to be no one as the line between death and the future evaporated and he slipped closer to the gods by obeying them, by adopting the hero's impassive mask? The fact is he looked like Edward G. Robinson, not Oedipus or Lear immortalized in the revelatory aftermath of cosmic self-discovery. Reticent, masochistic, mildly depressed all his life, he stood there, to me awesome and godlike because of his ordeal near death. "He'll never walk out of the hospital," the doctor had said, and here, five months later, he was, as fate would have it, a passerby about to act in a bad movie, about to play one of the gods as they are today. By now Elaine May was pacing the edge of the crowd inside the roped-off area, looking for extras, picking people by their faces to walk past under an arcade behind Falk during the bottle-throwing scene. She saw my father, nodded a questioning "Yes?" He ducked under the rope, which May lifted for him, and joined a group of eight people then moved to the outside of the crowd. By now I was standing beside him, listening. All were told to begin walking, briskly, scattered apart, just before Falk reaches the front of the hotel when the bottle hits. Over and over he walked, briskly, until we thought he would drop dead. Over and over I watched his gray speechless face, betraying nothing, glistening under his gray hat in the lights, while behind me, off to my right, where the camera was, pointed away from the hotel at Falk and the extras walking by—Falk ran past into the hotel, yelling something, after the bottle crashed, and a woman yelled back at him from the window. Gena Rowlands? Over and over. Finally they got it right and we went home. For months, I waited for the newspaper ads announcing the film so we could all pay to see you. When it finally played, and we went, that scene wasn't even in it. The film was so mediocre it ran less than a week. I tried buying a clip of the scene but they wouldn't sell the footage. Several years since your walk-on part, and it happens anytime: the muggy summer night, the family, kids and all, the gauzy air, you doing what you're told by the director—I'll be teaching, doing a chore, reading, writing, talking with Millie and the kids, a middle-aged man, your son, watching his old sick father, but not on the screen in a theater. It's still the street, the live, sweaty people, you doing it over and over, over and over the scene being shot, the bottle, the scream, the lights, "O.K.—try it again!" coming from behind faceless faces, from where the black weapon steel body and silent blank eye of the surrounded camera are pointed at us.

THE WEAVE

The blind black chair caner is leaning still against the Fidelity Bank building on 16th Street in Philly where I was born and live, a 2 X 2 inch hunk of woven cane is pinned on his lapel with a safety pin to advertise his trade, a dull tin cup is drooping hooked from his left hand's index finger; a beach chair, its green crisscross webbing, dangerously frayed, has been opened and set behind him in the doorway. Most of the time he stands and holds his cup; a lunch bag sits, usually, rolled closed on the chair; and when I pass him mornings I'll drop a coin in, hear "Thank you." About six years ago after my father died I was looking in a closet and found his charcoal-gray Tripler overcoat draped on a hanger, dumbly available, like new. He rarely wore it because it cost so much. When the nap caught the light, I recall, it glowed like pollen on a flower petal; the dull black buttons shone; the irregular hand-cut deeply-notched narrow lapels stood out. I'd wear it now and then but it stopped above my knees, my jacket and shirt-sleeves would show, the armpits were tight and high. Even in daylight the weave was almost invisible. It had a black-on-black pattern: each sixteenth of an inch something like a tiny dim snowflake or a miniscule ghost face appeared, but you couldn't see the flakes or the faces unless you stood nose to the coat and squinted and focused and told yourself—so you had words to help you see—that you were actually seeing those things, actually looking at that faint grid of signs, that mesmerizing text as if it were some spiritual design that had to be fathomed or a field of visual chanting as indecipherable as the self. You'd stare until the "it" and the "you" for one split second didn't exist. I remember looking into a mirror once, trapped in some personal hell, and not knowing who I was, terrified because the face in the glass seemed to disconnect from my knowledge of who it was and not be my face, the way a word can lose its meaning if you repeat it enough times, or an object seem uncanny if you keep staring at it, seem to look back at you. It was the morning after I decided to quit therapy, "give myself a Christmas present," I announced to my shrink. I woke up scared shitless, I didn't know why, and at the sink when I wet my beard and looked up to shave, lifting my soapy hands, I couldn't recognize myself, I felt I didn't exist, the face was flat, distant, a stranger's. ". . . a sudden inward flash." In the closet all there was was the thick good wool, smelling of damp and dust a little. There I was, staring at the coat, almost merged with the dark inside the closet: acid whiffs of old rubber boots and the musk of scarves and gloves floated out; my father dressed up in his coat floated back to me out of the darkness—we were in the grainy gray smoked-hazed lowlit air of Jimmy Ryan's in New York. I took him there one winter night to hear some of the jazz I love, the abrupt delicate wails and sighs of the de Paris Brothers, Edmond Hall, skinny and grinning "Pops" Foster, Davison, I forget who-all now, the brass-, ebony-, skin- and gut-drenched rhythms blasting, wheedling, dousing us with precise, sung, wordlessly voiced emotion. That one night my father and I sat across from each other in the dense light: now and then a word, a sentence: his drumming fingers: me saying, "Listen to this. . ." Most of the time it was him on his side, me on mine, in a silence between us as clear and moving as the music that shook the room. It was snowing then as it was when I stared into the closet at the coat. I carried it downtown and gave it to the black man, draped it over his arm, neatly folded, told him it had been my father's—they were about the same size—and he held the coat, gently it seemed to me, held it folded over his right arm while face to face we stood there in silence for a while. "Thank you. Thank you." And I walked away. Next day, instead of his flimsy raincoat, he was wearing my father's heavy coat. It was still snowing. I went by without speaking, without giving him any change. I kept my eyes half-closed against the big sloppy flakes. Phrases, unascending hymns to lost love, chords, pieces of stories that have nothing to do with coats, blind men, pity like static ripped through my head. For a block I followed my image in the windows—bank, men's store, travel agent, luggage, bar—blanked out between each by metal and stone, and heard "if you were here, if you. . ."—whoever the you is, in the pain of the impossibility of ending. I turned off 16th and went down Walnut Street, two shining little people—I'm sure of it—still standing in the lenses of the chair caner's dark glasses.

FOR JIM WRIGHT

"Begin with horses in adolescence, with how you'd ride and ride after a poor childhood in Newark, ride in South Orange; and end with Jim's death and your horse poem 'On Hearing of a Friend's Illness'"—Charlie, that's in my letter to you about your essay on influences, on what started you writing, on what makes you write the way you do. I have a fantasy of you—after your father made money and you moved—spending weekend after weekend obsessed with horses, loving the saddle and dung smell, loving the heat of their flanks, skinquivers, nostrils, size, but especially the lesson of their power, of how by staying close you got to know the animal, you could control and guide him under you until, in moments of ecstasy, the difference between you and the horse dissolved. The fantasy ends (after scenes of you covering hills and sunny fields) with the word "escape." The whole escapade of your horse-love might have been escape . . . from what I can't say. What follows is in Martin's Ferry, Ohio, a story Jim told me about working as a boy for a strip-mining company. His boss, when he'd get angry at Jim for doing something wrong, would lead Jim to one of the barns, lift a set of chains off a nail then beat the living shit out of a horse while he forced the boy to watch. Your horse poem as an elegy, Charlie, its impulse to escape the news of Jim's death, to not feel his death—who knows why the mind at such times can skip to something else, some act, which seemed at the time mere pleasure, that saves us? I remember—maybe it was 1965—Jim stayed with us on Pine Street. I thought anyone as wildly alive as he was must be insane. He'd wake and drink half a bottle of bourbon by eleven then stand at the kitchen window reciting to the sky Robinson or Donne or some anonymous poem, cursing politicians whose names would pop up between "So if I dreame I have you I have you," and "For all our joyes are but fantastikal," and "That there is more of unpermitted love/ In most men's reticence than most men think." Alcaeus's political fragment "between earth and snowy sky" comes to me, God knows why, probably because I'm not sure *why* it's political. But I believe it means political evil evaporates there, between earth and sky, in the unpeopled realm of earthlessness, of air. Those horses, yours and his, his death at fifty-two, his memory for poetry that would give out passage after passage as if the rugs and chairs and breakfast eggs weren't real, weren't nearly as real to him as "between earth and snowy sky," lines, passages, fragments of poems which he made solid with his passion, which he made happen to us where we are. And I don't know why, I don't know why Jim never wrote about that old boyhood punishment, or maybe he did, maybe this is his voice:

"Short, stocky and bald, my boss had developed the habit of morality that expressed itself only indirectly since he did not believe in showing anger to another person face to face, and if I were discovered loafing or having forgotten a chore or having worked too slow, he would 'invite' me after work at twilight into a barn to show me the little morality play he had staged in his mind as an object lesson. Twilight is a dramatic hour, with its failing light that softens the details of the world. The long hairy fields below us would be a chalky blue at that hour, almost a void you could step off into if you left the block of light that came from the company office window, that yellowed the ground. The barn was very dark until the man, holding me by the hand all the way as we walked there, reached up and jerked a cord that would bring on a single dangling bulb at the entrance to the runway between the stalls. There were damp stains and lumps of straw glistening, scattered along the concrete floor, and the familiar stink of dung and piss and hay. That light was the brightest light in the world, when we'd be standing there together. By now we were not holding hands. And just that lack of his hand made the difference in our heights clear and ominous—he was much taller than I, and so much heavier, bigger, bulkier—I must have sensed how the usual difference between man and boy is always weighted with the force of murder, and as the boy grows the force shifts and grows equal and winds up heavier on the other side. But anyhow, there we were, in the light. Two steps away were the chains on the nail slanted into one of the posts of a stall. Always before I knew it (because I could not bear to watch the transition between his not holding the chains and his holding them) one of the stalls was open in front of me and my boss was in it whipping the chains down against the hind quarters of a good horse. I tried to imagine the stars outside, where by now it must have been dark enough for them to show. I tried to see my mother, puttering in the kitchen, her dour, kind, heavily disappointed mouth open a little in unselfconscious ease because no one was in the room with her. I tried to see something as pitifully distant even as the tar-black dunce cap in one of my spelling books. But by now there were the strokes of blood shining on the brown flank and the echo of clanking and whinnying which, it seemed, I almost hadn't really heard, and a kind of shaking inside me, down, down very deep, like what you feel after some dreams, just as you wake, a shaking that resembles a heavy door being slammed in an old house several rooms away and you feel it vibrate through all those rooms and reach you and enter you, far from the door itself. That inner shock seems to be the universe shocked as well, both of you trembling. Then he pulled the light-cord again, and this time it was pure dark, the twilight gone now, and outside those stars I had tried to see—definite, flooding the sky. I watched them as we walked back through the night. Thank God they were there, exactly the way they looked in my mind, bluish, strongly vibrant, clustering in masses and little knots or alone, cold, absolute, exact, put there by nothing human. Then, there must be a part of my mind—that envisioned them while I watched in the barn— which is not human, which is beyond flesh, blood, warnings, punishments, goodness, and even love. Who was *I*, how could I understand those beatings, those lessons in right and wrong? Whose guilt was I feeling, and what was it about?"

Maybe Jim did write those words. Does it matter who wrote those words? What is it about his poetry—a human voice on a page that I read for pleasure, for comfort, for help—what is it that still draws me to his voice? What is it about his tone that can pity the tilt of an ancient statue's head, or redwings doomed by chemical spray, or an old man begging for sex, or find in any tiny natural thing the ecstasy of existence: the gift of being here to see, to despair, to be moral. Lucky redemption? Unwarranted remorse? He broke that "shameful and impotent privacy" that kills us; his voice has my voice in it, and yours; he believes Brodkey's dictum that you must keep in mind "the primacy of the audience's cry for help." Jim loved the word "Ohio." I know why: listen to it: Ohio. Repeat it. It has, like other words— especially nouns and place names—the gift of its own abstraction, of its ability not to be connected to the world. Say it enough times and it is music, pure music, not *beyond* pain or love or anything, but simply for a moment like those stars in a boy's mind, in the sky, or like that horse crying out, or like those chains wounding flesh and mind, or like the tone of Jim's voice—growly, sad, impassioned, utterly kind—a voice that loves us because it finds tenderness behind even the weirdest cruelty. I keep an image of those stars he saw as a boy, but, also— something I left out—the sweetness of his mother's humming at the sink, reaching, filling him in the barn, heard above the grunting, sweating, absolute body of the man. And the horse, standing quiet now, without a mark on it.

Note: "FOR JIM WRIGHT" originally appeared in a different version in *The Seattle Review.*

ABOVE AND ON FOLLOWING PAGES: PHOTOGRAPHS BY STEVEN D. FOSTER, FROM *THE LAKE SERIES* (1981–82). (*TQ* #55)

Had I a hundred mouths

William Goyen

for June Arnold

On Good Friday, in the warm afternoon, the two nephews lay huddled against their uncle's bony body, each nestled in the crook of an arm. Often the nephews would be left in their uncle's care and their habit was to take off their clothes because of the Gulf humidity and lie cool on the bed together and listen to his stories, which were generally about the joys and despairs of desire. It was a murmur they heard, a gruff whisper, a telling voice that the older nephew would hear all his life. The uncle smelled of whiskey which he drank from time to time from a bottle under the bed. "When you boys going to get you some?" he suddenly asked at each meeting, as though anything had changed since they had met before. "I don't know," the younger nephew would answer, eight. But the older nephew, eleven, was already bound and not free enough to give any answer to such a question.

The uncle nestled his two nephews against his frail breast (it was said that he had TB). He seemed lonesome, not a part of anything. He had stayed home in the little town all these years, while big cities bloomed up nearby and "offered opportunities," living on, after his mother and father had died, one after the other, of pneumonia, in the epidemic, and his brothers and sisters had left, moved to somewhere else or died somewhere else, stayed under the roof and shelter of the old house his father had built and never saying much, except when his sister and sister-in-law would come from Houston on holidays and bring their sons, his favorites. Then he would come alive and open his mouth and out would come stories. On this Good Friday afternoon it seemed like he might be getting ready to tell another story about a woman and a man.

The younger nephew lay like a blank-eyed doll nested in the uncle's embrace; he might even have been dozing; he seemed to be in some peace under his uncle's arm, in some kind of a haven, unthreatened. After all, he was a fatherless child. His mother, the uncle's sister, had run his father off, so all his kinfolks said, because he was lazy and couldn't make a living. She worked in a sewing room at a factory. Did

1982

479

his mother think she was making a living? They had no clothes. He wanted to go find his father in Shreveport. He'd heard them say he was there. When he got old enough he would, too. He told this to his cousin.

But the older nephew was feeling another thing. He was beckoned by some new feeling and he felt powerless before it; and, most of all, he didn't care. He felt that he would go all the way with some feeling, when it would soon come, and not hinder it because it was wrong, and not be afraid of it, not care what happened, overwhelmed. His story-teller uncle had something to do with this feeling, he was not sure what; but surely it was a feeling that had first come to him from his uncle; it seemed to be in the command of the man, it seemed called up in him by the man's very nurturing presence, something like what motherliness had been for him not so long ago but now pushed away forever; and by the seduction of storyteller, the surrender of listener to teller, almost in a kind of lovemaking, of sensual possession, yet within innocence and purity. A dark new life had started under the command of his uncle and the hot spell of the stories that boiled like steam, tolled like a bell, sang like a solemn singer's song out of his mouth. But he already knew the feelings of lust. And why wouldn't he? Later, in the wrestling with it, he figured that he had already come in lust long ago, born in it, that he had already inherited it in his flesh long before he laid his head on the naked breast of his uncle and heard his tales of barns and gins and woods and under bridges, already had it in his blood, had been waiting only to be brought to it when the time came. Then that would change everything, that coming of something. It had already come, in a dark way, to some men and women of his family: some ran far away in its seizure and never came back, leaving everything; Aunt Beulah, Louetta's mother, did, the uncle had told, with a man, ran away with him from everybody—mama, papa, husband, child—and he was a Mexican that had worked on the place, named Juan, the uncle had told, from the Rio Grande Valley, and Beulah's husband then disappeared and never returned, either, leaving Louetta an orphan in her grandparents' house; sometimes people just suddenly ran away from everything and never came back. Life seemed dark, and sad beyond any way to tell it: there seemed no mouth that could utter the pain, only eyes to shed tears of it, or heart ache of it. Where was there any comfort? Where was God? In Sunday School the nephew had been shown the picture of a sweet man gathering under his arms a crowd of little children and the words under the picture said COME UNTO ME. Where in this family, thought the nephew, was this comforter? And lying in the cradle of his uncle's naked arm, he felt as close to that man as to his uncle, and as in need of him, on that Good Friday afternoon.

But did the younger nephew? Who knew? He did not seem to hear.

Or did he hear and just not care? Who knew? All the older nephew knew was that the stories fell upon the ripe ground of his brain, as in the Bible, and were ripening there and one day might come, bountiful fruit, from his own mouth. Then, in that rich time it would seem that he had not enough mouths to tell—or to re-tell—the stories of his uncle, and his own, now, there would be so many and they would come so richly and so fast. But the younger nephew seemed deaf. Wasn't that peculiar? Why was that, the older nephew asked himself, asked God, others, for all his life. Some heard and some did not, though the same news fell on the ears of each. And he also asked himself which one had peace, the teller-on—the mouthed—or the silent one in whom the story stopped. But did telling-on make any difference, help anything? The older nephew already had little peace. At home, more was expected of him than he could fulfill. But he would never let them know of his inadequacy. He carried the world, boy Atlas. His father, his uncle's brother, could not make enough money from his job to give his family what they "deserved," whatever that was; but that was his father's cry, and especially when he was drinking, "I can't give you all what you deserve. I'm not good enough for you." The older nephew's mother reminded him of his mission, charged him to be the one who would give them their deserving. That was what he would have to look for, those apples of gold such as Hercules sought—as in the story in school—and temporarily took upon his shoulders the world so that Atlas, who knew where the golden treasures were, could go get them and bring them back. Who would relieve the older nephew of his weight so that he could go? Well it would surely be his uncle who would bring him this ease. It was with these feelings that he heard the uncle's suddenly solemn voice. What was this voice, this tone? What story?

It was in the dark afternoon on a November day of sleet, told the uncle. We waited and we waited for Louetta to get home from her trip into town. The darker it got the scareder we got. More sleet fell and sleet was all in the frozen grass and in the trees. At four o'clock it was getting like night, it was so dark. Ben, they said, you better go on to the woods and look for her, Louetta's bound to be lost. I'll take the big lantern, I said. And so I started out alone. It was freezing cold, and dark fallen, just about. The sleet cut at me. I got to the haunted woods of the old sawmill. They was so lonesome and you couldn't hear nothing but the dropping of the stinging rain, sleeting. Nobody ever went back there in the ruined sawmill woods, back in there where the ruined kiln was, and the old log pond. Black people said it was haunted and that bad spirits lived there in the deep pineland because of a terrible thing that happened once, back in the days when the sawmill was flourishing. A white foreman and his strawboss caught three niggers fucking a Cushata Indian squaw back in there and they cut off their nuts and roasted them in the kiln and made the Cushata woman eat 'em. But the white men had been fucking the Cushata squaws as long as there'd been a sawmill. Squaws'd come over from the reservation at Moscow to give the white men some for some salt pork from the Commissary, or for some coffee. Cushatas supposed to have put a bad spell over the sawmill, one day a man'd fall under the logs in the log pond and his head'd be crushed between the logs; next a man would lose a whole hand in the planing saw; and there was some bad fires. Course the Cushatas was thieves and come in and stole at the Commissary and from people's houses, couldn't trust one of 'em, black niggers hated red Indians, red Indians despised the black niggers, the white men didn't trust either one of 'em, black *or* red, so—the best thing to do was drink a little whiskey and stay away from all of 'em; 's what your granddaddy did and what I did. When the sawmill finally died out, some folks said that was why, that the Cushata curse had finally got its vengeance. I don't know much about those days and glad they're gone, by the time I was old enough to sneak out to the old sawmill 'twas a wild grown-over thicket man or boy could hardly stand up in, said was snakes in there big as a man, and the mill fallen down and the Cushatas just about all died out, starved to death mostly, or had TB.

Anyway, I was walking over the frozen leaves on the old sawmill road and calling for Louetta. It scared me to hear my call in the woods. Louetta! No Louetta. I went towards the old kiln where there was a cave made under the fallen trees that were hit a long time ago by the tornado come on us out of Oklahoma and made a cave out of brambling together the great clumps of tree roots; time had made walls and the living trees, living on with leaves and vines, made a sheltering cave, dark and cool—the kind of a thing you will sometimes see nature make better than any man could, 'twas something of nature, a beaver could have made it, or wind of a big storm could've, and natural roots and earth wrapped over and bound together, could last a hundred years of time. I started towards that, when I heard a soft wailing, and on top of that a man's low voice, agrowling. I went quiet as I could towards the cave and I heard more and more the growling and the wailing. And then I heard the words of the man growling low how good it was, and the soft wailing. I laid in the bush until it was over and quiet and then I saw the man, a big red nigger, seemed aglow with redness all around him—ever seen that in a nigger? I don't know why it 'tis—I saw him come out of the cave and go on off. I was so scared. I waited until his footsteps was gone and then I shone my light onto . . . Louetta, lying in the cave. I thought she was dead. Louetta! I said. When she saw my face in the lantern light she wailed and whispered, Ben, Ben, please don't look! Please go away, please don't tell anybody, just let me alone. What happened? I said. The Nigra ran out at me in the woods, Louetta whispered, and I couldn't stop him. In the dark cave was the warm smell of woman, and I knew what the nigger had done. Well I'm not going to leave you, Louetta, like this, I said. Then help me to the river, she said. In Trinity River I put her down and she told me to go away a little, and I stood in the bushes and saw her wash and I was seventeen and felt what it was, of a man and a woman, the growling and wailing, that the red nigger knew, and what Louetta, my cousin, knew now, what he'd showed her in the cave, even though she was softly awailing in the riverwater, as she washed herself. This all come on me. Even in my hate of the nigger I felt a wanting for the woman washing herself of him, and the smell of the cave was all in my nose and all over me, on my hands that had helped Louetta up and to the river, a smell of the nigger stuff and the woman. I didn't want to wash that off, life, but then I didn't want them to smell it on me when we got home so I bent down into the river and washed my hands; and then it seemed like I'd made love to Louetta and that we was both awashing ourselves of it. When Louetta come out of the river, I wanted her. And I grabbed her. And took what the nigger took. I was just like him. She was hot, and still crazy, and ready, and took me, wailing Oh no, Oh no, please don't; said not you, not you. Just like the Nigra. But I was naked in the river—who took off my clothes?—and I was all over her. I said you've already done it now, the nigger made you ready, give to me what you gave to him. I was just like the nigger. And then in the midst of her wailing I took her, soft and made good by the red nigger. And I heard my growling, too, but I couldn't stop and Louetta couldn't stop taking me. We was both seventeen. There's a wildness, once it starts, you can't stop. That's what happens with it, you get crazy with it, once you've had it, once you've started. You boys will see, one day; and you'll remember what your uncle told you of it. The uncle growled, and the nephews were afraid. But the uncle went on. Now he seemed different than he had ever been in the older nephew's memory. We washed together, the uncle went on, me and Louetta, cousins, and when we washed each other, we both felt damnation on us; the Cushatas had put damnation on us. And that was the beginning. From then on, Louetta just couldn't stop wanting it and whispering of it, was a crazy woman; and I wasn't any different. We did it in the cave, day and night, wild. We was lost.

When the black baby was born in the cave and I helped Louetta with it, black, and said Oh my God Louetta black, it's black, I took it to the Orphanage up at Longview. But they would not take it, black. All day I was wandering with the little black baby boy, through the woods and hiding in the deep groves, wondering what to do. It was a warm little thing with big white eyes and I hated to give it up cause I felt that it was part mine, you understand. Towards dark I took the baby to Aunt Kansas Tate, our washerwoman way back in the woods in Niggertown and begged her to take it, and she looked, black, at me, the way they do when they're stern like that, a kind of look of God, and I knew she thought the baby was mine. Who is its Mama? asked Kansas Tate. And I told her that I found the baby in the woods. Must be God's child, she said. And then she held the warm child and I saw her love, and she took the baby boy. She named him Leander.

Louetta and I watched the boy grow. When Kansas Tate came to our place to wash and iron, the little boy Leander played near the washpot, under the chinaberry tree. And I saw Louetta watching him from the window. Leander was different, 'twas in his eyes. After all, he was borned in a cave of tree roots that the tornado from Oklahoma had made in 1918, tore up half of the county. He was as light-complected as a light Mescan boy, and real different. Something of Louetta was on him and sometimes I'd catch her standing at the back door peeking and staring out at the little boy playing in the woodpile. Leander grew on. A look of Louetta was strong over him. But I never saw her talk to him. Sometimes I'd play with Leander and as he grew up I taught him marbles and we'd shoot 'em; and I showed a lot of things a father would have shown him—how to aim and shoot a beebee gun, how to whittle a slingshot; and we hunted rabbit once, back of the old road. Until the Klu Klux boys caught us and warned me not to do it again. This hurt me before the boy, because what could I say to the boy, that we couldn't be friends or that we would have to hide to be friends. And so we slipped out to the cave in the sawmill woods where nobody ever came and we hid in the cave and played jackknife and I told him stories and answered some of the questions thai he was beginning to ask. And Leander grew. Louetta and I had made love oh I guess a million times by that time. We'd never got enough since the first time. We did it back in the woodshed at night and sometimes in the barn in pure daylight. But the hiding was terrible and our feeling of sin was terrible. How could we stop? I guess nobody in the world has ever stopped something like that, once it's started. But Louetta said she felt doom, said something terrible was going to happen to us, and I worried for fear she would do something to herself, sometimes she was ahurting so. But then we'd want each other again and no suffering God made, I hate to say it, could keep us from that wanting. One day you boys might know that, hope to God you won't, but one day you might, and guess you will; because nobody's perfect and we all got flesh on us.

When Leander was twelve Louetta came one day to where he was, working and helping out on the place, and gave him a red ring for his twelfth birthday that he put on his finger. He loved that ring and kept it there. I don't know why but I felt Leander was part my boy, that I'd helped make him, I'd held him first of anybody in the world and carried him when he was just borned, so he was that much mine. But the boy had two fathers, one run away, black, and one keeping a secret, white. I loved Leander. The town was afraid of him, though, because he was so light-complected and carried something unusual over him, not like any others. Sometimes I would see Leander watching Louetta when she was in the yard and I saw him gazing at her with such a look, almost as if he knew.

And now I'm going to tell you something. One night Louetta was sitting in the hot dark on the gallery, a darkest night, black as ink, was over us, the way it is back here when the moon's away, black as ink. The rest of us had gone up the road to see about old Uncle Ned that was sick. And Louetta saw a shape coming in the dark and she could not see who it was; and before she could call out anybody's name the figure was on her and tore at her and she could see that it was black and she begged and she fought. This's what she told me, because when I came home I found Louetta torn and wild and I smelled the smell again and saw that she'd been taken again. And I said was it the red nigger come back and she said black black. I run in the dark to get my shotgun that I kept in the hall in the corner, but then I heard a terrible sound, one I'll never forget, one of broken well-water, the groan of the deep porch well, and Louetta had thrown herself in the well. And right then the others came back, Mama and you boys' mothers, Holly and Eva, and I run for the boys to come and help bring up the body of Louetta from the well. When I held the cold body of Louetta how could I show all the feelings I felt before the others, just for a cousin? I tried not to pull that frozen body to my flesh like I had done so many times, my secret to my own damnation, and then I saw that Louetta's blue hand was clutched as though it held something it would never give up; and when nobody saw me, I broke open Louetta's hand and there, what she clutched and held on to, to her very death, in all her feelings of shamefulness and her, I'll bet you, tenderness, and would not even now give up until I broke the very bones of her hand, was the red ring of Leander. Fighting his wild hands, Louetta must have clawed it off Leander's finger. My howling was so loud that they ran to see if a snake had bit me or a blue hornet stung me, and before they knew it or anybody ever saw, I swallowed the red ring. It burned down my gullet like a coal of fire. I didn't know how I was going to live with my feelings. I wanted to jump into the well, but I couldn't show my hurting; and I couldn't show my shamefulness for all these secrets; and I couldn't show my despisement of Leander for killing my own secret Louetta—too many feelings for one person ever to stand and I don't know how I did it. But so much was happening. The boys wanted to run to Niggertown and round up the men, and I don't know what kept them from it, God himself did, I guess, if He could be in such an infernal place; because we all begged them to wait until Louetta was buried and they agreed if we would bury her the next day. The whole town was roiling and bonfires were burning all night and the boys put on their sheets and burnt a cross on the hill; was like the end of the world. All the pore niggers in Niggertown hid in their houses.

At the funeral suddenly come from out of nowhere Leander and Kansas Tate and stood by me. Leander was dirty and wild and looked like he had been hiding in the thicket all night long and Kansas Tate was in her black strongness and with a face that dared everybody. And suddenly Leander broke from us and ran and fell in the dirt of the open grave of Louetta and wailed and wailed, and oh the sight of that boy in the dirt of his mother's grave made me cry like a baby. People thought it was all for Louetta, but some was for Leander. Leander's hurting was terrible to see. They couldn't get him off the grave, he clung in the dirt, but the pallbearers in their white hoods seized him and dragged him away. Kansas Tate cried out that the Lord would strike them dead for blaming an innocent Negro boy and making him pay for somebody else's evil deed and they had to hold her in her wildness and daring of everybody. But the Klu Kluxes shouted burn him, make him pay for the one that raped and killed a white woman, a nigger in the hand is worth five in the bushes; and Clarence McKay, an old friend of Kansas' but a leader of the Klu Klux, said Kansas I can't stop them, they'll have to have them a scapegoat. And Kansas Tate cried out, Scapegoat? Scapegoat? Leander's not a scapegoat! He's a Christian boy that loved Miss Louetta. But they dragged Leander on off into the woods. Back in the woods, no matter what I knew about it or what I felt, I couldn't lay a hand on Leander. The red ring laid in my gut and cut it like a claw. Most of the Klu Kluxes sympathized with my hurting for my cousin Louetta, but when they tore off his clothes from his brown young man's body they had to hold me to keep me from running to stop them and protect Leander; but then I rushed with them when they cut him clean as a woman and hung his young manhood on a tree branch. And I stood there crazy with the red ring of Leander and Louetta in me and saw them tar and feather Leander's brown young body, now neither man nor woman, and I vomited on my knees in the night. And there on the ground in the flare of the Klu Klux torches I saw the gleaming of the red ring, my damnation to curse me. I wanted to stomp it into my own vomit and crush it into the ground, but I took it and put it in my pocket.

And then they brought Leander into town and run him howling down Main Street on that funeral night and then they let him go, hollering to him to get out of town. That night Kansas Tate in her misery fell in a stroke and died, and I run far into the woods and drank my whiskey in the dark of the deep woods and laid like a log in the leaves. And then I crawled and hid in the dark of the cave.

The uncle took a long swallow of whiskey. And then he said, very low, I've never told a soul this story until now. Had I a hundred mouths I could not have told the story; it was too much of a story to tell. I've kept the tale of Leander and Louetta a secret all these years and have drank a ton of whiskey on it. And now I've told it to you boys, my brother's son and my sister's son, one just becoming a man and the other still adozing in his little boyhood. And the uncle reached again under the bed and brought up the bottle to his mouth. The golden fumes of whiskey spread over the nephews, and the carnality of that moment, the despairs of the flesh and the sorrows of the story of Leander brought life down upon the older nephew so heavily that it seemed unbearable; and he wondered how he would ever bear his feelings that his heart and his body were just beginning to give to him. He understood then his uncle's feelings and the ton of whiskey used to deaden them, but he vowed he would never deaden life, that he would feel his feelings full and that he would not fall under their burden as his uncle had, in hiding and numbness. He would feel and he would tell, even as his uncle had, finally, this afternoon.

But the uncle had more to tell. His voice went on, graver than the nephew had ever heard it. That day as I laid in the cave and wanting to die, I heard a sound, and it was Leander rolling on the ground in the leaves and grunting like an animal dying. He'd torn his flesh from the bone trying to get off the tar that had clung to him like another skin. He had skinned himself. And then I laid and watched him go to the river where his unbeknownst mother had washed herself of what had made him, and where I had washed myself, too. And there by the river I saw Leander, rising up out of the river, a scary figure, and I saw him tear at himself and I heard his wailings of pain. I'll drown him, I said to myself. But I heard myself call, Leander! Leander! I called. When he saw me, who I was, he howled at me like Satan the devil, white eyes flashing, and came out of the water, steaming and red like a young Satan and spit at me like a fiend. I saw his burnt face and I saw his clawed bleeding body and I saw him limp from a foot that had been bad hurt. Leander! I cried. I ought to kill you for what you done. But I can't help it I am your friend and I ask you to remember all our life together; sometime I'll tell you how I held you when you was just a little baby. I will help to heal you if you will let me. And then I held out the red ring and Leander fell passed out and I picked him up from the water like a raw piece of meat and took him to the cave and tied him to a root. Poor lonesome lost nigger boy, there's not any more can be done to you for what you did and I can't kill you, like somebody'd tell me to.

I kept Leander hid back in the cave, tied to the tree root, and nursed him, every day I'd come and feed and doctor and nurse him, right there in the deep cave of trees where he was borned and where he was made on the night I heard his maker crying out, sixteen years ago. He never asked one question, never said one word. I set and drank my whiskey. In the secret woods, in the cave, Leander was healing from the Klu Klux. He never told his feelings, never said a word. He hid his hate, and what love could he have? The foxes and the deer came to the cave and put their noses to his face, and the birds knew Leander. Summer and winter and spring Leander saw come over the woods; and Leander was seventeen. Every night I'd come and walk him out of the cave and in the light of the moon, I saw the terrible scars and patches of white on him. His beauty was ruined and all over his face was white scars and his torn mouth was healed crooked and his lips looked like they were burnt away. The healed skin on his face and on his arms and all over his body had turned white. In the moonlight I saw that Leander was striped and spotted like an animal. He limped because of his hurt leg some way, but he would never let me see what was the matter with it. His big eyes glared pure white, his hair was all coming back wild and long like a white man's and 'twas of a reddish color like his bedeviled father's. Who was this boy? Who could live like that, who would want to, you answer me that. And he never showed his feelings; no matter how many times I asked the question why would you do something like that, he would look at me with that terrible look as if he was asking, do what? When I finally held him up against the wall of the cave and said tell me, tell me why you would do something like that, and I almost told him about the red nigger his father and that he had done it to his own mother, but I couldn't, I couldn't do that, I guess I just loved Leander too much to kill his heart like that, if he had any of it left, and if any of his heart was left he was probably saving it for his mother and his father if ever he would find them. Anyway, when he didn't say a word I finally realized that he couldn't, that his voice must have been burnt out of his throat. Because when I finally held him by the throat he groaned a sound of ah-ah-ah and his breath smelled of old smoke of the Klu Klux Klan. Leander was burnt inside too. Poor lost nigger boy. So I just came and sat in the cave with him and drank my whiskey in the dark, quiet as he was. This was when I give him back the red ring and he put it on his burnt finger.

I begun some days to let Leander loose. He strayed from the cave more and more. I warned him not to, but he'd wander in the woods. I saw him begin to leap and to run, the way a cripple does—or a crippled animal. Because that's what he would have looked like to any hunter if any had come out there, and they would have shot him dead. Once when I came and could not find him and I was afraid to call out his name, I looked and looked and finally found him by the log pond where the old kiln was and heavy trees that vines crawled up to the top of and fell down, all blooming, morning glory and honeysuckle and muscadine vines, and trumpets; this was where I found Leander. I saw him sitting on the old walls of the kiln, looking into the pond. It was just at twilight. An owl begun to make its hurting sound. And I thought, who is this creature of the woods, borned in the woods and burnt in the woods and healed, and hiding in the woods from his persecutors and from all humanity? And at that time I was afraid for Leander and for myself, wondering what we would ever do. There was a road going to be built soon across the woods—that's the Highway now, I-17—and I heard talk of some kind of a plant going to be started—which is now of course the Dye Works—and I was scared. And I said to Leander, you muss not ever do that again, run off from the cave that far. But Leander didn't want to go on living hiding, I saw that, he wanted free, I could see that. And I knew that he had seen himself in the pond.

But he went on. Leander went on living, continued the uncle. Why? You'd have thought he'd just hang himself from a tree or drown hisself in the log pond—many times I expected to come and find that he had done that, killed himself by his own hand. Like his mother did. But Leander stayed alive and kept living, don't know why. And then one day when I came to the cave he was gone. I looked everywhere. I couldn't call because I didn't know who'd hear me. At first I run this way and then I run that way and then I was going around in circles. If even a branch of a tree cracked, I thought it was Leander. Then I got my bearings from the black piece of smokestack of the old sawmill that stuck up like a knife and I ran to the kiln and whispered Leander! I saw some birds that must have been his friends and I asked the birds, where's Leander? And I saw a doe and her fawn and they perked up and looked right at me and I said, please tell me where has Leander gone. Because he'll never make it all alone. And then when I shone a light into Leander's old dark corner of the cave, something gleamed. And there, on a tree root, dangling on a string, was the red ring, the sad red ring. The uncle reached under the bed, drew up the bottle of whiskey to his mouth and took a deep swallow from it, the deepest of all. Then he was quiet for a long time. Finally the older asked, What happened to Leander? and the uncle answered softly, I never saw Leander again. I went away and never came back again to the cave in the sawmill woods. Wasn't too long before bulldozers leveled the place and men came in and built the state highway through there: I-17.

And then they lay silent together for a long time, the uncle, the older nephew and the young one. And in a while the nephews heard their uncle sleeping. But the older cousin did not sleep. He lay fiercely awake and felt the flesh of his uncle against his side, the beat of his heart and the breeze of his breath, whiskey-laden, upon his cheek.

Some years later, the older nephew, who had long ago left the place, came back home to his uncle's funeral. He had died, they called and told him, alone in a drifter's mission, drunk on a cot, in Houston. And as he stood at the grave, unwelcomed by those of his kinfolks who were left, a group of hooded white figures came out from the trees and gathered around the coffin; and he saw, when one of them lifted for a moment his mask, the face of the young nephew. The older nephew felt a chill of terror and rage; but he held still until the preacher, who had stepped forward and was reading Galatians 6:8, "For he that soweth to his flesh shall of the flesh reap corruption," had finished. And then he turned his back to the place and left it—forever, he vowed.

And then more years passed and the older nephew had drunk his uncle's whiskey, had looked here and there, had lost love and speech, had been living hidden for nights and days away from life in a dark world of fear and dumbness, Leander's brother, bound back to the land of his uncle. And returning home late one night on a darkened street in a cold city, the older nephew heard a ghostly sound of breaking glass, and he saw coming towards him out of the darkness a startling shape of beauty and oddness. As if drawn together, the figure and the nephew moved toward each other; and when they confronted each other it was as though they had come together out of the ages, face to face. The nephew looked upon a phantom face, as if what face had been there had been burned away and this was the painted mask of it. The creature's head was covered with a rich mane of hair, and in the street light there appeared to be a red glow over it. The being was clothed in a glimmering garment of scales of glass; and colored feathers were reflected in their mirrors. And the nephew saw that gaudy rings glistened on scarred brown hands. Leander! he whispered. Why did he think that this was the burnt boy, the orphan child of lust, that on a long-ago Good Friday afternoon signaled the end of his boyhood? Leander! he called. But there was no sign of feeling in the shadowed ancient eyes which, for a searing moment, locked upon him. And then the phantom being moved around the nephew and went on, swathed in the delicate tinkling of glass.

Leander! he softly called, once more, Leander! And he was calling to his uncle and his uncle's sorrow and to all storytelling, all redemption: Leander, Leander. But the figure steadily moved away, as if it were made of glass and falling delicately to pieces in its ruined march, into the gloom of the night, farther and farther away from any recognition, any redemption, any forgiveness.

And all that night the nephew put this down and told again the story that his uncle told him, a story that he could not have told before had he had a hundred mouths to tell it with. In the morning, in the silver light of dawn over the old city of his miracles, miraculously refreshed he saw in the mirror his naked body, its skin, its haunch, its breast: the ancient sower's flesh, the reaper's.

from
Steht noch dahin
Marie Luise Kaschnitz

SISTER—SISTER

You've been dead eight years now, I say to my sister, would you like to know what's been happening? No, my sister says. Fine, I say, then I'll tell you. The Vietnam war still isn't over. I could have predicted that, my sister says. There's still no cure for cancer, I say. You've got to die of something, my sister says. There are planes now, I say, which have room for five hundred passengers and take a few hours to fly between Europe and America. That doesn't interest me, my sister says. All bills are figured by computers, I say. They store all the knowledge in the world, and you can ask them questions. I don't understand, my sister says. You've studied law, I say. Perhaps you'll be interested to know that the accused no longer rises before the judge and that the witnesses litter the courtroom. I condemn that, my sister says. Perhaps, I say, you'd also like to know that parents nowadays have great trouble bringing up their children. That the children talk back to their parents and even hit them. Serves them right, my sister says. Recently they flew around the moon, I say. They took pictures from there, and on the pictures the earth is as blue as a sapphire. I wish I could have seen that, my sister says.

Translated by Lisel Mueller

1982

Prayer for the dying

Willis Johnson

The day Yakov Kaputin died he managed to make the nurse understand that he wanted to see Father Alexey. Yakov had lived in America for thirty years but he did not speak English. He scribbled a faint, wiggly number on the paper napkin on his lunch tray and pointed a long knobby finger back and forth between the napkin and his bony chest. "You want me to call, do you, dear?" the nurse asked in a loud voice that made Yakov's ears ring. Yakov could not understand what she said but he nodded, "*Da.*"

When the telephone rang Father Alexey was just dozing off. It was July. Crickets were chirring in the long dry grass outside his window. The priest was lying in his underwear listening to a record of Broadway show tunes on the new stereo his mother had bought him. His long beard was spread out like a little blanket on his chest. The window shade was down and a fan was softly whirring.

He thought it was the alarm clock that rang and tried to turn it off.

"Mr. Kaputin wants you to come to the hospital," the nurse said with finality, as if announcing some binding decision from above.

He did not know how long he had slept. He felt shaky and unfocused.

"I can't," he said.

"Is this the Russian priest?"

"This is Father Alexey." His voice seemed to echo far away from him. "I'm busy just now."

"Well, we're all busy, dear," the nurse said. She paused as if waiting for him to see the truth in that and do the right thing.

"What is it this time?" Father Alexey said with a sigh.

"I just came from him," the nurse began to converse chattily. ("That's better now," her tone seemed to say.) "He's a real sweetheart. He wrote your number down. He didn't touch his lunch, or his breakfast. I don't think he feels well. Of course we can't understand a word he says, and he can't understand us. . ."

"He never feels well," Father Alexey said irritably. "You usually do not feel well when you have cancer."

"Well," the nurse said indignantly. "I've called. I've done *my* duty. If you don't want to come. . ."

Father Alexey sighed another large sigh into the receiver. He hated the hospital. He hated the way it smelled, the way grown men looked in little johnny coats, the way Yakov's bones were all pointed. Besides that, it was very hot out. During the entire morning service not even the hint of a breeze had come in the door of his little church. In the middle of a prayer he thought he might faint. He had had to go into the Holy of Holies and sit down.

"It's not a matter of 'not wanting,'" he said pointedly. "I'll have to adjust my schedule, and that's not always easy. I don't know when I can be there. I have to try to find a ride."

He lay for a while longer with the fan blowing on him, his hands clasped on his soft white stomach. The sheet under him was clean and cool. He looked tragically at the window shade. It was lit up like a paper lantern.

Father Alexey lived next to the church in an old house with a cupola, fancy molding and derelict little balconies. A rusty iron fence tottered around the unmowed yard. Once every seven or eight years one or two sides of the house got a coat of paint. The different shades of paint and the balusters missing from the little balconies gave the house a patched, toothless look. On rainy days water dripped down the wall next to Father Alexey's bed. He complained to Mr. Palchinsky, the president of the Union of True Russians, which owned the house. Mr. Palchinsky got the Union to provide each room with a plastic bucket. Father Alexey would have tried to fix the roof himself but he did not know how to do it. Yakov said he knew how to do it but he was too old to climb a ladder and besides they did not have a ladder.

Yakov's room was next to Father Alexey's. Each night after the old man said his prayers he would say good night to the priest through the wall.

Father Alexey did not always answer. Yakov was a nice man but he could be a pain. He was always talking, telling stories about himself. Yakov in the forest, Yakov in the Civil War, Yakov in the labor camp, Yakov tending flower beds for some big shot in White Plains. Father Alexey knew them all. And whenever he made an observation with which Yakov did not agree, Yakov would say, "You're young yet. Wait a while. When you're older, you'll see things more clearly."

The priest knew it was one of the things people in town said about him: he was young. He tried to look older by wearing wire-rimmed glasses. He was balding, and that helped. Not that it was a bad thing to say, that he was young. If people really wanted to be disparaging—as when the Anikanov family got mad at him because he forgot to offer them the cross to kiss at their mother's memorial service—they went around reminding their neighbors that he was not Russian at all but an American from Teaneck; if they knew about his mother being Polish they called him a Pole; they brought up the fact that he once had been a Catholic. If they wanted to truly drag his name through the mud, they called him a liberal, even though he almost always voted Republican.

Yakov had been to the hospital before, once when he had his hernia and once for hemorrhoids. This time, even before they knew it was cancer, he sensed he wouldn't be coming home. He was, after all, almost ninety years old. He carefully packed his worn suit, the photographs of his wife, his Army medal, some old books that looked as if they had been rained on, into cardboard boxes which he labeled and stacked in his room. He left an envelope with some money with Father Alexey and also his watering pail for his geraniums. When the car came he didn't want to go. Suddenly he was afraid. Father Alexey had to sit with him in his room, assuring him it was all right, he was going to get well. He carried Yakov's suitcase out to the car. Yakov was shaking. When Father Alexey waved good-bye the old man started to cry.

The hospital was in the city, fifteen miles away. Once a week the senior citizens' bus took people from the town to the shopping center, which was only a mile from the hospital, and you could get a ride if there was room. But if you did not have a car and it was not Thursday, you had to call Mikhail Krenko, the dissident. He had a little business on the side driving people to the city for their errands.

Krenko worked nights on the trucks that collected flocks from the chicken barns. He had arrived in town one day after jumping off a Soviet trawler. It was said that he offered a traffic policeman two fresh codfish in exchange for political asylum. People suspected he was a spy. They were almost certain he had Jewish blood. Why else, they asked each other, would the Soviets have given him up so easily? Why had he come to live in a godforsaken town that did not even have a shopping center?

Krenko was a short man with limp yellow hair and a round face like a girl. He chewed gum to cover the smell of his liquor, sauntered with his hands in his pockets and did not remove his hat upon entering a house, even with an ikon staring him in the face. In the churchyard one Sunday people overheard him call Mr. Palchinsky *Papashka*— "Pops." Anna Kirillovna Nikulin told of the time she rode to the city with him and he addressed her as Nikulina—not even *Mrs.* "Here you are, Nikulina," he said, "the drugstore."

Some female—an American; young, by the sound of her—answered when Father Alexey dialed his number.

"He's in the can," she said.

"Well, would you call him, please?" he said impatiently.

"Okay, okay, don't have a kitten."

She yelled to Krenko. "I don't know—some guy having a kitten," she said.

When Krenko came on the telephone, the priest said as sarcastically as he could, "This is Father Alexey—the 'guy' from your church."

"Hey, you catch me hell of time, with pants down."

"I called you," Father Alexey replied stiffly, "because one of my parishioners happens to be very ill."

He hung his communion kit around his neck and went to wait for Krenko in the sparse shade of the elm tree in front of the house. Only a few branches on the old tree still had leaves. In some places big pieces of bark had come off. The wood underneath was as dry and white as bone.

Across the street was the town's funeral home. Sprays of water from a sprinkler and a couple of hoses fell over the trim green grass and on the flowers along the walk. Father Alexey held his valise with his holy vestments in one hand and in the other his prayer book, a black ribbon at the prayers for the sick. He could feel the sweat already running down his sides.

He thought how it would be to strip off his long hot clothes and run under the spray, back and forth. He saw himself jumping over the flowers. He could feel the wet grass between his toes. Setting down his valise, he took off his hat and wiped his face and bald head with his handkerchief. He fluttered the handkerchief in the air. In a minute it was dry.

Then from behind him a window opened and he heard Mrs. Florenskaya call. He pretended not to hear. He did not turn around until the third time.

"Oh, hello, Lidiya Andreyevna," he said, holding the bright sun behind his hand.

"Somewhere going, *batiushka?*" the old woman asked in her crackly voice.

"Yes," the priest said reluctantly.

"Good," Mrs. Florenskaya said. "*Ich komme.*"

The Union of True Russians had bought the house as a retirement home (it had been a fine, sturdy house, the home of a sea captain; the church next door had been the stable for his carriage horses) and at one time all the rooms and flats had been occupied. Everyone was gone now, dead or moved away—mostly dead. The whole parish had grown older all at once, it seemed. Now with Yakov in the hospital, Father Alexey was alone in the old house with Mrs. Florenskaya. Every day she shuffled up and down the empty, echoing hallway in her worn slippers and Father Alexey would hear her crying. In nice weather she cried out on the porch. The first time he heard her—it was shortly after he had arrived to take over the parish a year ago (his predecessor, Father Dmitri, had started to drink and was transferred back to New York)—Father Alexey had run upstairs to see what was wrong. Mrs. Florenskaya listened to his beginner's Russian with a happy expression on her face, as if he were trying to entertain her. Then she had replied in a mixture of English and German, although he didn't know any German, that a bandit was stealing spoons from her drawer.

He no longer asked.

After a minute the front door opened and the little woman came spryly down the stairs carrying a cane which she did not seem to need. A paper shopping bag and an old brown purse hung from one arm. She was wearing a kerchief and a winter coat.

"Where going *Sie*, little father?" She came into the shade and smiled up at him.

When he told her about Yakov, she sighed heavily. "Old people just closing eyes," she said. Her chin started to wobble.

"Aren't you hot in that coat, Lidiya Andreyevna?" he asked.

She pulled a wadded tissue out of her pocket. "*Sie* young man, *Sie* can *arbeiten*. I am old." She wiped her nose, then lifted her chin in the air. "I *arbeiten* in Chicago," she said proudly. "In fine hotel."

Father Alexey looked down the empty street.

"He's late," he said.

"*Ja*," the old woman said emphatically, as if he had confirmed all she had said. "Many *zimmer* taken care of; wash, clean, making beds."

A short distance from where they stood the road dropped steeply to the river. Father Alexey could see the far bank and the dark pines of the forest beyond. The sky was blue and still. The leaves were motionless on the trees, as if they were resting in the heat. Above the brow of the hill, Father Alexey saw two heads appear then slowly rise like two plants pushing up into the sun. The heads were followed by two bodies, one long, one square. They came up over the hill and came slowly in the heat toward the priest and Mrs. Florenskaya. They were dressed for the city, the woman in a dress with flowers, the man in a suit and tie. The woman was the long one. The man was sheer and square like a block of stone. As they drew near, the man took the woman's arm in his thick hand and stopped her short of the shade. They looked back down the road. The man checked his watch.

Bending around the priest, Mrs. Florenskaya peered at them with curiosity.

"Good heavens," she said at last in Russian, "why are you standing in the sun? Come here, dearies, with us."

The man gave them half a smile. "It's all right," he said as if embarrassed. But the woman came right over.

"Thank you," she said as if the shade belonged to them. "That hill! We had to stop four times. Stepanka, come join these nice people."

She took him by the arm. "Now that's much better—no?"

Father Alexey introduced himself and said in Russian that the weather was very hot.

"Fedorenko," the man said but he did not offer his hand. He added in English: "My wife."

"Ach, Sie sprechen Englisch!" Mrs. Florenskaya said delightedly. "I, too!"

From time to time Father Alexey ran into them in the market or on the street. The man was Ukrainian, the woman Byelorussian. The woman would always smile. Once in a while the man nodded stiffly. On Sundays Father Alexey would see them pass by on their way to the Ukrainian church.

"Are you waiting for someone?" the man's wife asked, continuing the English. "We're supposed to meet Mr. Krenko here."

"He was supposed to be here ten minutes ago," the priest said.

"We're going to do a little shopping," the woman informed them. "Stepan's not allowed to drive. It's his eyes. They wouldn't renew his license. We're going to get some glasses for him. He doesn't want them. He thinks they'll make him look old."

"Not old," her husband said sharply. "Don't need it. What for spend money when don't need it?"

"You see?" she said hopelessly.

As they waited the sun grew hotter. They inched closer together under the tree. They could see the heat coming up from the road and from the black shingles of the roofs that showed above the hill. Mrs. Fedorenko fanned her face. Mrs. Florenskaya unbuttoned her coat. They stared longingly at the glistening spray of water across the way. There was a rainbow in the spray and the water glistened on the green grass and on the flowers and on the lawn sign on which the undertakers had painted in gold an Orthodox cross beside the regular Christian one.

Finally they heard an engine straining. Up over the hill through the waves of heat came Krenko's car. It was a big car, several years old, all fenders and chrome. Upon reaching level ground it seemed to sigh. It came up to them panting.

Krenko pushed open the front door.

"You're late," Father Alexey told him. With a look of distaste, he set his valise with his holy vestments on Krenko's zebra-skin seat. Mr. and Mrs. Fedorenko climbed into the back, followed by Mrs. Florenskaya, who nudged Mr. Fedorenko into the middle with her bony hip.

"Where is she going?" Krenko said.

"Ask her," the priest shrugged.

"Where you going, lady?"

"Never mind," Mrs. Florenskaya said.

"Not free, you know. Cost you money."

"Ja. Everything all time is money."

"Ten dollars," Krenko said.

"Ja, ja."

"You have?"

Mrs. Florenskaya took a rag of a bill out of her pocketbook and waved it angrily under Krenko's nose. She put it back and snapped her purse. "Everything is money," she said. Tears suddenly rolled out from under her eyeglasses.

"Crazy old woman," Krenko muttered.

"May we go?" Father Alexey said.

They drove around the block onto the main street of the town. On the street was the market, the bank, the hardware store, the laundromat, the boarding house where old people who did not belong to the Union of True Russians lived, and a variety store where they sold pizzas. Part way down the hill Krenko stopped and blew the horn.

"Another passenger, I presume?" Father Alexey said.

"Make it when sun is shining," Krenko winked.

From a door marked "Private" stepped Marietta Valentinova, the famous ballerina who lived over the hardware store. A white cap with green plastic visor kept the sun from her small severe face. Krenko got out and opened the front door, giving her a mock bow, which she ignored.

She had been at the St. Vladimir's Day service that morning at Father Alexey's church. Several members of the parish were named Vladimir, so there had been a good attendance in spite of the heat, more than a dozen. St. Olga's Day a few days earlier had not been nearly so successful, but then there was only one Olga in town, and she was sick and couldn't come. Marietta Valentinova had stood in her usual place in the center, where she was in range of any idle chatter, which she would silence at once with a scalding look. She also kept an eye on the ikon candles. She did not like to let them burn down more than halfway, and all during the service she was blowing them out and removing them from their holders. People who had lit the candles complained about it to each other but none dared say anything to her. On Sundays or saints' days, it didn't matter, she put a dollar in the basket. No one had ever seen her take back change. But she was very severe.

"Good afternoon, Marietta Valentinova," Father Alexey said. "Ya yedu v gospital."

The ballerina glanced at his valise. One corner of her small red mouth lifted slightly. "I thought you have been looking thin," she teased him in English. "That's the trouble with being monk: no wife to feed you."

"It's Yakov Osipovich," he said, reddening.

"Well," she said, "shall you move over or must I stand in sun all day?"

"Maybe you get in first, lady," Krenko said. "With such little legs you fit better in middle."

"I will thank you to pay attention to your own legs. And also your manner. Who do you think you are, blowing that horn?"

"Like joking with her," Krenko winked when the priest got out to let the ballerina in.

"How about the air conditioning?" Father Alexey said when Krenko got back behind the wheel.

"Okay. First got to put up all windows," Krenko said. Then he turned a switch. Air blew out from under the dashboard.

"I think that's the heat," said Father Alexey.

"Is okay," Krenko said. "Got to cool up."

They drove to the bottom of the hill and turned up along the river. The water lay flat and colorless between banks of colorless clay. Soon they were in the woods. The road ran over the tops of hills and down to stream beds filled with rocks. The undergrowth was dense and tangled and they could not see the river. They passed a farmhouse with a barn propped up by poles. In a clearing slashed in the woods a mobile home squatted like a gypsy, its children and its trash strewn round the yard.

The air was blowing out, but the car was stifling. They were squeezed together, Father Alexey with his valise on his lap. Marietta Valentinova smelled Krenko sweating. She moved a fraction closer to the priest, who had pulled out his handkerchief and was wiping his face.

"If I don't get some air, I am going to faint," Marietta Valentinova said.

Krenko moved the switch another notch. The hot air blew out harder.

"Sometimes takes couple minutes," he said.

"In a couple of minutes we will be cooked," the ballerina said. "Can't you see I'm dying?"

"Hold it!" Krenko said. He felt under the dashboard. "Now is coming."

Father Alexey wiggled his small white fingers in the air blowing on his knees. It was still hot.

"Now is coming," Krenko said confidently.

"Open a window," the ballerina commanded.

"You going to let air condition out. . ."

"Did you hear me?" she said in a voice so severe that everyone at once rolled down his window.

"Thank God," said the priest as the hot wind blew in on them. They put their hands out into it, groping for a current of coolness.

After a while Mrs. Fedorenko said, "It was very hot in New Jersey, too. That's where we lived."

"Hot like hell," Krenko agreed, although he had never been to New Jersey. "Here is not hot."

"I am very glad to hear that this is not hot," the ballerina said. She held a hanky over her mouth as they passed a chicken barn.

"More hot in California," Mr. Fedorenko said. "I been all over United States. Many Ukrainian people live in California. Many Russian, too," he added for the benefit of the ballerina who had cocked her ear toward him, showing him her profile, the raised eyebrow. "And many Ukrainian. Not same thing."

"Do tell us about it," the ballerina said haughtily. To Marietta Valentinova there was no such thing as a Ukrainian. That was modern nationalist nonsense. What was the Ukraine?—*Malorossiya*, Little Russia. They were all Russians.

"You are from New Jersey, *batiushka?*" Mrs. Fedorenko asked to change the subject.

"Yes. It is very hot in New Jersey. I haven't been to California."

"*I* in Chicago *arbeiten*," Mrs. Florenskaya said.

"You were saying something about the *malorossy*, I believe?" the ballerina said.

"Not Little Russians, lady. Ukrainian."

"All right, Stepanka. Did you hear? *Batiushka* also lived in New Jersey."

Mr. Fedorenko folded his heavy arms. "Don't call us *malorossy*."

"I don't call you anything," the ballerina smiled coldly.

"No?" Mr. Fedorenko pushed forward his big chin. "What are you calling ten million Ukrainians? The ones Russia starved?"

"If you are speaking of the Soviet Union, I'll thank you not to call it Russia," the ballerina said. "I even hate to say that word—*soviet*."

"Okay," Krenko said, "long time ago—okay?"

"I have a question," Father Alexey said.

"You, too," said Mr. Fedorenko accusingly. His face was very red.

"Me too, what?"

"Stepanka," Mrs. Fedorenko implored.

"I see you Four July parade. See you turn away when Ukrainian club marching. You don't remember, huh?"

"I didn't turn away."

"I wouldn't blame you if you did," the ballerina said. "I certainly would."

"I didn't."

"That's enough, Stepanka."

"Maybe I just looked somewhere else," the priest said. "There is a big difference between looking somewhere else at a given moment and turning away."

"Of course there is," Mrs. Fedorenko assured him.

"I know how is seeing," her husband said.

"All right, Stepanka. What were you going to ask before, *batiushka*? You had a question."

"I don't know," the priest said dejectedly. After a moment he said, "I guess I was going to ask why everyone is speaking English."

"You're absolutely right," Mrs. Fedorenko said. "You need to learn." And then she said something in Russian, or Ukrainian, or Byelorussian, which Father Alexey did not quite catch. In the conversation that followed, he heard many words he knew but there were many words in between—they spoke so quickly—which he could not understand.

Then there was silence.

He looked around and saw the others looking at him.

"*Nu?*" the ballerina said.

"*Shto?*" he asked.

"*Shto ti dumayesh?*"

"*Shto?*"

"Heavens, my dear Father Alexey," the ballerina changed to English. "We are talking about poor Mr. Kaputin. Haven't you been listening?"

"Of course I've been listening."

"Well, then?"

"Well, what?"

"Is he getting better? You did say you were going to see him?"

"Yes, of course, Marietta Valentinova. I know. I understand." He had picked out Yakov's name in the wash of words but assumed they were talking about the old man's geraniums. Yakov grew them in his window box. They were big and healthy flowers, all from pinchings from other people's flower pots, and it was the thing people saw when they walked past the house. Father Alexey shifted the valise on his lap. His clothes were stuck to him.

"The nurse said he wasn't feeling well," he said. "Who knows what that means? Last time they said the same thing and I went all the way there and there was nothing wrong with him. He was fine. He just wanted someone to talk to. I walk in and he says, 'I'm glad you came, *batiushka*. Have you paid my electric bill? I think I paid it before I came here, but I can't remember.' I told him everything was taken care of. 'That's good,' he says. 'I was worried. So how are you, *batiushka*? It's hot out, isn't it?' "

"How sweet," the ballerina said.

"Sweet? It cost me—the church—ten dollars."

"Don't blame me," Krenko said. "They don't give the gas away yet."

There were more farms, more rocky fields and unpainted houses that tilted one way and another. Then more woods broken by raw-cut clearings full of stumps and weeds and plastic toys and house trailers on cement blocks.

Of the farms and houses, Father Alexey could almost pick which was Russian, which American. None of the people in them had money, you could see that easily enough, but the American ones almost seemed to be the way they were out of stubbornness. There was something in a savage, defiant way willful about the broken porches, the rusty machinery outside the barns. The Russian yards were unkempt only with weeds and overgrown grass and the woods coming closer and closer. They had little gardens, just tiny patches, with flowers and a few vegetables. Father Alexey started to get depressed.

"Did you ever think," he said, looking out the window, "that you would be here?"

No one said anything.

"Are you speaking to me?" Marietta Valentinova said.

"Yes. To anyone."

"Think I would be here? Of course not. Who would?"

"Then why did you come?"

"We're getting personal, I see." But she wasn't angry.

"I'm sorry. I was just thinking. . ."

"You want to know? All right, I came for my health."

Mr. Fedorenko gave a guffaw. His wife pulled at his sleeve.

"It's true. Why would I leave New Jersey? I had a nice apartment. When I danced I got good write-ups. You should see the people who came to my ballets. You could barely find a seat. And it wasn't a small auditorium in that school, either. Only thing, the air was no good for my health. All that pollution. So where does a Russian go? You've got to have a church. So you go where there are Russians. At least there there were people with intelligence," she added over her shoulder. "Not like this godforsaken place."

"How many people lived in New Jersey!" Mrs. Fedorenko said before her husband could say anything. "We like it here, though," she said, patting Mr. Fedorenko's thick square hand. "We've had enough big things—the war, DP camp. After the camp we went to Venezuela. On Monday morning you turned on the radio and if there was a revolution you didn't have to go to work. Too many things. Here it's small and quiet. And Stepan always wanted to live near a river. He says that way you will never starve."

"I live in this place eighteen year," declared Mrs. Florenskaya. "*Achtzehn jahr,*" she added for Father Alexey's benefit. "All in this old house."

"Eighteen years," said the ballerina sadly. "I couldn't stand this place so long." But she already had been in the town more than half that.

Father Alexey calculated. Eighteen years ago he was nine years old. It was a whole year in his life, but all he could remember of being nine was being in the fourth grade and Sister Rita St. Agnes being his teacher, a stern little woman with thick black eyebrows who had seemed to take to him after his father died. "The boy with the laughing eyes," she called him affectionately. Sometimes he looked into the mirror to see why she called him that. The eyes belonged to a bald, not very old person who was expected to be full of answers for people far older than he, people who were afraid of getting sick and of nursing homes and hospitals and what was going to happen to them. He dispensed answers like the holy water he flung on heads and shoulders at a feast-day procession. Answers for death and fear and sadness and stolen spoons. And in all his life he had only lived in New Jersey with his mother and in the monastery in New York and now in a little town no one had ever heard of. How could he know?

In another eighteen years he would be forty-five. How much would he know then? Would he see things more clearly, as Yakov said? Krenko, the ballerina might still be around. Krenko probably would be in jail, he thought with some satisfaction, or in the real estate business or some scheme, making money one way or another. The ballerina would be an old woman if she were still alive. The others would surely be dead. Most of the people in the parish would be dead.

He was becoming more and more alone in the world.

The shopping center was on a long broad avenue that ran between the interstate and the city. It once had been a road of fine old houses with wide porches and broad lawns and beds of marigolds and tulips. A few remained. Dentists and lawyers had their offices in them. The rest had been torn down for the fast-food restaurants, gas stations and bargain stores that lined the road like a crowd at a parade. Krenko drove into the shopping center parking lot from the back road that came up from the river and discharged his passengers in front of the K-Mart. He'd be back in two hours, he said.

Father Alexey let the ballerina out and got back in the front seat. His cassock was wet and wrinkled where the valise had been.

"Look like you piss yourself," Krenko said and laughed.

In the hospital Father Alexey carried his valise in front of him to hide the wet place. Two teenaged girls snickered behind him on the elevator. A small boy who got on with his mother gawked up at him all the way to the seventh floor. "Hey, mister—you look like something," the boy said when the elevator stopped.

Father Alexey marched to the nurses' station and set his valise down hard. Then he remembered the wet place and covered it with his prayer book.

"You're here for Mr. Kaputin?" asked the nurse who was there.

"Yes," Father Alexey said curtly. "Are you the one who called?"

"No, Mrs. Dinsmore has gone." She came into the corridor. She was a tall woman with narrow shoulders and a tired face. Even before she said anything, Father Alexey knew that Yakov was going to die.

"The doctor has been in," she said.

He followed her to the room. Yakov was asleep, long and gaunt under the sheet. There was a thick sweet smell in the room. Yakov's bones looked as if they might pop through his face. With each breath his mouth puffed out like a frog's. On the stand beside his bed was an ikon of the Holy Mother of Kazan and a vase with daisies whose petals were falling off.

Father Alexey touched the old man's arm. His eyes blinked open. For a while he stared up at the priest. "It's you," he said.

"How are you feeling, Yakov Osipovich?" the priest asked in Russian.

"I saw my mother." Yakov's voice was hoarse and old. He took a long time between his words.

"Where did you see her?"

"She went away. There are fewer Russians, *batiushka*. . ."

He began to talk incoherently, something about apples in his father's orchard. The words came out in pieces that did not fit, as if something had broken inside of him.

The nurse brought a glass of tea. Father Alexey cooled it with his breath.

"Here, Yakov Osipovich," he said, raising the old man's head. The tea rose halfway up the glass straw, then sank back into the glass.

"Try again, Yakov Osipovich. Pull harder."

"Shall I try?" the nurse asked.

Father Alexey took his communion kit from around his neck. "I don't think it matters," he said.

The nurse went out quietly, leaving the door ajar.

Father Alexey arranged articles from his kit and others from his valise on the stand beside Yakov's bed and put on his holy vestments. He took the ribbon from the place he had marked in his book, then turned through the pages to the prayers for the dying.

He read quietly, occasionally making a cross over the old man's head. Yakov gazed up at him in silence and a kind of wonder, his mouth agape.

The priest softened a piece of bread in a little wine.

"Yakov Osipovich," he said, "are you sorry for your sins?"

The old man looked from the priest's face to the hand with the bread. Then his eyes closed. The priest shook him. "Yakov Osipovich," he said. "Say yes."

He tried to put the bread into Yakov's mouth but the old man's teeth were clenched. He slipped the bread between Yakov's lips, tucking it back into his cheek. Eventually Yakov's mouth began to move. He chewed fast, as if he were hungry.

Yakov opened his eyes just once more. Father Alexey was putting his things away. He heard Yakov's voice behind him. The old man was looking at him calmly.

"How did you come?" he said.

The priest came and sat beside him. "I found a ride. Are you feeling better?"

"Then you have to pay."

"Don't worry about it, Yakov Osipovich."

"Well, I'll straighten it out with you later, *batiushka*."

Krenko was parked outside the emergency door in a place marked "Doctors Only."

"You make me wait long time," Krenko said. Father Alexey could smell liquor on him.

"I'm sorry."

"Not me, I don't care. But little dancing lady going to be mad like hell."

Marietta Valentinova sputtered at them half the way home. Tiny drops of saliva landed on the dashboard. Father Alexey watched them evaporate, leaving little dots. At last she stopped. They became aware of his silence.

"*Batiushka?*" Mrs. Fedorenko said.

After a while Krenko said, "Well, you got to go everybody sometimes."

"Where going?" Mrs. Florenskaya said.

"Mr. Kaputin," Mrs. Fedorenko told her gently.

"*Ja, alles,*" the old woman said, "*alles kaput. Mein man, meine kinder. Alles* but me."

The sun was gone from the window shade when Father Alexey got back to his room and lay down on his bed. It was still light, it would be light for a while yet. He turned on his fan to move the air and looked at the wall through which Yakov had said good night. He heard Mrs. Florenskaya upstairs in the hallway. She was starting in again.

The priest switched on the stereo with the record from the afternoon. But he could still hear her.

"Christ," he said, and turned up the volume.

Don't they speak jazz?

Michael S. Harper

I was fortunate enough to be born at home, delivered by my grandfather, and so there was much lore attached to my birth, much signifying because I was marked for his father. My parents weren't rich, but they had a good record collection, and they prohibited me from playing any of their 78s, a guarantee that I'd investigate in my own time, always when they were out of the house. After dusting the records, and making sure the needle was in place, the records in the appropriate order, I'd forget not to hum the songs I'd heard, and get caught with a smile. I also had the habit of riding the subway trains on what we called off-days, days when we took off from school, all the Jewish holidays in particular; I'd been riding the subways since I was five, but my parents didn't know it, and it took them three years to catch me. On that fateful day I was illegally riding after school, and passed my father as he went to work; I knew he'd seen me, though he never let on, and I decided to get on the next train and continue riding. At the next express stop I got off intending to turn around and go back home to the inevitable whipping when I heard a tapping on a window of another train—it was my grandmother; she waved faintly with a hint of a smile. Music and trains! Coltrane. You learn most by getting caught doing the things you love; it leaves an impression.

I knew Bessie Smith and Billie Holiday from birth, but I was a horn man: President Lester Young; Coleman Superhawk Hawkins; Big Bad Ben Webster; Charles Chan Parker, alias the Bird; John William Coltrane, alias the Trane. There's a story that Trane was searching for a particular tone on his horn; he had what we thought was a perfect embouchure, but his teeth hurt constantly, so he searched for the soft reed which would ease the pain. After searching for a year, each session killing his chops, he gave it up completely; there was no easy way to get that sound: play through the pain to *a love supreme.*

I wrote, secretly, in high school, buried in the back of some English class for fear I'd be asked to stand and recite a memorized poem: Donne or Shakespeare, or John Keats; luckily I tore up all these efforts, switched to prose and short dramatic forms until I was almost through college. I was working on the postal facing table, the middle-class equivalent to the pool hall; almost everybody in sight had advanced degrees. It was there I learned about Tolstoy and *So What* Dostoevsky, as one of my partners used to call the Russian underground man; my partner had discovered Miles Davis. When I went to the Writers Workshop at the University of Iowa, I was the only blood in either fiction or poetry, and I was enrolled in both; several teachers asked me was I going to be another James Baldwin—one of the faculty members so obsessed with Baldwin he *knew* I'd known Mr. Baldwin— I had read his novels and essays, but hadn't met him personally. I began to specialize in retorts to affronts. You met Isaac Singer? You been hunting with Hemingway? But this kind of humor didn't go over very well. All the writers in the workshop at the time were victims of the New Criticism, the poets writing in rhyme and meter, the fiction writers reading James and Forster. I hung out with the football players; this was the era of Iowa's great dynasty. The best lineman on the team, Al Hinton, would creep over to my garage (most blacks had to live in the dorm) apartment behind one of the few black families in Iowa City, and ask me if I knew anyone who could teach him to draw. We were dancing to "Gypsy Woman" and playing tonk; I used to stay in the library until closing time, 2 A.M., to avoid the cold. My first and only poem on the worksheet in the poetry class was a poem dedicated to Miles Davis, "Alone," which I've since cut to three lines: "A friend told me / he'd risen above jazz. / I leave him there." Jazz was my bible. How would it be to solo with that great tradition of the big bands honking you on? Could one do it in a poem? I'd taken my survey courses, studied my Donne and Shakespeare, got hot at the Moor of Venice, "I have done the state some service and they know it," hotter at Prospero, me mad Caliban, and gone on to American literature, without Frederick Douglass, or DuBois, Johnson or Toomer. Richard Wright I remember most clearly because he was talked about in Brooklyn when I was a kid; I read all his books in one weekend because none of his books had ever been taken out of the school library. I took offense at O'Neill's Brutus Jones (as I'd despised Vachel Lindsay's "Congo" poem), and T.S. Eliot's remarks on the ending of "All God's Chillun Got Wings" (neither play large enough for the torso of Paul Robeson), and searched for the cadence of street talk in the inner ear of the great musicians, the great blues singers. This brings me to church. My mother was Episcopal, my father Catholic, I was a Baptist because of the great singing; each Sunday I had to *hit the meter* (put money in the collection box), hit the holy water, and take the subway to 52nd St. to catch Bird play. One morning, just after 9 A.M., Bird came out a side door, his ax in a triply-reinforced Macy's shopping bag; "Boy, how come you not in church?" he asked, but I was quick, told him I'd been, and took up his horn case, the handles raggedly stringed. He took us, three or four kids, all under ten, to the subway station, changed a quarter, gave us each a nickel, told us not to sneak on the train going home, and disappeared uptown.

I have images of musicians at their best and when they were down and out; their playing seldom faltered—the other musicians wouldn't tolerate anything less than a journeyman job, a little extra inspiration. My people were good storytellers; some of my personal kin walked north and west during the Civil War from North Carolina, South Carolina and Virginia; one ancestor came from Chatham, Ontario, Canada. I was surprised to find their images in books, not Stowe's *Uncle Tom's Cabin*, the play version differing greatly from the text of the novel, but Douglass' 1845 narrative, written by himself; Douglass' rhetoric, the notion of each slave having on his person an articulate pass, was my ticket to freedom.

I have gotten letters from "friends" praising my knowledge of history; I learned a little terminology from a zoology teacher in Los Angeles who had us count somites in his worms; he told me I shouldn't study because I'd never get into medical school; pick up a broom and forget the microscope. He, of course, was being scrutinized for future reference. As a new critic once wrote, "Nigger your breed ain't metaphysical," and of course I'm not; the poet, Sterling Brown, whose record I heard in the library in San Francisco fifteen years ago ("the strong men, coming on/the strong men, git stronger"), coined an infamous retort—"Cracker, your breed ain't exegetical."

I wrote about my "Grandfather" because he was a hero in the highest sense, though he sometimes waited tables in white clothes; he taught me to study Sugar Ray's left-hook technique, how to step inside someone's sense of time, of theater, off the stage and in the arena, and floor-show to one's own tune. Ellison called it *antagonistic cooperation*; Wright called it the switchblade of the movie screen. Language and rhetoric are essential power; why else were the slaves prohibited from reading, from learning to pen their own sagas? Most great art is finally testamental; its technical brilliance never shadows the content of the song: "Deliver the melody, make sure the harmony's correct, play as long as you like, but play sweet, and don't forget the ladies."

Some final notes on the blues: always say *yes* to life; meet life's terms but never accept them; "Been down so long that down don't worry me/road so rocky, won't be rocky long"; as Johnny Hodges must have said to Duke on tour: *you run them verbs* (in the key of G), *I'll drive the thought* (the rabbit on his own rainbow). A coda on the American audience: it is vast, potentially; "I wish you'd buy more books," said Huck to Tom—meanwhile Jim was bringing his family to freedom. The landscape of the poem is the contour of the face reading the Declaration of Independence; how many white Jeffersons are there in this country, anyway? When I interviewed for my present duty at

Brown University, all that slave trade money come back to haunt me once again, a man yelled out from the genteel back of the room that I was an impostor, borrowing from musicians; couldn't I do something about my accent? People were embarrassed for him, he was quickly ushered out, and the East Side returned to normal, good old Providence with its old money and the Mafia flair. I remembered that Douglass had been run out of Providence to New Bedford after an abolitionist meeting and it's rumored that John Brown (the fanatical one) came all the way from Oberlin, Ohio, to meet the best gunsmith in town, a black infantryman from the Black Regiment of Rhode Island. "Straight, No Chaser," said the musician; he must have meant the street corner and the library; this has been a riff in honor of my ancestors, with some lies thrown in, a little stretching of the truth to make the point. One more lie to make the audience sweet: when I was in South Africa in 1977 on an American Specialist Program, all by myself, I landed at Jan Smuts airport in Johannesburg at about 2:30 A.M.; I was carrying Sterling Brown's *Southern Road* and Robert Hayden's *Angle of Ascent* and some of my own, one book with Coltrane's image on the cover. I was first addressed in Afrikaans, but not being *colored*, I answered in American, "I'm from Brooklyn; you ever heard of Jackie Robinson?" It took me awhile to get through customs; I was staying at the Holiday Inn right at the airport so all I had to do was wait for the little van picking up customers. I stood there for a few minutes, a few whites not far away; when the driver, a black South African, approached, I got ready to board, I was first in line; the driver held up his hand to me, telling me to wait, boarded all the white passengers, and drove off. I stood there taking names, so to speak. When the driver returned, he apologized for not taking me in the van with the other passengers. He wanted to know where I was from and then he said—"What language do you speak when the white people aren't around?" I said, "English," and he said, "No, no." What language did I speak when the white people weren't around—the second time he asked I changed my response to "American." "Brother," he said, "when blacks are among themselves, don't they speak *jazz*?" I nodded, *right on*, brother. Send more Afro-Americans from the States; bring your record collections. The battle of the big bands begins.

1982

Aubade

Roland Flint

Afterward, lying still, sleepy again,
I say tell me to get up and you do
And I sit up, and say, Now tell me what to *do*,
And you smile and say, Go write a poem.
Well this is my poem of the morning
This morning, when we wake ready
And you say, Do you want me on top?
O yes, I say, and we begin.
My poem this morning is especially that
But also it is how you never
Close your eyes but look at me
As we move, even if I close mine, and
It is the way we smile as in a dream
And it is even the way, by now, we
Sometimes speak of this or that
Child or chore in the early going,
And my best poem of the morning,
Even better, I think, again by now,
Than our times and perfect timing,
Is the way of your long hair as it sways,
Touching my face, long and falling down
And smelling not like new-cut clover or hyacinth or fern,
But always like a woman's long, clean hair,
Soft across my face and open eyes
And smelling like our life together,
Like morning, this morning, after seven years:
We have written on and in our bodies, love,
The poem of the day, which this can but improve.

1982

The third count

Andrew Fetler

I am waiting for my sister Nina to drive up from Boston for our Saturday lunch in my house on Bay Road, an old country road near Dudleyville. For a bachelor of fifty-nine, I make good lunches, she says. I have covered the salad with Saran Wrap and put it in the fridge. She wants her lettuce crisp, with a tomato from my garden and a sliced boiled egg. Besides the salad, we will have chicken rice soup (we had chicken noodle last week), cold cuts, and toast with Diet Mazola. For dessert, fresh peaches and cottage cheese. She is dieting again.

For thirty years my sister Nina has been seeing psychiatrists and feeling better about herself. "It's a *process!*" She has discovered health foods, but won't refuse an offer of Bavarian cream pie. She has tried *est*, folk dances of many cultures (Roumanian dances are fantastic), protein powders for clearing her blood, sweetened calcium tablets for her puffy eyelids, and human potential encounters for raising her consciousness. But not until Jesus saved her, a year ago, could she forgive our father for having been a Christian.

Our father, Hamilton Crail, was a successful businessman and a founding father of the Full Gospel Church in Boston. As an elder of that church he practiced a mixture of Scottish Calvinism and American fundamentalism. He struggled continually against sins of the flesh. When my sister Nina was fourteen, for example, he marched her off to his study one night for bringing the devil into our home. I don't know how she could have provoked our father. Did he catch her fondling herself, or wearing a pretty dress, or smiling while wearing a pretty dress? Shamed and bewildered in his study, she sobbed and on command croaked the Repentance Song: "Just as I am, without one plea." Apparently not satisfied, he took her to his study again the following night, for closer questioning behind his locked door.

And then, two months after these curious interrogations in Nina's fourteenth year, she fell sick and had to be taken to the hospital. She

PETER DE SEVE. (*TQ #*

was brought home looking pale and wilted, cured of an "infection." Our father praised the Lord, and in church, as if inspired by Nina's recovery, he stirred up the congregation against our pastor for false preaching, and had him sacked. God, our father cried from the pulpit, holding up the Bible for his authority, could not use a modernist who doubted Creation Science and tolerated immoral books in public schools. Our false pastor, moreover, had done nothing to rescue from a mental hospital a young widow, a firecracker for the Lord, who had branded the foreheads of her two children with the emblem of the cross, to protect them from demons. The widow ought not to have used a heated knife, our father allowed, but her love and faith were great.

We were happy, Nina and I and our three brothers, when we could tiptoe through the day without attracting our father's attention. We scattered when we heard him coming, or froze in guilty attitudes when his figure loomed in the doorway. We could not live up to his standards. But we were not to despair. Our sins were God's opportunities. Hamilton Crail never hugged his children, flesh revolted him, but he worried about our souls. He believed in spiritual diagrams and drew pictures of our souls—a rectangle, say, containing circles and arrows going in and out.

Silent and withdrawn since her visit to the hospital, Nina found music harder to ignore than diagrams. Sometimes, when the church choir sang "Perfect submission, perfect delight," she was touched by the love of Jesus and wept. "Filled with His goodness, lost in His love."

But when the call to repent thundered from the pulpit, she did not go forward to prostrate herself before the elders, among whom Hamilton Crail stood waiting darkly.

My sister Nina is fifty-five years old now and very fat, and she has spent her life worrying about her weight. A year ago, at a meeting in Boston of charismatic youngsters who call themselves The Disciples, she found happiness, she tells me, that cannot be expressed in words. She gave herself to Jesus completely, without reservations—Nina insists upon her surrender by tapping her chest with her chubby fist—and in return Jesus has taken her burdens upon Himself. "The only word for it is bliss!" she says, chattering without stop—she who used to hesitate before speaking—and smiles at my wonder. She feels omnipotent, she could do anything, she declares, and looks around my living room for a mountain to move.

Nina has backslidden twice since her conversion a year ago. During these dark spells that test her faith, lasting two or three weeks, she looks miserable and mutters about our father. "He must have hated me," she says. Would I say she had been hateful as a little girl? She says he never forgave her for the "unspeakable secret" between them, which Nina has never revealed to me beyond its being her unspeakable secret. "I hope you never guess," she stammers, her intelligence lapsing strangely, and tears fill her eyes.

Poor fat Nina takes her backslidings to her overworked psychiatrist, who gives her two Valiums and sends her to The Disciples for another fix. The Disciples rally round her. Lovely youngsters with effulgent eyes. They chant and clap to the accompaniment of electric guitars and drums, and raise their hands, palms up, when the Spirit begins to move, drums beating, until Nina shudders and jiggles with hiccups, and the storefront resounds with jubilation. "I'm a Jesus junkie, there's no way without Him," she says happily, between backslidings, and has taken to quoting chapter and verse and using evangelical language not heard in our family since our father died in the Lord thirty-five years ago.

She is an honest soul, my sister, and frankly expresses doubts about The Disciples and their Apostle, who has spoken face to face with Gautama Buddha, Moses, and Jesus, and who will be translated bodily into heaven. Their Apostle sends pamphlets, tape cassettes, and instructions to his flocks from headquarters in Los Angeles. Her doubts are received with love and understanding by the joyful youngsters. They don't say much about Father, as they call their Apostle, to new converts. Her doubting is beautiful, they tell her. Her every opinion is beautiful. And after the meeting they have coffee and cake, and the elders (ages eighteen to twenty-six) organize the week's Outreach activities. Think of all the people who will be left behind, any day now. Next week, the Boston flock will divide for missionary forays into Worcester and Amherst, scheduled for the same Monday, a college holiday, and Nina has offered to transport a load of them in her Plymouth Volaré.

The minister is a twenty-six-year-old sweetie from Salt Lake City, Utah, for whom the Apostle picked a darling girl from Dallas, Texas. Nina has never seen such a happy couple, so in love with each other. The girl's parents tried to have the marriage annulled, spending more money on lawyers than they ever spent on their daughter. The Apostle limits the happy couple to spiritual intercourse for two years and may separate them in different missions far from home, to deepen their God-centered commitments to each other. His missions are nursing and foster homes in thirty-eight states—God's plan is to cover all fifty—into which are funneled federal and state moneys, only the Apostle knows how much and the Lord's work cannot have enough. The godless parents of that darling girl, Nina tells me with a mildly crazy look in her eyes, have not seen these kids at work, in prayer and praise.

At the meeting in their temple, a Boston storefront, Nina sits with the young minister, paper plate on her lap, styrofoam cup in her hand, and tells him how she relapsed from her slimming diet. Does her relapse signal another backsliding? "That's beautiful," says the attentive young man, and places his hand lovingly on her fat arm. "You're a beautiful person, Nina."

All this Nina relates with a full heart, her eyes shining. Her eyes are too old for clone-like effulgence and cloud over when she gives a scared smile of hope for me as well. We should be in this thing together, she says. Our three brothers rejected Jesus, she reminds me, and look at what happened to them. All dead. "You're all I have left, Jim," she says. Jesus takes pity on her backsliding and turns His face to her again, and pulls her to His forgiving bosom, and even lets her eat if she wants to. Eat or don't eat, but don't make such a big deal of it. "Look at the flowers of the field!" she cries. What am I going to do about Jesus? she wants to know. After all His suffering for us, will I accept Him or reject Him? If I accept Him He will accept me, and if I reject Him He will reject me.

The child's garden in her soul has had a long time to grow into a jungle. Lost in those senseless mazes, Nina is at last finding a way out, or believes that a way out is being found. I am glad for her and am almost grateful to The Disciples. Better than Valium, maybe. We were five once, four boys and one girl. Now Nina and I alone are left and our Saturday lunches are the last gasps of our family.

She forgoes some of our Saturdays for The Disciples. She lends them her car and gets it returned with a bashed fender. One Saturday she joined them in a street demonstration against Moonies, followers of a false prophet who claims that Jesus was hot to get married when He was killed, a doctrine the true Apostle in Los Angeles has pronounced unbiblical, inspired by Satan, leading to such Communist godlessness as the mass suicide-murder in Jonestown, Guyana. Full proof available on request, without cost or obligation.

Nina called last Monday to say that she would be free—*free?*—to visit me this Saturday, and suggested chicken rice soup for lunch. "Father says we should eat more rice, less potatoes." So the Apostle of The Disciples is her new father. She would arrive at noon, she said, and added that she had committed ten percent of her stock portfolio to The Disciples. The principal, not the income. That would come to $30,000, roughly. She sounded pleased with herself.

"The *principal?*"

"I knew you'd gasp. It's the tithe I owe them. I'm ashamed I didn't promise more. I owe them *everything!*"

Imagine owing anybody everything. Since her religious conversion, she has begun to talk like a fourteen-year-old. "Nina, you can't do that."

"I knew you wouldn't understand," she said with harrowing patience. "Just trust me, O.K.? I know what you think of The Disciples, but you're dead wrong. You're still blinded, like I was. Please don't bring it up again when I see you."

If it made me feel better, she said, the young minister talked her out of giving more than ten percent. She had to grow stronger in the Lord before her new father in Los Angeles would consider accepting her total commitment: Caesar could contest large donations in court if they were not done right. I felt a weakness in my knees and sat down by the telephone, at my kitchen table. "I'm sorry I mentioned it," she babbled. "Just fix the salad and I'll be there by noon. You know what it's like, Jim? Coming to Jesus is like coming home again!"

Right.

Ten percent to that fellow in Los Angeles—for a start. "A tithe," I said, "is a tenth of your *income*, not your *principal*, for Christ's sake!"

"I won't have you taking the Lord's name in vain!" But she allowed herself a pause, perhaps for the shadow of a doubt to cross her mind. "I don't care what a tithe is. I'd rather be dead than live without Jesus. It's called faith, if that still means anything to you. For all his faults, Father had *faith*. Now I'm sorry for every bad thought I ever had about him. I beg his forgiveness!" she began to yell. "I repent in dust and ashes! I *was* hateful! Yes, I love him! Do you hear me, Jim? I just can't hate him any more, don't you understand? I'm *tired*! I've made peace, and you're still ranting after all these years. Except now you are ranting at *me* instead of at Father."

Before The Disciples got to Nina we talked about lawn fertilizers and stock options, and walked in the woods, and came in for coffee and an oldie showing Fred Astaire and Ginger Rogers. Now Nina talks about Jesus. I had rather we talked about fertilizers and stock options again, and about a little elephant in our county.

I want to talk about a local inbred, Sloan Mudge, a spawn of incest who keeps a female dwarf elephant in his zoo. Sloan Mudge is physically and mentally deformed, and his elephant, recently acquired, resembles Nina in her obesity. I hold them in view when she talks about Jesus.

Last summer I took her out to Teewaddle Road for a look at Sloan Mudge and his dwarf elephant. Nina did not want to go, she loathes Mudge and his slithery ways. But she had not seen his elephant and came along.

Mudge sat askew on his crate, clutching a roll of zoo tickets, and greeted us with his professional "'Joy yourself, now!"

She ignored him, and she hated his dirty elephant standing in its own muck, regarding her with little eyes. Raising its trunk, it worked its prehensile lips an inch from her face. Nina would not stay another minute in that damned zoo. "Is *that* what you brought me out here for?"

On the telephone, Nina's voice quavered, suddenly plaintive. "Are you there, Jim?"

"Look," I said. "I don't mind your Disciples. They give me an idea to buy Sloan Mudge's elephant."

"What are you talking about?"

"If you can spend ten percent on Jesus, I can spend a few dollars on an elephant."

Her intake of breath was followed by a threatening silence.

"We could trade," I said. "You give me Jesus, I'll give you the elephant."

"Is that all you can feel about me now? Ridicule?"

She was crying. Kids in a Boston storefront, gone from pot to pushing an Apostle in Los Angeles, taking their guitars with them, attract a sad fat woman who has never married and loves children. They give her a Jesus-fix and she feels bright, a beautiful person with beautiful opinions. But there is a side to Nina that is not primitive: her backslidings will grow longer, darker.

"I'm sorry," she said, sniffling, when she'd had her cry. "I didn't mean that about you. God knows you're a sweetie. But listen. Are you listening?"

"I'm listening."

What she said next chilled me, as if she were offering lemonade and cyanide in Jonestown, Guyana. "Jim, you mustn't be afraid. I'm not afraid any more. I'll be with you, we'll go together. I *know* God will reclaim you, even if He has to break you first—remember? Father *was* right, after all."

He was right. All our brothers suffered diseases or accidents or bad marriages. The eldest was broken by all three, the second by suicide, the third by madness. Two to go, Nina and me. Hamilton Crail's ghost has been stalking his children and now has Nina cornered, a lonely woman too weary to keep running, a broken and a contrite heart. In a year she will be ready to give her last stitch to The Disciples, mop floors in a barracks in Beulah, and write, when permitted contact with the doomed world, of her fears for me, and send unbelievers to hell, and pray for my salvation. It would be too awful for Nina to go alone, as the Bible threatens: sister taken, brother left behind.

In parting, Nina said on the telephone, "I'll pray for you, Jim, and I won't stop praying for you. That's all Father could ever do for us."

"Thank you very much."

"Don't *trifle* with God! I can't ever, *ever*, allow you to use that tone again—praise the Lord!"

That did not sound like Nina but like the old Full Gospel Church.

Salad, cold cuts, peaches and cottage cheese—all is ready for Nina's arrival at noon. The table in my dining room is set with our father's silverware, his monogram engraved indelibly. In the kitchen I find a squat vase with narrow neck, for my glass flowers. I bought them yesterday at the Crafts Fair from two scrubbed members of a commune, a man and a woman—bare feet, Levis, plaid shirt, mop of hair, torpor common to both. These two were working out their salvation by selling handmade clay pipes, ceramic medallions on thongs, glass flowers with long metal stems, and home-sewn cotton tunics piled rumpled in a dirty cardboard box. Their eyes drifted and they gave me slack-jawed smiles.

At my kitchen window I can keep an eye out for Nina's car to appear on Bay Road, while I arrange the glass flowers in the vase. Blue, green, red, and yellow—two of each. I got them for my crystal collection, glass flowers for my crystal dancer. They are supposed to sway and tinkle.

In the living room the grandfather clock Nina picked up at an auction chimes the eleventh hour, a ghostly sonority recalling the ordered days and years of a family long gone. It occurs to me, with a spasm, that I need some disorder in my house, something alive and warmer than my crystal dancer. Nina's religious estrangement is cooling the weekly warmth she used to bring. Her voice has a hard edge when she talks about Jesus. Her face looks tight. She'll end up a missionary, if I know the signs. How keep myself warm? My incontinent old Airedale had to be put away last year. How about Sloan Mudge's dwarf elephant? A little madness would be nothing new in our family.

The owner of the elephant is of a race of New England inbreds still to be seen in our parts, a stunted little man with matted hair, low forehead, yellow eyes. At today's prices he could make a good living cutting firewood, but he can't stick to any one task. He sets up a stand of blackberries for the sparse traffic on his road, hires himself out to pick cucumbers at child-labor rates, patches car tires at the Mobil station in Dudleyville. Sometimes, he disappears for a month, nobody knows where. Life has taught Sloan Mudge to be secretive. Once, an alarming rumor compelled a Congregational minister to bear a gift of groceries to his shack, and ask the recluse if he kept a grown daughter chained to his bed. "Nope," said Mudge, and took the groceries. The minister did notice a fall of chain in the rubbish on the rickety porch, but no daughter in the shack or near it. "He *had* a daughter by his sister," Nina said when we gossiped, her belief unshaken. Nobody had ever seen a woman in his vicinity, and all other Mudges, young and old, were safely tucked away in Mildwood Cemetery.

Sloan Mudge put up signs for a quarter of a mile along his road, boards nailed to trees, reading "CAMPING $2" in whitewash and an arrow pointing to the sky. He had run a water pipe from his well to the camp, and clapped together an outhouse with boards from his collapsed barn. A few out-of-state explorers pulled in with their campers and were driven out by mosquitoes from Mudge's swamp. His camp fared no better the second summer, though an agent from a state agency in Boston, studying water resources, offered to drain the swamp and kill the mosquitoes. Government interference did not sit well with Mudge, but the threat may have fired his ingenuity to come up with a better idea for pulling in campers. His dream of the good life would not die, and, in the third summer of his camp's existence, below his amended "CAMPING $4" appeared a second sign: "ZOO." I did not drive out to Teewaddle Road for a look at his zoo until two college students stopped by my house soliciting signatures for a petition to free the animals. The Society for the Prevention of Cruelty to Animals had been alerted, and legal machinery had been set in motion to close Sloan Mudge's private enterprise.

Driving out on a hot summer Saturday, when Nina was serving The Disciples, I was touched to see that in his "ZOO" signs along Teewaddle Road Sloan Mudge had not availed himself of the adman's exclamation mark. His "ZOO" stated a fact, take it or leave it. I felt instinctive sympathy for Mudge, and rejoiced at the sight of cars pulled up by the zoo entrance, a classic example of Mudge architecture: gravel dumped over a culvert.

Here, Sloan Mudge himself sat on a crate, sweating and scratching himself, wearing a new T-shirt over stained pants, and guarded the entrance with a board reading "25" propped up beside him. He looked a happy man, his aches forgotten. Without raising his yellow eyes to mine, he snatched the coin from my hand before I could give it, and, turning to spy who else might be coming up the road, said, "'Joy yourself, now!"

Seven campers and two tents showed in the trees on the swampside, striped awnings unfurled. In the foreground, a dozen locals converged around a snack wagon featuring popcorn, Fritos, hot dogs, Table Talk pies, and sodas in the drifting dust.

Setting forth on my tour, I came upon a fox in a chicken wire enclosure, lying dusty beside a dusty tin plate. The fox was being urged to move—"Move it!"—by a man who had taken his denim shirt off in the heat, his paunch hanging over his belt. "Bet this critter's dead," he guffawed, jabbing me with his elbow, and tossed his crushed beer can at the fox, just missing the tail.

The next attraction was a coughing mongrel tied by a rope to a post. Atop the post was fastened a five-inch cage made of window screening, containing a spider watching flies trying to get in. Then the path forked, offering choices. The left path took me to the birds: a pintail duck sitting in the dust, a turkey in a swarm of flies, a ring-necked pheasant with a broken tail, and two chickens and transient sparrows, all in one enclosure. Chicken wire, strung between two pines and a young elm, housed a screech owl asleep on a truncated branch. Beneath this triangular cage, small bones and droppings littered the ground, and from the hexagonal mesh of the cage floor hung bits of rodent skins.

Returning to the spider's post, I took the more traveled path to the most impressive structure in Sloan Mudge's Zoo, a massive cage of four-by-fours, spacious enough for tiger or lion, but as yet vacant. Fortified with hot dogs and sodas, the locals had preceded me to a dwarf elephant beyond.

This captive, a spiritless female and the only animal in the zoo foreign to our parts, was no larger than a donkey. She was chained by a hind leg to an iron stake driven into the ground. Behind her lay the predictable dry bucket in the dust, overturned. Children reached out to slap her lethargic trunk—"Don't get too close!"—and the man with the beer paunch stood pelting her dusty hide with popcorn, expressing the general disapproval, for in her prolonged exposure to the hot sun the little elephant ignored her visitors. In the minutes I watched, she did not rest from her comatose swaying, back and forth, each forward motion forcing her chained hind leg off the ground as she pulled the chain taut. Her trunk hung unresponsive amid flying popcorn and candy wrappers.

When I left the zoo, Mudge called from his crate, "Come again, now!"

Three months later—I had taken Nina to the zoo in the interval—the SPCA succeeded in having Sloan Mudge's zoo closed and his animals impounded, including a knock-kneed pony I had missed seeing, an emaciated pony that had been kept in a narrow stall for such a long time (four years, the Dudleyville Gazette said) that its hooves had curled up like Turkish slippers. Mudge's domestic animals, except his coughing mongrel and spider, were taken to the university's Agricultural Station for documentation.

But for some legal reason the authorities could not impound his dwarf elephant, for which he was able to produce a dubious bill of sale. The elephant had to await separate legal action.

Yes, I am dwelling on Sloan Mudge. Arranging the glass flowers in the vase and keeping an eye out for Nina's car to appear on Bay Road, I sit at my kitchen table and dwell on Mudge. Consider. In town Mudge has been showing acquaintances his picture in the Gazette.

How, I wonder, given his material and mental resources, did he achieve so much in so little time? A zoo, no less, with an elephant and a screech owl and other birds and beasts, and maybe a lion or tiger on the way. A good idea builds. He had actually pulled it off, his greatest idea. He had looked happy that day, snatching the coin from my hand and wishing me joy in his paradise. He and his generations of inbred artists have always run afoul of the law; it is not his fault that the law wrecked his great zoo. Tenacious, ingenious Mudge has tried. He can rest now and feel in his weary bones the tug of millennia and the deliverance that lies in extinction.

In my mind I have christened Mudge's elephant Baby. What if I offered him $2,500 for her? Would he hold out for $3,000? I foresee problems with Baby, not the least of them local publicity. But the publicity will pass and Mudge inspires. Of course Baby would be better off in the Boston Children's Zoo—or would she? I could give her my love and a good home. Her bucket would never run dry. Hell, I'd give her a whole pool to play in, in a fine expansive paddock of upright railroad ties, even if I had to dip into my stock portfolio to do it.

Apparently Mudge does have title to Baby, though how he acquired her, with what money, where, remains nobody's business but Mudge's. His bill of sale for her, an incomprehensible German "Rechnung" on which Mudge's name is superscribed, was pictured on page 20 of *The Boston Globe*: "*Sie erhalten auf Grund Ihrer Bestellung als Postpaket: 1 Elephas africanus pumilio.*" Signed by one "G. Hagenbeck, Hamburg," the bill shows numbers for "*Postschekkonto*," "*Bankkonto*," "*Girokasse*," "*Girokonto*," and is originally addressed to "*Herrn, Frau, Frl., Firma* Nelly Billiard, Philadelphia, Pa., U.S.A." Did G. Hagenbeck ship the elephant to Nelly Billiard by parcel post? Beyond the "*Elephas africanus*," this bill of sale, in its every aspect and unimaginable connection with Mudge, or indeed with Nelly Billiard, is as unintelligible to me as my own life—those aspects and connections of my life that occupy my thoughts.

My main difficulty would be providing for Baby's comfort so late in the season. Fall is upon us, the leaves are turning, you can smell arctic regions in breezes from Canada. Winter is coming. Whoever has no house will not build one now. If I kept Baby in the garage I would need a shed for my tractor mower and workbench. I'd have to lay a drainpipe for hosing the garage floor, and run the pipe out to the septic tank. The garage would need enough insulation and heating to be warm as the Congo during snowstorms. All this needs planning, contracting, time. For this winter, I see, I would have to take Baby into my house. Needless to say. . .

Is it really impossible?

Who would consent to having a child if he foresaw in a flash all the expense and terrors which the rearing of his child would visit upon him? My sister Nina and I are vulnerable in this regard, our father's religion having tinted our souls with catastrophic expectations. I worry, for example, that Baby's progress through my house would punch holes in the floor, like tracks in snow. But stop and think. Look at her. This specimen of a pigmy Congo race is no larger than a donkey, which some Sicilians keep in their houses. She is no heavier than my Yamaha upright piano, which I have rolled about the house for a good acoustical spot, without cracking the floor. Baby could safely mount the two steps from garage to kitchen and find her own way to the running water, down the hall to the right.

I can see my little elephant sitting in the tub, filling her trunk with water and spraying it around the walls. I'll have the walls and doorway hung with plastic curtains, and the floor tiled toward a drainpipe, a simple job in the bathroom with its wealth of plumbing. Baby could easily climb in and out of the tub, for it is a modern tub, only twelve and one-quarter inches deep, designed for space calculated by efficiency engineers. She would not want to get out of the water, I would have to scold her through the plastic curtain, mop in hand, my view blurred by drops and rivulets on the curtain: "You've had all morning. Nina is coming. You don't want Nina catching you here, do you?"

Waiting for Nina to arrive for our Saturday lunch, I sit at the kitchen table turning the vase of prismatic glass flowers. The ceiling glitters with refracted sunlight. Outside, the wind has risen. The forecaster promised a calm day. I know a meteorologist who does not forecast; he marks the sweeping picture of the years. The prodigious elm tree on my lawn flutters in a frenzy of yellows and browns, seemingly on fire in a blizzard of elm seeds. In the light of this conflagration, Nina's car, sporting the fender bashed by The Disciples, turns into my drive at last.

"If I thought you were serious," Nina says when we have eaten the peaches and cottage cheese, "I'd commit you to a mental hospital."

She is taking my elephant fantasy more seriously than I expected. "Baby would be in the house only this winter," I say, testing Nina's credulity. "By spring I'd have the garage ready for her. The paddock would take no time at all. The big job would be the pool, but she could wait for that."

"Baby will certainly want to express her gratitude. She'll corner you one day, right there by the TV, and crush you to death."

Nina has gained weight again. She has exchanged her tweed suit for a loose batiste in penitent gray, resembling a maternity dress, too light for the season. Over her shoulders she has thrown a girlishly pink sweater, pink on gray like fall leaves awaiting winter.

A horrible thing happened when we sat down to lunch. She could not fit herself between the arms of her chair. Too fat. I hastened to substitute an armless guest chair. Seating herself precariously, she composed her face and said: "Disgusting, ain't I. Well, it's true. Why pretend?" It was a bad moment for me to go on spinning my elephant fantasy for my elephantine sister. But I would have done worse to drop the subject abruptly, after introducing it with such a toot for something a bit messy in my life.

We take our coffee to the couch in the bay window. I see the elm burning in the sun, positively on fire. Every fall Nina remarks on the turning colors, but for once I don't call her attention to my elm. A trick of light does something unpleasant to it, something other than pretty. I stand transfixed.

"Why don't you get a dog?" she says, impressing the couch enormously with her buttocks. Her body seems to be inflating before my eyes.

I sit beside her. "No dog," I say. "After Emmy"—my Airedale gone to glory—"there is no other."

"Get a cat," says Nina.

"Emmy was afraid of cats."

"You're beginning to irritate me. You're doing it on purpose, aren't you. To get back at me?"

"For what?"

"For Jesus," she says.

"I don't know Jesus. I know some people who know Jesus."

"Your joke is wearing thin. Why do you keep hammering away at it?"

"What makes you think I'm joking?"

"Because an elephant is unthinkable, even to you."

"The unthinkable can become thinkable. Jesus, for example."

"Jesus *unthinkable?*"

"Of course Jesus is unthinkable. Born of a virgin? Passing understanding. Why else would you need faith? If you can think about Jesus, why can't I think about an elephant?"

"Where in *hell,*" Nina explodes, "do you propose to keep your damned elephant! In the guest room?"

"The guest room is too small. So is the sewing room."

"You considered the sewing room?" she wails. "With all my things in the sewing room?"

"I wouldn't touch your things. You can come live here any time you want."

"Bay Road," she says with a moan. "I can't live on Bay Road. I need people. How can you live on Bay Road? You must have ice in your veins, like that crystal dancer of yours. Why don't you move to Boston?"

"I'd go crazy in Boston."

"You're going crazy on Bay Road, talking about elephants."

In the bay window the wind is subsiding, the elm stands burning like an iceberg.

"I couldn't keep Baby in this room, either," I say, pushing my fantasy. "I'd have to move the couch to your bedroom and the TV to the kitchen. But where would I put the piano? The kitchen isn't big enough for the piano."

Nina rolls her eyes, an expression she reserves for my inanities.

"The dining room," I say, "is long enough, but too narrow. The den is my library. I'm not giving that up, not even for Baby. The only room left is your bedroom, Nina. It's large enough for Baby, private bath and all. Just for this winter, remember. You could have my bedroom when you stay over. I'll sleep in my den."

She is stunned.

She says, "Why do you hate me?"

"I don't hate you."

"I have nobody."

I ought to hug her now, divert her with something light, affecting, a confection on Channel 3 or a home-fried gospel song to make her clap her hands with all the people, and let her have her cry, and sniffle, and smile again. But I shall not divert her from my fantasy. She will divert herself in a moment. I am thinking of the children of Hamilton Crail, no less than of a little elephant whose keeper shows doubters a mysterious bill of sale for his authority to chain her to an iron stake. Seeing God-appropriators pelting Nina with religious popcorn, I am brightening the corner where I am. "Stand thou on that side, for on this am I!" the Full Gospel Choir used to sing in transports of self-confidence. Here is my own song, about a little elephant.

Nina recovers, going from tearful to tough in twenty seconds. "You're not hurting me, James. What I can't understand is why you should want to hurt Jesus. Because that's what you are doing. After all He has done for us! Never mind me, but Jesus *does* matter." And she quotes John 3:16 to prove that Jesus matters. "Come with me to the temple," she says, referring to the Boston storefront of The Disciples. "Just once. Your eyes will be opened."

The elm on my lawn burns icily. Shall I ask her to look? She would not see the terrible tree. She would see God's glory in the fall colors. Nina is moved by nature. "That's the glory of God," she will say. She is learning or recovering pretty ideas about God. She knows as much about God as TV evangelists and Job's comforters. She knows how loving God is, for God is Love, and, though just, He is merciful, her loving Father.

Silent, we sit on the couch, and then she is crying.

"I want to pray," she says. "Will you pray with me?"

"You go ahead."

"It's something we can do together, Jimmy."

"I'm not stopping you. Go ahead and pray."

"I want to *help* you!"

I feel a double-take. She wants to help me. I live in perpetual astonishment, in a kind of low dread that does not respond to sing-alongs sung ardently off key. Nina must have happiness, warmed and passed through many hands.

Hurt by my resistance, she sits rocking back and forth like my little comatose elephant chained to the stake. With great effort she pulls herself up from the couch, her effort so great that her eyeballs show their whites as if she's gone blind. She lumbers out between couch and coffee table and turns uncertainly, casting about for a way to kneel on the rug.

Somehow, she lands softly and stands on hands and knees, on all fours like Baby, her huge bulk breathing, her loose dress flowing in gray folds from her buttocks, revealing a blotched, liver-spotted, awesome circumference of thigh one might glimpse in the jungle.

Her pink sweater has fallen from her shoulders and lies hooked on the coffee table. She rights herself from all fours to her knees and raises her hands for praying, her body cantilevered like that of a circus elephant.

And then, horribly, our old Repentance Song breaks from her throat in her sweet little-girl voice; and I see her bewildered at fourteen, locked up with our father in his study, humiliated at his feet: "Just as I am, without one plea. . . ."

But I have always *loved Jesus, even as a little girl,* Nina has told me since Jesus saved her, as if she were eager to please Jesus even in her memories.

"Jesus, my Lord and Savior," she says, swallowing a catch in her throat, and prays in whispers inaudible to me.

I sit on the couch studying her desolation. Thus have I known her since her fourteenth year. I can still see a vestige of that little girl in poor Nina, an outlined innocence in elbows and hands clasped in prayer. She is backsliding again and hanging on for dear life. Now and then my name rises from her slurred whispers, so she is praying for me too. Maybe I could help her by drawing the curtains: the light in which the tree stands is too harsh—too harsh altogether. I could play my stereo record of Mendelssohn's *Elijah*: "If with all your hearts ye truly seek me, ye shall ever surely find me." I'd like that myself, make no mistake. I'd need a hanky, hearing Elijah, and Nina would weep torrents and feel better, much better.

As Nina prays in her loneliness, I turn to look at the tree. The wind has fallen, the leaves are stilled, the great tree stands motionless like a crystal arrangement, not impressively colorful just now. It is a muted incandescence suffused with cold blue. I once sailed in a luxury liner dwarfed by a radiant iceberg that inclined my voyage, I know today, to this tree on my own lawn.

Yesterday, I happened to see the ruins of Sloan Mudge's Zoo. Stopping by his culvert, I got out of the car and scanned the blighted field for relics. A rank odor, sweetly putrescent, infected the air. A stark post stood where his zoo once stood. Rotting boards lay strewn about. A bit of window screening had curled and, with grass grown through, disguised itself as tumbleweed. The massive cage of four-by-fours, once intended for a miraculous lion or tiger, had vanished without a trace.

May not such a miracle live in the pilgrim's reverence, on evidence not seen?

Pilgrims not lacking. Three distinct truck tracks, made by vehicles heavy enough to churn up mud, snaked across the field to Mudge's swamp. There, where campers once camped in clouds of mosquitoes, I now discerned a scattering of industrial drums, indifferently concealed from the road. The drums led the eye beside the still waters of the swamp proper, a glimmering darkness streaked with silver and foam, such as may be painted by chemical wastes.

When Mudge gets caught he will be fined $50 for polluting his own drinking water, and admonished. "Yes, sir," he will say.

I drove on but slowed down and stopped again as Mudge's shack came in view on high ground, etched against the sky. He had prospered. In his weedy yard stood a new pickup and a horse trailer. A junked car lay on its back. Within the dark proscenium of his porch, a naked light bulb shone in an uncurtained window. Beside the shack stood the wreck of a barn, somehow keeping its feet, whole sections of walls missing, the roof caved in as if smashed by a fist. In a gaping hole in the barn I saw what I had not consciously come to see, the dwarf elephant.

Or was it a pony? I got out of the car for a better look. From the road I could not make out the animal's shape in the gloom. The head seemed too large for a pony, the body too thick. I could not see her trunk or judge which way she faced. She stood under the caved-in roof, a shadow.

A shadow, polluted waters, a stark post in a blighted field, relics—Sloan Mudge never disappointed. True to his generations of inbred artists, he continued to provide. The westering sun played its light on his old sign, a board nailed to a tree by the side of the road. The sign was weathered now, hung askew, the whitewash faded but still legible: "CAMPING $4" and an arrow pointing to the sky. And below, in witness of a bygone marvel: "ZOO."

He will never knock down these joyful tidings. If a traveler should ask, Sloan Mudge will steal a look at the out-of-state license plate, shift his yellow eyes to the swamp, and in time, with hindsight and fore-sight, spin a myth.

I felt tired approaching my sixtieth year and was struck by the similarity between Mudge's road and mine. Too far from shopping malls, schools, and churches, both roads were shunned by home builders. Abandoned farms on Bay Road had been reclaimed by woods, while Teewaddle Road favored swamps and thickets. At twi-light in October, roads more solitary than Mudge's and mine may not be seen in our parts, nor vistas more withdrawn from the human concourse. Such roads are sometimes pictured in tabloids. I could not loiter. A parked car on these desolate stretches suggested something less definable than lovers or bird watchers.

Nina's prayer smolders and goes out. It is hard to pray with an unbeliever in the room. I steady her as she reaches for the coffee table and maneuvers herself up from her knees. Having regained her feet, she pulls away from my supporting hand, recovers her pink sweater, and looks about for her overcoat.

"You're leaving?" I ask.

She is. She is going back to her friends in Boston. "I really must. We have an early meeting today."

My silly elephant fantasy has ruined our lunch. We'll not be walking in the fall colors and tart air promising winter. How pleasant it would have been, then, to come in for coffee and an oldie on TV, Basil Rathbone and Nigel Bruce this afternoon. *Great Heavens, Holmes!*

"What about *our* day?" I remonstrate. "There's a Sherlock Holmes movie today. Basil Rathbone."

"Really." She smiles in token that she has passed beyond such pabulum.

Besides losing our family hour with Sherlock Holmes, I have for-feited the moment for moderating Nina's caprice to squander $30,000 on The Disciples—her promised "tithe." Had I been sensible I might have nudged her to reconsider the sum for The Disciples. What possessed me to offer her bedroom to an elephant? I cannot reach her now, as she stands poking in her shoulder bag for the car keys.

"The chicken soup was great," she says. "Thanks for reminding me of my nothingness."

"That's not what I meant."

"That's exactly what you meant." She clasps her hands in mock gratitude. "Isn't that what you always meant—*all* of you? Didn't I get to wash the dishes while you played the piano? Nina the Moron?" And she stings herself three times with our childhood singsong: "'Nina the moron!'"

Is that what her prayer tossed up? As I move to mollify her, she wards me off and whimpers the old incantation through gritted dentures. I can't get near her. She is spitting hellfire.

I follow Nina out to her Plymouth Volaré.

Bay Road passes through woods here and my clearing is surrounded by woods. Summer and winter, my garden (now bedded in straw) stands in shadows well after sunrise and well before sunset. From the road my house, fieldstone and wood painted white, looks neatly tucked away in the woods. When the leaves turn, an occasional tourist car slows and sometimes the driver points at my house for his passengers to see. The sky is bright now but darkness abides in the underbrush.

As I hold the car door for Nina, she falls in expertly backwards. Then she pulls her thick legs in after her, one at a time. I wonder how she avoids collisions: she drives reclining at an angle of forty-five degrees. The seat belt is not long enough for her girth. I close the car door. She fumbles with the keys and rolls down the window. Her cheek does not respond to my kiss.

"Are you really going to a meeting?" I ask.

She sits touching up her hair before the rearview.

"You treat me like a stranger," she says, adjusting a curl. Satisfied, she turns to give me a parting shot. "I wanted to talk about something important to me, and you talk about keeping an elephant in my bedroom. You think that's funny? You think it's funny telling me to trade Jesus for your damned elephant?"

"I'm sorry. It was a stupid joke. You came to talk, let's talk. Come on, get out. It's time for our walk. Then we'll have coffee and Sherlock Holmes. Won't that be fun?"

"I've had quite enough, frankly," she says. The car engine sparks to life.

Reclining now in her fearful driving position, she shifts her automatic into Rear but keeps her foot on the brake pedal, hesitantly. "Giving money to The Disciples doesn't really do it, does it?" she says.

"I couldn't agree more."

"Money is not enough," she says, resolutely, and shifts back into Park. "I want to go to a Bible College. I've been thinking about Okeko in San Diego. But my friends say Okeko discriminates against fatsos. They say fatsos are cursed by God. Do you know anything about it? Is it true?"

Is this what Nina came to talk about, and I talked about an elephant?

Is it true that Okeko Bible College discriminates against fatsos, or that God has cursed fatsos, or cursed the lot of them?

"If Okeko says so," I say, "it must be in the Book."

"But that's only a human *interpretation*! Why can't they read the Bible like it's written!"

I stand looking at her. She is close to tears again. Unaccountably, Nina wears her hair short, effectively lowering her forehead to simian proportions, capped by stiff ringlets of thinning hair blasted by beauty parlors. Her hair is graying. The ringlets do not altogether conceal the curvature of her skull, when viewed against light.

"It's great your wanting to go to college," I say. "I wish you'd told me sooner. I'll find a perfect little college for you. Just don't do anything in the meantime—all right?"

"I know all about your perfect little colleges. No thanks. But find out about Okeko. If I can't go to Okeko, I'll try Father. It's just that I'm not worthy of him yet."

"Worthy of Father?"

"Our Apostle," she says curtly, and seems to regret having blurted that much to an outsider. A guarded expression veils her eyes.

"Does that mean you will leave The Disciples, if you go to Okeko?"

"Why do you pretend interest? You're not interested. You haven't the faintest idea what it takes to be worthy of Father. What can you know on this deserted island of yours?"

"Are you coming next Saturday?"

"Are you inviting me?"

"Of course. Always."

"Not next Saturday," she says. "We're doing Outreach. I'll call you when I can."

So she leaves. Her car passes my roadside mailbox and glides out of my clearing into the woods.

Will she pay $30,000 to be found worthy of Father, and boil her brains into the bargain, in some Bible College that teaches Creation Science in the name of truth, *avoiding profane and vain babblings, and oppositions of science falsely so called: which some professing have erred concerning the faith?* . . . Nina would have made a good horticulturist, or a good pastry chef. She has a green thumb, can talk to plants, and her pleasure in sweets would impress an effendi in Istanbul.

Silence flows back. Bay Road is a quiet old country road, traffic having abandoned it for a better one. From the lawn bench under my elm I contemplate the empty road and hear a soft wind in the trees and the raucous slang of a blue jay, a bird whose insolence is bred by violent dislike of predators. A hawk is about, or a roosting owl. Inhaling the cool air, I return to myself on this deserted island of mine.

I have never known a man whose agonies about the sins of his children matched my father's intensity. His after-dinner Bible Hour brought the Full Gospel Church into our home every day between Sundays, and when he judged we needed more he summoned us to the living room at bedtime, or later. On such occasions, while waiting for him to appear, we sat without speaking, as ordered, and scowled accusations at each other. Who among us had transgressed?

Hamilton Crail did not account himself the most blameless man in Boston, only the most God-loving. Shortly after Nina's "infection" in her fourteenth year, his rage for glory tortured him to confess himself the Chief of Sinners.

I do not recall what else he said that night. Our family meetings were all alike, indistinguishable from church services and the Radio Gospel Hour, without the latter's pitch for a Free Grace-Faith ("golden metal") Prosperity Cross prayed over according to God's promises in Deuteronomy and Matthew. My father had indeed prospered, he could not love God enough, and he used to conclude our family meetings with a swing of the evangelical cudgel: "Pray with me!"

What I remember lucidly is my falling into a troubled sleep after one of those meetings, a sleep that conjured up the meeting in the form of a dream. It is my dream of the event, rather than the event itself, that has stuck in my memory through the years. From time to time I dream that dream again.

In my dream, the five of us have been summoned and sit waiting in the living room for our father to appear. My two younger brothers grow restive and pull at me to climb up on a ladder-back chair. They want to sled me around the room. I mount the chair, our eldest brother watches to see if we dare, and just then the door opens and a gigantic stranger enters, instead of our father.

Our summons is explained by the stranger's cropped hair and uniform of a prison guard from a 1930s melodrama. Massive neck and shoulders, blunt nose, stump of chin. He surveys the room with an air of authority. Much has happened behind the scenes last night while we slept, his manner tells us. We have all broken the law, and our father has had to go to the authorities and do his duty. The guard advances heavily into the room, an immoderate hulk suggesting restrained force, and speaks without raising his voice: "You all get ready to move, now."

He will brook no disobedience, it is clear. All except Nina rise to their feet. She slumps on the floor by the bookshelf, a dropped puppet in a pretty dress, her face that of an old woman, oddly darkened.

The guard seats himself in a Windsor chair and looks us over. His eyes rest on Nina and move on, unconcerned. Oblivious of my elevated position on the ladder-back chair, I remain standing on it, guessing that we will be marched out to a wagon and taken to our destination. I face the guard with confidence in my alacrity to obey. Hypocritical obedience is my strong suit. I will hop on one leg when ordered, fling myself to the ground when ordered. What can't I do, when ordered? I shall be a model prisoner, I shall win over the guard and get a commendation for good behavior, and maybe privileges.

"Now," says the guard, after he has scrutinized us. "When I count to three, you all start running out that door."

He will see what a good boy I am. Standing on my chair, I brace myself as for the start of a race. I want to be the first in the wagon.

"One . . . two. . ."

As the guard holds off the third count, I become aware of his watching me narrowly to see if I jump the gun. I will not jump the gun, never never. I will make for the door on the third count precisely, not a split second before or after.

I keep this promise to myself, inspired by fear of the unknown and by my need to survive. I don't jump the gun. And the third count never comes.

The guard sits scanning the room. All stand frozen like dummies.

We wait for the third count, and the guard's silence persists. My forward knee begins to tremble with the effort of holding still. I can't abandon my feeling that he is only doing his job, an elementary humanity behind the functionary must respond to my good will. I read in his eyes, as he returns my look, that he understands my sentiment. But he appraises me with an animal's vacant regard, and then I see that his skull is empty but for an implacable, unqualified, impersonal hatred, hatred without sense, directed not at transgression or trans-gressor but simply there like a reptile.

The third count never comes. But for a moment the pain of its not coming is transcended. My two younger brothers, ages nine and eleven, below the age of reason, one could plead, suddenly give the chair I stand on a shove, and, as I catch my balance, sled me around the room. In an eruption of play they push me in a delightful circle over the carpet, to the far end of the room and back. I feel securely fixed on the careering chair, and with the momentum gained I steer myself as on skis to the guard and come to a stop with a happy little flourish.

He leans sideways and holds me in his reptilian gaze. He can't punish me, I'm sure. Technically, I did not disobey him, I did not leave the chair, I remained standing on it, waiting for his third count, I was shoved and the chair slid about by itself.

"Having fun?" he says, and turns to the room at large. "You all accept Jesus, now. There's no other way. By the time I count three it will be too late."

Who could have invented such an instrument?

In the cemetery
where Al Jolson is buried

Amy Hempel

for Jessica

"Tell me things I won't mind forgetting," she said. "Make it useless stuff or skip it."

I began. I told her insects fly through rain, missing every drop, never getting wet. I told her no one in America owned a tape recorder before Bing Crosby did. I told her the shape of the moon is like a banana— you see it looking full, you're seeing it end-on.

The camera made me self-conscious and I stopped. It was trained on us from a ceiling mount—the kind of camera banks use to photograph robbers. It played our image to the nurses down the hall in Intensive Care.

"Go on, girl," she said, "you get used to it."

I had my audience. I went on. Did she know that Tammy Wynette had changed her tune? Really. That now she sings "Stand By Your *Friends*"? Paul Anka did it too, I said. Does "You're Having *Our* Baby." He got sick of all that feminist bitching.

"What else?" she said. "Have you got something else?"

Oh yes. For her I would always have something else.

"Did you know when they taught the first chimp to talk, it lied? When they asked her who did it on the desk, she signed back Max, the janitor. And when they pressed her, she said she was sorry, that it was really the project director. But she was a mother, so I guess she had her reasons."

"Oh, that's good," she said. "A parable."

"There's more about the chimp," I said. "But it will break your heart."

"No thanks," she says, and scratches at her mask.

*   *   *

We look like good-guy outlaws. Good or bad, I am not used to the mask yet. I keep touching the warm spot where my breath, thank God, comes out. She is used to hers. She only ties the strings on top. The other ones—a pro by now—she lets hang loose.

We call this place the Marcus Welby Hospital. It's the white one with the palm trees under the opening credits of all those shows. A Hollywood hospital, though in fact it is several miles west. Off camera, there is a beach across the street.

She introduces me to a nurse as "the Best Friend." The impersonal article is more intimate. It tells me that *they* are intimate, my friend and her nurse.

"I was telling her we used to drink Canada Dry Ginger Ale and pretend we were in Canada."

"That's how dumb *we* were," I say.

"You could be sisters," the nurse says.

So how come, I'll bet they are wondering, it took me so long to get to such a glamorous place? But do they ask?

They do not ask.

Two months, and how long is the drive?

The best I can explain it is this—I have a friend who worked one summer in a mortuary. He used to tell me stories. The one that really got to me was not the grisliest, but it's the one that did. A man wrecked his car on 101 going south. He did not lose consciousness. But his arm was taken down to the wet bone—and when he looked at it—it scared him to death. I mean, he died.

So I didn't dare look any closer. But now I'm doing it—and hoping I won't be scared to death.

*   *   *

She shakes out a summer-weight blanket, showing a leg you did not want to see. Except for that, you look at her and understand the law that requires *two* people to be with the body at all times.

"I thought of something," she says. "I thought of it last night. I think there is a real and present need here. You know," she says, "like for someone to do it for you when you can't do it yourself. You call them up whenever you want—like when push comes to shove."

She grabs the bedside phone and loops the cord around her neck. "Hey," she says, "the End o' the Line."

She keeps on, giddy with something. But I don't know with what.

"The giveaway was the solarium," she says. "That's where Marcus Welby broke the news to his patients. Then here's the real doctor suggesting we talk in the solarium. So I knew I was going to die.

"I can't remember," she says, "what does Kübler-Ross say comes after Denial?"

It seems to me Anger must be next. Then Bargaining, Depression, and so on and so forth. But I keep my guesses to myself.

"The only thing is," she says, "is where's Resurrection? God knows I want to do it by the book. But she left out Resurrection."

She laughs, and I cling to the sound the way someone dangling above a ravine holds fast to the thrown rope.

We could have cried then, but when we didn't, we couldn't.

"Tell me," she says, "about that chimp with the talking hands. What do they do when the thing ends and the chimp says, 'I don't want to go back to the zoo'?"

When I don't say anything, she says, "O.K.—then tell me another animal story. I like animal stories. But not a sick one—I don't want to know about all the seeing-eye dogs going blind."

No, I would not tell her a sick one.

"How about the hearing-ear dogs?" I say. "They're not going deaf, but they are getting very judgmental. For instance, there's this golden retriever in Jersey, he wakes up the deaf mother and drags her into the daughter's room because the kid has got a flashlight and is reading under the covers."

"Oh, you're killing me," she says. "Yes, you're definitely killing me."

"They say the smart dog obeys, but the smarter dog knows when to disobey."

"Yes," she says, "the smarter *anything* knows when to disobey. Now, for example."

She is flirting with the Good Doctor, who has just appeared. Unlike the Bad Doctor, who checks the I.V. drip before saying good morning, the Good Doctor says things like "God didn't give epileptics a fair shake." He awards himself points for the cripples he could have hit in the parking lot. Because the Good Doctor is a little in love with her he says maybe a year. He pulls a chair up to her bed and suggests I might like to spend an hour on the beach.

"Bring me something back," she says. "Anything from the beach. Or the gift shop. Taste is no object."

The doctor slowly draws the curtain around her bed.

"Wait!" she cries.

I look in at her.

"Anything," she says, "except a magazine subscription."

The doctor turns away.

I watch her mouth laugh.

*   *   *

What seems dangerous often is not—black snakes, for example, or clear-air turbulence. While things that just lie there, like this beach, are loaded with jeopardy. A yellow dust rising from the ground, the heat that ripens melons overnight—this is earthquake weather. You can sit here braiding the fringe on your towel and the sand will all of a sudden suck down like an hourglass. The air roars. In the cheap apartments onshore, bathtubs fill themselves and gardens roll up and over like green waves. If nothing happens, the dust will drift and the heat deepen till fear turns to desire. Nerves like that are only bought off by catastrophe.

"It never happens when you're thinking about it," she observed once.

"Earthquake, earthquake, earthquake," she said.

"Earthquake, earthquake, earthquake," I said.

Like the aviaphobe who keeps the plane aloft with prayer, we kept it up till an aftershock cracked the ceiling.

That was after the big one in '72. We were in college; our dormitory was five miles from the epicenter. When the ride was over and my jabbering pulse began to slow, she served five parts champagne to one part orange juice and joked about living in Ocean View, Kansas. I offered to drive her to Hawaii on the new world psychics predicted would surface the next time, or the next.

I could not say that now—next. Whose next? she could ask.

Was I the only one who noticed that the experts had stopped saying if and now spoke of when? Of course not; the fearful ran to thousands. We watched the traffic of Japanese beetles for deviation. Deviation might mean more natural violence.

I wanted her to be afraid with me, but she said, "I don't know. I'm just not."

She was afraid of nothing, not even of flying.

I have this dream before a flight where we buckle in and the plane moves down the runway. It takes off at thirty-five miles an hour, and then we're airborne, skimming the tree tops. Still, we arrive in New York on time. It is so pleasant. One night I flew to Moscow this way.

She flew with me once. That time she flew with me she ate macadamia nuts while the wings bounced. She knows the wing tips can bend thirty feet up and thirty feet down without coming off. She believes it. She trusts the laws of aerodynamics. My mind stampedes. I can almost accept that a battleship floats, and everybody knows steel sinks.

I see fear in her now and am not going to try to talk her out of it. She is right to be afraid.

After a quake, the six o'clock news airs a film clip of first-graders yelling at the broken playground per their teacher's instructions.

"*Bad* earth!" they shout, because anger is stronger than fear.

*   *   *

But the beach is standing still today. Everyone on it is tranquilized, numb or asleep. Teenaged girls rub coconut oil on each other's hard-to-reach places. They smell like macaroons. They pry open compacts like clamshells; mirrors catch the sun and throw a spray of white rays across glazed shoulders. The girls arrange their wet hair with silk flowers the way they learned in *Seventeen*. They pose.

A formation of low-riders pulls over to watch with a six-pack. They get vocal when the girls check their tan lines. When the beer is gone, so are they—flexing their cars on up the boulevard.

Above this aggressive health are the twin wrought-iron terraces, painted flamingo pink, of the Palm Royale. Someone dies there every time the sheets are changed. There's an ambulance in the driveway, so the remaining residents line the balconies, rocking and not talking, one-upped.

The ocean they stare at is dangerous, and not just the undertow. You can almost see the slapping tails of sand sharks keeping cruising bodies alive.

If she looked, she could see this, some of it, from her window. She would be the first to say how little it takes to make a thing all wrong.

*   *   *

There was a second bed in the room when I returned. For two beats I didn't get it. Then it hit me like an open coffin.

She wants every minute, I thought. She wants my life.

"You missed Gussie," she said.

Gussie is her parents' 300-pound narcoleptic maid. Her attacks often come at the ironing board. The pillowcases in that family are all bordered with scorch.

"It's a hard trip for her," I said. "How is she?"

"Well, she didn't fall asleep, if that's what you mean. Gussie's great—you know what she said? She said, 'Darlin' just keep prayin', down on your knees.'"

She shrugged. "See anybody good?"

"No," I said, "just the new Charlie's Angel. And I saw Cher's car down near the Arcade."

"Cher's car is worth *three* Charlie's Angels," she said. "What else am I missing?"

"It's earthquake weather," I told her.

"The best thing to do about earthquakes," she said, "is not to live in California."

"That's useful," I said. "You sound like Reverend Ike: 'The best thing to do for the poor is not be one of them.'"

We're crazy about Reverend Ike.

I noticed her face was bloated.

"You know," she said, "I feel like hell. I'm about to stop having fun."

"The ancients have a saying," I said. "'There are times when the wolves are silent; there are times when the moon howls.'"

"What's that, Navajo?"

"Palm Royale lobby graffiti," I said. "I bought a paper there. I'll read to you."

"Even though I care about nothing?" she said.

I turned to page three, to a UPI filler datelined Mexico City. I read her "Man Robs Bank With Chicken," about a man who bought a barbecued chicken at a stand down the block from a bank. Passing the bank, he got the idea. He walked in and approached a teller. He pointed the brown paper bag at her and she handed over the day's receipts. It was the smell of barbecue sauce that eventually led to his capture.

The story made her hungry, she said, so I took the elevator down six floors to the cafeteria and brought back all the ice cream she wanted. We lay side by side, adjustable beds cranked up for optimal TV viewing, littering the sheets with Good Humor wrappers, picking toasted almonds out of the gauze. We were Lucy and Ethel, Mary and Rhoda in extremis. The blinds were closed to keep light off the screen.

We watched a movie starring men we used to think we wanted to sleep with. Hers was a tough cop out to stop mine, a vicious rapist who went after cocktail waitresses.

"This is a good movie," she said, when snipers felled them both.

I missed her already; my straight man, my diary.

A Filipino nurse tiptoed in and gave her an injection. She removed the pile of popsicle sticks from the nightstand—enough to splint a small animal.

The injection made us sleepy—me in the way I picked up her inflection till her mother couldn't tell us apart on the phone. We slept.

I dreamed she was a decorator, come to furnish my house. She worked in secret, singing to herself. When she finished, she guided me proudly to the door. "How do you like it?" she asked, easing me inside.

Every beam and sill and shelf and knob was draped in black bunting, with streamers of black crepe looped around darkened mirrors.

*   *   *

"I have to go home," I said when she woke up.

She thought I meant home to her house in the Canyon, and I had to say No, *home* home. I twisted my hands in the hackneyed fashion of people in pain. I was supposed to offer something. The Best Friend. I could not even offer to come back.

I felt weak and small and failed. Also exhilarated. I had a convertible in the parking lot. Once out of that room, I would drive it too fast down the coast highway through the crab-smelling air. A stop in Malibu for sangria. The music in the place would be sexy and loud. They would serve papaya and shrimp and watermelon ice. After dinner I would pick up beach boys. I would shimmer with life, buzz with heat, vibrate with health, stay up all night with one and then the other.

Without a word, she yanked off her mask and threw it on the floor. She kicked at the blankets and moved to the door. She must have hated having to pause for breath and balance before slamming out of Isolation, and out of the second room, the one where you scrub and tie on the white masks.

A voice shouted her name in alarm, and people ran down the corridor. The Good Doctor was paged over the intercom. I opened the door and the nurses at the station stared hard, as if this flight had been my idea.

"Where is she?" I asked, and they nodded to the supply closet.

I looked in. Two nurses were kneeling beside her on the floor, talking to her in low voices. One held a mask over her nose and mouth, the other rubbed her back in slow circles. The nurses glanced up to see if I was the doctor, and when they saw I wasn't, they went back to what they were doing.

"There, there, honey," they cooed.

*   *   *

On the morning she was moved to the cemetery, the one where Al Jolson is buried, I enrolled in a Fear of Flying class. "What is your worst fear?" the instructor asked, and I answered, "That I will finish this course and still be afraid."

I sleep with a glass of water on the nightstand so I can see by its level if the coastal earth is trembling or if the shaking is still me.

What do I remember? I remember only the useless things I hear—that Bob Dylan's mother invented Wite-out, that twenty-three people must be in a room before there is a fifty-fifty chance two will have the same birthdate. Who cares whether or not it's true? In my head there are bath towels swaddling this stuff. Nothing else seeps through.

I review those things that will figure in the re-telling: a kiss through surgical gauze, the pale hand correcting the position of the wig. I noted these gestures as they happened, not in any retrospect. Though I don't know why looking *back* should show us more than looking *at*. It is just possible I will say I stayed the night. And who is there that can say I did not?

Nothing else gets through until I think of the chimp, the one with the talking hands.

In the course of the experiment, that chimp had a baby. Imagine how her trainers must have thrilled when the mother, without prompting, began to sign to the newborn. Baby, drink milk. Baby, play ball. And when the baby died, the mother stood over the body, her wrinkled hands moving with animal grace, forming again and again the words, Baby, come hug, Baby, come hug, fluent now in the language of grief.

ON FOLLOWING PAGE: DRAWING BY PETER DE SEVE. (*TQ* #56)

June harvest

W. S. Di Piero

They've all come down. And for reasons
I should know by now but don't,
another vision of you caught me up.
I saw you at the kitchen table,
one year before you died, head fallen
on your arms, crossed as if to shield you
from the heart's loosening terror.
The air shone all around, facsimile
of the formica top. What was that terror
after all? To reckon that no nerve
sustains us in the need to be effectual
and good, that we can't be both at once.
Husband, father, worker, perfecting
what? And so the casing broke in grief
so general, pure, and brittle, no elemented
mind could sort or shape its meaning,
no words could spell or justify the guilt
of lost sense. You wept in that knowledge.

And now they've all come down. The poplars'
lazy fuzzballs loosed in absent wind,
the shaggy maple fruit and box-elder
wings, all collapsed upon the dandelions
shrunk to seed, spongy camomile, and clover.
So my daughter and I went gathering
while two swallows looped overhead,

quickened points of midday shade.
Fists full of elm castings, we sat
and slowly peeled each one, ripping down
the paper sheath from the clean notched mouth.
As the seeds squirmed loose we set them
in neat files. That's when the vision came.
The little pause, seen, stuns me now
as my laughing child tugs my arms and begs me
not to hide my head, to speak to her.
Having this, I feel a wild gladness
for you, that you were soon done with life.

Ambush

John Morgan

A light with the richness
of cream pours over the bar.
Slack night. I sip a glass
of beer remembering who I think
I am and then forgetting.
"Killing's more direct than talk,"

he says, says he could do it still
but what's the use? His breath's
a heavy metal stink about like dirt
or the wide circles
of waiting he pledged allegiance to
before his birth.

Camped in the Asian dark,
sick on his first patrol,
he tells me how they wouldn't
talk to him, his alien platoon
that first night out. Then
something like a finger beckoning.

He turns, hears in his middle ear
a bird's frail tune,
thick eons shouldering over oceans of recall.
With hardly time to think
he's off his stool, rolling
in a fit of peanut shells and drool.

1983   543

The mind at war
has got its reasons. Plunging
in a sink of need,
he's there as well as here,
hands tensed around his snub-nosed
sharp-toothed pet,

and suddenly I could do
with one less beer. Tomorrow
if he lives he'll burn
a village, be a vet.
All wars are fought by country
boys used to this long road.

Instructions to be left behind

Marvin Bell

I've included this letter in the group
to be put into the cigar box—the one
with the rubber band around it you will find
sometime later. I thought you might
like to have an example of the way in which
some writing works. I may not say anything
very important or phrase things just-so,
but I think you will pay attention anyway
because it matters to you—I'm sure it does,
no one was ever more loved than I was.

What I'm saying is, your deep attention
made things matter—made art,
made science and business
raised to the power of goodness, and sport
likewise raised a level beyond.
I am not attaching to this a photograph
though no doubt you have in your mind's eye
a clear image of me in several expressions
and at several ages all at once—which is
the great work of imagery beyond the merely
illustrative. Should I stop here for a moment?

These markings, transliterations though they are
from prints of fingers, and they from heart

and throat and corridors the mind guards,
are making up again in you the one me
that otherwise would not survive that manyness
daisies proclaim and the rain sings much of.
Because I love you, I can almost imagine
the eye for detail with which you remember
my face in places indoors and out and far-flung,
and you have only to look upwards to see
in the plainest cloud the clearest lines
and in the flattest field your green instructions.

Shall I rest a moment in green instructions?
Writing is all and everything, when you care.
The kind of writing that grabs your lapels
and shakes you—that's for when you don't care
or even pay attention. This isn't that kind.
While you are paying your close kind of attention,
I might be writing the sort of thing you think
will last—as it is happening, now, for you.
While I was here to want this, I wanted it,
and now that I am your wanting me to be myself
again, I think myself right up into being
all that you (and I too) wanted me to be: You.

Gill boy

Dennis Schmitz

for John, my son

The toys I bought for you
splash down in your brothers' tub,
are rubbed paintless,
protean, in the 15 years coming down:

the space vehicle Apollo,
the rubbery aliens,
the tooth-scarred astronaut
who trails air-hose,
prepared to go breathless

into the child's world.
You lived only five days,
unable to surface, cyanotic

in the isolette, then cold—
the way I've learned to accept you
when I wash your two brothers real,
when I shape each
of their small parts over

& over again with soap.
I tried to forget, to sublimate,
but under seven inches of bathwater,
out of reach,

you learned to breathe.
The suds your brothers leave,
the soapy waste

webs galls & scaly eyelets
all over your skin
so cruel no one could love you

& want to survive.

From A *minor apocalypse*

Tadeusz Konwicki

Translated by Richard Lourie

Here comes the end of the world. It's coming, it's drawing closer, or rather, it is the end of my own world which has come creeping up on me. The end of my personal world. But before my universe collapses into rubble, disintegrates into atoms, explodes into the void, one last kilometer of my Golgotha awaits me, one last lap in this marathon, the last few rungs up or down a ladder without meaning.

I woke at the gloomy hour at which autumn's hopeless days begin. I lay in bed looking at a window full of rain clouds but it was really filled with one cloud, like a carpet darkened with age. It was the hour for doing life's books, the hour of the daily accounting. Once people did their accounts at midnight before a good night's sleep, now they beat their breasts in the morning, woken by the thuds of their dying hearts.

There was blank paper close at hand, in the bureau. The nitro-glycerin of the contemporary writer, the narcotic of the wounded individual. You can immerse yourself in the flat white abyss of the page, hide from yourself and your private universe, which will soon explode and vanish. You can soil that defenseless whiteness with bad blood, furious venom, stinking phlegm, but no one is going to like that, not even the author himself. You can pour the sweetness of artificial harmony, the ambrosia of false courage, the cloying syrup of flattery onto that vacant whiteness and everyone will like it, even the author himself . . .

The first sounds of life could be heard in the building. This building, this great engine, moved slowly into daily life. And so I reached for my first cigarette. The cigarette before breakfast tastes the best. It shortens your life. For many years now I have been laboring at shortening my life. Everybody shortens their existence on the sly. There must be something to all that. Some higher command or perhaps a law of nature in this overpopulated world.

I like the misty dizziness in my head after a deep drag of bitter smoke. I would like to say some suitable farewell to the world. For ever since I was a child I have been departing from this life but I can't finish the job. I loiter at railway crossings, I walk by houses where roof tiles fall, I drink until I drop, I antagonize hooligans. And so I am approaching the finish line. I am in the final turn. I would like to say farewell to you somehow or another. I long to howl in an inhuman voice so that I am heard in the most distant corner of the planet and perhaps even in neighboring constellations or perhaps even in the residence of the Lord God. Is that vanity? Or a duty? Or an instinct which commands us castaways, us cosmic castaways, to shout through the ages into starry space?

We've become intimate with the universe. Every money-hungry poet, foolish humorist, and treacherous journalist wipes his mouth on the cosmos and so why can't I too hold my head up high to where rusted Sputniks and astronaut excrement, frozen bone-hard, go gliding past.

And so I would like to say farewell somehow. I dreamed of teeth all night. I dreamed I was holding a pile of teeth like kernels of corn in my hand. There was even a filling in one, a cheap Warsaw filling from the dental cooperative. To say something complete about myself. Not as a warning, not as knowledge, not even for amusement. Simply to say something which no one else could reveal. Because before falling asleep or perhaps in the first passing cloud of sleep, I begin to understand the meaning of existence, time, and the life beyond this one. I understand that mystery for a fraction of a second, through an instant of distant memories, a brief moment of consolation or fearful foreboding and then plunge immediately into the depths of my bad dreams. In one way or another everyone strains his blood-nourished brain to the breaking point trying to understand. But I'm getting close. I mean, at times I get close. And I would give everything I possess, down to the last scrap but, after all, I don't own anything and so I would be giving a lot of nothing, to see that mystery in all its simplicity, to see it once and then to forget it forever.

I am a biped born not far from the Vistula River of old stock and that means I inherited all its bipedal experience in my genes. I have seen war, that terrible frenzy of mammals murdering each other until they drop in exhaustion. I have observed the birth of life and its end in that act we call death. I have known all the brutality of my species and all its extraordinary angelicalness. I have traveled the thorny path of individual evolution known as fate. I am one of you. I am a perfect, anonymous *homo sapiens*. So why couldn't a caprice of chance have entrusted me with the secret if it is, in any case, destined to be revealed?

These words have a sort of day-off quality, the luxury of an idler, the twists of a pervert. But after all, all of you who from time to time put the convolutions of your own lazy brains into gear are subject to these same desires and ambitions. The same fears and self-destructive reflexes. The same rebellion and resignation.

Two drunken deliverywomen have knocked over a tall column of crates containing milk bottles. Now, standing stock-still, they are observing the results of the cataclysm, experiencing the complicated and yet at the same time simple process which transforms a mess into some light-minded fun. The transparent rain has caught its wing on our building, which is rotting with age. A Warsaw building built late in the epoch of Stalinism, when Stalinism was decadent and had become Polonized and raggedy.

I have to get up. I have to rise from my bed and perform fifteen acts whose meaning is not to be pondered. An accretion of automatic habits. The blessed cancer of tradition's meaningless routine. But the last war not only took the lives of scores of millions of people. Without intending to, accidentally, the last war shattered the great palace of culture of European morality, aesthetics, and custom. And humankind drove back to the gloomy caverns and the icy caves in their Rolls-Royces, Mercedes, and Moskviches.

Outside, my city, beneath a cloud the color of an old, blackened carpet. A city to which I was driven by fate from my native city, which I no longer remember and dream of less all the time. Fate only drove me a few hundred kilometers but it separated me from my old unfulfilled life by an entire eternity of reincarnation. This city is the capital of a people who are evaporating into nothingness. Something needs to be said about that too. But to whom? To those who are no longer with us, who are sailing off into oblivion? Or perhaps to those who devour individuals and whole nations?

The city was beginning to hum like a drive belt. It was stirring from the lethargy of sleep. Moving towards its fate, which I know and which I wish to avoid . . .

I am free. I am one of the few free people in this country of patent slavery. A slavery covered by a sloppy coat of contemporary varnish. I have fought a long and bloodless battle for this pitiable personal freedom. I fought for my freedom against the temptations, ambitions, and appetites which drive everyone blindly on to the slaughterhouse. To the so-called modern slaughterhouse for human dignity, honor, and of something else, too, which we forgot about a long time ago.

I am free and alone. Being alone is a small enough price to pay for this none-too-great luxury of mine. I freed myself on the last lap when the finish line could already be seen by the naked eye. I am a free, anonymous man. My flights and falls occurred while I was wearing a magical cap of invisibility, my successes and sins sailed on in invisible corvettes, and my films and books flew off into the abyss in invisible strongboxes. I am free, anonymous.

And so I'll light up another cigarette. On an empty stomach. Here comes the end of my world. That I know for certain. The untimely end of my world. What will be its harbingers? A sudden, piercing pain in the chest beneath the sternum? The squeal of tires as a car slams on its brakes? An enemy, or perhaps a friend?

Outside, those women were still discussing the catastrophe with the milk. They sat down on the old, dark gray, plastic cases, lit up cigarettes and were watching the watery milk trickle down the catch basin, which was belching steam because, no doubt, hot water from the heat and power plant had again gotten into the water main by mistake. And then I suddenly became aware that no one had delivered milk for years, that I had forgotten the sight of those women workers of indeterminate age pushing carts of milk bottles long ago and in my mind that image was associated with those distant green years when I was young and the world was too.

They're probably making a period film, I told myself, and pressed my forehead against the damp windowpane. But all I saw was an everyday normal street. Small crowds of people hurrying by the buildings on the way to work. As usual when the temperature rises in the morning, a crumbling block of stone facing tore loose from the Palace of Culture and flew crashing down into the jagged gulley of buildings. It was only then that I noticed the eagle on the wall of that great edifice, an eagle on a field of black—that is, on a field of red blackened by rain. Our white eagle is not doing too badly because it is supported from below by a huge globe of the world, which is tightly entwined by a hammer and sickle. The gutter spoke with the bass of an ocarina. Then the wind, perhaps still the summer wind or maybe now a winter wind, came tearing from the Parade Field and turned the poplars' silver sides to the sun, which was confined in wet clouds.

I was out of cigarettes. And when you run out of cigarettes you are suddenly seized by a desire to smoke. And so I opened the next drawer of my treasure chest where I keep outrageous letters and old accounts, broken lighters and tax receipts, photographs from my youth and sleeping powders. And there, among tufts of cotton batting and rolls of bandages from the good old days when it was still worth my while to submit to operations, in those age-encrusted recesses I found a yellowed page from many years ago, a page like a cartouche on a monument or a gravestone, a page where I once began a piece of prose I have not finished yet. I began this work in that wonderful time around New Year's, right after New Year's Eve, with a nice hangover still throbbing healthy in my head. I began on New Year's Day because I had indulged in superstition and wanted to celebrate the new biological and astronomical cycle with some work. Later I realized that my own New Year's begins at the end of summer or the beginning of fall and so that is why I stopped writing and have not written a word since.

And so there was that page, once white, now yellow, for long months, seasons, years, never finished, never completed, with its faded motto which was to bless the wistful scenes, the exalted thoughts, the lovely descriptions of nature. I blew the dust from Warsaw's factories off that waxen corpse of my imagination and read the words, which were the credo of an old Polish magnate in the nineteenth century: "If Russia's interests permit, I would gladly turn my feelings to my original fatherland." What was it I had in mind then? Did I want to read that avowal every morning to my children before breakfast? Or did I intend to copy it out at Christmas to be sent to the magnates of science, literature, and film, my contemporaries? Or was I trying to win the favor of the censor for a piece that had come stillborn from an anemic inspiration?

The windows rattled painfully. Hysterical police sirens leapt from some side street. I glanced at the watch my friend Stanislaw D. had once brought me back from a trip to the Soviet Union. It was going on eight. I knew what that meant. Each day at that hour, an armored refrigerator truck carrying food supplies for the ministers and the Party Secretaries raced through the city escorted by police vans. The cavalcade of vehicles flashed past my building splashing the puddles of milk on the street. The archaic milk deliverers, let out of some old-age home for the day, ground out their butts on the muddy sidewalk, exchanging furtive goodbyes.

Suddenly the gong by my door rang. I froze by the window, not believing my ears, certain that device had not been working for years. But the elegant, xylophone-like sound was repeated, and more insistently this time. Pulling on an old robe, a present from my brother-in-law, Jan L., I moved guardedly toward the door. I opened the door. Hubert and Rysio, both wearing their Sunday best, suits which reminded me of the carefree middle seventies, were standing at the top of the stairs.

Hubert was holding a cane in his right hand and in his left a sinister-looking black briefcase. My heart began beating rapidly, and not without cause, for they came to see me only about twice a year and each of their visits marked a radical change in my life.

"May we come in? It isn't too early?" asked Hubert jovially.

I was well acquainted with those artificial smiles of theirs which concealed attacks on my comfort.

Now smiling freely myself, I opened the door hospitably and, as they entered with much ceremony on their part, I instantly divined the purpose of this visit. Thanks to them, I had signed dozens of petitions, memorials, and protests sent over the years to our always taciturn regime. A few times it cost me some work, and many times I was secretly dispossessed of my civil rights; practically every day I was subjected to some petty, invisible harassments which are even shameful to recall but which, adding up over the years, helped estrange me greatly from life. So, we exchanged cordial hugs, smiling all the time like old cronies, but I was already quite tense and my throat had gone dry.

Finally we found ourselves in my living room and we sat down in the wooden armchairs, all in a row as if we were on an airplane flying off to some mysterious and exciting adventure.

"You look good," said Hubert, setting the sinister-looking briefcase down beside him.

"You seem to be holding up too," I said in a friendly tone.

For a moment we looked at each other in embarrassment. Hubert was resting his sinewy hand on his cane. His one blind eye was motionless, the other kept blinking and regarding me with something between affection and irony. Once long ago he had been tortured, perhaps by the anti-Communist underground or perhaps by investigating officers of the Security police and, because of that incident, now long forgotten by everyone, he walked with a cane and was in poor health. Rysio, whom I remembered as a blond angel, was now balding and had put on weight, the high priest of the plotless allegorical novel without punctuation or dialogue.

We looked good, for old fogeys, that was true. But then the moment of silence lengthened out a bit and something had to be said.

"Would you like a drink?"

"A drink couldn't hurt," said Hubert. "What do you have?"

"Pure vodka. Made from potatoes. Imported potatoes."

"All the more reason not to refuse." Hubert's voice was thunderous, as if he were in some space larger than my cluttered room.

While I was getting the bottle and the glasses from the cupboard, they were both looking discreetly about the room. The liquid made from imported potatoes began to gurgle as I cowered at the edge of my chair. A cigarette on an empty stomach is bad for you but a hundred grams of potato vodka is death itself. Or maybe it's better. I raised my glass.

"Good luck."

"Your health." Rysio finally said something, and quickly tossed off the contents of his glass.

Outside, the wind had died down for the moment and the poplars had turned their solid green toward us. My building was, as bad luck would have it, exceptionally quiet and our silence was becoming increasingly louder. But I made a firm decision not to speak and to force them to show their cards.

Hubert set his glass aside with a certain deliberation.

"You're not going out much," he said.

"That's right. Autumn puts me out of sorts."

"A little depression?"

"Something like that."

"Are you writing?"

"I had just started."

He seemed to be looking at me in disbelief. Rysio poured himself another glass.

"What's it going to be?"

"No revelations. I just felt like writing a little nonsense about myself."

"You always wrote about yourself."

"You could be right. But I wanted to write about other people."

"It's high time you did."

"To drown myself out."

The whole thing looked like an examination. And I felt like a high school senior taking his finals. But, after all, I had felt that way my whole life, a student at best.

"Well, Rysio," said Hubert all of a sudden. "Time to get down to business."

Rysio nodded.

"Something to sign?" I hazarded a guess, squinting accomodatingly over at the black briefcase.

"No, this time it's something else. Perhaps you might begin, Rysio."

"Go on, go on, since you started," said Rysio eagerly.

A sort of goofy warmth was rising in me. I reached for the bottle automatically, wanting to pour Hubert a glass while I was at it.

"Thanks, that's enough." He stopped me with a somewhat official tone. I took that as a bad sign.

Really I was indifferent. I am a free person who has been suspended high above this city and who from a distance and with serene amazement observes the strange humans and their strange doings. Without thinking, I turned on the television on the table. I heard the sound of wind howling, the flutter of cloth, but after a moment, the image of a festively decorated airport emerged out of the silvery dots. An honor guard was frozen across the screen, some civilians were shielding themselves against the wind with their overcoats while, above the honor guard and the civilians, red, sail-like flags swelled in the wind, and shyly interspersed among them were red and white Polish flags.

"Well now," said Hubert, deciding to break the silence. "We haven't spoken with you for some time now."

I took a deep breath, which made me feel ashamed, and I sank deeper into my chair.

"Yes, we lost contact with each other," I said in a worldly tone.

"We're a vanishing breed."

"Everyone's out for himself," added Rysio.

"But I've been observing your activities."

"What activities," said Hubert with a dismissive wave of one hand. "We're keepers of a dying flame."

"That's a fact. I have the impression that this country is really dying," I said, without knowing what they were driving at.

"So many years of struggle. We've grown old, we've gone to pot putting out those semilegal bulletins, periodicals, appeals which are read by next to no one. Of course the young people read them. But young people get married, have babies, buy little Fiats, give up on action and start growing tomatoes. We've been overrun by the bourgeoisie, a Soviet bourgeoisie.

"It's the end, the grave," added Rysio, pouring himself another glass.

Water was dripping onto the floor through the leaky balcony doors. I should have looked for a washcloth to prevent any damage but I didn't much feel like it and I would have been a little embarrassed to do it in front of my colleagues. Our conversation was not going well. It was hard to chat about the things we thought about all day long and which we even dreamed about in our lousy sleep. Things had looked better at one time. We were children of the nineteenth century. Our fathers had been members of Pilsudski's Legions or his secret army, and during World War II we had been in the Home Army or the Union of Fighting Youth. That means, how to say it now, that means, how to explain it after all those years, that means, the hell with it, that doesn't mean anything, now, at the end of our splendid twentieth century, a century of tyranny and unbridled democracy, foolish holiness and brilliant villainy, art without punch and graphomania run rampant.

I saw Hubert's good eye fixed on me.

"Are you listening?" he asked.

"Yes, of course."

"We have a proposition for you. On behalf of our colleagues."

My spine went cold and very slowly I put my unfinished glass aside.

"What is it you wish to propose?"

"That today at eight p.m. you light yourself on fire in front of Central Party Headquarters."

Nothing had changed on the screen—wind, the violent flapping of the flags, the waiting. Only then could the reverent, solemn music broadcast from the studio be heard.

My throat gulped saliva mixed with vodka.

"Are you joking, Hubert?"

"No, I'm not joking." He wiped some invisible sweat from his brow.

"But why me? Why are you coming to me with this?"

"Who else? Somebody has to do it."

"I understand, I understand everything, I just don't understand why me."

Hubert glanced over at Rysio. "I told you this would happen." Rysio looked down at the floor.

"Listen," he finally said in some anguish, "we've been discussing this for a long time. We've analyzed all the possible candidates. And it came out you."

My tree of happiness stood by on the windowsill. Only then did I notice how much it had shot up lately and grown thick with young, strong leaves. It was sickly for many years and now, suddenly, without any external cause, it had surged upward, sending out a large number of powerful, knotty branches.

"You see," said Hubert softly, "an act like this can only make sense if it shakes people here in Poland and everywhere abroad. You are known to the Polish readers and you have a bit of a name over there in the West too. Your life story, your personality, are perfect for this situation. Obviously, we can't talk you into it and we won't even try— it's up to you and your conscience. I only wish to pass on an opinion which is not only mine or Rysio's, but that of the entire community which is attempting to put up some resistance. You'll pardon me for my lack of eloquence."

"I doubt whether my death would play the part you expect. I know people whose sacrifice would become a symbol the world over."

They looked at me with curiosity. Hubert rubbed his fingers, which were turning insistently bluish.

"No doubt you're thinking of Jan?" he asked.

"Naturally. The whole world knows his films and his books are read in many countries in courses on world literature. Every year we're on tenterhooks waiting to see if he'll win an Oscar or the Nobel."

A barely perceptible smile appeared on Hubert's face.

"That'd be too high a price to pay. Too high a price for the country and our community. You've answered your own question."

"All right. But what about our filmmakers, our composers? I can give you a few names better than mine right off."

"You're the one, old man," said Rysio and reached for the bottle. He clearly felt I was weakening, which gave him heart.

"Life and blood have to be disposed of intelligently," said Hubert wearily. "Those others have a different role to play. Every nugget of genius possesses the highest value in this massacred nation. Their deaths would not enrich us very much and would impoverish us terribly."

"But why not you, or Rysio?"

They glanced at each other with distaste. My blubbering embarrassed them.

1983

"Then why would we have come to you?" asked Hubert. "Let's be frank. Your death will be spectacular, another order up. Don't you see that?"

"You're the one, old man," added Rysio, who was softhearted and was now suffering along with me.

"Listen to me, Hubert. I never interfered in the functioning of our artistic life. I never butted into your affairs, the affairs of a careworn opposition in a country no one cares about. But now I must tell you what I think. You have bred blind, deaf demiurges, who in their marvelous artistic passions create beautiful, universal art but do not notice us crawling in the mud or the daily agonies of our society. They worked hard at guarding the flame of genius that burned in them and gladly exploited the claque of the regime's mass propaganda which boasted of them every day and fed its own complexes with their world renown. You, the emaciated opposition, did not spare them the claques either, anointing them with the charisma of moral approval. They grew fat on our exile, our humiliations, our anonymity. They hopped freely from one sacred grove of national art to another, for we had been driven out of them or had left of our own free will. When you went around pleading with them to sign even the most modest of humanitarian appeals which would displease our team of wanton rulers, they arrogantly sent you packing empty-handed, winking at their coteries to say that you were provocateurs, secret police agents. Their greatness came from our being voluntarily dwarfed. Their genius sprang from our graves as artists. Why shouldn't one of them pay for their decades of solemn, superhuman greatness with a cruel, physical death?"

I turned off the television, where the civilians and soldiers were impatiently waiting for someone. A sudden downpour flew past the balcony, knocking a condom withering on the iron balustrade off into the abyss. Those condoms—bouquets of lillies of the valley, presents to me from my neighbors on the upper floors from their days off.

"We're all racked by envy to one degree or another," said Hubert, somewhat taken aback. He was pale and strenuously rubbing his fingers, which were turning blue. "But let's not talk about that today. Maybe some other time."

"But when are we going to talk if I carry out your command?"

"But, old man, you know," said Rysio, setting his glass aside, "these arguments are indecent."

"I never said anything even though my guts were turning. Hubert, do I need to tell you the names of the people who spent their whole lives walking hand in hand with the government while pretending to go their own way? And their works, which the more clever ones clothed in the garb of universal fashion, world frustration, western melancholy and what is a sort of the neuralgia of the left. And when we became Sovietized to such a degree that a cult of the illicit erupted here, an ambiguous desire for a lick of the forbidden, a pitiful delight in political pornography dressed in the lingerie of allusion, when there arose in Poland that aberration, that scheming contest of self-justification for all the sins of collaboration, they were the first, greedy for applause, anxious for success, they fastened onto the new state of affairs and littered art with the phony gestures of cunning Rejtans, they muddied our poor art, they stomped out the last of their own conscience in it. Why do you fall down before them when they climb on your crosses looking for the golden apples which feed their pride? Why do you pour admiration on them when their fate is opposed to yours?"

"You chose your own fate. This is not the time for that sort of discussion. Rysio, isn't it time for us to be going?" Hubert bent forward heavily and drew the black briefcase out from under the table, the briefcase which could contain an appeal for the abolition of the death penalty, a volume of uncensored poetry, or an ordinary homemade bomb.

"Wait a minute, Hubert." I stopped his hand. "Tell me here, in private, man to man, why have you designated me?"

He tore his hand from mine.

"I don't designate. I have the same rights as you do. And the same duties."

"But there must be something about me that makes me suitable and others less so."

The rain had hazed the windows over. Nearby a child was playing a melody with one finger, a melody which I remembered from years back, many years back.

"After all, you've always been obsessed with death," whispered Hubert hoarsely. "I never treated your complex as a literary manner-ism. You are the most intimate with death, you shouldn't be afraid of it. You have prepared yourself and us for your death most carefully. What were you thinking about before we arrived?"

"Death."

"You see. It's at your side. All you have to do is reach out."

"Just reach out."

"Yes, that's all."

"Today?"

"Today at eight o'clock in the evening when the party congress is over and the delegates from the entire country are leaving the building."

"What about the others?"

"Who?"

"The people necessary to the nation."

"In sin and holiness, in conformism and rebellion, in betrayal and redemption, they will bear the soul of the nation into eternity."

"You're lying. You're choking on that garbage, your eyes are popping out of their sockets."

Rysio leapt from his chair, knocking over his glass.

"Leave him alone!" he shouted and began rummaging in Hubert's shirt. Hubert had gone stiff and extended his legs as if he wanted to look at his muddy boots. Rysio began pushing pea-like pills through his lips, which had turned blue. He forced a few drops of water between his clenched teeth. Hubert moved his jaw, closed his eyes then bit one pill in half and tried to swallow it.

Someone rang the bell. I opened the latch with trembling hands. A man, a bit on the drunk side, stood in the doorway, holding onto the doorframe.

"You should run yourself some water because we're going to turn it off," he said, belching a cloud of undigested alcohol.

"I don't need any water."

"I suggest you run your tub and your other faucets. We'll be cutting it off for the whole day."

"Thank you. So did a main burst then?"

"Everything burst. May I sit down here for a minute? I'm dead on my feet."

"I'm sorry but my friend isn't feeling well. I have to go fetch an ambulance."

"No one's feeling good these days. I won't bother you then. Stay well."

"The same to you."

He went off to knock on my neighbors' doors. I returned at a run down the hall. Now Hubert was sitting up straight in his chair. He smiled painfully to hide his sudden panic.

"Should I call a doctor?"

"No need to. I'm all right now. Where were we?"

A swath of sunlight moved across the rooftops of the city like a great kite. My friend the sparrow hopped onto one bar of the balustrade and was surprised that I did not greet him.

"Hubert, is there any sense to all this? Do you really believe there is?"

"Now you're asking?"

"Why have you been so unrelenting all your life? In all ways. Is it hormones or some higher force commanding you?"

"Leave him alone, he has to go home." Rysio pushed me away.

"Isn't it a short way to the party building?"

"Not all deaths are the same, you see," said Hubert in a muffled voice. "We all need the elevated, the majestic, the holy. That is what you can offer us."

"For your sins, old man," added Rysio and attempted a smile.

"You have plenty of yours, and ours, on your conscience."

"But they have just as many," I said in despair, affected by the hysteria of that foul autumn day.

"They're not here. You're all alone with God or, if you prefer, with your conscience."

"And where are they?"

"Far away on a small, unhappy planet."

"Hubert, what a stupid joke. Someone put you up to it."

"No, it's not a joke. You know that perfectly well yourself. You've been waiting for us for years. Be honest for once and admit you were waiting."

He looked at me for a long moment with his one good eye and then began searching for his briefcase, which he had kicked under the table during his attack.

"Hubert, answer me—do you believe this is necessary?"

He walked heavily over to me, put his arms around me, and kissed both my cheeks with his cold lips.

"Be at number sixty-three Vistula Street at eleven. Halina and Nadezhda will be waiting for you there. They're in engineering."

"The engineering of self-immolation?"

"Don't make things more difficult, old man," interjected Rysio.

A sudden fury seized me. "And what are you supposed to be, just one of the guys? You better start using commas and periods, goddammit."

At a loss, Rysio began retreating toward the door.

"The lack of periods bothers you?" he said uncertainly.

"If you used punctuation, then maybe we wouldn't need to show deaths in this country."

A lazy peal of thunder rolled from one end of the city to the other. The wind drove the balcony doors groaning open. I would have closed them but the handle had come off.

"Lend us five thousand for a taxi. It's too much for him to walk home in this weather." Rysio took Hubert's enchanted briefcase from him and then glanced out into the dark corridor.

I dug a five-thousand-zloty note out of my pocket. They took it without thanking me and started for the front hall. And then we were greeted by a sort of a droning, the high-pitched sound of telephone wires presaging bad weather. They had been making that glassy moan for years now, since the days when the world had still been a calm and normal place.

Hubert stopped before a heap of old slippers which had somehow or other accumulated over the course of a lifetime.

"When did you stop writing? I can't remember anymore," he said, looking askance and unseeing at the junk strewn about the floor.

"But I'm still writing."

"You've started writing again now. You're writing your testament. But I was asking about your fiction."

"I don't recall. Maybe five, maybe seven years ago. That's when I rid myself of two censors in one fell swoop, my own and the state's. I wrote a story for some little underground journal and that was my last piece. After that I was free and impotent."

"You were born to be a slave. Slavery emancipated you, it lent you wings, it made you a provincial classic. And then to punish you, it took everything away like some evil witch."

"Slavery has always perished at the hands of slaves," said Rysio. "You see what I mean, old man?" . . .

For some reason they loitered when leaving. Hubert began reading my neighbor's calling card tacked beside his bell. They were always a bit curious about my life though good form required contempt for my existence. So he read that card, the shop sign of a Secretary on the Central Committee, without knowing that behind that door an old pensioner had been dying for ten years, had been trying to die day after day but with no success. From above, drops of dirty water dripped from the steps and the edges of the stairs. Our janitor, or as he is to be called these days, the building superintendent, an incorrigible lunatic, was washing the landing. He had already been on television and been written up in the papers and still on he went washing our stairs, the only building superintendent in the country still doing it.

"Don't punk out, old man," said Rysio.

"I have to think it over."

"They're expecting you at eleven, Halina and Nadezhda," added Hubert.

"And if I don't do it?"

"Then you'll go on living the way you've lived till now."

They began down the stairs, supporting each other like two saints, like Cyril and Methodius. And naturally I remembered Rysio from those years long ago when we both were young. I remember one mad drunken night on some farm near Warsaw, the two of us sleeping side by side on a bed of straw. At that time Rysio was something between a critic and a filmologist. There was a drunken girl lying between us, a girl I never saw again. We were both lying semiconscious on my green poncho which I had obligingly spread out for us. The girl was moaning in her deep, drunken sleep. Rysio was fooling around with her, panting hoarsely with sudden desire and so she turned her back to him. Then she was facing me and I could feel her damp, sleepy breath on my cheek. Rysio did not give up; unconscious but hard at work, he was fumbling at her, tearing at her clothes, slipping under her inert body, breathing wildly. And then, when I was already falling into a delirious fever, Rysio clearly achieved his end, for he suddenly began moaning and pulling himself free on the frantic hay. Unaware of his ecstasies, she breathed her light, calm breath on me. It was only in the morning when, hungover, we were all collecting ourselves on that rustic bed, that I struggled into my raincoat and automatically put my hand in the pocket and to my horror discovered that in the darkness of the night, my pocket had been the victim of Rysio's passion, that he had made love to my pocket with a fierce and youthful love, perhaps even the first of his life.

Now Rysio wrote unpunctuated, amorphous prose, played adjutant to Hubert, and was a venerable figure in the literary world. I returned to my room to watch them through the window. Just then, by some miracle, an empty taxi happened by, but they missed it and walked off with dignity toward Nowy Swiat. I was curious if they were being followed. But no car pulled away from the curb and no one came running out from the half shadows of any neighboring building.

At one point Hubert had hanged himself in his wardrobe; he had been mercilessly baited during one campaign, for at that time, toward the end of the sixties, the regime still had strength enough for cruel spectacles and sinister campaigns. So, Hubert hanged himself, but of course it was the first time he had ever done it and he didn't have the knack yet. The rod broke, the wardrobe turned over, and Hubert survived. Yes, he survived so that years later he could bring me my death sentence.

There was another peal of thunder in the low, cramped sky. I went to the bathroom to wash up. The pipes began gurgling something awful, they hiccupped, but what was left of the water came out. I washed mechanically, wondering if it were right to wash and dress, considering what was in store for me. But, after all, one should take death like communion, neatly dressed and with reverence. But did I have to die? Was someone going to force me off a bridge or douse me with gasoline? The decision was mine, wasn't it? I could die with honor or go on living dishonorably.

The gong resounded again. I thought that Rysio and Hubert had forgotten something or were returning to call off the sentence. Dripping with the little water there was, I ran to the door. An old man with a large, leather bag was sitting on the steps.

"Are you here to see me?" I asked.

"Yes, I am. I've been instructed to turn off the gas."

"But you've already turned it off three times this year."

"What do I know, first they tell me turn it off, then they tell me turn it on. They don't know what they're doing. Every day a house blows up, so to make it look like something's being done about it, they tell me to turn off the gas. It's a lucky thing your apartment's still here because I've got the numbers here of places which are gone." He showed me a dirty slip of paper.

"Well, then why don't you turn off the electricity while you're at it? It doesn't matter to me."

"It doesn't matter to you," said the old man with a sly smirk, and he sprang nimbly into the bathroom. "But it matters to me. I've only got authority for the gas."

And indeed, in a fraction of a second, he had turned the valve, had taken apart the grate on the heater and was already sitting on the edge of the bathtub, lighting up a cigarette that was coming unglued.

"It's nice to take a warm bath, if only to wash your butt, you'll pardon the expression," discoursed the old man, glancing about the bathroom. "But what can you do, orders are orders. Maybe you should have a little talk with the manager, you know what I mean. Speak to his hand."

"I don't feel like talking with the manager. I'm going to die today."

The old plumber began chuckling merrily.

"Why'd you think that one up for today, isn't there enough going on? That Russian Secretary's coming today. They've got the whole town decked out. There's been bands playing everywhere since this morning. They say there's a sort of festival going on, some big holiday of theirs, maybe it's one of ours too. They've filled up the stands with goods, everywhere, by the Palace of Culture, down by the Vistula, people have been standing in line since early this morning and you're getting set to die."

"I'll be dying to spite them."

The gray-haired tradesman wiped away tears of joy.

"You're a funny man. If we started dying to spite them, there'd be no Poles left. You know what, I'll connect up your gas, but I'll seal up the valve handles. I'll leave it open wide enough so you can use the gas, just you be careful."

"I don't have need for gas. Why don't you take the little heater as a souvenir?"

"You're pretty touchy. If you don't want to, you don't have to. Sign here please."

I accompanied him back to the hall. He took the opportunity to feel my coat, which was hanging by the door.

"Nice wool. Foreign."

"Take it. Wear it in good health."

"What are you talking about? I can pay you. I'll give you fifty thousand."

"I'll give it to you for nothing. The only thing is, when you put it on, give a sigh for my soul, would you?"

"You must be an artist, right? You like a good laugh, right?"

But he rolled the coat up skillfully, packed it in his bag and then was already at my neighbor's door, pressing the doorbell, a severe look on his face.

1983

The belly of Barbara N.

Wiktor Woroszylski

from *Diary of internment* (Darlowko, 1982)

In the dark warm shelter
carefully vaulted
out of the body and blood of this young woman
there is hiding
before the grating pursuit of the padlock
before the yellow sign blocking the way
before the pitfall of despair
before the flaming mountain of hatred
the yet unborn prisoner
begotten between the release of his father
and the arrest of his mother
not figuring in the register of internees
a future citizen and soldier of this country

Translated by Boguslaw Rostworowski

1983

Two poems

Stanislaw Baranczak

Along with the dust

Along with the dust on the books,
the fingerprints on all the glass (fragile—
do not drop), along with
a ration coupon for sugar and a cross to bear
(fragile—this side up) I'm moving
along with the writing in my lap, the thousands
of terms in my head (fragile—remember with care),
with an extra thousand zlotys just in case
(fragile—do not worry too much), along with a mask of
    self-confidence
and a wound in my back, along with an empty promise and
    an ill-
fitting hope (fragile—do not trust), along
with maybe finally and quick hurry up,
along with you can depend on it and I'm sick to death
(fragile—do not die) along with let's begin at the beginning
and knock on wood and what's the use,
and along with this love that's
all that will stay with me for better, for worse,
and forever, it's fragile, you movers,

and it's all a lot heavier than it looks

Translated by Reginald Gibbons and the author

1983

If china

If china, then only the kind
you wouldn't miss under the movers' shoes or the treads
    of a tank;
if a chair, then one that's not too comfortable, or
you'll regret getting up and leaving;
if clothes, then only what will fit in one suitcase;
if books, then those you know by heart;
if plans, then the ones you can give up
when it comes time for the next move,
to another street, another continent or epoch
or world:

who told you you could settle in?
who told you this or that would last forever?
didn't anyone tell you you'll never
in the world
feel at home here?

Translated by Reginald Gibbons and the author

LESZEK SOBOCKI. LINOCUT. (*TQ* #57, VOL. 1)

MIGUEL HERNANDEZ ESPAÑA
DESDE AHORA Y DESDE SIEMPRE
TE HA QUERIDO COMO A UN HIJO
DE SU RAZA Y DE SU LECHE

JOSÉ LUIS DELGADO. FROM SERIES ON STREET MURALS BY SPANISH NEIGHBORHOOD ASSOCIATIONS. (*TQ* #57, VOL. 2)

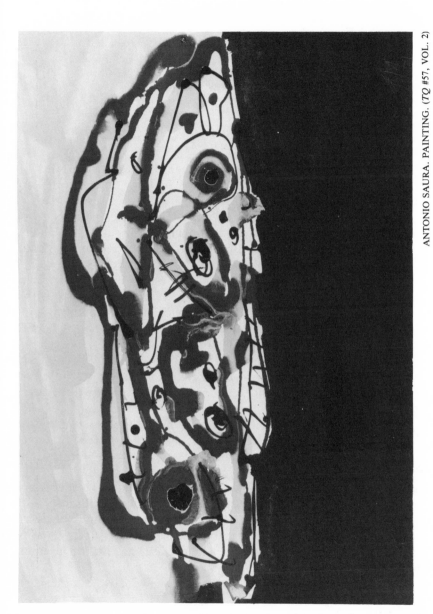

Isaac Babel

R. D. Skillings

> Surely the reckoning will be made
> After the passing of this cloud.
> We are the people without tears,
> Straighter than you ... more proud ...
>   Anna Akhmatova

To honor him I wanted to write a story named "Isaac Babel" after his "Guy de Maupassant," but material for such an imitation did not exist, and I was unwilling or unable to invent.

The wish grew into an obligation, yet a year went by without giving me an inkling of how to proceed, though I wearied my brains and ransacked my journal. And as time passed nothing seemed less plausible than to write a story about a story—or more necessary.

Babel's terrible paradigms obsessed me, especially his masterpiece about a penniless Odessa Jew who goes to Petersburg in 1916 with a forged passport and his ancestors' injunction to enjoy, and gets a job translating Maupassant for the voluptuous wife of a profit-maddened munitions supplier, owner of a publishing house.

Three of Maupassant's stories—"Miss Harriet," "Idyll," and "The Confession," all tales of Eros—are sketched in Babel's tour de force about famished youth, at once a panegyric, a treatise on writing, and a deadly foreboding.

Drunk one night, exuberant with his genius, the translator tries to seduce his patroness, then returns singing to his garret and reads a biography, learning that Guy de Maupassant, born in Normandy in 1850, was Gustave Flaubert's cousin, lived a profligate life and developed syphilis at twenty-five. At first his prodigious energy and joie de vivre withstood the onslaughts. He struggled furiously, fled around the Mediterranean in a yacht, going crazy and blind, but always writing. He attained fame, at forty cut his throat, survived to be confined and die two years later in a madhouse, crawling on all fours, eating his feces.

The disciple closes the book and goes to the window, but the world is hidden in fog.

In 1969, sick of the city and its constantly shrieking sirens, Abigail and I had moved to Provincetown and found ourselves part of an influx of refugees. Normally moribund in the winter, the resort

STORY ILLUSTRATED BY MATTHEW OWENS. (*TQ* #58)

boomed year-round, and the Selectmen refused to sign the census since it was clear many more were living here than had been counted. Draftdodgers, self-seekers, the gay, idle escapists, mystical dreamers, astrologers, artists, the rich in rummage, welfare-getters, junkies, hopeless hedonists, the cracked, the numb, dropouts, copouts, hippies and even a handful of native sons, like inner émigrés, congregated nightly at a dance bar named Piggy's, formerly the Pilgrim Club.

A cesspool, according to one familiar, it was like a large dim living room with paintings of monsters devouring women on the driftwood walls, stained glass windows, Tiffany lamps, mirrors and oak pews. The tables were old cable spools, the stools nail kegs with cloths trussed over their padded tops like little ragged sheiks. The masterful owner sat in one corner with a cigar, legs crossed, enjoying his scene— a noisy, noxious nuisance in the view of respectable people. Twice a night the cops stood grimly in the doorway looking from crime. One night they appeared with American flags sewn on their sleeves and I wanted to kill them. Once they arrested a boy dressed only in the flag. The worse the war raged, the wilder the dancing got, a moiling mass, sweaty and glad. The night Nixon mined Haiphong it reached a frenzy, and later in our beds the cold fear of chaos gripped us.

It was during these apparent portents that I met Lasiter, the pornographer. He, too, spent his nights at Piggy's watching the dancers, and I leaned at the rail beside him. He was a curious figure with his white mustache, shaven skull, red eyes and face wrinkled beyond his fifty years. In summer he wore old army clothes, in winter a bulky silvery gray woman's fur coat that made him look like a moth.

He eked out a living writing sex books which he signed with pseudonyms and which he boasted contained no two couplings alike. To represent the true extremities of pleasure required a fatiguing amount of research, he said, but I dismissed this as fustian. I read five or six; they all had tropical settings and a tinge of despair.

He had been leaving town for the past few years, but at the last minute always got a new lover instead. His wife Sylvia no longer cared what he did, if only he wouldn't drink himself into dependence on her. They had come from the beatnik life of San Francisco an epoch ago, and he had left her umpteen times already. She continued to look after him intermittently, as they lived apart now and had different schedules. She got up at 4:30 in the morning to waitress. He had a room with a hot plate, lived out of a suitcase and always seemed in a quandary. He would wipe a trembling finger across his brow and say, "This amuses you."

Inspired by the bourbon he bought by the quart, I told him the stories of Isaac Babel, including the one named "And Then There Were None," circa 1923, long suppressed in Russia, about the murder of nine Polish prisoners by a wounded Cossack over the protests of a

Jewish supply officer who next day takes his diary into an untouched garden of hyacinths and blue roses to make notes on the dead, but immediately is interrupted by fellow-soldiers with coats over their heads and a smoking torch, plundering the beehives.

He lays down his pen, horrified at the number of memorials still to be written.

No iron can stab the heart with such force as a period put at exactly the right place, Babel says in "Guy de Maupassant," and adds, *A phrase is born into the world both good and bad. The secret lies in a slight, almost invisible twist. The lever should rest in the hand, getting warm, and can be turned only once, not twice.*

With a certain enjoyable malice, I divulged to Lasiter the gist of "Rue Dante," a tale about a Parisian prostitute who cuts her boyfriend's throat when he jilts her.

The corpse is carried from the brothel by the gendarmes at six in the evening, the hour of love, when the hotel soars through the air on groans. Men with unlaced boots are lined up in the halls. Half-dressed women are restoring their lipstick and rouge.

A chorus of old women gathers—mounds of wry and goiterous flesh, bewhiskered, stertorous of breath, with walleyes and purple blotches—and pronounces God's punishment on those who do not love.

Darkness falls. The squat crowds of the Latin Quarter scuttle into their crevices and a burning breath of garlic wafts from the courtyards. Danton had lived here a century and a half before; the same scene, the blind, close-pressed hovels, the bridges cast lightly across the Seine, had met his eyes. Jostled by the wind, the rusty trusses of the inn signs creak.

Lasiter read only pornography, plagiarized freely and composed ignoble debaucheries in flowery prose. Virtue Undone, Vice Rewarded was his soothing, mournful theme. The relief of the dear, distressed flesh and the degradations of the spirit that flowed from his pen seemed devised to suborn the reader. "You think all art is affirmative," he once complained. "Unlike you blocked esoterics who get grants to produce driblets no normal wretch wants to read, I aggravate a need."

All the same, he was a humble soul compared to me, who, drinking while drunk, railed at the gods. Shakespeare? Shakespeare quit writing and went back to Stratford! Shakespeare retired! How could that be?

I couldn't conceive of such a desire. Lately impelled to record other people's stories in their words—so much easier to find than mine—I was jumping out of my skin, rid of my old fear of the insignificance of everything I knew well enough to put on paper. Other tellers, other tales, released me, though I still felt a copyist of a reality too casual for magnitude, too unique to matter.

1983

573

I wrote on my wall, Forget all forms. Trust only in truth, in only what happened, in the real.

But what was that? And was it enough? Wanting the tragic, I produced only the dreadful. Upon examination, reality appeared to be lacking, and stories remained lies.

But once I had written out the true events, and used up the phenomena I had observed, as often as not I needed an ending life had yet to provide. A danger lay in the temptations of the future, the desire for conclusions. Having a work underway, one might suspend the pen to watch, to wait—or worse, meddle in the elements, trying to induce an outcome. Otherwise, patience, endless patience, was required, and the nine lives of the cat.

I told Lasiter my ambition—once I had completed my belated apprenticeship and returned to fiction—to write an unreadable story, and a long one at that. I even had a first sentence: We were going through the village killing everyone.

Lasiter loved shoptalk: it cheered him up. Many happy, harmless hours we spent in this way, reeling around his desk, repeating ourselves, while the year wheeled by.

Between books, when he was not scrawling chapters for Sylvia to decipher, edit and type, seduction addicted him. Women were his Mount Everest and Dismal Swamp. His custom was simply to solicit every female he met, bow at rebuffs, with due humility renew all offers as time went on, and never give up. His manner was ingratiatingly grave, rueful, kind and warm, without a trace of irony, and he never touched anyone, nor spoke a lewd word.

August disgust mellowed in dark winter, he allowed, and indeed he had no end of confidantes. But whoever he was with, he was always on the lookout for the next, and he was hardly tenderhearted about parting from someone once she had ceased to inspire his pen.

By the second year I knew him he was in a bad spell. He could not find a lover, he could not write, he was drinking a lot and sleeping all day and going broke. The thought that he might have to move back with Sylvia depressed them both. His bags were packed, his typewriter was in its case, friends in half a dozen cities had been alerted to his arrival, but when it came time to get on the bus he would have a drink for the road and wind up too drunk to go.

It was February, the deadly month, when he said, "All women are the same."

"Even Esmeralda?" I said, with my evil genius.

"Who's she?" he said, lifting his eyes at the name.

So I took him to her house. I was surprised he did not know her, but in fact she had stopped going out. She could no longer stand the grim world or any of its manifestations, and people thought her affected, and she thought them mad.

She spent hours in her velvet-hung, perfume-heavy bedroom, sitting before a mirror propped on a desk covered with cosmetics, changing her makeup and nails. She wore flowing, flimsy black gowns or a clinging slip and her large round breasts moved like moons as she arose or reclined on the pillow-strewn couch in her narrow living room. A parallel length of marble on milk crates always offered vials of various drugs and a hookah. Coffee brewed in the kitchen. At that time her life was a search for new highs.

It was like Breughel's "Land of Cockayne" there, where the dim lights were never turned off, with everyone and everything afloat timelessly, and fancies, thick as thieves, crowded the tongue, an abstract world where one ate standing up, alone, at all hours, staring out at the bare briars and empty parking lot.

Lately she had suffered a languid indifference to one lesbian lover after another and was surely Lasiter's jaded equal. "Why don't you go back to men?" I would say, but it was a political issue with her.

The introductions made, Esmeralda said with her gargantuan horror, "You actually write pornography?" and brought out a bottle of brandy.

His eyes turned bright red as he said, "Yes."

"Then you're practically the perfect personification of the enemy," she said.

"I don't know what I am," he said, and there was an eerie treble in his voice.

"I know what I am," Esmeralda said with her implacable gravity. "I spent my infancy on top of a bar where my mother served drinks to workingmen. My father was an unemployed Marxist and read Bakunin to me. When he was drunk he would beat my mother because the revolution refused to come. She died of a heart attack at thirty-two, and then he lost hope and died himself. He was a degenerated Anglo. She was a Guatemalan peasant, and in spirit so am I. But foremost, above all else, I am a woman."

She caught my eye and her glowering gloom dissolved in delighted laughter at the outlandishness of it all. "But I think I like you," she said to Lasiter, who bowed. "How is that possible?" He bowed more deeply yet.

I went home to Abigail and my blank page. How the unending hours must have flown on the voluminous couch, what exquisite tinglings must have been sustained, what disturbing astonishments, what fearful inklings of submission!

I saw little of them for the next month and did not enter Esmeralda's house, as she never answered her door. In March, meeting her on the street, I went home with her and found a new world. Lasiter was reeling around, his eyes red as a sunrise. "I can drink," he said, "all day long and never get drunk, and I hardly need a wink at night."

On the left-hand corner of the kitchen table was a mug full of pens and a pile of scrawled foolscap. His typewriter was set up at the end of the living room, and beside it stood a battered wire basket with half an inch of finished manuscript.

"About Esmeralda?" I said.

He looked at me with shock.

"I may write one about him," she said, and her rippling, tumultuous laughter engulfed us.

"I'm writing my autobiography," he said.

"Dear Jesus!" I said.

"It seems to be writing itself," he said with dignity. "Knock on wood."

I did so with goodwill and skinned my knuckles on the edge of what turned out to be a formica table. I hit the wall and some plaster fell. I bent, hurting my back, and beat on the floor.

"Actually I've decided to finish my thesis," Esmeralda said, and her eyes roamed the magnificent ranges of her books.

Over dinner I related "Di Grasso," 1937, the penultimate of Babel's published works, a tale of the Odessa theater, in the unhappy year the opera flopped.

Things looked desperate indeed with the arrival of a Sicilian tragedian and his shabby gypsy troupe. Even at half price, tickets wouldn't sell. Opening night, they staged a folk drama as trite as the succession of night and day. A peasant girl is engaged to a shepherd. A city slicker steals her love. In the second act she hands the shepherd back his ring. In the third the city slicker meets his end. Having a shave at the barber's, he fidgets in his chair, feeling the shepherd's burning gaze. Finally he sits up and in a shaking voice shouts for a policeman to clear the square of all gloomy, suspicious-looking persons.

The shepherd, played by Di Grasso himself, stands lost in thought, then gives a smile, leaps aloft, sails across the stage and sinks his teeth in his rival's throat, growling and squinting and sucking the blood as the noiseless, ominous curtain falls, confirming that there is more justice in outbursts of noble passion than in all the joyless rules that run the world, and saving the impresario's shirt, filling his erstwhile empty house nightly thereafter, inspiring his wife to badger him into returning—albeit with a pinch—the pawned watch of one of the ticket sellers, a boy who, having swiped it from his father, was just on the verge of fleeing to Constantinople, but who now, saved from paternal wrath, suddenly sees his surroundings as they really are: frozen in silence and ineffably beautiful.

Lasiter and Esmeralda were happy. At the end of a day he was too tired to talk and listened rapturously, restfully, to her utopias and indignations, which touched forgotten chords of his psyche. He was reminded that the rest of the world still existed. She was fascinated by his blind stare and voluptuary's hands always in play like those of the deaf.

At eleven I asked the rhetorical question, "Is it time for Piggy's?"

They looked at me as if I had proposed a novelty. They hadn't, I discerned, ever been out together at night, but they showed not a doubtful moment, gaily getting into their boots, scarves, mittens, and turning out the lights.

So well was Lasiter feeling that he was quite changed for the better, he who heretofore considered cats a species of cockroach. I forgot to mention Esmeralda's large, fluffy, severe-faced Angora with glittering eyes that brooked no familiarities except exactly the ones it wanted. One mistake and the hand got a scratch that itched for days.

As we were going out into the alley he spied a slinking feline. "Kitty, kitty!" he called and bent down. The cat cast a startled glance over its shoulder and ran faster, its tail low to the ground. Laughing, we walked rapidly arm-in-arm to Piggy's, panting with the cold, a stinging, bitter wind in our faces off Shankpainter Pond.

At closing time few were ready to leave—the canny crowd having stocked up at Last Call—and for almost an hour we watched the slow exodus. Doubtless it was an ordinary night, but to Lasiter and Esmeralda, wanting nothing, with their warm bed and morrow's work awaiting them, it felt like an epitome of good vibes, all aspects of everything being perfectly apt, various and comprehensible. The Rolling Stones had rocked the smoky air. The oblivious pool game had played on off to one side under a lone lamp while the dim mob milled around. The beautiful dancers luxuriated. Everybody's good qualities could be seen and none of their bad.

The last to leave, we sailed home on a strong wind that carried us warmly along. The geese gabbled as we passed and the cat that lives in the laundromat was waiting in the window for someone to let it out.

"I think I'll work just a minute or two," Lasiter said.

"I'll get in bed and read another chapter," Esmeralda said.

This bliss persisted deep into a harsh spring. Blizzards buried the crocuses, melted under the rains and came again.

I was stupefied, next time I met Esmeralda, to learn that she was pregnant. "These devices!" she said with scornful disgust.

But it was no misfortune. At thirty-seven it was not too late for her to raise a Socialist child, a desire long suppressed. "Not an age one would want to bring children into," she had lamented for years, but now her pessimism failed. She suddenly felt at home in the world, whose injustices she detested; she resolved to be of use.

Lasiter vacillated. Now that he had found happiness he felt old and the possible solace of a daughter intrigued him. Perhaps the end of eroticism was a generous life. He threw away his collection of keep-sakes, but could not quite get himself to give up his room and went on paying rent, though he never went there and nothing was left in it but a bed. All the same he swore he wholly intended to embrace the rounded responsible life his new nature now allowed.

He went to get Sylvia's assent and assure himself of their future collaboration. It occurred to him the child would want an aunt. Sylvia had renounced children for art even before she met Lasiter, but the ideal had faded, and she had little to show for the years. Her pride was in his books, so hard won from him that she well might have put her pseudonyms on them, beside his, as in their old joke.

Grim and remote, she wished him bad luck in an unfamiliar, insinuating tone. She was bent on divorce, a resort he had often offered her, and was arranging to move to New York and hunt for a loft. She had lost weight and looked intent.

He left her calm apartment profoundly amazed and got drunk by himself. At closing time, when he wondered where to go, his heart shrank at the touch of an irremediable truth. He slept in his room for the first time in two months and awoke with the spring sun prickling his face.

He went back to Sylvia's day after day, but in spirit she had already gone. Once she left him sitting at the kitchen table while she did errands, then asked him to leave upon her return.

Esmeralda lost her laughter and sudden lines masked her face. Her friends were disbelieving, then appalled, finally mocking or silent. Groups of women visited her like delegations, but she was steadfast in her decision and braced for Lasiter's defection.

His mouth warped, he walked with eyes upon the ground while the zero days approached—Sylvia's departure and the date too late for an abortion. He could not endure either Sylvia or Esmeralda for need of the other, and he could abide neither, since both damned him.

Next I knew he had retreated to his bare room to think, as he put it, but what he mostly did was drink. His book had come to an end, too vile to write, nor could he face the mirror of the future. "Change, change!" he muttered. "But what ever changes?"

"Time to leave town," I said with a grin, not meaning it.

The following Thursday I read in the *Advocate* that he had been found near the wharf, eaten to a skeleton by crabs, his pockets full of rocks.

I ran to Esmeralda's. She was just leaving for Boston. "I've decided to have the abortion," she said.

It was an evil era. A spate of untimely wakes swelled the binge. Jill Marley, model and mistress of the famous, died in the hospital, hitched to a machine to sustain her drink-destroyed pancreas. Camille said, "Veedon's next," but died herself of cigarette cancer. Jade O'Grady dropped dead on his doorstep and Busty had a heart attack and died when she couldn't obtain his ashes because they weren't

married. All were in their forties, as was the portrait artist, Barky Darnell, a family man, also a heart victim.

Esmeralda went back to Texas. Sylvia became a white ghost of herself and never left town. I clung to Abigail and betrayed her.

A year later, coming home one night from Piggy's, I found my downstairs neighbor sitting up with two travelers. Both had beards and packs. One kept the pot-pipe filled while the other told how he made his living selling pens. "This pen," he said, "will write what you want, when you want it to."

He took the cap off, wet his lips and began to play Bach. The candle flame wavered in the dim room, the vodka in the bottle went down. His long, tremulous fingers held the cap to his swelling lips and he nodded time, swaying from side to side. I have never been happier.

None of them had heard of Isaac Babel. I started to tell the little I knew but to my amazed shame cried uncontrollably and couldn't talk. They all nodded sympathetically, it did not matter at what, some stranger bursting into tears late at night. After a while the musician took up his pen cap and began to play. He switched to jazz, then ragtime parodies of sentimental tunes. The evening ended in torpor and exhaustion. We shook hands, hoping to meet again. I climbed to my porch in the cloudy dawn and cursed the invisible stars.

Isaac Babel was born in the Moldavanka district of Odessa in 1894, the only child of Fanya Aronovna Shvevel and Emmanuel Isaakovich Babel, a shopkeeper. Sprung from a maelstrom of pogroms, revolution and war, the protégé of Maxim Gorki, he achieved international renown with his youth's books, *Red Cavalry* (1926) and *Odessa Stories* (1932), after which new works were announced, never to appear. He apologized, wrote his quota of journalism and movie scripts, supported a tribe of dependents, befriended pariahs, hid from editors, joked that he had become a past master of the genre of silence.

His stories in their impossible drafts piled up on his shelves. His wife, mother and sister emigrated; a daughter was born abroad. Still, in spite of sinister gossip, he was the very figure of the Soviet writer. The government gave him a villa, let him leave the country three times, and three times he returned alone, unable to persuade his family to follow. His phenomenal joie de vivre never flagged, he believed in the triumph of man and mind, belonged to the Revolution, loved his country and language. Greedily curious, a powerful optimist, he visited the Chief of the Secret Police to sniff the smell of the store where, he told Osip Mandelstam, the only merchandise was death. Awesome in early achievement, cautious and clever, revered by all, he endured the censorship, mastering his terror, till his arrest in May 1939. Entering Lubyanka Prison, he is said to have smiled and said, "I wasn't given time to finish."

His unpublished works were burned with the police archives in December 1941, as the Germans approached Moscow.

Sage of the ghetto, cast up by the titanic times, he crowed that only Odessa could beget a national Maupassant, a poet of the sun to celebrate the Black Sea and bronzed bathers, the various fructifying South and all its colorful life, not old Russia's cold ancestral gloom— the muddy road, the drunken drudge's shout.

Inexhaustible giant in chains, brave at his desk, the frail myopic boy become a Cossack, he laughed with his whole body, was called wise, an awkward customer, fond of cornering pomp. Hacks fled his quips. Only one thing he couldn't understand: humdrum anti-Semitism, the crippled ragman that children loved who tore the head off his dove.

Horse lover, explorer of women's handbags, asthmatic twister of string—prolixity was not in his nature. *Deeper*, he said. *Deeper. The unexpected is the essence of art.*

Did the eye wither, the ear crack, as day by day, year on year, the new dark age came in?

The Nazis burned *Red Cavalry.* Dostoyevsky and Gogol grew dangerous in Moscow. He praised late Tolstoy and the proletarians when interviewed. I honor his steady nerve and long survival. I mourn his lost stories.

No one knows among the millions how Isaac Babel died, or why. Even the mad Czar was bereaved, the last Father of all, who had banished tragedy but wanted immortal praise and knew of him, knew of everyone. Monstrous, inconceivable Russia!

All we ask is a natural death, beyond the reign of bombs. War and revolution are done for, finished—or we are. May Babel still have believed in the future when the bullet hit or he lay unwakable in a barracks, typhus-ridden, one with his silence, done with the polished oar of his beloved slavery, done with Russian, while his camp mates mustered outside for their dawn march to field or canal, road or mine, in the stifling charnel house where he had long since ceased to distinguish the living from the dead.

The storytellers

Fred Chappell

Uncle Zeno came to visit us. Or did he?

Not even the bare fact of his visit is incontestable. He was a presence, all right; he told stories, endless stories, and these stories worked upon the fabric of our daily lives in such manner that we began to doubt our own outlines. Sometimes, walking in the country, one comes upon an abandoned flower garden overtaken by wild flowers. Is it still a garden? The natural and the artificial orders intermingle, and ready definition is lost.

But the man who effected such transformation seemed hardly to be among us. He was a slight, entirely unremarkable man given to wearing white shirts with frayed cuffs and collars. That is, in fact, how my memory characterizes him: a frayed cuff, a shred, a nibbled husk. If he had not spoken we might have taken no more notice of him than of one of the stray cats which made our barn a sojourn between wilderness and wilderness. His hair, his face and hands, I cannot recollect. He was a voice.

The voice too was unremarkable, except that it was inexhaustible. Dry, flat, almost without inflection, it delivered those stories with the mechanical precision of an ant toting a bit of leaf mold to its burrow. Yet Uncle Zeno had no discernible purpose in telling his stories, and there was little arrangement in the telling. He would begin a story at the beginning, in the middle, or at the end; or he would seize upon an odd detail and stretch into his stories in two or three directions at once. He rarely finished a story at one go; he would leave it suspended in mid-air like a gibbeted thief or let it falter to a halt like a stalled car blocking the road. And he took no interest in our reactions. If the story was funny our laughter made no more impression upon him than a distant butterfly; when we were downcast at a sad story, he did not seem to realize it. His attention was fixed elsewhere. My father and I got the impression that he was not remembering or inventing his stories, but repeating words whispered to him by another voice issuing

STORY ILLUSTRATED BY MATTHEW OWENS. (*TQ* #58)

from somewhere behind the high, fleecy clouds he loved to stare at.
That puts me in mind of . . .

These six flat monosyllables will be spoken at break of Judgment Day; they are the leisurely herald notes which signal that time has stopped, that human activity must suspend and every attention be bent toward discovering the other leisurely country words which follow. This is the power that beginnings have over us; we must find out what comes next and cannot pursue even the most urgent of our personal interests with any feeling of satisfaction until we do find out. The speaker of these words holds easy dominion.

That puts me in mind of—Uncle Zeno said—Lacey Joe Blackman. You know how proud some folks are of what they've got—he said—cars and fine houses and such. Some folks are proud of their wonderful hunting dogs, like Buford Rhodes was, but I ain't talking about him but about Lacey Joe Blackman. Lacey Joe was proud of a watch which come down to him from his daddy and Lacey Joe kept it on him for fifty years or better, and he couldn't say how long it had been in the family before his daddy. It was real old-fashioned, a big fat bib watch in a silver casing and been around so long the silver had wore thin on it like a dime. Even when he got to be seventy-five years old, Lacey Joe was liable to tug his watch out and flip up the lid and give you the time of day, you didn't need to ask.

Lacey Joe had a well-known name as a hunter, maybe only Turkey George Palmer had killed more brutes, and Lacey Joe would go on a hunt anytime night or day, deer, bear, groundhog, you name it. Go a-hunting pissants I reckon if they was in season. They ain't much bear hunting in these parts any more, I remember the last time Lacey Joe went.

Setback Williams had sold his big farm down on Beaverdam, as he was getting on in years, and him and Mary Sue had bought a little homestead that butted up against the Smoky National Park. No farming on it, Setback was past doing any heavy labor, but there was a little apple orchard in the back, maybe two dozen trees, and old Setback liked his apples and apple trees.

But there was a troublesome bear ranging in those acres and he liked the apples and the apple trees powerful well too. You know how it is with a bear and the apple trees, gets all excited and he'll go to sharpening his claws like a cat with a settee. Go around and around a tree ripping at the bark and pretty soon he's girdled it and that tree is doomed to die.

Setback had done already lost two trees to this bear and he didn't know what to do. Can't shoot a bear anymore even if he's on your property unless you get permission from the Park Service and they won't hardly never give permission no matter what cussedness a bear had been up to. But Setback called anyhow over there to the Ranger

Station I don't know how many times and kept deviling them and finally they were out to his place and allowed as how maybe he had a problem.

What they done was put up a fence, but the Park Service won't put you up no barbwire fence because it ain't what they call rustic-like, they don't want no tourist looking at a barbwire fence. They put up a heavy peel-log fence around the orchard about six foot high, ten times as much work as a good barbwire fence, and Setback took one look at it and declared, Boys, that ain't going to keep no bear off of my apple trees. And it wasn't two days later he went out and there was a bear setting in a tree, looking down like he owned that tree and the U.S. Park Service too. Setback raised a holler and the bear scuttled down and lickety-split into the forest right over the fence. Didn't make no more of that fence that you would a plate of peach cobbler.

So he called the Rangers again and they dawdled and cussed awhile and finally come over and built another peel-log fence, never seen anything like it. This one was fourteen foot high if it was an inch and strong as a fort. Kind of awesome to look at, think about the work them fellers had put into it. But Setback wasn't nothing only suspicious, and a week later he looks out and there was that same bear up in that same tree. Like the King of England on his throne all of gold. Setback ran out and hollered and the bear jumped down and run to the fence. When he got there he stretched up like a man reaching down a jug off of a tall shelf and took hold of a middle log about seven foot high and leapt up and then he was over. It was plumb pretty to look at, Setback said, except he was so mad.

He was on the telephone in a jiffy and told them he was going to shoot that bear, National Park or no National Park, and they said No he wasn't. He told them a man has a right to protect his property, especially the apple trees, and also besides his wife was getting scared, that bear coming in on them all the time. That was where he was stretching it because Mary Sue never took fright of nothing, stouthearted she was. Finally they said they'd let him trap the bear as long as he used the trap they'd bring him, and he could hold it and they'd come and pick the bear up and carry it to the farthest-back part of the forest and it wouldn't wander out as far as his apple trees again. He suspicioned that wouldn't work neither, but he was willing to try anything.

The trap they brought him didn't have no teeth, smoothed off so it wouldn't hurt a bear's leg much, but it was awful big and heavy, Setback said he never seen one that big.

He pegged it in the ground out there amongst the trees. Used a locust stake must have been five foot long and a big old drag chain. Covered it over with leaves all proper.

Might be another week passed before Setback and Mary Sue heard the awfulest row and tearing-around and uproar. It was the early hour of the morning, not what you call sunlight yet. Bothersome to be woke up like that, but when it come to Setback they must have caught the bear, he hustled into his clothes and went out to have a look.

But there was nothing to see but some tore-up leaves and rassled-around dirt. Not one other blessed thing. That bear had pulled that five-foot stake plumb out of the ground. Hadn't left nothing, toted off the trap, the drag chain, and the locust stake, and gone over that fourteen-foot log fence. Hard to believe his eyes, Setback said.

He was back on the phone to the Rangers again, telling them what he was going to do and them saying Yessir right along. Because you couldn't leave the animal with the trap on his leg, him in pain like that. Then he called up me and five others and Lacey Joe Blackman who still kept his bear dogs and always had such a name for bear hunting. And we met over at his place it must have been about eight o'clock in the morning.

The dogs got the scent right in a hurry, all barking to beat Joshua, and we set off in a trot. We kept an eye on Lacey Joe, him going on eighty years of age, but he was hale and spry and after a little bit we figured he would wear us down and the dogs too. Didn't have far to go, though, maybe two miles and the bear was already treed.

Might not even have been the dogs, might have treed hisself, worried kind of crazy toting that iron and wood on his leg. Whatever, he was sure enough treed, the pack yipping and jumping around the bottom of the tree.

An awful big tree too, sixty foot tall anyhow, and spindly at the top where he was at. He was right in the very tip-top, and the tree was bowed way over with him. If it wasn't a pine tree you'd think it might bust. And just enough wind to sway it, and the bear in it, that was some sight. We stood just a-looking for a long time.

Till Setback says, Well, Lacey Joe Blackman, I believe it's up to you to take the first shot. Him being the oldest, and us all thinking he was about half sand-blind and one of us would get the kill. I'll do her if that's what you want, he says, and steps out and raises up his rifle. Which we seen was an old thirty-aught-six must've belonged to Nimrod and didn't even have a front sight. We was all thinking, that bear ain't got no worries just yet, and he steps out and raised up his rifle and didn't take no aim and killed that bear stone dead. Bullet we found out later went in right between the eyes.

The bear dropped plummet. Down about thirty foot and then jerked up again. That locust stake he'd been dragging got caught crossways in the fork of a big old limb and held him up there. The tree was bending way over. And the bear hung up like that went back and forth like a pend'lum on a grandfather clock. Back and forth, and back and forth. It was a sight made us all stand there quiet as pallbearers.

And so Lacey Joe Blackman, he pulls that silver-case watch of his out and opens it up. He squints at that bear swinging back and forth and he looks down at his watch, up at the bear, down at his watch. And he says, Boys, if this-here old watch of mine is still keeping right, that bear is swinging just . . . a mite . . . slow . . .

"Just a mite slow?" My father frowned. "I don't get it. A bear is not hanging in a tree to be keeping time. What does he mean, a mite slow?"

But that was the end of the story, and the end too of Uncle Zeno's talk. He only told stories, he didn't answer questions. The voice he listened to, the voice beyond the world, gave him only stories to report; any other matter was irrelevant..Uncle Zeno turned to my father but his gaze was so abstracted that the chair my father sat in at the supper table might as well have been empty.

That was part of the trouble. Uncle Zeno lived in a different but contiguous sphere that touched our world only by means of a sort of metaphysical courtesy. So how was he able to tell stories? He seemed to absorb reality, events that took place among people, without having to be involved.

"Was Homer blind because he was a poet?" my father asked me next day. "Or was he a poet because he was blind?"

"I don't know what you mean."

"I'm thinking about Uncle Zeno," he said.

"Oh," I said.

"You remember I told you the story of the *Iliad*? Well, Homer couldn't have been a soldier, of course, because he was blind. That's how he came to know so much. If he'd been a soldier, he couldn't have told the story. If Uncle Zeno ever struck a lick of work, if he ever had any dealings with people at all, maybe he couldn't tell his stories."

I could recall vividly my father's retelling of the *Iliad*. He found a magazine photograph of Betty Grable and propped it on the mantelpiece by the gilt pend'lum clock and said that Miss Grable was Helen of Troy and had been stolen away by a slick-hair drugstore cowboy named Paris. Were we going to stand for that? Hell no. We were going to round up a posse and sail the wine-dark seas and rescue her. He flung himself down on the sagging sofa to represent Achilles loafing in his tent, all in a sulk over the beautiful captive maiden Briseis. He winked at me. "These women can sure cause a lot of trouble." The account ended ten minutes later with my father dragging three times around the room a dusty sofa cushion which was the vanquished corpse of Hector.

His excitement enticed me to read the poem in a Victorian prose translation, and I found it less confusing than his redaction, its thrills ordered.

That was the trouble with my father's storytelling. He was unable to keep his hands off things. Stories passed through Uncle Zeno like the orange glow through an oil-lamp chimney, but my father must always be seizing objects and making them into swords, elephants, and magic millstones, and he loved to end his stories with quick, violent gestures intended to startle his audience. He startled us, all right, but never by the power of his stories, always by the sharpness of his violence.

He had grown jealous of Uncle Zeno's storytelling and decided he would tell a suppertime story involving a mysterious house and a haunted shotgun. But his brief tale was so perplexed that we couldn't follow it at all. We were, however, disagreeably shocked when the haunted shotgun fired because he illustrated this detonation with a swift blow of his fist on the edge of the table which caused the insert prongs of the inner leaf to break, catapulting a bowl of butter beans onto my father's shirtfront.

My mother and grandmother and I stared at him in consternation as he mumbled and began plucking beans from his lap, but Uncle Zeno, sitting directly across the table, took no notice, gazing past my father's downcast confusion into his portable Outer Space. "That puts me in mind of . . ." he began, and proceeded to tell of a haunted house of his knowledge, atop which the weather vane pointed crosswise to the wind, in which fires flamed up without human agency in the fireplaces, and the cellar resounded with a singing chorus of lost children. We turned with grateful relief from my father's predicament and were soon enrapt by Uncle Zeno's monotone narrative, which now began to include sealed doors that sweated blood, a bathtub that filled up with copperhead snakes from the faucet, a vanity mirror that gave back the images of the dead, a piano whose keys turned into fangs whenever "Roses of Picardy" was attempted. My father too became enthralled and sat motionless among his butter beans until Uncle Zeno concluded. His ending, if that is the correct term, was, "Anyhow—"

That jerked my father awake. "Anyhow?" he cried. "What kind of climax is that? Did this Willie Hammer ever find the forbidden treasure or didn't he?"

But Uncle Zeno was not to speak again until possessed by another story, and he merely looked at my father with an expression of vacant serenity. My father gave up in disgust and began again to drop his lapful of beans into the bowl one at a time, plunk plunk plunk.

His jealousy grew. He was going to learn to tell stories that would shade Uncle Zeno's the way a mountain overtowers a hill of potatoes. He ransacked his memory, and he begged stories from the loafers down at Virgil Campbell's grocery store, and he began to delve into the volumes of fairy tales and folklore scattered about the house. He borrowed my book of Norse mythology and committed a good half of it to memory. All to no avail. My father was simply too entranced with mischief and effect, and the stories he managed to begin in leisurely fashion soon careered into wild gesticulation and ended with an unpleasant loud noise. "Wham!" he would shout. "I've gotcha!"

But he didn't have us, not in the way he wanted to, and he looked into our startled faces with an expression of expectancy quickly sagging to disappointment. "Well, maybe I left out some stuff," he would say, "but it's still a damn good story. Better than some I've heard lately."

Uncle Zeno said: That puts me in mind of Buford Rhodes and his coonhounds. Buford was a good old boy anyway you want and kind of crazy about raising coonhounds and was an awful smart hand at it. Lived out there in Sudie's Cove in a tin-roof shack with his wife and six younguns and must have been a good dozen dogs. All kinds of dogs, Walkers and Blue Ticks and Redbones and lots of old hounds with the breeding mixed in like juices in soup. One of them named Raymond, you couldn't never figure out, must have been a cross between a bloodhound and a Shetland pony. Kids rode that dog all day like a pony, he was that good-natured.

But it was the dog called Elmer that Buford was most proudest of, though Elmer wasn't much bred either, just an old sooner dog. Still he was the brightest dog anybody ever heard tell of. Buford was selling his hides to Sears and Roebuck for a dollar apiece. He'd catch them coons by the score and skin them and tack their hides up to cure. Got so after a while there wasn't a inch of wall on Buford's house or milkshed not covered with coon hides. So Buford always kept an eye out for old scrap lumber and kept piling it underneath his house to cure them hides on.

That was where Elmer's smartness come in. That dog Elmer was so smart that if Buford showed him a piece of oak board or a joint of pine siding, he'd take off and tree a coon which when the hide was skinned off and stretched would exactly fill out that length of wood. That was what made him so smart and valuable and caused Buford to think the world of him, rather have Elmer than the jewels of Sheba and the wisdom of Solomon.

But then they got into trouble one Tuesday about the middle of September. Elmer happened to wander inside the house while Buford was off somewhere and his wife had left the door open by mistake. Buford wouldn't never of let him in, ruins a good dog to lay around in a dwelling house. But Elmer wandered in this time and seen Buford's wife there ironing the laundry. He took one look at that ironing board and just lit out down the road as fast as he could go and heading west as far as you could point. Buford said later on he didn't know whether Elmer already had a coon that big somewhere he knew about or it just sparked his ambitions.

Whatever, Elmer had set hisself a journey and when Buford got home and heard what happened he took off after him. Dog like Elmer, that smart, can't afford to lose a dog like that. So Buford was traveling west now, trying to track him down, asking questions of anybody he came to, and for a long time he could tell where he'd been. Folks will remember a dog that's got something on its mind. But then the houses got scarcer and not many people to ask, and Buford was getting worried—

My father nodded sagely. "And I'll bet you're not going to tell us any more. You're just going to leave it hanging there, aren't you, Uncle Zeno?"

Uncle Zeno gazed into his placid abyss.

My father leaned over the table toward him. "Well, I've got your number now. I don't know any Willie Hammer or Lacey Joe Blackman or Setback Williams or those other people you've been telling us about. But it happens that I do know Buford Rhodes. Hired him one time to do some house painting. I know right where he lives, down there on Iron Duff, and I can drive right to his house. That's what I'm going to do, Uncle Zeno, and check your story out."

This possibility made no impression upon the old man. Why should it? We didn't care whether the story was true and Uncle Zeno didn't care about anything. But the idea that he could actually track down Buford Rhodes and talk to him seemed to give my father gleeful satisfaction.

It occurred to me that my father was preoccupied with the problem of Homer's blindness. Homer had lived in history and told his stories about real soldiers and described in grisly detail battles he could not have seen. But, like Uncle Zeno, Homer had left no trace in the world.

Patient scholars were forced to debate whether the poet had actually ever lived. My father was not much interested in getting the details straight about coonhounds; he wanted to see if Buford Rhodes had ever met and talked to Uncle Zeno. The old man was living with us, eating our food and sleeping in the upstairs bedroom, but he was hardly present except as a voice. Like Homer, he was leaving no trace.

And so my father, in the disinterested pursuit of knowledge, was going to interview Buford Rhodes, the actual subject of one of Uncle Zeno's stories. Schliemann, unearthing the first traces of a Trojan site, must have felt something of the excitement my father felt.

My grandmother muttered that it seemed pure foolishness to her, traipsing down to Iron Duff for no good reason, but my father, leaning back in his chair and blowing a happy smoke ring, said, "That's just exactly where I'm headed first thing tomorrow morning."

Actually, he didn't get underway until midmorning, some five hours after rosy-fingered Eos had streaked the sky with orient pearl and gold. I realize now that he had other necessary errands to perform, but of course he wouldn't give my grandmother the satisfaction of knowing that he was doing something useful. He preferred for her to think he was off lollygagging after Uncle Zeno's story.

His absence left me with idle time and, since it was a lovely August morning and not yet sweltering, I decided to forgo reading and wander the hills of the farm until lunchtime. A favorite place for lonesome cowboy games was in a glade behind one of the farther hills of the pasture. An awesome storm had blown over a great oak there and I loved to clamber among the fallen branches and look at the jagged tears wrought in the trunk and see what new animal life had come to inhabit.

But when I arrived I found the tree already occupied. Uncle Zeno was sitting perched in an easy place on a big limb. His back was toward me and over his left shoulder protruded the end of the gnarly staff he sometimes used for walking. Never had his figure seemed so insignificant, his shoulders slumped and his head craned forward away from me so that I knew he was once again looking deep into his private void.

He was talking too, out here in the grassy knolls under the soft blue sky where there was not a living soul he could have been aware of to listen to him. I crept up as noiselessly as I could. I wanted to hear what he told himself in private, thinking that maybe the old man was revealing secrets of the earth he alone was privy to.

Here is what Uncle Zeno was saying: —but finally he was lost and he had to admit it. Hated it like poison, he'd never been lost in the woods before and he was hoping none of his buddies would ever hear about it, Buford Rhodes lost in the woods. He had give up on his good dog Elmer and he thought he'd be lucky if he could get back alive hisself.

But right then he heard a baying he knew was Elmer and he begun to take heart. Happened though that he was down in a box cove with steep flanks on both sides and an anxious-looking rock-face cliff at the upper end. The sun was a-going down and the moon not coming up yet. And echoed in there till he couldn't say where the baying was coming from. He started climbing but by the time he was halfway up the mountainside Elmer lost the scent and hushed. Or maybe Elmer wasn't following no scent, just lost and worrying about it like Buford, but anyhow he shut up and not another sound out of him.

So now Buford was loster than before. He was going to swaller his pride and call out for help, but he seen they wasn't no use, he wasn't close to nothing but mossy rocks and sawbriars. He set down there on a rotten pine log and waited and he was feeling about as bad as a man can feel.

Didn't know how long he set there. It got cooler and the moon come up, turning the green leaves as white as snow, and it was as quiet as the bottom of a well. And then he seen somebody, or he thought he seen somebody, the moonlight deceiving. It was a Indian woman. She come at him smiling with her arms down at her sides, and he was awful happy to see her except when he tried to talk he found out she didn't speak nothing but Cherokee, which he didn't speak none of, not a speck. They tried to talk together but soon had to give it up as a bad job. She finally just reached out and took his hand and led him off with her, deeper and deeper into the woods, Buford feeling worse and worse. He was content he'd go with her wherever she wanted, he couldn't do no better.

It was a cave she lived in that she took him to and wasn't a bad cave, nice and dry, with some crevices for smoke to get out, and there was stuff to eat, berries and roots and herbs and squirrel meat. Wasn't the most comfortable place in the world but must have suited ole Buford all right because he lived there in that cave with the Cherokee woman two year or more. Turned out not such a bad life after all, because

Indian women don't like for their menfolks to do no work, and Buford just laid around and let her wait on him hand and foot. Ever once in a while at night he'd hear that fine hound dog Elmer start up baying somewhere off in the dark and Buford would get up and go scouring around the ridges, thrashing through blackberry briars and laurel hells. But then after a few months he didn't even bother to get up and look, didn't see much point in it anymore.

Went along like that two whole years, till one morning in spring he happened to wake up just when the woman was stepping over him to poke up the fire for breakfast and he took notice of a part of her he hadn't looked at close before and he wasn't what you called pleasured. Looked like a big ole crow had swallered a redbird there. He shut his eyes, and laying there with his eyes shut it come to him how awful ugly this woman was. He never thought about that before and now it started to bother him right much. After breakfast he sneaked away to a clearing where he had a favorite sandstone rock that he liked to sit on and think.

He set there and thought till he was pure gloomy. Here he was, lost in the woods and living with the ugliest woman creation ever made and he couldn't even talk to her. Well, he had plumb sunk into being a forsaken savage, all there was to it. Seemed to him there wasn't no hope for Buford Rhodes in this world anymore, he was lost to the sight of God and mankind. It was a black study he was in, but just right then when he was thinking his darkest thoughts, he heard a rustling over in the bushes—

At this point Uncle Zeno ceased. The story impulse had died in him, or maybe the story flew from this roosting-place across the world to another storyteller, Chinese or Tibetan, who sat waiting for inspiration. Uncle Zeno's audience—the white clouds and fallen tree, the blue daylight and sweet green grass—listened patiently, but the story was over for now. Yet here in the glade was the best setting for his stories, and I felt that I understood him now in a way I hadn't before. He was some necessary part of nature we hadn't recognized, seeing him only as a windy old man. But he was more than that, and different. What was he doing now that the story had ended in him? Why, he was sitting on the tree, giving audience to the story of its regal life and calamitous downfall, a story I couldn't hear. I would have to wait until Uncle Zeno was possessed by the impulse to repeat it to us.

I hoped he would never find out I'd been there to overhear him. I turned away quietly and went back to the house and made a lunch of bread and cheese and buttermilk from the icebox. I ate alone. My mother and grandmother had walked over to pay their respects to a shut-in friend, my father was down in Iron Duff playing archeologist-detective, and Uncle Zeno was in the pasture telling stories to the mica rocks and horse nettles.

After lunch I took a book of science out to the porch to read, learning that Sirius was the most luminous star in our heavens and was thought in old times to bring on madness in people and fits of poetic frenzy. I didn't care to read fiction; I'd had enough stories for a while.

My father returned about four o'clock and came into the porch to sit and chat with me. He looked haggard.

"What did you find out?" I asked him.

He rubbed the back of his neck and looked at the pine ceiling. His tone was mournful, puzzling. "Nothing," he said.

"Couldn't you find Buford Rhodes?"

"Couldn't find him, couldn't find anyone who knew him, couldn't find the least trace of him."

"Maybe you went to the wrong house. You might have forgot where he lived."

"Drove right to his front door, where he used to live. House was empty and run-down. Windows broken, doors off the hinges. Holes in the roof. Looked like nobody had lived in it for twenty years."

"Did you ask the neighbors?"

"They never heard of him. Walked down to Hipps' grocery, and nobody there ever heard of him either."

"You must have got the wrong place. Somebody would know him."

"I drove down to ask Virgil Campbell. He knows everybody that was ever in the county. At first he thought he sort of did remember a Buford Rhodes, but the more he thought about it the less he could remember."

"Maybe you got the name mixed up," I said. "Maybe the man you hired to paint had a name like that but different."

"I know Buford Rhodes," he said. "Know him anywhere. Uncle Zeno described him to a T." He snapped his fingers. "I'm glad you mentioned that. I recall I paid Buford with a check. I'll have a record in my check stubs. Paid him seventy-seven dollars exactly. Wasn't but three years ago, I'll go look that up." He rose and walked to the door.

"Where did you eat dinner?" I asked.

He gave me another harried look. "I haven't been hungry lately, Jess," he said and went in to pore through his records.

But this research, too, proved disappointing. He found a check stub for the amount of seventy-seven dollars, and its date would fit it into the period of the house painting, but he had failed to list whom he'd written the check to.

When the women returned from their errand of charity, he asked my mother about it. "See, here's the check stub," he said, waving it under her chin. "You remember Buford Rhodes, don't you?"

She backed away from the flapping paper. "We had three or four painters working about that time. I don't remember any of them."

"You'd remember Buford, though. Had the kind of beard that gives you a blue face. Always cracking jokes and talking about his hound dogs. Always had a drink or two under his belt no matter what time of day it was."

"That describes every house painter I ever met," she said.

"You ought to remember him, though. Uncle Zeno has got him down exactly. He was some kind of character."

"All I ever meet are characters," she said. "I don't believe that normal human beings show up in this part of the country."

Exasperated, he flung down the booklet of stubs and stamped on it. "How could anybody not remember Buford Rhodes?" he shouted.

"Calm down," she said. "It's not important."

But it was important to my father, and his shouting indicated the intensity of his feelings. I almost spoke up then. I almost told him that the last I'd heard Buford Rhodes was lost in the forest and living in a cave with an ugly Indian woman. I realized, however, that I'd better not speak; this information would only cause more confusion.

I was assailed by a wild thought and a goosy sensation. What if Buford Rhodes had ceased to exist upon the earth *because* Uncle Zeno told stories about him? I had entertained odd fancies since overhearing the old man this morning. What if Uncle Zeno's stories so thoroughly absorbed the characters he spoke of that they took leave of the everyday world and just went off to inhabit his narratives? Everything connected with them would disappear, they would leave no more sign among us than a hawk's shadow leaves in the snow he flies above. The only place you could find Achilles these days was in the *Iliad*. Had he ever existed otherwise? Had any of those heroes left evidence behind?

I cried out, "What about Agamemnon?"

My father gave me a peculiar look. "What about him?"

"Didn't you tell me they found his death mask? Didn't you say it was a mask made out of gold and they put it in a museum?"

He answered in a vexed tone. "That's the name they give it, but they can't really prove it belonged to Agamemnon, of course."

"Well, it ain't his," I said. "They've got the wrong man." Because now I was convinced of my notion. Homer and Uncle Zeno did not merely describe the world, they used it up. My father had said that one reason Homer was reckoned such a top-notch poet was you couldn't tell where the world left off and the *Iliad* began . . . . No wonder you couldn't tell.

My theory was wild enough to amuse my father; it was just the sort of mental play-pretty he liked to entertain himself with. But I decided not to tell him about it. He was earnestly troubled by the problem of Buford Rhodes and obviously in no mood for metaphysical speculations in the philosophy of narrative. I could read that much on his face. Then he said, "Come on, Jess. We'd better get the milking chores done."

I rose and followed him willingly. I looked forward to getting the evening chores out of the way and sitting down to supper. I was hungry, with nothing but bread and cheese for lunch, and I was eager to hear Uncle Zeno tell another story. I felt like a scientist now that I'd hit upon my brilliant idea, and I wanted to watch the process at work.

Sure enough, as soon as my grandmother had got through one of her painfully detailed supper prayers, Uncle Zeno began talking, without excuse or preamble, as always.

—and out of the bushes there, Uncle Zeno said, come a gang of six kids, looked to be eight, ten years old, and dressed in washed overalls and pinafores. They kept staring at Buford and he begun to think for the first time how he might look awful strange, dirty and bearded from living in the woods so long. But he kept hisself soft-talking and gentled them kids along until they agreed to lead him back to civilization. These here kids belonged to the Sunday-school class of a hard-shell Baptist church back up that way and they'd run into Buford while they was hunting Easter eggs. Turned out he hadn't been as lost as he thought he was, no more than two miles from a little old settlement there, and the congregation had come up here for an Easter picnic. It was just that Buford's mind had been occupied, thinking about that Indian woman and worrying about his good dog Elmer that he hadn't heard bay in more than a year now. Buford just hadn't been taking no proper interest, that was all.

So the kids led him out of the woods down to the settlement and he got started on the right road a-going home. He was dreading to arrive, figured his place must have gone to rack and ruin while he was gone and his wife and children probably in the poorhouse a long time ago. He didn't know what he was going to tell folks and whether anybody would believe him or not.

But when he came in sight of his house, well, he was mighty surprised. The place was all fixed up and just a-shining, better than he ever done for it. There was a spanking new tin roof, and them old coon hides had been tore down from everywhere and the house was painted up nice and white and there was a new Ford car setting by the edge of the yard.

So he reckoned his wife had took up with another man while he was gone and they wouldn't have no use for him around there no more. But he went on up anyhow and rapped at the door. It took his wife a minute or two to recognize him but when she did she was happy fit to bust and reached out and hugged him tight and his kids run out in fine new clothes and jumped around, it was the best welcome-home you'd ever want to see.

After they settled down a little bit he got to questioning her. How come you're doing so good, with the house all fixed up and a Ford car in the front yard? And she said it was Elmer. Elmer had found his way finally back home a year ago and seen how the family was doing poorly, so he went out and got hisself a job. Buford said that was awful good news, he was proud of that dog, and what kind of job did he have? She said Elmer got him a job teaching over at at the high school, arithmetic and natural science, and drawed a pretty good salary considering he didn't have no experience to speak of. And Buford said a dog that smart didn't need no experience, what he was going to do was get Elmer to show him how to smell the ground and track coon and they'd switch off, Buford would be the dog and Elmer could be the man because maybe that's the way it should have been in the first place—

"All right," my father said. "I'm glad to hear some more of that story." He kept rubbing the back of his neck. "But what I want to know is, Where does Buford live now? I've been looking for him all day and can't turn up hide nor hair. Speak, Uncle Zeno. Tell us where Buford Rhodes has got to."

But of course there was no answer. Uncle Zeno looked calmly into his vast inane, contemplating the nothingness that hung between stories. He probably wasn't aware that my father spoke to him. He lifted a slow spoonful of creamed corn to his mouth.

My father leaned back, his sensibilities sorely bruised. "No, you're not going to tell us. I know that. I wish I hadn't asked." He heaved a sorrowful sigh and looked down at his lap. "Well, now I'll tell a story," he said. "It's my turn." He leaned forward again, placing the palms of both hands flat on the table, and stared intently into Uncle Zeno's face. He looked like a bobcat ready to spring. "Once upon a time there was a pretty good old boy who never did anybody any harm. I won't say his name, but he was a pretty good old boy. It happened that he fell in love with a fine mountain girl and married into her family and they lived there in the hills and he worked the farm for them. That was all right, everything was just fine. Except that in this family there was an army of strange uncles who were always dropping by, and they were an interesting bunch, most of them. This good old boy—let's just call him Joe—got along O.K. with these strange visitors. He liked to talk to them and find out about them. He was interested, you know, in what makes people tick. . . . But there was this one weird uncle—we'll call him Uncle Z.—he couldn't figure out to save his life. Truly he couldn't. And it began to prey on his mind until he couldn't make himself think about anything but this Uncle Z. and how queer he was. . . . I'm sorry to tell you, Uncle Zeno, that I don't know the end of this story. But I think that this good old boy started worrying so much that he finally just went crazy and they carried him off to the funny farm in a straightjacket." He gazed morosely into the plate of food he had hardly touched. "But like I say, I don't really know the end of the story."

My grandmother reprimanded him, in a tone gentler than usual. "Now, Joe Robert, you don't want to be unmannerly."

He stood up. "No, of course I don't," he said. "If you-all will excuse me, I think I'll go out on the porch and have a cigarette. Maybe clear my head. I don't know what's the matter with me." He fumbled a moment with the knob, then stepped through the door and closed it.

My mother and grandmother looked at each other, and my grandmother said, "Joe Robert's acting kind of peculiar, seems to me. He ain't ailing, is he?"

"He doesn't seem to be ill," my mother said.

"It's Uncle Zeno's stories," I told them. "They get him all worked up. He wants to do something, but he don't know what to do."

"They're only stories," my mother said. "No one is supposed to do anything *about* them."

I wanted to reply, but I couldn't very well tell my mother that she didn't understand my father, that he always had to be doing things, changing the order of the world in some way, causing anarchy when he could or simple disorder if he couldn't do any better.

"Just seems peculiar to me," my grandmother said, "somebody getting all worked up about a few harmless windies." She looked at our visitor with a fond expression. "Why, Uncle Zeno wouldn't harm a fly."

The three of us looked at him, an inoffensive old man who hardly appeared to occupy the chair he sat in. He seemed ignorant of our regard, and it was clear that what she said was true. He wouldn't harm a fly.

Then his drifting abstraction formed into a voice and he began to speak again. "That puts me in mind of," Uncle Zeno said, "Cousin Annie Barbara Sorrells that lived down toward the mouth of Ember Cove. Had a right nice farm there, about a hundred acres or so, but didn't have nobody to work it, her oldest son dying when he was eight and her other boy, Luden, gone off to California on a motorcycle. But she had her a son-in-law, Joe Robert his name was, and he was a pretty fair hand at farming, she didn't have no complaints to speak of, except that Joe Robert was ever the sort to dream up mischief. . . . Well, it happened one time that her boy Luden had sent Annie Barbara a present, which was a box of fancy candies he'd bought in St. Louis—"

This was too much.

Uncle Zeno was telling a story about us. I knew what he was going to say; I'd lived through those events, after all. His story focused on my father, and that fact disturbed me. My father didn't seem to get along too well with Uncle Zeno as it was, and perhaps he wouldn't be happy to hear that he was now a character in the old man's stories.

I jumped up without even saying Excuse me and went out to the porch. It was as dark as the dreams of a sleeping bear; rain clouds blocked off the starlight and there was only a dim light coming through the dining-room drapes. My father was not smoking, but just sitting in a chair shoved flat against the wall of the house.

"Are you here?" I asked.

He paused a long time before answering. "Yeah, I'm right here, Jess."

"Are you feeling O.K.?"

Another pause, and I could hear Uncle Zeno's mumble drone through the door.

"I'm all right, I guess. Maybe I'm catching a cold. I've been feeling kind of light-headed. Feel a little weak all over, like I'd lost a lot of weight in a hurry."

"Come on back in and have a piece of apple pie. Maybe it'll make you feel better."

He sat motionless. There was no wind sound, no sound at all except for the low, indistinct mutter of Uncle Zeno's story.

"Apple pie," he said softly. "Well, that's not bad medicine." He didn't move for a while yet. Finally he rose slowly from the chair. But when he took a step he walked directly into darkest shadow and I couldn't see him at all and at that moment Uncle Zeno's story concluded and all the night went silent.

Night traffic near Winchester

Dave Smith

Through tall ash, through stunning cidery air,
under winesaps bobbing on every hill,
past leaf-littered fieldstone walls
mute as farmwomen bent in rows,
around weathered clapboard barns,
those veterans leaning casually,
quaint as postcards from the dark
drugstore that never closes,
catching the sour gargle of trucks
headed the other way, we descend

into the Valley, slow, ease our stop-and-go
route through painted brick cottages
huddled more than a century, and speak
of heartpine floors sloped so badly
everyone leans toward the fetid creek.
Each foundation, like ancestors' hips,
is cracked, patched, and recracking,
but still holds its house along
the street that keeps a false yellow
front on the place used by Jackson
to plot raids dashing and thunderous
as the tattering Bible he slept with.
It's darker than a mapcase now, closed.

I promise we'll stop another time, stay
long enough to see boots, old orders,

the grim portraits like Puritan ghosts,
but now we climb, car straining until
we top the northern ridge and halt
where my father stopped years back.
Stepping out, the crackle of leaves,
the chill, high night air drifts
me into the smell of his coffee.
This is the way to grandmother's,
he says, so I say it now, feeling
this dark is a friend, the roof
I seem to have lived under, or below
where the city boils all Friday night,
as if teamsters, hearing a rumor—
"Grant's passed Charlottesville"
—beat hell out of tardy recruits.

Leaving our girls asleep in the car, my son,
old as I was with my father, steps off
to the overlook's lipfall I don't
need to see, that historical dark,
and I come quick to take his hand.
His varsity jacket shines, absorbing
this gay bowlful of the thousands
of tiny lights we never stop bearing,
yellow caution, gold houses, blue K mart,
and across a gulf of breath that hill
steady with taillights like campfires.
What army there? I asked my father,
confused. The people's, he said, just
men, and any man's fire makes a short
night when you're afraid. I'm afraid
at this edge where fathers have stood
pulling at dark hands that always ask
"How far have we come?" Hours staring
off headlights rising the old road,
I hear the voice I had thought lost
say far, but not far enough yet. Up
ahead they will be sleeping, a few
lights lit, coffee hot, ready for news.

1983

Sweet sixteen lines

Al Young

You bet it would've made a tender movie!
If only someone had been flighty enough
to capture the shape of what turned out to be
our last days alone, the end of a rough
journey that dulled every sense but touch.
Heroically juvenile, lighter than light,
we talked what we felt, but never thought much.
We were Romeo and Juliet night after night.
It was like we'd sailed from heaven in a jet,
copilots, cool but glorious, and landed
our sullen craft too artfully—poets yet;
runaways on life's slick runway of expanded
unconsciousness. Maybe. Who knows for sure?
But Ruby and the Romantics came out that year
with a sweet-nothing single: hot, airy and pure
enough to hold us aloft by heart and by ear.

1983

Father and son

Morton Marcus

His body is long,
his face is long and thin.
Overhung eyebrows and smoke-black eyes,
and darkened hollows beneath cheekbones and chin.
His teeth are white, and fanged,
and even when he is seventy-one, they are all his.
When he smiles, those teeth
slide into view,
and the boy will cringe:
the old man has a wolf in him.

The old man's eldest son
looks much the same:
beard too heavy; mouth too grim.
There is something definitely foreign in each of them.
Angered, they'll growl and snap,
pinch the offender's arms or ears
and fling him toward another room
with a boot in the buttocks or a final slap.

That's for family, inside the house.
For the bickerers and bargainers on the street,
There are the smoke-dense eyes and the toothy grin.
And should those outsiders cheat or curse,
there's the knife in the boot
or the knobby knuckles hurtling toward their chins.
To others the world is "dog eat dog,"
but the old man and his eldest son are wolves
and they'll hear none of that.

Besides, they're taking care:
the family and all its heirlooms

1983

are in their charge: brooches and tarnished spoons,
a pearl necklace from a great-aunt's will,
several silver plates and cups.
They are neither kind nor heroic men:
They mean to survive.
That's what the old man's parents taught to him,
and he teaches it to his daughters and sons
with such ferocity, they cannot look him in the eye.
Love is not the point, it never was.
Joy and ecstasy are bearded men in black
who caper through the streets like laundry flapping on a line.
Power, control—that's what he's after.
The saliva sluices through his teeth, his eyes flash.
When he dreams of God, he tells his eldest son,
he envisions a Hand that holds the world like a rock
about to be thrown at a noise in the dark.
The portion of stone covered by this Hand
is shadowy: night. The portion that isn't—
all that birdsong and light—"Vell,"
the old man says, "who cares about dhat."

His happy hour

Alan Shapiro

The gregarious dark is shifting
when she puts her second drink,
the free one, half on the coaster.
The tipped wine poised at the brim
is the beginning of the bad girl
she'll promise never to be again
tomorrow, who can taunt him now
to prove he doesn't love her
and never could: her hand slides
up his thigh until he tenses—
"My little prig, don't you want
to fuck me?," the bad girl
she couldn't be at home, his wife on ice.
All he can do is smile back
as though she's made a harmless
good-natured joke, and struggle
not to look around to see
who's heard, who's watching. He wants
to smash the wine glass in her face
so he can know for once
exactly what he's done wrong;
but he places it instead
back safely on the coaster
quickly before she sees.
Never cautious enough, he is prepared
even if she knocks it over
to go down on his hands and knees
and wipe it up, kind and forgiving.

1983

In all ways careful to acquit himself
so that tomorrow when she says
she doesn't deserve him, he's too good,
he can believe her. Tomorrow
will be *his* happy hour. There won't be
anything she wouldn't do for him.

RAFAEL ALBERTI. DRAWING FOR INVITATION TO CELEBRA-
TION OF ALBERTI'S 80TH BIRTHDAY. (*TQ* #59)

The last class

Ellen Bryant Voigt

Put this in your notebooks:
All verse is occasional verse.
In March, trying to get home, distracted
and impatient at Gate 5 in the Greyhound station,
I saw a drunk man bothering a woman.
A poem depends on its detail
but the woman had her back to me,
and the man was just another drunk,
black in this case, familiar, dirty.
I moved past them both, got on the bus.

There is no further action to report.
The man is not a symbol. If what he said to her
touches us, we are touched by a narrative
we supply. What he said was, "I'm sorry,
I'm sorry," over and over, "I'm sorry,"
but you must understand he frightened the woman,
he meant to rob her of those few quiet
solitary moments sitting down,
waiting for the bus, before she headed home
and probably got supper for her family,
perhaps in a room in Framingham,
perhaps her child was sick.

My bus pulled out, made its usual turns
and parted the formal gardens from the Common,
both of them camouflaged by snow.

1983

And as it threaded its way to open road,
leaving the city, leaving our sullen classroom,
I postponed my satchel of your poems
and wondered who I am to teach the young,
having come so far from honest love of the world;
I tried to recall how it felt
to live without grief; and then I wrote down
a few tentative lines about the drunk,
because of an old compulsion to record,
or sudden resolve not to be self-absorbed
and full of dread—
                    I wanted to salvage
something from my life, to fix
some truth beyond all change, the way
photographers of war, miles from the front,
lift print after print into the light,
each one further cropped and amplified,
pruning whatever baffles or obscures,
until the small figures are restored
as young men sleeping.

Two poems

C. K. Williams

Neglect

An old hill town in northern Pennsylvania, a missed connection
 for a bus, an hour to kill.
For all intents and purposes, the place was uninhabited; the
 mines had closed years before—
anthracite too dear to dig, the companies went west to strip,
 the miners to the cities—
and now, though the four-lane truck route still went through—
 eighteen-wheelers pounding past—
that was almost all: a shuttered Buick dealer, a grocery, not even
 a McDonald's,
just the combination ticket-office, luncheonette and five-and-
 dime where the buses turned around.
A low, gray frame building, it was gloomy and run-down, but
 charmingly old-fashioned;
ancient wooden floors, open shelves, the smell of unwrapped
 candy, cigarettes and band-aid glue.
The only people there, the only people I think that I remember
 from the town at all,
were the silent woman at the register, and a youngish teenaged
 boy standing reading.
The woman smoked and smoked, stared out the streaky
 window, handed me my coffee with indifference.
It was hard to tell how old she was: her hair was dyed and teased,
 iced into a beehive.
The boy was frail, sidelong somehow, afflicted with a devastating Nessus-shirt of acne

boiling down his face and neck—pits and pores, scarlet streaks
and scars; saddening.

We stood together at the magazine rack for a while before I
realized what he was looking at.

Pornography: two naked men, one grimaces, the other, with a
fist inside the first one, grins.

I must have flinched: the boy sidled down and blanked his face
more—I left to take a walk.

It was cold, but not enough to catch or clear your breath:
uncertain clouds, unemphatic light.

Everything seemed dimmed and colorless, the sense of surfaces
dissolving, like the Parthenon.

Farther down the main street were a dentist and a chiropractor,
both with hand-carved signs,

then the Elks' decaying clapboard mansion with a parking space
"Reserved for the Exalted Ruler,"

and a Russian church, gilt onion domes, a four-horned air-raid
siren on a pole between them.

Two blocks in, the old slate sidewalks shatter and uplift, gnawed
lawns, aluminum butane tanks,

then the roads begin to peter out and rise: half-fenced yards
with scabs of weeks-old snow,

thin, inky, oily leaks of melt insinuating down the gulleys and
the cindered cuts

that rose again into the footings of the filthy, disused slagheaps
ringing the horizon.

There was nowhere else. At the depot now, the women and the
boy were both behind the counter.

He was on a stool, his eyes closed, she stood just in back of him,
massaging him,

hauling at his shoulders, kneading at the muscles like a boxer's
trainer between rounds.

I picked up the county paper: it was anti-crime and welfare
bums, for Reaganomics and defense.

The wirephoto was an actress in her swimming suit, that
famously expensive bosom, cream.

My bus arrived at last, its heavy, healthy white exhaust pouring
in the afternoon.

All aboard Carbondale, all aboard Pittston, all aboard Nanticoke,
Tamaqua, La Plume.

Glancing back, I felt a qualm, concern, an ill-heart, almost parental, but before I'd hit the step
the boy'd begun to blur, to look like someone else, the woman had already faded absolutely.
All that held now was that violated, looted country, the fraying fringes of the town,
those gutted hills, hills by rote, hills by permission, great, naked wastes of wrack and spill,
vivid and disconsolate, like genitalia shaved and disinfected for an operation.

MATTHEW OWENS. (*TQ* #58)

Waking Jed

Deep asleep, perfect immobility, no apparent evidence of consciousness or of dream.

Elbow cocked, fist on pillow lightly curled to the tension of the partially relaxing sinew.

Head angled off, just so: the jaw's projection exaggerated slightly, almost to prognathous: why?

The features express nothing whatsoever and seem to call up no response in me.

Though I say nothing, don't move, gradually, far down within, he, or rather not *he* yet,

something, a presence, an element of being, becomes aware of me: there begins a subtle,

very gentle alteration in the structure of the face, or maybe less than that, more elusive,

as though the soft distortions of sleep-warmth radiating from his face and flesh,

those essentially unreal mirages in the air between us, were modifying, dissipating.

The face is now more his, Jed's— its participation in the almost Romanesque generality

I wouldn't a moment ago have been quite able to specify, not having its contrary, diminishes.

Particularly on the cheekbones and chin, the skin is thinning, growing denser, harder,

the molecules on the points of bone coming to attention, the eyelids finer, brighter, foil-like:

capillaries, veins; though nothing moves, there are goings to and fro behind now.

One hand opens, closes down more tightly, the arm extends suddenly full-length,

jerks once at the end, again, holds: there's a more pronounced elongation of the skull—

the infant pudginess, whatever atavism it represented, or reversion, has been called back.

Now I sense, although I can't say how, his awareness of me: I can feel him begin to *think*,

I even know that he's thinking— or thinking in a dream perhaps— of me, watching him here.

Now I'm aware— again, with no notion how, nothing indicates it— that if there was a dream,

it's gone, and, yes, his eyes abruptly open although his gaze, straight before him,

seems not to register just yet, the mental operations still independent of his vision.

I say his name, the way we do it, softly, calling one another from a cove or cave,

as though something else were there with us, not to be disturbed, to be crept along beside.

The lids come down again, he yawns, widely, very consciously manifesting intentionality.

Great, if rudimentary pleasure now: a sort of primitive, peculiarly mammalian luxury—

to know, to know wonderfully, that lying here, warm, protected, eyes closed, one can,

for a moment anyway, a precious instant, put off, the lower-specie onsets, duties, debts.

Sleeker, somehow, slyer, more aggressive now, he is suddenly more awake, all awake,

already plotting, scheming, fending off: nothing said but there is mild rebellion, conflict:

I insist, he resists, and then, with abrupt, wriggling grace, he otters down from sight,

just his brow and crown, his shining, rumpled hair, left ineptly showing from the sheet.

Which I pull back to find him in what he must believe a parody of sleep, himself asleep:

fetal, rigid, his arms clamped to his sides, eyes screwed shut, mouth clenched, grinning.

MATTHEW OWENS. (*TQ* #58)

Recovering

William Goyen

The story—and travail—of two brothers has been on my mind: Jacob and Esau, twins. Esau was born first, "coming forth red and all his body hairy, like a mantle," and Jacob followed, clutching onto his brother's heel. As though he wanted to hold back Esau, pull him back and go on ahead of him, "supplant" him. For this Jacob was called "The Supplanter." I suppose we've all felt the grabbing hand, the clutch on the heel as we were making our own natural headway, at some time or another; something—not good—pulling us back, stumbling us, even: a grasper, a potential supplanter. This is what Esau felt.

These brothers were, then, struggling brothers from the start, contending, even, for very birthright and blessing, as you may remember. Esau was a hunter and a man of the field, Jacob a quiet, indoors man. At a time in their youth their brotherhood became murderous out of jealousy and disharmony—as though they had been cursed; and Rebekah, Jacob's mother, heard of Esau's vow to kill his brother and advised Jacob to leave home. Once, Esau, the red and hairy, had been so hungry when he came in from the fields that he offered his birthright to his quieter, domestic brother for some soup he was making. The brother, Jacob the Supplanter, accepted the bargain and so took his brother's birthright. And another time—this time by deceit—the wild, red brother of nature lost his father's blessing to his softer, more cunning brother. When the brothers' father Isaac was an old, failing blind man (he'd been sixty when his twin sons were born), he craved some good venison soup once more before he died and begged Esau,

This lecture was delivered at the Writer at Work Series, Gallatin Division, New York University, on April 13, 1983, sponsored by New York University, The Rockefeller Foundation, and the New York State Council on the Arts. The other speakers were Joan Rodman Goulianos, Joyce Johnson, and Eileen Simpson. William Goyen died on August 29, 1983, in Los Angeles.

his favorite, to provide it. Esau's mother, Rebekah, whose favorite was Jacob, overheard the request and made the soup herself. Take the soup to your father, she urged, and thereby gain his blessing. A blessing was a powerful gift and coming from venerable beings or from certain people of unusual power was carried by the blessed person for a lifetime like an anointing, a protective benediction, a redemption, sacred. So Rebekah, Jacob's mother, hoping for the blessing of Isaac upon her favorite son, made this suggestion to Jacob. "But he'll feel my hands and see that they are smooth where my brother's are hairy," said Jacob, "and know that I am not his beloved Esau; and then he'll curse me instead of bless me." "We'll dress you in Esau's clothes and cover your hands and neck with the bristling skin of an animal," the mother said. When Jacob brought the soup to his father, his father said, "The voice is Jacob's voice but the hands are the hands of Esau." So Jacob ate the venison and gave his impersonating son the vaunted blessing: it said that nations might serve him and peoples bow before him, receiving obeisance from his mother's sons. Jacob, again the supplanter, had stolen his brother's blessing.

But soon came Esau with *his* dish of venison. "Bless me, father," asked Esau. "Who are you?" cried his father. "Who was it who has already brought me venison? I've eaten my fill and given *that* one my blessing, and on him the blessing will come. Thy brother, coming in disguise, has snatched thy blessing from thee." "He's rightly named the Supplanter!" cried Esau. "First he took away my birthright and now he has stolen my blessing. Father," he implored, "have you no blessing left for me?" "No," answered Isaac, "I have designated your brother your master, I have condemned all his brothers to do him service; I have assured him of corn and wine; what claim have I left myself to make for you, my son?" "But," Esau pled, "have you only one blessing to give, father?" Esau wept. Then Isaac was moved and said, "All thy blessings shall come from earth's fruitfulness, and from the dew of heaven. Thy sword shall be the breath of life to thee, but thou shall be subject to thy brother until the day comes when thou wilt rebel and wilt shake off his yoke from thy neck." Esau begrudged this blessing and made a plan to kill his brother as soon as his father died. When Jacob's mother heard of this threat, she sent her son Jacob away from home. Thus the hostile separation of the two brothers began, fed by deceit and jealousy and contention. But Jacob, the heel-clutcher, had got ahead of his brother.

Years passed and Jacob had seen the fruits of his blind father's misplaced blessing: he was very rich with cattle and sheep, wives and servants and eleven children. He had not seen his estranged brother Esau for a long time, but now a meeting was at hand. It was time to go home again, to reenter the promised land of home and to meet his brother, to make amends. Jacob was returning as a prosperous and successful man and sent ahead to Esau gifts of abundance, cattle and sheep and camels and corn and oil. This returning home again is hard when there has been no increase, no fulfillment, no "success"; it is often bitter; as such a returnee I remember well some empty-handed homecomings; but Jacob came back covered in glory. But his fear was great. He had wronged his brother and was afraid of him and had amends to make. His brother had vowed to kill him. He hoped to disarm his anger with gifts sent ahead, but he was going to have to face his brother whom he had cheated, deceived, swindled, impersonated, "supplanted."

The story, in the book of Genesis (32: 22–32), of Jacob's return home to meet his brother, encloses the ancient and beautiful incident of an angelic encounter by a river. It is concerned with the themes of loss and recovering of self, of wounding and healing, of discovery of true self through spiritual struggle. It is about an all-night, mysterious wrestling between two silent men, opponents; or one silent man, *himself* his own contestant: which is it? The silent wrestling is broken only by the approaching dawn, when each asks the other's name and by one wounding, crippling—"halting"—the other in order to subdue him, and by the subduer asking the subdued to bless him! The passage reads: "The same night Jacob arose and took his two wives, his two maids, and his eleven children, and crossed the ford of the Jabbok river. He took them and sent them across the stream, and likewise everything that he had. And Jacob was left alone; and a man wrestled with him until the breaking of the day. When the man saw that he did not prevail against Jacob, he touched the hollow of Jacob's thigh; and Jacob's thigh was put out of joint as he wrestled with him. Then the man said, 'Let me go, for the day is breaking.' But Jacob said, 'I will not let you go, unless you bless me.' And the man said to him, 'What is your name?' And he said, 'Jacob.' Then the man said, 'Your name shall no more be called Jacob, but Israel; that is, He who strives with God and prevails. For if you have held your own with God, how much will you prevail over men?' Then Jacob asked him, 'Tell me, I pray, your name.' But he said, 'Why is it that you ask my name?' And there he blessed him. So Jacob called the name of the place Phenuel (that is, the face of God), saying, 'For I have seen God face to face, and yet my life is preserved.' The sun rose upon him as he passed Phenuel, limping because of his thigh."

Jacob's recovering his name and spirit, his redemption by the night river, is one of the most mysterious and enigmatic scenes of literature and has meant a great deal to me in the experience of recovering. Relating to my work it is direct metaphor. I've limped out of every piece of work I've done. It's given me a good sock in the hipbone in the wrestling. My eyes often open when I see a limping person going down the street. That person's wrestled with God, I think. I don't know when I ever rose from that contest as hale and whole as when I began. For me every accomplishment of work has been a wounding that brought new strength, new vision. I've always felt new, changed when the work was done. And in a new—or different—relation with life. Work, for me—writing, that is—has been that renewal through wrestling, that naming, that going home, that reconciliation with old disharmony, grief, grudge. For me that was recovery. Now I am not here—thank God—to define functions and meanings of literature, of the art of writing for anybody but myself—and that only by way of sharing my experience in living the life of an artist, in creating fiction (which is and has long been a way of life for me). I am sharing my own very personal experience in writing life, in recovering life. I am speaking of recovery of spirit where it had been lost, of finding again, as though it were new, fresh, what had been thought to have gone; of renewed vitality where there was debilitation; of replenishment where there had been emptiness. That kind of wrestling. "Recovery" involves a transformation. It is not simply a dead replacement, a lifeless exchange of one thing for another. And the transformation I speak of is spiritual—of the spirit. Art recovers life through spirit—that is, not through physical action. Nostalgia, the use of flat memory, in recalling the thing itself, calling back what once was, and in self-pity, is not what I'm talking about when I speak of recovery, of recovering life as art. In nostalgia, the element of lifeless longing is present, and so it is sentimental in that it wishes, yearns for things to be once again the way they used to be, exactly—a dead transference from then to now, stamped down. The Now, the present moment, the livingness of life, the world of "lived, ordinary lives," are dammed back, buried over by grieving over what was. I speak entirely from my own feelings and my own experience, from my own personal adventures. Everything is autobiography for me. Long ago I knew that another could not give me my life, only help to find it. I could only know life through myself, or recover it myself. I continue to be astonished by my own history. My own experience keeps justifying living. Others' experience in history has supported and inspirited me; but finally my own has got me through. The most I have been able to offer others and can now is this self-consciousness, ferocious protection of personal feeling. I am astonished by what has happened to me. More than anyone else, I am most curious about myself, my own hidden behavior, the secret services of my mind. Of all people, I am the person closest to my own feelings. It is, above all, my journey, that long and close association with myself that has been the signal value of my existence. The journey with myself is more remarkable than any other journey I have ever taken. Therefore, writing life for me is (and has been) a spiritual endeavor, and is transforming and redemptive. Wrestling and getting named and demanding "blessing," I limp.

1983

In speaking of the writer recovering, one can ask, why recover? Why not just give back what was, as it was, what is as it is? Why recover? Why not just let everything alone? Why wrestle, why not surrender; why not die? The unhealed must think this. In the fifties there was a vogue of the unhealed and unhealable. The poet was mad and lost. Some feared that "getting well" might mean the loss of poetry. If addictions were removed, by the grace of God, would art be removed along with them? Did a poet's songs live in speed and gin? These poets were exalted as lost and damned. Could writing heal them? Were poems cures? The recovering poet was the creating poet, the fertile, producing poet. I've sat in university halls and listened to visiting unrecovering poets who could not be understood behind drunkenness and dope. Could new poems heal them? If they could again in clear head write their poems, would they get well? Could the will, the willingness to make new poems, heal them? *Ex opera operandis*. In the power of the work itself, the power of the person.

The unhealed. I have not only known the unhealed but have been among them and one of them. The unhealed will not let go of the sickness, that is, come awake. The unhealed choose the hypnotism of illness and will not only not wrestle with it but certainly not ask a blessing of it. But pain and affliction do carry a blessing in them, I believe. Illness is a spiritual condition. It brings us to see something we had not seen before—seeing the meaning of our suffering. Thus, being healed—recovering—in this manner can cause great joy and even gratitude over having been sick. "Ordinarily, people feel sorry for themselves for having suffered," writes Dr. Thomas Hora in *Dialogues in Metapsychiatry*; "but in cases where real healing takes place, there is a sense of gratitude for the experience because it has brought about a realization which is of great value to the individual. Once we understand the true nature of healing, there is a valuable lesson in it for us all. If we have a problem, we do not have to seek fast relief, or even a quick healing to get rid of the problem as soon as possible. We may embrace the problem and say the same thing that Jacob said: 'I will not let thee go, except thou bless me.' If we quickly get rid of a problem and find relief, we are missing an opportunity to learn something vitally important. The mode of being-in-the-world changes and our character undergoes a transformation. That's the greatest healing." I will not let thee go, except thou bless me. Dr. Hora and others have shown me that in my stricken life and in my recovering life there has been a deep change within me; I am no longer the same person; I am somewhere made new. And I make new things out of this vision and out of this reality. In no longer holding onto my sickness in isolation and self-nursing, I have let go and have found new prowess, a new relationship to life and to others.

Which brings to mind, again, my friend the Greek archer:

Philoctetes, about whom I have spoken before. Philoctetes was, you'll remember, given a bow of great power—a blessing in terms of what we have been saying. On a wild island where he and his fellow warriors had stopped to pray to a local god, Philoctetes was bitten by a snake. A person with a magical gift had been wounded, lamed, "halted." The wound was incurable, and what's more, gave off an unbearable odor, which drove the gifted youth's friends from him. More than that, seizures periodically rendered Philoctetes frightening—he looked and acted crazy. He was abandoned on the forlorn island. He hid himself further away from the world in a cave by the ocean. He limped.

Philoctetes was so concerned with his wound that he forgot his bow. He knew utter loneliness. But he had his wound, morbid companion. Years passed. Suddenly he was urgently needed by others: a crucial war could be won if he would come again among his family and his fellows, return to his homeland with his bow. But, the young man reasoned with himself, there is this wound. Philoctetes refused to return; he was of no use. A famous doctor was offered. He would heal the wound. He asked to be left alone; he rejected the healing physician. Philoctetes was now in a position of power. A person with a handicapping wound and a priceless gift in demand by his society! He could sleep on, in self-pity and sickness, or accept healing and come back to the use of his gift, doubly empowered by his long suffering, by the long contest with himself, by his wrestling. You know the rest of the story, or can find it. It is the situation of the unhealed that serves us here.

For as I see it, the singer is the song; the poetry is the poet; the archer is the bow. In the power of the work itself, the power of the person. The two conditions are inseparable. I do not mean that a person must be wounded in order to use his gift. Isolate either the bow or the archer and you have no whole, a fatal division, a fragment. A person who sees life and others exclusively in terms of his own affliction is out of a literature we all know, and a seductive literature at that: we can name poets and novelists who have lured us into the darkness, given us opiate visions that have seemed to be life itself. Exclusive self-nursing, tending the "curse," the "difference" that separates, produces darkness, a sunless, festering creation. Exclusive magic produces sentimentality, heartlessness, silvery confection, a doll. At any rate, there is a conversation I must have with Philoctetes, my brother. For it is clear that he and I have met with the same choice, suffered together that crucial struggle, lain day after day, night after night, in the same haunted cave, "unhealable," dozing undelivered in the uterine glow, held by sucking death from pushing out into the explosion of life, heel in the grasp of a seductive supplanter. The deadly wound was all. The life-robber, the death sore, had taken over life. The radiant, the life-thrusting—the bow—lay untouched in the darkness. But brother Philoctetes, your healer arrived, the wound was closed, the bow won the battle; and O brother of the cave and the pain, I too have once again shaken free, flipped like a fish from the hand that stretches toward me; I kick towards light, but the finger-touch is on my heel. Lend me your bow! Come before me!

From what I have said, it is clear that writing—recovering life—for me is a spiritual task. No matter what the craft of it, writing for me is the work of the spirit. Style for me is the spiritual experience of the material of my work.

Art and Spirit endure together. Art heals, puts the precious bow in our hands again; binds up and reconciles; recovers the dignity and the beauty in us that keep getting wounded by the wrestling with the angel in us, with the God in us, or—in the absence of angels or God—with the mystery in each of us, waiting in the night by the river that we shall surely come to, on our way home to meet our brother.

William Wilborn

On welfare

We have two ways to aid the poor
Down here in Jackson City:
A white-draped basket at the door;
A similar committee.

Two poems
William Heyen

The new American poetry

It is the poetry of the privileged class.

It inherits portfolios.

It was born in the Ivy League, and inbred there.

Its parents filled its homes with bubbling Bach,
    silver and crystal brightnesses for its surfaces
    which do not sweat to wring meaning from paychecks.

It does not hear the cheap and natural music of the cow.

Its vases hold platinum-stemmed roses, not ponds with logs
    from which turtles descend at our approach, neckfold
    leeches shining like black droplets of blood.

It swallows Paris and Athens, tracks its genes to the Armory
    Show.

As it waits by their coffins in the parlor, it applies rouge
    to Poe and Beau Brummell.

Its father is Gertrude Stein, not Whitman, who despises it,
    though it will not admit it.

Old women with children do not live in it.

It does not harvest thought, or associate with farmers.

It does not serve in the army, or follow a story.

It revels in skewed cubes, elliptical appositions.

It is inviolate, buttressed by its own skyhook aesthetics.

Ultramarine critics praise it, wash their hands of subject matter.

It is tar-baby without the baby, without the tar.

Its city is not the city of pavement or taxis, business or bums.

It dwells on absence and illusion, mirrors refulgent flames.

Deer that browse beneath its branches starve.

Its emotions do not arise from sensible objects.

It passes rocks as though they were clouds.

It sustains itself on paperweight petals.

It does not flood out its muskrats.

It does not define, catalog, testify, or witness.

It holds models before the young of a skillful evasion,
   withering heartlessness.

It lifts its own weight for exercise, does not body-block,
   or break up double plays, or countenance scar tissue.

It flails in the foam, but has no body and cannot drown.

In his afterlife, Rimbaud smuggles it along infected rivers.

Memorial Day, Brockport, 1981

We stand under cemetery maples.
The high school band has played Keyes' questioning anthem.
Seven veterans stand at parade rest, the oldest
from WWI, the youngest from Vietnam.

A minister prays aloud for the dead,
for those who survived, for peace for us all.
I close my eyes, inhale scents of flowers on the graves,
drift in remembering shadows through the day. . . .

A wavery trumpet remembers "Taps." The vets fire blanks.
Our small town shivers in the sound.
Then, a minute's silence while an undecided sky
goes on with sun and clouds

as though for this, for something here
impossible to say, as soldiers raise our flag again.
God bless these living soldiers, and the dead. Sometimes,
we needed them. Now, we live with what they've done.

MARK GODFREY. *KHE SANH, VIETNAM* (1971). (*TQ* #59)

The hooded legion

Gerald McCarthy

> *Let us put up a monument to the lie.*
> Joseph Brodksy

There are no words here
to witness why we fought,
who sent us or what we hoped to gain.

There is only the rain
as it streaks the black stone,
these memories of rain
that come back to us—
a hooded legion reflected in a wall.

Tonight we wander weaponless and cold
along this shore of the Potomac
like other soldiers who camped here
looking out over smoldering fires into the night.

What did we dream of
the summer before we went away?
What leaf did not go silver
in the last light?
What hand did not turn us aside?

Snowy egret

Bruce Weigl

My neighbor's boy has lifted his father's shotgun and stolen
Down to the backwaters of the Elizabeth
And in the moon he's blasted a snowy egret
From the shallows it stalked for small fish.

Midnight. My wife wakes me. He's in the backyard
With a shovel so I go down half-drunk with pills
That let me sleep to see what I can see and if it's safe.
The boy doesn't hear me come across the dewy grass.
He says through tears he has to bury it,
He says his father will kill him
And he digs until the hole is deep enough and gathers
The egret carefully into his arms
As if not to harm the blood-splattered wings
Gleaming in the flashlight beam.

His man's muscled shoulders
Shake with the weight of what he can't set right no matter what,
But one last time he tries to stay a child, sobbing
Please don't tell. . . .
He says he only meant to flush it from the shadows,
He only meant to watch it fly
But the shot spread too far
Ripping into the white wings
Spanned awkwardly for a moment
Until it glided into brackish death.

I want to grab his shoulders,
Shake the lies loose from his lips but he hurts enough,
He burns with shame for what he's done,
With fear for his hard father's
Fists I've seen crash down on him for so much less.

1984

I don't know what to do but hold him.
If I let go he'll fly to pieces before me.
What a time we share, that can make a good boy steal away,
Wiping out from the blue face of the pond
What he hadn't even known he loved, blasting
Such beauty into nothing.

Three epigrams

Elder Olson

Returning a knife to a "friend"

Here: this thing belongs to you
—A favorite tool you must not lack—
Sharp, bright, and clean, as good as new,
Quite undamaged by my back.

Revenant

The ghost who came back to terrify
Fled in horror from our world.

Mad girl

Because I shrieked out "Murder! Rape!"
You called my terrors dreams, and you
Locked me in a windowless cell
So that such dreams should not escape
Into a world not half as true,
A thousand times more terrible.

1984

ABOVE AND FACING PAGE: PHOTOGRAPHS BY MARK GODFREY. *CONGRESS, 1974; A POR-TRAIT OF GEORGE WASHINGTON, IN THE HOUSE OF REPRESENTATIVES CHAMBERS AT THE CAPITOL AND CAMPAIGN '76; JIMMY CARTER CAMPAIGNS IN A NEW HAMPSHIRE LIVING ROOM DURING THE PRESIDENTIAL PRIMARY. (TQ #59)*

Interview with Saul Bellow

Rockwell Gray, Harry White and Gerald Nemanic

The text of this interview has been prepared from the transcript of a two-hour conversation taped on March 12, 1983, in Mr. Bellow's office at the University of Chicago. Mr. Bellow subsequently emended the transcript, clarifying his replies and providing further context for them. As much as possible, the conversational quality of the dialogue has been retained.

TQ: What are your reflections on the relationship between physical place and the sense of identity sought by a writer and his characters? Would you say, for example, that a city like Chicago becomes, in fiction, more a central metaphor for self-definition than a merely reportorial or naturalistic backdrop?

BELLOW: I don't really know what to make of Chicago—a mysterious place and also much maligned. When people ask whether I have roots here I say that tangled wires would be more like it than roots. One's attachment to a place is seldom understood. People always want to know for regional-patriotic reasons why I am attached to this heath, which is not my native heath. I arrived here when I was nine years old and have spent most of my life here.

Chicago has earned the right to be considered the center of American materialism—the classical center. It has cultural pretensions, of course, and has had since the great Fair of 1893. These pretensions aren't very significant. They are associated with boosterism. The rich, growing more boorish and ignorant with every decade, put up money for museums, orchestras, opera companies, art associations, arty clubs and so on. *Poetry* magazine has had its headquarters here since the days of Harriet Monroe. Banks and big corporations recognize art as a sort of asset, but Chicago's wealth is not in culture. The universities have absorbed almost everything that resembles cultural life. The newspapers have a thousand times more pork, sex and scandal in their pages than they do painting and literature. The pulse of culture beats thinly in the "media." We have one fat, glossy, squalid magazine—a big money-maker. The universities give sanctuary for delicate people who need it. And the universities also have their sassy con-artists and noisy promoters. I never had much use for sanctuaries. I did need a certain amount of conversation, and that, after diligent search, I could eventually find in the university. And from students I could learn where the U.S.A. was heading. But I couldn't be described as an academic. When I was younger I thought I needed "protection." I was wrong. I wasted much time in looking for the great good place. American artists, for more than a century were determined to find it, traveling to Europe, dreaming of an environment friendly to writers. They were on a wild-goose chase. Certain of them had a good time. In Paris towards the end of the last century, from, say, the Whistler-Henry James period until the middle of the Depression, they were very happy. They had little to do with Paris itself. But for nearly a century France was the center of a powerful international culture. It was hospitable to the Picassos, Modiglianis, Rilkes, Apollinaires, Joyces, Marinettis, Brancusis—a multitude of foreign geniuses. For political reasons Paris, too, began to be corrupted in the thirties. The struggle of the two totalitarianisms, reaching its climax in the Spanish Civil War, infected Paris with a violent and dulling disease. Politics took over. Postwar Paris was dominated by Sartre. Marxist *ratatouille* was served to all visitors. After the Second World War all the action seemed to be on our side of the Atlantic. No getting away from it. Paris was no longer the home (or locus, if "home" is too sentimental a word) of an international culture. You had to reconcile yourself to life in commercial-technological-etc. America. Here you would stay put, and make silk purses out of pigs' ears—or other organs.

TQ: Some of that of course you grasped right away as a boy, I take it.

BELLOW: Yes. It was possible to grasp it, but it isn't easy to understand what your connection to this business society signifies. You can't understand when you're very young—and few understand in middle age—what the situation really is. The underlying fact is that in the modern democracies a contract was offered to the majority. It's plainly spelled out in many documents—in the *Federalist Papers*, for instance. It reads as follows, in my own summary:

"We will provide for your real needs. You will be fed and protected, you will live in peace. As for the life of the imagination, unfortunately we can't do much for you in that respect. Scientific imagination, yes. That must and will thrive, but as for esthetic imagination—forget it." Bear this in mind and you can begin to understand the isolation of the great American writers of the nineteenth century. They were great solitaries.

TQ: The Customs House syndrome.

BELLOW: Yes, the Customs House, or Edgar Allan Poe's desperate queerness and boozing, the self-incarceration of Emily Dickinson. Many young writers of my generation protected themselves as a mass of sensibilities, or tics, tried to make special provision for their special needs, took measures to armor themselves. Meaningless. Foolish. To the romantic French, up to and including Malraux, the artist made war on bourgeois philistinism. "Sensibility" had political implications. This can mean very little to Americans whose French history comes from textbooks. For Americans the question is what

1984   633

can be done by writers, painters, etc., in a country which has so little use for artists. That old devil "environment."

TQ: Achieve through feeding off it sometimes, I would take it, by observing it carefully.

BELLOW: Well, yes. It's important, though, to avoid the cliché of artist vs. bourgeois. It's true that the rich were forever aping the artists, looking for nicer ways to be rich, or more interesting ways to spend money. Today the "life-style" trend has deprived the artist of his influence. He is no longer interestingly imitable, not part of a compact, exclusive clan attractive to people with money. To put the whole matter briefly, it's extremely important not to be drawn into futile struggles with the Situation, not to be in opposition on principle, and not to try to convert hostility into friendliness—not to think that you have to edify the unedified masses or try to prevent them from becoming irretrievably sodden. For that's a mistake, too, one that almost everybody makes. Henry James, when he said that his business as a writer was in part the cure of souls, was making it. The "cure of souls" isn't the writer's business. The writer works, or cultivates, certain permanent human impulses and capacities. I take it for granted that such cultivation is good for the soul. To have a soul, to *be* one—that today is a revolutionary defiance of received opinion. But the cure of souls—writers as priests or would-be priests? No.

TQ: When you talk about the would-be priests, whom are you thinking of, especially?

BELLOW: Most American writers of the nineteenth century were guides, teachers, counselors, spiritual advisors. Emerson and Thoreau preached. Whitman added illustration to preaching. He made it quite explicit that in a democracy it was the business of the poet to create models of manhood and womanhood. He did a wonderful job of it, although his models, when you find them today, are more degenerate than inspiring. Edification was big in England, too—the Carlyles, the Ruskins—Dickens, too, up to a point (of course he was freed from mere teacherism by his genius).

On the other side were the counter-edifiers who proclaimed that the condition was irredeemably decadent: the negative romantics, Baudelaire, Flaubert—Joyce, for that matter. Finally we reach the *Waste Land* outlook—despair over the withering of all the great things and the flourishing of all the trivial things. At this extreme, a higher edification is invoked, or hinted at, or prayed for. Democrats, naturally, were edifiers. The anti-edifiers were, as writers, more powerful. The nihilists expressed what the majority of civilized mankind thought and felt. They were more truly representative than the edifiers, hence their greater power.

TQ: You mean that the doctrines of the edifiers have worn too thin or that the current fix is simply an impossible one to address?

BELLOW: Well, writers don't seem to understand the situation. Not long ago I picked up *Junkie* by William Burroughs. He states in the introduction that his purpose in writing the book is to warn people about narcotics. Well, people won't read him for the moral lesson. They want to know about dope. But one must edify. Even Burroughs accepts that rule.

TQ: You mentioned that the writer is ignored in this country. Does this help the writer insofar as he is thus unencumbered, that he doesn't have to live up to any particular standards?

BELLOW: It helps if he isn't damaged, if his feelings aren't too badly crushed. One needs *some* attention. It's all or nothing in the U.S., and if you don't make the celebrity circuit you are wretchedly ignored.

TQ: The would-be edifiers as well?

BELLOW: Very often. In their own way. It's very hard to escape edifying – a social duty in which everybody has been drilled. The public will say, "What are you doing for us? How do you justify your existence?" As I see it, the writer's obligation, insofar as he has one, is to liberate his imagination, to write as he lives, to live as he writes.

TQ: But the writer is praised or faulted instead for his ability to edify or not to edify. Those become the terms by which he is measured.

BELLOW: Most often. Edification is part of the populist tradition. Read Carl Sandburg's collected poems and what you see as you turn the pages is one instruction after another: this is what a guy ought to be like, this is the attitude he ought to have towards personal freedom, towards children, towards standards of success. The poetry affirms certain principles. Sandburg's celebrated title sums it up: *The People, Yes.*

TQ: I was thinking of those who are in the profession of edifying, the critical establishment or the university professors. They write gobs of material measuring the artist in those terms. They want somebody whom they can submit to their own edification-mills. And they come to evaluate literature in terms of the excitement of the ideas it presents. That's the particular nature of that kind of beast.

BELLOW: The nature of the beast is to turn a cognitive profit on imaginative activities. You read a poem and then you talk about its cognitive equivalents – really a kind of translation. After much travail you obtain an "intellectual" result, and such "intellectual" results enjoy the very greatest prestige. In my student days a professor might claim, "I've examined George Herbert's theology, his political background, the cultural history of his times, and I am therefore able to tell you what his poem means." He would set before you an intellectual shadow, highly pleasing to all parties. We feel very much at home with what one of my profs was fond of calling "the cognitions."

In my day, the ruling cognitions were those of Rousseau or Marx (Lenin), whose books had inspired revolutions. Interpretations of painting and literature followed the same revolutionary path, producing a body of doctrines (Malraux will serve as an example) whose binding power we are only now beginning to feel—when I say "we," I refer to those of us who resist the power of the victorious cognitions. Not all the conquering stereotypes are political. Freud is one of our conquerors. In many branches of thought his authority is supreme. We must reckon also with the "behavioral scientists," the philosophers (existentialists and logical positivists), historians, theologians—bands of academics, critics and pundits, creators of "schools." Taken altogether, the body of "thought" created by these "intellectuals" is a huge affliction. Its effects are deadly. Few are strong enough to ward them off. Writers can't afford to draw their premises from this stock of "ideas"—idées reçues is a more suitable expression. The unhappy fact is, however, that they do—even the best of them draw major premises from the cliché stockpile. "Are you an Antihumanist, Brother? Have you squared yourself with Malraux? With the Structuralists? Are you on truly bad terms with the prevailing ethos?" You couldn't be a real writer if you hadn't estranged yourself from the culture and the society of your time.

Whereas the older generation of academics were sworn edifiers, their younger successors are proud of their "estrangement." They enjoy the esthetic prestige of the "estranged" (the only real) "artist." At the same time, they control the departments (philosophy, English, etc.) in which they have tenured appointments. In the name of "deconstruction," they have taken over not only these departments, but literature itself, operating in the cockpit side by side with Shakespeare, Milton, etc., as copilots. These academics—good God! Suppose that a dwarf sitting in Shakespeare's lap were to imagine that he was piloting the great Shakespearean jet!

TQ: We came quite a way from the original question about the city as metaphor. Is there any interest in picking up that original thread, or not?

BELLOW: Yes, why not? I've spent most of my life in Chicago. A glance from the window in the morning is enough to set off endless trains of associations. The weather alone will do it—sixty years of chill, darkness, rain, ice, smoke, winter blue, summer blue. Structural steel or the brick walls of six-flats send messages to me. Inevitably, you invest your vital substance in familiar surroundings. That's why they are called "familiar." Chicago is one of the larger provinces of my psychic life. I refer, of course, to the old Chicago, which is now in full decay. A new, proud, synthetic Chicago has begun to spread outwards from the Loop.

TQ: You seem to suggest that it's simply an accident that you wound up in Chicago, that although Chicago has certain associations for you there is nothing unique about it. Some kind of vitality . . . ?

BELLOW: I was brought here by my parents at the age of nine. Accident? I am reluctant to speak of "my karma." Yet I do sometimes feel that I was stuck here, assigned to the place, shackled to it by one of those phantom intelligences that Thomas Hardy invokes, his "Spirits Sinister and Ironic." Mine would be a Spirit Comedic. In my late sixties I am able to share the joke with my tutelary Spirit.

TQ: I wonder if, when we see Chicago portrayed in the work of an imaginative writer, we are seeing the "real" Chicago so much as a metaphor of the city. In other words, aren't we sensing Chicago as a kind of concrete manifestation of the emotions of the writer's characters? In the novels of Dreiser, for example, are we being shown what Chicago of 1900 was really like or what Dreiser felt he had to show us?

BELLOW: Dreiser was the star-struck country boy madly excited by the provincial capital. I find it very agreeable, at times truly moving, to read books like *Sister Carrie* or *Dawn*. How deeply the Hoosier kid feels the power of the great city—the purposeful energy of the crowds. Everything fascinates him—factories, horse-cars, hotel lobbies, a machine which makes keys, a hardware warehouse, luxury shops, fast women, plausible salesmen, exponents of social Darwinism and other bookish ninnies, sturdy railroad men. He's drunk with all this, thinks The Windy City the most marvelous thing that ever happened. When I read him I am inclined to think so, too. In his Cowperwood novels the play of power behind the scenes inspires a similar excitement. Who's got the money? Who controls the streetcar lines, the newspapers, the city council? What sort of women do these money titans marry, what sort of mistresses do they keep? Dreiser loves to speak of the animal "effrontery" of his magnates, and to theorize clumsily about their motives, the "chemisms" that drive them. He's crammed himself with T. H. Huxley, Herbert Spencer, Darwin and a heavy diet of "artistry," but he's such a passionate materialist that he carries you with him even while you are dismissing his theories and his clumsy artiness. For he was a big man, and the humanity of his characters was large. Dreiser's old Chicago, the Chicago of 1900, is gone; few traces of it remain. The old materialistic innocence has disappeared—florid bars, good carriage horses, substantial Victorian virtues, substantial carnality; German, Irish, Polish, Italian Chicago bursting with energy—the Protestant businessmen, bankers and empire builders. The crass, dirty, sinful, vulgar, rich town of politicians, merchant princes and land speculators, the Chicago of Yerkes and Samuel Insull, has vanished. Suddenly the "Hog Butcher for the World" was there no longer (I've never been able to decide whether Sandburg's "Chicago" was a poem or an advertising-man's effusion). Vitality—I suppose that means a passionate release of the energies which had been restricted in the old country. Here Europeans—even New Englanders—were able to let themselves go. And now a new population of Third World immigrants has settled in. Also internal immigrants from the South.

TQ: Then you think that the new immigrants coming to the city are having an experience significantly different from the one you had when you came here as an immigrant?

BELLOW: Of course they are. Chicago is a far more dangerous place now.

1984   637

Black politicians and white city-council crooks who have taken over the old Daley Machine have between them divided the city on racial lines. Has the crime rate increased? The police fiddle with the records on orders from our mayors, so it is impossible to obtain reliable figures. Impossible also to get an accurate breakdown of the statistics. Newspapers, when they report abominable crimes, do not refer to the race of the suspects. The public, which understands only too well, is resigned to the imposition of this taboo. Right-thinking liberal citizens, hoping for future improvements, recalling past injustices, counsel themselves to be patient. "Patience" sounds better than "intimidation" or "surrender," and nicer than "cowardice." Perhaps there are not more muggings, knifings, shootings and murders than there used to be, but the crimes seem to be more outlandish—committed in a more demonic spirit. You are robbed, and locked in the trunk of your car; raped, and also forced to go down on the rapist; or sodomized. Consider the hazards new immigrants must now face. Different? Of course Chicago is different! The public schools are now eighty-five or eighty-seven percent Negro and Hispanic. What sort of democratic education do you suppose such schools afford? There's no way to compare the experience of old and new ethnic groups—the Central Americans, Koreans, Pakistanis, Iranians come here seeking employment, peace, stability. A refugee from the terrors of Beirut opens a grocery store in Chicago, thrives, and then is shot in a holdup. Not an uncommon story. The funny misfortunes and torments of *Candide* are the literal facts of modern experience. The older "ethnics," the Poles, Czechs, the Italians, the Irish, the Germans and the Scandinavians, live in heavily-defended districts, clinging to the properties in which their parents and grandparents invested so much labor. They organize neighborhood watch-groups, and they buy arms. But the division into blacks and ethnics is a disaster. A second disaster is the swift rise of the demagogues in both factions. They expose each other's corruption and criminal connections. But the more the public learns, the more its paralysis increases.

TQ: Are you saying that the traditional image of Chicago from the 1920s and 1930s—Chicago as a violent place—is rather superficial?

BELLOW: In the twenties the Capone guys shot up the O'Banion guys. Only one innocent died in the Valentine's Day massacre. You knew when a body was found in a sewer which gang the victim belonged to. The circulation wars sometimes affected the newspaper guy on the corner because he might lose all his teeth if he carried the *Examiner* instead of the *Tribune*. Most ordinary citizens—civilians, if you like—were not greatly affected. By contrast, over a recent Thanksgiving weekend no less than nine murders were reported.

TQ: The picture of Chicago—circa World War I—in the fiction of a writer like Sherwood Anderson emphasizes his sense of shock at the amount of violence and the press hype of this kind of activity in the city. Anderson seemed to think of Chicago as a kind of dreadful sin bin.

BELLOW: Yes, but he was an artistic small-towner. He had left the provinces because his sensibilities required more culture, more ideas, conversation and refinement. In Winesburg he found only psychopathology in Freudian (sexual) forms. Anderson was characteristic of the small-town American with esthetic inclinations, circa 1910. That doesn't mean that he lacked talent, only that he was a provincial, craving big-time esthetic and cultural horizons. That Chicago should seem awful to him is easy to understand.

TQ: He simply couldn't have known enough about the city to be able to apprehend the whole of it?

BELLOW: Right. And he applied to it standards of "refinement" and "art" which today make us a bit uncomfortable.

TQ: To another topic. Your fictional vision of how a genuine man comes to be appears to have much in common with European predecessors like Dostoevsky and Mann. I refer partly to the traditional form of the *Bildungsroman*—the novel of education—as it embodies the process of authentic character formation and partly to the emphasis you all (that is, yourself, Dostoevsky, and Mann) place on family influence, or lack of it, in the formation of character. The question then is: Do you feel that there is an essential difference between the way a contemporary writer needs to approach the problem, "How do I live genuinely?" and the way such earlier writers as Dostoevsky and Mann approached that problem?

BELLOW: First of all, I would make a distinction between Dostoevsky and anybody else because he was the greater writer by far, a man struggling to justify his Christianity against his own skepticism and nihilism. Mann was more ready to play; rather, to make a game of examining the bourgeoisie against a background of nihilism, and to exploit the opportunities for historical painting that this offered. In *Buddenbrooks* the bourgeois order in which the family had been rooted was decaying, falling into pessimism (Schopenhauer) and decadence. My own situation was that of a person who early understood that, like it or not, he was an exotic among other exotics. The children of immigrants inherited no "bourgeois stability." This may be a little difficult to interpret. Stability, if we were to have any, must be found or created. The word for this was "Americanization." The masses that came from Europe in the great wave of immigration between 1870 and 1930 wanted to be as American as possible. I was quick to recognize how hard the immigrants were trying to be something that they were not. They had excellent reasons for making themselves over. The distortions they suffered in Americanizing themselves also charged them with a certain energy. It was this energy that built the great cities. "Traditionalists" disliked—no, despised—this, but what American cities did "tradition" build? When FDR said on the air one night during a Fireside Chat that we are all aliens here, that this was a nation of aliens, he could safely, generously, advantageously, say it because he obviously was not an alien. He was a rich country squire who belonged to a famous family, but he was picking up a lot of votes by speaking plainly about the others. Though everybody wished to be an American, everybody's secret was that he hadn't succeeded in becoming one. My friend Lillian McCall, in her forthcoming memoirs, develops this theme in an original manner. The immigrant might have changed his name and his clothing and denied his native Italian or Russian or Yiddish, but the mark of the alien was upon him – you could see it. I picked *that* up, and that's why I don't know whether a book like *The Adventures of Augie March* is so much a *Bildungsroman* as it is a piece of ethnography. And I understand now why Augie March himself was such an *ingénu*: he didn't want to acknowledge the worst; the fact is, he wanted to enjoy his situation, wanted to play the American naïf. There was a price to pay. He was unwilling to pay it.

TQ: Paying for it would have meant recognizing the unfinished quality of his world?

BELLOW: Yes, and its wickedness, rawness and vulgarity. He wanted to relish it, I think. He was that kind of *ingénu*. He didn't want to be bitter about it. Sad, yes. I think he expressed what was probably very genuine just then for adolescent Americans of immigrant background: the desire to embrace everybody, the desire for fraternity, the wish to be the lover of experience for its own sake, the lover of novelty. At any rate, he did not intend to be disappointed. He was very much like the young man Dreiser described – the one who had just arrived in Chicago, the young Theodore of *Dawn*.

TQ: Does Augie March's desire for fraternity differ very much from that which Dostoevsky describes in *The Brothers Karamazov*?

BELLOW: Yes, because Dostoevsky's fraternity has to overcome, first of all, a heavy dose of neurosis, and secondly, a kind of deadly accurate sadistic insight into the motives of people. *The Brothers Karamazov* is not brimming with lovable human beings. Here and there, yes – a child, or an Alyosha, or a Zossima. Can Americans swallow Father Zossima?

TQ: I was thinking about how somebody like Augie relates to his brother Simon. It's a very difficult relationship for him, and then when Simon reveals, at one point, his terrible hatred of the parents: "Well, Augie, you know who our father was, don't you? He abandoned us; he wasn't even here. And you know what our mother was like, don't you? A simpleton. The two of them craved sex, and that's how we came to be." That's something difficult for Augie to overcome, it would seem to me. Augie sees the power of his brother and somewhat understands the wild suffering Simon is undergoing. Simon's suffering, and who knows? The absent father's suffering, the mother's . . .

BELLOW: Well, I think that Augie's attitude is: "Nevertheless, I am personally free. No matter how I happened to get here." There is a kind of light-hearted equality about the book which is – well, inaccurate. It's not really the way it was; it's just the way Augie wanted it to be.

TQ: But accurate in terms of the dreams that young people had at that time?

BELLOW: Right. And I think *Augie March* also reflected the spirit of Chicago during the Depression – a feeling remarkably widespread and now gone, leaving hardly a trace. What everyone felt then was that a terrible thing had happened – something like an earthquake, a natural disaster. Everybody had been stricken by it. You were called upon to pitch in and help. Then Happy Days would presently be Here Again. Never mind the disgrace; never mind that educated people were digging in the city dump, that M.D.'s and engineers had become scavengers or worked on the roads for the PWA or the WPA. Everything was going to turn right-side-up.

TQ: Are you referring now especially to the immigrant neighborhoods rather than those of the middle class?

BELLOW: Many middle-class Americans felt that the Depression was a hideous disgrace, that they had fallen to the level of the immigrants. Were now indistinguishable from greenhorns.

TQ: It was the middle-class Americans who felt they had suffered dramatic reversals, who, as a consequence, sometimes took drastic actions like stepping out of high windows.

BELLOW: That wasn't so common, really. I think the country then was at its best and was unified by a spirit which disappeared with World War II, when the country had a visible enemy to fight and hate. Pearl Harbor was a terrible shock. We heard songs about going out to slap "the dirty little Jap." Vile songs. Rationing made people very angry, and the black marketing made them angry. There were currents of racism which hadn't been felt before. There certainly was a surge of Jew-hatred during the first days of the war. And the internment of the Japanese. And so on. A great deal of ill nature, just then. You heard people complaining: "We can't get tires for our cars, or meat, or Lucky Strikes." All these articles were easy enough to find on the black market.

TQ: Why would the war necessarily have brought on anti-Semitism and other forms of racism?

BELLOW: While most people approved of the War in the Pacific there were those who didn't like the War in Europe. Many did not. They said, "Why should we go to war with Hitler? Let the Germans fight the Bolsheviks. It's the Jews who want us to fight Hitler."

TQ: You think the change was permanent after the war?

BELLOW: No, it wasn't permanent. When the war ended, the boys were brought home. And then the country soared into a state of pig-heaven prosperity. Everybody had two cars, unskilled workers could afford campers, speed boats, Florida condominiums, trips to Hawaii.

TQ: Americans were going to hell in a hand-basket.

BELLOW: Very quickly.

TQ: Wasn't that basking in prosperity an antidote to the anxiety previously brought on by the Depression and the war?

BELLOW: America found itself a superpower, at the heart of world politics. Americans were understandably uneasy. They turned to money and property with a heightened intensity. Wealth in the twenties had been snobbish (Fitzgerald); in the fifties it was democratized, more widely shared, more infected with anxious disorders, more consciously or ideologically hedonistic, sexually more open and also more troubled.

TQ: Getting back to literature a bit. In your concern with the comic mode in fiction, you've been interested over the years in the role of the fool or the *schlemiel*, if the two can actually be linked. Could you comment a little for us on the continuing vitality of this figure for the fiction writer now?

BELLOW: Well, I don't really know much about that.

TQ: I guess we could say about fools in general. I'm sure you know a lot about that [laughter]. No names please, but presumably real fools are the models or inspiration for literary fools.

BELLOW: Well, I think that something else is going on, and it has to do with increasing literacy and the forced growth of a mental life, of cleverness. On a large scale, in modern societies, you also have a sense of reduced personal scope. Dostoevsky, in *Notes from Underground*, anticipated this in the last century. His Underground Man, a creature of resentful, impotent intelligence, is aware that the world is darkened by a metaphysical shadow, and that one can no longer easily and clearly distinguish good from evil. Existence is a minefield. Civilized consciousness is anarchic. *Schlemiels*, when their hats blow off, chase them across minefields. Your typical *schlemiel* will seldom theorize.

TQ: I was thinking, too, of some of the positive connotations that could be given to the term, in the sense of one who somehow becomes a survivor, who is bumbling almost, but he realizes that he can't cope with it, and in some way rolls with it or bounces with it—that this is one dimension of the fool.

BELLOW: Your modern "Fool" has a sharply comic sense of himself. He is not a bumbler, simply. The bumbler has no pattern, no structure. Your Fool—not your *Schlemiel*—holds well-defined ideas.

TQ: Some wit?

BELLOW: Some wit. He is an astute observer. He is a Cassius who will never stab his Caesar. I think of somebody like Herzog. People were frightened by *Herzog* because they thought it was a serious book. It was a funny book—

642   1984

TQ: [Laughter.]

BELLOW: Well, it's true—

TQ: No, no, of course. I wouldn't argue.

BELLOW: It intimidated readers because it was so full of "ideas." It was really, I think, in the twentieth century, the first portrayal (naturally comic) of the American intellectual trying to come to grips with life. My *intellectual* has been educated out of his senses. He has received an utterly useless education and breaks down as soon as he faces a real crisis. Simply doesn't know what to do. He starts to drag books from the shelves to see what Aristotle advises, or what Spinoza has to say. It's a joke. To his credit, he quickly understands this. His blindness ends when he begins to write letters. By means of these letters the futility of his education is exposed. On Job's dunghill, and scraping himself with a potsherd, he recognizes (with joy!) how bad an education he has had. And this was what I was after in my book. I was investigating the so-called culture of a new powerful class—the professors. Professors did all right for themselves, but humanly they were as dumb as they come. Their ignorance doomed them to a kind of hysteria at the first touch of pain and suffering. Herzog didn't really know what to do when his wife took a lover and pushed him out of the house. He therefore played the fool. He played out all the fine roles that his education had acquainted him with—intellectual, lover, abused husband, longing father, pitiable brother, armed avenger—all of that. And finally he found himself at square one again. What is square one? Square one is the square in which you resume your first self, with its innate qualities. You recover (or almost recover) your original sense of life and your original powers of judgment return. Lucky to have a second opportunity. Herzog is thus a negative *Bildungsroman*. It goes in reverse.

TQ: That somehow must relate to the idea of the axial lines in *Augie March*, those pages late in the book having to do with rediscovering your true self again and again in your life, if you stay quiet enough.

BELLOW: When the noise dies down you'll find yourself with the "I" you first knew when you came to know that you were a self—an event which occurs quite early in life. And that first self is embraced with a kind of fervor, excitement, love—and knowledge! Your formal schooling is really a denaturing of that first self.

TQ: You know that wonderful quote out of Thoreau's *Journals* where he poses the question, "What does education often do?" And he answers it by saying, "It makes a straight-cut ditch of a free, meandering brook."

BELLOW: I think we would have to agree with him. In a recent article my colleague Allan Bloom has written that a modern education removes the created soul and implants an artificial one.

TQ: As you were talking I thought of Ivan Karamazov, who confesses to Alyosha before launching into his great world-denouncing diatribe, "But I love the sticky green leaves that come in the spring," as if that elemental feeling is enough, almost to say, "Well, I know this is all rubbish, but as an intellectual I feel bound to the rubbish."

BELLOW: Yes, the sticky leaves—the melancholy love that your intellectual, ruled by a critical intelligence, cannot enjoy—but cannot quite forget. Ivan is a romantic intellectual. It is his fate to suffer from the development of a "higher consciousness" which separates him from the common life and leads him into hubris and madness, etc. Higher consciousness, Western-style, deprives him of his true—his Russian—identity. You cannot expect a Jewish reader, however sympathetic, to grow enthusiastic over Slavic nationalism and the anti-Semitism that goes with it. Let's descend from the heights a bit. My own temperamental preference is for comedy. To return to my book, I discovered as I was finishing it that Herzog had played out all the roles he had learnt in order to demonstrate their bankruptcy.

TQ: In what way bankrupt?

BELLOW: Bankrupt because inapplicable. Bankrupt because we revere "thinking," but know so little about real thought. I was reading the other day Lord Moran's reminiscences of Winston Churchill, and Moran records a conversation with a professional soldier, a brave man who led a guerilla group in Burma. This man tells Moran, "People like me should be teaching in the universities. I can remember my own university education, and there was nobody to teach me anything real because everybody there was trained in books and was the product of a long course of professional instruction and didn't really know anything about what matters." The brave solider was quite right. I can remember two sociology courses in "Marriage and the Family" taught by Professor Ernest Burgess, a dear, mild, touchingly gentle bachelor. What had he to tell us about women or sexual love? We should have been instructed by someone burnt in love's fires, by a Laclos, a Casanova, a Stendhal. What had poor Burgess to tell us? From his classes we were sent directly into the lines. No, to the shooting gallery. Of the real things we learned nothing, nothing that mattered.

I realize now that I loved some of my teachers—loved them for their innocence, mainly, or for their eccentricities. For they hadn't much to tell us. Thank God for the formative affections they elicited! And I am grateful also to certain academics whose classrooms anticipated the Theater of the Absurd. Mortimer Adler had much to tell us about Aristotle's *Ethics*, but I had only to look at him, even as an undergraduate, to see that he had nothing useful to offer on the conduct of life. He lectured on Prudence, or Magnanimity. It was—well, tomfoolery. True, we did read Aristotle. And Mortimer Adler gave good value in his way. But we should have had Jimmy Hoffa as well. He was often at the Shoreland, within walking distance of the campus. Such, at any rate, was the liberal education we received. I wonder whether the professional schools were any better. Were there courses in the

Law School on the venality of judges? Was there a bagman seminar? It was only after you had been admitted to the bar and went downtown to practice that you learned the facts of life.

TQ: You made the statement that Herzog is a reverse *Bildungsroman*. . .

BELLOW: As a matter of fact, before this interview I never thought of *Herzog* as a non-*Bildungsroman*. I see it now, thanks to you.

TQ: But doesn't he know at the end a great deal more than he knew at the beginning? You say he does go back in a sense to first things, but yet he goes back to those first things with the memory of what's gone in between.

BELLOW: Well, he's learned from his false education that he didn't have an education. Maybe this is the moment at which education begins. As in *The Way of All Flesh*.

TQ: I was wondering if you chose the name Herzog because it suggests a kind of natural monarchy. You do talk of the "marvelous Herzog," a person trying to get back to a sense of being marvelous.

BELLOW: Well there were lots of tough kids in Chicago called "Duke" [laughter]. And even their dogs were called "Duke."

TQ: I was thinking also about the root etymology of the word, *Herz*, and was wondering if Herzog also went back to that person who had pledged his heart in a sense.

BELLOW: It may have had something to do with that.

TQ: You've talked repeatedly about the need to affirm and have suggested that the very act of writing is in itself affirmative—

BELLOW: I don't know about affirmation, but if a man writes an excellent sentence, he has performed a valuable action, one which teaches you something. Even if the sentence has no direct moral application, he's done something of value. That in itself is a good thing. It increases love in some ways. It certainly increases the love of literature for anyone who has the heart to feel it. But it's not a question of resolute edification or affirmation.

TQ: But in specific terms of the novel, or any work of fiction or poetry, how can this affirmation be given without seeming, as it were, out of touch with the times or that one is edifying or prettifying?

BELLOW: One has no business to be out of touch with the times. What I dislike about Augie March is that he was too often out of touch, that he selected those things that might be enjoyed, and dropped the others. He was a kind of ethical hedonist, accepting the pleasures of an ethical life, but without looking too closely at the facts.

TQ: So this complicates talking about affirmation a great deal, doesn't it? You look back on that and say it was a certain kind of error, I mean insofar as you still would hold to that feeling about what it is that moves you or moves others when they read your work. It gets pretty tricky, doesn't it, to trace how affirmation could come about?

BELLOW: Yes, it gets tricky. I can remember when I wrote that book in Paris in '48 and '49, being perfectly aware that the Nazis had just left. And I knew that when I took a deep breath I was inhaling the crematorium gases still circulating in the air, and that was more immediate than my recollections of Chicago in the thirties. In Paris I enjoyed a nostalgic Chicago holiday. I didn't at all know how to cope with the more demanding modern theme. I was too American to do it. *Augie March* may be an interesting book, but it's not a true book, not fully true. I had read my Céline, and I knew what the modern theme was. But it wasn't the kind of thing that would have come naturally to a kid who had grown up in Chicago in the twenties and thirties.

TQ: When is that attitude adopted, or should I say, when does the confrontation with these modern pains begin in your works?

BELLOW: It begins to begin with what I wrote immediately after *Augie March*, a novella called *Seize the Day*. In that short book I examined a man who *insisted* on having a father, who demanded that his father *be* a father to him. But Wilhelm's father had no use for the failed "father" ideology embraced by his son—the seedy *ingénu* son.

TQ: All the larkish aspects of *Augie* have collapsed in the novel.

BELLOW: Right. The only "fun" in the book is to be found in the exploitations of Wilhelm the dupe by Dr. Tamkin, a clumsy charlatan.

TQ: Those feelings of wanting to get along and not being able to—do you associate those feelings with your being in Paris after the occupation and the death camps? That one couldn't get along in the world after this?

BELLOW: I needed to work this matter out within an American frame of reference. I was not going to embrace European nihilism because, after all, I was in no position to do it. The only language that I use is the language of Americans, of people whose premises are very different from those of Europeans—the promises of a democratic, if not anarchic, crowd. Theirs was the mild populist anarchism of wise guys, boxing fans, bleacher-bums, gladhanders, go-getters. Decent enough Americans (as portrayed by themselves). The "decent American" is at the heart of Wilhelm's vision of the human average. Tamkin the "realist" says to him, "You don't know how crazy people are, how twisted." Wilhelm protests, "No, no, there are wonderful people of all kinds." And when Tamkin asks where they are to be found, Wilhelm says,

"Well, they're out there, in the country." I guess you have to go further west. [Laughter.] But Wilhelm has no evidence for his claim. And there I move into deeper gloom. But an American writer of the fifties could not assume the attitudes of a European. These would have been entirely artificial.

TQ: It seems to me that you wanted to repudiate the other stuff as you felt it being exported from France.

BELLOW: Damn influential stuff, nevertheless. And as a Jew who knew what the Final Solution was I might have done otherwise. A kind of blindness to the greatest of evils is an important by-product or result of Americanization. As a nation we prefer the milder, the vaguer, view. Dreiser was a fiercer analyst than most. He knew that your enemies would cut your throat—wouldn't flinch from applying the knife, even plucking a few hairs from your neck first to test the sharpness of the blade.

TQ: A kosher slit, testing the blade like the rabbis.

BELLOW: But that was a Darwinist conception applied to capitalism. Anyway, Augie avoided all this. And Wilhelm, the bon enfant making his last hopeless stand, cheated by Tamkin, rejected by his father, enters a funeral parlor to have a good cry over the death of his cherished ideals. You can get took. You can die of it, lie in a coffin. So much for Tommy Wilhelm, who trustingly (or lazily) surrendered his soul to the milder, vaguer view.

TQ: And is Herzog avoiding this with his imported, fashionable despair?

BELLOW: Herzog is fortunate enough to recover the power to judge for himself. His despair is neither imported nor fashionable, but quite genuine. He is an intelligent man and his comic gifts are anything but superficial.

TQ: In terms of the kind of confrontation you're speaking of, Sammler seems to be the first major figure to have actually suffered through the war. Does he represent a further step in that direction?

BELLOW: In Sammler [Mr. Sammler's Planet], I was trying to write about the United States from a European perspective. My parents, my brothers, my sister were European-born. I was the first of the American Bellows— Canadian by birth, but an American nevertheless. And the family left— fled—St. Petersburg in 1913. I grew up among European uncles and cousins and neighbors. And after the war—in Paris, London, Warsaw and Rome—I met survivors of the older generation who were very like Artur Sammler.

TQ: And yet Sammler doesn't appear to be as despairing a soul as Herzog would like to be. Sammler is still interested in a utopian like H. G. Wells.

BELLOW: You are being hard on poor Herzog. Herzog's pains are quite real. I have often wondered why readers were put off by him. He was an intellectual and people felt that their education was being tested by him;

perhaps they were grinding their teeth as they read, like students sitting for a comprehensive examination, tense and therefore also humorless, resentful. Herzog's high earnestness was intended to be part of the fun. But let us leave that. You ask about Sammler and H. G. Wells. Wells' utopianism went sour towards the end of his life. His last book, Mind at the End of its Tether, is relentlessly pessimistic. His final judgment on civilization is that men destroy one another like rats in a sack. Sammler had read this book.

TQ: A few moments ago you talked, with reference to Seize the Day, about going deeper into the gloom. Relating that back to the Paris Review interview in which you spoke about earlier modern literature as having an elegiac bent (though somehow this going into the gloom was not intended to or does not end up repeating that mode), I wonder, however, whether you feel some of that earlier mode is renewed and updated in your later writing?

BELLOW: Ah, T. S. Eliot, I presume.

TQ: Yes, you mentioned The Waste Land.

BELLOW: But that was not for me. You see, I've always been devotedly faithful to my own history, and I've never struck attitudes that didn't suit it. I am not a WASP trained on the classics, the stray descendant of a golden age of gentlemen lost in the modern abysses, and all the rest of that. That's not me. I am not about to take that viewpoint. My Jewish history gives me an entirely different orientation. The heavens in all their glory can open up above the ghetto sidewalk, and one doesn't need Gothic or Renaissance churches, Harvard University, or any of these places, in order to condemn the nihilism of the modern age from a viewpoint sufficiently elevated. That's what I disliked about The Waste Land. It was the elevation, the nostalgia for things that probably never were, the longing for distinctions that ruled out those who would never be eligible for them. And I knew about those pre- scriptions for eligibility. I had read my Henry Adams, my Spengler, and T. S. Eliot's The Idea of a Christian Society; and I knew there would be no place for me as a Jew in that kind of civilization. Therefore all the greater was my enthusiasm for embracing this American democracy with all its crudities, which nevertheless granted me an equality which I felt was mine by right. I wasn't going to be ruled off the grounds by those WASP hotshots; and so I rejected all of that. On the contrary, I saw "traditionalism" as a further descent into the nihilistic pit. "Traditionalists" had gone deeper into the night, with their fascism and anti-Semitism.

A writer has no choice but to be faithful to his own history. I was not born into the American Protestant Majority. But I was never at all persuaded to view that majority as an exclusive club. I assume American democracy to be a cosmopolitan phenomenon. I see it as liberation, not as decline and fall. What has my Jewish history to do with Eliot's "classicism," "royalism," or with "tradition" as the term is defined by those who feel that they have suffered a great fall? My generation of students was bowled over by The Waste Land and I went down together with the rest, but I was on my feet again quite soon. I thought it an excessively "educated" poem. Joyce's *Ulysses* has been called a "summa of its age." Behind *The Waste Land* there is a summa, too. Despite my great admiration of Eliot, and even more of Joyce, I have never been able to agree with the comprehensive schemes on which they base themselves. Dedalus as a philosopher is not convincing with his "diaphane" and "adiaphane" and the "ineluctable modality." And behind Eliot I always glimpse Frazier's *Golden Bough*, and other collections of what we have now come to know as Comparative Religion. Perhaps because I am an amateur myself, I am quite good at seeing through other amateurs of myth. I could never for a moment take Freud's Egyptology seriously. I read his *Moses* as a novel and was sorry he had burdened his story with scientific baggage. Eliot protested that he was a "classicist." To me, however, *The Waste Land* was a work of romantic *sehnsucht*. Joyce, to his great credit, worked painfully and honestly through the modern age, while Eliot was horrified at the pollution of Spenser's "sweet Thames." Perhaps the most gifted of our Environmentalists. Here again was the romantic "far away and long ago." To turn this against the modern age did not make him a classicist. The modern age is our given, our crushing *donnée*. No, Eliot is not for me. I much prefer Nietzsche. Much more strengthening to the soul—the soul of a Jew, I should add.

TQ: Perhaps related to the question of gloom, there is a sense, ever stronger since *Mr. Sammler's Planet*, of leave-taking from this world, which seems to be exhibited as ever more forbidding and hostile. There's not the sense of embracing life that one gets in *Augie March*, not even the quiet achieved at the end of *Herzog*. The concerns seem more otherworldly.

BELLOW: No great mystery here. With everything I write I draw a little closer to whatever it was that made me wish to be a writer. Recently I was surprised, in reading Philip Roth's latest Zuckerman novel, at the horrors he experiences in writing. Why, with his great gifts, has Roth nothing but difficulties to report? Can it be because he believes with Freud that we write in order to get money and women? In America any clever man can make money. As far as *getting* women!—well, Freud had no way to anticipate how much the sexual revolution would simplify that. But isn't writing a spiritual activity? I seem always to have assumed that it was.

TQ: I must admit to having been stumped as to what to make of all these excursions into theosophy and Rudolf Steiner by Citrine in *Humboldt's Gift*.

BELLOW: *Humboldt's Gift*, a comic novel whose true theme is death, seems to have thrown a good many readers. Theosophy, by the way, is what Mme. Blavatsky and Annie Beasant did. Steiner called himself an anthroposophist. And you may be interested to learn that the anthroposophists, with few exceptions, disapproved of the irreverence of *Humboldt's Gift*. But no disrespect was intended. Steiner was a very great man indeed. Whether he was an Initiate I am not qualified to say. Hostile critics who attacked *Humboldt* were not qualified to say, either. They had not found it necessary to read Steiner to try to learn why he had made so great an impression on Charlie Citrine. They might have discovered that he was a great visionary—they might even have been moved by his books. This, however, is not the proper place for a defense of Steiner. I can only try to explain what it was that drew Charlie Citrine to him. It was, in a word, the recognition that everything which Charlie had taken to be commonsensical, realistic, prudent, normal—his ambitions, marriage, love affairs, possessions, business relations—was a mass of idiocies. "A serious human life? This! You've got to be kidding!" And from demonic absorption in the things of this world, he turns to an invisible world in which he thinks his Being may be founded. Is there, in fact, any basis for religion other than the persistence of the supersensible? "Science" with the aid of modern philosophy—what we call the positive outlook—has driven "the invisible" into the dark night where enlightenment says it belongs. Together with it, in our simplemindedness, we drive away revelation as well, and with revelation we drive out art, also we drive out also dreaming. Dreams are readmitted only through the Ellis Island of science, by officials qualified in the legitimate interpretation of dreams. Music we bootleg. We bring it across the threshold surreptitiously.

The moral law also has a precarious existence among us. Now, what is to prevent a writer from imagining that we exist without revelation, without music and poetry, without the moral law, without the Gods, *only* in our present depleted and restricted quotidian consciousness, and that in fact life-giving forces sustain us from beyond, and also from within—in sleep, in dream, through imagination, by means of intuition? That the true Unconscious is a much bigger thing than the dark, libidinal province established by Freud, which we enter with the passport of "science." Charlie Citrine does not accept being intimidated by the representatives of "scientific" respectability. I'm a bit that way myself. I can't remember going out of my way to be heterodox. But I was born into an orthodox family, and detested orthodoxy from the first.

ON FACING PAGE: STEPHEN DEUTCH. *WABASH AVENUE AT RANDOLPH STREET, CHICAGO.* (*TQ* #60)

1984

Fulfilling the Promise

Lisel Mueller

1

A man I know named Booker
runs a second-hand bookstore.
My florist's name is Fiore.
Formica designs kitchens
in California, and Richard Hazard
sells real estate and insurance.
We can change our names
or grow into them.

2

Except the unlucky ones.
Even their murderers knew
the children of the Czar
were innocent. But they could not kill
the name Romanoff
without killing its bearers.

3

Today, in the hospital nursery,
I visit Grace, asleep
under a pink blanket,
her hands still curled into shells.
She lies between Tiffany
and Marvella, who soon must wear
the heavy crowns of their names.
Her mother named her Grace
in spite of her red skin
and her head like an egg. She likes
the old-fashioned sound. "Give her time
to fulfill the promise," she says.

4

At her wedding, a woman gave up
half of her name
and exchanged it for another.
Half of her is public,
subject to trade; the other
private, treasure and loneliness,
what he thinks of as *her*,
what she would share, if she could.

5

And the man who testified
for the State, who named the mobster,
how does he manage the old self
behind the new glasses
and the removable beard?
Under the memorized name
on the false documents
the container and spinner of memory
endures uninterrupted.
At night, with the lights out
and the TV turned up,
a woman whispers his secret name:
it frightens and excites him,
like the hundredth name of God.

1984

The Aragon Ballroom

John Dickson

I could hear the music as I waited to be born—
Wayne King the Waltz King and his golden sax
rolling across the roofs and through the alleys
and into our windows down the street
making my feet move, making me wonder
what sort of planet I'd come to, anyway.
And later as I crawled through Persian patterns of the rugs
and later still as I memorized my night paths
behind the stores and through the shadowy streets,
clarinets and trumpets heralded my way.

But in less time than you'd think I learned that place—
by day how it slept through roars of the passing 'L's,
through sooty pigeons cooing at its windows.
And by night how it turned to plaster Spain inside—
gold statues of caballeros and their señoritas
and the thick red carpet stretching from the ticket taker
into the illusion paradise of yellow balconies
with vines and bright balloons and tiled roofs
that scraped the Spanish sky of faint electric stars.

And all the Lorettas and Teresas, Margies and Maries—
half floozie, half madonna in their first high heels,
the smell of soap, the smell of sharp cologne,
drawn there on those nights to come alive
with some Sam or Tony, Mario or Fred,
lanky, muscle-bound, or Mr. Five-by-Five,
but necessarily capable of serious dancing—
either to the organ shuddering through the building
or to a wispy saxophone, snare drum and brushes
for drifting and weaving around the crowded floor.

And off in the haze beyond the dancers
or up in the shadows of the balcony
the crew cuts and greasers busy as scheming roosters,
surveying the crop, considering anything fair game —
girls who lived for their mothers
or those with whom no one would dance,
girls still homesick for small-town families
or those who could barely look up from their shyness
lost in their loneliness of makeup and corsage,
blaming themselves for even being there.

And always on the fire escape of summer nights
the bright dress and dark suit of quiet intermission.
And always at the tables of the soft-drink stand
those long conversations of serious intent.
And always the ultimate weddings of relatives and wine
held in the Halls For All Occasions,
always the painted wedding photographs
of responsible grooms and basic brides —
eyes blue, lips red, and cheeks unnatural pink.

But now only the whisper of those lives
rushes through the empty building
with echoes of "Old Black Magic" and "Small Hotel,"
"Take the A-Train," "Adios," and "Blue Room."
And all those nights, as though embedded in amber,
kept safe or worn as charms
through hospitals or wars or drudgery
as a reminder of those nights in Spain
or just of partners who could really dance.

NATHANIEL C. BURKINS. *MICHIGAN AVENUE, CHICAGO, 1980. (TQ #60)*

The City

Lorraine Hansberry

From *All the Dark and Beautiful Warriors*

The Christmas season stormed snowily into Chicago a few weeks later and Son found himself hopping about the garage almost always at double speed; the rush hour had become rush hours. All day long people poured into the Loop garage and rushed off and returned with great bulging armloads of packages that they had to be helped with so that his tips soared.

For the first time he found himself with a little extra money after he paid his bills. He bought himself a bright plaid heavy mackinaw and a cap that let down over both ears and some high thick rubber boots. Even so outfitted he was astonished to feel, when he strolled down Michigan Avenue looking in airline offices and luggage-shop windows, the incredible wrath of the winds which came in over Lake Michigan. He did not ever remember being so cold in his life. There was something special about this wind: it did not seem to exhaust itself and die down like other winds he had known, it was like a constant sheet of ice against his legs. And yet, he liked it. There was some-how a freedom in it—a bite that made him feel exhilarated, oddly clean and curiously strong.

He took, therefore, to wandering about the Loop a great deal on his off-hours, drawing from time to time into the great department stores to relieve himself of the cold and to see the wonders that they held. No one paid him much attention, except once when, riding the escalators and eating a hot dog, he wandered into one of the more heavily carpeted salons on the upper floors, where women, with blue-gray hair and dark furs slung back over their chairs, arched their backs and turned amazed eyes on him. He did not return to that floor.

But he enjoyed the city, all of it. Sometimes he crossed the ramparts that led out to a curving drive which edged the great and furious winter lake; he would stand there scanning its immensity, wondering what oceans there might really be in the world more vast. Then he would turn inland suddenly, in a way he had learned to do, and surprise his eyes with the great skyline, cut out and pasted against some mood of the sun; it always gave him a thrill and he went often to the water's edge.

Still, for all of its wonders, faithful to a tradition, the season brought its own sudden, smarting, special loneliness.

When it was worst, the loneliness, he directed his wandering to the South Side. He had never seen that many black people all at one time in his life and the city within a city intrigued him. He took bus rides to its far south corners where the rich Negroes lived, to watch them getting in and out of their cars, to see their houses, their careful lawns, their brushed and shiny children. He learned that they were not friendly as were the people in the neighborhood where his room was; here people hardly broke their step if one engaged them in the streets and seemed suspicious of a stranger's smile.

One Sunday he found a pretty church tucked into a quiet street in Woodlawn; the pastor stood at the door greeting the congregation, a heavy-set man in black robes with red piping on them, who smiled at Son. The boy took off his cap and passed into church with the others. He had liked the sermon very much: it had been a lecture on the meaning of the spirituals and very interesting, the minister being learned and generous in his humor. But people had stared at his mackinaw and his boots and the singing was done mainly by a choir that sang music by men with strange names and even the spirituals in a strange way; he liked better the churches he had found in the bowels of the ghetto, huge and packed and Baptist, where people shouted just as they did down home and patted their feet and clapped their hands when the music got to them. He went to these churches often; sometimes the singing there and the good food at the Wednesday-night suppers that the sisters set out made such an assault on his loneliness that for a few hours he was warm inside and possessed of joy.

Best of all, he found Forty-seventh Street. All manner of life surged there, business people and secretaries and nurses and merchants and housewife shoppers—not rushing about the way people did downtown but, it seemed to him, more at home, taking their time—and here and there, sprinkled among them, sober-faced salesmen jumping in and out of their cars at lunchtime, going off to find someplace to eat outside the ghetto. On Halloween, he was told, the entire South Side gathered on this street to promenade in costume or merely watch, because on that night the ghetto unleashed its imagination and that was a furious and hilarious thing.

And it was here, too, on Forty-seventh Street, that he found the South Center—a department store staffed entirely by Negroes—and he saw the people who came by the thousands to wander at Christmastime, in the toy department especially: big strong-looking men with tired eyes, in clothes much like his own, and weary brown women in worn cloth coats swatting at the little ones pulling at their skirts to demand one of almost everything if only Santa could be so informed. Son studied them: all with determined lips in this season of hope, making the rounds of the toy displays to touch, to feel and smile and shake their heads and move away and be drawn back again, figuring this much for the middle children and so much for the oldest boy and so much for the baby: weighing, arguing, risking in each purchase the promise of at least *one* magic morning of beauty to widen the eyes of the young.

One especially cold Thursday evening, two days before the Holiday, he found himself at Forty-seventh and Cottage Grove Avenue, peering out at the crowds from a blurry, dirty streetcar window. At the far corner he saw an old man wheeling a little cart through the snow and his heart leaped. The shakily-lettered sign read: "HOT SKINS – 10¢." He jumped off the car at the next stop and ran back down the street to the cart.

"Where you from, boy?" the old man asked, shaking hot red sauce on the bacon rinds.

"Tennessee."

"That so? Ain't too many Tennessee or Kentucky folks in Chicago. Practically everybody you meets here is from Mississippi. And if they ain't they mamas and papas is. This here town ain't nothing but Mississippi done come North." He gave Son his skins and collected his coins.

With the first taste of the hot rinds on his tongue, a measure of contentment flooded Denmark Williams: the meat and the sauce tasted of home, of his father's curing shed.

"Very few owns up to it though," the old man was saying. "Tell you in a minit: 'I was born in Cleveland or Harlem!'" he mimicked wildly and slapped his thigh thinking of how hilarious it was the way Southern Negroes lied about where they were from. Son laughed too, and went on eating and enjoying his skins and listening to the old man.

"Me," the vendor said, "I'm from North C'lina. My granddaddy was jet black and had hisself sixty slaves and that's a fact, yessuh! In North C'lina!"

"Sure enough," Son said easily, falling instinctively into the polite acceptance he knew was to be assumed with old people. It seemed to him that he had already met a lot of old men like this one, old men full of fancy and true memory all mixed up in their heads. He had known men like that down home; he had met them among the pickers and, of course, there was Irving Brown at the garage. He smiled at the vendor and said sure enough again and went on eating and nodding his head up and down at the things the old man told him.

"Yes, Lawd!" the vendor said, "We still got the old house down there now. I be goin' back directly. My mama, she down there. Waitin' for me."

Denmark saw that the man was no longer talking to him at all, only to himself. An alien emotion seized Son and the food went dead in his mouth as he watched the old man standing in the snow speaking of North Carolina in his shapeless ragged sweater and sagging worn trousers, with a peppery pad of beautiful white hair showing from under his hat. Son stared at him, amazed at the strange new feeling which gripped him; it was a curious mixture of rage and association. He had never heard the word "compassion" in his life and he only felt fear at its first thrust and he turned on his heel and walked swiftly away from the vendor, who went on talking to himself in the falling snow.

Hours later, wandering on Thirty-fifth, he went into a bar, where he met a fat and pretty young woman named Lottie, who took him where she lived when he had almost passed out from the drinking and put him to bed. The next day she fed him and bathed him and sent him off to work. That night he brought ribs and beer and two hot sweet-potato pies to her place and they ate them and listened to good music from a South Side disc-jockey program and made love and slept well.

The second morning that he awakened in Lottie's room, he lay for a long while and stared at the water-marked ceiling and listened to the sounds of Thirty-fourth Street coming in through the walls. Then, finally, he rose and dressed, thinking of the woman. Folks spoke little of this part in the world, they talked mainly of the other, the bitter, the cruel things. He had found those parts aplenty, but of this, these pauses in the hurting parts — why did folks speak so seldom of that? For several weeks he had almost strangled on his loneliness and then, in a bar, there was Lottie who, for two days, had shared with him. A strangling feeling of affection rose in his throat and he did not look at the woman as he fumbled with his clothes.

She sat by the window with a cup of coffee at her fingers. He had noticed several times how beautiful her hands were: golden brown and fleshy and dimpled but tapered and carefully cleaned and polished with bright happy polish.

"Lottie," he said finally, "is there some place where you can get a letter?"

The woman hummed to herself and kept on looking out of the window. "Just my mama's house in Gary. That's 'bout all they has to do with me now'days is to send me my mail when they knows where I is. But I don't get too much mail. And I don't hardly stay in one place."

"Then write down the Gary number for me."

The woman did not move. "You don't have to pretend nothing like that, Baby. Once you out that door you be done forgot 'bout Lottie."

"Write it down for me, Lottie."

She looked at him for a second and then got a small nubby pencil from a drawer and wrote something down carefully on a tiny piece of paper. He took it and left and, as far as she could see him, she watched after him from her window.

STEPHEN DEUTCH. *BENCH SITTER, NORTH SHERIDAN ROAD, CHICAGO.*
(*TQ* #60)

The Address

Marga Minco

"Do you still know me?" I asked.

The woman looked at me, inquiring; she had opened the door a crack. I came closer and stood on the front step.

"No," she said, "I don't know you."

"I'm the daughter of Mrs. S.," I said.

She kept her hand on the door as though she wanted to prevent it from opening further. Her face didn't betray any sign of recognition. She kept looking at me silently.

Maybe I'm wrong, I thought, maybe she isn't the one. I had only seen her once in passing, and that was years ago. It was quite likely that I had pushed the wrong doorbell. The woman let go of the door and stepped aside. She was wearing a green hand-knitted sweater. The wooden buttons were slightly faded from laundering. She saw that I was looking at her sweater and again hid partly behind the door. But now I knew that I was at the right address.

"You knew my mother, didn't you?" I asked.

"Did you come back?" said the woman. "I thought that no one had come back."

"Only I," I said. In the hall behind her a door opened and closed. A stale smell came out.

"I'm sorry," she said, "I can't do anything for you."

"I've come here especially on the train. I would have liked to speak with you for a moment."

"It's not convenient now," said the woman. "I can't invite you in. Another time."

She nodded and carefully closed the door, as though no one in the house should be disturbed. I remained on the front step for a moment.

The curtain of the bay window moved. "Oh, nothing," the woman would say, "it was nothing."

I looked at the nameplate once more. It said "Dorling," with black letters on white enamel. And on the doorpost, a little higher, the number. Number 46.

While slowly walking back to the station, I thought of my mother, who had once, years ago, given me the address. It was during the first half of the war. I had come home for a few days, and it had struck me right away that something had changed in the rooms. I missed all sorts of things. My mother was surprised that I'd noticed it so quickly. Then she told me about Mrs. Dorling. I had never heard of her before, but she seemed to be an old acquaintance of my mother's whom she hadn't seen in years. She had suddenly turned up and renewed the acquaintance. Since that time she had been coming regularly.

"Every time she leaves she takes something home with her," my mother said. "She took all the silver flatware at once. And then the antique plates which hung over there. She really had a tough job lugging these big vases, and I'm afraid that she hurt her back with the dishes." My mother shook her head with compassion. "I would never have dared to ask her. She suggested it herself. She even insisted. She wants to save all my beautiful things. She says that we'll lose everything when we have to leave here."

"Have you arranged with her that she'll keep everything?" I asked. "As though that were necessary," my mother exclaimed. "It would be an insult to agree on something like that. And think of the risk she takes every time she leaves our house with a full suitcase or bag!" My mother seemed to notice that I wasn't totally convinced. She looked at me reproachfully, and after that we didn't speak of it again.

Without paying too much attention to the road I had arrived at the station. For the first time since the war I was walking again through familiar districts, but I didn't want to go further than absolutely necessary. I didn't want to torment myself with the sight of streets and houses full of memories of a cherished time. In the train back, I saw Mrs. Dorling before me again, the way I had met her the first time. It was the morning after the day my mother had told me about her. I had gotten up late, and as I went downstairs I saw that my mother was just seeing someone out. A woman with a broad back.

"There is my daughter," said my mother. She motioned to me.

The woman nodded and picked up the suitcase which stood under the coatrack. She was wearing a brown coat and a shapeless hat.

"Does she live far?" I asked after seeing how laboriously she left the house with the heavy suitcase.

"On Marconistraat," said my mother. "Number 46. Do try to remember."

I had remembered. Except that I had waited quite a long time before going there. During the first period after the liberation I felt no interest at all in all that stored stuff, and of course some fear was involved. Fear of being confronted with things that had been part of a bond which no longer existed; which had been stored in cases and boxes and were waiting in vain until they would be put back in their places; which had survived all these years because they were "things."

But gradually everything had become normal again. There was bread which was steadily becoming lighter in color, there was a bed in which you could sleep without being threatened, a room with a view which you got more and more used to every day. And one day I noticed that I was becoming curious about all the possessions which should still be at that address. I wanted to see them, touch them, recognize them. After my first fruitless visit to Mrs. Dorling's house, I decided to try it a second time.

This time it was a girl of about fourteen who opened the door. I asked whether her mother was home. "No," she said, "my mother is just on an errand."

"That doesn't matter," I said, "I'll wait for her."

I followed the girl through the hall. Next to the mirror hung an old-fashioned menorah. We had never used it because it was much more cumbersome than candles.

"Wouldn't you like to sit down?" asked the girl. She held open the door to the room and I went in past her. Frightened, I stood still. I was in a room which I both knew and didn't know. I found myself among things I had wanted to see again but which oppressed me in the strange surroundings. Whether it was because of the tasteless manner in which everything was arranged, because of the ugly furniture or the stuffy air, I don't know, but I scarcely dared look around me anymore. The girl moved a chair. I sat down and stared at the woollen tablecloth. I touched it carefully. I rubbed it. My fingers got warm from rubbing. I followed the lines of the design. Someplace on the edge there should be a burn hole which had never been repaired.

"My mother will be back very soon," said the girl. "I had already made tea for her. Would you like a cup?"

"Please," I said. I looked up. The girl was setting out teacups on the tea table. She had a broad back. Just like her mother. She poured tea from a white pot. There was a gold edge just around the lid, I remembered. She opened a small box and took some teaspoons out of it. "That's a lovely little box." I heard my own voice. It was a strange voice. As though every sound in this room had another ring to it.

"Do you know much about that?" She had turned around and brought me my tea. She laughed. "My mother says that it is antique. We have lots more." She pointed around the room. "Just look."

I didn't need to follow her hand. I knew which things she meant. I kept looking at the still-life above the tea table. As a child I had always wanted to eat the apple that lay on the pewter plate.

"We use it for everything," she said. "We've even eaten from the plates which hang on the wall. I wanted to. But it wasn't anything special."

I had found the burn hole at the edge of the tablecloth. The girl looked at me inquiringly. "Yes," I said, "you get used to all these beautiful things at home, you hardly look at them anymore. You only notice when something is not there, because it has to be repaired, or, for example, because you've lent it to someone."

Again I heard the unnatural sound of my voice, and I continued: "I remember my mother once asking me to help her polish the silver. That was very long ago, and I must have been bored that day, or maybe I had to stay home because I was ill, for she had never asked me to do that before. I asked her which silver she meant, and she answered me, surprised, that she was of course talking about the spoons, forks, and knives. And that was of course the odd thing, I didn't know that the objects with which we ate every day were made of silver."

The girl laughed again.

"I bet you don't know that either," I said. I looked at her intently.

"What we eat with?" she asked.

"Well, do you know?"

She hesitated. She walked to the buffet and started to pull open a drawer. "I'll have to look. It's in here."

I jumped up. "I'm forgetting my time. I still have to catch my train."

She stood with her hand on the drawer. "Wouldn't you like to wait for my mother?"

"No, I have to leave." I walked to the door. The girl opened the drawer.

"I'll find my way." When I was walking through the hall I heard the clinking of spoons and forks.

At the corner of the street I looked up at the nameplate. It said Marconistraat. I had been at Number 46. The address was right. But now I no longer wanted to remember it. I would not go there again, for the objects which in your memory are linked with the familiar life of former times suddenly lose their value when you see them again, torn out of context, in strange surroundings. And what would I do with them in a small rented room in which shreds of blackout paper were still hanging along the windows and where in the narrow table drawer there was room for just a few dinner things?

I resolved to forget the address. Of all the things I should forget, that one would be the easiest.

Translated by Jeannette K. Ringold

1984

Departures

Linda Pastan

They seemed to all take off
at once: Aunt Grace
whose kidneys closed shop;
Cousin Rose who fed sugar
to diabetes;
my grandmother's friend
who postponed going so long
we thought she'd stay.

It was like the summer years ago
when they all set out on trains
and ships, wearing hats with veils
and the proper gloves,
because everybody was going
someplace that year,
and they didn't want
to be left behind.

1984

He, She, All of Them, Ay

John Peck

In only a few days they will change houses,
the counselor and his wife, daughter, maid, adopted son,
so I work my way around their patio, momentary cousin
loosening stanchions and a green wire trellis.
Eleven o'clock, the Limmat shines below,
gulls glide to the rapids, plop in, drift down, and skim back,
prospecting where a trail threads budding poplars.
The consulting room gapes onto foggy sun,
a drained fishbowl, the drapes not yet unhooked.
More than half of the bolts have frozen fast.
I use the hacksaw and roll the trellis into tumbleweed.
Crows preen among tips of the shore forest.
Across the river, more poplars, then a sprawling factory,
then a multilane, and then hazy mountains.
Cloudy glass flung wide, cockpit of aid vacant,
steady cello twang of the road washing over.
A spider blows from the trellis to go the wind's way.
Don't worry, Brother Eight-legs, God cleans house without
    fussing.
The last time I did this I carried the owner's clavichord
like a fairy coffin out to the front lawn
and, weary, laid it across two chairs
to pick through the F-minor fugue by Sebastian Bach.
Halfway through the second countersubject I found
the upper voice in my left hand, the lower in my right.
May we always be so lucky. And may we only half notice.
Packing my own house, pushing our girl on her swing,
I saw in her brave face more than I thought could break there.
No instrument this time, but there's a river, there are mountains.
Facing them, the gardener walks towards the brink.
He unbolts the jagged scimitar from his pruning grip

and slips in a larger, shinier scimitar.
He swipes down through the first wiry rank of brush
to grasp the lanky trunk of a golden sapling.
The top branches wiggle, and then sway, and plunge over.
He descends further, another one falls like a flail,
and two crows flap up. It is nearly noon.
He takes off his red shirt, folding it like a flag,
and begins the climb back uphill, wiping his steel.
He will sit down and eat. Midday veils the mountains.
And so, tell us again: why this endless spring wind?
Why do we cross the river?

ABOVE AND ON FOLLOWING PAGE: PHOTOGRAPHS BY DENIS CAMERON. FROM *AFRICAN SERIES, 1968. (TQ #61)*

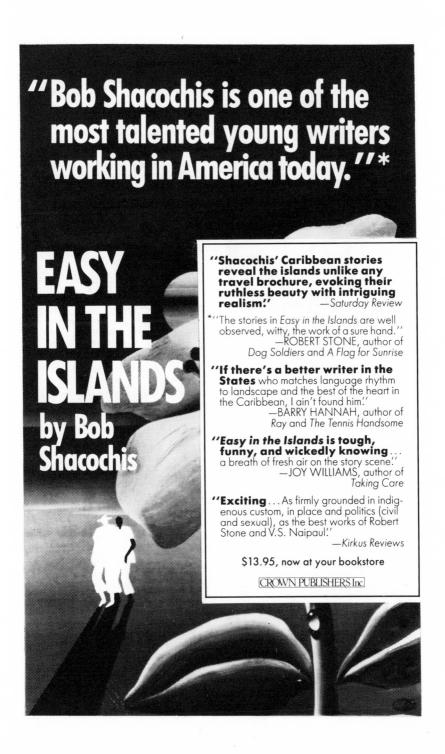

CHICAGO

STRANGERS
DAVID FERRY

"This is a lovely work from a voice which has neither attenuated with long silence, nor coarsened with inevitable darkenings."
— John Hollander, *Yale Review*
Phoenix Poets series
Paper $5.95   Cloth $12.95
64 pages

THE COURTESY
ALAN SHAPIRO

"Alan Shapiro's *The Courtesy* is a collection of poems balancing a wry and altogether individual sensibility with and against an unobtrusive technical control; a young poet whose work . . . is full of humor and acquaintance with pain."
— Howard Nemerov
Phoenix Poets series
Paper $5.95   Cloth $12.95
69 pages

THE SOLITARY SINGER
A Critical Biography of Walt Whitman
With a new Preface
GAY WILSON ALLEN

No genuine competitor to Allen's monumental biography of Walt Whitman has emerged since it was first published. In the words of Justin Kaplan, it "remains indispensable and has set the standard for all subsequent Whitman scholarship."

"For thirty years [*The Solitary Singer*] has been the standard life. Now, in this paperback edition, it can be welcomed by a new generation of readers." — Malcolm Cowley
Paper $15.95   640 pages
11 b&w illustrations

FISH
MONROE ENGEL

Harry Karp is "Fish" — cautious divorcé, deferential lover, meticulous observer, the narrator of a wry contemporary romance.

"What I especially admired about *Fish* was the full confidence of Monroe Engel's control, his handling of a very dense, complex and suggestive language colored by his personality and doing exactly what he told it to do." — Saul Bellow
Phoenix Fiction series
Paper $6.95   224 pages

The University of CHICAGO Press
5801 South Ellis Avenue, Chicago, IL 60637

TriQuarterly
Twentieth Anniversary Back-Issue Offer

#25 **Prose for Borges:** a special issue with an anthology of writings by Borges and essays and appreciations by Anthony Kerrigan, Norman Thomas di Giovanni and others. 468 pp. $6.00

#26 **Ongoing American Fiction I:** features Stanley Elkin, Robert Coover, Thomas McGuane, Russell Edson, Alain Robbe-Grillet, Joyce Carol Oates and Philip Stevick. 420 pp. $5.00

#29 **Ongoing American Fiction II:** stories by John Gardner, Joseph McElroy, Joy Williams, Gilbert Sorrentino, William Kittredge and others. 216 pp. $4.00

#31 **Contemporary Asian Literature:** coedited by Lucien Stryk. With Lu Hsun, Chairil Anwar, Ho Chi Minh, Shinkichi Takahashi, Yasunari Kawabata and others. 244 pp. $3.50

#33 **Ongoing American Fiction III:** James Purdy, David Kranes, Alan Sillitoe, Paul Bowles, Daniel Halpern, Morris Dickstein, Robert Alter and more. 340 pp. $3.50

#34 **Ongoing American Fiction IV:** Charles Newman, Ian McEwan, Robert Creeley, Gilbert Sorrentino, Ron Sukenick, Joseph McElroy, Robert Scholes and nine others. 256 pp. $3.50

#36 **Ongoing American Fiction V:** Robert Coover, Ursule Molinaro, Paul West, Ian MacMillan, Joyce Carol Oates, Peter Michelson. 256 pp. $5.00

#52 **Freedom in American Art and Culture:** Theodore Lidz, Robert Coles, Jonathan Schiller, Richard Schechner, David Hayman, Peter Gena, Greil Marcus and others. 296 pp. $5.95

#53 **General issue:** fiction by Arnost Lustig, Stanley Elkin, Arturo Vivante, Joseph McElroy and others; interview with Robert Stone; essay by Thomas LeClair. Photographic portfolio of sculpture by Magdalena Abakanowicz. 280 pp. $5.95

#54 **A John Cage Reader:** color etchings by Cage plus contributions celebrating his 70th birthday from Marjorie Perloff, William Brooks, Merce Cunningham and others; fiction by Ray Reno, Arturo Vivante and others; poetry by Teresa Cader, Jay Wright and Michael Collier. 304 pp. $5.95

#55 **General issue:** fiction by Paul West, Willis Johnson, David Plante, Joe Taylor and others; poetry by Pamela White Hadas, Roland Flint, Theodore Weiss and others; nonfiction by Janet Lewis, Phyllis Rose and Michael S. Harper; photographs by Steven D. Foster. 240 pp. $5.95

#56 **General issue:** New work by and an interview with William Goyen plus fiction by Frederick Busch, Amy Hempel, Stephen Dixon, Andrew Fetler and others; poetry by Mairi MacInnes, Marvin Bell, Joyce Carol Oates, W.S. Di Piero, Lucien Stryk and others. A selection of The Small Press Book Club. 288 pp. $5.95

#57 **A special two-volume set—Vol. 1, A Window on Poland:** featuring essays, fiction and poems written during Solidarity and martial law. Konwicki, Brandys and others, with twenty-two photos and graphic works. 128 pp. **Vol. 2, Prose from Spain,** featuring recent fiction and essays, plus an interview with Juan Goytisolo and eight color pages of street murals. 112 pp. $3.95/each vol., $7.90/set

#58 **General issue:** stories by Fred Chappell, Janet Kauffman, Perry Glasser and others; poetry by George Starbuck, C.K. Williams, Dave Smith and others; essays by William Goyen and Alan Shapiro; illustrations by Stan Washburn and Matthew Owens. 224 pp. $6.95

#59 **The American Blues:** fiction by Ward Just, ~~Jo~~ Carol Oates, Gayle Whittier, Rodney Jones and ~~oth~~ Bruce Weigl, John Ciardi, Joh~~n~~ ~~umin~~ and others; photogra~~ph~~ ~~American~~ political figures ~~~~ and Others," a supplement of poetr~~y~~ ~~~~mplementing *Prose from Spain* (#57, Vol. 2). 272 p~~p.~~ ~~~~

#60 **Chicago:** interviews with Saul Bellow and Norman Maclean; fiction by Lorraine Hansberry, Harry Mark Petrakis, Richard Stern and others; memoirs by Karl Shapiro and Gwendolyn Brooks; poetry by Paul Carroll, Lisel Mueller and others; photographs by Stephen Deutch, Arthur Shay and others. 444 pp. $10.95

#61 **General issue:** fiction by Kobo Abé, Dino Buzzati, Stephen Dixon and others; essays by Alan Shapiro and Josephine Jacobsen; poems by Hayden Carruth, Reynolds Price, Linda Pastan and others; photographs by Denis Cameron. 224 pp. $6.95

For orders of two or more books, deduct 20% from total price.
We pay postage on orders of three or more copies. (For orders of one or two books please add $1.00 for postage and handling.)
Note: While supplies last, an index to issues 1-50 is available on request, free of charge, with any order.

TriQuarterly, Northwestern University
1735 Benson Ave., Evanston, IL 60201

Please send me the following back issues of **TriQuarterly:**

_____ _____ _____ _____

I enclose $_____ ☐ *VISA* ☐ MasterCard #_____

Signature: _____ Expires:_____

Name _____

Address _____

City_____ State_____ Zip_____

"Charles Newman's **The Post-Modern Aura** *is a real eye-opener, the best thing I've read on the state of American culture in a long time, and grounded, moreover, in a tough-minded analysis of the economics of publishing—something unheard of in the annals of literary criticism."*
Christopher Lasch, author of *The Minimal Self*

Charles Newman, *The Post-Modern Aura: The Act of Fiction in an Age of Inflation*

This brilliant meditation on Post-Modernism in fiction, the arts, and culture is an irreverent combination of cultural criticism, literary analysis, and economic-historical forecast. Newman argues that "an age of inflation" renders obsolete the standard categories in which literary-cultural debate has been conducted. Most striking and original are the connections Newman draws between high literary theories of the Death of the Novel and low economic realities of publishing. Cloth $18.95, Paper $7.95

*Newman, novelist (**The Promisekeeper, White Jazz**) and editor, offers a brilliant, wide-ranging, often scathing analysis of "post-modernist" culture here—focusing on contemporary fiction, with economic inflation as a metaphor...important reading for those concerned with the esthetics of contemporary culture—and fiction in particular.*
Kirkus Reviews

"I found **The Post-Modern Aura** *remarkably free of partisan folly, and so sane as to shame the rest of us who write about these matters. Newman knows the art; he knows the business; he understands the culture game; and all aspects are brilliantly illuminated and brought together here."*
William H. Gass, author of *Fiction and the Figures of Life*

"This is an intellectually bold and provocative discussion of some major cultural questions which deserves to be widely read and thought about."
Bernard Bergonzi, *University of Warwick*

Northwestern University Press
1735 Benson Avenue
Evanston, IL 60201
312-491-5313

Crain's Chicago Business

SALUTES

TriQuarterly

for 20 years

of excellence

in writing and graphics

CONGRATULATIONS!